LEAVING CERTIFICATE
GEOGRAPHY TODAY

BOOK 1
CORE UNITS 1, 2, 3

Liam Ashe and
Kieran McCarthy

The Educational Company of Ireland

First published 2017
The Educational Company of Ireland
Ballymount Road
Walkinstown
Dublin 12
www.edco.ie

A member of the Smurfit Kappa Group plc

© Liam Ashe, Kieran McCarthy, 2017

All rights reserved. No part of this publication may be reproduced, stored in a retrieval system, or transmitted in any form or by any means, electronic, mechanical, photocopying, recording or otherwise, without either the prior permission of the Publisher or a licence permitting restricted copying in Ireland issued by the Irish Copyright Licensing Agency, 63 Patrick Street, Dún Laoghaire Co. Dublin.

ISBN 978-1-84536-717-6

The paper used in this book comes from Managed Forests in Northern Europe. For every tree felled, at least one new tree is planted

Editor: Sarah Butler
Design and Layout: Identikit
Illustrator: Compuscript
Indexer: Jane Rogers
Proofreader: Kristin Jensen
Cover Design: Identikit
Cover Photography: Shutterstock/Liu Zishan

Acknowledgements

The authors wish to extend a sincere word of gratitude to Kristin Jensen and Sarah Butler for their attention to detail and support throughout the project. They also wish to thank Frances Ashe, Conor McCarthy, Rose McCarthy, Shane McCarthy, Michael Kelly, Edel Handley, CSO, Dublin City Council, Dublin Docklands, Fáilte Ireland, IDA, Met Éireann and Transport Infrastructure Ireland.

Photograph acknowledgements

Alamy, Barrow Coakley Photography, Conor McCarthy, DigitalGlobe, Geological Survey of Ireland, Getty, INPHO, John Herriott (Ireland Aerial Photography), NASA, Ordnance Survey Ireland, picsaboutspace.com, Science Photo Library, Shell Ireland, Shutterstock, USGS

Ordnance Survey Ireland
National Mapping Agency - www.osi.ie

Ordnance Survey Ireland Permit No. 9087
© Ordnance Survey Ireland/Government of Ireland

While every care has been taken to trace and acknowledge copyright, the publishers tender their apologies for any accidental infringement where copyright has proved untraceable. They would be pleased to come to a suitable arrangement with the rightful owner in each case.

Web references in this book are intended as a guide for teachers. At the time of going to press, all web addresses were active and contained information relevant to the topics in this book. However, The Educational Company of Ireland and the authors do not accept responsibility for the views or information contained on these websites. Content and addresses may change beyond our control and pupils should be supervised when investigating websites.

09S23

CONTENTS

CORE UNIT 1 PHYSICAL GEOGRAPHY

Chapter 1	The Earth's Structure	2
Chapter 2	Plate Tectonics	8
Chapter 3	Folding, Faulting and Doming	23
Chapter 4	Earthquakes	35
Chapter 5	Volcanoes	50
Chapter 6	Rocks and the Rock Cycle	72
Chapter 7	Denudation: An Introduction	90
Chapter 8	Weathering	92
Chapter 9	Karst Landscapes	101
	PREAMBLE TO CHAPTERS 10–13	118
Chapter 10	Mass Movement	119
Chapter 11	River Processes	134
Chapter 12	Coastal Processes	161
Chapter 13	Glacial Processes	185
Chapter 14	Landscape Cycle and Isostasy	208

CORE UNIT 2 REGIONAL GEOGRAPHY

Chapter 15	The Concept of a Region	220
Chapter 16	The Dynamics of Regions 1	251
Chapter 17	The Dynamics of Regions 2	295
Chapter 18	The Dynamics of Regions 3	341
Chapter 19	The Complexity of Regions	372

CORE UNIT 3 GRAPH SKILLS AND GEOGRAPHICAL INVESTIGATION

Chapter 20	Ordnance Survey Maps	392
Chapter 21	Aerial Photographs	419
Chapter 22	Satellite Images	438
Chapter 23	Weather Charts	454
Chapter 24	Interpreting Graphs	463
Chapter 25	Geographical Investigation	473
Appendix:	Exam Terminology	479
	Index	480

PREFACE

Geography Today 1 meets the demands of the Leaving Certificate geography syllabus at both Higher and Ordinary Level. It covers the three core units of the course:

- Patterns and processes in the physical environment
- Regional geography
- Geographic investigation and skills.

The material is as up to date as possible at the time of writing. Special care has been taken with the text to ensure that it is easy to read and presented in an interesting way. The authors were very conscious of the nuances of examination questions during the writing process.

Full colour is used throughout the book and the presentation of the material is visually appealing. A wide range of up-to-date maps, diagrams, photographs, statistical data and satellite images has been used to supplement the text.

Material that is Higher Level only is clearly shown where relevant, as are the choices within some topics.

Each chapter opens with a list of keywords and learning objectives. There is a major focus on geographic skills. A wide range of activities and short questions are included in the margins to test students' skills and understanding of the material. An end-of-chapter summary map is also provided to facilitate revision and further understanding of the topic. Each chapter ends with both short and long Leaving Certificate examination questions at both Higher and Ordinary levels.

Up-to-date, exam-focused case studies appear throughout the book. The material in the Regional Geography section reflects the changing economic circumstances in the regions studied. Two Irish regions and two European regions are examined as well as Brazil as the sub-continental region. The challenge posed by Brexit is examined in the final chapter of this unit.

This core book links closely with the settings in the Elective and Optional units in *Geography Today 2* and *Geography Today 3*. These links help students to deepen and reinforce their knowledge of material relating to a particular topic or theme.

Digital resources

The *Geography Today 1* digital resources will enhance classroom learning by encouraging student participation and engagement.

To provide guidance for the integration of digital resources in the classroom, animations, videos and PowerPoints are **referenced in the student textbook** using the following icons:

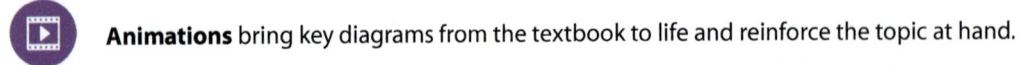

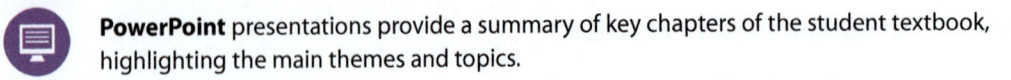

Animations bring key diagrams from the textbook to life and reinforce the topic at hand.

A series of stimulating **videos**, covering a variety of different topics, allows students to observe geography in action.

PowerPoint presentations provide a summary of key chapters of the student textbook, highlighting the main themes and topics.

Teachers can access the *Geography Today 1* e-book, plus the animations, videos and PowerPoints, at www.edcolearning.ie.

CORE UNIT 1 PHYSICAL GEOGRAPHY

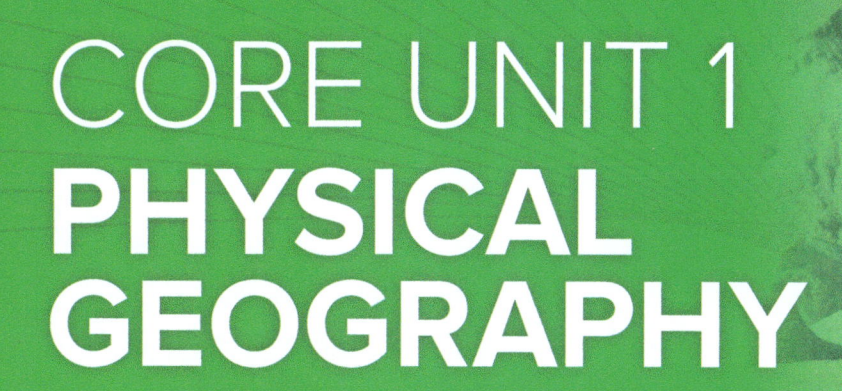

Chapter 1	The Earth's Structure	2
Chapter 2	Plate Tectonics	8
Chapter 3	Folding, Faulting and Doming	23
Chapter 4	Earthquakes	35
Chapter 5	Volcanoes	50
Chapter 6	Rocks and the Rock Cycle	72
Chapter 7	Denudation: An Introduction	90
Chapter 8	Weathering	92
Chapter 9	Karst Landscapes	101
	PREAMBLE TO CHAPTERS 10–13	118
Chapter 10	Mass Movement	119
Chapter 11	River Processes	134
Chapter 12	Coastal Processes	161
Chapter 13	Glacial Processes	185
Chapter 14	Landscape Cycle and Isostasy	208

Chapter 1
The Earth's Structure

> **KEYWORDS**
>
> - the Earth
> - core
> - mantle
> - crust
> - oceanic crust
> - continental crust
> - lithosphere
> - asthenosphere

> **LEARNING OBJECTIVES**
>
> By the end of this chapter, you should be able to understand:
> - The internal structure of the Earth
> - The make-up of the crust.

The Earth's layers

The Earth is about 4.6 billion years old. It was formed from a large cloud of dust and gas. This cloud gradually cooled, shrank and solidified to form the planet that we have today.

As the Earth cooled, the heavier materials, such as iron and nickel, sank to the centre. The lighter, rocky materials floated upward. Due to this, the Earth is made up of a number of different layers.

The Earth's crust

There are two different types of crust: thin oceanic crust under the oceans and thicker continental crust under the continents. They differ in age, thickness and the minerals they are made of.

Oceanic crust

- **Oceanic crust** is 6–10 km thick.
- On top is a thin blanket of sedimentary rocks. It consists of sands, clays and shells.
- Beneath this blanket, the oceanic crust contains ancient, heavy igneous rocks such as basalt.
- The rocks of the oceanic crust are often referred to as **sima**. This is because the most abundant minerals in it are silica and magnesium.

> **ACTIVITY**
>
> **Skills**
>
> Examine Figure 1.1. Identify each of the following layers:
> (i) The hottest layer
> (ii) A fully solid layer
> (iii) The widest layer.

> **GEOFACT**
>
> If the Earth was the size of a football, the crust would only be about 0.5 mm thick.

Crust

The outermost layer, made of solid rocks and minerals, is called the crust. It consists of two zones: oceanic crust and continental crust.

The crust is broken into sections called plates.

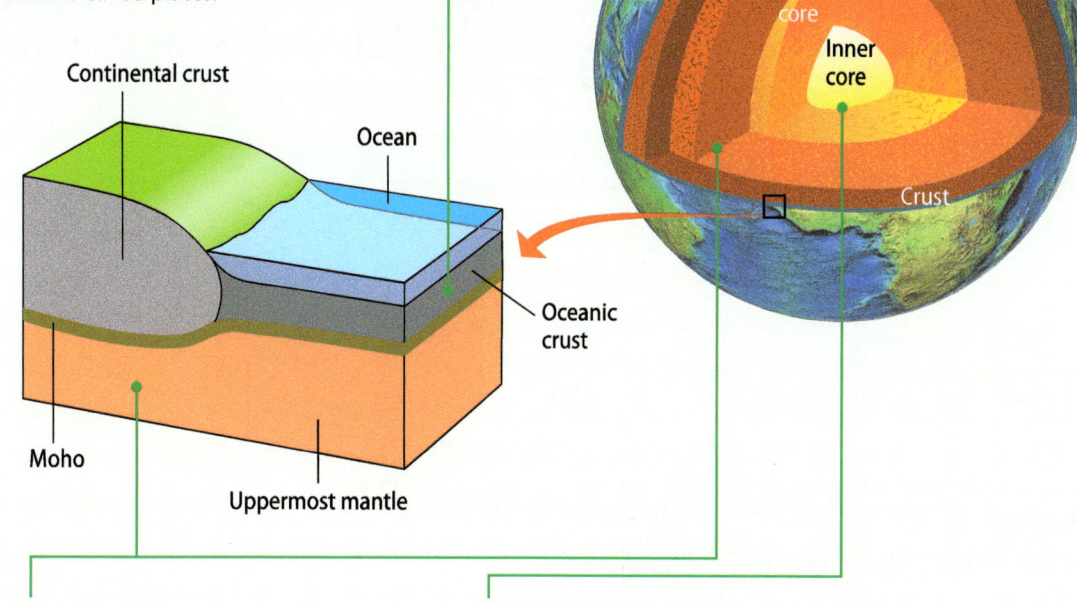

Mantle

The mantle makes up over 75% of the Earth's volume and consists of several layers of rock.

It is rigid at its uppermost section (see Figure 1.3). As it goes deeper, it varies from semi-molten to molten. Thus, it is able to flow.

Core

The core is made up of two sections: a liquid outer core and a solid inner core. Both consist of iron and nickel. Each core is also extremely hot, with temperatures ranging up to 6,000°C.

The **outer core** is in a molten or liquid state. The **inner core** is solid because it is under intense pressure.

Figure 1.1 The structure of the Earth

Continental crust

- **Continental crust** varies in thickness. It is 30 km thick where the continents have been stretched and over 60 km thick in the mountain belts where the continents have been squashed together.
- It is made up of younger, lighter rocks such as granite.
- The rocks of the oceanic crust are often referred to as **sial**. This is because the most abundant minerals in it are silica and aluminium.
- The continental crust does not begin at the coastline, but in ocean water far beyond the shore. This submerged area of continental crust is known as the **continental shelf**.

DEFINITIONS

The boundary where the crust meets the uppermost mantle is called the **Moho**.

Continental shelf: The edge of a continent that lies under relatively shallow water. The shelf descends towards the ocean floor by the continental slope.

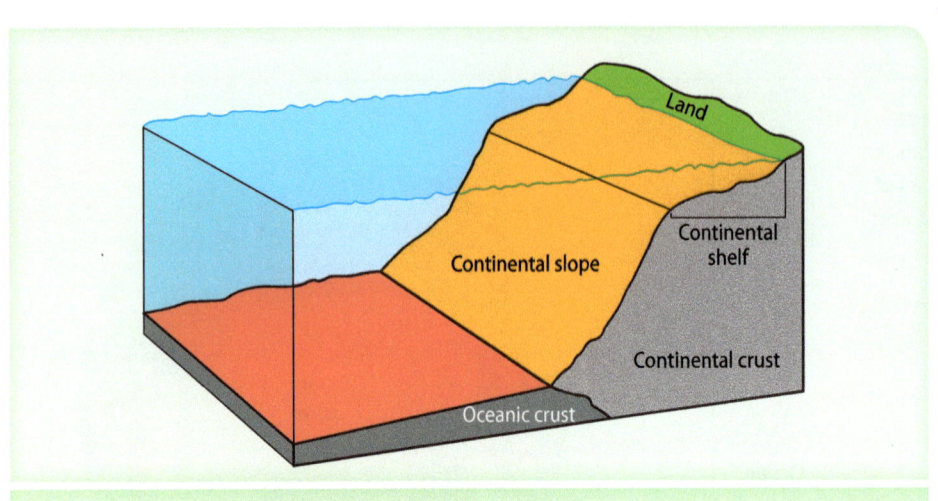

Figure 1.2 The continental crust stretches out past the shoreline. It extends under the ocean as far as the edge of the continental shelf and the continental slope.

ACTIVITY

Research

Look up images of the continental shelf in Europe on the internet.

The lithosphere

The **lithosphere** is the solid, outer part of the Earth.

> It is composed of the crust and upper section of the mantle.
> It forms a solid and relatively rigid shell, averaging about 100 km in thickness.
> The rocks here can bend but they cannot flow.

The **asthenosphere** is the section of the mantle that is found just below the lithosphere.

> The rocks here are hotter and have partially melted. This gives them the texture of putty.
> As a result, they are able to flow, setting the lithosphere floating on them into motion.

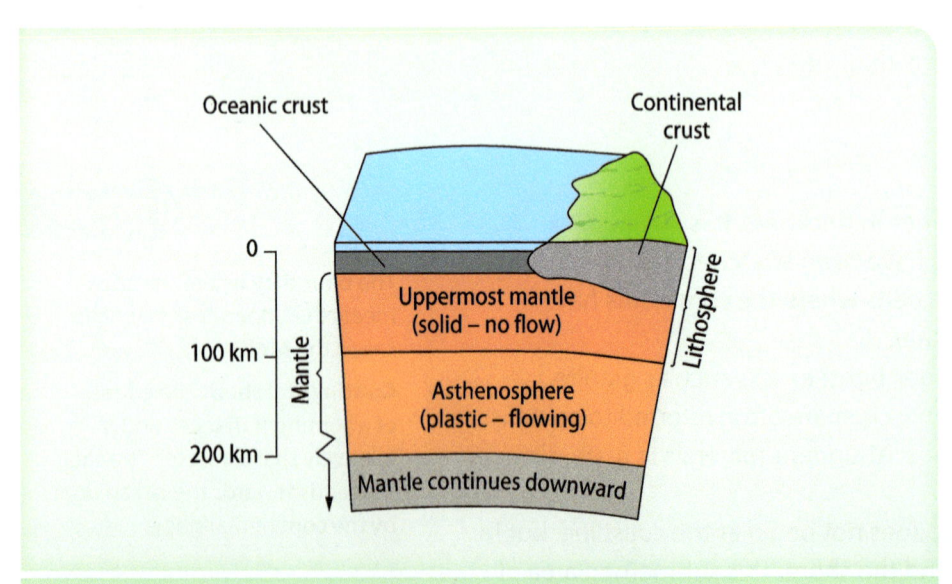

Figure 1.3 The lithosphere consists of the crust and the uppermost layer of the mantle

GEOGRAPHY TODAY

PowerPoint Summary

SUMMARY CHART

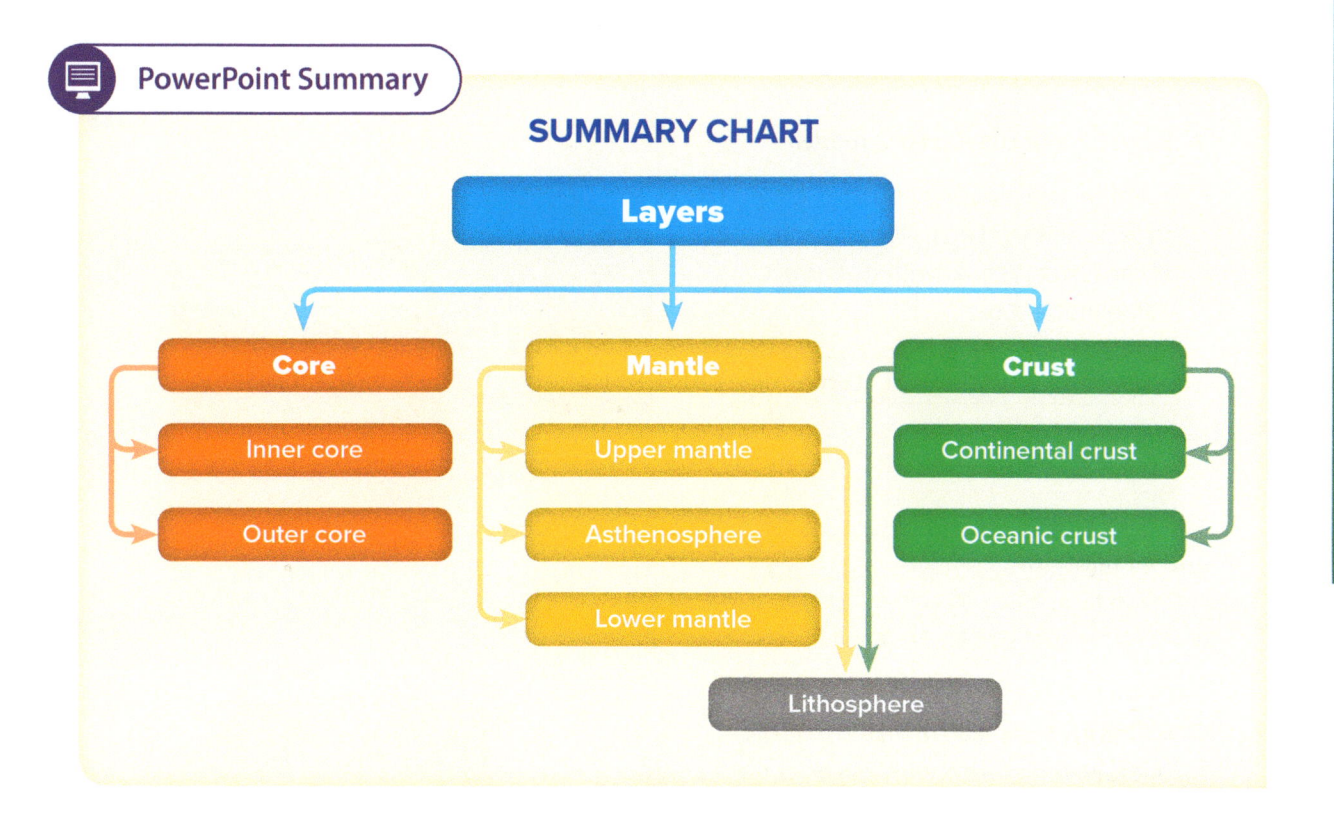

Layers

- **Core**
  - Inner core
  - Outer core
- **Mantle**
  - Upper mantle
  - Asthenosphere
  - Lower mantle
- **Crust**
  - Continental crust
  - Oceanic crust

Lithosphere

Leaving Cert exam questions

SHORT QUESTIONS: HIGHER LEVEL

1 Structure of the Earth (8 marks)

Examine the diagram of the structure of the Earth. Match each of the following terms with its correct letter in the diagram.

Mantle	E
Outer core	
Oceanic crust	
Continental crust	
Inner core	

2 Structure of the Earth (8 marks)

Examine the diagram of the structure of the Earth. Match each of the letters **A** to **D** with its correct name in the table.

Name	Letter
Mantle	
Asthenosphere	
Core	
Crust	

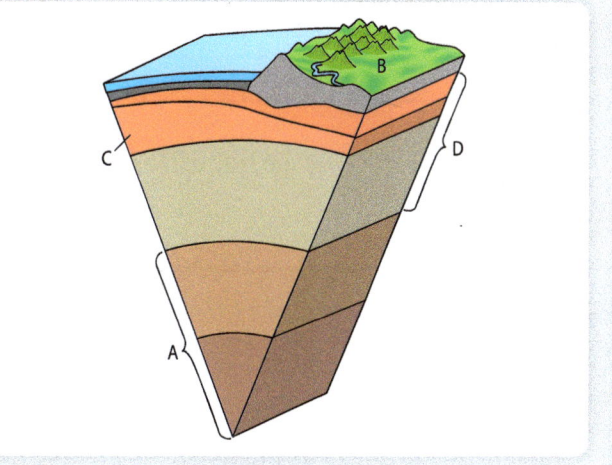

CHAPTER 1 · THE EARTH'S STRUCTURE 5

UNIT 1 · PHYSICAL GEOGRAPHY

3 Structure of the Earth (8 marks)

Examine the diagram of the structure of the Earth. Match each of the letters **A** to **D** with its correct name in the table.

Name	Letter
Ocean	
Continental crust	
Upper mantle	
Oceanic crust	

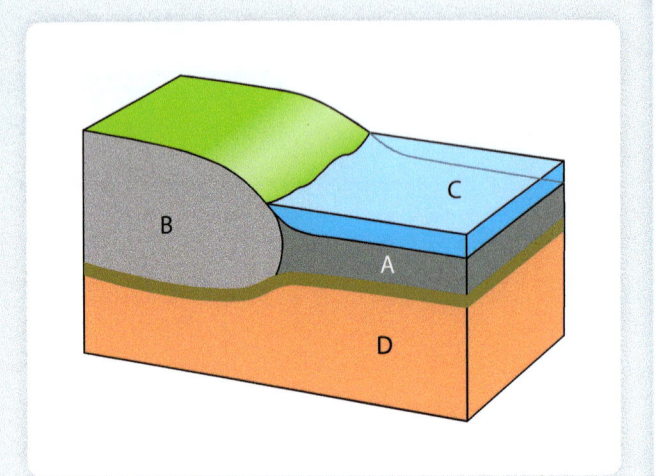

4 Structure of the Earth (8 marks)

Examine the diagram of the structure of the Earth. Match each of the following terms with its correct letter in the diagram.

Name	Letter
Lithosphere	
Upper mantle	
Oceanic crust	
Continental crust	

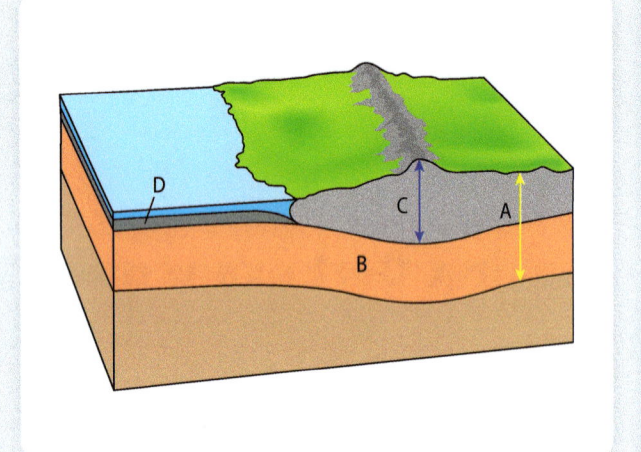

SHORT QUESTIONS: ORDINARY LEVEL

1 Structure of the Earth (10 marks)

(i) Examine the diagram and match each of the letters **A**, **B**, **C** and **D** with one of the terms in the table.

Term	Letter
Mantle	
Outer core	
Inner core	
Crust	

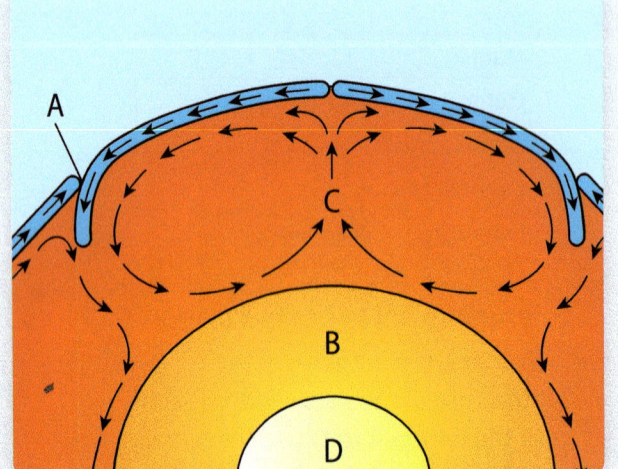

(ii) Which letter shows the hottest layer?

LONG QUESTIONS: HIGHER LEVEL

1 Internal structure of the Earth
(20 marks)

Examine the diagram showing the internal structure of the Earth and answer each of the following questions.

(i) Name each of the layers of the Earth **A**, **B**, **C**, **D**, **E** and **F**.

(ii) Describe briefly the main difference between the composition of layer **C** and layer **D**.

(iii) Explain briefly why plates move.

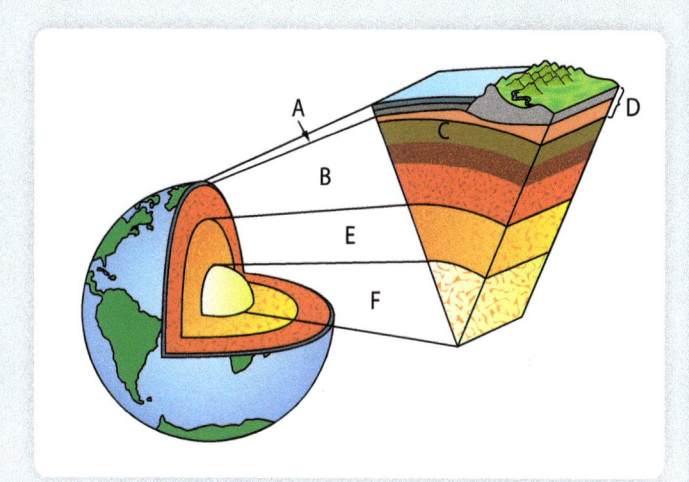

LONG QUESTIONS: ORDINARY LEVEL

1 Internal structure of the Earth
(20 marks)

(i) Examine the diagram. Name each of the layers of the Earth labelled **A**, **B** and **C**.

(ii) Explain briefly what is meant by the term *crust*.

(iii) Describe **two** differences between continental crust and oceanic crust.

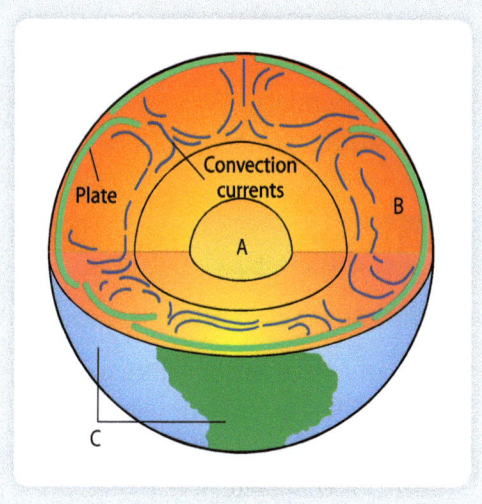

Chapter 2
Plate Tectonics

KEYWORDS

- plate
- plate tectonics
- continental drift
- sea-floor spreading
- plate boundary
- transform boundary
- divergent boundary
- mid-ocean ridge
- convergent boundary
- subduction
- ocean trench
- volcanoes
- San Andreas Fault
- earthquakes
- active plate margin
- trailing plate margin

LEARNING OBJECTIVES

By the end of this chapter, you should be able to understand:

- The theory of plate tectonics
- How plates are able to move
- What happens at the margins of plates
- The position of Ireland in relation to plate boundaries now and in the past.

Plate tectonics

The lithosphere is divided into large, rigid sections called **plates**. Plates float on the asthenosphere, the semi-molten section of the mantle (see Figure 1.3 on page 4). The movement of these plates and the activities that result from it is called **plate tectonics**.

The theory of plate tectonics combines two earlier ideas: continental drift and sea-floor spreading.

> **DEFINITION**
>
> **Plates:** Very large sections that the outer layers of the Earth are broken into.

The Earth's plates

There are seven major plates and several minor plates. They move slowly as they float on the asthenosphere. As a result, they collide, separate and slide past each other. Most earthquakes, volcanoes, oceanic trenches and mountain building occur at plate boundaries.

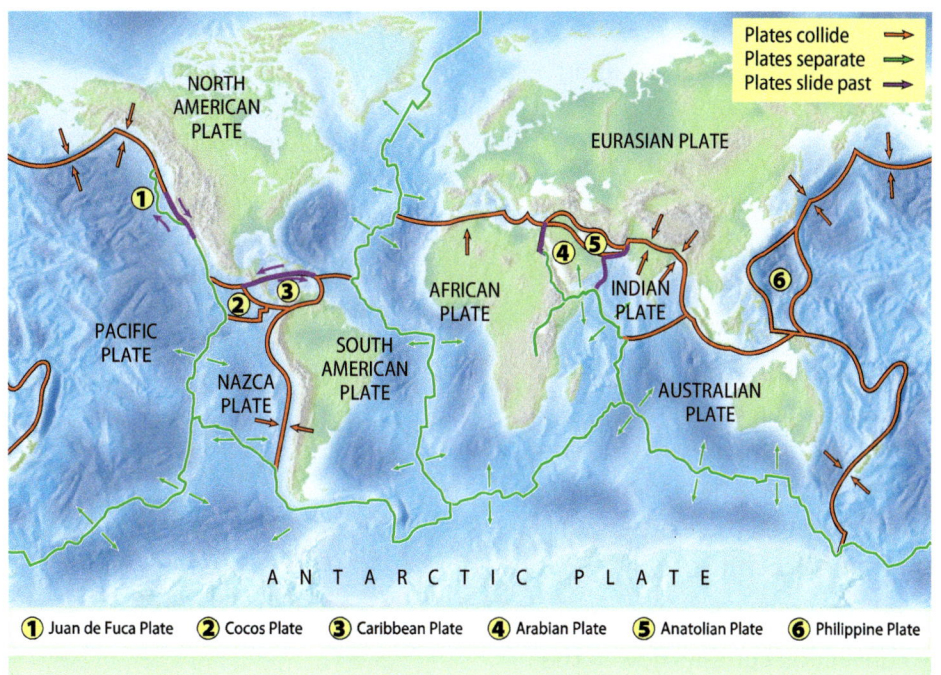

Figure 2.1 The Earth's crust is broken into seven large plates and several minor ones

① Juan de Fuca Plate ② Cocos Plate ③ Caribbean Plate ④ Arabian Plate ⑤ Anatolian Plate ⑥ Philippine Plate

ACTIVITY

Skills

Examine Figure 2.1.

(i) What plate does Ireland lie on?

(ii) Which plate is named after an ocean?

(iii) What two continents make up the Eurasian Plate?

The break-up of Pangaea

The plates have not always been in their current locations and the Earth did not always have seven continents. Instead, it had one massive supercontinent, called **Pangaea**, which was surrounded by a single ocean.

About 200 million years ago, Pangaea began to break up into several pieces, called plates. These plates then slowly drifted away from one another. As they moved, the continents on them moved too. They continue to move today. This process is called **continental drift**.

Scientists believe that in about 250 million years, they will join together again to form a new, different supercontinent.

ACTIVITY

Discussion

Examine Figure 2.2. Why will the Mediterranean Sea disappear about 100 million years from now?

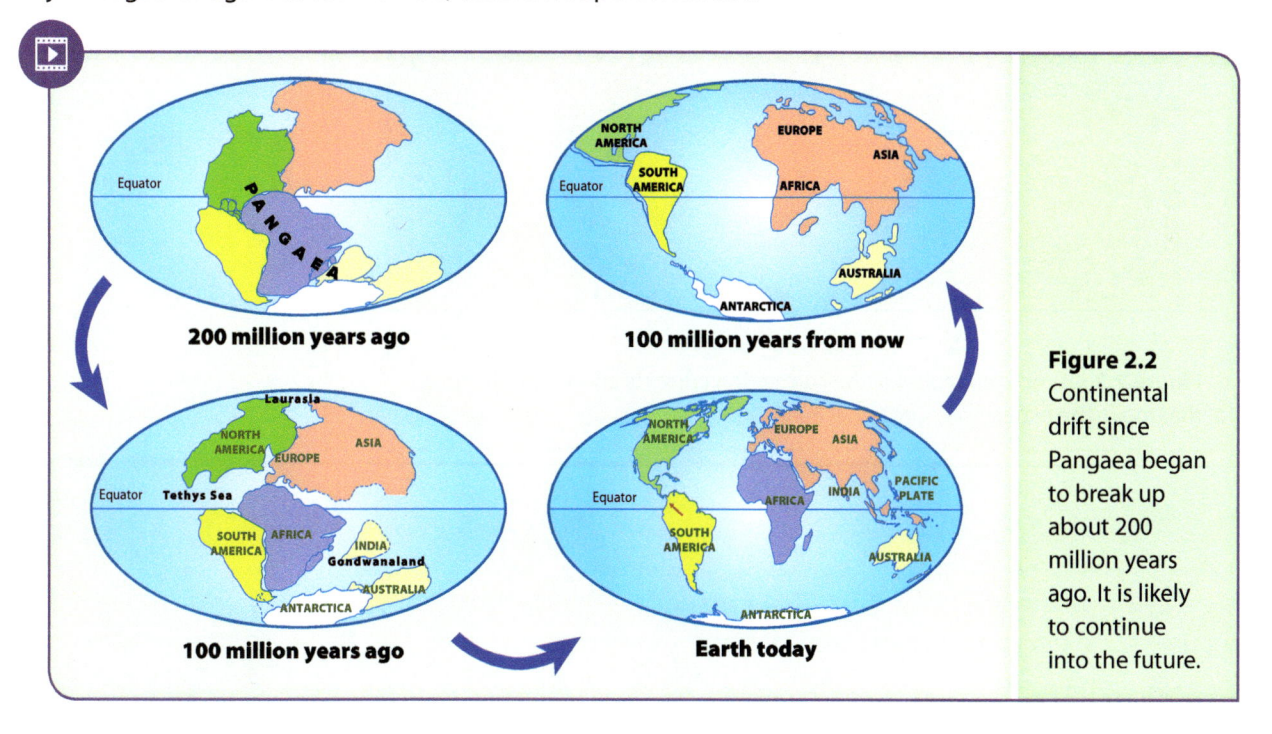

Figure 2.2 Continental drift since Pangaea began to break up about 200 million years ago. It is likely to continue into the future.

CHAPTER 2 · PLATE TECTONICS

How do the plates move?

The movement of the plates is driven by heat escaping from the core and lower mantle.

The core is extremely hot. It transfers some of this heat outwards towards the rocks of the lower mantle. As these are heated, they begin to rise slowly towards the Earth's surface in the form of currents of magma.

By the time the magma comes close to the asthenosphere, it has begun to cool down and begins to move in a sideways direction. When it cools down some more, it begins to sink back down towards the core, where it is once again heated. This cycle has led to the development of **convection currents**. There are about twenty of these currents within the Earth.

There is friction between the plates and the convection currents. Thus, when the convection currents flow in the mantle, they also move the plates.

The movement of the plates is also assisted by **slab-pull** force. When one edge of a plate begins to sink into the mantle, it then pulls the rest of the plate after it. (See *Subduction*, page 16.)

GEOFACT

The theory of continental drift was first suggested in 1912 by Alfred Wegener, a meteorologist with an interest in geology. His ideas were dismissed by geologists, mainly because he was unable to explain how or why the continents drifted.

HINTS

For convection currents, think 'lava lamp'.

For slab-pull, think 'duvet sliding off a bed'.

ACTIVITY

Research

Look up images of 'evidence of continental drift' on the internet. List two pieces of evidence that you found.

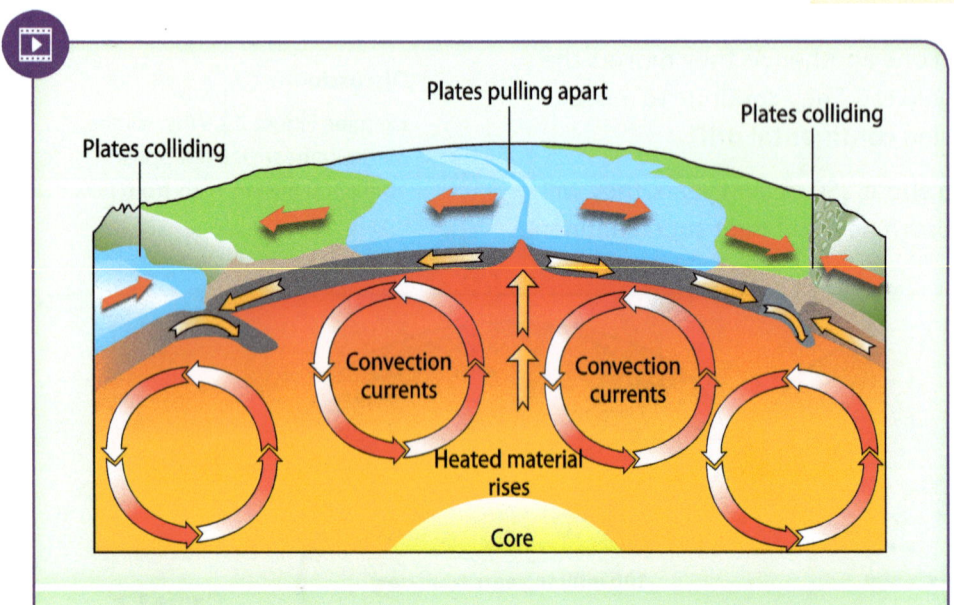

Figure 2.3 A simplified model of the convection currents and slab-pull forces that move the plates

Plate boundaries

As plates move, most activity takes place at their boundaries or margins. Rocks are created here as plates separate, collide or slide past one another. While the plates are moving in several different directions, there are only three types of plate boundary:

> Transform plate boundaries
> Divergent plate boundaries
> Convergent plate boundaries.

Transform plate boundaries   **Divergent plate boundaries**   **Convergent plate boundaries**

A **transform plate boundary** occurs when two plates slide or grind past one another. Since rock is neither formed nor destroyed, these are **passive** boundaries.

An example of a transform boundary is:
- The boundary between the Pacific Plate and the North American Plate in California.

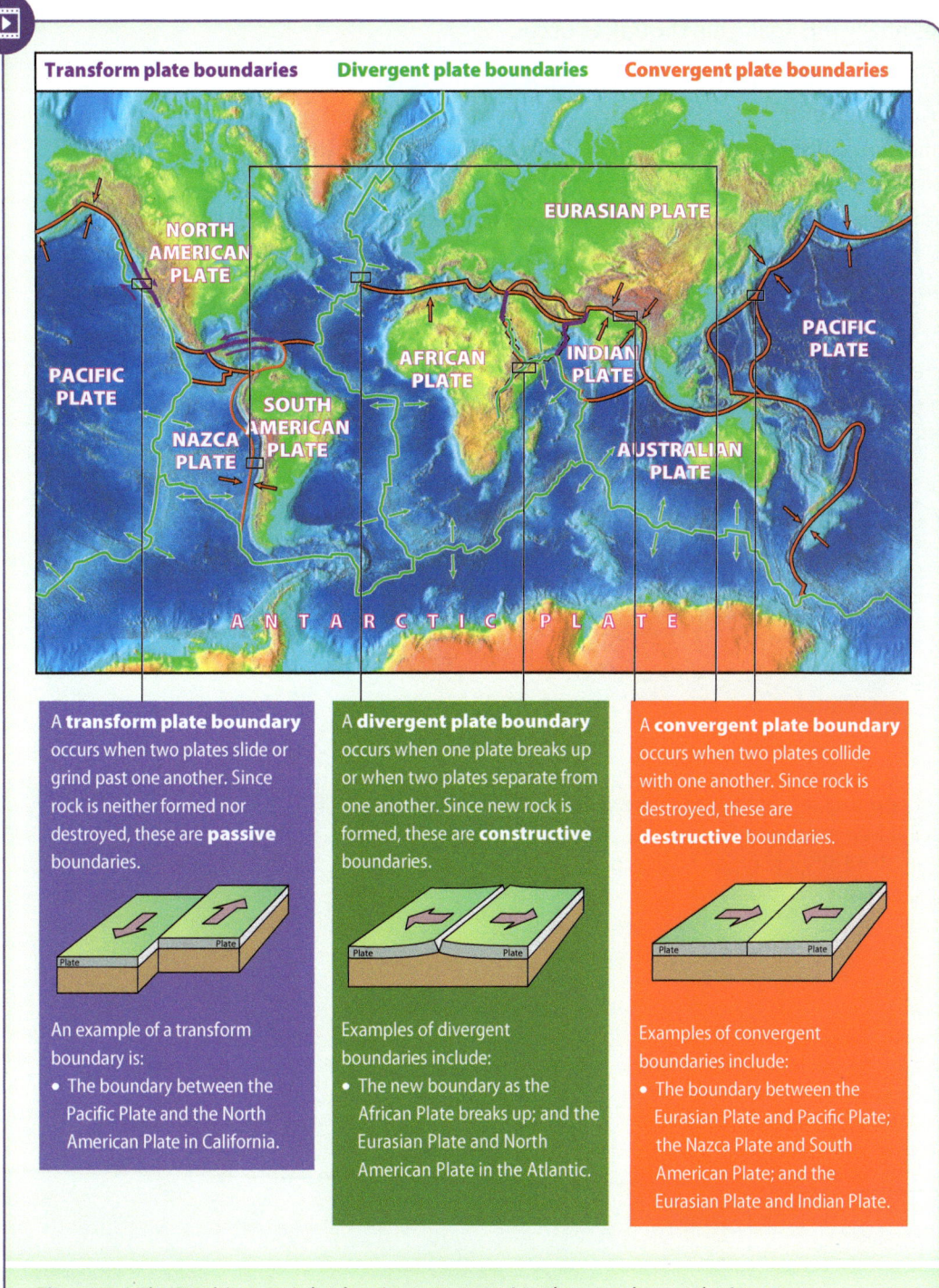

A **divergent plate boundary** occurs when one plate breaks up or when two plates separate from one another. Since new rock is formed, these are **constructive** boundaries.

Examples of divergent boundaries include:
- The new boundary as the African Plate breaks up; and the Eurasian Plate and North American Plate in the Atlantic.

A **convergent plate boundary** occurs when two plates collide with one another. Since rock is destroyed, these are **destructive** boundaries.

Examples of convergent boundaries include:
- The boundary between the Eurasian Plate and Pacific Plate; the Nazca Plate and South American Plate; and the Eurasian Plate and Indian Plate.

Figure 2.4 The Earth's crust is broken into seven major plates and several minor ones. These plates separate, collide and slide past one another.

CHAPTER 2 · PLATE TECTONICS

UNIT 1 · PHYSICAL GEOGRAPHY

Transform plate boundaries

When two plates slide past each other, it is called a **transform boundary**. The boundary is marked by a transform **fault line**. The plates may move in different directions, or in the same direction but at different speeds.

At transform plate boundaries no new crust is formed, nor is any old crust destroyed. Thus, these boundaries are also called **passive** boundaries.

However, movement of the plates is not smooth due to friction between the rocks of the two plates. The plates may get 'stuck' and lock together for decades. This leads to an enormous build-up of pressure (energy). When the plates finally slip again, **earthquakes** occur.

Most transform faults are found on the ocean floor. A few, however, occur on land. The **San Andreas Fault** is the best known. It runs through California, where the Pacific Plate and the American Plate move parallel to each other. Both plates are moving in the same direction, but not at the same speed. The Pacific Plate is moving faster by a rate of about 5 cm per year (see pages 36 and 37).

Process
> Plate movement

Type of boundary
> Transform (passive)

Landform
> Fault line

Figure 2.5 If plate movement at the San Andreas Fault continues at its present rate, Los Angeles should be on an island offshore of San Francisco in about 10 million years

Satellite image of a transform fault. The plates have moved a distance of over 4 km.

Divergent plate boundaries

Divergent plate boundaries are found where the lithosphere is separating or breaking up. These boundaries are the locations of some of the youngest parts of the Earth's surface, where new crust is continuously being created. Thus, they are called **constructive boundaries**.

There are two situations where divergent plate boundaries occur:

> Continental break-up
> Sea-floor spreading.

Continental break-up

The early stages of a continental plate separating or breaking up can be found in Eastern Africa.

The crust in this region was damaged when the African and Eurasian plates collided. Rising currents (plumes) of magma caused the crust to warp upwards. This weakened the crust and as a result, it fractured.

> Faults began to open and various sections of the plate began to move apart. Due to this, the Arabian Peninsula has split from Africa, opening up the Red Sea and Gulf of Aden. These seas may eventually widen to become a new ocean.
> The faults to the south are still widening slowly. The central block has dropped down and a series of rift valleys have developed. These are occupied by lakes.
> In time, the rifting may become slower and stop. However, if it continues, Eastern Africa will break away from the rest of the continent. A new sea floor will form and a new continent will be created. (See *Rift valley*, page 28.)

Process
> Plate break-up

Type of boundary
> Divergent (continental)

Landforms
> Rift valley
> New seas

GEOFACT

Australia and New Zealand were part of the same plate until it broke up (rifted) and New Zealand floated away.

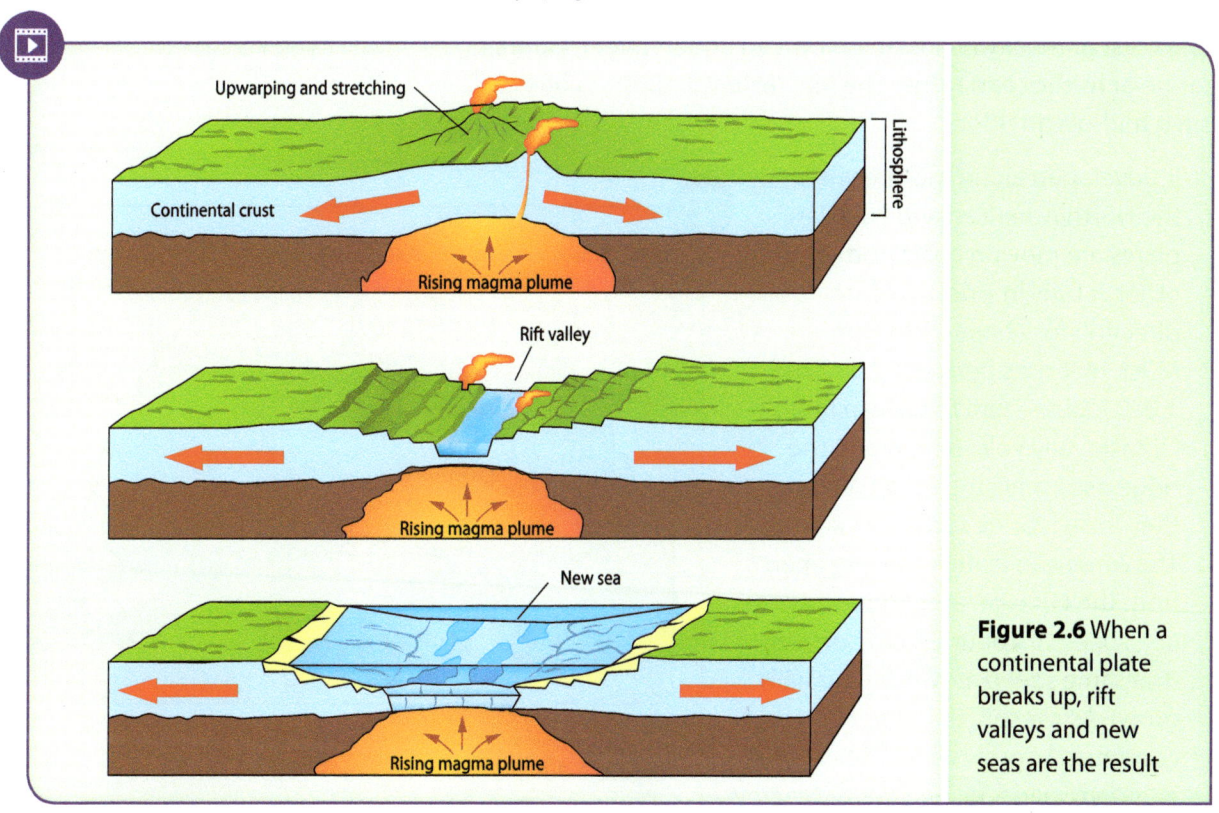

Figure 2.6 When a continental plate breaks up, rift valleys and new seas are the result

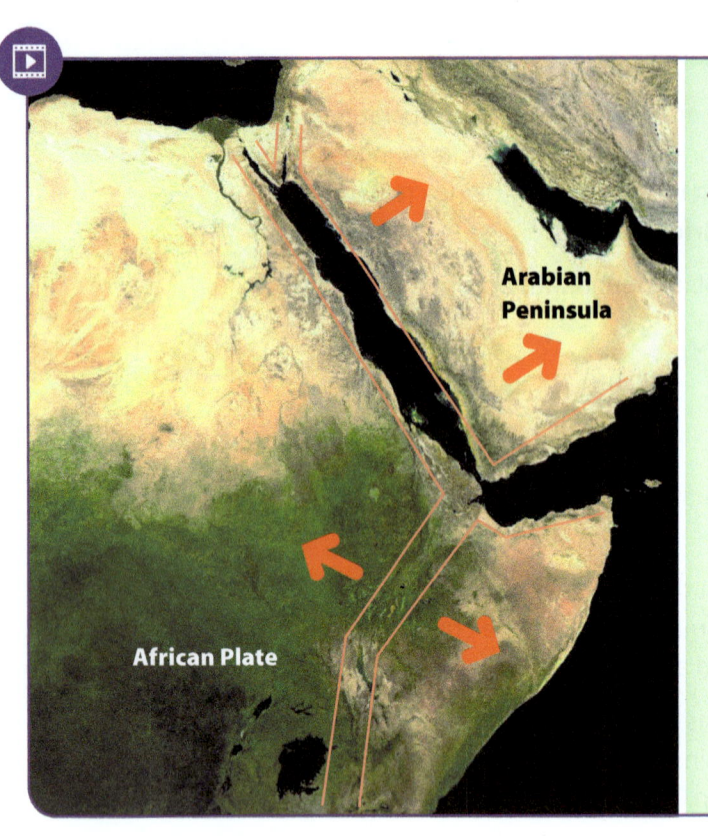

The East African Rift Valley represents the initial stage of the break-up of a plate. The Red Sea and the Gulf of Aden represent a later stage of the break-up. The Arabian Peninsula has already been torn from the African Plate and a 'new' ocean is forming.

Sea-floor spreading

A mid-ocean boundary is the next step after continental break-up. The convection currents in the mantle continue to force the plates to pull apart. This process is called **sea-floor spreading**. Magma then rises from the mantle and moves up through the crack. When it reaches the ocean floor, it is cooled by the seawater and it solidifies to form new oceanic crust.

The crust gradually builds up to form an underwater mountain range or **mid-ocean ridge**. The **Mid-Atlantic Ridge** is one such mid-ocean ridge.

Process
› Sea-floor spreading

Type of boundary
› Divergent (oceanic)

Landforms
› Mid-ocean ridges
› Volcanic islands

› It developed along the line where the North American and Eurasian plates are moving apart from each other. It runs in a north–south direction for about 15,000 km.
› Much of it rises between 2,500 and 3,000 metres from the ocean floor. Occasionally volcanoes along the ridge rise above the ocean, where they form islands such as Iceland.
› The American Plate is moving apart from the Eurasian and African plates at a speed of about 2.5 cm per year (the same speed at which your nails grow). As a result, the Atlantic Ocean continues to grow wider. (See *Fissure eruptions*, page 55; *Geothermal energy in Iceland*, page 66.)

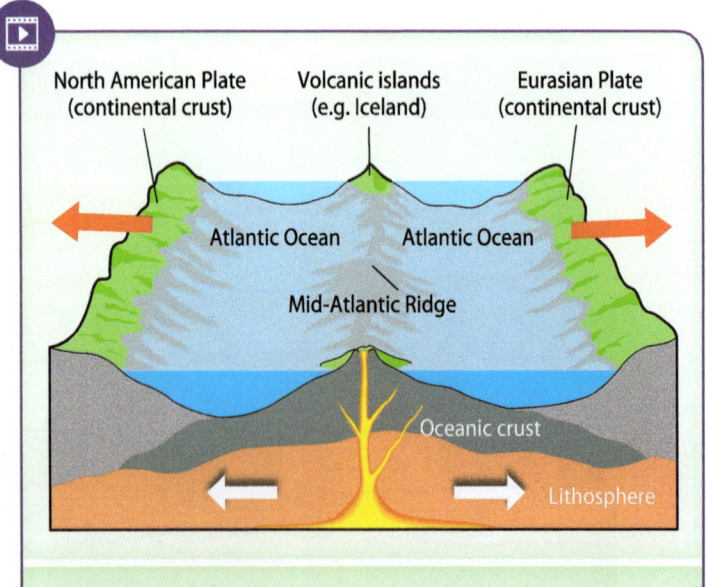

Figure 2.7 A mid-ocean ridge develops as plates pull apart and new crust is created

A road passing through the rift between the North American Plate (left) and the Eurasian Plate (right) in Iceland

GEOFACT

One-third of all the lava that reached the Earth's surface over the last 500 years can be found in Iceland.

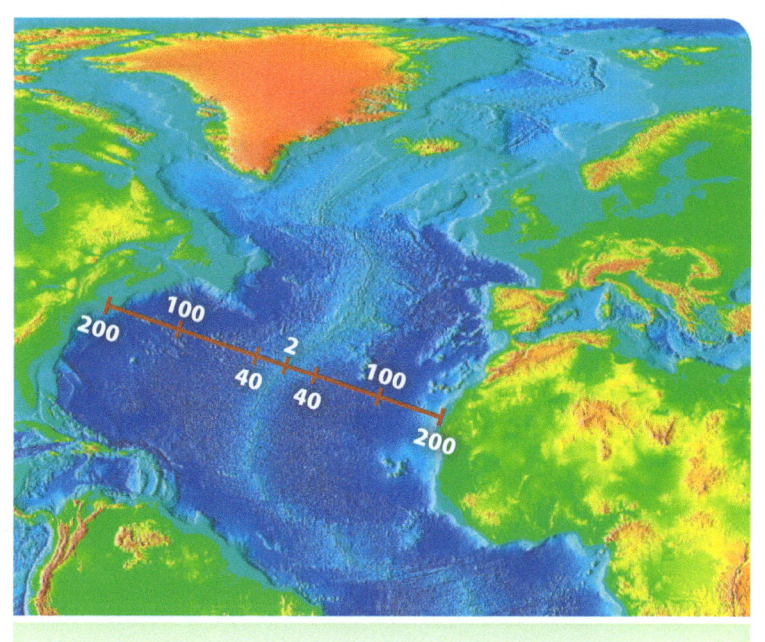

Age of the Atlantic Ocean floor (in millions of years).
The youngest oceanic crust is at the mid-ocean ridges. The crust gets gradually older away from the ridges. This shows that new rocks form in the middle of the ocean. In the diagram above, this line of new rocks is known as the Mid-Atlantic Ridge.

QUESTION

Explain the following terms:
(i) Plate
(ii) Pangaea
(iii) Plate tectonics
(iv) Continental drift
(v) Sea-floor spreading.

GEOFACT

When geologists accepted the idea that sea-floor spreading created new crust, they also realised something else. If the size of the Earth is to remain the same, some crust must also sink back into the mantle and be destroyed.

ACTIVITY

Skills

Examine the false-colour satellite image above. Identify each of the following:
(i) Eurasian Plate
(ii) Continental shelf
(iii) Mid-Atlantic Ridge.

CHAPTER 2 · PLATE TECTONICS   15

Convergent plate boundaries

Convergent plate boundaries occur where the lithosphere is being compressed because two plates are colliding. As a result, one plate is forced down under the other. The plate that is older and heavier will slowly slide under the younger, lighter plate, aided by slab-pull. This process is called **subduction**. Since some lithosphere is lost, these are called **destructive boundaries**.

> **DEFINITION**
>
> **Subduction:** The process where the heavier plate slides beneath the lighter plate and slips down into the mantle.

There are three situations where convergent plate boundaries occur:

> Oceanic plate collides with oceanic plate
> Oceanic plate collides with continental plate
> Continental plate collides with continental plate.

Oceanic–oceanic plate convergence

Oceanic–oceanic convergent boundaries are mostly hidden under the sea. When two oceanic plates collide, the older, heavier plate is subducted beneath the younger, lighter plate. The friction between the plates and the convection currents pulls the plates along, helped by slab-pull force.

> **Process**
> > Plate collision
>
> **Type of boundary**
> > Convergent (oceanic–oceanic)
>
> **Landforms**
> > Island arc
> > Ocean trench

> A long, deep, narrow **ocean trench** develops at the point of subduction. The descending plate is heated as it slips down into the asthenosphere. The heat comes from the hot magma in the asthenosphere and also because the descending plate is being compressed. The plate eventually melts, which produces magma.

> As the new magma starts to make its way to the surface, volcanic activity begins. Over millions of years, the erupted lava and volcanic debris pile up on the ocean floor. Eventually the submarine volcanoes rise above sea level to form island volcanoes. Such volcanoes normally appear in chains called **island arcs**.

> **QUESTION**
>
> Explain the following terms:
> (i) Destructive boundary
> (ii) Ocean trench
> (iii) Island arc.

> Japan is an example of an island arc. It results from the collision of the Eurasian Plate with the Pacific Plate.

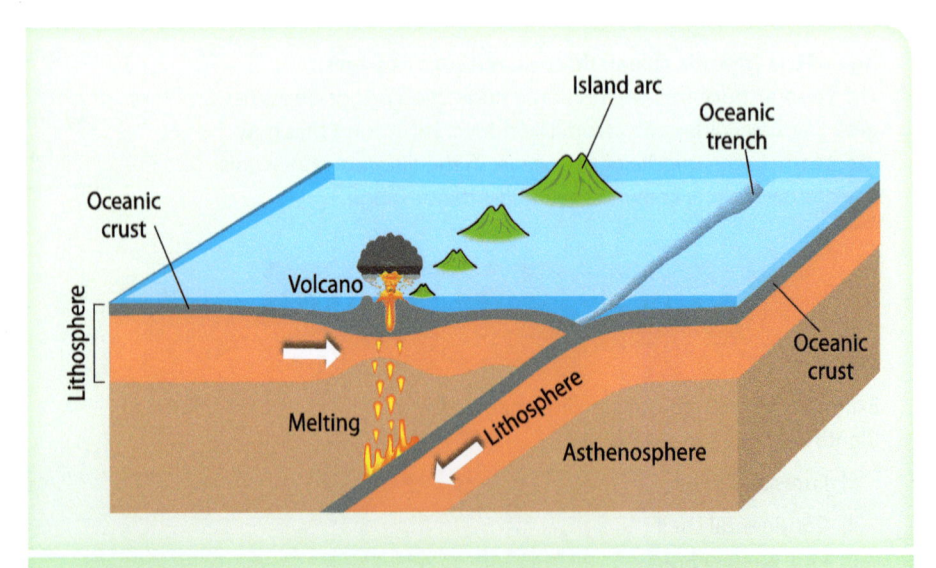

Figure 2.8 An island arc and ocean trench develop when two oceanic plates collide

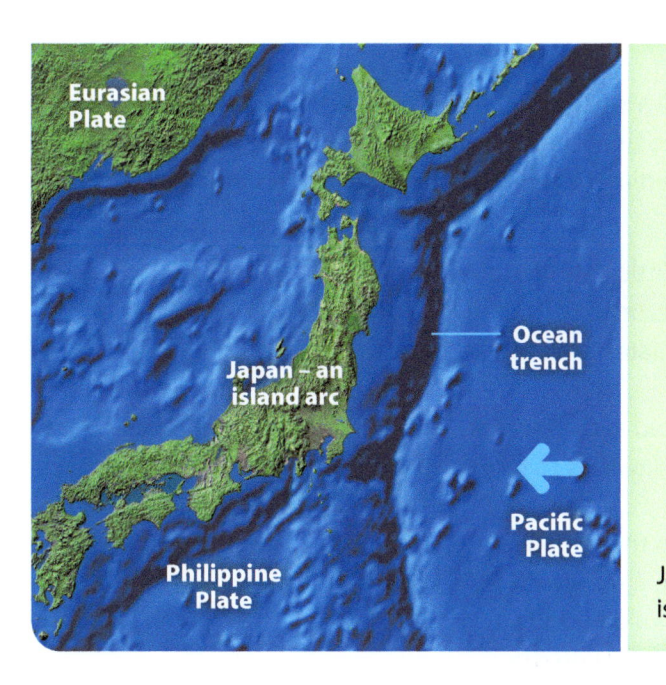

Japan is an island arc

LINK

See the case studies on the Japan earthquake (2011) and the Tibet earthquake (2015) on pages 42–44.

GEOFACTS

> There are more than 2,000 active volcanoes in the Chilean Andes.
> The Peru–Chile ocean trench runs parallel to the coast of South America for almost 6,000 km.

Oceanic–continental plate convergence

Continental crust is much lighter than oceanic crust. When these plates collide, the heavier oceanic plate **subducts** under the continental plate. The friction between the plates and the convection currents pulls the plates along, helped by slab-pull force. As the oceanic plate subducts, an **ocean trench** is formed.

> The stresses that result from the collision cause the edge of the continental plate to buckle upwards and a range of **fold mountains** is created. As the oceanic plate descends, it is heated and eventually melts. This produces magma.
> As the new magma begins to rise to the surface of the continental plate, **volcanoes** are formed. Sometimes the subducting plate becomes locked in place for a long time before moving suddenly, resulting in strong **earthquakes**.
> A good example of this type of boundary is found along the west coast of South America, where the Nazca Plate is being driven under the South American Plate. The **Andes** fold mountains have formed as a result.

Process
> Plate collision

Type of boundary
> Convergent (oceanic–continental)

Landforms
> Fold mountains
> Ocean trench
> Volcanoes

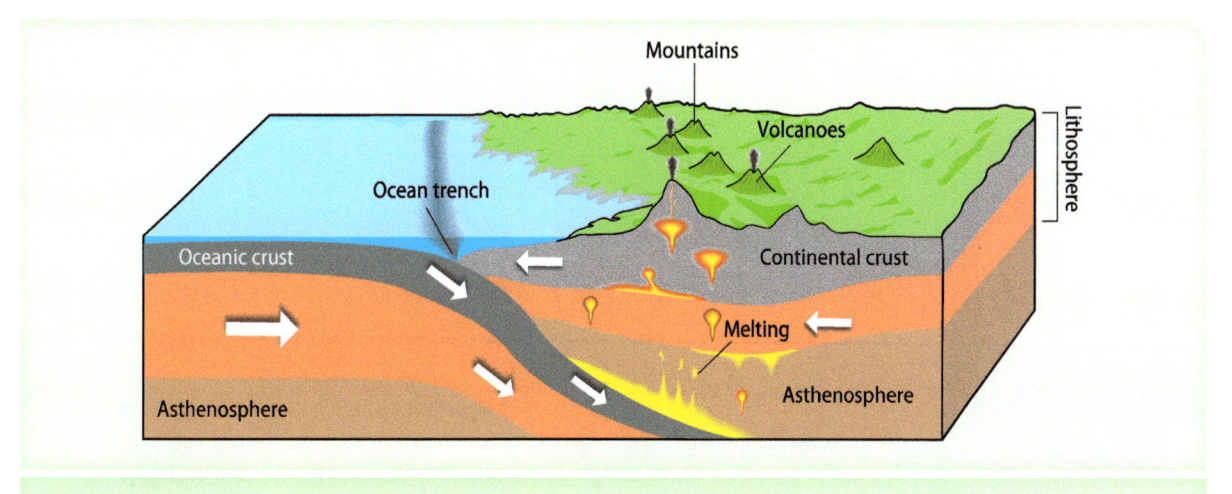

Figure 2.9 The Andes Mountains, along with a string of volcanoes, were formed when the Nazca Plate was subducted beneath the South American Plate

CHAPTER 2 · PLATE TECTONICS

UNIT 1 · PHYSICAL GEOGRAPHY

Continental–continental plate convergence

Continental–continental convergence begins with a sea between two continental plates. As the plates move closer, the ocean between them begins to close or shrink as the sediments on the seabed are compressed and buckled upwards.

> When two plates meet head on, there is very little subduction because both continental plates are very thick. Instead, the intense pressure fractures the edges of both plates and forces them to buckle upwards.
> As a result, a range of **fold mountains** is formed in the interior of a new continent. Material is also forced downwards to form deep mountain roots.
> This type of plate convergence occurred when the Indian Plate moved northwards and collided with the Eurasian Plate. After the initial collision, the two plates continued to drive into one another. Over millions of years, this has pushed up the Himalayas and the Tibetan Plateau to their present heights.
> Today, the Indian Plate continues to push into the Eurasian Plate at a rate of about 3 cm per year and the Himalayas continue to grow higher.

Process
> Plate collision

Type of boundary
> Convergent (continental–continental)

Landforms
> Fold mountains
> Plateau

ACTIVITY

Thinking
Why, in your opinion, are the Himalayas so high?

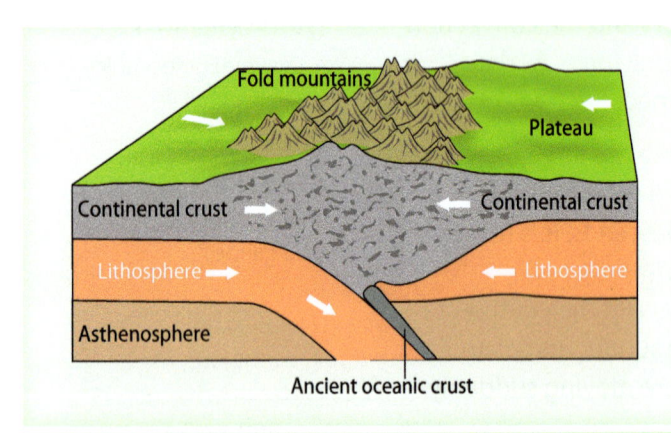

Figure 2.10 A continental–continental plate collision. The continental crust and its sediments are crumpled and thickened. This helps to create high mountains and a wide plateau.

Tibetan Plateau in the foreground, with the Himalayas in the background

Figure 2.11 Since it broke away from the African Plate about 90 million years ago, the Indian Plate has moved north. It eventually collided with the Eurasian Plate, leading to the formation of the Himalayas.

CASE STUDY

Ireland on the move

Plate movement has played a major part in shaping the Irish landscape.

1

About 800 million years ago (MYA): North-west Ireland and Scotland were part of the North American Plate and lay close to the equator. Southern Ireland, England and Wales lay almost as far south as the Antarctic Circle. Both plates were moving towards one another.

2

500–300 MYA: Ireland lay south of the equator. The ocean between the two sections closed. The collision of the plates resulted in folding, faulting, metamorphism and volcanic activity.

› See *The Leinster Batholith*, page 65.
› See *Caledonian folding*, page 26.

Sediments were eroded from uplands and washed into shallow seas, where they eventually formed sandstone.

› See *Old red sandstone*, page 76.

Sea levels later rose and Ireland was covered by a shallow tropical sea. This period saw the formation of limestone.

› See *Limestone*, page 77.
› See *The Burren*, page 110.

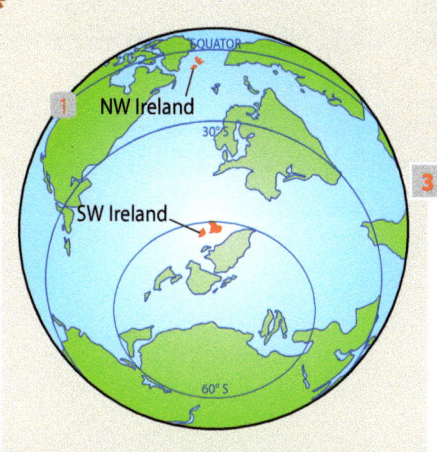

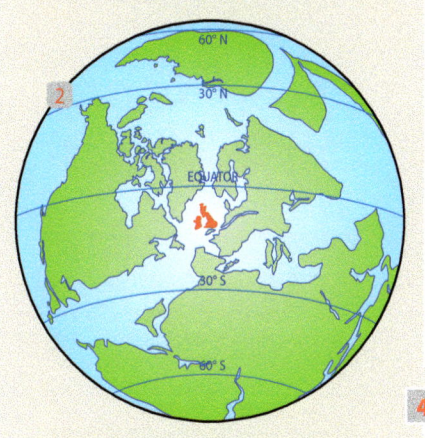

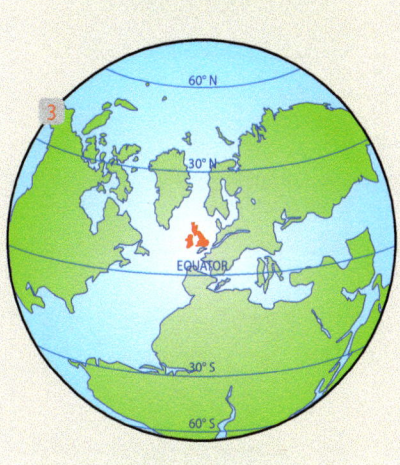

3

300–100 MYA: Continental drift continued. The Eurasian and African plates collided. This resulted in folding in the southern half of Ireland. Ireland was now part of the supercontinent Pangaea.

› See *Armorican folding*, page 26.

Pangaea began to break up. Marine sediments, rich in organic matter, were laid down. Over time, this matter transformed itself into oil and natural gas.

› See *Natural gas in Ireland*, page 83.

4

100 MYA–present: The European and American plates began to move apart and the Atlantic Ocean was born. As the rocks were stretched and cracked, volcanic activity resulted.

› See *The Antrim–Derry Plateau*, page 64.

All the above, and more, provided the foundation for the Irish landscape. Over time, mass movement, weathering and erosion have shaped the distinctive landscape that we have today. These processes are ongoing.

› See Chapters 7–14.

UNIT 1 · PHYSICAL GEOGRAPHY

PowerPoint Summary

SUMMARY CHART

- **Supercontinent Pangaea** → **Continental break-up** → **Tectonic plates**
- **Tectonic plates** → **Plate movement** → **Convection currents**
- **Plate movement** → **Plate boundaries**
- **Plate boundaries** → **Other terms**: Continental drift, Subduction, Slab-pull

Plate boundaries branch into:

Transform boundaries
- Plates slide past one another (Passive boundary)
  - Fault line
    Earthquakes
    (Pacific and American plates)

Divergent boundaries
- Plates break up or separate (Constructive boundary)
  - Plate break-up
    - Rift valley
      New seas
      (East Africa)
  - Mid-ocean separation
    - Mid-ocean ridge
      Volcanoes
      Volcanic islands
      (American and Eurasian plates)

Convergent boundaries
- Plates collide (Destructive boundary)
  - Oceanic–oceanic
    - Island arc
      Ocean trench
      Earthquakes
      (Pacific and Eurasian plates)
  - Oceanic–continental
    - Fold mountains
      Ocean trench
      Volcanoes
      (Nazca and South American plates)
  - Continental–continental
    - Fold mountains
      Plateau
      (Indian and Eurasian plates)

20 GEOGRAPHY TODAY

Leaving Cert exam questions

SHORT QUESTIONS: HIGHER LEVEL

1 **Plate tectonics** (8 marks)

   Examine the diagram and answer each of the following questions.

   (i) Name the type of plate boundary shown in the diagram.

   (ii) Name the type of plate at **A**.

   (iii) Name the process taking place at **B**.

   (iv) Name the part of the mantle at **C**.

2 **Plate tectonics** (8 marks)

   Examine the map and answer the questions that follow.

   (i) Name each of the plates **A**, **B**, **C** and **D**.

   (ii) Name the type of plate boundary at **E** and **F**.

   (iii) Name two plates that are colliding at **G**.

3 **Plate tectonics** (8 marks)

   Examine the diagram and answer each of the following questions.

   (i) Name the type of plate boundary illustrated.

   (ii) Name the feature at **A**.

   (iii) Name an igneous rock formed at **B**.

   (iv) Name the upper part of the mantle at **C**.

4 **Plate tectonics** (8 marks)

   Examine the diagram and answer each of the following questions.

   (i) Name the plates at **A** and **B**.

   (ii) Name the type of igneous rock most frequently found at **C**.

   (iii) State the age range of the crust at each of **C** and **D**.

   (iv) Explain briefly why the ocean crust at **D** is older than the ocean crust at **C**.

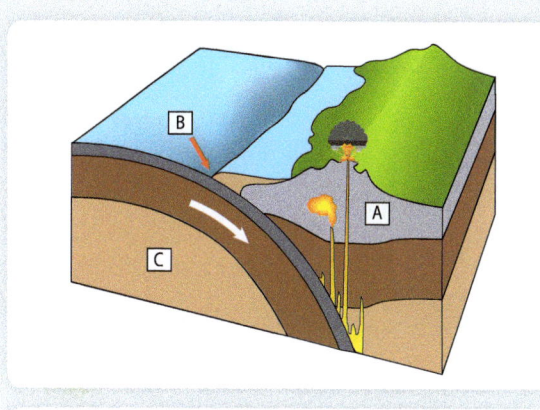

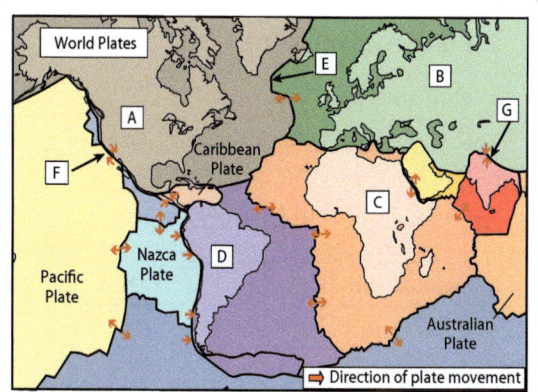

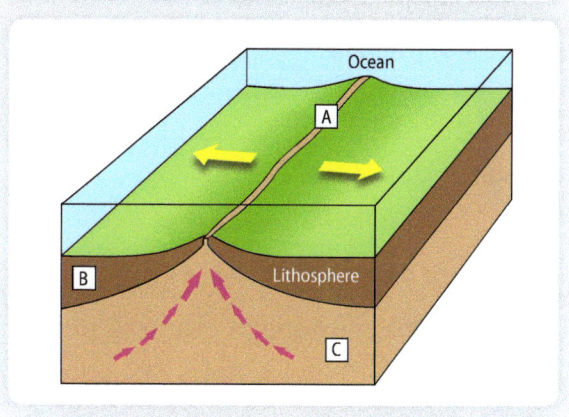

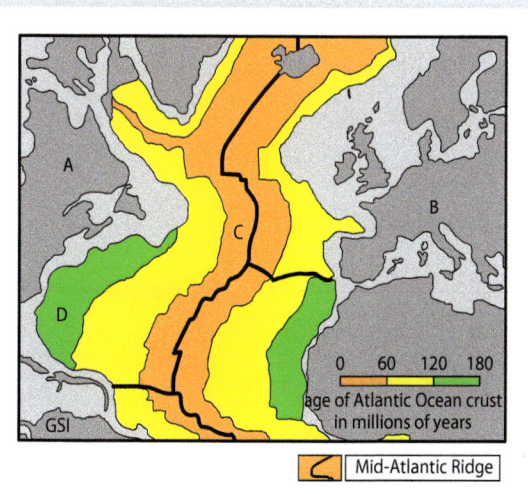

CHAPTER 2 · PLATE TECTONICS

UNIT 1 · PHYSICAL GEOGRAPHY

HL

5 Subduction zone (8 marks)

Examine the diagram and then match each of the named landforms in the table.

Feature	Letter
Asthenosphere	
Lithosphere	
Subduction zones	
Volcanic intrusions	

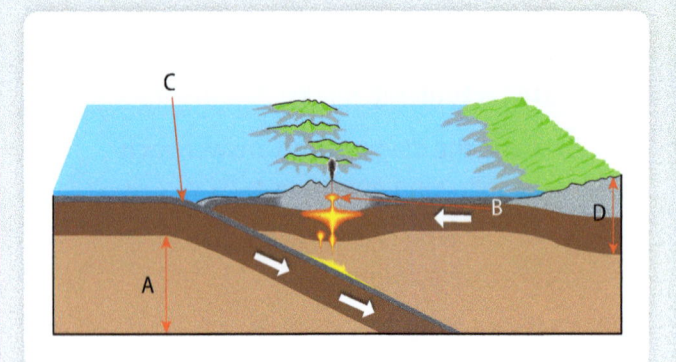

OL

SHORT QUESTIONS: ORDINARY LEVEL

1 Plate tectonics (10 marks)

Examine the diagram and then match each of the named landforms in the table with its correct letter in the diagram.

Landform	Letter
Volcanoes	
Mid-ocean ridge	
Subduction zone	
Rising magma	

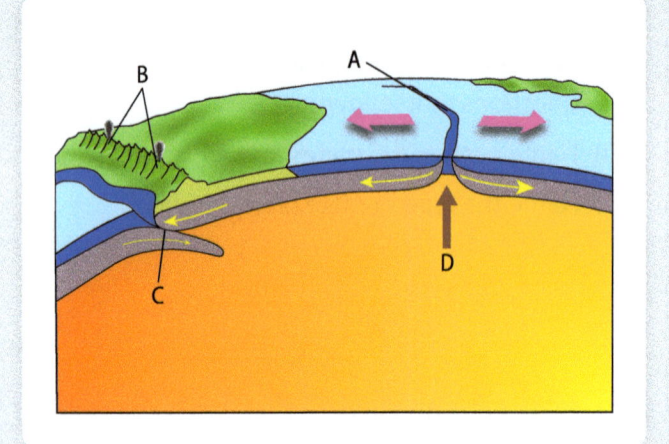

Name any volcano.	

HL

LONG QUESTIONS: HIGHER LEVEL

1 Plate boundaries (30 marks)

Describe and explain destructive plate boundaries.

OL

LONG QUESTIONS: ORDINARY LEVEL

1 Plate boundaries (30 marks)

Describe and explain the theory of plate tectonics.

2 Plate boundaries (30 marks)

Describe and explain what happens at plate boundaries.

3 Plate tectonics (40 marks)

Use this diagram to help explain plate tectonics.

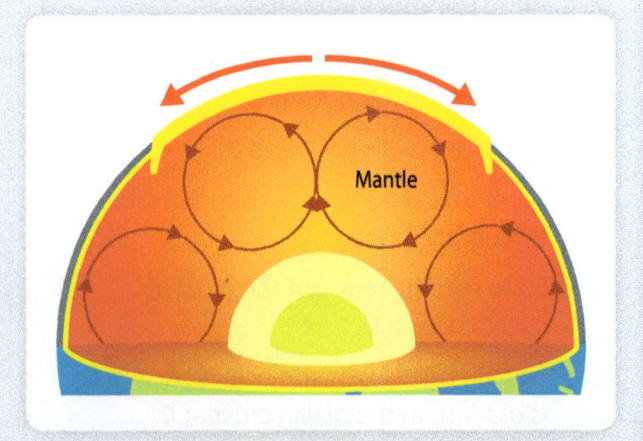

22 GEOGRAPHY TODAY

Chapter 3
Folding, Faulting and Doming

KEYWORDS

- deformation
- folding
- faulting
- compression
- tension
- shearing
- anticline
- syncline
- ridge and valley
- orogeny
- Caledonian
- Armorican
- Alpine
- block mountain
- rift valley
- normal fault
- tear fault
- reverse fault
- thrust fault
- doming

LEARNING OBJECTIVES

By the end of this chapter, you should be able to understand:

- The forces of rock deformation
- How rocks are deformed by folding, faulting and doming
- The structures that develop as a result of rock deformation
- The impact of these processes on the Irish landscape.

Deformation

Deformation refers to any change in the shape or size of rock as a result of stress. The solid rocks of the Earth's crust are deformed when force is applied to them during tectonic activity (plate movement). This deformation may take place at plate margins or within plates. It results in **folding**, **faulting** and **doming** in the rock body.

DEFINITIONS

Fold: A bend or curve in the stratified rocks of the Earth's crust.

Fault: A crack or fracture in the Earth's crust.

Dome: A structure shaped like an upturned bowl.

Forces of deformation

There are three types of forces involved in rock deformation:

- **Compression** squeezes and shortens the rock. It is associated with convergent plate movement. It results in folding and/or faulting in the rock.
- **Tension** stretches a body of rock. It is associated with divergent plate movement. It results in faulting in the rock.
- **Shearing** fractures the rock and pushes sections past one another. It is associated with both convergent and transform plate movement. It results in faulting in the rock.

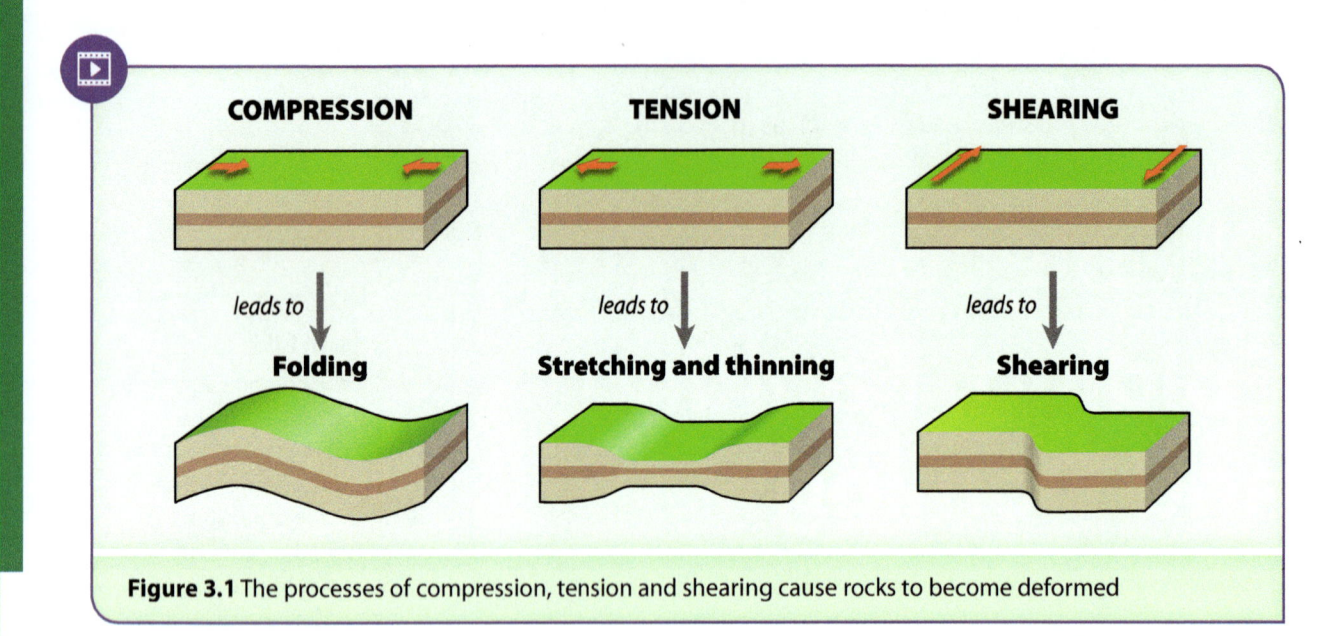

Figure 3.1 The processes of compression, tension and shearing cause rocks to become deformed

Folding

Most folding is linked with convergent plate margins. As the plates collide, the rocks are slowly compressed or squeezed together at the boundary. The crust crumples, forming **folds**. These folds can range from a few centimetres across to many kilometres across. Most folding occurs in sedimentary rocks because they are weaker and more flexible.

When the rocks are compressed, the layers are pushed up to form **anticlines** or pushed down to form **synclines**. Strong pressure and high temperatures over a long period of time can enable rocks to fold without breaking.

Processes
› Compression
› Folding

Type of boundary
› Convergent

Landform
› Fold mountains

QUESTIONS

1 What force is involved in the formation of fold mountains?
2 What type of plate boundary does folding occur at?

ACTIVITY

Thinking
1 Explain the following terms:
  (i) Fold   (ii) Fault.
2 Explain how the following forces deform rocks:
  (i) Compression   (ii) Tension
  (iii) Shearing.
3 Explain the difference between the following:
  (i) Fold   (ii) Anticline
  (iii) Syncline   (iv) Limb.

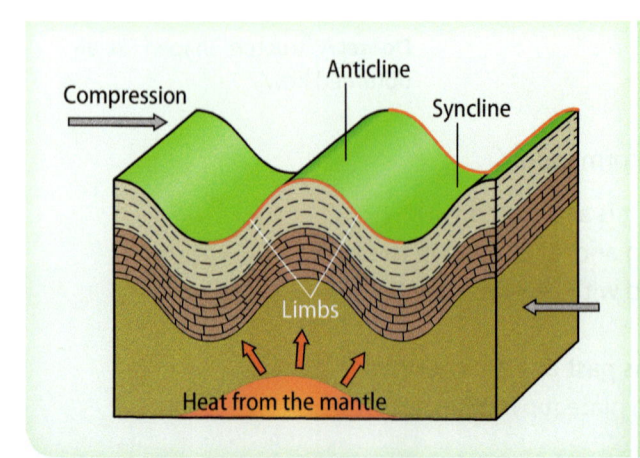

Figure 3.2 An upfold is called an **anticline**. A downfold is called a **syncline**. The sides or flanks of each are called **limbs**. Folding may lead to a so-called 'ridge and valley' landscape.

Types of folds

Where compression is more intense, such as in mountain belts, the rocks are further deformed into a series of different fold shapes.

GEOFACT

These forces are most obvious in sedimentary rocks because most sedimentary strata are horizontal when they are laid down.

Simple fold
This fold has two limbs of equal steepness because compression is applied equally from both sides. It is also called a **symmetric fold**.

Asymmetric fold
One limb is steeper than the other in this fold because greater compression is applied to one side of the fold than the other.

Overfold
When compression from one side is much greater, one limb is pushed over the other limb.

Recumbent fold
As the compression continues, the folds eventually lie almost horizontally on top of one another.

Overthrust fold
Finally, the compression force is so great that the rock strata fracture (fault) and one limb is pushed up and over the other limb. As a result, the strata are no longer continuous. (See Figure 3.10 on page 31.)

Figure 3.3 Various types of folds develop as the pressure from compression becomes more intense

Fold mountain building

There have been three major phases of fold mountain building (or orogeny). These are the Caledonian, Armorican and Alpine orogenies.

DEFINITION

Orogeny: The term used to describe a period of mountain building.

Severe folding in a body of sedimentary rocks

Caledonian folding

Caledonian folding took place about 400 million years ago when the American and Eurasian plates collided at a continental–continental boundary. Because of the directions the two land masses travelled in, the folds have a SW–NE trend.

> When they were first pushed up, the Caledonian mountains were probably higher than today's Alps. They have since been reduced by weathering and erosion, exposing the igneous rocks that lay under the sedimentary strata. Caledonian fold mountains include the Highlands of Scotland and the Appalachians of North America.

> In Ireland, Caledonian folding is found in the west and north-west (Maamturk Mountains, Twelve Pins, Bluestack Mountains) and in the east (Dublin Mountains and Wicklow Mountains).

Armorican folding

Armorican folding occurred about 250 million years ago following a collision between the Eurasian and African plates. The pressure came from the south as the African Plate drove into the Eurasian Plate.

> As a result, these mountains have an E–W trend. Armorican fold mountains are found in England, France and Germany.

> The so-called 'ridge and valley' landscape of Munster is also the result of Armorican folding.

Alpine folding

Alpine folding is the most recent period of mountain building. It reached its peak about 30 million years ago but still continues slowly today.

> It occurred when the African and Indian continental plates collided with the Eurasian Plate. As these are 'young' fold mountains, they are very high and have not yet been lowered by weathering and erosion.

> Alpine mountain ranges include the Himalayas, Rockies and Alps. This period of folding is not represented in Ireland.

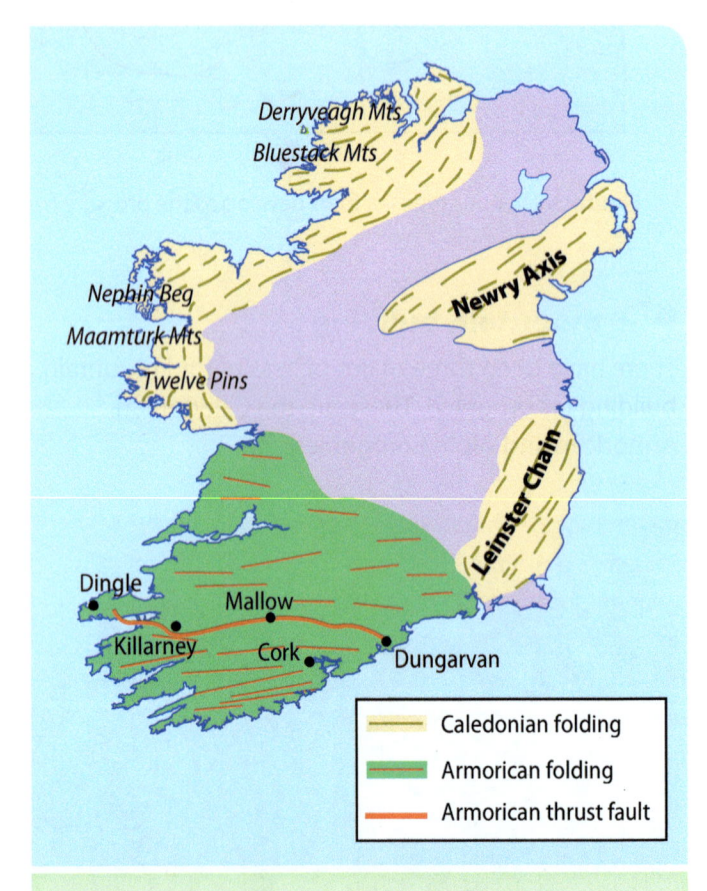

Figure 3.4 Two periods of fold mountain building are represented in Ireland. The older Caledonian folds have a SW–NE trend. The more recent Armorican folds have an E–W trend.

CASE STUDY

Armorican folds in Ireland

Ireland lay north of the main collision zone of the African and Eurasian plates. Most of the folding that occurred was confined to Munster. Since the compression came from the south, these mountains have an E–W trend.

Horizontal strata (layers) of shale, sandstone and limestone were buckled and folded into anticlines and synclines. The result is a 'ridge and valley' landscape that runs from Kerry through Cork and into West Waterford.

The mountain ranges that make up this landscape include the Macgillycuddy's Reeks, Galtee Mountains and Comeragh Mountains.

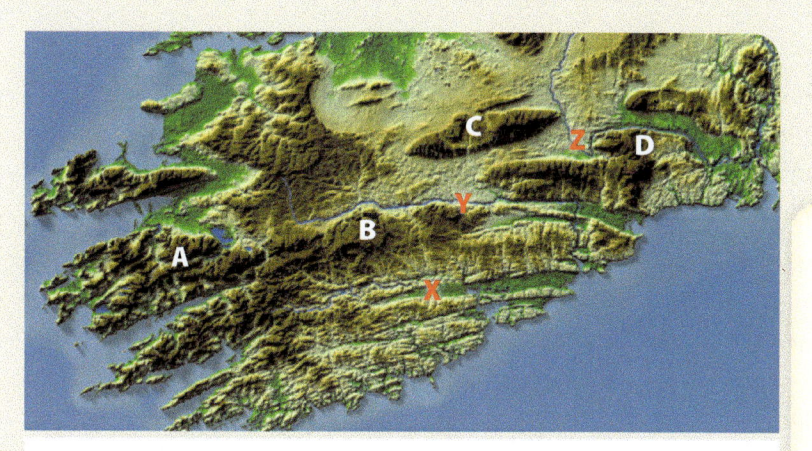

A ridge and valley landscape has developed in Munster following the Armorican period of folding. Note the E–W trend.

ACTIVITY

Research

With the aid of an atlas:
(i) Identify the mountain ranges marked **A**, **B**, **C** and **D**.
(ii) Identify the rivers that occupy the valleys at **X**, **Y** and **Z**.

Over millions of years, the overlying folds of limestone and chalk have been removed from the ridges by weathering and erosion. This has exposed the underlying old red sandstone (ORS). The valley floors still have their cover of limestone and shale. Rivers, including the Blackwater, Lee and Bandon, occupy the valley floors and form a trellis drainage pattern (see page 136).

The Bandon River (here at Innishannon) occupies the floor of an anticline formed during the Armorican period of folding

ACTIVITY

Discussion

Refer to the photograph on the right.

1 Give two pieces of information that suggest the village is located in an anticline.
2 Why did the village of Innishannon develop back from the river?

CHAPTER 3 · FOLDING, FAULTING AND DOMING

UNIT 1 · PHYSICAL GEOGRAPHY

27

Faulting

When rocks are subjected to too much stress, they eventually fracture. When there is movement of rock along one or both sides of the fracture, it is known as a **fault**. Faulting usually takes place along zones of weakness in the crust. The movement of rock may be vertical or horizontal or a combination of both. The rock may slip as little as a centimetre in a single fault movement. Over time, this can add up to hundreds of kilometres.

Faults are classified according to the type of movement that takes place. The three main types of fault are:

> Normal fault
> Tear fault
> Reverse fault.

Processes
> Compression
> Tension
> Shearing

Type of boundary
> Convergent
> Divergent
> Transform

Landforms
> Faults
> Scarps

Normal fault

A **normal fault** results from tension stress in the crust. The crust is extended until a fault eventually occurs. The movement is mainly vertical, where one block of crust slips downwards relative to the other. It results in a very steep fault slope. The exposed section is called a **scarp**.

> Sometimes two or more parallel faults occur in the same area as a result of the stretching of the Earth's surface. If the block between the two faults slips down, a long, narrow trough called a **rift valley** (or graben) is formed. Lough Neagh is in a rift valley. It lies between the same two parallel faults that formed the Scottish Rift Valley. These faults merge at Killary Harbour (see Figure 3.8 on page 30).
> If the surface on the outside of the faults slips down, a structure called a **block mountain** (or horst) is left standing above the general level. The structure may take the form of a plateau or mountain mass with two steep, straight sides.
> In Ireland, the Ox Mountains, formed of igneous rock, stand above the surrounding landscape. The limestone to the north and south has slipped down. Rift valleys and block mountains can occur separately or side by side. (See *Continental break-up*, page 13.)

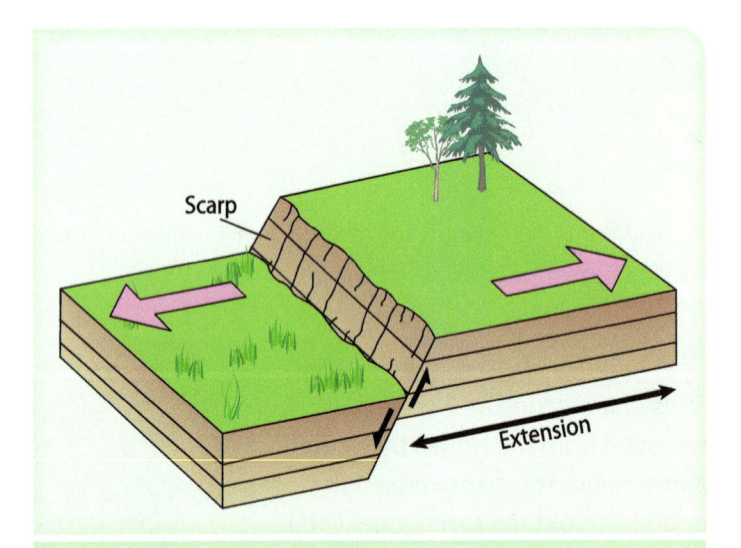

Figure 3.5 A normal fault. One block slips down as the crust is stretched by tension.

This scarp developed following an earthquake along a fault in California

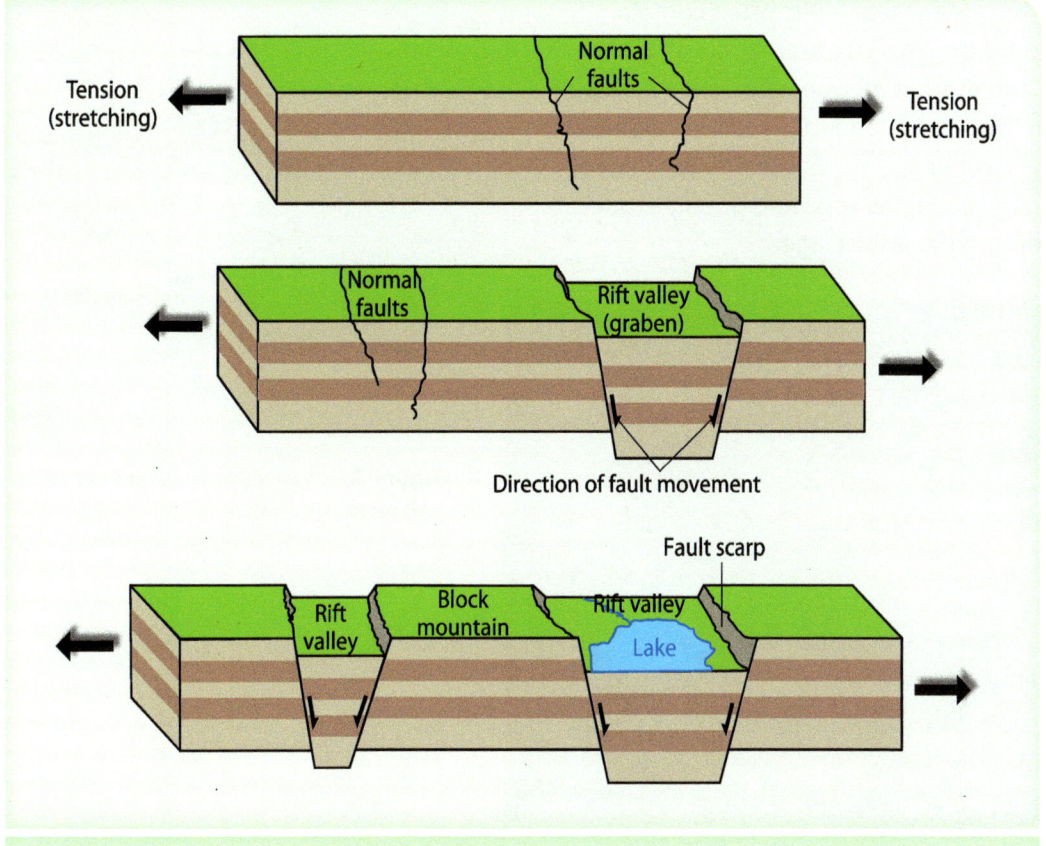

Figure 3.6 Block mountains (horsts) and rift valleys (grabens) occur where parallel faults have developed. They may occur separately or together.

Tear fault

A **tear fault** is a fracture in the rock. It happens when one block moves sideways or horizontally past another block instead of up and down. Rocks on either side of the fault may move in opposite directions or in the same direction but at different rates.

- The San Andreas Fault is the best-known and largest tear fault system in North America. Here, the Pacific Plate and American Plate grind past one another at an average rate of 5 cm per year. (See *Transform plate boundaries*, page 12.)
- The Leannan Fault (Co. Donegal) is thought to be an extension of the Great Glen Fault in Scotland. It is estimated that the block north of this fault has moved in a SW direction for about 100 km relative to the rock on the south side of the fault.

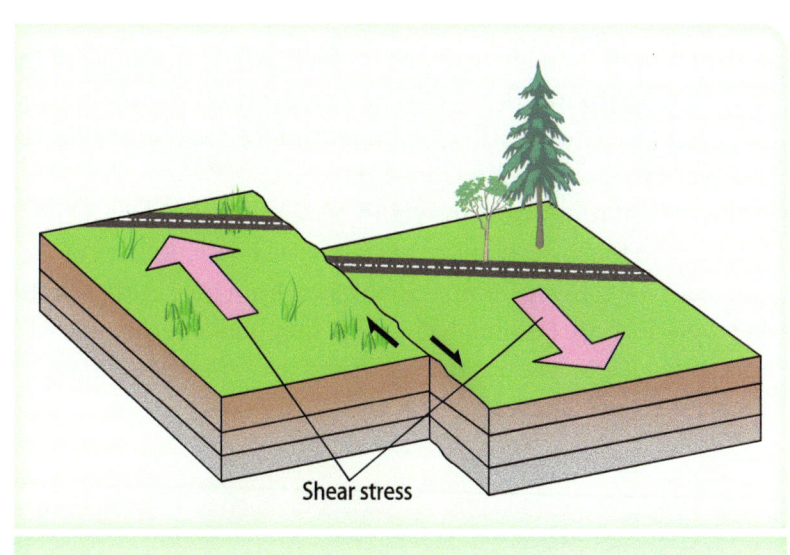

Figure 3.7 Rocks are moved in a horizontal direction by a tear fault

CHAPTER 3 · FOLDING, FAULTING AND DOMING

› Zones on either side of tear faults often contain badly crushed rocks. This creates a situation where weathering and erosion are very effective. As a result, the Leannan River has cut deeply into the Leannan Fault. Killary Harbour and the Eriff Valley (Co. Mayo) lie along similar fault lines and were deeply eroded by glaciers during the last ice age.

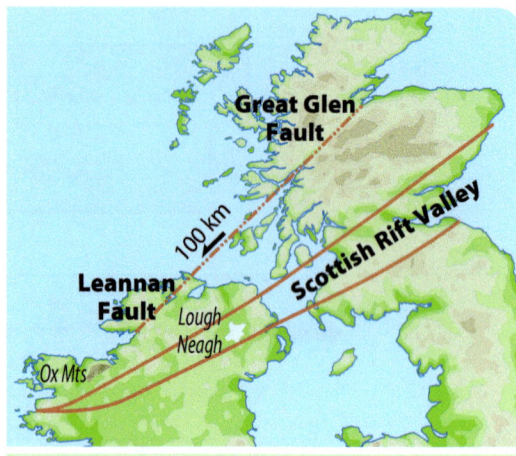

Figure 3.8 Rift valleys and tear faults in Ireland and Scotland

The Great Glen in Scotland is the result of a tear fault. Long, narrow lakes, including Loch Ness, occupy the fault floor.

Reverse fault

A **reverse fault** is the opposite of a normal fault. It results when rocks in the crust are subjected to compression during earth movements. The compression is so great that the folded rocks fracture. One block is forced forward and up. It rides over the other block and there is an overall shortening of the crust.

› A **thrust fault** is one type of reverse fault, where the angle of the fault is almost horizontal. The overlying rock layers can be pushed forward for great distances. Blocks of younger surface rocks are buried beneath the block that was pushed forward.
› A thrust fault runs across the south of Ireland, roughly in a line from Killarney to Mallow. For much of its length, it follows the course of the Blackwater River. Compression came from the south, resulting in severe folding. Eventually the folds snapped and the old red sandstone (ORS) was pushed north and over the carboniferous limestone. (See Figures 3.3 and 3.4.)

ACTIVITY

Discussion

Why are reverse faults and thrust faults similar?

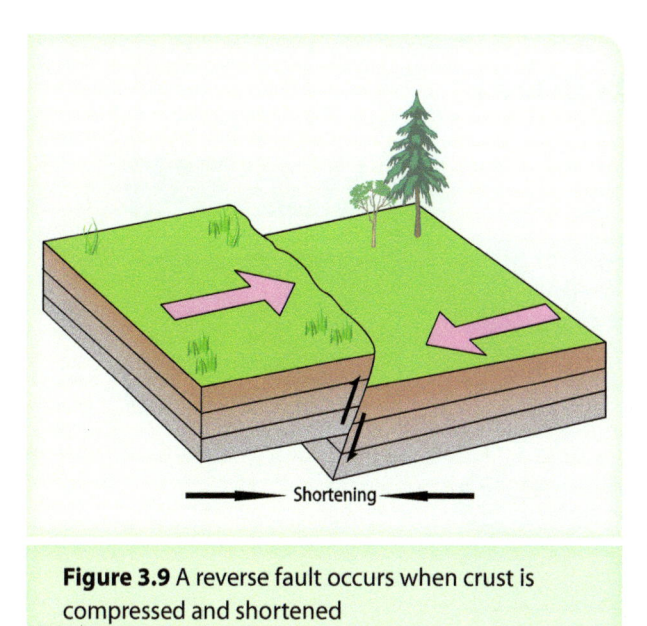

Figure 3.9 A reverse fault occurs when crust is compressed and shortened

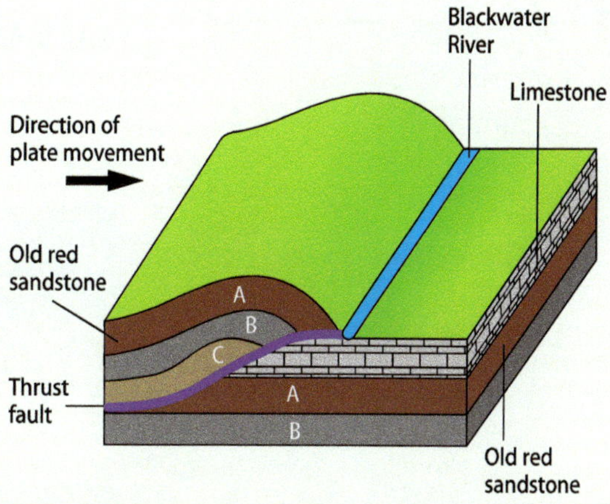

Figure 3.10 A thrust fault runs right across the south of Ireland, roughly in a line from Killarney to Mallow. For much of its length, it coincides with the course of the Blackwater River.

Doming

A **dome** is a structure that is shaped like an upturned bowl. It slopes out in all directions from the highest point.

› The original structure was either a bed of flat-lying sedimentary rocks or an anticline. Great amounts of molten magma then pushed up under the Earth's crust. The rising magma forced the overlying rock layers further upward to form the dome. The rock layers of the surrounding area remained flat.
› Over time, the highest part of the dome faced the effects of weathering and erosion. As a result, the older rock layers in the centre of the dome were exposed. The younger rocks then formed its outer rim.
› The **Slieve Bloom Mountains** (Laois–Offaly) were formed by doming. Weathering and erosion have removed the highest parts of the dome. We now see the oldest shale and slate exposed in its centre, while the sandstone and limestone form its outer rim.

ACTIVITY

Thinking

Why are rocks at the centre of a denuded dome older than the rocks that surround it?

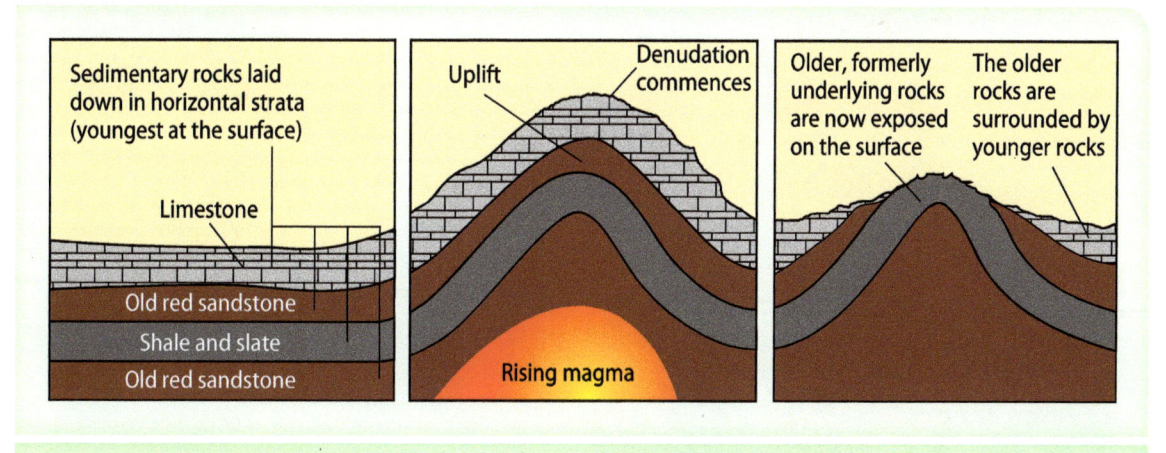

Figure 3.11 Cross-section showing the development of a sedimentary dome

CHAPTER 3 · FOLDING, FAULTING AND DOMING

31

UNIT 1 · PHYSICAL GEOGRAPHY

PowerPoint Summary

SUMMARY CHART

Deformation of rocks → **Forces of deformation**
- Compression
- Tension
- Shearing

Deformation of rocks → **Impacts of deformation**

Impacts of deformation branches into: Folding, Doming, Faulting

Folding
- **Types of folds**: Simple, Asymmetric, Overfold, Recumbent, Overthrust (fault), Blackwater Valley
- **Periods of folding**: Alpine, Armorican, Caledonian
  - 400 MYA, SW–SE trend, Leinster Chain, NW Ireland
  - 250 MYA, W–E trend, Munster ridge and valley, Magillicuddy's Reeks, Comeragh Mountains

Doming
- Sedimentary dome
- Slieve Bloom Mountains

Faulting
- **Types of faults**: Normal, Tear, Reverse, Thrust
- **Landforms**: Scarp, Rift valley (graben), Block mountain (horst), Ox Mountains, Scotland Lough Neagh

GEOGRAPHY TODAY

Leaving Cert exam questions

SHORT QUESTIONS: HIGHER LEVEL

1 Faultlines (8 marks)

Examine the diagrams showing four types of fault. In the space provided, write each of these labels in the appropriate space: **Transform** (twice), **Reverse** and **Normal**.

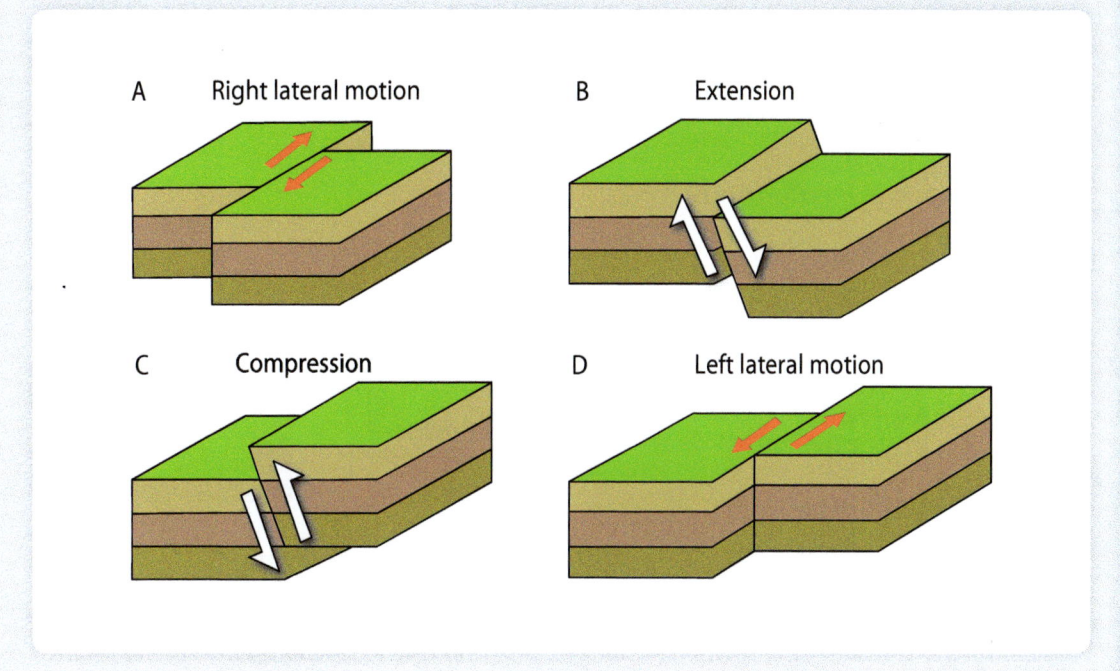

A — Right lateral motion
B — Extension
C — Compression
D — Left lateral motion

Letter	Fault type
A	
B	

Letter	Fault type
C	
D	

SHORT QUESTIONS: ORDINARY LEVEL

1 Folding (10 marks)

(i) Examine the diagram and link each of the letters **A**, **B**, **C** and **D** with one of the terms in the table.

Term	Letter
Block mountain	
Compression	
Extension	
Rift valley	

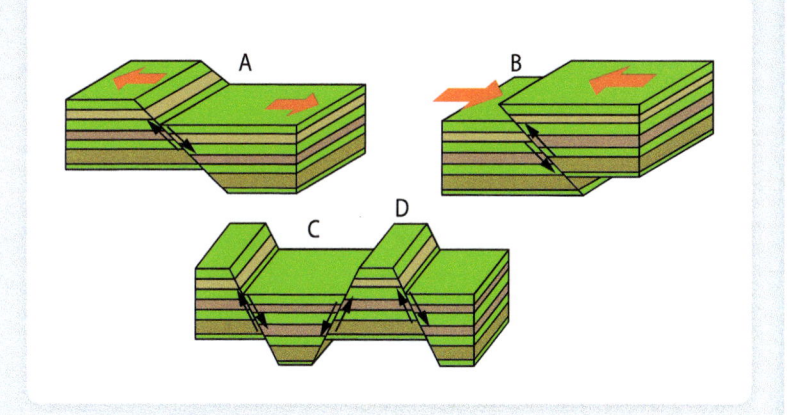

(ii) Name **one** range of fold mountains found in Ireland.

CHAPTER 3 · FOLDING, FAULTING AND DOMING

LONG QUESTIONS: HIGHER LEVEL

1 Landform development (30 marks)

Examine how one of the following influences the development of landforms:

> Folding
> Faulting.

2 Folding (30 marks)

Explain, with reference to examples you have studied, how folding impacts on landscape development.

3 Faulting and landforms (20 marks)

Examine the diagram and answer the following questions.

(i) Name the type of fault at **A** and the type of fault at **B**.

(ii) Explain briefly what causes the faulting at **A** or **B**.

(iii) Name the landform at **C** and the landform at **D** that results from faulting.

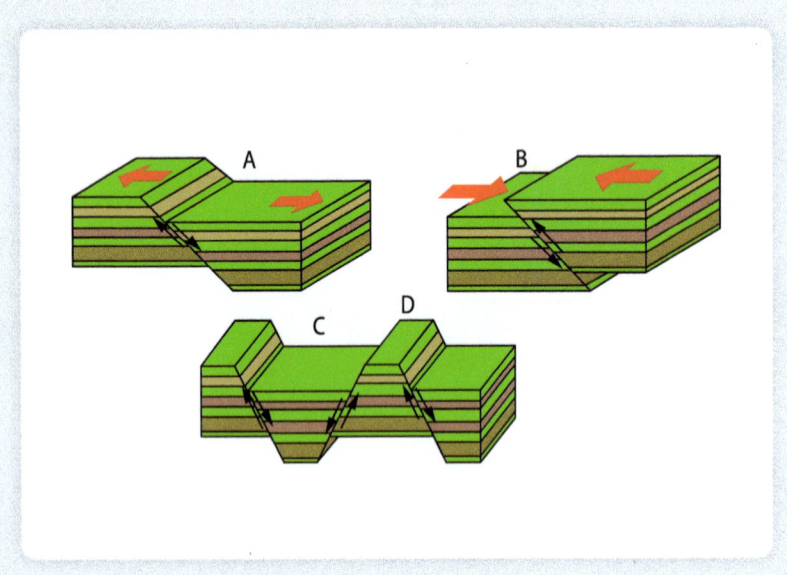

4 Tectonic activity – Irish landscape development (30 marks)

Examine the impact of tectonic activity on the development of the Irish landscape.

5 Structures of deformation (30 marks)

Examine the impact of folding and faulting on the landscape. In your answer, refer to **one** landform in each case.

6 Folding (30 marks)

Explain how the study of plate tectonics has helped us to understand the global distribution of fold mountains.

LONG QUESTIONS: ORDINARY LEVEL

1 Fold mountains (30 marks)

(i) Name **one** example of fold mountains.

(ii) With the aid of a diagram(s), explain how fold mountains are formed.

Chapter 4
Earthquakes

KEYWORDS

- tremors
- aftershocks
- focus
- epicentre
- seismic waves
- body (P and S) waves
- surface waves
- seismograph
- Richter scale
- magnitude
- Mercalli scale
- intensity
- seismic gap
- liquefaction
- tsunami

LEARNING OBJECTIVES

By the end of this chapter, you should be able to understand:

- What an earthquake is
- Why earthquakes occur
- The global pattern of earthquakes
- How earthquakes are located and measured
- How earthquakes may be predicted
- How earthquake damage may be limited
- The impacts of earthquakes.

What is an earthquake?

An **earthquake** is a sudden movement or shaking of the Earth's crust. This releases a large quantity of energy in the form of **seismic waves**. The waves then race through the crust, giving off a series of shocks called **tremors**.

While most major earthquakes occur without warning, some may be preceded by small bursts of shaking called **foreshocks**. Major earthquakes are usually followed by many lesser-scale earthquakes called **aftershocks**.

The place where the energy is first released deep below the Earth's surface is called the **focus**.

The point on the Earth's surface directly above the focus is called the **epicentre**. This is the point where the tremors first reach the surface. The effects of the earthquake are usually at their strongest and the most damage is done here.

> **DEFINITION**
>
> **Seismology:** The study of earthquakes.

What causes earthquakes?

The plates of the Earth's crust are constantly moving. Since the edges of the plates are rough, the plates sometimes jam or stick together. This puts the rocks in the plates under enormous **stress**. A build-up of energy occurs and this energy is stored in the rocks.

When there is too much stress, the plates slip. The built-up energy is suddenly released. It spreads outward from the fault in all directions in the form of **seismic waves**, like ripples on a pond. An earthquake has occurred!

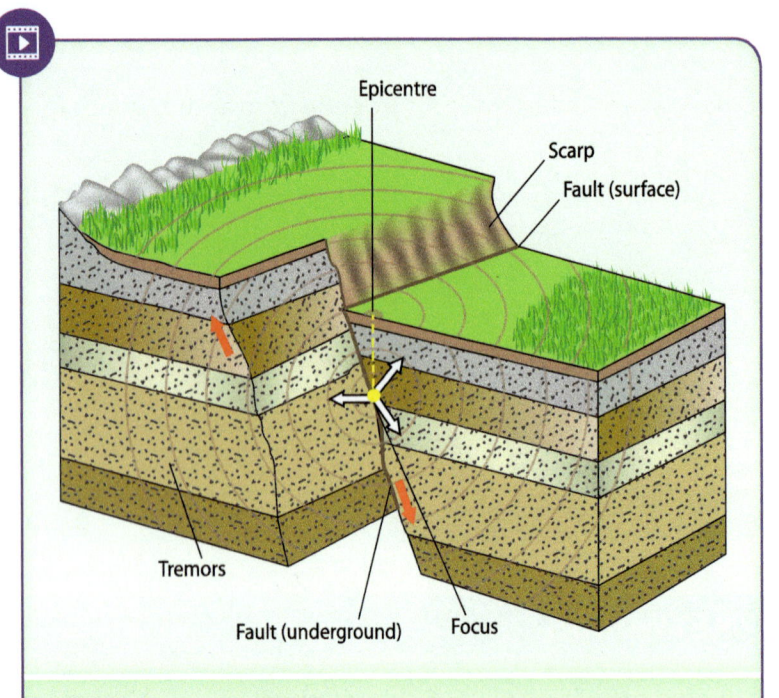

Figure 4.1 As seismic waves move further away from the epicentre, they get weaker

Transform plate boundaries	Divergent plate boundary	Continental collision boundary	Subduction zone boundary
Earthquakes tend to be shallow but powerful	Earthquakes tend to be shallow and weak	Most earthquakes are deep and also very powerful	The deepest and the most powerful earthquakes occur at subduction zones

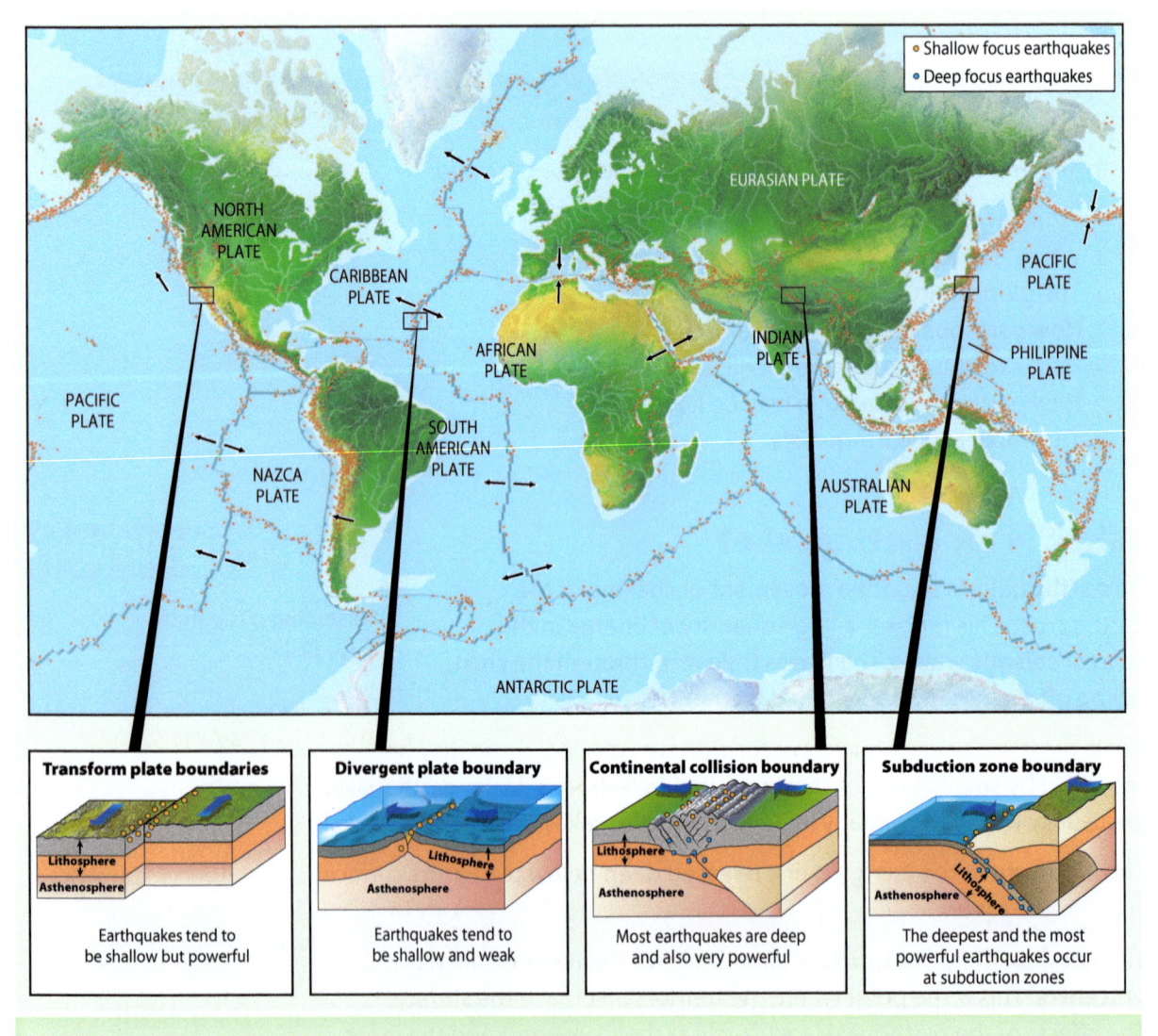

Figure 4.2 Most earthquakes occur along plate margins

Depth and distribution of earthquakes

Earthquakes can happen at any depth, from at the surface to about 700 km deep.

- **Shallow focus** earthquakes occur when the focus is close to the surface (less than 80 km deep). They are much more common than deep focus earthquakes. Unfortunately, they cause most damage on the surface of the Earth. This is because they are closer to the surface and therefore produce stronger shaking.
- **Deep focus** earthquakes have a focus greater than 300 km and up to 700 km deep. They rarely cause damage on the surface because their energy is lost before it reaches the surface.

Most earthquakes occur at **plate boundaries**, where plates collide, diverge and slide past one another. The most obvious earthquake zone is the Pacific belt. This is a zone of seismic activity that almost circles the Pacific Ocean. It overlaps with zones where continental and oceanic plates are in collision.

- The **subduction** zone off the coast of Japan is the most earthquake-prone area in the world. Here, the Pacific Plate is subducting beneath the Eurasian and Philippine plates. In March 2011, an earthquake occurred off the coast of Japan that resulted in a major **tsunami** that devastated the region (see *Japan earthquake*, page 42).
- Massive earthquakes also occur when two continental **plates collide**. The Himalayan mountain range is the best active example of this type of plate boundary. Major earthquakes hit Nepal in 2015 and India in 2016 (see *Nepal earthquake*, page 42).
- Many earthquakes occur at **transform fault boundaries**, where plates slide past one another. The most famous is California's San Andreas Fault. Other transform boundaries are more destructive, such as the plate boundary that runs through Haiti and other Caribbean countries.
- Earthquakes also occur at **divergent** plate boundaries, such as near the Mid-Atlantic Ridge. These are few in number and not very strong.

ACTIVITY

Thinking

Explain the following terms:
(i) Transform plate boundary
(ii) Convergent plate boundary
(iii) Subduction zone.

GEOFACTS

- Although more than half a million earthquakes occur each year, only about fifty are strong enough to cause damage.
- The largest earthquake ever reported in Ireland occurred off the coast of Anglesey (the Welsh coast) in 1984. It measured 5.4 on the Richter scale.

The San Andreas Fault runs through California and is an earthquake zone (see Figure 2.5 on page 12)

Seismic waves

Earthquake energy travels in **seismic waves**. These waves are classified according to where and how they move. There are two basic groups of waves:

› Surface waves
› Body waves.

Surface waves

Surface waves are the slowest type of waves. They travel close to the surface of the Earth and cause it to shake side to side as well as up and down. The latter is similar to the way a boat is tossed about in a body of water. Surface waves are very destructive as they generally have the strongest vibrations.

Body waves

Body waves pass through the interior (or body) of the Earth.

› **P waves** (P stands for primary) are fast waves that travel through the mainly molten interior of the Earth. As they travel, they compress and expand the material, causing it to vibrate back and forth. This is similar to the movement of a toy slinky spring.
› **S waves** (S stands for secondary) follow more slowly. As they travel, they cause the material to vibrate at right angles to the wave. This is similar to the way a rope moves when it is tied at one end and shaken.

Except in the most powerful earthquakes, body waves generally do not cause much damage.

ACTIVITY

Discussion

Why are surface waves more powerful than body waves?

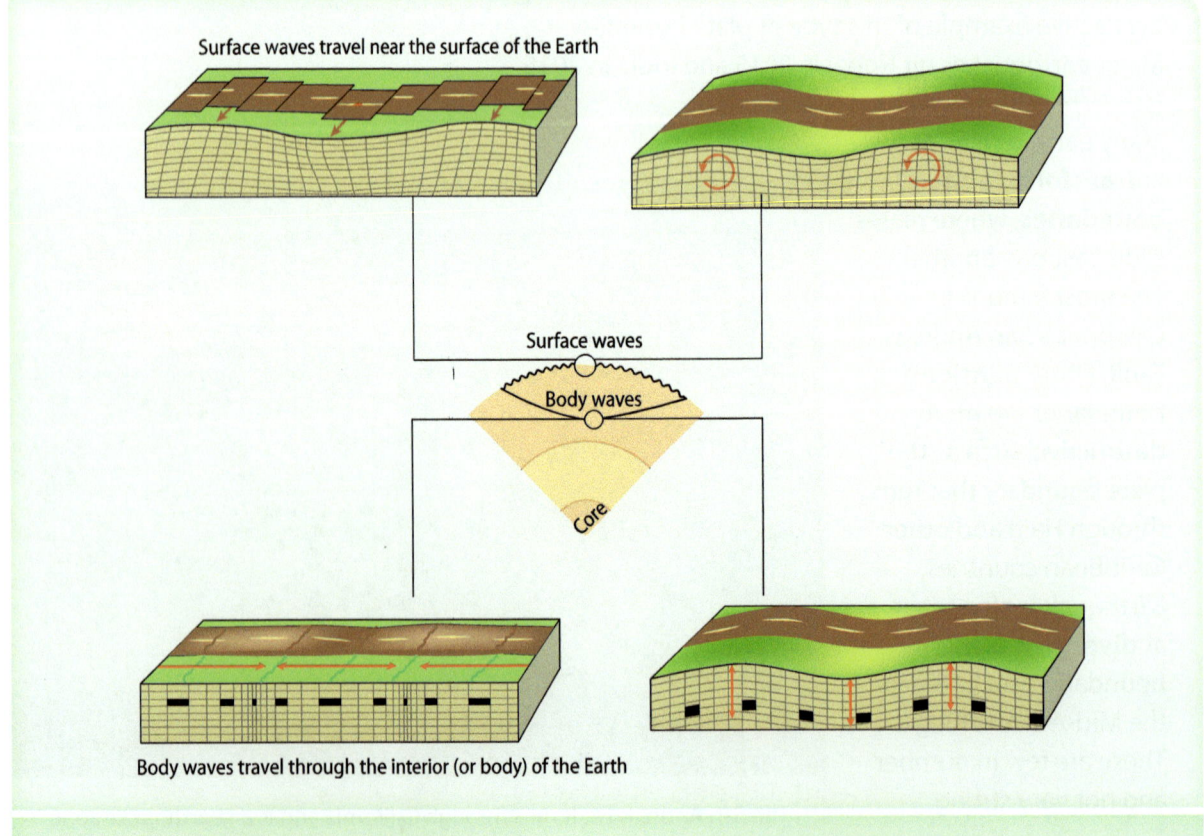

Figure 4.3 The different types of seismic waves

Recording and measuring earthquake data

How is the data recorded?

A **seismograph** measures and records earthquake (seismic) waves. It does this by recording the motion of the ground during an earthquake.

A simple seismograph works by having a pen attached to a weight and hanging it from a spring. When the ground shakes, the drum moves with it. The weight on the pen keeps it from moving. The pen then graphs this movement on the drum. The more violent the quake, the greater the width of the graph.

Three seismographs are required to gather a full set of measurements. Two are used to measure horizontal movement (E–W and N–S). A third is used to measure vertical movement. These readings are transmitted from a global network of more than 150 recording stations. Many of these stations are located in remote regions.

Figure 4.4 A simple seismograph. This model measures horizontal (side-to-side) motion.

Figure 4.5 Seismic waves travel at different speeds

What data is recorded?

The two main characteristics of an earthquake that are measured are:

› Magnitude
› Intensity.

Magnitude

Magnitude is a measure of the amount of energy released during an earthquake. This is sometimes referred to as the *size* of the earthquake. It remains unchanged with distance from the earthquake's epicentre.

› Magnitude is determined by using measurements from seismographs. It is described by the **Richter scale**. This is a logarithmic scale, which means that for each unit increase on the scale, seismic waves are ten times as large. For example, an earthquake that measures 7 on the Richter scale has seismic waves that are ten times larger than an earthquake that measures 6 on the scale.
› However, the energy released by an earthquake increases at an even greater rate. For each unit increase in the Richter scale, the amount of energy that is released is more than thirty times greater. Thus, an earthquake of magnitude 8 has about 900 (30 x 30) times more destructive energy than an earthquake of magnitude 6.

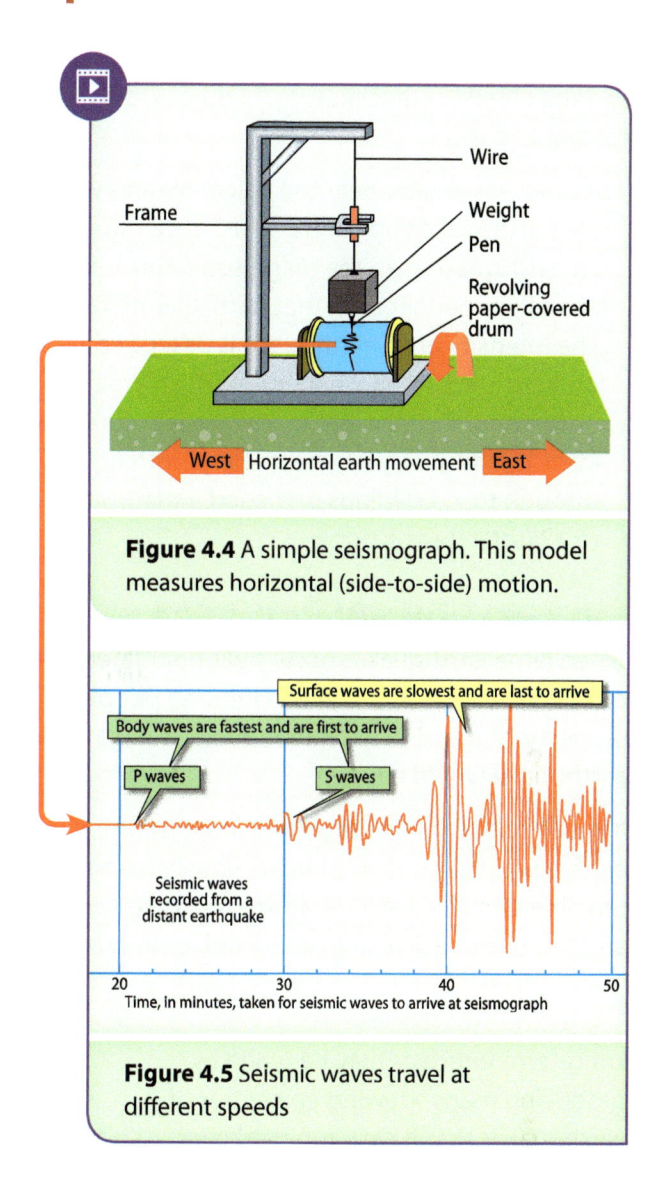

ACTIVITY

Research

Look up 'introduction to earthquakes video' on the internet.

Intensity

Intensity refers to the effect of an earthquake on the Earth's surface. It describes the degree of shaking caused by an earthquake at a given place and the effects of that shaking. In other words, intensity is how *strong* the earthquake was.

> Intensity is greater near the epicentre and weakens with distance from the earthquake's epicentre. Thus, it is a more meaningful description of an earthquake than the magnitude. This is because it refers to the effects actually experienced at that particular place.
> The intensity of an earthquake is described by the **Mercalli scale**. It is based on what people in an area feel and their observations of damage to buildings around them. It ranges from 1 (felt by very few people and with no damage), through to 7 (buildings damaged and furniture overturned) to 12 (total destruction).

ACTIVITY

Research

Look up Mercalli scale on the internet.

Forecasting earthquakes

When large earthquakes occur near populated areas, they have catastrophic results, killing and injuring people as well as destroying property. Much of this could be avoided if we knew where and when an earthquake would happen.

It is possible to make **long-term** forecasts, for example saying that an earthquake will probably hit San Francisco in the next 100 years. It is still not possible to make accurate, **short-term** predictions, for example saying that an earthquake will hit a particular place in Japan within the next two days.

Long-term forecasts

Long-term forecasts may be made by producing maps showing epicentres of earthquakes that have happened over a period of time. The assumption is that a region that has had earthquakes in the past is likely to experience more earthquakes in the near future. Due to this, seismic zones are regions that have greater seismic risk.

A **seismic gap** is a region along a fault where stress is building up because no earthquakes have occurred there recently. Seismic gaps are often flanked by areas that have experienced earthquakes in the near past. The plates at the gap are locked and stress is building up. Seismologists believe that these gaps are the most likely locations for a big earthquake in the future. The **Guerrero Gap** in Mexico is one such location.

Figure 4.6 A large earthquake in the Guerrero Gap would flatten the tourist resort of Acapulco. It would also cause significant damage in Mexico City (because it is built on the dried-out mud of a dried-up lake bed).

Short-term forecasts

Seismologists want to be able to make accurate short-term forecasts, but so far this has not been achieved.

The best that has been achieved is a system that might give a 10-second to 100-second **early warning**. It is based on monitoring foreshocks, the seismic waves that come ahead of the main event. While earthquake tremors travel at the speed of sound, the seismometers that initially detect the tremors can send a message even faster, at the speed of light. This warns residents farther away that the tremors are coming. This advance warning can allow people and systems to take actions such as evacuating buildings, stopping transport and shutting down power stations. Warnings for the general public can be provided by TV and radio broadcasts. A similar warning text service is enabled by default on new mobile phones in Japan. Unfortunately, very few countries have invested in this system due to the expense.

> **QUESTION**
>
> Explain two reasons why it is so difficult to accurately predict earthquakes.

The Chinese have monitored **animal behaviour** in an attempt to predict earthquakes in the short term. Some animals may behave strangely before an earthquake. This is because very few humans notice the smaller primary waves that arrive first. Animals, with their keen senses, are often able to feel them. So far, two major earthquakes have been predicted. However, this is easier in rural areas, where people have a closer association with animals. Unfortunately, this is not of much benefit for urban areas.

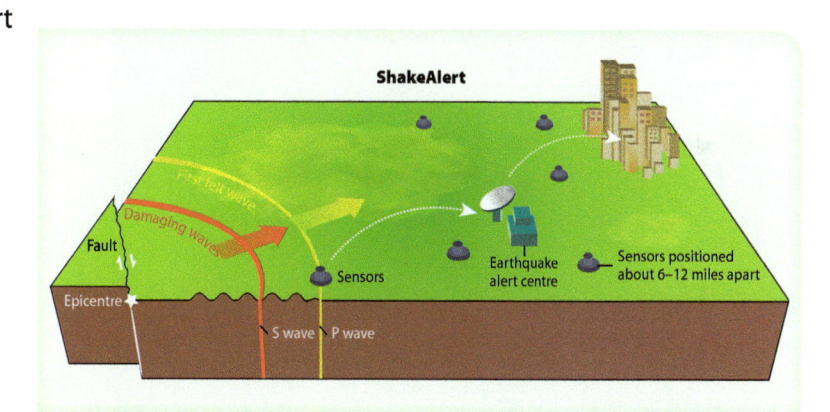

Figure 4.7 ShakeAlert is an early warning system that is being developed for California

Effects of earthquakes

Most of the damage from an earthquake is caused by the ground shaking. The level of damage depends on a number of factors, including:

› **Magnitude of the earthquake:** Larger-magnitude earthquakes release much more energy.
› **Distance from the epicentre:** The strength of seismic waves decreases as they move through rock.
› **Level of development:** This impacts on the quality of materials and construction standards used in buildings, roads and bridges.
› **Population density (rural or urban area):** The more densely populated an area, the more deaths and injuries there will be.

The effects of earthquakes can be classified as:

› **Primary effects:** These are the things that happen immediately as a result of the earthquake.
› **Secondary effects:** These are the after-effects of the earthquake – the things that happen in the longer term (hours, days and weeks) following the earthquake.

CASE STUDY

Two countries, two earthquakes

In this case study, you will learn about the effects of two earthquakes in two different countries.

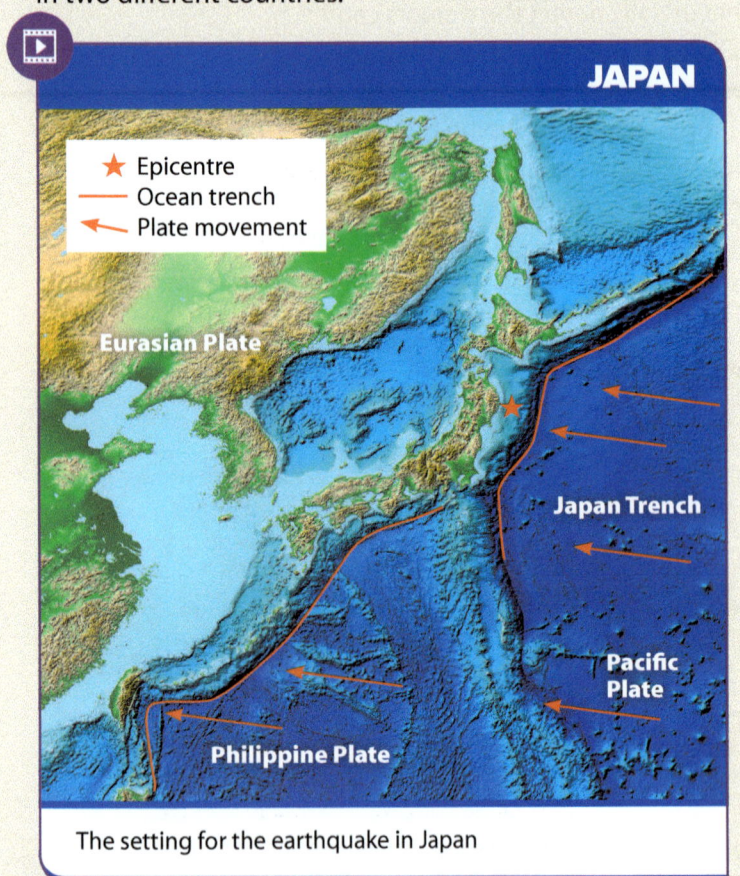

Japan is an island arc in the Pacific Ocean. Its capital city is Tokyo. It is classified as a more economically developed country (MEDC). It has the third largest economy in the world.

ACTIVITY

Research

Look up '2011 earthquake Japan' and '2015 earthquake Nepal' on the internet.

Nepal is located in the high Himalayas, wedged between China to the north and India to the south. It is classified as a less economically developed country (LEDC). The size of its economy is just 0.5% of Japan's.

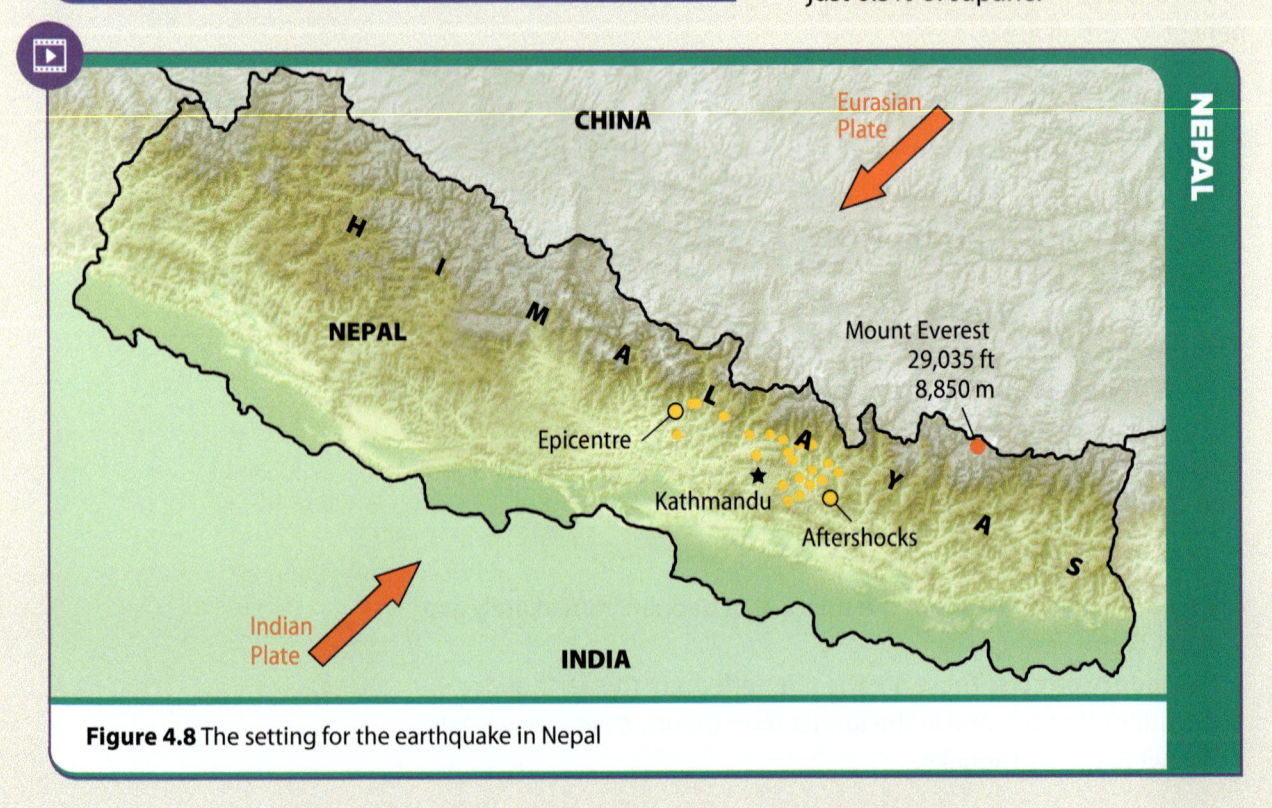

The setting for the earthquake in Japan

Figure 4.8 The setting for the earthquake in Nepal

Japan, March 2011

- The earthquake occurred on a convergent plate boundary where the Pacific Plate is subducted under the Eurasian Plate.
- It registered 9 on the Richter scale.
- Its epicentre was only 60 km from the coast.
- The earthquake had a shallow focus, about 25 km beneath the surface.
- The seabed was thrust upwards by up to 8 metres over a distance of 180 km.
- The earthquake was followed by more than 5,000 aftershocks over a two-month period.

Japan: Primary effects

- The earthquake generated a large wave called a tsunami. It spread out in all directions, both across the Pacific Ocean as well as towards the coast of Japan. The tsunami varied in height between 4 metres and 10 metres, depending on the shape of the coastline. It was highest when it was channelled into narrow valleys and harbours.
- Parts of Japan were shifted more than 2 metres further east as the plates slipped.
- A 400 km stretch of coastline dropped vertically by 0.6 metres. This allowed the tsunami to flow over defences, travelling further and faster inland.
- Soil liquefaction occurred in areas of reclaimed land around Tokyo, damaging more than 1,000 buildings.

Japan: Secondary effects

- The tsunami reached the Japanese coast within an hour of the earthquake. Authorities had not expected a tsunami of this height and had based their precautions and warnings accordingly.
- The official count of the dead and missing was almost 25,000 people.
- Entire towns were wiped off the map. Houses and cars were washed away. At least another 200,000 houses were damaged.
- Roads, bridges and railways were washed away. Airports were flooded.
- One nuclear power plant was damaged, leading to radiation leaks. This resulted in large evacuations, as well as concern over the pollution of food and water supplies.
- Millions of houses were left without electricity and water.

Nepal, April 2015

- The earthquake occurred on a fault that divides the Indian and Eurasian plates. The Indian Plate is pushing north, causing a build-up of stress. (See Figure 2.10 on page 18.)
- It registered 7.8 on the Richter scale.
- Just one hour later, an aftershock caused as much damage as the earthquake itself.
- Its epicentre was only 75 km from the capital, Kathmandu.
- The earthquake had a shallow focus, just 18 km beneath the surface.
- Two weeks later, the earthquake was followed by a second earthquake with a magnitude of 7.3 on the Richter scale.

Nepal: Primary effects

- An area of the crust about 120 km long was moved forward by about 2 metres.
- The death toll was almost 9,000 and nearly 20,000 people were injured.
- More than 800,000 homes were destroyed or damaged.
- Many hospitals were damaged, schools were destroyed and telecommunications were cut.
- Roads and railways were badly damaged, mostly by landslides and avalanches.
- Several UNESCO World Heritage Sites and monuments were damaged.

Nepal: Secondary effects

- Almost 3 million people were left homeless.
- More than 1 million people were in immediate need of food assistance.
- Displaced people moved into tents and temporary shelters.
- It was difficult to provide immediate aid or distribute food efficiently. This was because of the damage to transport infrastructure, the remoteness of many villages and the mountainous terrain.
- People were vulnerable to diseases such as cholera because of unsafe water and lack of sanitation facilities.
- The economic cost to the country is equivalent to about 25% of its gross domestic product (GDP). Tourism in particular has suffered a huge drop.

Japan: Immediate responses

> A tsunami warning was issued three minutes after the earthquake.
> The Japanese government is among the best prepared in the world for disasters. Planned responses involving the military, police and medical staff were activated.
> While many MEDCs offered aid, the Japanese government only requested help in areas such as search and rescue teams and sniffer dogs.
> Other nuclear power plants were shut down as a precaution. A 20 km exclusion zone was put into place around the damaged Fukushima reactor.
> Modern innovations such as Twitter kept people up to date on the situation far earlier than the regular media.

Japan: Longer-term responses

> Within six months, all damage to air, rail and road systems had been repaired.
> Within nine months, all electricity, water and communications systems had been repaired.
> Leaks from the damaged nuclear station were contained. Issues still remain about removing the radioactive contamination from the surrounding air, water and land.
> The Japanese government offered financial and tax incentives to businesses to reinvest in the affected areas.

Nepal: Immediate responses

> National and local governments were ill-prepared to deal with a disaster of this scale.
> Neighbouring countries, including China and India, provided emergency aid and medical supplies.
> Within days, emergency rescue teams arrived from many countries, most under the UN flag. They helped to rescue those trapped in the rubble and set up field hospitals.
> Many organisations, such as the Red Cross, sent personnel to help with the rescue operations and food distribution.
> Fundraising was organised internationally by humanitarian organisations.

Nepal: Longer-term responses

> One year later, most of those who needed shelter were still living in temporary tent cities or unsafe accommodation that offered little protection against the cold.
> Some 200,000 people have received cash or food for public work such as clearing rubble.
> The World Bank and UN provided money to support reconstruction and recovery programmes. Much of this work has been hindered by local bureaucracy. For example, most families have yet to get a grant of €1,500 to build houses.
> Many other organisations also pledged money, but much of it did not arrive.
> Agriculture appears to have escaped relatively unscathed. It remains Nepal's principal economic activity, providing a third of the GDP.

DEFINITION

Liquefaction: Soil liquefaction occurs when clays and sands mix with groundwater during an earthquake. This turns the ground into a quicksand-like material in minutes.

GEOFACT

Tsunamis are sometimes incorrectly called tidal waves. Tides are not involved at all.

Limiting earthquake damage

While it is impossible to prevent an earthquake, it is possible to prepare for one. Areas of preparation include:

> Early warning systems
> Improved construction standards
> Awareness programmes.

Early warning systems

Technology exists to detect earthquakes so quickly that an alert can reach some areas before strong shaking arrives. One example is the ShakeAlert system in California. It is hoped that this will deliver an advance warning of an impending earthquake of between 10 and 100 seconds (see Figure 4.7 on page 41).

An advanced early warning system for tsunamis, involving twenty-eight countries, is in place in the Pacific. The system aims to detect and locate earthquakes in the region and then to determine if they have the potential to generate a tsunami.

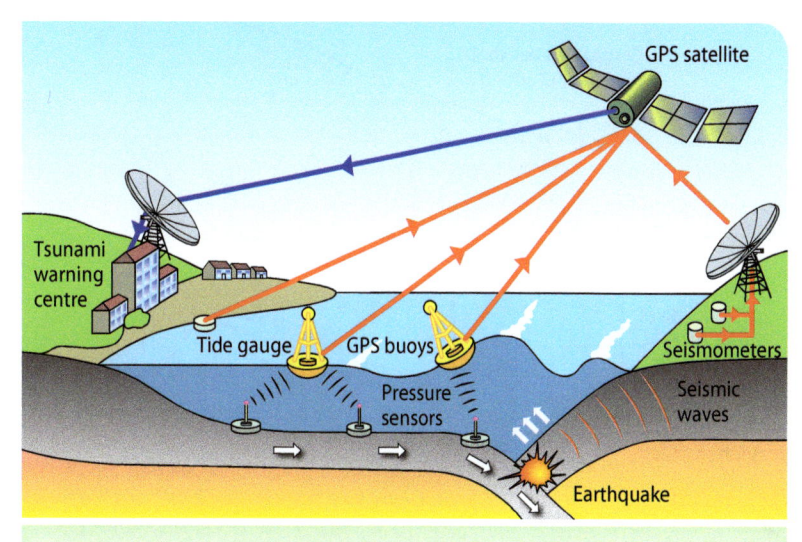

Figure 4.9 A tsunami early warning system

Improved construction standards

It has been said that earthquakes don't kill people; buildings do. Building collapse is the major cause of death and injury, especially in urban areas.

Developed economies

Countries with developed economies, such as Japan and the USA, have applied a high standard of earthquake proofing to buildings, roads and bridges. Planning permission is not granted for new buildings in fault zones or areas where liquefaction is likely to occur. Older buildings and structures are retrofitted to survive earthquakes by wall and foundation reinforcement.

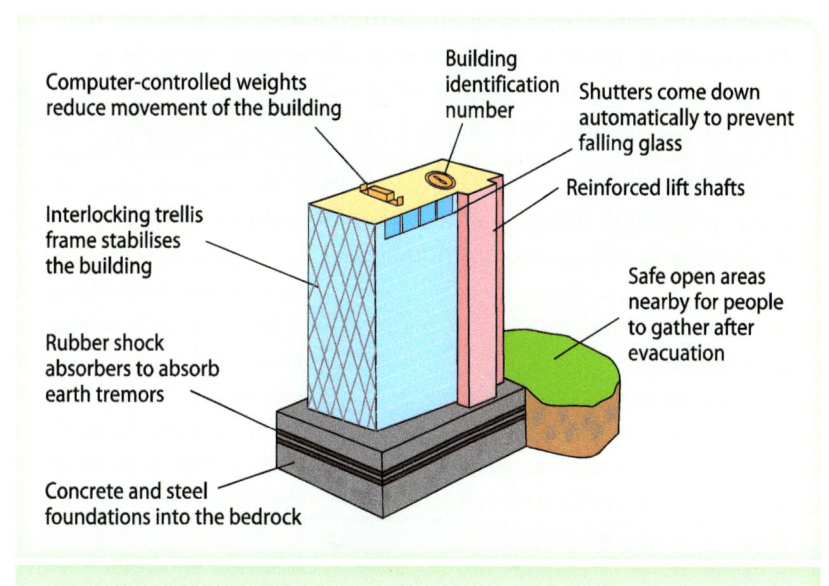

Figure 4.10 New buildings in earthquake zones in MEDCs have many design features that prevent or limit earthquake damage

Less-developed economies

Countries with less-developed economies, such as Nepal and Haiti, do not have the money to introduce high-tech regulations. Instead, they now impose basic building regulations to ensure that buildings will not collapse. Key elements include the use of lighter materials that are flexible and readily available.

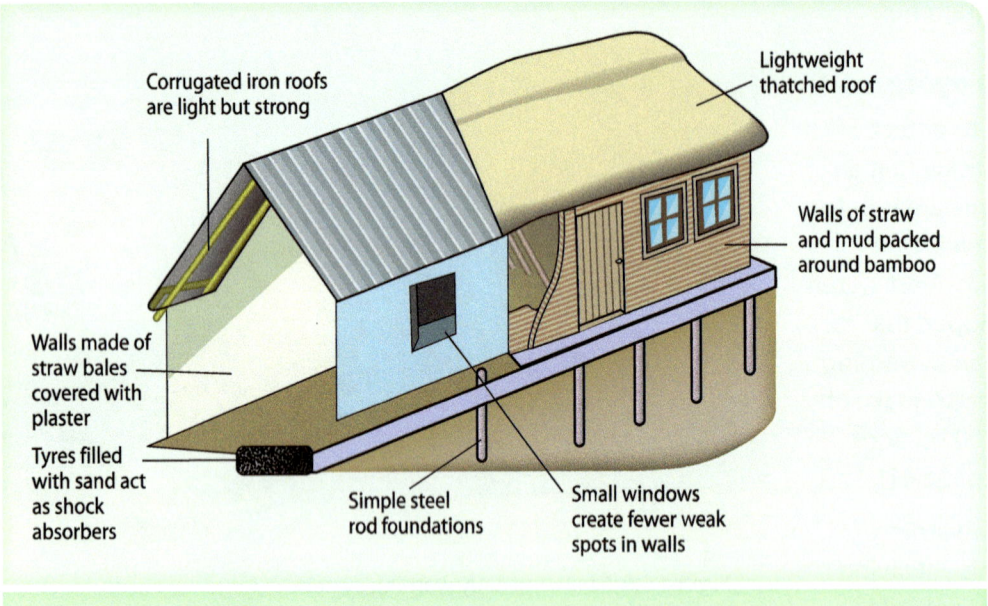

Figure 4.11 Techniques that enable people in rural communities in LEDCs to build their own earthquake-resistant, low-cost housing

Awareness programmes

People living in earthquake zones can prepare for the arrival and impact of an earthquake.

- Families and schools can hold earthquake drills to practise what to do during and after an earthquake.
- They can put together emergency kits (food and medicines) and store them in their homes.
- They can make their homes safe by securing anything that can move, fall or break during an earthquake.
- They can plan to link with and get support from neighbours and family following the earthquake.

ACTIVITY

Discussion

Explain why a country's ability to limit the effects of earthquake damage may be linked to its level of economic development.

📺 **PowerPoint Summary**

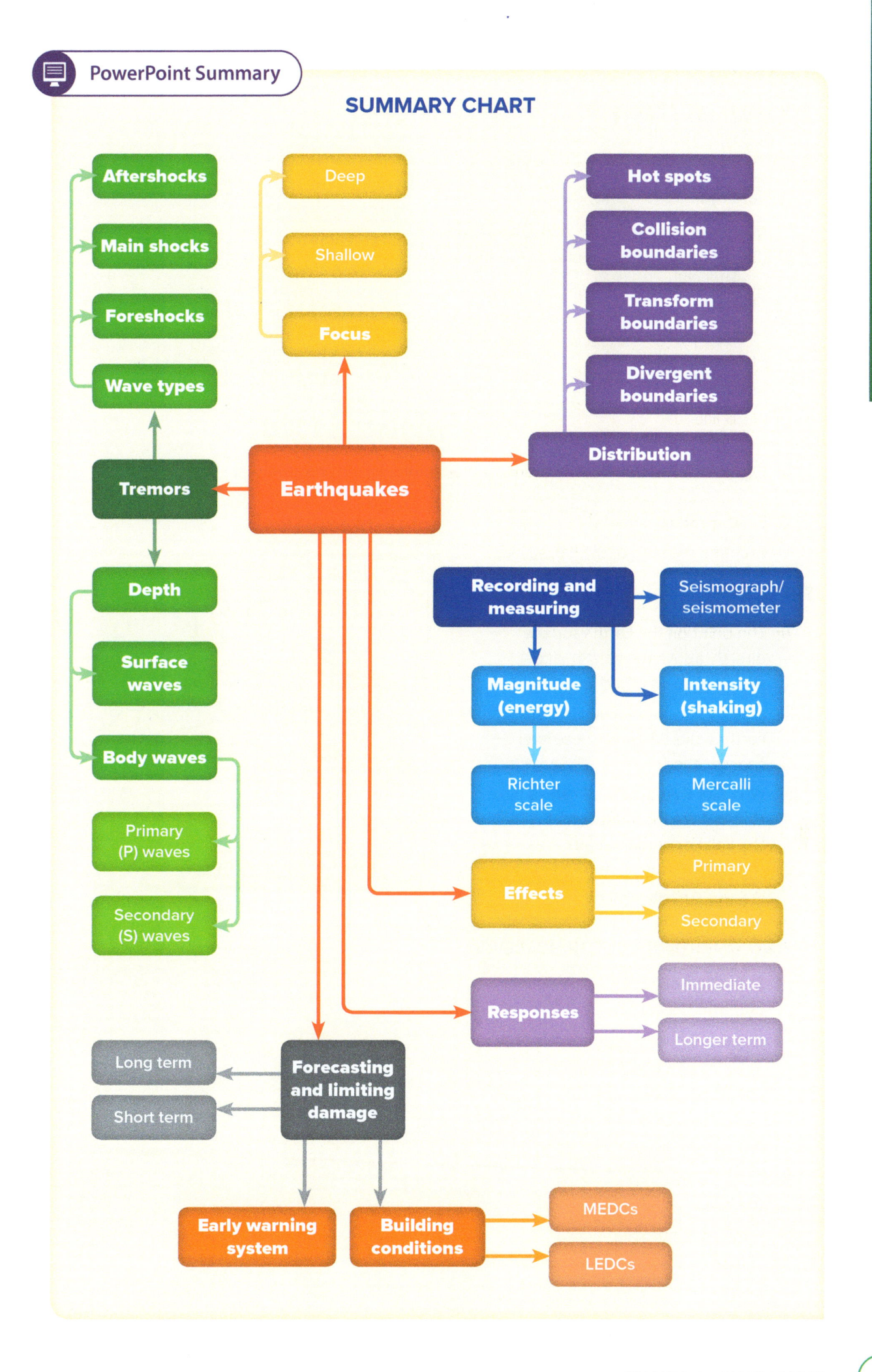

SUMMARY CHART

Earthquakes

- Aftershocks
- Main shocks
- Foreshocks
- Wave types
  - Tremors
    - Depth
      - Surface waves
      - Body waves
        - Primary (P) waves
        - Secondary (S) waves

- Focus
  - Deep
  - Shallow

- Distribution
  - Hot spots
  - Collision boundaries
  - Transform boundaries
  - Divergent boundaries

- Recording and measuring → Seismograph/seismometer
  - Magnitude (energy) → Richter scale
  - Intensity (shaking) → Mercalli scale

- Effects
  - Primary
  - Secondary

- Responses
  - Immediate
  - Longer term

- Forecasting and limiting damage
  - Long term
  - Short term
  - Early warning system
  - Building conditions
    - MEDCs
    - LEDCs

UNIT 1 · PHYSICAL GEOGRAPHY

CHAPTER 4 · EARTHQUAKES

Leaving Cert exam questions

SHORT QUESTIONS: HIGHER LEVEL

1 Earthquakes (8 marks)

(i) Match each of the letters **A**, **B**, **C** and **D** on the diagram with the correct feature in the table.

Feature	Letter
Focus	
Epicentre	
Seismic waves	
Fault line	

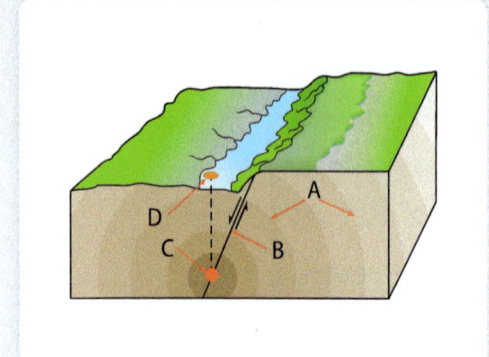

(ii) Explain each of the following terms: (a) seismologist (b) seismometer.

2 Earthquakes (8 marks)

Examine the map of the Pakistan–India border region and answer the following questions.

(i) The point on the Earth's surface directly above the earthquake – shown at **A** – is called what?

(ii) Smaller shocks followed the main earthquake. What are these later shocks called?

(iii) Which of these cities is likely to have suffered the most damage: Uri, Balakot or Islamabad?

(iv) To what scale does the term '7.6 magnitude' refer?

A 7.6 magnitude earthquake killed thousands and left millions homeless in the Himalayan region of Pakistan and India.

SHORT QUESTIONS: ORDINARY LEVEL

1 Satellite imagery – tsunami (10 marks)

The satellite image shows an area of Thailand before and after the tsunami of December 2004.

(i) What is a tsunami?

(ii) State one cause of a tsunami.

(iii) Name three problems caused in Thailand by the tsunami.

LONG QUESTIONS: HIGHER LEVEL

1 Plate tectonics – earthquakes (30 marks)

Explain, with reference to examples that you have studied, how the theory of plate tectonics helps to explain the distribution of earthquakes around the world.

2 Plate tectonics – earthquakes (20 marks)

Examine the map and answer the following questions.

(i) Name the plates **X** and **Y**.

(ii) What is the annual average movement of the Indo-Australian Plate?

(iii) Given that the epicentre of the earthquake shown on the map is offshore, name and briefly explain the main effect of this earthquake at sea.

(iv) Name **two** scales that measure the magnitude/intensity of an earthquake.

3 Earthquakes (30 marks)

Examine, with reference to actual examples, the measurement and effects of earthquakes.

LONG QUESTIONS: ORDINARY LEVEL

1 Earthquakes (40 marks)

(i) Name **one** location where an earthquake has occurred.

(ii) Name a scale used to measure the force of an earthquake.

(iii) Describe how earthquakes occur and describe their main effects.

2 Earthquakes (30 marks)

Read the adapted newspaper article and answer each of the following questions.

(i) What direction from Dublin was the epicentre of the earthquake and how far, in kilometres, was the epicentre from Dublin?

(ii) Name **two** locations in Ireland where the earthquake was felt.

(iii) What is the term given to the smaller tremors which follow the main earthquake?

(iv) State **two** effects of earthquakes.

(v) Explain briefly why Ireland has not experienced major earthquakes.

3 Impact of earthquakes (30 marks)

Describe **one** short-term effect and **one** long-term effect of an earthquake which you have studied.

Earthquake in the Irish Sea

A 3.8 magnitude earthquake struck this morning. The epicentre was located approximately 2 km off the coast of the Lleyn Peninsula in Wales and was 97 km south-east of Dublin. The quake was followed four minutes later by a smaller 1.7 magnitude tremor. Moderate shaking was felt in Carlow, Kildare, Wicklow, Wexford and Dublin. Earthquake stations as far away as Valentia, Donegal and Galway also recorded the earthquake.

Adapted from an *Irish Independent* article, 28 June 2013

Chapter 5
Volcanoes

KEYWORDS

- volcano
- eruption
- active
- dormant
- extinct
- magma chamber
- basic lava
- acidic lava
- pyroclastic material
- extrusive
- crater
- central vent eruption
- fissure eruption
- plateau
- hot spot
- intrusive
- pluton
- batholith
- lahar
- geothermal energy

LEARNING OBJECTIVES

By the end of this chapter, you should be able to understand:

- Why volcanic activity occurs
- The global pattern of volcanoes
- How volcanic activity shapes the landscape
- How volcanic activity may be predicted
- The impact of volcanic activity on the Irish landscape
- Geothermal energy production.

Volcanic activity

Volcanic activity, along with earthquakes, is capable of causing sudden and massive change in the Earth's surface. The most obvious evidence of volcanic activity is when molten rock (magma) forces its way up to the surface of the Earth. However, most volcanic activity takes place deep underground.

Volcanic zones

Volcanic activity tends to be concentrated in specific **zones**. While most volcanic activity takes place at plate boundaries, it can also occur in plate interiors.

Most volcanic activity takes place:

- At convergent plate boundaries (subduction)
- At divergent plate boundaries (sea-floor spreading)
- Where plates are breaking up (rifting)
- At hot spots.

GEOFACT

There is an almost complete absence of volcanic activity at transform faults.

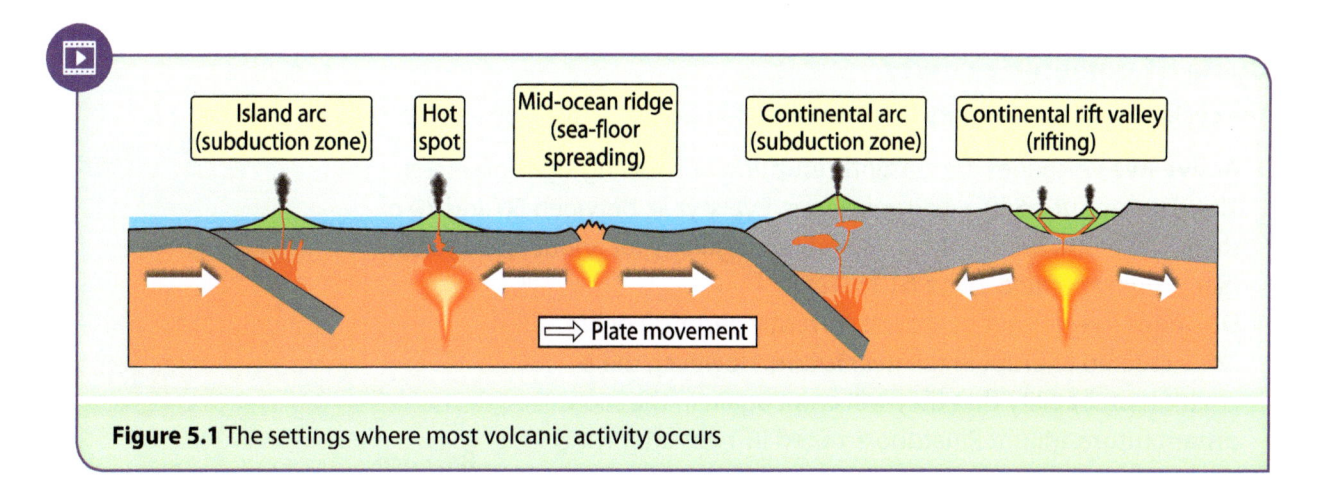

Figure 5.1 The settings where most volcanic activity occurs

The largest and most active volcanoes are on plate boundaries, such as those on the boundary of the Pacific Plate and its surrounding plates. This belt of volcanoes is known as the **Ring of Fire**. It contains about three-quarters of the world's active and dormant volcanoes. It stretches from New Zealand along the eastern edge of Asia and across to Alaska, and south along the coast of North and South America.

ACTIVITY

Thinking

What do all the volcanic settings in Figure 5.1 have in common?

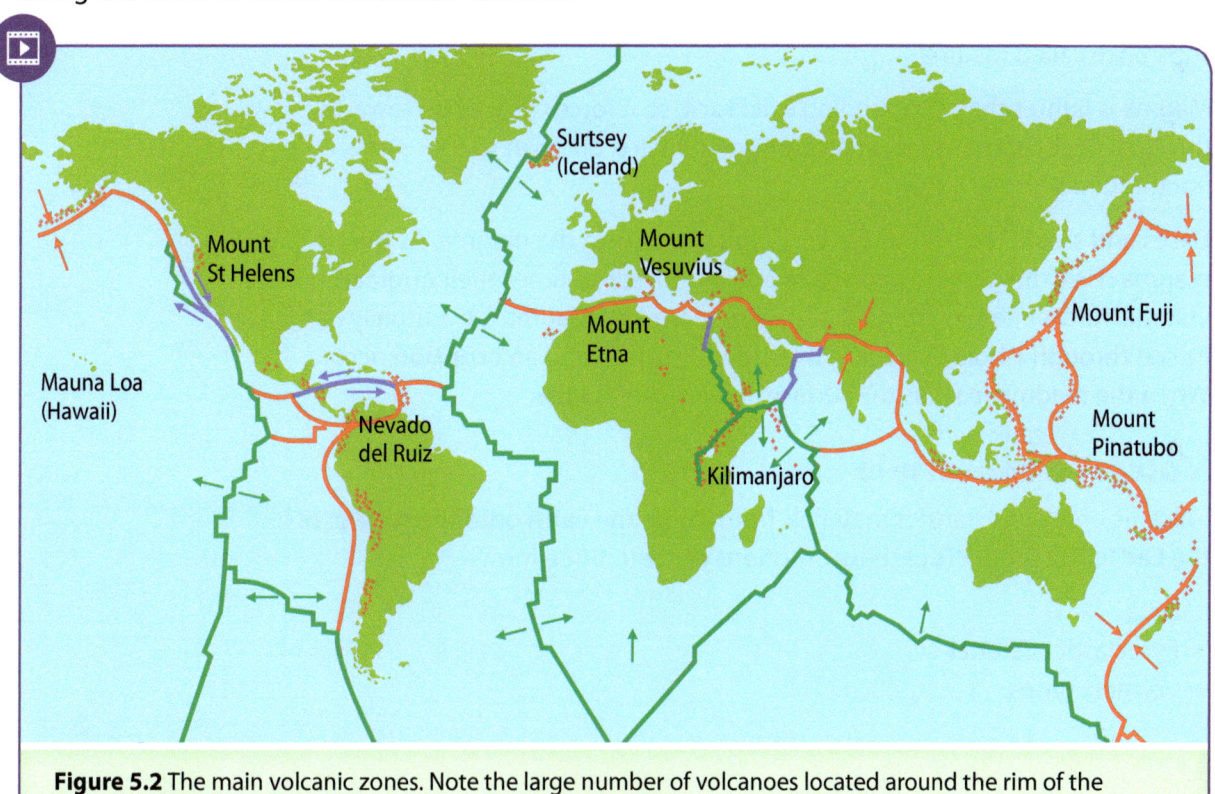

Figure 5.2 The main volcanic zones. Note the large number of volcanoes located around the rim of the Pacific Ocean (the Ring of Fire).

ACTIVITY

Discussion

With the aid of Figures 5.1 and 5.2, identify a volcano at each of the following zones:

(i) Subduction
(ii) Sea-floor spreading
(iii) Rifting
(iv) Hot spot.

CHAPTER 5 · VOLCANOES

Cycle of volcanic activity

The **cycle of volcanic activity** falls into three categories: active, dormant or extinct.

> **Active live** volcanoes are currently erupting or showing signs of unrest. There are about 1,500 active volcanoes. Every year, between 50 and 70 of them will erupt. Mount Etna has erupted regularly for about 3,500 years. (See *Mount Pinatubo*, page 61.)
> **Dormant live** volcanoes are not currently erupting or are not expected to erupt in the near future. However, there is a high probability that they will erupt again in the more distant future. Mount Pinatubo erupted in 1991 after lying dormant for almost 500 years.
> **Extinct (dead)** volcanoes, such as Slemish Mountain in Antrim, have not erupted in historical times. Geologists think that they probably won't erupt again because the volcano no longer has a lava supply.

ACTIVITY

Research

Look up 'Yellowstone supervolcano video' on the internet to examine a worst-case scenario.

Why do volcanoes erupt?

It is so hot in the upper mantle that the rocks there, including sections of plates that have been subducted, slowly melt. They become a thick, flowing substance called magma.

Magma is lighter than surrounding solid rock, so it forces its way up towards the crust. It collects in a **magma chamber**, which is an open space or area of fractured rock in the lithosphere.

Gases and steam are held under very high pressure in the magma. As the magma rises, the gases expand to several hundreds of times their original volume, further helping to drive the magma up. The magma is eventually forced through a hole or crack in the ground surface and an **eruption** occurs. When the magma reaches the surface, it is known as **lava**.

Volcanic materials

Volcanic eruptions transfer materials from inside the Earth onto the surface of the Earth. The products of these eruptions come in three forms:

> Lava
> Pyroclastic material
> Volcanic gases.

Lava

Lava is the main output of volcanoes. The type of lava coming out of a volcano depends on its silica content.

> **Basic lava** is low in silica content and very runny. It can flow out of a volcano in great rivers that travel for dozens of kilometres before solidifying. As a result, it forms extensive but gently sloping landforms. (See *The Antrim–Derry Plateau*, page 64, and *Hot spot eruptions*, page 56.)
> **Acidic lava** is high in silica content and is pasty (viscous). It flows for only a short distance before cooling and hardening. As a result, the landforms that it produces tend to have steep sides. (See *Mount Pinatubo*, page 61.)

Lava flow moving in to cover farmland following a fresh eruption

Pyroclastic material

Pyroclastic material is the group name for the airborne debris that erupts from a volcano. It includes ash, dust, cinders, pebbles and rocks. The heavier particles fall to the ground close to the volcano. The lighter particles are carried long distances.

> A **pyroclastic flow** is a mixture of dry rock fragments and hot gases that moves away from the vent of a volcano and flows down its flanks at hurricane-force speeds, often over 700 km/hr. This is the deadliest of all volcanic events.

> A **pyroclastic cloud** consists of dust and ash that are blasted high into the sky during an eruption. It can remain there for a long time and can be transported around the world by winds. A volcanic ash cloud resulting from the eruption of a volcano in Iceland disrupted air traffic across Northern Europe in the spring of 2010.

> A **lahar** is a kind of volcanic mudflow. If the ash and dust get mixed up with rain or steam from melted snow, a flow of thick mud results. This can flow down slopes at speeds of up to 200 km/hr. (See *Mount Pinatubo*, page 61.)

GEOFACTS

Will it flow or will it blow?

> **Basic lava** is very runny. The gas bubbles can easily escape from the lava. As a result, the eruptions tend to be relatively gentle.
> **Acidic lava** is very pasty. As the gas bubbles expand, they are unable to escape from the lava. As a result, eruptions tend to be violent.

Volcanic gases

Magma contains **gases**, which are the driving force that causes most volcanic eruptions. Large eruptions can then release enormous amounts of gas into the atmosphere in a short time. Water vapour (steam) is by far the most abundant volcanic gas and it is harmless. Others, including carbon dioxide, sulphur dioxide and chlorine, are hazardous. Acid rain can be produced when large amounts of these gases are washed out of the atmosphere. A cloud of heavier-than-air gases that escaped from a crater lake in Cameroon killed all the people and animals within a 25 km radius.

Volcanic landforms

When magma makes its way to the surface of the Earth, it is known as lava. It cools and solidifies to form various structures. Because these structures are formed on the surface of the Earth, they are known as **extrusive landforms**.

Some of the magma involved in an eruption does not reach the surface. Instead, it invades faults and forces its way into folds in the rocks of the crust. It then cools deep underground to form **intrusive landforms**.

Extrusive landforms

Extrusive landforms vary in shape as a result of the type of lava and the conditions under which it erupted. There are three main types of eruption:

- Central vent eruption
- Fissure eruption
- Hot spot eruption.

Central vent eruptions

Central vent eruptions occur when volcanic material spews from a **vent** or opening on the Earth's surface. The central vent is connected at depth to a magma chamber, which is the main storage area for the volcanic material. Most occur at destructive boundaries where plates collide.

Lava and other volcanic materials, including ash and cinders, pour out and build up around the vent. With successive eruptions, a **cone-shaped mountain** is formed. A steep-sided depression called a **crater** is found at the top of the volcano. It formed during the eruption as the last of the erupted material drained back into the vent. Its floor may consist of a lava lake or solidified material from the previous eruption.

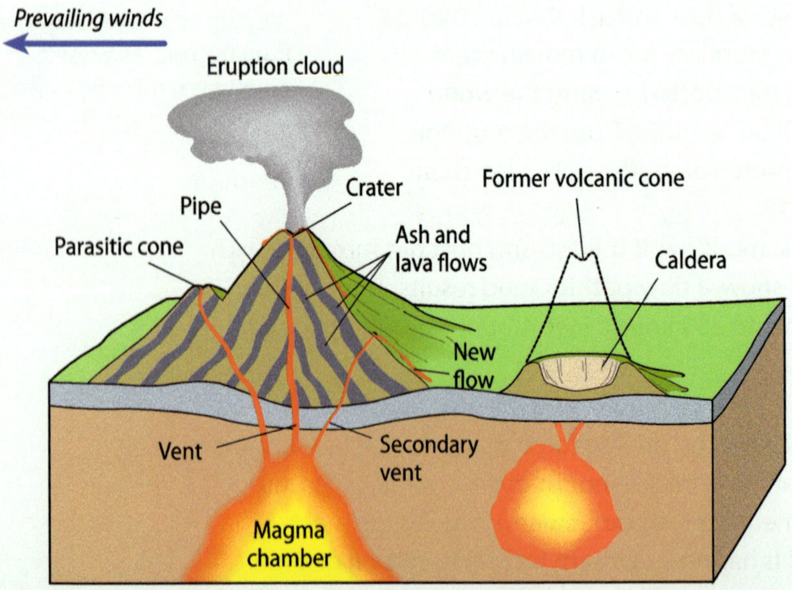

> **QUESTION**
>
> Explain the following terms:
> (i) Intrusive
> (ii) Extrusive
> (iii) Acidic lava
> (iv) Basic lava.

Figure 5.3 A central vent eruption. Magma accumulates in the magma chamber before it erupts onto the surface through a central vent. Successive flows build up to form a volcanic cone.

> **ACTIVITY**
>
> **Skills**
>
> Draw a labelled diagram to show the main elements of a typical volcano.

Volcanic cones and calderas along the Ring of Fire

A **parasitic cone** forms from material that erupts through secondary vents. These smaller vents form at fractures on the sides of the main volcanic cone.

The shape of the volcanic cone depends on the type of material it is made of.

› A **composite volcano** consists of alternate layers of lava and pyroclastic material (ash and cinders). As most of these materials fall near the vent, a steep cone begins to build up. The lava helps bind the loose pyroclastic material. The high volcanic cone that results is the classic image most people have of a volcano. Mount Etna and Mount Vesuvius are examples of composite volcanoes.
› A **lava dome** forms when acidic, viscous lava erupts. As it is so pasty, it is unable to flow very far before it cools and solidifies. The lava piles up around the vent and forms a dome shape with high, steep sides. Lava domes can explode violently, releasing a huge amount of hot rock and ash. A new lava dome has built up in the crater of Mount St Helens since its last major eruption.
› A **caldera** forms when large quantities of molten magma and gases are blown out onto the surface during violent eruptions. If enough magma is ejected, the magma chamber may become partially emptied. If this happens, the chamber is unable to support the cone above it, which collapses into the chamber. A large depression, called a caldera, results. Yellowstone National Park consists of three calderas, one of which is 45 km across.

Fissure eruptions

As magma rises, it will find the easiest route to reach the surface. If it rises up through a long crack or fissure, fountains of lava can form a curtain of fire. This is a **fissure eruption**.

Fissures can be up to tens of kilometres long. The eruption often takes the form of a curtain of fire, with the lava barely rising above ground level.

Fissure eruptions produce large quantities of basic (runny) lava and are less explosive. As the lava spreads out, it covers large areas of land. Individual flows can be up to 50 metres thick and spread more than 50 km from their source. Successive flows build up to form a flat landscape called a **lava plateau**, a flat-topped landform that rises above the surrounding area. The **Antrim–Derry Plateau** was formed in this way about 65 million years ago (see page 64).

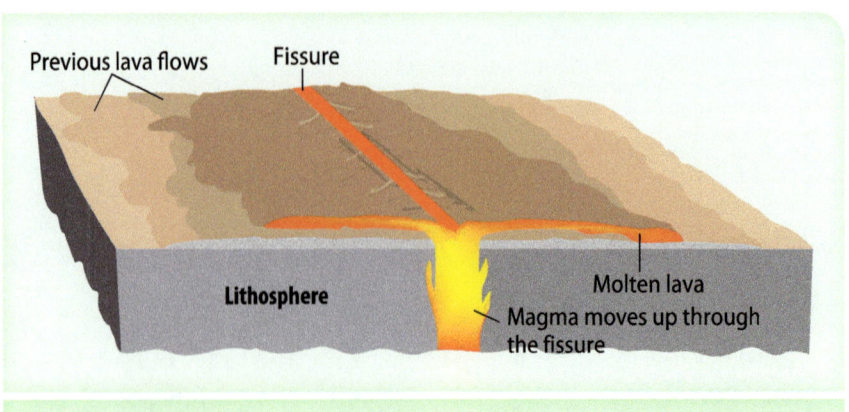

Figure 5.4 The formation of a lava plateau such as the Antrim–Derry Plateau

Fissure eruptions also take place where two plates are pulled apart. This is currently happening on the floor of the Atlantic Ocean, where the American and Eurasian plates are separating.

Magma wells up to fill the gap between the plates. When it meets the seawater, the magma cools and solidifies. Over time, it has built up to form a chain of underwater mountains known as the **Mid-Atlantic Ridge**. The ridge stands between 2,500 and 3,000 metres above sea level. It even rises above the surface of the ocean in a number of locations, including Iceland (see page 14).

ACTIVITY

Discussion
Identify two differences between a central vent eruption and a fissure eruption.

Part of an 8.5 km fissure eruption in Iceland

Hot spot eruptions

Volcanic activity also occurs away from plate boundaries. Zones where there is unusually hot mantle beneath the plates are known as **hot spots**. A column of hot molten rock, called a **plume**, rises from deep within the mantle. Acting like a giant blowtorch, the plume eventually breaks through the crust.

Lava erupts and builds up into a large **volcanic cone plate** directly above the hot spot. Built of runny **basic lava**, the cones are wide and have gently sloping sides.

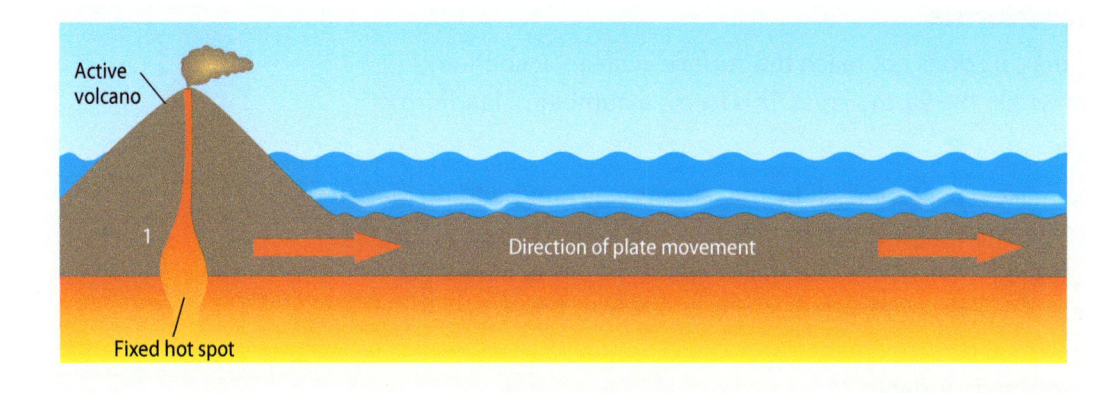

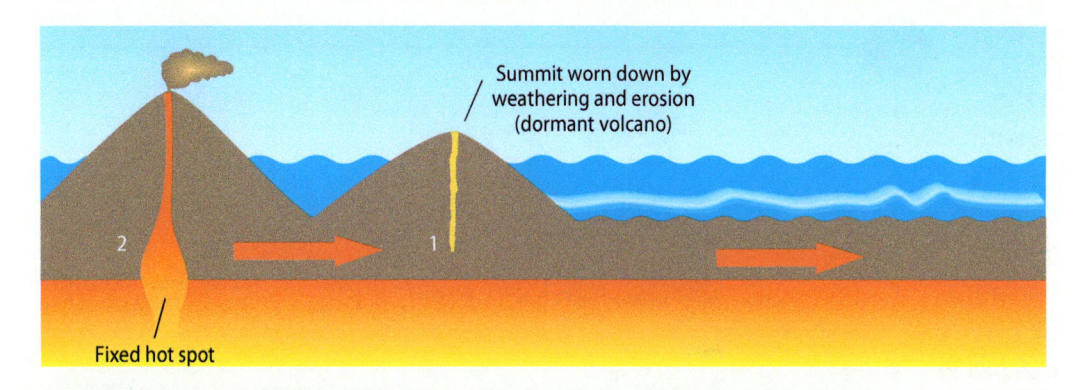

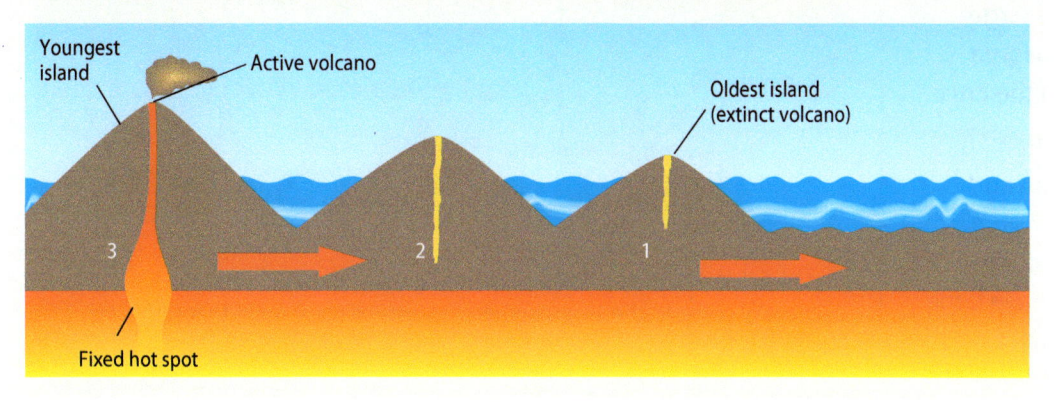

Figure 5.5 The Hawaiian Islands are hotspot volcanoes. The hot spot is fixed and the crustal plate moves over it.

The plume stays still while the plate above it moves. Like a giant conveyor belt, the plate carries older volcanoes away from the hot spot. These eventually become extinct while the hot spot continues to create new volcanoes. Thus, the volcanoes increase in age with their distance from the hot spot.

The **Hawaiian Islands** chain was formed when the Pacific Plate slowly moved over the stationary hot spot. Hawaii itself is less than half a million years old, but Kauai, the oldest island, was formed about 5 million years ago. New underwater volcanoes are already forming as the Pacific Plate continues to move over the hot spot.

GEOFACT

Mauna Loa is an active volcano on the island of Hawaii. Its highest point is almost 4,200 metres above sea level, but the flanks of Mauna Loa continue for another 5,000 metres to the seabed.

Thus, from its base on the seabed to its summit, Mauna Loa is higher than Mount Everest.

Intrusive landforms

Some molten magma does not reach the surface. Instead, it cools and solidifies deep within the Earth's crust. This forms a number of landforms called **plutons**.

> The magma makes space for itself by pushing its way into bedding planes and forcing them to bulge apart. It also penetrates cracks and fractures in the rock, wedging them open. Finally, it melts some of the parent rock.

> Plutons are classified according to their shape, size and direction. Many plutons are visible on the surface today because the overlying rocks have been removed by denudation.

Batholiths

Batholiths are the largest plutons, with a surface area greater than 100 km². They have a domed shape with steeply sloping sides. They were formed many kilometres below the surface as large volumes of magma intruded into the crust.

Since the molten magma cooled and solidified very slowly, the rocks are coarse grained and have large crystals. The main rock type is granite. (See *The Leinster Batholith*, page 65.)

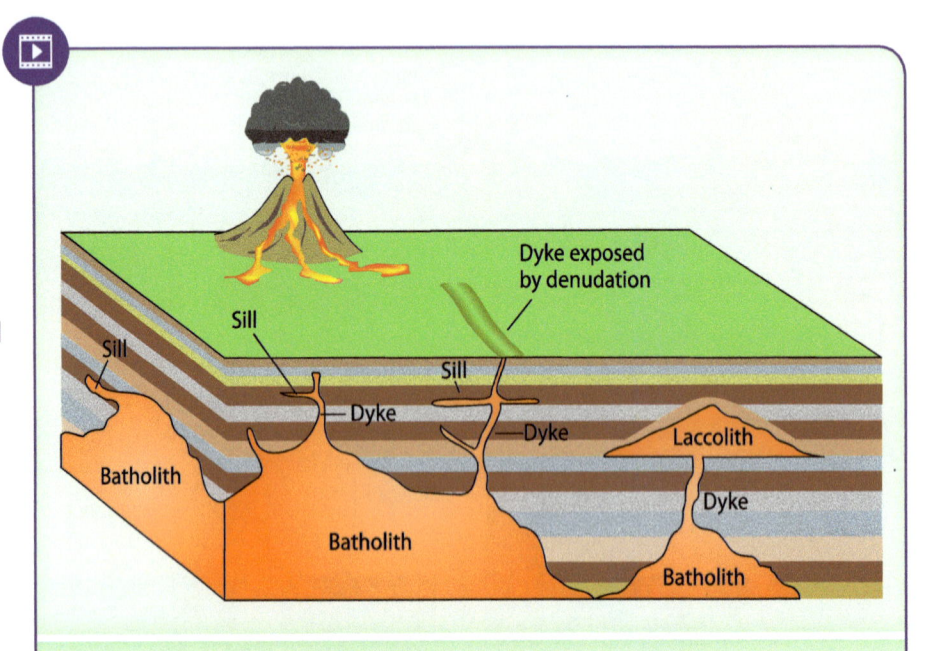

Figure 5.6 Intrusive volcanic landforms. Many of these landforms eventually come to the surface when the less resistant rocks that surround them are eroded.

Laccoliths

Laccoliths are dome-like structures with a flat floor. They were formed when magma pushed its way in between the rock strata. The pressure forced the overlying strata to bulge upwards. The magma then cooled and solidified.

Sills

Sills are horizontal sheets of volcanic rock that run parallel to the rock strata. They were formed quite close to the surface where there was less pressure from overlying rock. The magma forced its way into the bedding planes, where it cooled and solidified.

Dykes

Dykes are thin, vertical sheets of volcanic rock that run perpendicular to the rock strata. They were formed when magma was forced into vertical fractures or faults in the rock, where it cooled and solidified.

Predicting volcanic activity

Scientists are constantly trying to predict volcano eruptions so that authorities have time to evacuate surrounding areas and prevent loss of life. Most of the active volcanoes in the world are monitored regularly, some around the clock.

While it is very difficult to pinpoint exactly when an eruption will happen, predictions are becoming more accurate. Scientists were able to accurately predict the 1991 eruption of Mount Pinatubo. Most people living in the region heeded the warnings and fled to safety. This included about 20,000 people who lived in the immediate vicinity of the volcano and would have been affected by the pyroclastic cloud. (See *Mount Pinatubo*, page 61.)

Changes in the shape of a volcano

Before an eruption, magma moves into the area beneath the volcano. As it rises into the cone, it pushes outwards and can cause the surface of the volcano to bulge. Even a slight bulge or change of slope in the side of a volcano may indicate that an eruption is likely. Scientists use laser beams and satellite images to take accurate measurements of any changes that occur.

Heat and gases

The presence of hot magma increases the temperature of the surrounding rock. This may cause snow or ice on the volcano to begin to melt, triggering floods or lahars.

As the magma rises closer to the surface, the gases expand and begin to escape. The main volcanic gases include sulphur dioxide and steam. Any large increase in the amount of gases means that there is more magma close to the surface and that a volcanic eruption could be expected.

Seismic activity

As magma collects in a magma chamber, it generates great heat. This cracks the surrounding rocks, giving off small tremors. These tremors can be monitored by seismometers. Any sudden increase in the number or strength of these tremors can indicate that an eruption is about to occur.

History of eruptions

Scientists are now better able to interpret the record of past eruptions. They use this to predict when a new eruption is likely. Studying the history of volcanoes in this detail only began after the eruption of Mount St Helens in 1980.

Scientific equipment set up to monitor volcanic activity in Iceland. Note the ash cloud in the background and ash deposits in the foreground.

Effects of volcanic eruptions

Many of the effects of volcanoes are negative, but volcanic activity also has positive effects.

Positive effects

> Volcanic materials can produce **fertile soils**. Ash and cinders are rich in minerals and act as a natural fertiliser. Since these soils do not take long to support vegetation, people move back to volcanic regions soon after an eruption. Lava, when weathered and eroded, also makes for a fertile soil. Soils of volcanic origin support thriving agriculture in places such as the Brazilian Plateau (coffee), the Deccan in India (cotton), Java (tea) and New Zealand (dairying and kiwi fruit).
> Volcanoes are important **tourist attractions**. They have a positive effect on local economies by generating revenue and providing employment in accommodation, transport, guiding and souvenir production. Notable volcanic attractions include Yellowstone National Park (Old Faithful Geyser), Mount Vesuvius (Pompeii), Mount Etna (volcano viewing in summer and skiing in winter) and Iceland (hot springs).
> Volcanic activity is also a source of **geothermal energy**. (See *Geothermal energy in Iceland*, page 66.)

Negative effects

> Volcanoes can cause large-scale destruction and death. The eruption of Nevado del Ruiz (Colombia) in 1985 melted ice and snow on the mountain. This resulted in a **mudflow** (or **lahar**) that buried several villages and killed over 21,000 people in the town of Armero. This town was located at the head of a valley at the foot of the mountain.
> When a fissure in Iceland erupted throughout the spring and summer of 2010, air traffic was disrupted. Thousands of flights were cancelled, not only in Europe, but also flights from Asia, America and other continents. Hundreds of thousands of air travellers were left stranded for up to a week. The cause of the disruption was a huge **ash cloud** that posed a risk of damage to jet engines.
> Volcanic activity can release **poisonous gases** that can cause death. Lake Nyos sits in the crater of a volcano in Cameroon. In 1986, volcanic rumblings triggered the release of vast amounts of carbon dioxide. Carbon dioxide is odourless and heavier than air. It flowed down into the nearby valleys, displacing oxygen. Over 2,000 people and tens of thousands of animals died, most of them in their sleep.

ACTIVITY

Research

Investigate two impacts of the ash cloud that followed the volcanic eruption in Iceland in 2010.

CASE STUDY

Mount Pinatubo

Mount Pinatubo is a volcano located on a destructive (convergent) plate boundary where the Philippine Plate is subducted under the Eurasian Plate. This zone is part of the **Pacific Ring of Fire**, which has almost 200 active volcanoes.

By 1991, Mount Pinatubo had been **dormant** for almost 500 years. It was covered in tropical forest and was home to more than 30,000 people who lived in villages on its slopes. In June of that year it erupted, producing by far the largest and most destructive volcanic eruption of the last 100 years.

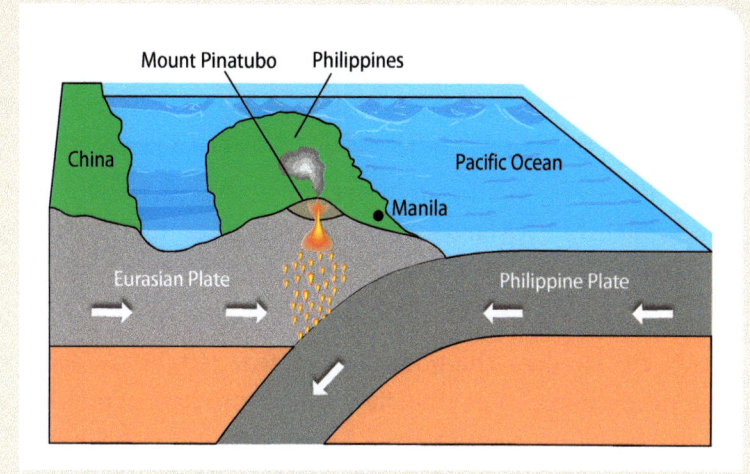

Figure 5.7 Mount Pinatubo is one of many volcanoes found along the convergent plate boundaries that ring the Pacific Ocean

The build-up

Even though it was dormant, the volcano was regularly affected by seismic tremors and steam emissions. Because of this, it was monitored by a team of vulcanologists.

However, in the months leading up to the eruptions, the number of earthquakes increased to several hundred per day, steam emissions increased and poisonous **sulphur dioxide** also began to escape. Small bulges were noticed on the mountain. These were all signs that magma was beginning to rise and that pressure was building up. As long as the gas was escaping, Mount Pinatubo was not likely to erupt or explode.

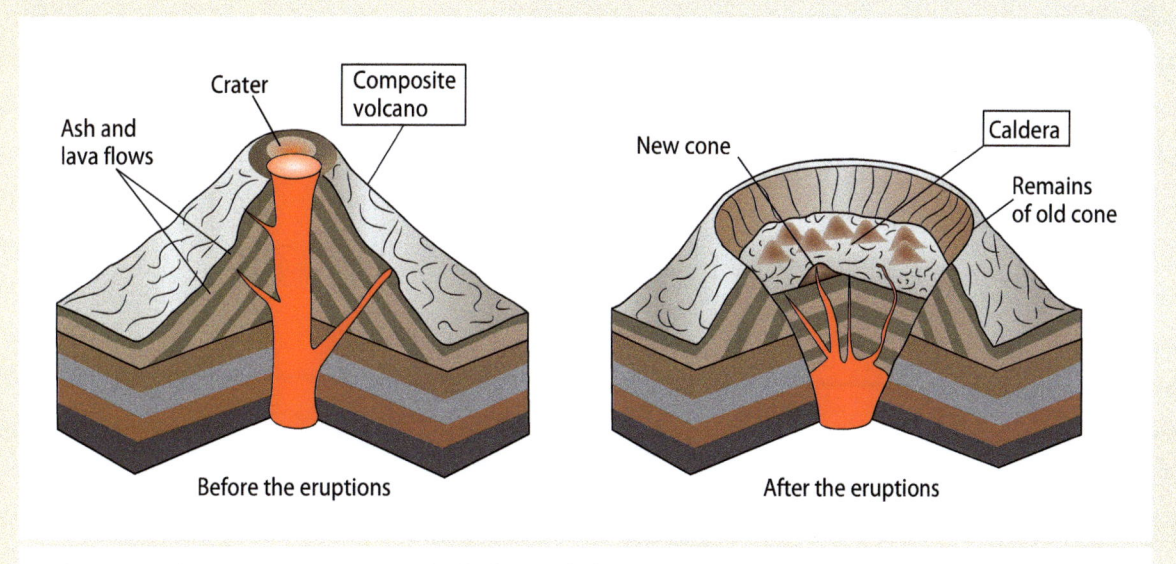

Figure 5.8 The cone at Mount Pinatubo before and after the eruptions

Soon, up to 1,500 **earthquakes** per day were being recorded. Ash began to escape into the atmosphere, suggesting that magma was very close to the surface. Small lava flows appeared.

In early June, the decision was taken to declare a state of emergency and **evacuate** everybody living within a 20 km radius of the volcano. Some 15,000 people were also evacuated from a US air base just outside this zone.

The eruptions

The eruptions continued for almost a week, climaxing with the final violent explosion.

In the first eruption, large volumes of magma reached the surface and erupted quite violently. Lava flowed down the slopes of the volcano and a cloud of ash rose more than 20 km into the atmosphere. Similar eruptions continued on the following days. However, the most violent eruption was yet to come.

In this, viscous **lava**, charged with **gas**, reached the surface and erupted with extreme violence. More than five cubic kilometres of material was ejected from the volcano. An ash cloud rose 35 km into the atmosphere. A **pyroclastic flow** consisting of hot ash, gases and pumice was blown down the mountainside in all directions. A typhoon hit the region at the same time and its rainfall turned much of the dry volcanic materials into a mudflow (**lahar**). This flowed downslope through the valleys.

So much lava and other materials had been blasted out of the volcano that its inside was practically empty. The summit began to collapse inwards to form a large depression, called a **caldera**, that was more than 2 km wide. The eruption had lasted for more than 9 hours.

Several weaker eruptions of ash and lava followed over the next few months as the volcano began to build new cones in the caldera.

> **QUESTION**
>
> Explain the difference between a pyroclastic cloud and a pyroclastic flow.

> **GEOFACT**
>
> The eruptions did not directly cause any deaths due to the well-organised evacuations that had taken place beforehand.

A pyroclastic cloud of hot gases and solids descending the flank of the volcano at speed

The consequences

The consequences of the eruptions were felt both globally and locally. Nearly 20 million tons of gases and ash clouds escaped into the atmosphere.

> It affected air traffic.
> It caused global temperatures to drop temporarily by about 0.5°C as it absorbed energy from the sun.
> Some gases destroyed ozone. The hole in the ozone layer reached its largest size in the year following the eruption.

Vast amounts of ash and other volcanic debris blanketed the countryside.

> Almost 800 people died, most when roofs collapsed due to the weight of ash that had fallen on them. The others died from diseases that they contracted in temporary camps.
> Two million people were affected due to damage to their property and to farmland that was rendered useless. Production of sugar cane and rice ceased.
> Relief operations were hindered because roads, railways and bridges were destroyed.
> Valleys were filled with ash and lahar sediments up to a depth of 200 metres. This also resulted in wide-scale flooding.
> Ironically, Mount Pinatubo has become a major tourist attraction, offering employment to locals.

Cars and people crossing a silt-filled river after the mudflows washed away the bridges

Extrusive and intrusive volcanic activity in Ireland

Ireland lies far from the margins of the Eurasian Plate, but this was not always so. We can find evidence of volcanic activity over many ages in the Irish landscape. Among these volcanic landscapes are:

- The Antrim–Derry Plateau
- The Leinster Batholith.

The Antrim–Derry Plateau

The **Antrim–Derry Plateau** is a basalt plateau extending to over 4,000 km^2 in area and rising above 350 metres in height. It is the result of volcanic activity that began about 65 million years ago and lasted for up to 15 million years. (See *Ireland on the move*, page 19.)

- At this time the Eurasian-American Plate began to split apart, creating a constructive plate boundary. The crust was stretched and thinned. Great cracks or **fissures** opened up. Lava poured out onto the surface, flow upon flow, to form a fairly flat, featureless landscape. These eruptions occurred without much violence because the ash, gases and other materials associated with violent volcanic activity were absent.
- The individual flows, varying in thickness from 5 metres to 40 metres, cooled to form the igneous rock **basalt**. In the process, the original chalk-covered landscape was covered up. As the plates drifted further apart, new continental crust was formed and the Atlantic Ocean began to open up. Volcanic activity moved with it and eventually ceased in the Antrim–Derry region. The most spectacular features associated with this period of volcanic activity are best seen today along the north Antrim coast. The different lava flows and the chalk that they covered up can be seen on the cliffs that rise to 150 metres in places.
- The **Giant's Causeway** is the most distinctive part of the plateau. Its 60,000 basalt columns attract the most attention. These formed when molten magma cooled very slowly after becoming trapped in a river valley. As the lava cooled, it contracted around regularly spaced centres. This caused the rock to break into hexagonal columns. The lower columns, buried deeper, cooled more slowly and formed a more uniform pattern than the upper flows. The lower columns are now exposed as a result of coastal erosion.

GEOFACTS

- As recently as 1700, there was debate as to whether the Giant's Causeway had been made by people with picks and shovels, due to the efforts of a giant or created by nature.
- Sixty million years ago, the landscape of the Antrim–Derry Plateau would have resembled that of Iceland today, where the American and Eurasian plates are separating.

Hexagonal blocks of basalt at the Giant's Causeway. Note the flat-topped Antrim–Derry Plateau in the background, showing evidence of several lava flows.

ACTIVITY

Thinking

Why did the basalt columns form into hexagonal shapes?

The Leinster Batholith

The **Leinster Batholith** is the largest batholith in either Great Britain or Ireland. It occupies over 1,500 km² of the landscape and includes the Dublin Mountains, the Wicklow Mountains and the Blackstairs Mountains.

> The Leinster Batholith was formed when molten magma was forced up into the crust. It pushed the original sedimentary rocks out of the way and occupied the great arched folds that this created. The magma cooled very slowly to form the great **granite** batholith.

> As the hot molten magma came into contact with the surrounding sedimentary rocks, the intense heat and pressure changed them to metamorphic rocks, such as **quartzite** and **schist**. Weathering and erosion have removed much of the overlying rock, exposing the gently sloping, dome-shaped mountains. Some are topped by **tors**. These are large blocks of granite with joints that have been enlarged by weathering (see page 97).

> Lugnaquilla, at 925 metres, is the highest peak in the Wicklow Mountains. It still has its capstone of resistant schist. This protected the underlying granite from erosion and has given it a steeper slope than the surrounding landscape.

DEFINITION

An **aureole** is the zone of metamorphic rock that surrounds an igneous intrusion.

Most of the Leinster Batholith is now exposed. This has produced a landscape of gently rounded hills, as seen here in the Blackstairs Mountains in Co. Carlow.

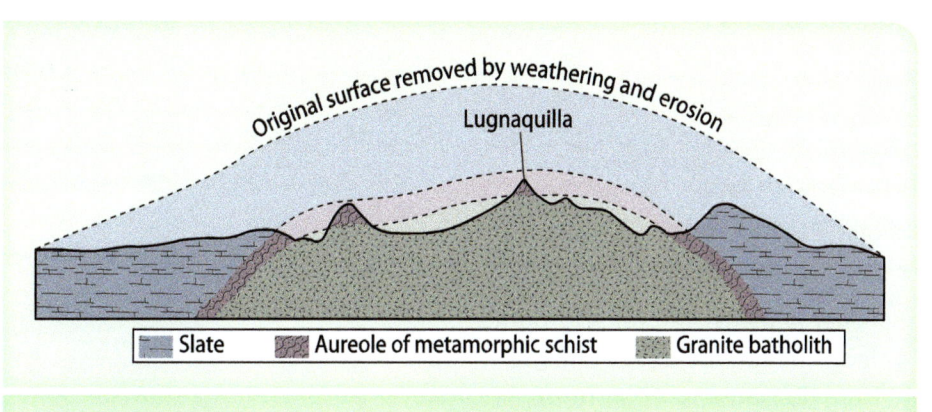

Figure 5.9 Weathering and erosion over the last 400 million years have eroded much of the overlying rocks of the Leinster Batholith

CASE STUDY

Geothermal energy in Iceland

Iceland's position on the Mid-Atlantic Ridge means that it is the location of much volcanic activity. Molten magma rises close to the surface. As a result, most of the country's energy needs are met by geothermal energy. Geothermal energy is energy derived from the heat of the Earth.

The groundwater in such areas absorbs heat from the rocks and becomes hot. As the water is heated, its temperature rises well above boiling point to become superheated. The water often reaches temperatures up to 200°C.

Wells are drilled into the rock and hot water is pumped out of the ground. If there is a shortage of groundwater, cold water is pumped into the rock via another series of wells. When the superheated water reaches the surface, the pressure drops and it turns to steam. The steam is then used to drive turbines and **generate electricity**.

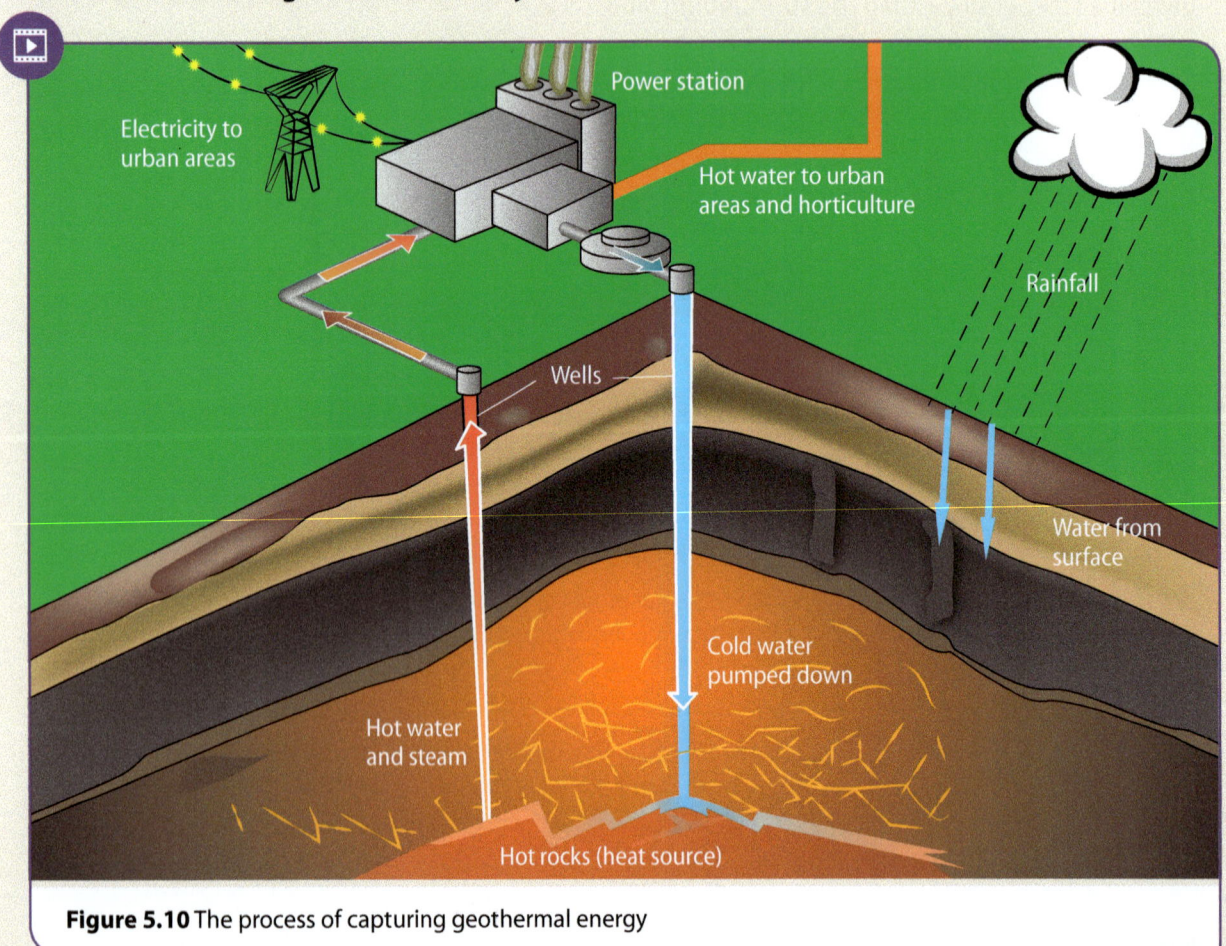

> **DEFINITION**
>
> **Geothermal:** Comes from the Greek works *geo* (earth) and *therme* (hot).

Figure 5.10 The process of capturing geothermal energy

Iceland has five geothermal energy plants and these produce over 75% of the country's electricity requirements. The main demand for energy comes from households. Apart from domestic uses, this source of clean, cheap energy has attracted energy-hungry industries such as aluminium smelting.

> **QUESTION**
>
> Why does Iceland have access to so much geothermal energy?

The country is now considering building an underwater connector to Scotland to export clean energy to the United Kingdom. This would help the UK to meet its renewable energy targets.

After being used to generate electricity, the still-hot water is then piped to nearby urban areas, where it is used for **central heating** in homes, offices and industry. Over 90% of homes in Iceland are heated by geothermal energy. Since the change from energy produced by coal to geothermal energy, Reykjavik, the capital of Iceland, has become one of the cleanest cities in the world.

At this stage, the water is now much cooler. It is then pumped through pipes that have been installed under the soil in **greenhouses**, enabling flowers and vegetables to be grown throughout the year. It has also replaced oil as the energy source used by growers.

Tourism is the fastest-growing section of the Icelandic economy. Most tourists are attracted by features that are related to volcanic activity. These include volcanoes, geysers and hot pools.

The **Blue Lagoon** is one of the best-known hot pools or spas in Iceland. Water heated by geothermal energy is pumped from 1,600 metres below the surface. Having been used to generate both heat and electricity, the excess (which is absolutely clean) is pumped into the lagoon. A major leisure complex has been developed and is now a key tourist attraction.

GEOFACT

In some parts of Iceland, hot water runs from geothermal power plants under pavements and roads to help melt ice.

The Blue Lagoon resort, with a geothermal power plant in the background

UNIT 1 · PHYSICAL GEOGRAPHY

PowerPoint Summary

SUMMARY CHART

Volcanic activity

- **Zones of volcanic activity**
  - Hot spots
  - Plates rifting
  - Divergent plate boundaries
  - Convergent plate boundaries

- **Cycle of volcanic activity**
  - Active volcanoes
  - Dormant volcanoes
  - Extinct volcanoes

- **Predicting volcanic activity**
  - Change in shape
  - Heat and gases
  - Seismic activity
  - History of eruptions

- **Volcanic materials**
  - Lava
    - Basic lava flow
    - Acidic lava flow
  - Pyroclastics
    - Ash, Dust, Cinders, Rock
      - Flow
      - Cloud
      - Lahar

- **Landforms of volcanic activity**
  - Intrusive
    - Batholith
    - Laccolith
    - Sill
    - Dyke
    - Cones, Dome, Caldera
  - Extrusive
    - Central vent eruption
    - Fissure eruption
    - Lava plateaus
    - Hot spot eruptions
    - Cones

- **Volcanic activity in Ireland**
  - Antrim–Derry Plateau
  - Leinster Batholith

- **Impacts of volcanic activity**
  - Positive
    - Soils, Tourism, Geothermal energy
  - Negative
    - Death, Destruction, Climate change

68 GEOGRAPHY TODAY

Leaving Cert exam questions

SHORT QUESTIONS: HIGHER LEVEL

HL

1. **Volcanic activity** (8 marks)

   Examine the photographs and answer each of the questions that follow.

   (i) Match each of the photographs **A**, **B**, **C** and **D** with the feature or process that best matches it in the table below.

Feature	Letter
Pyroclastic flow	
Lava fissure eruption	
Ash cloud	
Lava vent eruption	

   (ii) Indicate whether each of the following statements is true or false.

Basic lava has a very high silica content.	
Lava with a high silica content is most associated with explosive eruptions.	

2. **Structure of a volcano** (8 marks)

   Match the letters **A** to **H** in the diagram with the correct volcanic feature in the table below.

Feature	Letter
Vent	
Crater	
Ash cloud	
Secondary cone/parasitic cone	
Lava flow	
Magma chamber	
Volcanic bombs/lava bombs	
Subsidiary vent	

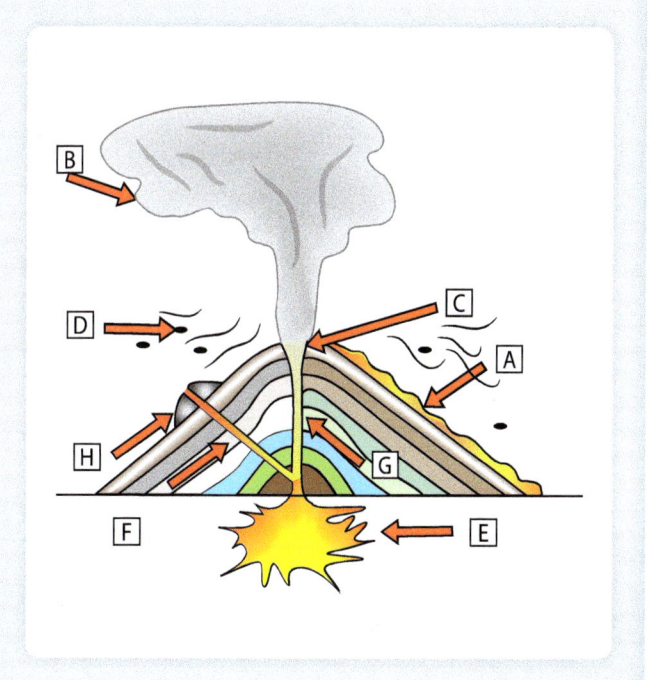

UNIT 1 · PHYSICAL GEOGRAPHY

CHAPTER 5 · VOLCANOES   69

UNIT 1 · PHYSICAL GEOGRAPHY

OL SHORT QUESTIONS: ORDINARY LEVEL

1 Volcano (10 marks)

Match each of the letters **A**, **B**, **C**, **D** and **E** in the diagram with the correct volcanic feature in the table.

Term	Letter
Magma chamber	
Vent	
New lava flow	
Old lava flow	
Crater	

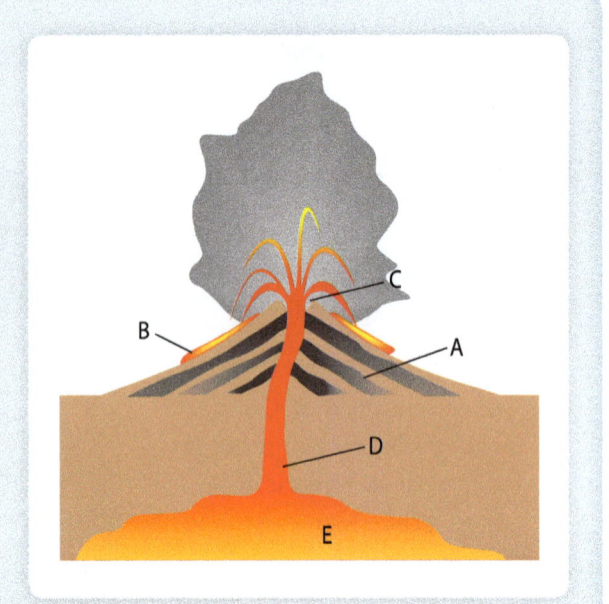

HL LONG QUESTIONS: HIGHER LEVEL

1 Volcanoes (20 marks)

Examine the map and legend showing the extent of the materials deposited as a result of the eruption of the Mount St Helens volcano. Answer the questions that follow.

(i) What were the most extensive deposits as a result of the eruption?

(ii) What was the direction of the pyroclastic flow deposits?

(iii) What distance did the pyroclastic flow deposits extend to?

(iv) Name **two** examples of pyroclastic materials.

(v) Explain briefly why some volcanoes erupt violently.

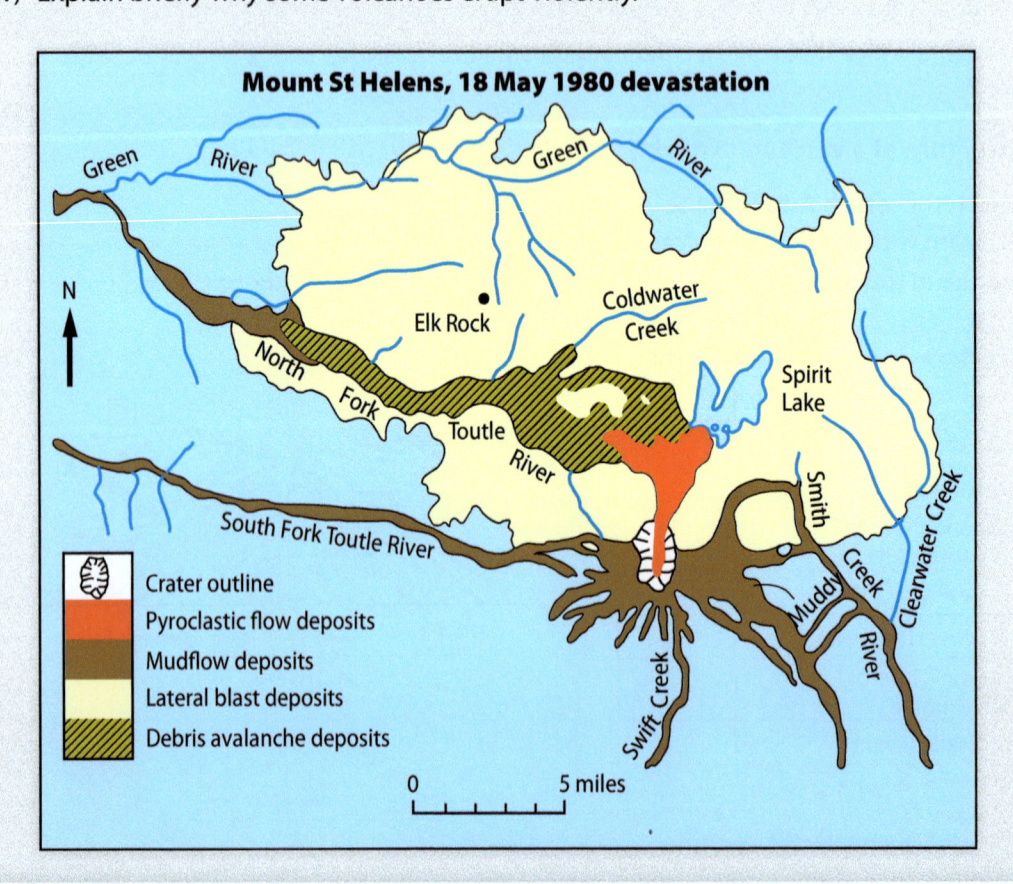

Mount St Helens, 18 May 1980 devastation

Legend:
- Crater outline
- Pyroclastic flow deposits
- Mudflow deposits
- Lateral blast deposits
- Debris avalanche deposits

GEOGRAPHY TODAY

HL

  2 Volcanoes (30 marks)

    Examine the processes that have led to the formation of any **two** volcanic landforms.

  3 Volcanoes (30 marks)

    Discuss the positive impacts of volcanic activity.

  4 Human interactions with rocks (30 marks)

    Examine how humans react with the rock cycle with reference to geothermal energy production.

OL

LONG QUESTIONS: ORDINARY LEVEL

  1 Volcanoes (40 marks)

  (i) Define and name an example of each of the volcano types listed below:
- Active volcano
- Dormant volcano
- Extinct volcano.

  (ii) Explain in detail how volcanoes occur.

  2 Volcanoes (40 marks)

  (i) Name **two** examples of volcanoes.

  (ii) Describe the negative effects of volcanoes.

  (iii) Describe the positive effects of volcanoes.

  3 Volcanoes (30 marks)

    Explain, with the aid of a diagram(s), how volcanic eruptions occur.

  4 Volcanoes (40 marks)

    Volcanoes can have both negative and positive effects on the landscape and on people. Explain **one** negative and **one** positive effect of volcanoes.

UNIT 1 • PHYSICAL GEOGRAPHY

Chapter 6
Rocks and the Rock Cycle

KEYWORDS

- mineral
- igneous
- sedimentary
- metamorphic
- granite
- basalt
- lithification
- organic
- inorganic
- chemical
- sandstone
- conglomerate
- limestone
- chalk
- thermal metamorphism
- regional metamorphism
- marble
- quartzite
- active plate margin
- trailing plate margin
- rock cycle

LEARNING OBJECTIVES

By the end of this chapter, you should be able to understand:

- How the different rock groups are formed
- How the rock cycle operates
- How variations in the rock type influence the physical landscape
- How humans interact with the rock cycle.

Rocks and minerals

Rock is the hard, naturally occurring material that makes up the Earth's crust. Rocks are composed of one or more **minerals** that have been cemented together. With about 4,000 different minerals found on the Earth, can you imagine how many rock types there are?

Rock groups

Rocks vary in colour, texture, hardness, age and mineral content. However, they are classified into three groups according to the way they were formed. These three groups are:

- Igneous (Latin *ignis* = fire)
- Sedimentary (sediments or remains)
- Metamorphic (Greek *meta* = change, *morphe* = form).

Quartz is the most common mineral on the Earth and is a part of almost every rock type

DEFINITION

Mineral: A naturally occurring inorganic substance that has its own unique properties.

GEOGRAPHY TODAY

Igneous rocks

Igneous rocks are formed when molten rock cools and solidifies. This can be either deep within the crust or on the surface. As a result, two groups of igneous rocks can be recognised.

> **Intrusive (or plutonic) rocks** are formed when molten magma forces its way into rock cavities or between layers of other rocks. It then cools and solidifies deep within the Earth's crust. Intrusive rocks eventually come to the surface as a result of uplift and the removal of overlying rocks. **Granite** is the most widespread type of intrusive igneous rock.

> **Extrusive (or volcanic) rocks** are formed when lava erupts from volcanoes or sea floor fissures. It then cools and solidifies on the Earth's surface. **Basalt** is the most widespread type of extrusive igneous rock.

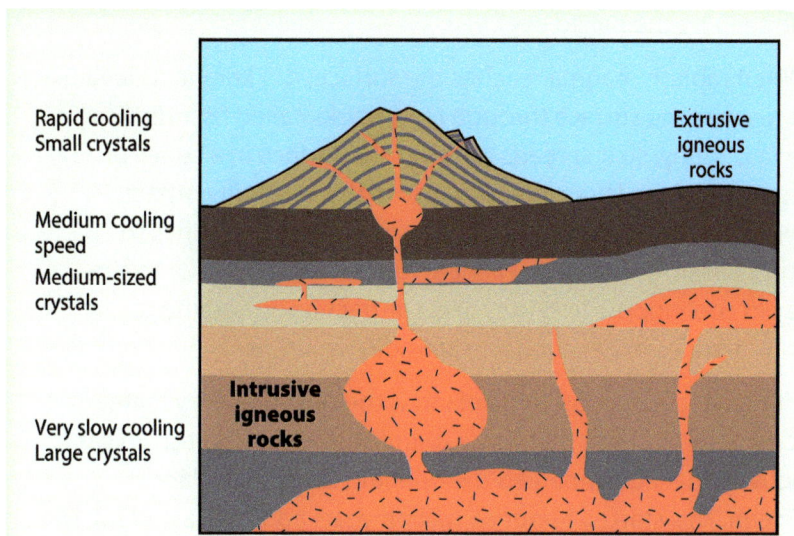

Figure 6.1 Igneous rocks can be divided into two groups, intrusive and extrusive, depending on where cooling and solidifying took place

Granite

Granite consists of three minerals: feldspar, mica and quartz. It normally has a dark grey colour. Variations in its mineral content can also lead to a range of colours, including pink-brown. It is **coarse grained** and has **large crystals**. It is very resistant to erosion.

Granite was formed when molten magma forced its way (**intruded**) into existing rocks on the Earth's crust. Over millions of years it cooled slowly underground, forming large structures called batholiths. The surrounding layers of rock acted like an insulating jacket and the magma cooled very slowly. As a result, crystals were given time to develop and grow.

The Connemara lowlands, the mountains of Donegal and the Leinster Batholith consist mainly of granite. They owe their origin to volcanic activity that took place about 400 million years ago, during the Caledonian folding. The overlying rock has been removed over time by weathering and erosion, exposing the granite to the surface (see *The Leinster Batholith*, page 65).

GEOFACT

Granite is one of the strongest building stones. It is used for the exterior of buildings, monuments and gravestones. It must be highly polished to prevent weathering.

When granite is broken down by weathering, it produces **kaolin** or **china clay**. These are used in the porcelain industry.

Basalt

Basalt is the most common type of rock in the Earth's crust and makes up most of the ocean floor. It is dark in colour, varying from black to dark green depending on its mineral content. It is **fine grained** and has **small crystals** (too small to be seen by the naked eye).

When molten magma reaches the surface, it is known as lava. It reaches the surface through long cracks called fissures. The lava is runny, so it spreads out over the surface in a series of flows to form a lava plateau. Because the lava is in contact with the atmosphere, it cools very quickly and solidifies to form basalt. The crystals that are formed are small due to the rapid cooling. The lava may also contract upon cooling to form a series of hexagonal or six-sided columns.

The main area of basalt in Ireland is the Antrim–Derry Plateau. It consists of basalt that came to the surface during the volcanic activity that accompanied the opening up of the Atlantic Ocean. This started about 65 million years ago and lasted for 15 million years (see *The Antrim–Derry Plateau*, page 64).

GEOFACT

Because it is so resistant to erosion, **basalt** is suitable for use as a road surfacing material. Its dull nature makes it unsuitable as a building stone.

When basalt is weathered in hot climates, it eventually breaks down to form a deep, fertile soil. This is suited to activities such as growing coffee.

ACTIVITY

Discussion

Describe two differences in the way that granite and basalt are formed.

Basalt (left) and granite (right). Describe two ways in which they differ.

Sedimentary rocks

Sedimentary rocks are formed on or near the Earth's surface. They may form on land, on lake beds or beneath the sea.

Sedimentary rocks generally develop in layers called **strata** (hence the term stratified rocks). This is because the sediments are deposited over time and at different rates. Successive strata are separated by bedding planes. The layers of sediments are converted into solid rock by the process of **lithification**.

Sedimentary rocks are usually classified by the origin of the sediments that they formed from.

DEFINITION

Lithification: The process that converts sediments into solid rock. It occurs in two ways:

> **Compaction:** The grains are squeezed together by the weight of overlying sediments.
> **Cementation:** Individual particles are bonded to one another by a cementing agent, such as silica or calcium carbonate.

- **Inorganic** sedimentary rocks were formed from sediments that were broken down by the weathering and erosion of pre-existing rocks. **Sandstones** and **conglomerates** are the most common inorganic sedimentary rocks.
- **Organic** sedimentary rocks were formed from the remains of once-living organisms, such as sea creatures and plants. **Limestone** and **coal** are the most common organic sedimentary rocks.

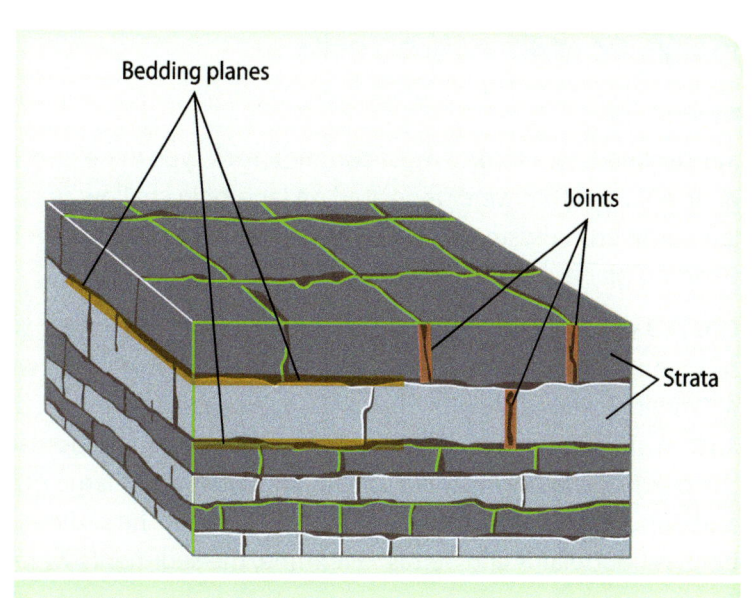

Figure 6.2 Many sedimentary rocks, including limestone and sandstone, form layer upon layer. These layers are called strata. The division between any two layers is called the bedding plane. They may also have vertical cracks called joints.

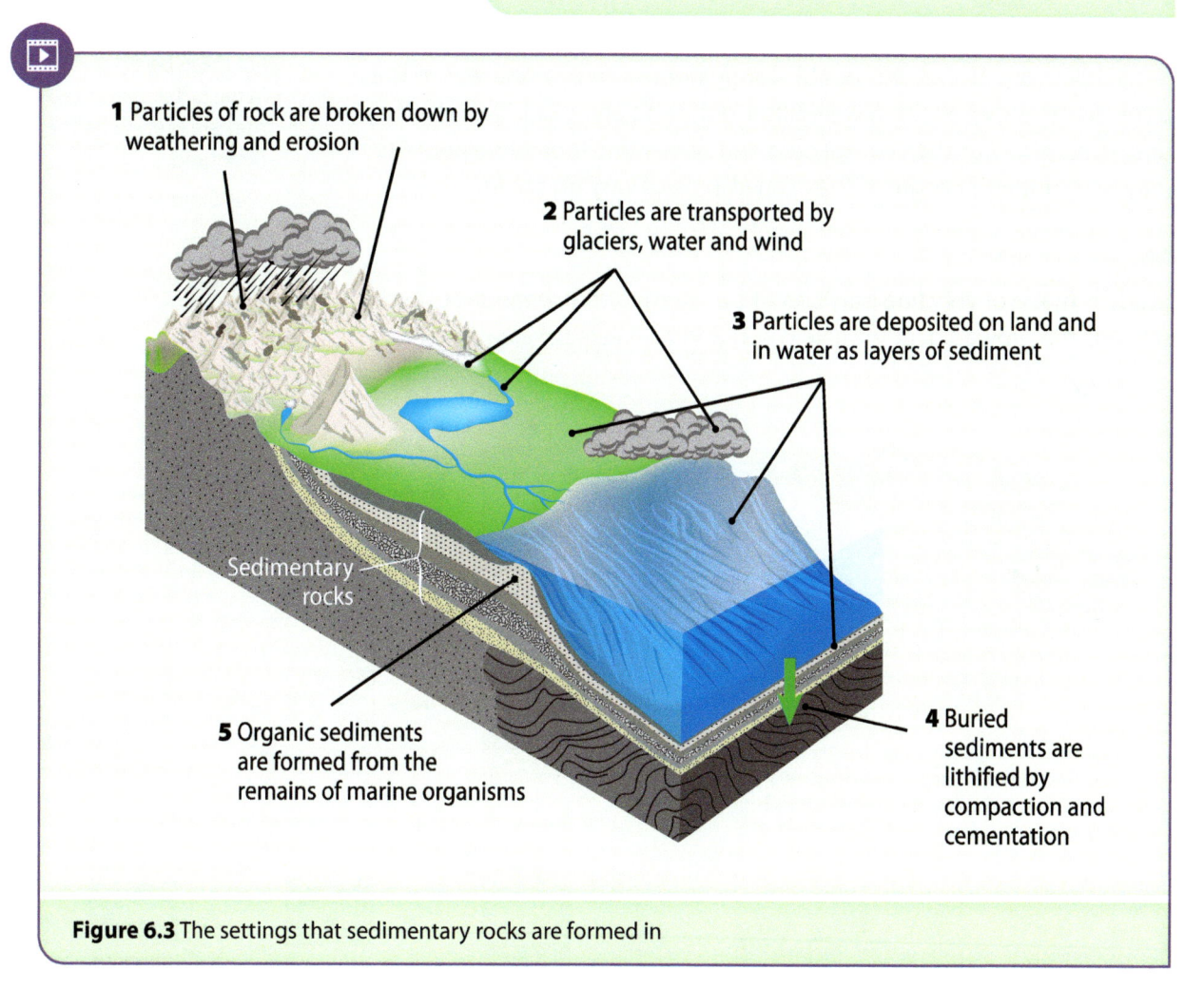

1 Particles of rock are broken down by weathering and erosion

2 Particles are transported by glaciers, water and wind

3 Particles are deposited on land and in water as layers of sediment

4 Buried sediments are lithified by compaction and cementation

5 Organic sediments are formed from the remains of marine organisms

Figure 6.3 The settings that sedimentary rocks are formed in

CHAPTER 6 · ROCKS AND THE ROCK CYCLE

Inorganic sedimentary rocks

Sandstone

Sandstone is the second most common rock type in Ireland. It was formed from grains of sand that were deposited on land or in shallow seas. These deposits were later lithified. Sandstone is a stratified rock, with the strata or layers separated by bedding planes.

Old red sandstone (ORS) has a brown-red or purple colour because the sediments contained particles of iron that later rusted. ORS was laid down almost 400 million years ago, when Ireland had a desert climate. At that time, weathering and erosion were wearing down the newly formed Caledonian fold mountains of the northern half of Ireland. Flash floods transported large quantities of sediments and deposited them on the bed of a shallow sea. The sediments were deposited here as floodplains and deltas. Over time, the sediments were lithified.

ORS can be found in locations as far apart as the Comeragh Mountains, Macgillycuddy's Reeks and the Galtee Mountains.

Conglomerates

Conglomerates are found in association with sandstone and were formed in a similar way. Stones and pebbles were deposited by flood water. The pore spaces between them were filled with sand and mud. The whole unsorted mass was then compacted and cemented. Individual pebbles may be rounded or angular. They can also be of varying colours.

Shale

Shale is made of very fine particles of clay or mud that were deposited by streams that flowed gently. Shale is soft and its layers flake easily.

> **ACTIVITY**
>
> **Thinking**
>
> Put these particles in the order that they are likely to be deposited:
>   (i) Sand
>   (ii) Clay
>   (iii) Gravel.

Conglomerate made of stones and pebbles cemented together

> **QUESTION**
>
> Explain each of the following terms:
>   (i) Strata
>   (ii) Bedding plane
>   (iii) Lithification.

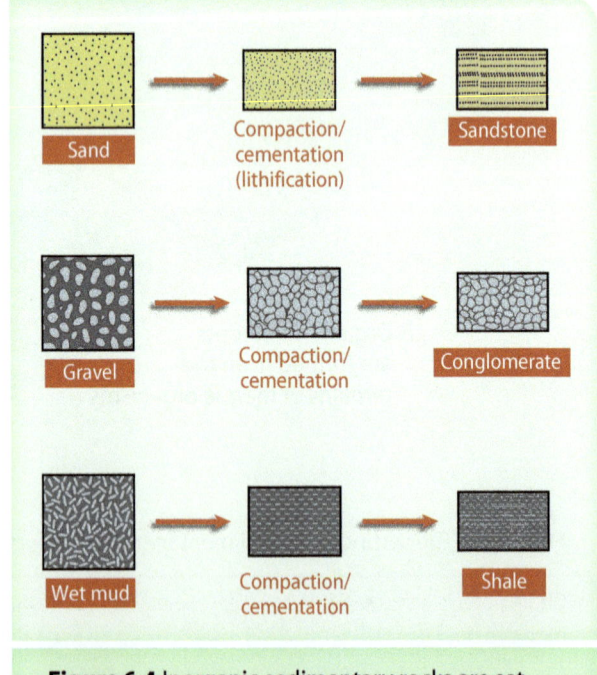

Figure 6.4 Inorganic sedimentary rocks are set apart by the size of the particles that they are formed from

Organic sedimentary rocks

Limestone

Limestone is composed almost entirely of calcium carbonate, but varies widely in appearance.

Limestone is a stratified rock laid down on the bed of a warm, clear, shallow sea. In the case of Ireland's limestone, this took place about 350 million years ago, when Ireland was located to the south of the equator.

Limestone is formed from the skeletal remains (teeth, bones, shells) of marine creatures. These include fish, sea urchins and coral. Great depths of these sediments were deposited. Over time they were compressed by their own weight and cemented by calcium carbonate to form solid rock. Some of these remains can still be seen embedded in the rock as **fossils**.

There are many types of limestone, including carboniferous, dolomite and chalk. Pure limestone is almost white. Carboniferous limestone is hard, grey and consists of at least 50% calcium carbonate. It gets its grey colour from impurities in the rock, such as clay, sand and carbon. It is well jointed, allowing for the development of a distinctive type of landscape called **karst** (see page 101).

Limestone is the most common rock in Ireland. It is exposed in regions such as the Burren and the Aran Islands. It is covered by peat and boulder clay in regions such as the Central Plain.

Chalk

Chalk is a pure, soft, white-coloured limestone. It was laid down far away from sediments that originated on land and so was not contaminated by them. It once covered most of Ireland, but has been eroded. This excludes where it is protected by a covering layer of basalt in the Antrim–Derry Plateau.

> **GEOFACT**
>
> Limestone is found in thirty-one of the thirty-two counties of Ireland. Wicklow is the exception.

> **ACTIVITY**
>
> **Discussion**
>
> Identify and describe two differences between organic and inorganic sedimentary rocks.

Chalk (left) is a soft, white, powdery limestone. Limestone (right) has colour variations due to impurities in the rock.

Metamorphic rocks

Metamorphic rocks are formed from igneous rocks or sedimentary rocks that have changed as a result of **heat** and/or **pressure**. These changes can be physical (change in appearance) or chemical (change in make-up). They take place at a great depth below the surface.

There are two types of metamorphism: **contact** and **regional**.

> **Contact (or thermal) metamorphism** occurs where there is an intrusion of molten magma into the crust. As a result, the rocks are changed by heat alone. Contact metamorphism is localised, as the intrusion 'cooks' only the surrounding band of rocks. This band of metamorphic rock that surrounds the intrusion is called an **aureole**.

> **Regional metamorphism** occurs when heat and pressure are applied over a large area (hence the term regional). This occurs at zones of fold mountain building or at subduction zones. Rocks are subjected to extreme pressure by the colliding plates. They are also exposed to high temperatures as magma rises into the buckled rock.

Most of Ireland's metamorphic rocks were formed about 400 million years ago during the Caledonian folding period, when the American and Eurasian plates collided (see page 26). Since then, many of the overlying rocks have been eroded, exposing the metamorphic rocks next to the igneous rocks that changed them.

QUESTION

Explain two ways in which regional metamorphism and contact metamorphism differ.

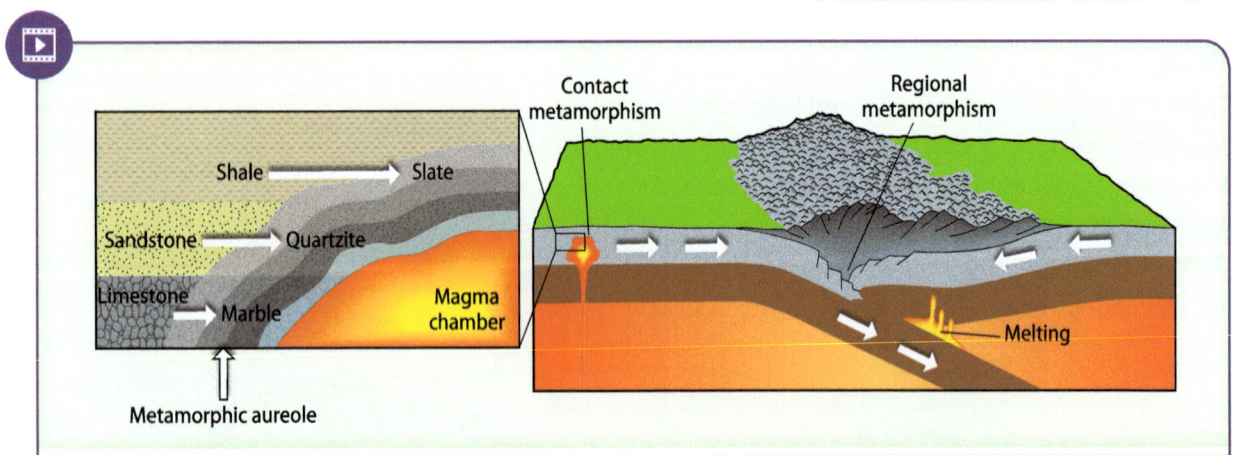

Figure 6.5 Metamorphism occurs in two ways: contact metamorphism and regional metamorphism. Contact metamorphism occurs closer to the surface, but regional metamorphism produces the greatest quantity of metamorphic rock.

Marble

> **Marble** is a coarse-grained rock whose parent rock was either limestone or chalk.
> Most marble is formed as a result of regional metamorphism, where the limestone was changed by both pressure and heat. The structure of the limestone is destroyed as fossils and other organic material trapped in the limestone are broken down. Crystals are melted by the heat. They are then reformed as large crystals in the new marble.

Unpolished lump of Connemara marble

- Pure marble is white. Quarries at Carrara (Tuscany) supplied the marble for Michelangelo's most famous sculptures.
- The limestone that marble is formed from often contains impurities, which give various colours to the marble. The presence of iron oxide produces a red or pink marble, while serpentine produces a green marble.
- Marble has many uses, most of which are ornamental. They include sculptures (headstones and statues) and building material (columns and floor tiles).
- Ornamental marble is found in many locations in Ireland, including Connemara (green), Cork (red) and Rathlin Island (white).

Quartzite

- **Quartzite** is made from its parent rock, sandstone, that has been metamorphosed. The change occurred during periods of folding, when sandstone came into contact with deeply buried magmas.
- Extreme heat and pressure then caused the quartz and silica grains in the sandstone to 'cook' and melt. This also destroyed the stratified structure of the sandstone. As the material cooled it fused together, creating a new rock with larger grains than the sandstone.
- Quartzite varies in colour, depending on the impurities in the original rock. It is a non-porous rock that is much harder than its parent rock. As a result, it is used for kitchen worktops.
- Quartzite is extremely resistant to weathering and erosion. It remains as a cap on some of Ireland's most distinctive mountains. These include Croagh Patrick (Co. Mayo), Mount Errigal (Co. Donegal) and the Sugar Loaf (Co. Wicklow).

ACTIVITY

Thinking

Why is limestone sometimes called the parent rock of marble?

GEOFACTS

- The so-called black marble of Kilkenny, used for headstones and monuments, is in fact a type of polished limestone.
- The Taj Mahal in India is built from white marble.

The resistant quartzite peak of Mount Errigal stands out above the Co. Donegal countryside

Distribution of rocks in Ireland

This simplified geological map of Ireland (Figure 6.6) shows the regional distribution of the three rock groups. Each group is broken down into its most commonly occurring rock types.

The rock cycle

The **rock cycle** is the repeated formation and destruction of rocks and minerals on the Earth's crust.

The elements that make up rocks are never lost. Thus, all the rocks on the Earth today are made of the same material as the rocks that dinosaurs and other ancient life forms walked, crawled or swam over.

Although the material that rocks are made from stays the same, the rocks themselves do not. Instead, over millions of years they are constantly changed or recycled into other rocks. This happens due to the forces that operate not just inside the Earth, but also on its surface.

The rock cycle shows that the three rock types are related to one another. It also explains the processes that continually change rocks from one type to another type and back again.

Rocks are:

> Formed when magma and lava cool and solidify to form igneous rocks.
> Broken down by weathering and erosion into sediment particles. These sediments can turn into sedimentary rocks.
> Changed by heat and/or pressure to form metamorphic rocks.
> Turned into molten magma and recycled. This molten material will again cool and solidify to form igneous rocks.

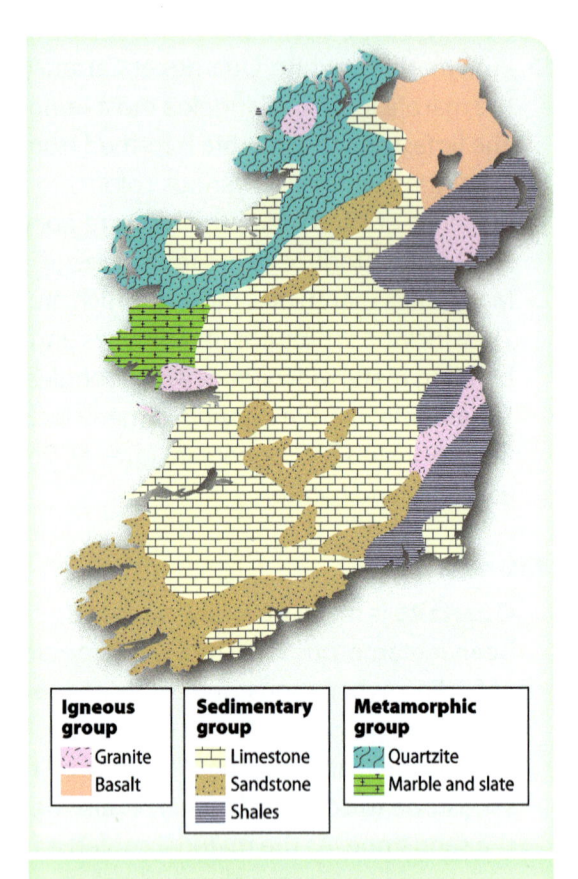

Igneous group: Granite, Basalt
Sedimentary group: Limestone, Sandstone, Shales
Metamorphic group: Quartzite, Marble and slate

Figure 6.6 Geological map of Ireland showing the locations of the main rock types

ACTIVITY

Skills
Examine Figure 6.6. Name the two most common rock types in Ireland.

GEOFACT

All rocks on the Earth were originally igneous.

ACTIVITY

Thinking
If an igneous or sedimentary rock gets so hot that it melts completely, why does it not become a metamorphic rock?

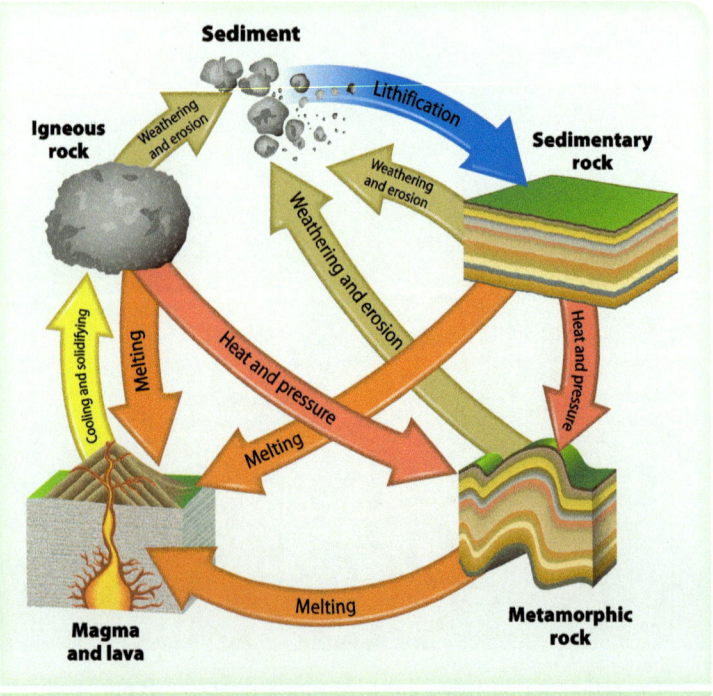

Figure 6.7 The rock cycle

CASE STUDY

Active and trailing plate margins in North America

There is a link between the processes that are active in a zone and the geology of that zone. This can be seen in North America, where:

> An **active plate margin** occurs along the western edge of the continent
> A **trailing plate margin** occurs along the eastern coastal plain of the continent.

Active plate margin

> The American Plate is colliding with the Pacific Plate at a plate boundary.
> This is an active plate boundary where ocean crust is being subducted under continental crust.
> There is a narrow continental shelf.
> The margin is associated with volcanic activity, earthquakes, folding and faulting.

This is reflected in the geology of the area:

> North America's newest igneous and metamorphic rocks have been formed here.
> Many of the older, overlying sedimentary rocks have been removed by weathering and erosion. This exposes the igneous and metamorphic rocks.
> Valuable mineral deposits (ores, gold and diamonds) are found here.

Trailing plate margin

> The American Plate is moving away from the Eurasian Plate.
> This is not on an active plate boundary. Instead, new ocean floor is being created.
> There is a very wide continental shelf. Gentle uplift is raising it above sea level.
> There is little or no seismic or volcanic activity.

This is reflected in the geology of the area:

> Sediments have been eroded from the mountains in the interior and deposited offshore. They have been lithified to form sedimentary rocks.
> Limestone is being formed in the warm, shallow seas further offshore.
> The region has enormous oil and gas reserves due to the burial and decay of organic materials.

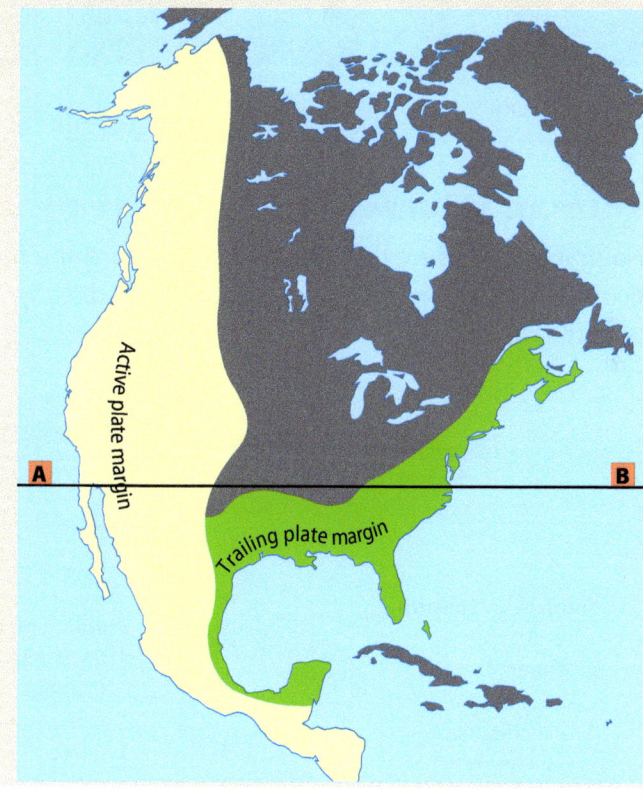

Figure 6.8 Active and trailing plate margins in North America

Rock type and landscape

Variations in rock type may lead to the development of distinctive landscapes. This is particularly true in the case of some rocks. In Ireland, these landscape include:

> The **basalt landscape** of the Antrim–Derry Plateau and Giant's Causeway (page 64)
> The **granite landscape** of the Wicklow Mountains (pages 65 and 97)
> The **limestone (karst) landscape** of the Burren (page 101).

Basalt landscape of the Giant's Causeway

Granite landscape of the Wicklow Mountains

Limestone (karst) landscape of the Burren

Human interactions with the rock cycle

Natural resources are those that occur in nature and have economic value. Most are linked, directly or indirectly, with the rock cycle.

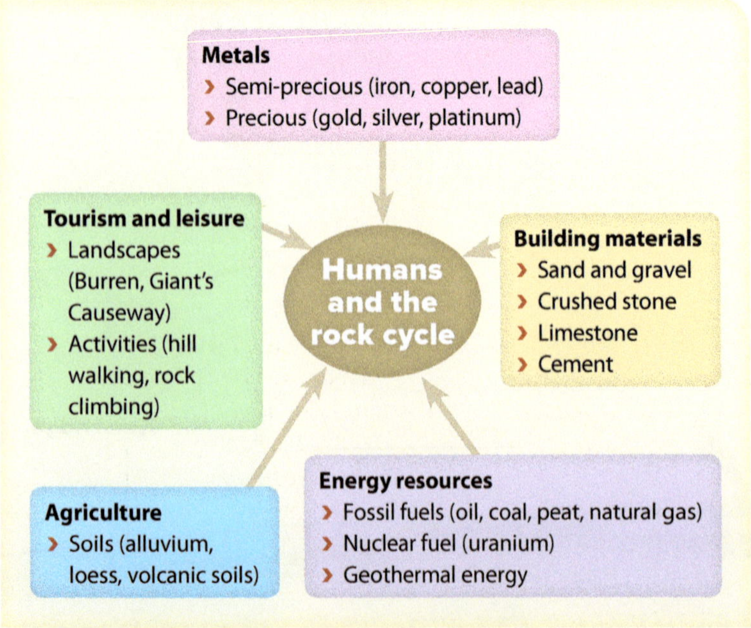

HINT

You must study **one** human interaction with the rock cycle.

Select from:
> *Geothermal energy* (page 66)
> *Natural gas* (page 83).

ACTIVITY

Discussion

Outline three factors that a mining or drilling company should consider before it starts a project.

Metals
> Semi-precious (iron, copper, lead)
> Precious (gold, silver, platinum)

Tourism and leisure
> Landscapes (Burren, Giant's Causeway)
> Activities (hill walking, rock climbing)

Humans and the rock cycle

Building materials
> Sand and gravel
> Crushed stone
> Limestone
> Cement

Agriculture
> Soils (alluvium, loess, volcanic soils)

Energy resources
> Fossil fuels (oil, coal, peat, natural gas)
> Nuclear fuel (uranium)
> Geothermal energy

Figure 6.9 Human interaction with the rock cycle

CASE STUDY

Natural gas in Ireland

Formation of natural gas

- **Natural gas** is part of a family of chemicals that also includes oil. Both are formed from the decayed remains of very small plants and animals.
- As these microscopic plants and animals lived, they absorbed energy from the sun. When they died, they were buried beneath layers of mud and sand in a marine environment where there was little oxygen. Over millions of years, bacterial action broke down the organic materials into tiny droplets of oil or gas. The amount of pressure and the degree of heat determined if the material became oil or natural gas.
- After the natural gas was formed, it tended to migrate up through tiny pores in the surrounding rock. Some migrated all the way to the surface and escaped. Other natural gas deposits migrated until they were caught under impermeable layers of rock, where they were trapped. These traps are where we find natural gas deposits today.

Tiny sea plants and animals die and sink to the ocean floor.

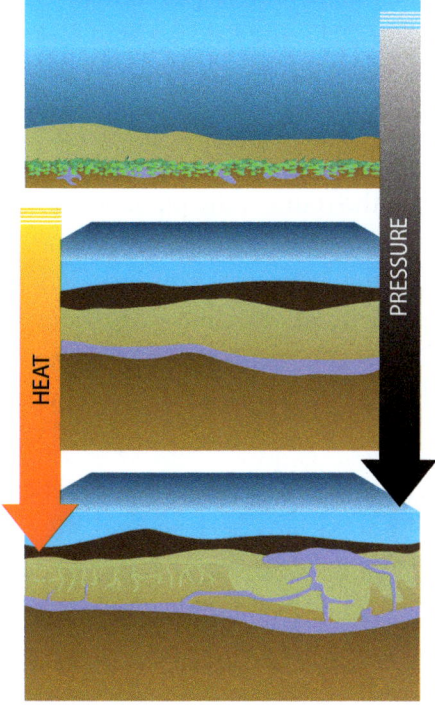

Over time, the plant and animal layer is covered with layers of silt and mud.

The layers are buried under more layers of sediment. Heat and pressure turn them into natural gas (and oil).

The gas migrates upwards until it is held in a trap beneath a layer of impermeable rock.

Figure 6.10 Natural gas collects in a trap, where it remains until it is discovered

Exploring for natural gas

- The search for natural gas begins with geologists locating rock structures (anticlines and faults) that are known to contain gas and oil deposits. Small explosions are used to create seismic waves, like tiny earthquakes. These allow for accurate three-dimensional mapping of underground formations.
- Rock samples are drilled and examined. If it seems that a gas deposit is present, an exploratory well is drilled. If the presence of gas is confirmed, further tests take place to determine its extent and rate of flow.

GEOFACT

Natural gas is mainly made up of methane, which is colourless and odourless. As a result, methyl mercaptan (with a smell like sulphur) is added as a safety device.

Natural gas production in Ireland

Ireland has two known sources of natural gas. Both are located offshore.

Kinsale Head

The **Kinsale Head gas field** was discovered in 1971 and the field has been in production since 1978. The main platform is located in 100 metres of water. It pumps gas from a depth of 1,000 metres below the seabed. It is pumped ashore via an underwater pipeline, reaching land at Cork Harbour. After production began, two other gas deposits were discovered in the area and were linked to the Kinsale Head pipeline. However, rates of flow have been much lower than expected. Gas reserves in these fields are now almost exhausted.

Corrib gas field

Natural gas was discovered in the **Corrib gas field** in 1986 but did not enter production until December 2015. The field is about 80 km offshore in waters that are over 350 metres deep. The gas trap is about 3 km beneath the seabed. Pumping takes place at the seabed and is remotely controlled.

Production of gas was originally due to start in 2005 but was delayed by planning issues regarding the route of the pipeline and the location of the processing terminal. Further delays occurred as opponents of the scheme cited concerns. These concerns included health as well as the safety and environmental impact of the onshore aspects of the project. These concerns led to part of the pipeline route being changed and some of the pipeline being enclosed in a tunnel.

The gas is processed at an onshore terminal at Bellanaboy Bridge. As with the gas from the Kinsale Head field, the gas will be distributed throughout Ireland via the Gas Networks Ireland (formerly Bord Gáis Networks) national grid.

> **GEOFACT**
>
> When gas production is complete, the Kinsale Head field is estimated to have the potential to store up to 330 million tonnes of carbon dioxide. This could reduce Ireland's greenhouse gas emissions to the atmosphere by 6% annually.

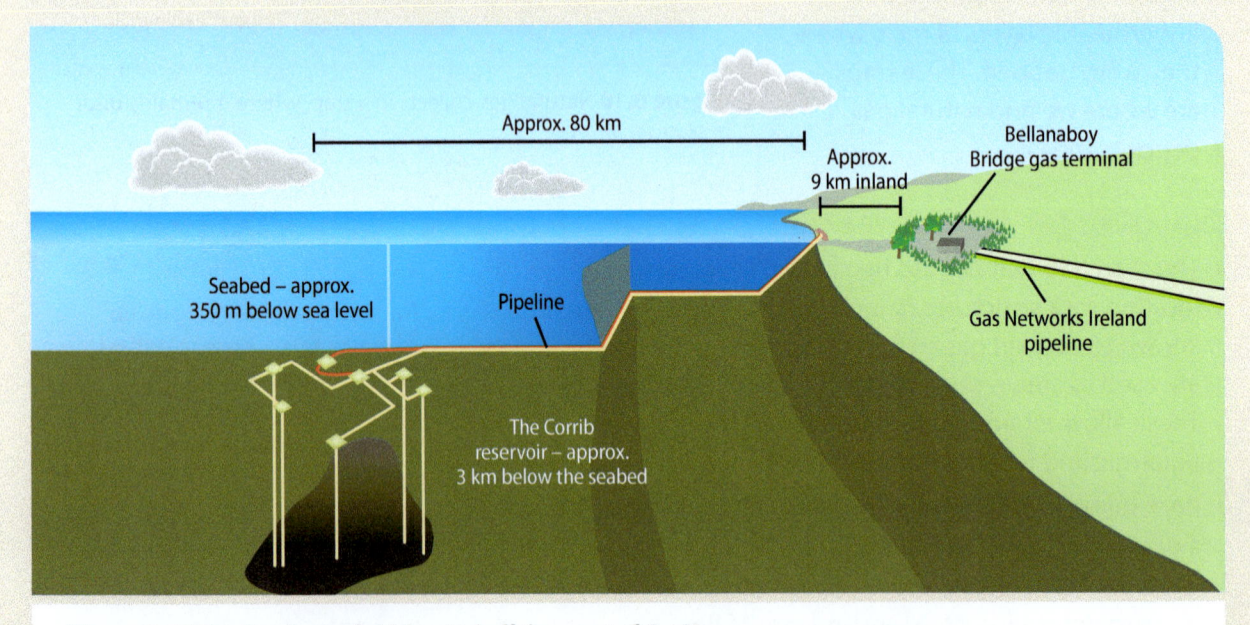

Figure 6.11 The Corrib gas field, located off the coast of Co. Mayo

Natural gas usage in Ireland in 2016

> Natural gas accounts for approximately 25% of the total energy demand in Ireland.
> The Irish gas market uses less than 1% of the total EU gas consumption.
> It is expected that at peak production, the Corrib gas field will provide up to 60% of Ireland's annual gas requirements. Supplies at the field are expected to last for fifteen to twenty years.
> The Irish market currently sources the rest of its gas supplies via sub-sea interconnector pipelines with Scotland.
> The gas supply market in Ireland has been gradually opened to competition in recent years. Business users and residential customers are now able to choose their own gas provider.
> Gas is used in the generation of about 60% of Ireland's electricity.
> Gas is also being used directly as an energy source by the industrial sector.
> More than half a million households have now been connected to the pipeline network.

Economic impact

Natural gas has benefited the Irish economy.

> It has generated revenue as well as reducing imported fuels. This will benefit our balance of payments.
> It will also provide a greater guarantee (security) of gas supply into the future.
> It offers direct employment in the two terminals as well as indirect employment in areas such as pipe-laying, etc.
> The arrival of the Corrib gas should also help to attract more industry to the West of Ireland.

Environmental impact

Natural gas is the cleanest of all fossil fuels. It is also the most efficient (less energy is wasted) of the fossil fuels used in electricity generation. However, drilling for natural gas and building pipelines to transport it have damaged some sensitive environments.

Figure 6.12 Ireland's natural gas pipeline network

UNIT 1 · PHYSICAL GEOGRAPHY

PowerPoint Summary

SUMMARY CHART

Plate margins
- Active (leading)
- Trailing (passive)

Rock cycle
- Cooling and solidifying
- Melting
- Heat and pressure
- Lithification
- Weathering and erosion

Rocks → **Rock types**

Rock types:
- Igneous
- Sedimentary
- Metamorphic

Igneous:
- Volcanic activity → Extrusive / Intrusive
- Extrusive: Basalt — Fast cooling — Small crystals — Volcanic cones, Fissure eruptions, Mid-ocean ridges
- Intrusive: Granite — Slow cooling — Large crystals — Leinster Batholith

Metamorphic:
- Processes: Heat and pressure
- Settings/types: Contact (thermal), Regional
- Marble — From limestone — Connemara, Donegal
- Quartzite — From sandstone — Errigal, Croagh Patrick

Sedimentary:
- Characteristics: Stratified, Bedding planes, Impermeable
- Lithification: Compaction, Cementation
- Inorganic: Sandstone/conglomerate — Grains of sand/stones and sand — Mountains of Munster
- Organic: Limestone/chalk — Remains of sea creatures — Burren, Antrim

Rock type and landscape
- Basalt (Giant's Causeway)
- Granite (Wicklow Batholith)
- Limestone (The Burren)

Human interaction
- Mining
- Extraction of building materials
- Oil/gas exploration
- Geothermal energy

86 GEOGRAPHY TODAY

Leaving Cert exam questions

SHORT QUESTIONS: HIGHER LEVEL

1 Rocks (8 marks)

(i) The list below contains a number of source materials from which rocks are formed and a number of metamorphic rocks.

- Sand
- Marble
- Shells and fish bones
- Gneiss
- Magma
- Quartzite

Complete the table below by inserting the correct terms from the list, to match each of the rocks named in the table with:

(a) The source material most associated with it
(b) The metamorphic rock most associated with it.

Rock name	(a) Source material	(b) Metamorphic rock
Sandstone		
Limestone		
Granite		

(ii) Name the rocks most associated with each of the following Irish locations.

(a) The Antrim Plateau
(b) The Burren

2 Rocks (8 marks)

The table below contains information on rocks regarding their name, category, location in Ireland and the name of the metamorphic rock they can become following metamorphosis.

Complete the table by inserting the correct term from the list below in its correct position in the table. One row of the table is completed for you.

- ~~Sedimentary~~
- ~~Central Plain of Ireland~~
- Sandstone
- Gneiss
- Igneous
- ~~Marble~~
- Wicklow Mountains
- Granite
- Mountains of Munster
- Quartzite
- ~~Limestone~~
- Sedimentary

Name of rock	Category of rock	Location in Ireland	Metamorphic rock
Limestone	Sedimentary	Central Plain of Ireland	Marble

3 Rock type (8 marks)

Link each of the following locations to one of the rock types below:
Wicklow Mountains, Galtee Mountains, the Giant's Causeway and the Burren.

Rock type	Location
Basalt	
Limestone	

Rock type	Location
Sandstone	
Granite	

CHAPTER 6 · ROCKS AND THE ROCK CYCLE

SHORT QUESTIONS: ORDINARY LEVEL

1 Rocks (10 marks)

Examine the photographs and answer each of the following questions.

(i) Indicate whether each of the following statements is true or false.

(a) The rock type in photograph A is limestone and it is a permeable rock.

(b) The rock type in photograph B is slate and it was formed from lava cooling.

(c) The rock type in photograph C is marble which was once limestone or chalk, but was changed by great heat and/or pressure.

(d) The rock type in photograph D is basalt and it can be found in Co. Antrim.

(ii) Is basalt an igneous, sedimentary or metamorphic rock?

2 Rocks (10 marks)

(i) Match the name of the rock with the location most associated with it by writing the correct letter in each case in the table below.

Letter	Rock type
A	Limestone
B	Marble
C	Basalt

Location	Letter
Giant's Causeway	
The Burren	
Connemara	

(ii) State whether each of following rocks is an igneous **or** sedimentary **or** metamorphic rock.

(a) Marble (b) Basalt

LONG QUESTIONS: HIGHER LEVEL

1 Rocks (30 marks)

Explain the formation of **one** igneous rock and **one** metamorphic rock, with reference to Irish examples.

2 Sedimentary and metamorphic rocks (30 marks)

Describe the formation of **one** sedimentary rock that you have studied **and** briefly explain how this rock may be transformed into a metamorphic rock.

3 Rock cycle (20 marks)

Examine the diagram of the rock cycle and answer the questions that follow.

(i) Name the category of rock formed at **A** and name **one** example of this category of rock.
(ii) Name the category of rock formed at **B** and name **one** example of this category of rock.
(iii) Name **one** example of an igneous rock which is formed at **C**.

The rock cycle

HL
(iv) Name **one** example of an igneous rock which is formed at **D**.
(v) Briefly explain the difference between the process of weathering and the process of erosion.

4 Rocks (30 marks)

Explain the formation of igneous rocks **or** sedimentary rocks **or** metamorphic rocks with reference to Irish examples.

5 Rocks and landscapes (30 marks)

Examine how different rock types produce distinctive landscapes, with reference to examples that you have studied.

6 Rock type and landscape (30 marks)

Examine, with reference to an example that you have studied, the formation of **one** rock type and how it produces a distinctive landscape.

7 Human interaction with the rock cycle (30 marks)

Describe any **one** of the following examples of how humans interact with the rock cycle:

> Quarrying
> Mining
> Oil/gas exploration
> Geothermal energy production.

8 Human interaction with the rock cycle (30 marks)

Explain, with reference to **one** human interaction with the rock cycle that you have studied, how humans benefit economically from this interaction.

LONG QUESTIONS: ORDINARY LEVEL

OL

1 Rocks (40 marks)
(i) Name **one** example of an igneous rock **and** name an Irish location where it can be found.
(ii) Describe how igneous rocks are formed.
(iii) Name **one** example of a metamorphic rock **and** name an Irish location where it can be found.
(iv) Describe how metamorphic rocks are formed.

2 Rocks (40 marks)
(i) Name any **two** examples of sedimentary rock.
(ii) Name any **two** uses of the sedimentary rocks named above.
(iii) Describe how sedimentary rock is formed.

3 Rock cycle (30 marks)

With reference to the circles labelled **A**, **B** and **C** showing the rock cycle, which letter represents each of the following?

> Sedimentary
> Metamorphic
> Igneous

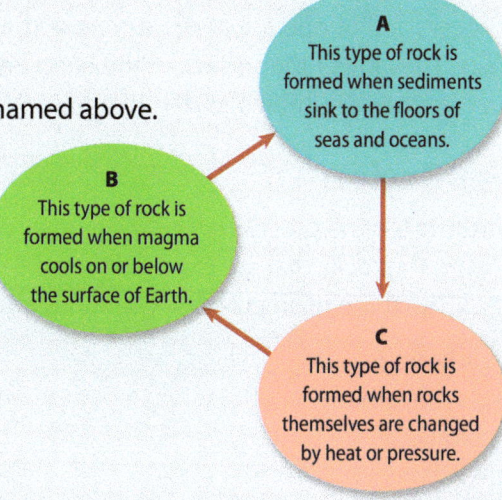

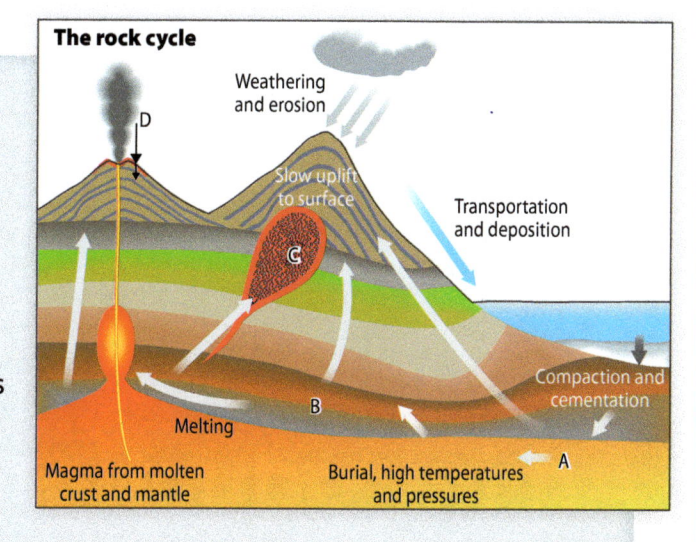

A This type of rock is formed when sediments sink to the floors of seas and oceans.

B This type of rock is formed when magma cools on or below the surface of Earth.

C This type of rock is formed when rocks themselves are changed by heat or pressure.

CHAPTER 6 · ROCKS AND THE ROCK CYCLE   89

Chapter 7
Denudation: An Introduction

KEYWORDS

- endogenic
- exogenic
- denudation
- weathering
- mass movement
- erosion

LEARNING OBJECTIVE

By the end of this chapter, you should be able to understand:
- That the surface of the Earth is shaped by weathering, mass movement and erosion.

Introduction

In previous chapters we dealt with the processes where rocks have been formed and modified by **endogenic** processes. These are processes where the energy originates from **within the Earth**. They include:

- Plate tectonics
- Volcanic activity
- Rock formation and the rock cycle
- Folding and faulting
- Earthquakes.

When rocks are exposed at the Earth's surface, they are modified or destroyed by **exogenic** processes. These are processes that operate **at or very near the Earth's surface**. They lower the surface of the Earth and, taken together, are known as denudation.

Denudation

Denudation is the process of breaking up and removing the rocks that are exposed on the Earth's surface. The three main processes of denudation are:

- Weathering
- Mass movement
- Erosion.

ACTIVITY

Discussion

Identify two differences within each pair of terms:
(i) Denudation and mass movement
(ii) Weathering and erosion.

GEOFACT

The rate of denudation is greater today than at any time in the Earth's history. About 20 billion tons of regolith are removed annually. Denudation is made easier due to land clearing, deforestation, crop farming and overgrazing.

PowerPoint Summary

Denudation
Occurs by weathering, mass movement and erosion.

Weathering
Weathering is the breakdown and decay of rocks that are exposed to weather.

There are two types of weathering:
› Mechanical weathering
› Chemical weathering.

Mass movement
Mass movement is the movement of loose material (**regolith**) downslope under the influence of gravity.

There are two categories of mass movement:
› Slow (creep)
› Rapid (slides, flows, falls).

Erosion
Erosion is the wearing away of rocks and the removal of the materials that results.

The main agents (causes) of erosion are:
› Moving water (rivers and sea)
› Moving ice (glaciers)
› Moving air (wind).

Figure 7.1 The processes by which denudation occurs

The impact of weathering on the landscape

Chemical weathering in the Burren

Mechanical weathering at Yosemite

The impact of mass movement on the landscape

Slow mass movement in Co. Clare

Rapid mass movement in South America

The impact of erosion on the landscape

Rivers: Waterfall in Wales

Ice: Valley glacier in New Zealand

Waves: Some of the Twelve Apostles, Australia

Wind: Sandy desert in Death Valley, California

CHAPTER 7 · DENUDATION: AN INTRODUCTION

Chapter 8
Weathering

KEYWORDS

- weathering
- physical weathering
- freeze-thaw
- scree
- exfoliation
- chemical weathering
- carbonation
- hydrolysis
- kaolin clay
- tor

LEARNING OBJECTIVES

By the end of this chapter, you should be able to understand:

- How to identify the different types of weathering
- How the processes of weathering operate
- How to identify landforms associated with weathering.

Weathering

Weathering is the process by which rocks on or near the Earth's surface are broken down or decayed in situ (in their original position). Weathering processes can produce distinctive landscapes.

Weathering is influenced by the following factors:

- **Rock type:** Rocks that contain bedding planes, faults and folds will weather more quickly than those that do not. Rocks that have minerals that react when mixed with water will weather more rapidly.
- **Climate:** Climate decides which type of weathering will be more active and the speed it takes place at.
- **Topography:** Upland areas are more exposed to weathering than lowland areas.

Types of weathering

Rocks are likely to be weathered when they are exposed to water, the gases of the atmosphere, changing temperatures or the release of pressure.

There are two main types of weathering:

- Physical (or mechanical) weathering
- Chemical weathering.

Although these types of weathering are different, some of them work together.

Physical weathering

Physical (or mechanical) weathering is the breakdown of rock by physical forces into smaller particles. There is no change in the chemical make-up of the weathered material.

Physical weathering is concentrated along weaknesses in the rock. Sedimentary rocks, such as sandstone, have layers, or strata. Some rocks, such as limestone, have joints or cracks. Others, such as conglomerates, have spaces between the grains they are made from. Physical weathering acts to widen these gaps.

Physical weathering is most likely to occur in areas that have little or no vegetation and extremes of climate, such as deserts and mountains. The two main types of physical weathering are both the result of **temperature change**.

They are:
- Freeze-thaw
- Exfoliation.

> **QUESTION**
>
> Give another name for each of the following:
> (i) Mechanical weathering
> (ii) Freeze-thaw
> (iii) Exfoliation.

Freeze-thaw

- **Freeze-thaw (or frost wedging)** is the most common form of physical weathering. It is most effective in cold or upland regions where the temperature moves above and below freezing point (0°C). For example, arctic and alpine environments have hundreds of freezing and thawing cycles per year.
- Water fills the spaces in the rock during the daytime, when temperatures are warmer. The water freezes at night when temperatures drop below freezing point. As the water turns to ice, its volume expands by about 9%. This puts pressure on the rock, forcing the gaps to open up. The pressure can be as great as two tons per square centimetre. When the water melts during the day, the pressure is released.
- This sequence of freeze followed by thaw slowly weakens the rock and widens the gaps. Eventually, particles of rock break off. These particles are called **scree** or talus. They may collect at the base of a steep slope under the influence of gravity. Scree particles are sharp and angular in shape, suggesting that they formed from sudden splitting.

> **ACTIVITY**
>
> **Thinking**
>
> Why is freeze-thaw unlikely to occur near the summit of Mount Everest?

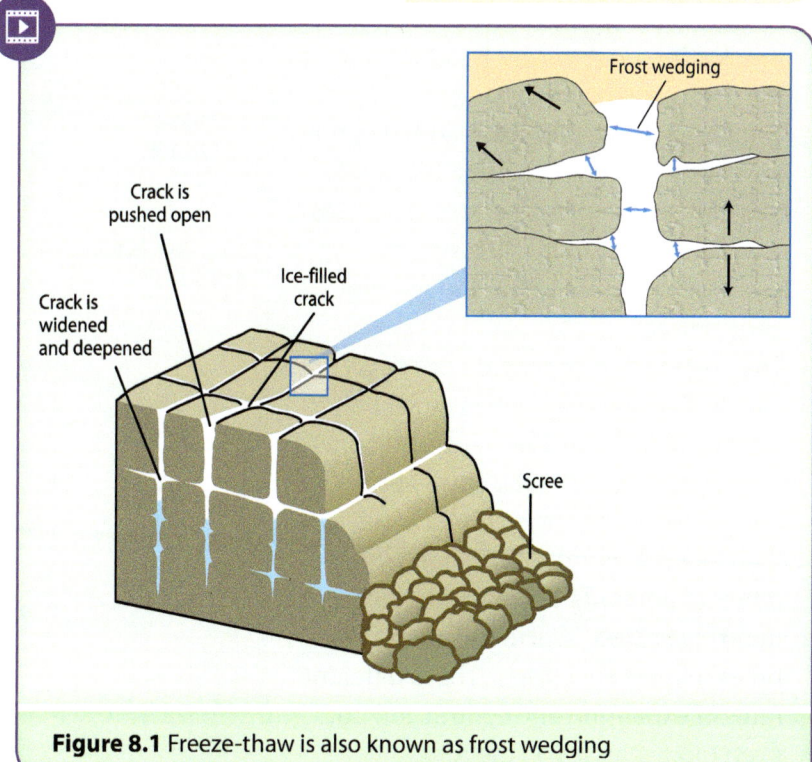

Figure 8.1 Freeze-thaw is also known as frost wedging

› Most scree accumulations in Ireland were formed at the end of the last ice age. Freeze-thaw still occurs in Ireland, mainly in mountainous areas in winter. Scree accumulations can be seen on the sides of Croagh Patrick (Co. Mayo), the Great Sugar Loaf (Co. Wicklow), Carrauntoohil (Co. Kerry) and Slieve League (Co. Donegal).

Scree accumulation at the foot of a slope in the Rockies

ACTIVITY

Skills

Examine the photograph on the right. What evidence is there to show that freeze-thaw has occurred?

Exfoliation

› **Exfoliation (or onion weathering)** is a form of physical weathering that is caused by temperature changes. This process helps to strip off the outer layers of rocks. It is most effective where the rocks have strata or joints that lie parallel to or are open to the surface.
› Exfoliation occurs in areas with a great daily (diurnal) temperature range, including hot deserts such as the Sahara and Death Valley. Daytime temperatures are high, frequently above 40°C. This is due to the absence of cloud cover and the position of the sun high in the sky. This heats the rock surface during the day, causing it to expand.
› The absence of cloud cover added to the absence of vegetation leads to a rapid loss of heat at night, when temperatures may fall close to 0°C. As a result, the layers of rock close to the surface cool and contract.
› The heating and cooling do not occur evenly. The outer layers heat and cool much more quickly than layers that are further in. Dark-coloured rocks absorb heat faster than light-coloured rocks. The minerals in the rocks expand by different amounts. For example, when quartz is heated, it increases in size three times more than feldspar. These different rates of expansion and contraction put even more stresses on the rock.

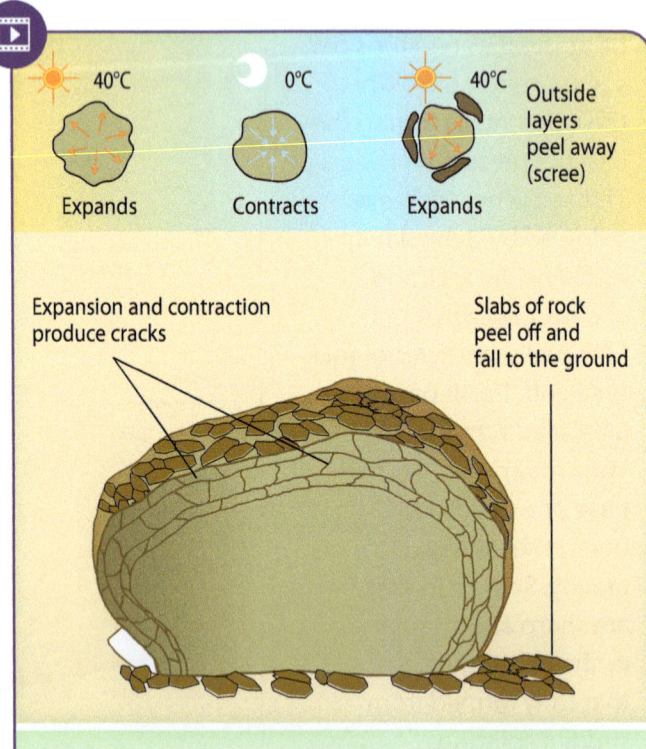

Figure 8.2 Exfoliation causes the outer layers of rock to peel off like the layers of an onion

> Fractures and flaking begin to occur. The outer layers of rock peel off like the layers of an onion and collect as a pile of scree at the base of the slope.
> As more layers of rock are removed, there is less pressure (weight) on underlying layers. This allows them to expand and as they do so, they fracture. This then begins the next cycle of exfoliation. The Half Dome in Yosemite National Park is a spectacular example of an exfoliation dome.

ACTIVITY

Thinking
Why does exfoliation mainly occur under desert or semi-desert conditions?

Exfoliation near the summit of the Half Dome in Yosemite National Park. Note the climbers on a wire walkway to the left of centre.

Chemical weathering

Chemical weathering refers to the decomposition or decay of rocks. In chemical weathering, the make-up of the rock is changed. Minerals are dissolved or they are changed to new minerals.

Chemical weathering involves a number of processes, all of them associated with moisture. Thus, it is most common in locations where there is a lot of precipitation. Temperature is also an important factor in the rate of chemical weathering. It occurs much more quickly in warm, wet conditions such as those found in the tropics than it does in deserts or near the poles.

Although there are many different chemical weathering processes, two that have helped shape the Irish landscape are:

> Carbonation
> Hydrolysis.

Carbonation

> **Carbonation** is one of the most common and effective forms of chemical weathering. Rainwater absorbs carbon dioxide as it falls through the atmosphere. As water passes through soil, it absorbs even more carbon dioxide from organic matter. The water and carbon dioxide combine to form a weak carbonic acid. This acid reacts with minerals in the rocks and either dissolves them or turns them into other minerals.

$$CO_2 + H_2O \rightarrow H_2CO_3$$
carbon dioxide in the atmosphere — water — carbonic acid

$$CaCO_3 + H_2CO_3 \rightarrow Ca(HCO_3)_2$$
limestone — carbonic acid — calcium bicarbonate

Figure 8.3 Carbonation weakens the rock and removes the weathered materials

- Rocks such as chalk and limestone contain calcium carbonate. The calcium carbonate reacts with weak carbonic acid to form calcium bicarbonate, which is soluble. It is then removed in solution. Carbonation is extremely effective at weathering limestone landscapes because limestone has lines of weakness in its bedding planes and joints. Carbonation is concentrated on these weaknesses.
- Carbonation produces distinctive limestone landscapes, called **karst** topography. Karst has characteristic landforms both on the surface and underground. In Ireland, these include the Burren in Co. Clare and the Marble Arch Caves in Co. Fermanagh. (See Chapter 9 for more on limestone landscapes.)

QUESTION

Why is limestone so readily affected by carbonation?

Carbonation has created a distinctive karst landscape in the Burren

Hydrolysis

- **Hydrolysis** is a form of chemical weathering where water reacts with chemicals in the rock and breaks them down. It produces a new substance that is nearly always softer and weaker than the original material.
- Fine-grained rocks generally weather faster than more coarse-grained rocks because they have a larger surface area that is open to weathering.
- Hydrolysis happens much more quickly in hot, wet conditions, such as those found in the tropics. Here water percolates (trickles down) to a considerable depth, so hydrolysis often occurs far below the surface. It also works best when the water is slightly acidic.

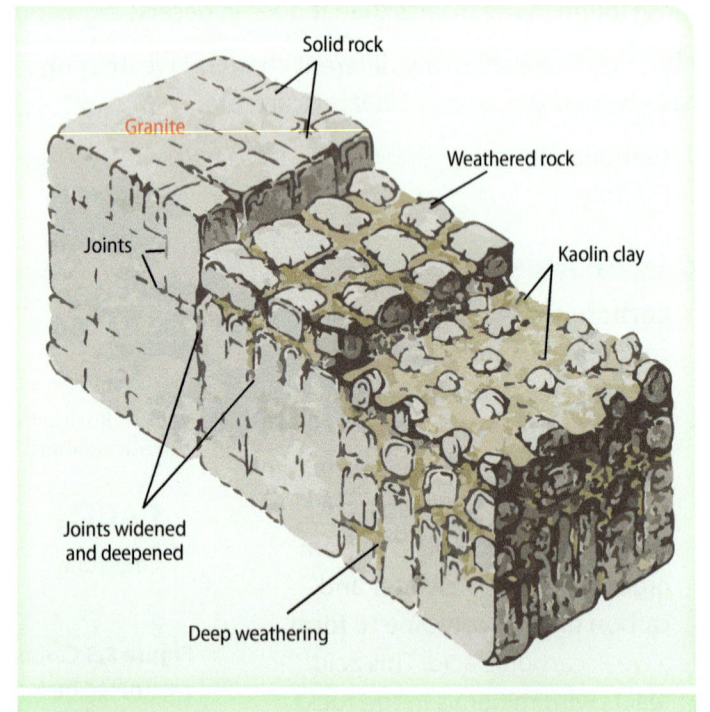

Figure 8.4 Granite is weathered both on and beneath the surface

- Hydrolysis is very effective in weathering rocks such as granite. **Feldspar** is one of the minerals that make up granite. It easily absorbs water. In the chemical process that takes place, the feldspar decays to a new clay-like mineral called **kaolin**.
- While feldspar is very good at bonding minerals in the rock together, kaolin is very poor at bonding. It crumbles easily, weakening the rock and causing it to break down and disintegrate. The more resistant minerals in the granite, such as quartz and mica, are no longer held together and remain as loose, sand-like debris.
- Hydrolysis is important in the soil-forming process because most soils contain a high proportion of clay minerals.
- Hydrolysis has helped shape the granite of the Leinster Batholith. The process took place when Ireland had a warmer climate, when the process was more effective.

> **GEOFACT**
>
> Kaolin clay, also known as china clay, is used in the pottery and cosmetics industries.

CASE STUDY

Weathering in the Wicklow Mountains

The Wicklow Mountains are part of the Leinster Batholith and consist mainly of granite.

The original rock cover of slate, schist and quartzite was gradually removed by denudation, exposing the granite. Over the ages, the granite has been shaped by running water, ice and weathering.

Unfractured granite is impermeable. However, with the weight of the overlying rock removed, the granite began to expand upwards. This caused it to crack and it developed both horizontal and vertical fractures. These lines of weakness were exploited over time by both freeze-thaw and hydrolysis. While these processes are very different, they often operate together, depending on the rock characteristics. Granite is one such rock.

> **DEFINITION**
>
> **Batholith:** An area of molten rock that cooled very slowly within the crust, creating a rock with large crystals.

The result is a series of roughly rectangular blocks called **tors**. These resistant rock outcrops stand out on the landscape because they have weathered less rapidly than the rock that surrounds them. With their horizontal joints, they resemble a series of flat rocks piled on top of one another. (See *The Leinster Batholith*, page 65.)

Tors on a granite upland landscape

PowerPoint Summary

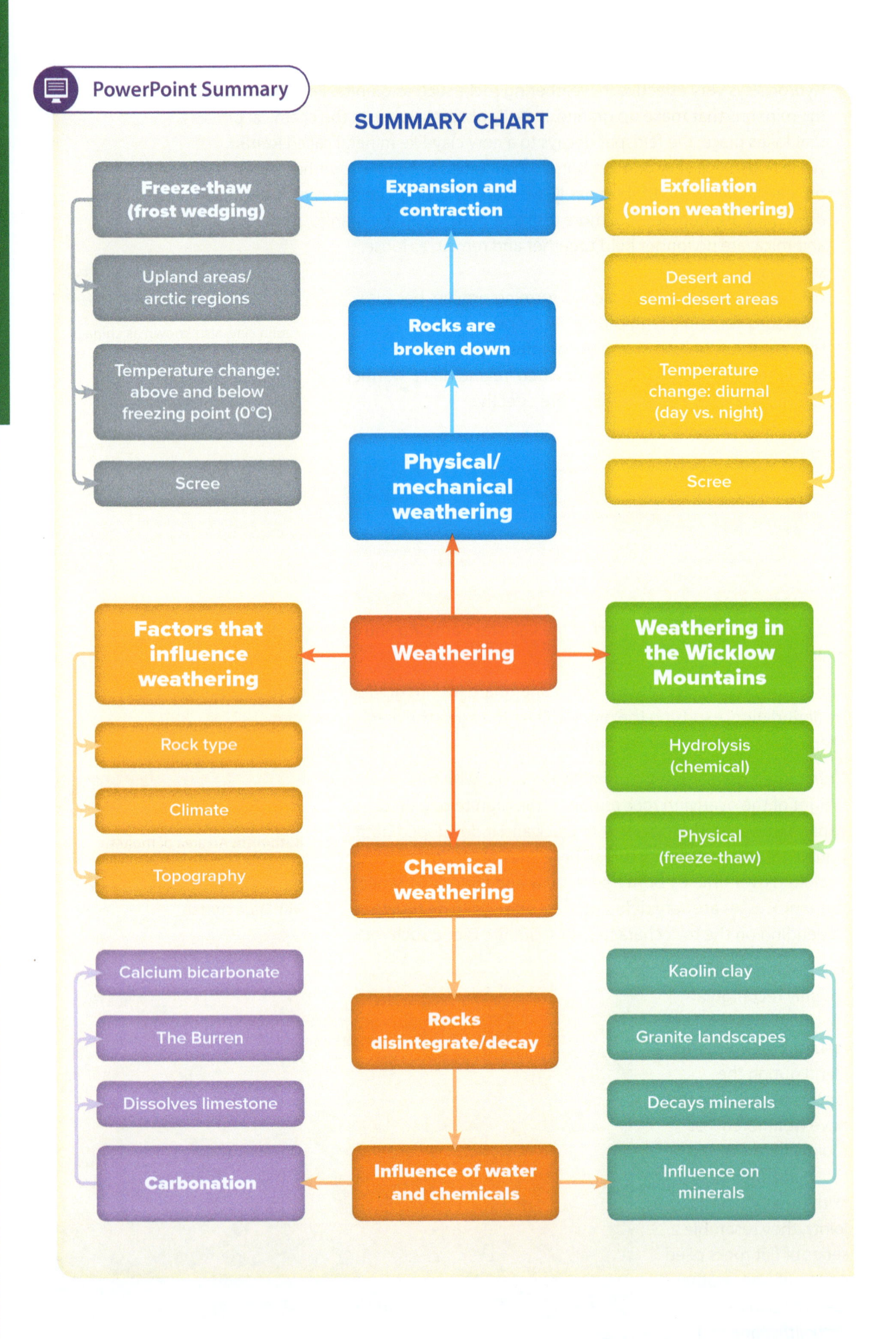

SUMMARY CHART

Weathering

- **Physical/mechanical weathering**
  - Rocks are broken down
  - Expansion and contraction
    - **Freeze-thaw (frost wedging)**
      - Upland areas/arctic regions
      - Temperature change: above and below freezing point (0°C)
      - Scree
    - **Exfoliation (onion weathering)**
      - Desert and semi-desert areas
      - Temperature change: diurnal (day vs. night)
      - Scree

- **Factors that influence weathering**
  - Rock type
  - Climate
  - Topography

- **Weathering in the Wicklow Mountains**
  - Hydrolysis (chemical)
  - Physical (freeze-thaw)

- **Chemical weathering**
  - Rocks disintegrate/decay
  - Influence of water and chemicals
    - Calcium bicarbonate
    - The Burren
    - Dissolves limestone
    - Carbonation
  - Influence on minerals
    - Kaolin clay
    - Granite landscapes
    - Decays minerals

UNIT 1 · PHYSICAL GEOGRAPHY

98 GEOGRAPHY TODAY

Leaving Cert exam questions

SHORT QUESTIONS: HIGHER LEVEL

1. **Weathering** (8 marks)

   Examine the diagram and write down the correct answer for each of the following.

   (i) Identify the weathering agent active at **A**.

   (ii) Is this agent an example of mechanical (physical) or chemical weathering?

   (iii) Which of the following best describes temperatures at **A**?

   (a) Always below freezing point (0°C)

   (b) Varying above and below freezing point

   (c) Never below freezing point

   (iv) What name is given to the rock particles at **B** that gather at the foot of the slope?

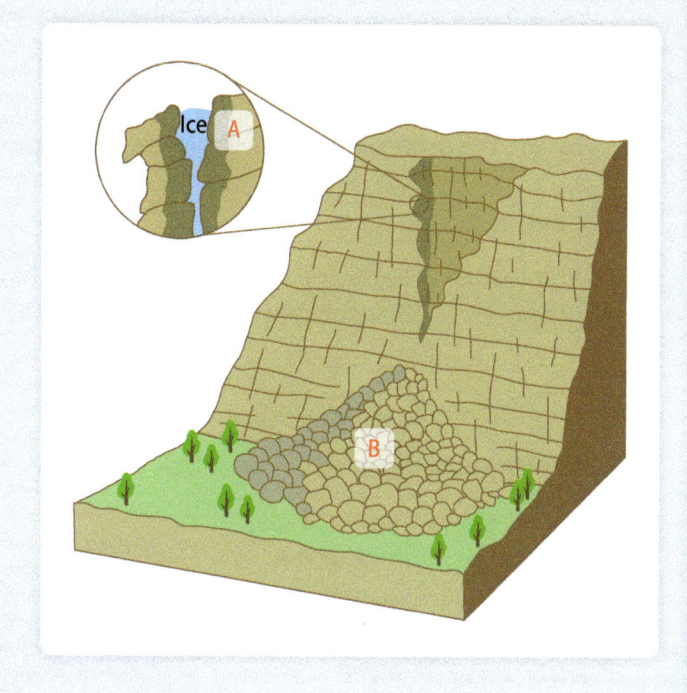

SHORT QUESTIONS: ORDINARY LEVEL

1. **Freeze-thaw** (10 marks)

   Insert each of the numbers **1**, **2**, **3**, **4** and **5** in the correct space in the table to indicate the order in which the process of freeze-thaw occurs. One line has been done for you.

Process	Order (1 to 6)
When the temperature goes below 0°C, the water freezes and expands.	
Repeated expansion and contraction weaken the rock and bits break off.	
The ice thaws during the day and contracts. Water goes deeper into the crack.	
Water collects in a crack in the rock.	
This puts pressure on the rock and the crack is widened.	
The particles of rock fall down the slope as scree.	6

CHAPTER 8 · WEATHERING

LONG QUESTIONS: HIGHER LEVEL

1 Weathering (30 marks)

Explain **one** process of physical weathering and **one** process of chemical weathering.

2 Weathering (30 marks)

Explain the process(es) of physical weathering **or** the process(es) of chemical weathering.

3 Weathering (30 marks)

With reference to the Irish landscape, examine how the processes of weathering have influenced the development of any **one** landscape feature.

LONG QUESTIONS: ORDINARY LEVEL

1 Weathering (30 marks)

(i) In your answer book, match each of the photographs **A** and **B** with the weathering process most associated with it from the list below:

> Carbonation
> Freeze-thaw action.

(ii) With the aid of a diagram(s), explain how rocks are weathered by freeze-thaw action.

2 Weathering (30 marks)

Describe and explain any **one** of the following weathering processes that you have studied:

> Freeze-thaw action
> Carbonation.

Chapter 9
Karst Landscapes

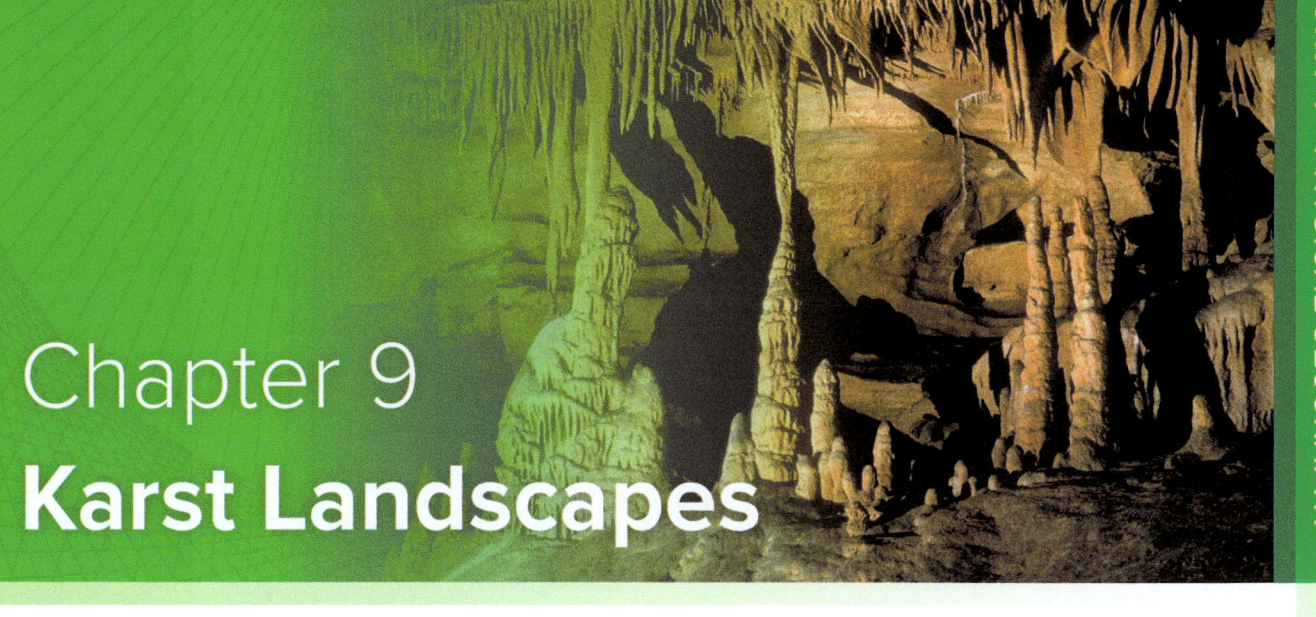

UNIT 1 · PHYSICAL GEOGRAPHY

KEYWORDS

- karst
- weathering
- carbonation
- solution
- limestone pavement
- clints
- grikes
- karren
- fluting
- swallow hole
- dry valley
- emergent stream
- closed depression
- doline
- uvula
- polje
- cave and cavern
- calcite
- stalactites
- stalagmites
- pillars
- curtains
- karst life cycle
- Burren

LEARNING OBJECTIVES

By the end of this chapter, you should be able to understand:

- How weathering interacts with rock characteristics to produce a distinctive landscape
- The formation of surface and underground landforms
- The life cycle of a karst landscape.

Characteristics of limestone

The development of landscapes is sometimes influenced by the characteristics of the bedrock. This is the case in a limestone landscape.

The following characteristics of limestone affect its weathering:

- It was laid down in horizontal **strata**, separated by **bedding planes**.
- It has fractures called **joints** that run at right angles to the bedding planes.
- Some limestone is porous. It contains small gaps between the solid fragments and these can hold water.
- It is **permeable**, enabling water to pass down through the joints and bedding planes.
- Weathering and erosion are concentrated on these lines of weakness.
- It is composed mainly of calcium carbonate, which is **soluble** in rainwater.

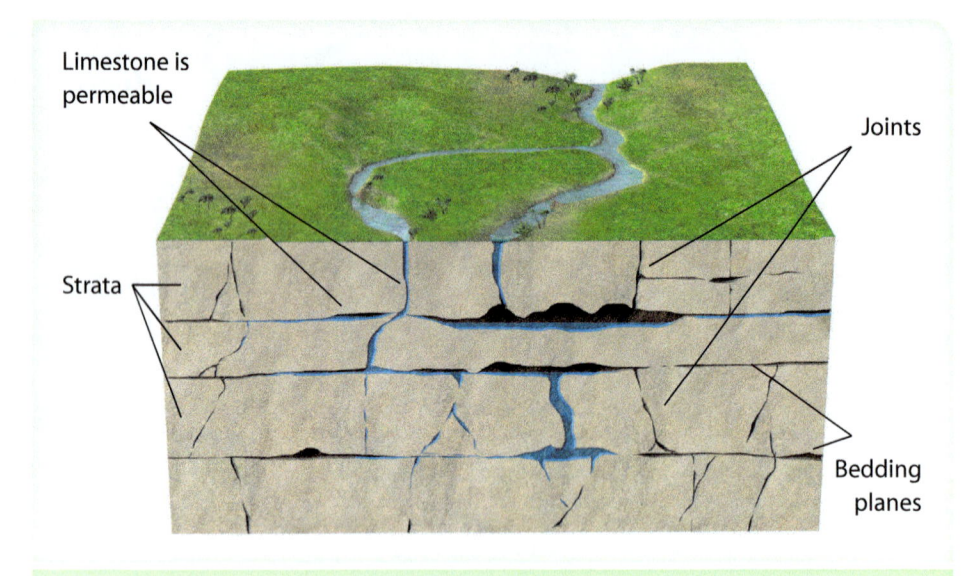

Figure 9.1 The characteristics of limestone that make it prone to weathering

When limestone is weathered, it develops a distinctive stony landscape, with both surface and underground features. This is called a **karst landscape**, after the karst region of Slovenia, where this type of landscape and landforms are well developed.

Shaping a limestone landscape

For a limestone landscape to develop, there needs to be a plentiful supply of rainfall. The water table should be well below the surface of the limestone. This enables the water to flow down. This is important because moving water shapes a limestone landscape.

The most important process in shaping a limestone landscape is **carbonation**. This is a chemical weathering process. It occurs when rainwater falling through the air absorbs carbon dioxide, turning it into a weak carbonic acid. Rainwater that passes through soil before reaching the limestone becomes even more acidic. The carbonic acid reacts with the calcium carbonate, changing it to soluble calcium bicarbonate. This is dissolved and removed from the rock in **solution**. Limestones that are relatively pure and hard with a high percentage of calcium carbonate tend to develop the best karst features.

Where the vegetation cover of a limestone landscape is thin or absent, **freeze-thaw** may occur in winter. This enlarges and widens the joints in the rock, increasing the surface area that is open to carbonation.

As the joints and bedding planes are enlarged, more water is able to enter and flow through them. This erodes the limestone by **hydraulic action** and **abrasion**.

The effects of carbonation are seen best in areas of exposed bare limestone, such as the Burren in Co. Clare. These landscapes lack surface drainage but have a range of distinctive **surface** and **underground** landforms.

ACTIVITY

Skills

Examine Figure 9.1. Identify two differences between bedding planes and strata.

DEFINITION

Solution: Where a solid (e.g. calcium carbonate) is dissolved in a liquid (e.g. acidic water).

Surface landforms of a limestone landscape

Limestone pavement

> A **limestone pavement** is a large, flat area of limestone that has had its soil cover removed and has been exposed at the surface over a long period of time.

> Limestone is a stratified and well-jointed rock. As a result, rainwater is able to percolate (trickle) freely down through the joints and bedding planes.

> **Carbonation** is concentrated in these areas. The joints are widened and deepened to form a series of fissures, called **grikes**. These can be up to 30 cm wide and 100 cm deep. The rest of the limestone is more resistant to weathering. It remains as a series of flat-topped blocks called **clints**. Since the joint pattern in a limestone region is often regular, the result is a landscape that appears to be covered in paving slabs.

> Carbonation also takes place on the surface of the clints, where the acid rainwater may lodge in pools or run over the edge. The result is that small solution hollows, called **karren**, develop on the clints. As the rainwater runs off the clint, it cuts small furrows or channels into its edges. This is known as **fluting**.

> The shaping of the limestone pavement was also influenced by freeze-thaw action. Water percolating into the joints would freeze and expand during winter, putting extra pressure on the rock.

> The Burren is Ireland's best-developed limestone pavement. Most of its soil cover was probably removed during the last ice age. Deforestation and over-cultivation resulted in the remaining soils being eroded. The bare rock surface was then shaped by carbonation over thousands of years.

Processes
> Carbonation
> Solution
> Some freeze-thaw and hydraulic action

ACTIVITY

Thinking

Why is the feature shown in the photograph called a pavement?

Clints and grikes on a limestone pavement. Minor features include karren and fluting.

Swallow holes and dry valleys

Processes
› Carbonation
› Solution
› Hydraulic action
› Abrasion

› A **swallow hole** (or sinkhole) is an opening in the bed of a river through which the river disappears from the surface to flow underground. Many swallow holes are found at a point where the river, having flowed across impermeable rock, meets a zone of limestone.

› As the river flowed over its limestone bed, some of the water percolated down through the joints. There was a greater flow of water at the points where a number of joints intersected. These joints were widened by **carbonation**. The soluble limestone was weathered by the slightly acidic water. The widening of the joints was also aided by hydraulic action and abrasion. In time, the joints became sufficiently wide to form a downward passage, called a **swallow hole**. The river then flowed into the swallow hole and left the surface. It began to follow a new underground course.

› The section of river valley that lay downstream of the swallow hole had now lost its water supply and became a **dry valley**. Thus, a dry valley is one that was carved out by the force of running water but does not have a river flowing through it now.

› The river eroded its valley by the usual processes of **hydraulic action** (the force of moving water) and **abrasion** (erosion by the load carried in the water). The process of creating the valley was also helped by **carbonation** and **solution**.

Surface stream disappearing into a swallow hole to flow underground

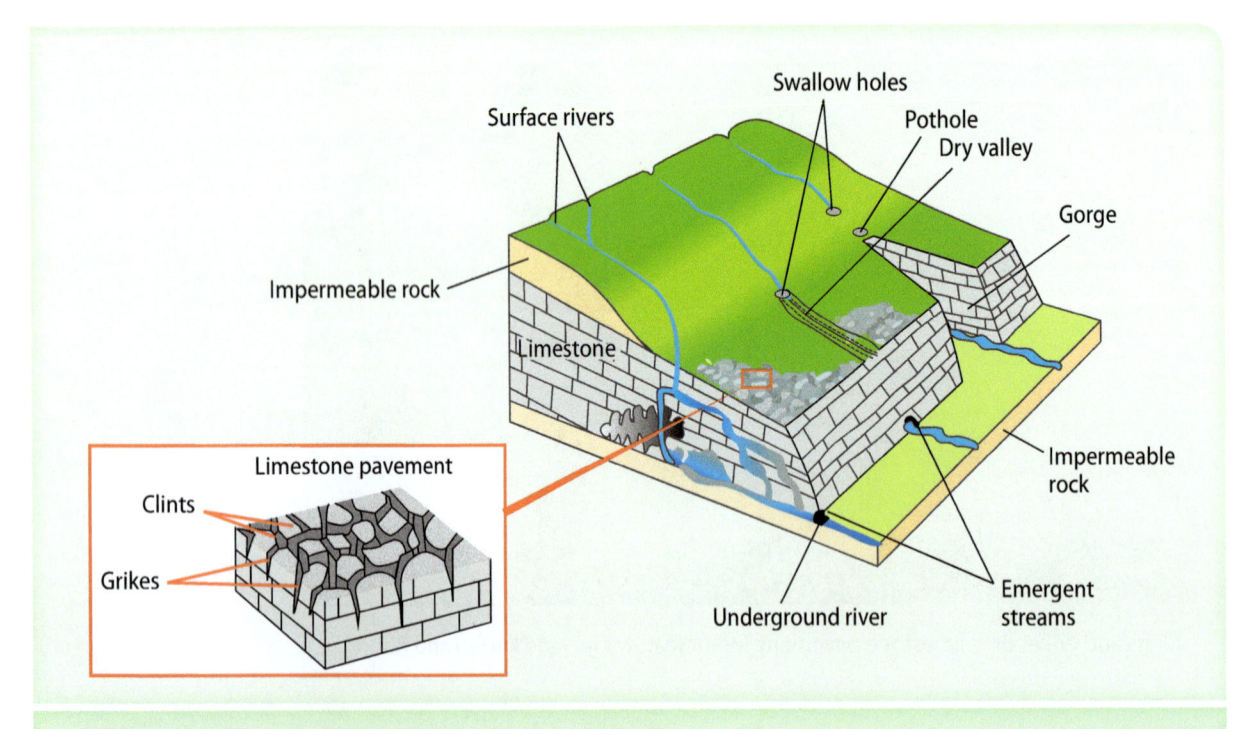

Figure 9.2 Surface landforms of a typical karst landscape

- Many swallow holes lose their supply of water as new swallow holes form further upstream. These are sometimes called potholes. This in turn lengthens the distance of the dry valley.
- If the limestone has a layer of impermeable rock underneath it, the river will again come to the surface as an **emergent stream**.
- Swallow holes and dry valleys can be found in the Burren. Many swallow holes (or potholes) have the prefix *Poll* or *Poul*. Examine the OS map on page 112.

GEOFACTS

- The Cong Canal, which links Lough Corrib with Lough Mask, was constructed in the 1840s as a Famine relief project. It leaked like a sieve as water disappeared through fissures in the limestone. As a result, the canal was never used.
- A **gorge** is a narrow, steep-sided valley. Gorges are common in karst regions, where they may be formed when the roof of an underground cave system collapses. Cheddar Gorge in England was formed this way.
- Seasonal lakes, called **turloughs**, occupy hollows in the limestone areas of East Galway and the Burren. The lakes form during winter, when the water table rises, but they disappear during the drier summer as the water table falls. (See the OS map on page 112.)

Closed depressions

- **Closed depressions** are enclosed hollows in the ground. They can range from a few metres in depth and diameter to hundreds of metres in depth and several kilometres in diameter.
- The smallest closed depression is the **doline**. A doline can develop in a number of ways. Joints and bedding planes near the surface of the limestone are widened by carbonation and the rock is dissolved downwards. At the same time, a cave may be enlarged by carbonation.
- Gradually, the overlying layers of rock become thinner and weaker. Eventually, the roof becomes unstable and collapses. Any surface material slumps into the opening and a doline is formed. It is usually circular and its sides and floor are blanketed with soil.
- When several swallow holes or dolines expand and come together, a larger depression called an **uvula** is formed. An uvula may also form when the roof of a large cavern collapses.
- The largest closed depression is the **polje**. It has steep sides, a flat floor and may occupy several square kilometres in area. There are two suggestions as to how it is formed. It may have formed when a number of uvulas expanded and came together. However, it is more likely that it developed as a result of downfaulting in the limestone following tectonic activity. The resulting depression was then enlarged by solution and erosion.
- The presence of glacial deposits on the floor of a polje suggests that it may also have been deepened or enlarged by glacial erosion.
- The Carran Depression is the largest polje in Europe. It is one of the oldest features in the Burren landscape and may have begun to develop millions of years before the last ice age. (See the OS map on page 112.)

Processes
- Carbonation
- Solution
- Collapse
- Faulting

QUESTION

Identify and describe any three surface landforms found on a limestone pavement.

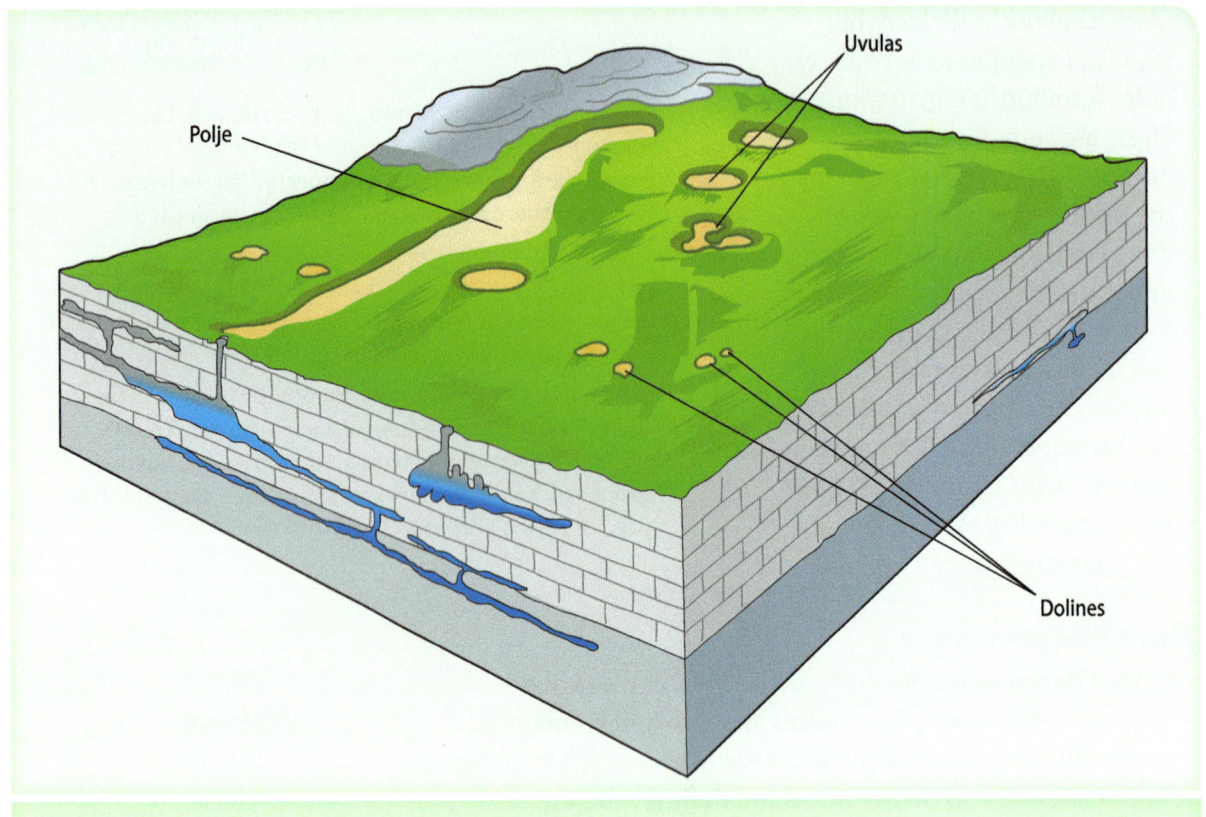

Figure 9.3 Closed depressions are classified by their size

Underground landforms of a karst landscape

Caves and caverns

- A **cave** is a naturally formed underground passage that is large enough to enter. It acts as a channel for water flowing underground from a swallow hole.
- Most caves are formed at or below the **zone of saturation**. As it flows underground, water follows the joints and bedding planes. These are lines of weakness in the rocks. The acidified water dissolves the limestone by the processes of **carbonation** and **solution**. As the rock is dissolved, the cavities are enlarged. They eventually join to form an underground passage called a cave.
- As the cave is enlarged, the water begins to flow more quickly. This moving water continues enlarging the cave by the processes of **hydraulic action** and **abrasion**. If the flow of the water is turbulent, sections of the roof of the cave collapse to form large chambers or **caverns**.
- If the level of the water table falls, new caves begin to develop at a lower level and those at the upper level are abandoned and left dry. These are the caves that we are so familiar with as tourist attractions.
- Fast-flowing underground water tends to open single-channel caves such as Aillwee Cave, Mitchelstown Cave and Dunmore Cave. If the water flows more slowly, it will attack every fissure in the rock to develop a maze of caves, such as those in Cloyne, Co. Cork.

Processes
- Carbonation
- Solution
- Hydraulic action
- Abrasion

QUESTION

Explain how the process of carbonation weathers a limestone landscape.

DEFINITION

Zone of saturation: The area of soil or rock below the water table, where the ground is totally saturated with water.

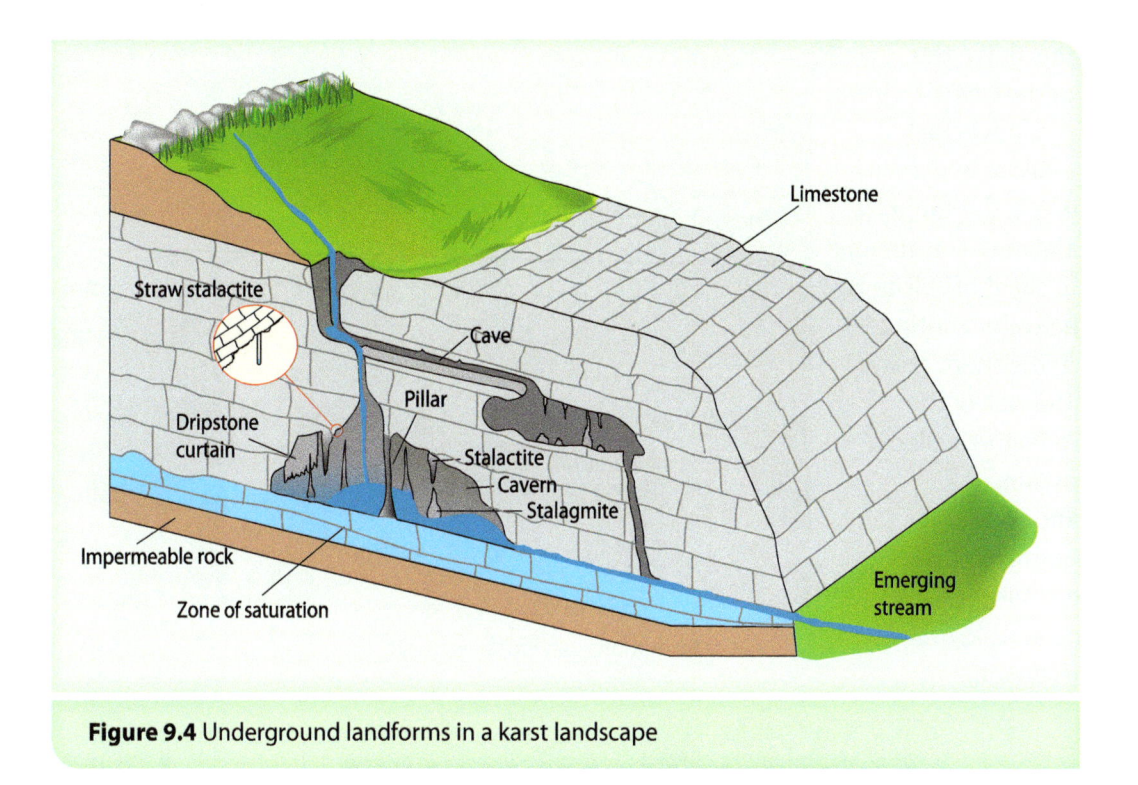

Figure 9.4 Underground landforms in a karst landscape

Calcite formations

› Weak carbonic acid reacts with calcium carbonate in limestone as it passes down through the rock. This forms calcium bicarbonate, which is removed in solution. When the water seeps through the joints to the roof of a cave or cavern, it hangs or drips from the ceiling. Some of the carbon dioxide is lost by evaporation. The remaining water is unable to hold all the calcium bicarbonate in solution. Tiny amounts of pure limestone, called **calcite**, are left behind. This forms various shapes on the roof, walls and floor of the cave. They are known as **dripstone features** because of the way they formed.

› Pure dripstone features should be white due to the colour of the calcite. Impurities in the water discolour the calcite. Copper gives it a greenish colour and iron oxide (rust) gives it a reddish colour.

› A **stalactite** is an icicle-like mineral formation that hangs from the ceiling of a cave. It is formed when water saturated with calcium carbonate hangs from the ceiling of a cave or cavern for a few seconds. When some of the carbon dioxide evaporates, a tiny ring of calcite, taking the shape of the water droplet, is left behind and solidifies. As the process continues, the calcite begins to grow down. This process continues over thousands of years and a hollow **straw stalactite** forms. If the straw becomes plugged by debris, the water flows down the outside. Over time, the calcite deposits thicken into the traditional carrot-shaped stalactite.

› When the drops of water hit the floor, more carbon dioxide evaporates and deposits of calcite build up from the ground. Soon they form domed shapes called **stalagmites**. These are thicker and more shapeless than stalactites due to the splashing effect of the water.

› As time passes, stalactites and stalagmites continue to grow until they join to form columns or **pillars**.

Processes
› Carbonation
› Solution
› Evaporation

CHAPTER 9 · KARST LANDSCAPES 107

- If the water runs down the sloping wall of the cave or seeps out of a narrow crack in the ceiling, calcite is also deposited there in the same way as for stalactites. This time, though, a thin sheet of calcite is formed. As the water continues to flow over it, the sheet grows down along the wall of the cave to form a feature called a **dripstone curtain**.
- Calcite formations can be seen at Mitchelstown Cave (Co. Tipperary), Aillwee Cave (Co. Clare) and Marble Arch Cave (Co. Fermanagh).

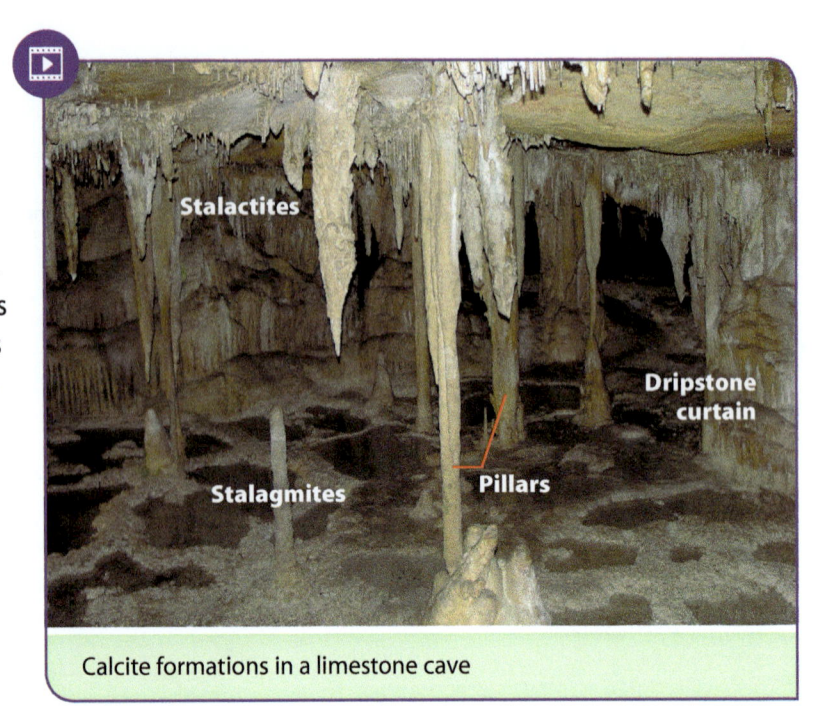

Calcite formations in a limestone cave

QUESTIONS

1. Explain the term *dripstone*.
2. Explain how any one dripstone feature is formed.

Life cycle of a karst landscape

The **life cycle** describes the sequence of changes that a landscape goes through as a result of the action of rivers. There are three stages in the life cycle:

- Youthful stage
- Mature stage
- Old age.

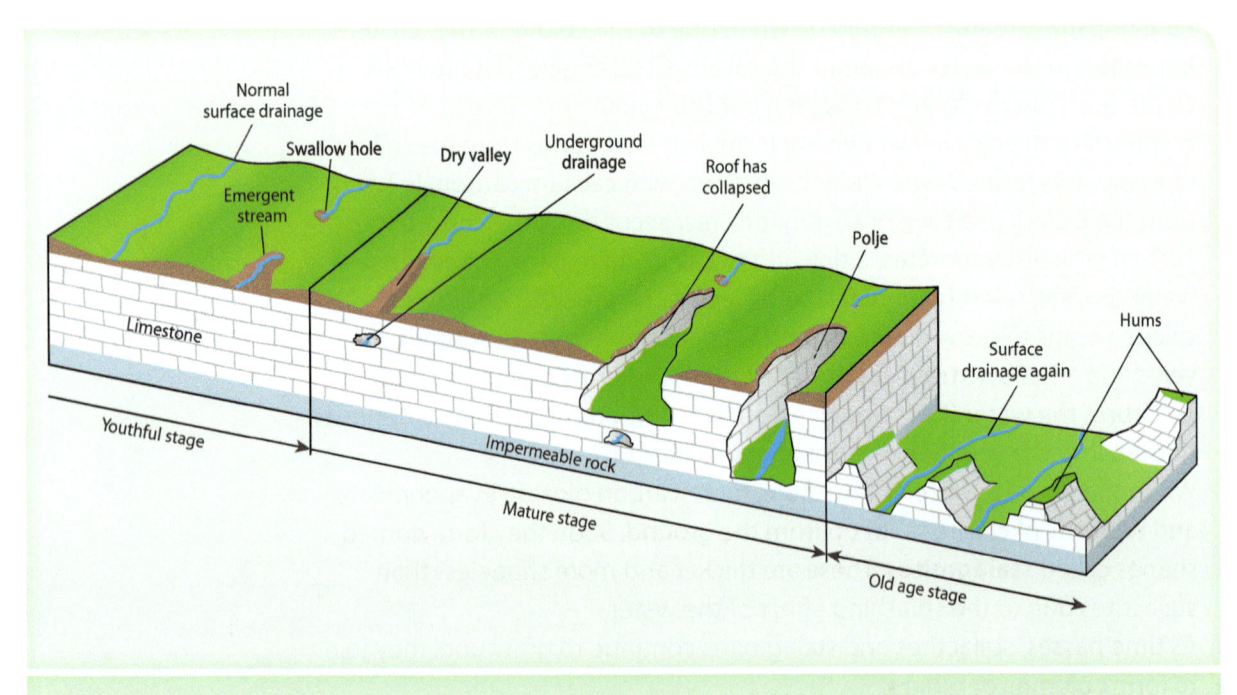

Figure 9.5 The life cycle of a limestone landscape passes through youthful, mature and old age stages

1 Youthful stage

- Rivers flow on the surface on a bed of impermeable rock.
- The rivers erode through this layer and expose the limestone.
- The weaknesses in the limestone are opened up by weathering and erosion.
- Some streams disappear underground through swallow holes.

2 Mature stage

- The karst landscape is fully developed with surface features. These include limestone pavement, swallow holes, dry valleys and enclosed depressions.
- Surface drainage is almost non-existent.
- An underground drainage system is fully established.
- A huge system of caves and caverns is established. In late maturity, their roofs begin to collapse.

3 Old age stage

- Most of the limestone has been removed by weathering and erosion, revealing the underlying layer of impermeable rock.
- Only the older, more resistant outcrops of limestone, called **hums**, remain.
- All evidence of underground drainage, such as caves and caverns, is removed.
- As rivers reach the underlying impermeable rock, surface drainage starts again.

The hums of the so-called Stone Forest in China. This is an example of a limestone landscape in its old age.

CASE STUDY

The Burren

The Burren is a limestone plateau that covers approximately 360 km² of North Co. Clare. It is the finest example of a **karst** landscape in Ireland.

The structure of the Burren is quite simple. It is composed of beds of limestone that were laid down during the Carboniferous period 300–350 million years ago. The rocks were uplifted and slightly folded during the period of Armorican folding. This folding can be seen in the saucer-like layers of rock at Mullaghmore Mountain.

At 344 metres, Slieve Elva is the highest point of the Burren. Here the limestone has a cap of impermeable shale and sandstone. This suggests that the whole Burren region was covered by these rocks at some stage. Most of them have been eroded over time, thus exposing the limestone.

Drainage

> Since limestone is a permeable rock, most of the drainage system is underground. The short streams that drain the impermeable slopes of Slieve Elva disappear underground through swallow holes as soon as they reach the limestone landscape. Some later come to the surface as emergent streams on the underground shale and sandstone.
> Some also emerge as springs, such as St Brendan's Well near Lisdoonvarna. They provide the main source of water for animals on an otherwise arid upland region.

Surface landforms

> Over 60% of the Burren consists of bare rock or rocky pasture. One of its main characteristics is the limestone pavement, much of which has a clint and grike surface.
> There are spectacular swallow holes and dry valleys. These are the result of streams disappearing underground.
> There are also seasonal lakes called turloughs in the lower regions. They appear during winter when the water table is near the surface. They may dry up in summer when the water table falls.

Underground landforms

> Most of the Burren's drainage is underground. These rivers have carved out caves and caverns. Ireland's longest cave is Pollnagollum in Co. Clare, where over 15 km of passageways have been explored to date.
> Aillwee is a dry cave. The stream that formed it now flows at a deeper level. The cave has been opened as a show cave and is one of the Burren's main tourist attractions.

Limestone pavement at Mullaghmore Mountain in the Burren. The strata were slightly folded as they were uplifted. Note the turloughs (seasonal lakes) in the middle background.

GEOFACT

The Burren is now entering the mature stage in the life cycle of a karst landscape.

ACTIVITY

Discussion
Identify and explain two reasons why the Burren is a distinctive landscape.

UNIT 1 · PHYSICAL GEOGRAPHY

CHAPTER 9 · KARST LANDSCAPES

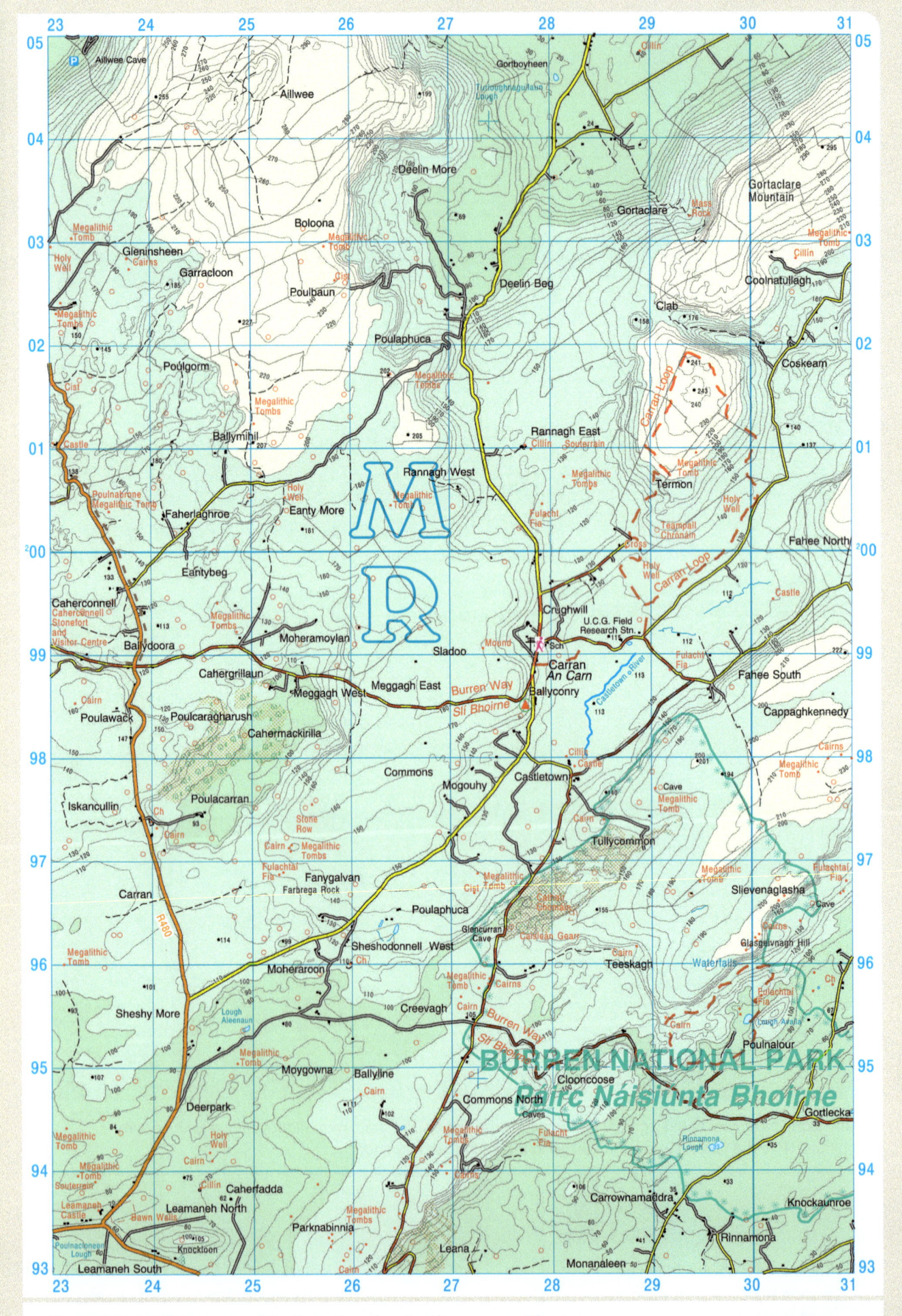

Figure 9.6 Identifying some of the Burren's surface landforms on an OS map

The Burren on an Ordnance Survey map

1

Turlough (M 28 04)

This seasonal lake is located in a low-lying area. Its name indicates that it is a turlough. There is another turlough at R 288 992.

2

Limestone cave (M 23 04)

Aillwee Cave has been developed as a tourist attraction. Note the parking area and the access road. There is a complete absence of surface drainage on Aillwee Mountain. Caves are also found at R 291 977 and R 278 945.

3

Swallow hole (M 26 02)

A stream that has disappeared underground. Many are now dry, as the drainage system is completely underground. The prefixes '*poll*' and '*poul*' mean hole. Swallow holes can be found at M 265 021 and R 245 974.

4

Dry valley (R 27 96)

A dry valley runs in a SW–NE direction for about 1 km. The presence of Glencurran Cave indicates that it was once occupied by a stream. There is another steep-sided dry valley at M 295 021.

5

Emerging/disappearing river (R 28 98)

The Castletown River emerges from underground, only to disappear underground again. It is hard to estimate the direction of flow because the contours and spot heights do not give any indication of the gradient.

6

Polje (R 24 97 and R 25 98)

This is a large, closed depression about 2 km long, 1 km wide and 80 metres deep. It has a bed of glacial drift, which suggests that its formation was also aided by glacial activity. Because it is low lying, it is at risk of flooding after heavy winter rainfall.

ACTIVITY

Research

Look up 'Burren video' on the internet.

PowerPoint Summary

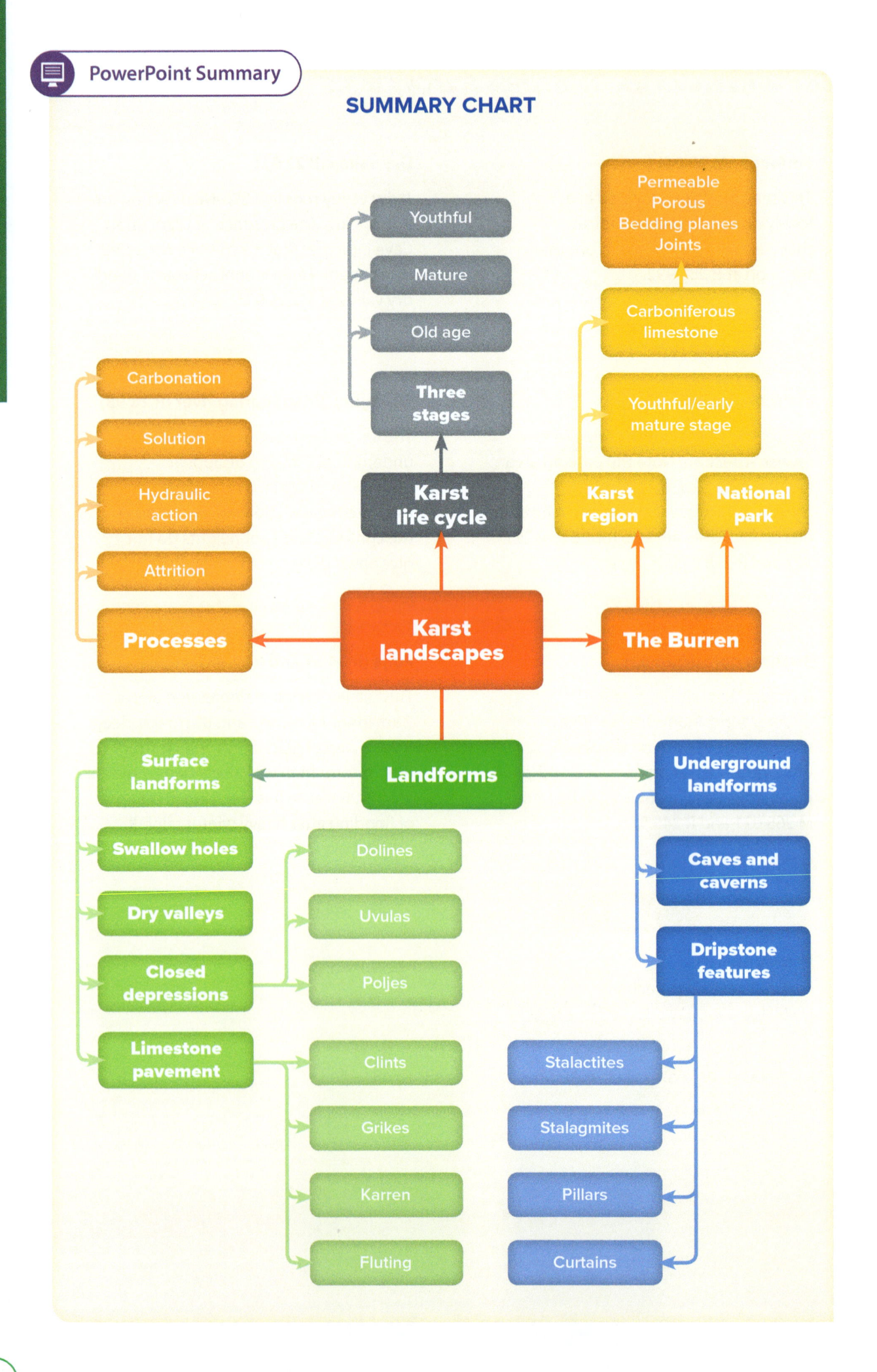

SUMMARY CHART

Karst landscapes

- **Karst life cycle** → Three stages
  - Youthful
  - Mature
  - Old age

- **Processes**
  - Carbonation
  - Solution
  - Hydraulic action
  - Attrition

- **The Burren**
  - Karst region → Carboniferous limestone → Permeable, Porous, Bedding planes, Joints
  - Youthful/early mature stage
  - National park

- **Landforms**
  - **Surface landforms**
    - Swallow holes
    - Dry valleys
    - Closed depressions → Dolines, Uvulas, Poljes
    - Limestone pavement → Clints, Grikes, Karren, Fluting
  - **Underground landforms**
    - Caves and caverns
    - Dripstone features → Stalactites, Stalagmites, Pillars, Curtains

UNIT 1 · PHYSICAL GEOGRAPHY

114 GEOGRAPHY TODAY

Leaving Cert exam questions

SHORT QUESTIONS: HIGHER LEVEL

1 Limestone pavement
(8 marks)

Examine the photograph and link each feature of a limestone pavement, labelled **A**, **B**, **C** and **D** with its correct name in the table.

Feature	Letter
Karren	
Grikes	
Fluting	
Clints	

SHORT QUESTIONS: ORDINARY LEVEL

1 Karst landscape (10 marks)

Examine the diagram of a karst landscape and answer each of the following questions.

(i) Match each of the letters **A**, **B** and **C** in the diagram with the landform that best matches it in the table below.

Landform	Letter
Pillar/column	
Clint	
Stalactite	

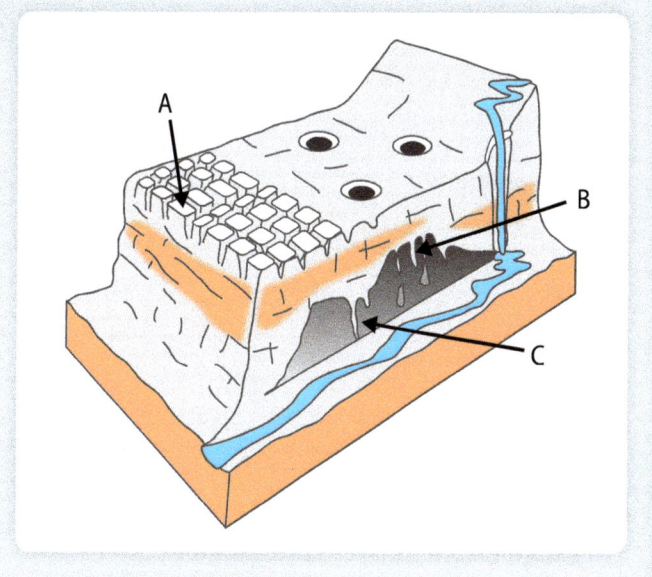

(ii) Indicate whether each of the statements below is true or false.

(a) The Giant's Causeway is an example of a karst landscape.

(b) Permeable rock allows water to pass through it easily.

CHAPTER 9 · KARST LANDSCAPES 115

UNIT 1 · PHYSICAL GEOGRAPHY

OL

2 Karst landscape (10 marks)

Examine the photograph showing a section of a limestone pavement and answer the following questions.

(i) Name the limestone features at **A** and **B**.

(ii) Name **one** location in Ireland where features like these are found.

(iii) Name **two** underground features which can be found in karst regions.

3 Karst regions (10 marks)

Examine the photograph.

(i) Which of the following rocks is found in the area of the photograph: granite or basalt or limestone?

(ii) Give the name of a region in Ireland where the rock named in part (i) can be found.

(iii) Link each of the following landforms with the correct location (surface or underground).

Landform	Location (surface or underground)
Cave	
Clints and grikes	
Stalactite	
Limestone pavement	
Stalagmite	

HL

LONG QUESTIONS: HIGHER LEVEL

1 Limestone pavement (30 marks)

With the aid of a diagram(s), explain how chemical weathering has shaped the limestone pavement in a karst region.

2 Karst landscape (30 marks)

With reference to the Irish landscape, examine the processes that have influenced the development of any **one** underground landform in a karst region.

3 Karst landscape (30 marks)

With reference to the Irish landscape, examine how the processes of weathering have influenced the development of any **one** limestone feature.

LONG QUESTIONS: ORDINARY LEVEL

1 Karst landscape (40 marks)

Examine the photographs of karst landscape features and answer each of the following questions.

(i) Name **one** surface karst feature evident in photograph **A** and explain, with the aid of a diagram, how this surface feature was formed.

(ii) Name **one** underground karst feature evident in photograph **B** and explain, with the aid of a diagram, how this underground feature was formed.

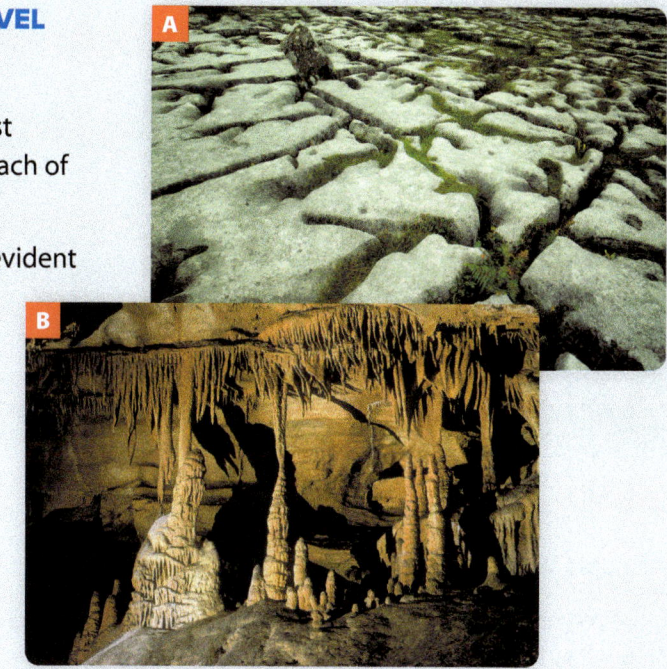

2 Karst landscape (40 marks)

Study the diagram of a karst landscape and answer the following questions.

(i) Name the three features marked **A**, **B** and **C**.

(ii) Name **one** other feature found in karst landscapes.

(iii) Explain, with the aid of a diagram, how any **one** feature in a karst region is formed.

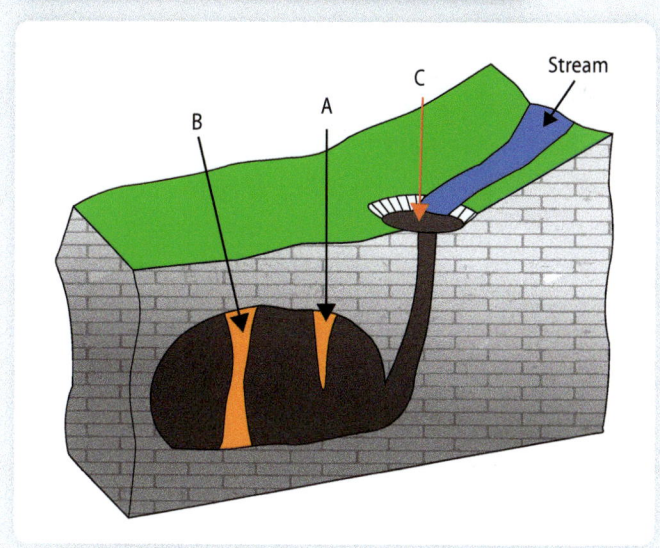

3 Karst landscape (30 marks)

Explain, with the aid of diagrams, how any **two** underground landforms found in a karst region such as the Burren are formed. Give a named example of each in your answer.

PREAMBLE TO CHAPTERS 10–13

Syllabus statement 1.5

You are required to study all of the surface processes listed in the following four chapters. You should then **focus in detail on one of them**.

- Mass movement processes and the factors governing them (Chapter 10)
- Fluvial processes, patterns and associated landforms (Chapter 11)
- Coastal processes, patterns and associated landforms (Chapter 12)
- Glacial processes, patterns and associated landforms (Chapter 13)

You are expected to study all the listed processes.

You should have a general understanding of all the processes. You should be familiar with the terminology and be able to recognise the resultant landforms in diagrams, maps and photographs.

You are required to make a detailed examination of **one** of the processes.

Syllabus statement 1.7

Students should study **one** of the following topics. They examine how human activities can influence the surface processes that they have already studied.

- Mass movement processes and the impact of overgrazing, overcropping and deforestation (Chapter 10, pages 128–130)
- River processes and the impact of hydro-electric dams, canalisation and flood control measures (Chapter 11, pages 152–156)
- Coastal processes and the impact of recreational pressures, coastal defence work, conservation and management measures (Chapter 12, pages 177–181)

Chapter 10
Mass Movement

KEYWORDS

- mass movement
- regolith
- soil creep
- terracettes
- landslide
- rockslide
- slump
- earthflow
- bogflow
- mudflow
- rockfall
- avalanche
- overgrazing
- deforestation
- overcropping

LEARNING OBJECTIVES

By the end of this chapter, you should be able to understand:

- The factors that influence mass movement
- How to describe and explain the processes of mass movement
- The impact of some human processes on mass movement.

Mass movement

Mass movement is also known as mass wasting. It is the process where material moves downslope under the direct influence of **gravity**. It is one of the most active processes in modifying the landscape.

Mass movement is aided by weathering, especially freeze-thaw, as it usually weakens slope materials. These materials include rocks, soil and mud.

Mass movement can be triggered by natural processes (earthquakes, rainfall, etc.) or by human activity (construction work, deforestation, etc.).

> **DEFINITION**
>
> **Regolith** is the loose material (soil and rocks) on the Earth's surface that results from weathering and erosion.

Factors that influence mass movement

Although gravity is the factor that controls mass movement, a number of other factors can influence the type of mass movement and the rate it occurs at.

- **Slope** (or gradient) is probably the major influence on mass movement. Generally speaking, the steeper the slope, the less stable it is. Therefore, steep slopes are more likely to experience mass movement than gentle ones. The material will also move more quickly on steeper slopes.

- **Water content** controls the speed of mass movement. Small amounts of water slow down mass movement, as it helps to bind particles together. When water is present in large quantities, it acts as a lubricant as well as adding weight to the material. As a result, mass movement is most likely to occur following periods of heavy rainfall.
- **Vegetation cover** helps to make slopes more stable. This is because roots help to bind soil particles together, preventing erosion. Vegetation also absorbs much of the rainfall that might otherwise make the slope unstable.
- **Tectonic activity**, especially volcanoes and earthquakes, can trigger mass movement. Tremors from earthquakes can cause material to dislodge and move downslope. Volcanic materials can melt ice and snow. This provides water to assist mass movement, especially in the form of lahars.
- **Human activities** can trigger mass movement in areas where it might not occur naturally. They can do this by deforestation, allowing overgrazing or construction activity. Examples of the latter include creating steep cuttings for roads and railways as well as building large heaps of mining waste. Vibrations from traffic and machinery can also trigger mass movement.

ACTIVITY

Thinking

Which of these factors is least likely to influence mass movement in Ireland?

Classifying mass movements

Mass movements are grouped according to the speed of the mass movement (fast, slow), the water content of the material (wet, dry) and the type of material (rock, soil, mud, etc.). This produces four types of mass movement:

- Creep
- Slide
- Flow
- Fall.

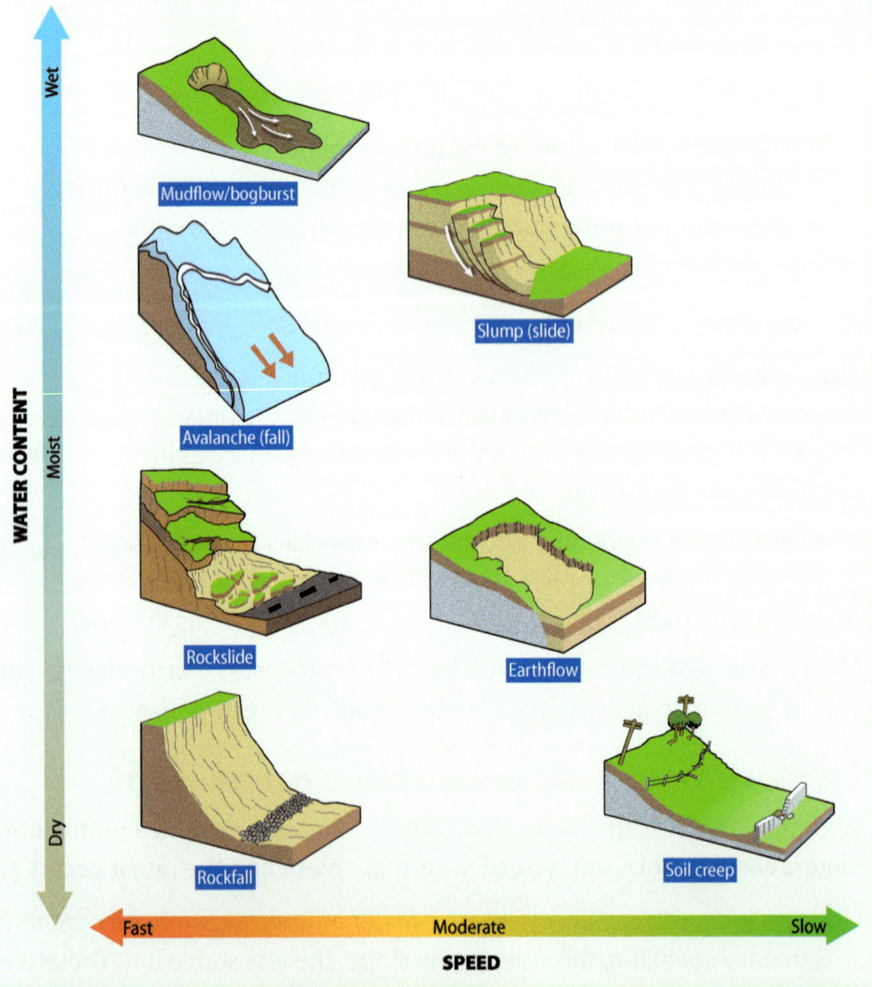

Figure 10.1 Classifying mass movement

ACTIVITY

Skills

Examine Figure 10.1. Which type of mass movement is:

(i) Slow and dry
(ii) Fast and dry
(iii) Fast and wet?

Processes of mass movement

Creep

Soil creep is the gradual movement downslope of individual particles of loose soil and rock (regolith) under the influence of gravity.

It is the slowest type of mass movement. It takes many years of gradual movement before its effect on a slope can be noticed. Soil creep usually occurs on slopes that have a gentle to moderate gradient.

The rate of movement is generally less than 0.5 cm per year and is almost impossible to measure over short periods of time. Vegetation cover slows it even further, binding the soil particles together and hindering mass movement.

The influence of gravity is the obvious cause of soil creep, but the presence of water is generally required. **Freeze-thaw** influences soil creep. When water between grains of sediment is frozen, it expands by about 9%, forcing particles of soil up. When there is a thaw, the particles are set back down, not in the same place as before, but further forward.

Creep is also influenced by the **wet-dry cycle.** During periods of rainfall, grains of sediment absorb moisture by hydration. This causes them to expand and move up. As they dry out they contract, especially if the soil is rich in clay. Gravity then pulls the grains down, to settle just a little farther downslope than where they started from.

Soil creep produces a series of parallel ridges called **terracettes** as well as a build-up of soil at walls and fences at the foot of the slope. The movement is greatest at the surface, declining to zero at the bedrock. The evidence for this is that vertical objects bedded in the soil, such as fences and telegraph poles, eventually tilt downslope. Trees that continue to grow after they have been tilted display a pronounced curve at their base.

Processes
- Gravity
- Freeze-thaw
- Wetting and drying

QUESTION

List two reasons why soil creep is so slow.

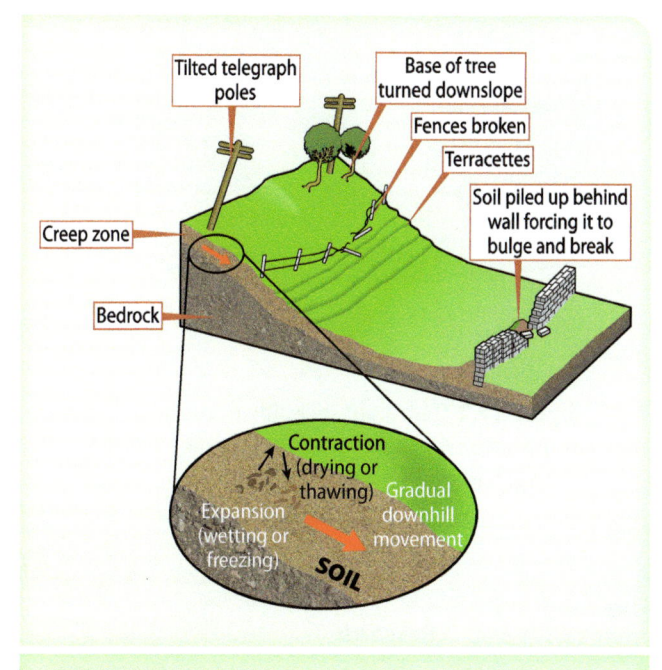

Figure 10.2 How soil creep occurs and its effects on the landscape

Terracettes on a slope as a result of soil creep

Slides

Slides are sudden and rapid downward movements of masses of blocks of bedrock and regolith under the influence of gravity.

They usually occur where the rock strata dip downslope in the same direction. They also occur when the rock is jointed and fractured. The mass of material moves along distinct surfaces such as bedding planes.

Slides occur when a slope fails. Most slope failures occur:

› Along bedding planes between rock strata
› Where rocks have been weakened by weathering
› Where the slope is undercut, either by nature (coastal cliffs) or human activity (road building)
› Following earthquake tremors.

Heavy rainfall may act as a lubricant. The underlying rock loses friction and is unable to hold the overlying rock in place.

There are several different types of slide, including **rockslides** and **slumps**.

Rockslides

Rockslides occur when blocks of bedrock break loose and slide down a slope. Sometimes the fractures develop when rocks have been weakened by weathering.

Rockslides can be triggered in a number of ways. If the slope is undercut at the base, it loses support and the rock gives way.

Processes
› Gravity
› Freeze-thaw
› Natural triggers
› Human triggers

CASE STUDY

The Vaiont Dam rockslide

A major rockslide occurred at a reservoir near Vaiont in Northern Italy in 1963.

The valley sides consisted of steeply sloped layers of limestone. Surveys failed to notice a thin layer of clay and shale that was sandwiched in the limestone. The construction of a dam went ahead and the dam filled up.

Following days of rain, the layer of shale and clay became saturated. The groundwater was unable to escape to the valley floor due to the lake. The slope became unstable and failed. The surface layer eventually slid off the face of the mountain along the layer of clay and shale and into the new lake.

Over 200 million tons of limestone became detached from the valley side and slid into the reservoir at speeds of up to 100 km/hr. The entire landslide lasted for less than one minute.

It displaced massive amounts of water. Some swept up the opposite bank, destroying a village.

Most, however, swept over the dam and down towards villages in the valley below. It was not the landslide itself but rather the waves that it created that killed more than 2,600 people.

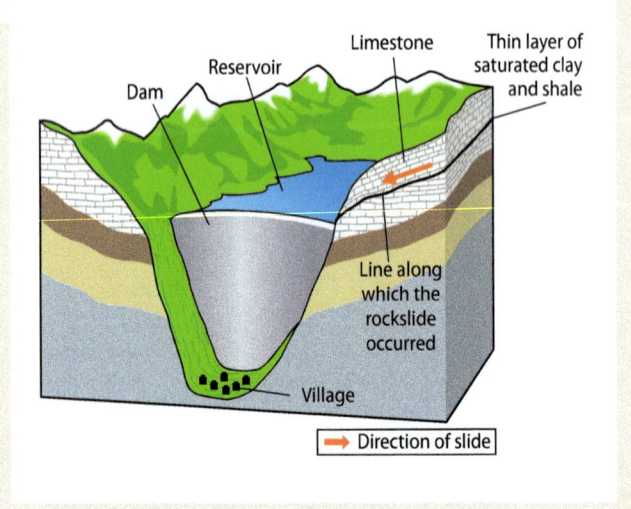

Figure 10.3 The Vaiont rockslide occurred when the slope failed. It was triggered by a combination of natural and human factors.

ACTIVITY

Research

Look up 'rockslide video' and 'rockslide video China' on the internet.

Slumps

Slumps occur when regolith (soil and loose rock) moves or rotates down along a curved surface. The upper section of the moving material tilts down and back, while the lower section moves up and out. This type of movement is called a **rotational slump**. The material in a slump tends to remain undisturbed as it rotates. A cliff-like scarp is left behind at the head of the slump.

Most slumps occur where material is relatively loose, for instance in the case of boulder clay.

Slumps can be caused by a variety of factors. The most common cause is erosion along the base of a slope, which removes support for the overlying material. This may be caused naturally by river erosion along the outer bank of a meander or by wave action at the base of a coastal cliff. Slopes can also be caused by human activity. These include the construction of highways and housing, when regolith is removed to leave a steep slope. In many cases, the slumps can be set off by heavy rainfall as the regolith becomes saturated.

Slumps are common along the limestone coast of Antrim and the boulder clay coastline of Wexford.

> **ACTIVITY**
>
> **Discussion**
> Identify two differences between a rockslide and a slump.

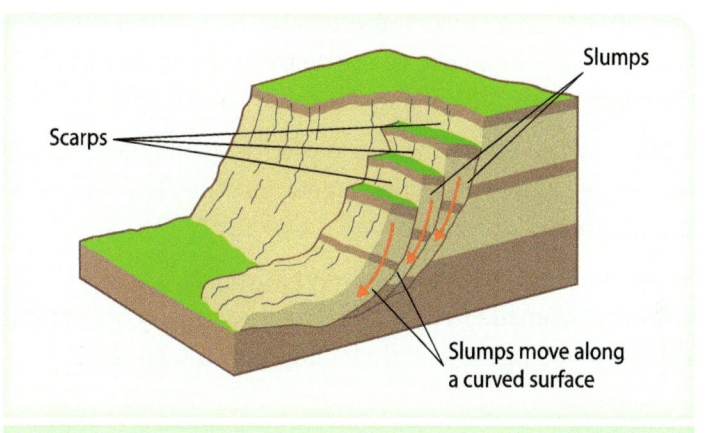

Figure 10.4 A rotational slump occurs when material slips down a slope along a curved surface

Several individual slumps have occurred in this area

Flows

A **flow** is a downhill movement of soft, wet material (soil, clay, silt, peat, etc.) that has been made fluid (or liquid) by rain or melted snow. There are three main types of flow:

> Earthflow
> Bogflow
> Mudflow.

Processes
> Gravity
> Natural triggers
> Human triggers
> Heavy precipitation/ snow melt

Earthflows

An **earthflow** occurs when a section of slope moves downhill for a limited distance following heavy rainfall.

Earthflows occur on hillsides and valley sides. It is most common where regolith lies on a bed of impermeable rock. Water saturates the soil and is unable to soak into the underlying rock. It then acts as a lubricant and the soil is able to flow.

If the flows are short, they simply leave small bulges on the landscape. If they break the vegetation, they leave scars on the landscape.

They can block roads and railways as well as cause extensive damage to property. They are usually not serious threats to life because of their fairly slow movement.

GEOFACT

Liquefaction is a type of earthflow. It occurs when vibrations, such as those that result from an earthquake, cause the soil particles to lose contact with one another. As a result, the soil behaves like a liquid. It loses the ability to support weights and can flow down gentle slopes.

Bogflows

A **bogflow** (also called a bogburst) is another type of flow that affects blanket bogs in upland areas. It occurs when peat, which has the ability to absorb large quantities of water, becomes saturated and begins to flow downhill.

CASE STUDY

Derrybrien bogflow

A bogflow occurred at Derrybrien in the Slieve Aughty Mountains in 2003. It was triggered by a number of factors. Excavation work was being carried out for the construction of a wind farm.

This involved removing large amounts of peat and piling it up at the edge of the site. The previous summer had been hot and dry. The peat dried out and contracted. Cracks developed in the peat and it lost its grip on the bedrock.

When heavy rain came, it increased the weight of the peat and quickly penetrated to its base. Following two weeks of heavy rain, the peat was turned into a liquefied mass. It flowed downhill, under the influence of gravity, through a river valley. It contaminated the water, leading to a fish kill. It also uprooted trees, blocked roads and damaged property.

The bogflow at Derrybrien resulted from a combination of human and natural factors

Mudflows

A **mudflow** is the most extreme form of flow. It has a very high water content and can occur after very heavy rainfall or snow melt. The water adds both volume and weight to the solid materials. It also acts as a lubricant to reduce friction.

Most mudflows start out on high, steep slopes where there is not enough vegetation to hold the soil in place. Streams of mud, like thin slurry, pour downhill following existing river channels. As the flow grows it may pick up debris, including boulders and trees. Boulders as large as houses have been moved by mudflows.

Mudflows may rush down a mountainside at speeds as fast as 100 km/hr and be up to 5 metres deep. When they reach lowlands, they spread out and slow down.

> **ACTIVITY**
>
> **Research**
>
> Look up 'epic mudslide caught on camera' on the internet.

CASE STUDY

Lahar at Nevado del Ruiz

One of the deadliest forms of mudflow is the **lahar**. It may follow a volcanic eruption. The most destructive lahar in history occurred after the eruption of Nevado del Ruiz in the Andes Mountains in 1985.

Lava and volcanic ash from the eruption melted snow and ice on the flanks of the volcano, releasing vast quantities of water. This picked up the ash and regolith on the slope of the volcano, turning it into mud. The lahar moved downslope. When it reached the town of Armero, it covered the region in mud and debris to a depth of up to 30 metres. It caused the deaths of 22,000 people in Armero and destroyed over 5,000 homes.

One other factor in the high death toll was that the lahar hit at midnight, when people were at home asleep.

> **DEFINITION**
>
> **Lahar:** A rapidly flowing mixture of rock debris, soil and water that originates on the slopes of an erupting volcano.

> **ACTIVITY**
>
> **Research**
>
> Look up 'Armero lahar – human cost' on the internet.

Devastation at Armero following the lahar that flowed downslope through the valley in the background

Falls

Falls are a sudden and rapid fall of materials from steep slopes or cliffs. The materials fall through the air and land at the bottom of the slope.

Rockfalls

A **rockfall** is an extremely rapid mass movement in which rocks of any size fall through the air. It can range in size from single rocks to massive falls that involve millions of cubic metres of debris.

Rockfalls can be triggered in a number of ways. If there is extreme physical weathering in mountainous areas, freeze-thaw will enlarge cracks and joints in the rock, eventually breaking them off. The rocks then fall down the slope under the force of gravity, collecting at the foot of the slope. Here they build up into a pile of jagged rocks, called **scree**. The largest rocks in the pile tend be located farthest from the slope face because of their greater size and momentum.

Rockfalls are rarely hazardous to people because they occur in relatively isolated locations.

Rockfalls also occur along coastal cliffs when undercutting by waves creates an overhang. If the overhang is unable to support itself, it breaks off and a rockfall takes place.

Human activity can trigger rockfalls. When roads or railways are built in mountainous areas, cuttings are created. If the sides of these are too steep they may become unstable, leading to rockfalls. Many of these cuttings have a covering of mesh wire to trap rocks as they fall and prevent them from landing on the roadway or railway.

Skellig Michael, a UNESCO World Heritage Site off the coast of Co. Kerry, is sometimes closed to tourists due to the risk of rockfalls.

Processes
> Gravity
> Weathering
> Natural triggers
> Human triggers

ACTIVITY

Research

Look up 'massive Cornwall rockfall' on the internet.

Rockfall blocking a road in the Alps. Note the steep cutting that was created when the road was built.

Avalanches

An **avalanche** is a mass of snow and ice that suddenly falls down a mountain slope, often taking regolith with it. Travelling at speeds exceeding 200 km/hr, it is the fastest form of mass movement. The falling snow also pushes air ahead of it as a strong avalanche wind.

Snow masses in mountain areas are loose and unstable. The snow is in layers, with older compressed snow covered by newer snowfalls. If a weak layer within the snow is unable to support the weight of the newer snow, it will collapse. This causes the overlying snow to break free and flow downhill. The collapse can be triggered by thawing, earth tremor or human activity.

Most snowfalls happen during the winter but most avalanches occur in spring. When a thaw comes, the upper layer of snow begins to melt. Meltwater seeps down through cracks towards the hard, lower layers of snow. It acts as a lubricant. Bit by bit, the loose upper layers of snow lose their grip, just like snow on the roof of a house. Eventually, the snow spills down the slope as an avalanche.

Any sudden movement can cause the loose surface snow to break away and start an avalanche. When even the smallest earthquake hits a snow-covered region, avalanches result. The weight of just one person can sometimes be enough to break a fragile layer of snow. This is why skiers and snowboarders sometimes trigger avalanches.

Avalanches kill almost 100 people in the Alps each year. Most are snowmobilers, skiers and snowboarders. Avalanches have also destroyed forests, roads, railroads and even entire towns.

> **QUESTION**
>
> Describe two ways in which human activities trigger rockfalls and avalanches.

> **GEOFACT**
>
> The most effective way to control avalanches is to cause an artificial avalanche with the help of explosives. This triggers relatively small flows of snow, thus preventing a much bigger avalanche later.

Snow avalanche in the Mount Everest region. Note the piles of snow-covered scree in the foreground, the result of weathering and rockfalls.

CHAPTER 10 · MASS MOVEMENT   127

CASE STUDY

Human influences on mass movement

Mass movement rarely occurs as a direct consequence of human influences. However, human influences can increase the likelihood of mass movement occurring. They can also cause the consequences of mass movement to be more severe.

The risk of mass movement is increased where human activities put too much pressure on the land available. These activities include:

- Overgrazing
- Deforestation
- Overcropping.

Overgrazing in Ireland

- **Overgrazing** by sheep became a major problem in upland regions of Ireland when the EU changed its system of aid to farmers in 1980. By the 1990s, sheep numbers had trebled to 9 million, with one-third of them in counties Donegal, Mayo and Galway.
- The increase was mainly due to the EU system of subsidy payments. Farmers were given grants based on the number of sheep that they carried on their land. As a result, the farmers increased their sheep numbers considerably, often beyond the limit that the land could support. This led to overgrazing of the land.
- Blanket bog is one of the most sensitive habitats to grazing. This is because of the slow rate at which the vegetation grows. Over time, overgrazing by sheep can lead to the loss of vegetation cover, especially as they close-crop the grasses and heathers.
- One of the worst-affected areas was the commonage grazing lands of the Nephin upland region in Co. Mayo. By the mid-1990s, satellite images suggested that 30% of these uplands were at risk from overgrazing. The loss of grasses and heathers meant that there was very little to hold the peat and soil in place on steep upland areas. It had by then become a fragile landscape.

> **DEFINITION**
>
> **Overgrazing** occurs when too many animals are allowed to graze in an area to the point where the vegetation cover is damaged.

Loss of vegetation cover in an upland area of blanket bog

- Up to 80 mm of rain fell on the mountains of North Mayo in a two-hour period in September 2003. The soil and peat cover became saturated. This triggered mass movement on the steep slopes.
- More than forty individual **mudflows and bogflows** occurred. Three kilometres of road was washed away, bridges were destroyed, houses were cut off and graveyards were damaged. River channels were blocked and fish stocks were damaged.
- Over the last twenty years, changes in EU policy have led to a sharp reduction in sheep numbers. This has allowed the vegetation to recover from the damage caused by overgrazing, thereby reducing the risk of further mass movement. Indeed, the risk now is that some of this land will be undergrazed and abandoned!

Deforestation in Haiti

- **Deforestation** leaves a bare landscape that is without a cover of protective vegetation. Trees act as a barrier to slow water as it runs off the slopes. Roots bind the soil and prevent it from being washed away. The trees also absorb excess water. Thus, deforestation can lead to **soil erosion** and **mass movement**.
- Haiti has the highest rate of deforestation in the world. A mere 2% of Haiti's original forests remain. Much was cut down to create farmland. Many of the country's people, the poorest in the Americas, have also routinely cut down trees for fuel, either to burn 'raw' or turn into charcoal.
- Hurricanes with torrential rain hit the country each summer during the so-called rainy season and soil quickly becomes saturated. About two-thirds of the country is mountainous, with steep slopes. Haiti is also located on a plate boundary, making it an earthquake zone. All are triggers for mass movement.
- When these factors act on a deforested landscape, mass movement events are both regular and serious. The most common are **landslides** and **mudflows**.
- People have been killed, property destroyed, farmland covered and communications disrupted as the landslides and mudflows run down the steep slopes. Tens of thousands of people lose their homes each year and are displaced.

ACTIVITY

Discussion

Why are the people of Haiti so dependent on wood for fuel?

Following deforestation, the slopes of Haiti's mountains are left without a protective covering of vegetation. As a result, any soil covering can be removed by mass movement following heavy rainfall.

Overcropping in the Sahel

- **Overcropping** occurs when too many 'robber crops' are grown by farmers in an area over and over again. These crops, including cotton, peanuts and maize, rob the soil of minerals and nutrients. The soil becomes so infertile that no vegetation can grow on it, leaving it open to the impact of the weather and natural processes.
- The Sahel is a narrow, semi-arid region of Africa that lies between the Sahara Desert to the north and equatorial forests to the south. The natural vegetation is grassland and open woodland. In the past, the region supported nomadic tribes that moved with their herds of cattle and goats.
- High birth rates in the Sahel led to high population growth in recent decades. Farmers were forced to change their traditional pattern of nomadism. They began to settle and use the land more intensively to grow crops. The increase in the demand for these crops soon meant that the fallow year was abandoned. Many farmers also concentrated on growing a single crop (**monoculture**).
- This overcropping meant that the soil was soon sapped of its nutrients, thereby reducing crop yields. The land became less productive. Soon crops failed and the soil was left exposed to the elements.
- Rain is irregular and infrequent, but when it does come it is often in the form of heavy downpours. The water acts as a lubricant and also adds extra weight for the soil. Soil erosion, **landslides** and **mudflows** follow, especially where the soil is exposed on steep slopes. This has resulted in the loss of life, the loss of livestock and the destruction of homes and food stores. Again, in this instance, a combination of natural forces (heavy rain) and soil exhaustion caused by human activities have led to mass movement.

> **DEFINITIONS**
>
> **Deforestation:** Clearing all or most of the trees in an area.
>
> **Robber crop:** A crop that uses up (or robs) the soil's fertility.

The exposed soil is open to removal by both erosion and mass movement in Mali

PowerPoint Summary

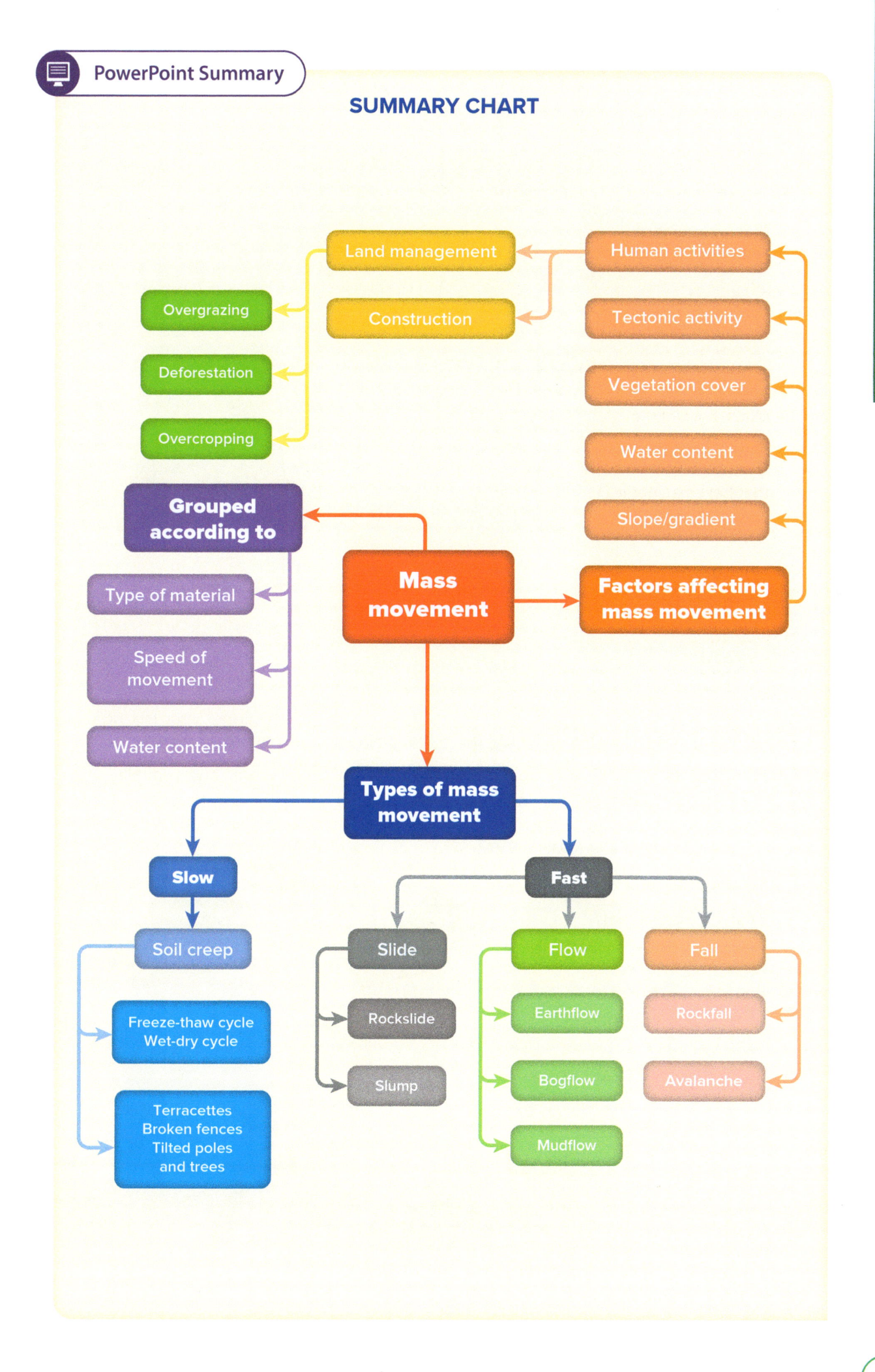

SUMMARY CHART

- **Mass movement**
  - **Grouped according to**
    - Type of material
    - Speed of movement
    - Water content
  - **Factors affecting mass movement**
    - Human activities
      - Land management
        - Overgrazing
        - Deforestation
        - Overcropping
      - Construction
    - Tectonic activity
    - Vegetation cover
    - Water content
    - Slope/gradient
  - **Types of mass movement**
    - **Slow**
      - Soil creep
        - Freeze-thaw cycle / Wet-dry cycle
        - Terracettes / Broken fences / Tilted poles and trees
    - **Fast**
      - Slide
        - Rockslide
        - Slump
      - Flow
        - Earthflow
        - Bogflow
        - Mudflow
      - Fall
        - Rockfall
        - Avalanche

CHAPTER 10 · MASS MOVEMENT   131

UNIT 1 · PHYSICAL GEOGRAPHY

Leaving Cert exam questions

SHORT QUESTIONS: HIGHER LEVEL

1. **Mass movement** (8 marks)

   Examine the photographs and answer each of the following questions.

   (i) Match each of the letters **A**, **B**, **C** and **D** with the process that best matches it in the table below.

Process	Letter
Rotational slump	
Soil creep	
Landslide	
Mudflow	

   (ii) Name any **two** factors that influence the operation of mass movement processes.

   (iii) Name **one** example of a very rapid mass movement process and name **one** example of a very slow mass movement process.

SHORT QUESTIONS: ORDINARY LEVEL

1. **Mass movement** (10 marks)

   Examine the diagrams and link each type of mass movement labelled **A**, **B**, **C**, **D** and **E** with its correct name in the table.

Mass movement	Letter
Soil creep	
Mudflow	
Avalanche	
Slump	
Rockfall	

132 GEOGRAPHY TODAY

LONG QUESTIONS: HIGHER LEVEL

1 Mass movement (30 marks)

Describe and explain **one** process of mass movement that you have studied.

2 Mass movement (30 marks)

Describe and explain the factors governing the operation of any **one** mass movement that you have studied.

3 Human interaction with mass movement (30 marks)

Examine the impact of human activity on mass movement.

LONG QUESTIONS: ORDINARY LEVEL

1 Mass movement (40 marks)

Describe and explain any **two** processes of mass movement.

2 Human interaction with mass movement (30 marks)

Examine how humans interact with mass movement.

3 Human interaction with mass movement (30 marks)

Describe and explain how humans attempt to take control of the surface process of mass movement.

4 Mass movement and weathering (30 marks)

Study the images of mass movement and weathering and answer the questions that follow.

(i) Match each image with the correct term.

Term	Letter
Scree	
Soil creep	
Avalanche	

(ii) State whether each image is as a result of mass movement or weathering.

Term	Process
Scree	
Soil creep	
Avalanche	

Chapter 11
River Processes

KEYWORDS

- drainage basin
- watershed
- discharge
- velocity
- gradient
- turbulent flow
- drainage pattern
- dendritic
- radial
- trellis
- deranged
- hydraulic action
- cavitation
- abrasion
- attrition
- vertical erosion
- lateral erosion
- headward erosion
- traction
- suspension
- saltation
- solution
- long profile
- youthful course
- middle course
- old course
- base level
- V-shaped valley
- interlocking spurs
- waterfall
- meanders
- floodplain
- oxbow lake
- levees
- delta
- dams
- canalisation

LEARNING OBJECTIVES

By the end of this chapter, you should be able to understand:

- How rivers form patterns on the landscape
- The processes that are active along the course of a river
- How to describe and explain how landforms develop along the course of a river
- How to identify river landforms on an Ordnance Survey map
- The impact that human activities have on the processes that take place along the course of a river.

Running water

Running water, in the form of rivers, contributes more to shaping the landscape than ice, wind and waves combined. The main river processes, also called **fluvial** processes, are erosion, transportation and deposition.

Drainage basins

A **drainage basin** is the area of land that is drained by a river and its tributaries. It is separated from the next drainage basin by a ridge of high land, called a **watershed**. The precipitation on opposite sides of a watershed will flow into different drainage basins.

All the precipitation that falls within a drainage basin will eventually find its way to a stream, either by surface run-off or by flowing through soil. All these streams will eventually come together and lead to the final large river that will empty into a sea or ocean.

QUESTION

Explain each of the following terms:
  (i) Source
  (ii) Tributary
  (iii) Confluence
  (iv) Drainage basin.

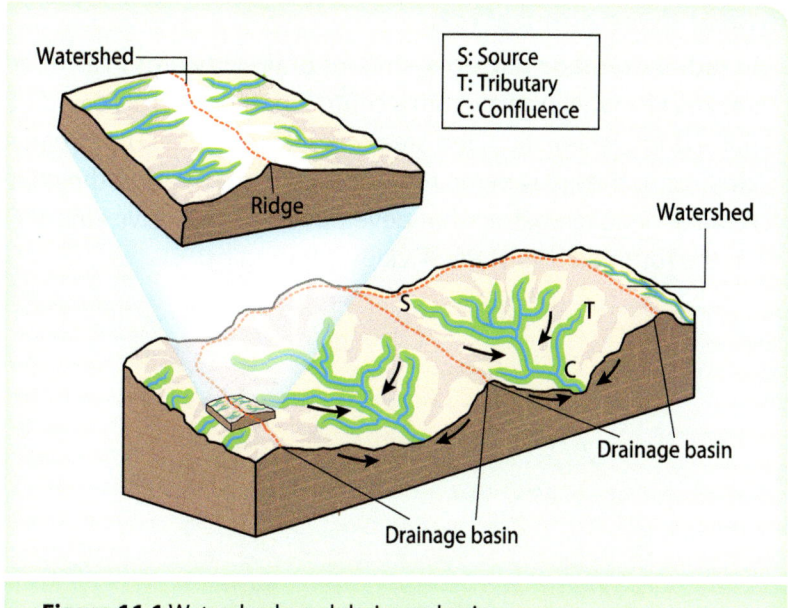

Figure 11.1 Watersheds and drainage basins

Drainage patterns

A **drainage pattern** is the overall layout that a river and its tributaries make in an area. Drainage patterns vary greatly due to differences in the rock type, rock structure and the slope of the land the river developed on. The main drainage patterns in the Irish landscape are:

› Dendritic pattern
› Radial pattern
› Trellised pattern
› Deranged pattern.

Dendritic drainage pattern

› The **dendritic drainage pattern** is the most common drainage pattern. The word dendritic comes from the Greek word for tree (*dendron*). The main river looks like the trunk of a tree. The tributaries of the main river resemble the branches and the small streams are like twigs.
› It develops on gently sloping land where the rock type is uniform. As the tributaries are small, the valleys that they cut are small and not very wide. The main river has the greatest volume of water, so it has the widest and deepest valley.
› The Shannon River system is a good example of a dendritic drainage pattern.

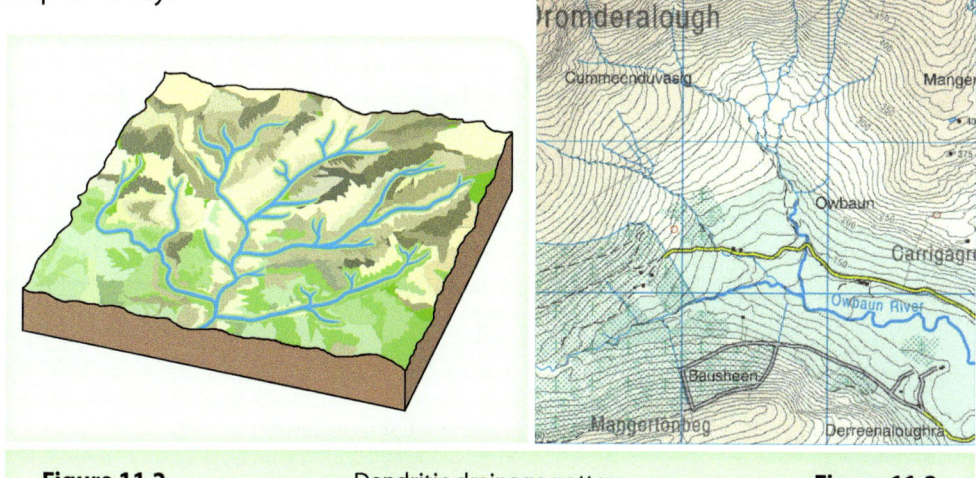

Figure 11.2 Dendritic drainage pattern **Figure 11.3**

Radial drainage pattern

> In **radial drainage patterns**, streams drain outwards in all directions (like the spokes of a wheel) away from a central high point. This could be an isolated hill, a dome-shaped upland area or a volcanic cone. The streams may be single streams or they may begin to form other patterns after they flow downslope.
> A radial drainage pattern has developed on the Twelve Pins in Co. Mayo and on the rounded hills of the Wicklow Mountains.

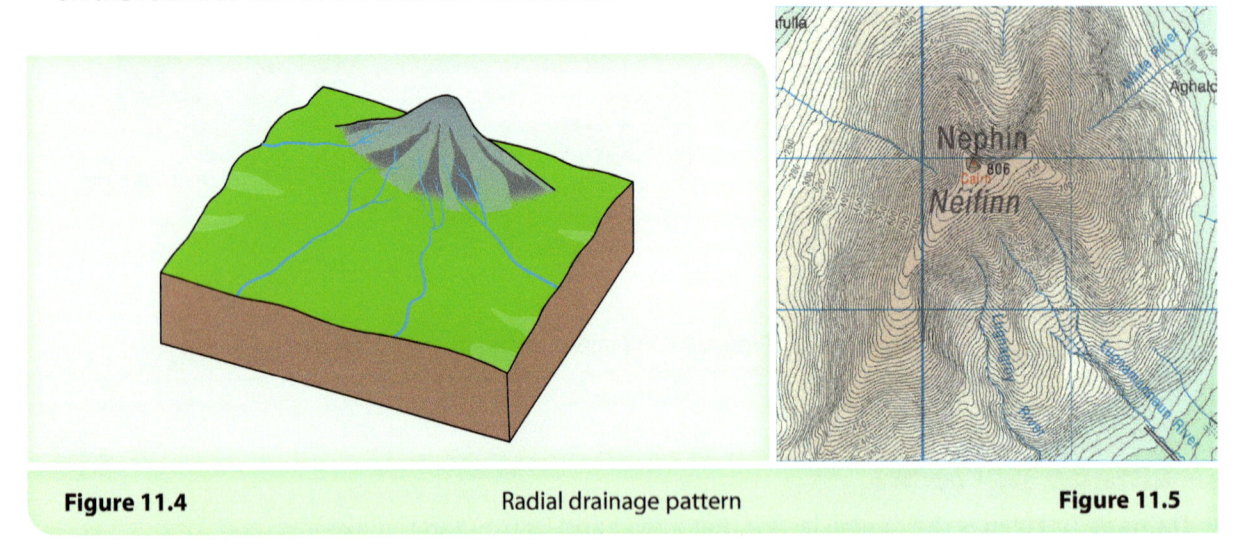

Figure 11.4   Radial drainage pattern   **Figure 11.5**

Trellised drainage pattern

> A **trellised drainage pattern** forms when the tributaries join the main river at right angles.
> It is best developed in a ridge and valley landscape, such as in Munster.
> The less resistant limestone that occupied the synclines was eroded more quickly than the more resistant sandstone in the anticlines. As a result, the main river occupied a deep valley floor. Tributaries now flow down from the anticlines to join the main rivers in the synclines.
> The rivers Bandon, Lee and Blackwater have a trellised pattern.
> The rivers that occupy many glaciated valleys may also have a trellised drainage pattern as tributaries flow down the steep valley sides to join the river in the main valley floor. This pattern has developed in the Gap of Dunloe and Glenveagh in Co. Donegal.

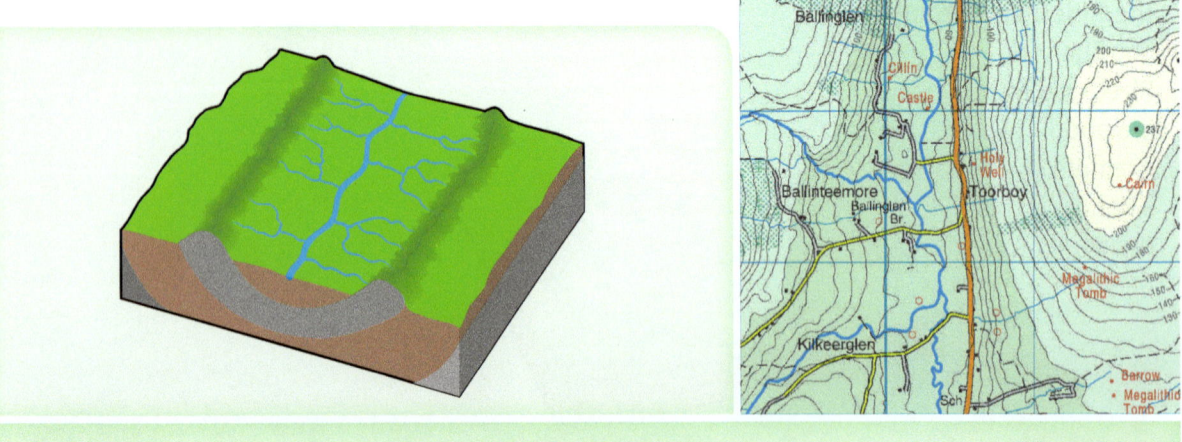

Figure 11.6   Trellised drainage pattern   **Figure 11.7**

Deranged drainage pattern

> A **deranged drainage pattern** has a chaotic appearance. Rivers flow in a random pattern, often doubling back and intersecting with one another and with small lakes in the area.
> This pattern is associated with marshy or boggy lowland landscapes where surface water is slow moving. It also develops in glaciated landscapes.
> Much of the Connemara landscape has a deranged drainage pattern that developed when the landscape was stripped of its soil cover and had small lakes gouged out.
> Rivers that flow on the heavy clay soils and between the drumlins of Cavan and Monaghan have also developed a deranged pattern.

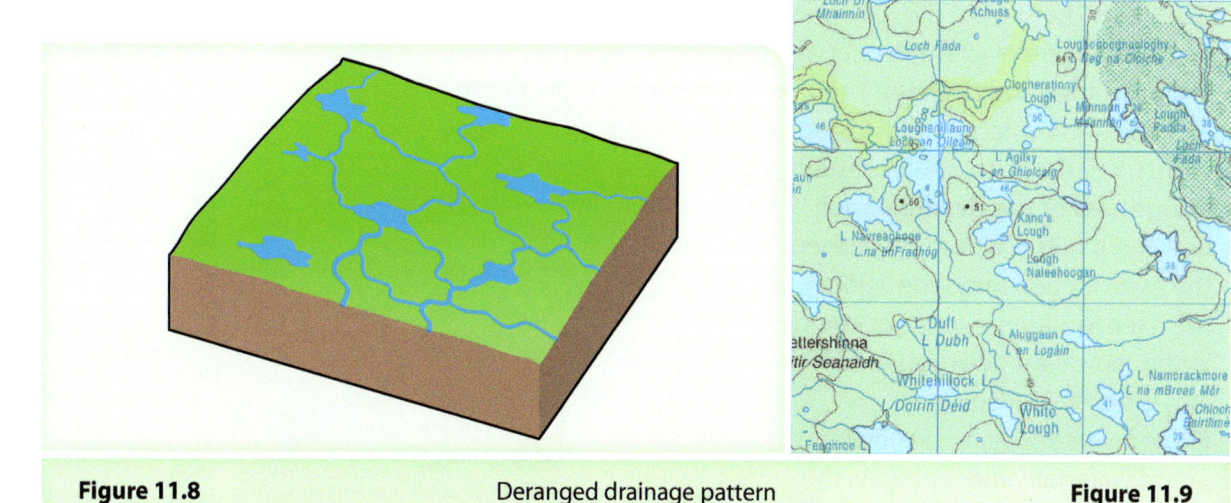

Figure 11.8 Deranged drainage pattern **Figure 11.9**

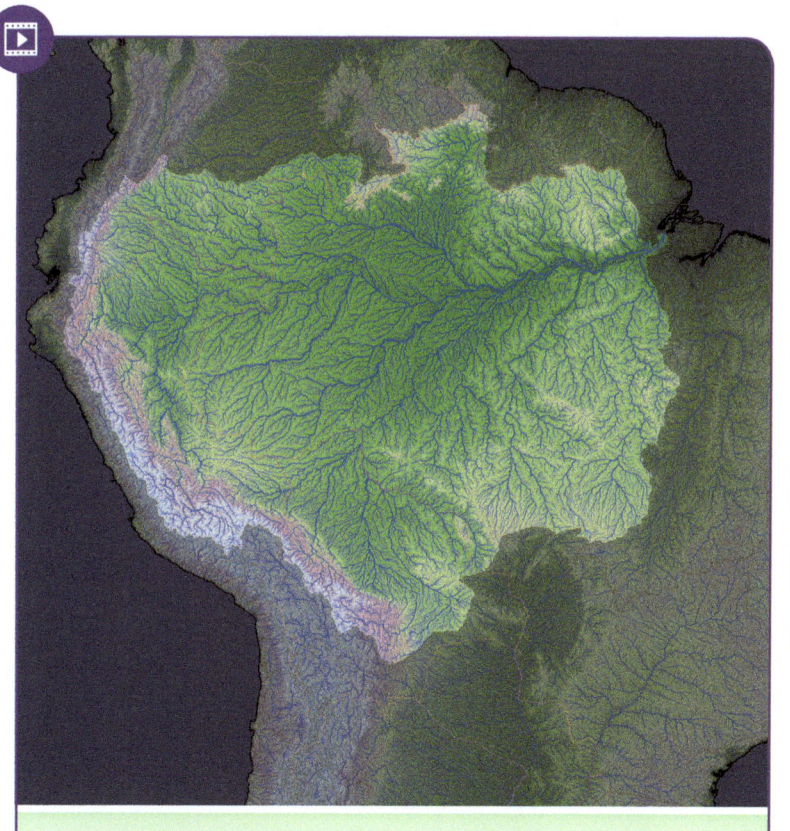

ACTIVITY

Skills

Examine the OS map extract of Dungarvan on page 410. Identify and locate with a four-figure grid reference any three drainage patterns.

GEOFACT

The Amazon River and its tributaries have a drainage basin that is more than 80 times larger than Ireland.

Satellite image showing the drainage basin of the Amazon River. Note the dendritic drainage pattern of the river.

CHAPTER 11 · RIVER PROCESSES 137

The work of running water

Running water uses its **energy** to shape the landscape by:

> **Erosion:** The removal of rock and regolith from their original positions.
> **Transportation:** Moving the eroded material to a new position.
> **Deposition:** Setting down the material further downstream.

The amount of energy that a stream has in order to shape the landscape is influenced by:

> **Discharge:** This is the volume of water that is carried by a river at a given time. The greater the discharge, the greater the ability of the river to erode and transport material.
> **Gradient:** The steeper the gradient of a river, the faster it should flow and thus the more energy it should have.
> **Shape of the river channel:** The wetted perimeter is the length of bed and banks in contact with the water. A bigger wetted perimeter creates more friction with the water, resulting in a loss of energy.
> **Roughness of the river channel:** If the bed and banks of a river are uneven, the extra friction slows the velocity of the river, resulting in a loss of energy. In the same way, tree roots or boulders also increase friction.
> **Flow:** Rivers appear to be flowing fast at waterfalls and rapids. As the water flows, it is mixed and thrown about. This may also occur where the riverbed is rough due to potholes and boulders. This type of flow is described as **turbulent flow**. It is important for erosion and transportation.

QUESTION
Describe three factors that affect the amount of energy that a river has.

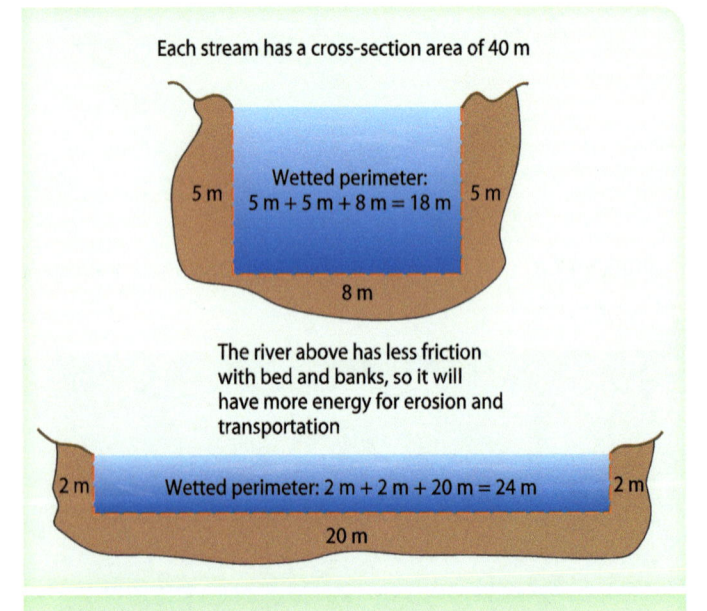

Figure 11.10 The shape of the channel influences the amount of energy that a river has for erosion and transportation

Each stream has a cross-section area of 40 m

Wetted perimeter: 5 m + 5 m + 8 m = 18 m

The river above has less friction with bed and banks, so it will have more energy for erosion and transportation

Wetted perimeter: 2 m + 2 m + 20 m = 24 m

Processes of erosion by rivers

Erosion is a collection of processes that wear away the landscape and produce a load for transportation. Most erosion takes place in the river's youthful stage, when the flow is at its most turbulent.

Rivers erode by hydraulic action, abrasion, attrition and solution.

Hydraulic action

Hydraulic action is caused by the force of moving water. It is strongest where the water has a fast flow. It is capable of dislodging particles of clay and gravel from the river's bed and banks. Some water is forced into cracks in the rocks. The air in the cracks is compressed. This puts extra pressure on the banks and bed of the channel. This slowly weakens them.

Cavitation is also a form of hydraulic action. It occurs when air bubbles in the water collapse. This sends out tiny shock waves that weaken the banks of the river and loosen particles of material.

Abrasion

Abrasion occurs when the river uses the force of its load to erode. Pebbles, sand and gravel carried by the river (its load) are hurled against the bed and banks of the river in a sandpapering effect. Most abrasion takes place when the river is in flood and capable of carrying a much larger load. It is the main process by which the river cuts down into its bed (vertical erosion).

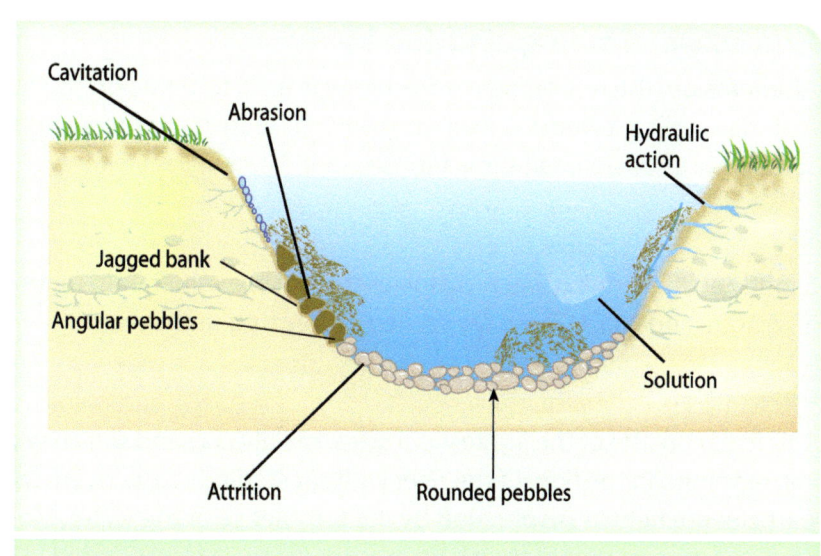

Figure 11.11 Rivers erode by the processes of hydraulic action (including cavitation), abrasion, attrition and solution

Attrition

Attrition is a way of eroding the river's load rather than the bed and banks. It takes place through small collisions between the particles of the river's load. The particles rub against one another as they are transported. The sharp edges are smoothed. The particles become smaller and more rounded as a result.

Solution

Solution is the chemical weathering of rock surfaces by water. When rivers flow on soluble rocks such as limestone and chalk, carbonic acid in the water dissolves minerals in the rock. The dissolved particles are then removed in solution.

Directions of erosion

Erosion takes place in three directions:

- **Vertical erosion:** A river makes its valley deeper by cutting down into its bed. It is most common in a river's youthful (upper) course. (Think V for vertical.)
- **Lateral erosion:** A river erodes on the outside of its channel. It eventually leads to the widening of the valley. It occurs mostly in the mature (middle) and old (lower) stages of a river.
- **Headward erosion:** A river erodes upstream from its source. It lengthens the river valley in an upstream direction. It also occurs when a waterfall retreats.

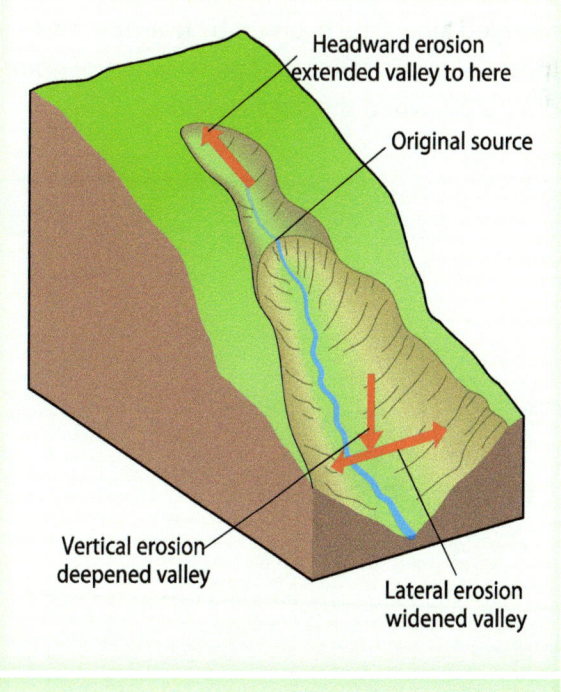

Figure 11.12 Vertical, lateral and headward erosion help shape a river valley

Processes of transportation by rivers

After erosion, the rest of the river's energy is used to transport various materials, called its **load**. A river transports its load in the following four ways: solution, suspension, saltation and traction.

Solution

Slightly acidic running water dissolves the soluble minerals in rocks such as limestone and chalk. These are carried in **solution** in the water.

Suspension

This load consists of the lightest particles, mainly clay and silt. They are carried along in the flow of the river without settling to the riverbed. The particles are held in **suspension** by the turbulence of the water. Most rivers carry the greater part of their load in suspension. The suspended load is the cause of the brown colour of a river, especially towards its mouth or when it is in flood.

Saltation

Particles of sand, gravel and small stones that are too heavy to be carried in suspension are picked up by the water and carried forward, only to fall back to the riverbed further downstream. As these particles land, they in turn dislodge other particles upwards, causing more such movement to take place. This bouncing process is known as **saltation**.

Traction

The largest stones and boulders are too heavy to be picked up by the water. Instead, they are rolled or dragged along the riverbed by **traction**. This requires the most energy. It mainly happens during periods of high discharge (when the river is in flood).

> **DEFINITION**
>
> **Bedload:** The load that a river moves along its bed by saltation or traction.

> **ACTIVITY**
>
> **Skills**
>
> Draw a simple labelled diagram to show how a river transports its load.

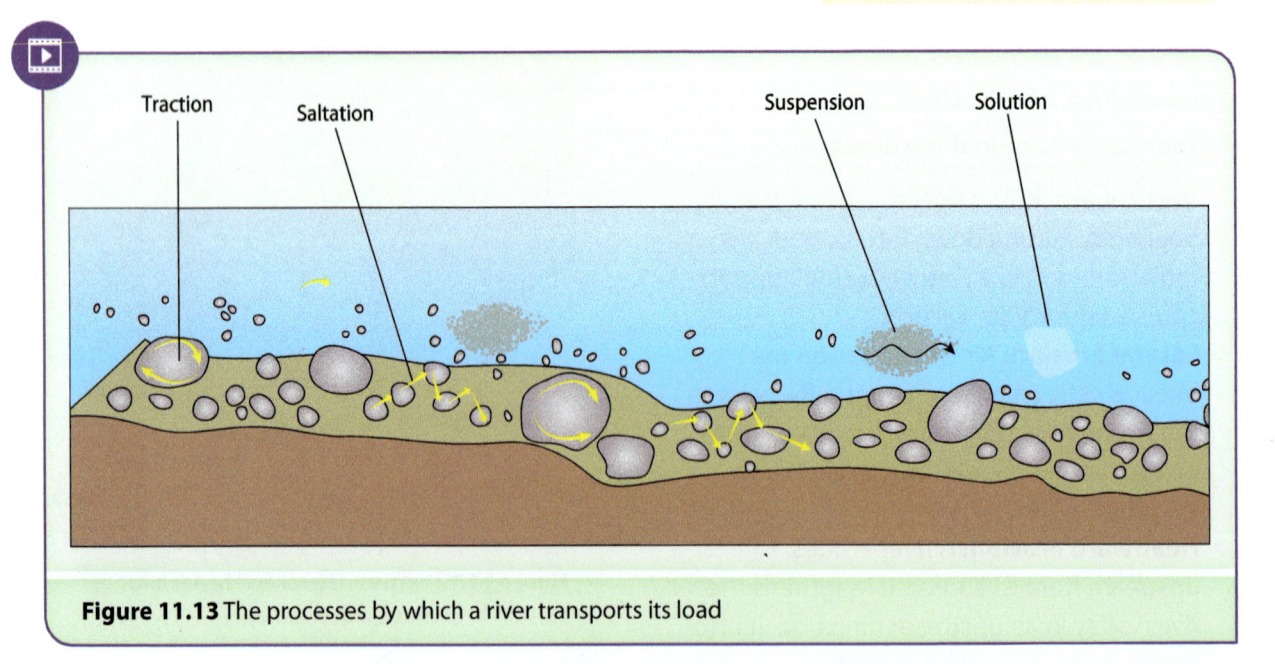

Figure 11.13 The processes by which a river transports its load

The Hwang Ho is also known as the Yellow River. It got its name because of the fine sediment that is being transported in suspension by the water. Each year, more than 1.6 billion tons of soil flow into it, making it the world's muddiest river.

Processes of deposition by rivers

When a stream loses energy, it is unable to transport its entire load and begins to deposit some of it. The material is sorted as it is deposited. The heaviest material is deposited first, followed by smaller particles of gravel and sand. The finest material, consisting of clay and silt, is carried furthest before being deposited.

GEOFACT

If the velocity of a river is doubled, perhaps during a flood, it can transport particles that are 2^6 (64) times heavier than previously.

Deposition occurs when:

> **Velocity (speed) is reduced:** When a river overflows its banks onto its floodplain, the water spreads out and slows down. If the course of the river is interrupted by a lake or reservoir, the river loses velocity when it enters the still body of water. The same happens at its mouth, when it flows into the sea.
> **Discharge is reduced:** If the river's discharge is reduced, then the river will lose energy because it isn't flowing as quickly anymore. This can occur when the river flows through a desert where there is increased evaporation. It can also occur following a period of reduced precipitation or if water is taken from a river for irrigation or urban usage.
> **Load is increased:** This may be caused when there is increased soil erosion following heavy rainfall. It can also occur when a fast-flowing tributary joins the main river and adds new load to it.

The finest particles may not be deposited until the river reaches the sea. Even then, the load may not be deposited but carried out to sea.

DEFINITION

Alluvium: The general term for the sorted sediments (sand, clay and silt) that are deposited in layers (strata) by rivers.

Changes along the course of a river

As we follow the course of a river from its source to its mouth, we can identify three distinct stages. They are the **youthful** (upper) course, **mature** (middle) course and **old** (lower) course. Each stage of the river's course is formed by different processes and has its own distinctive shape and landforms.

The long profile

The **long profile** shows how a river's gradient changes as it flows from its source to its mouth. In general, it has a concave shape. The upper part of the profile has a steep gradient, while closer to its mouth the gradient is very gentle and almost level.

A long profile is normally uneven. This is because there are points where the gradient of the river changes suddenly because of landforms like waterfalls, rapids or lakes. Rivers gradually remove these irregularities over time.

If all irregularities were to be removed, the long profile would become smooth and concave shape, creating a graded profile. However, it is highly unlikely that this state will ever be achieved.

The valley cross-section

In the **youthful course** of the river, the gradient is steep and the river channel is narrow. Erosion is the dominant process. The river cuts vertically into the landscape. This, combined with weathering and mass movement, results in a narrow, steep-sided valley along with other distinctive landforms.

In the **mature course**, the river has more energy and volume than in the upper course. The gradient is more gentle and the river channel has become deeper. Vertical erosion becomes less dominant. Instead, lateral erosion has widened the valley. The valley sides also have a gentler gradient. Some of the load, mainly the coarser material, is deposited.

Finally, at its **old course**, the volume of water in the river is at its greatest, mainly due to water from tributaries.

> **ACTIVITY**
>
> **Discussion**
>
> Identify three ways in which the cross-section and gradient of a river change from source to mouth.

> **DEFINITION**
>
> **Base level** is the level below which a stream cannot erode vertically. Sea level is the final base level. A river may also have temporary or local base levels where it flows into a lake or reservoir.

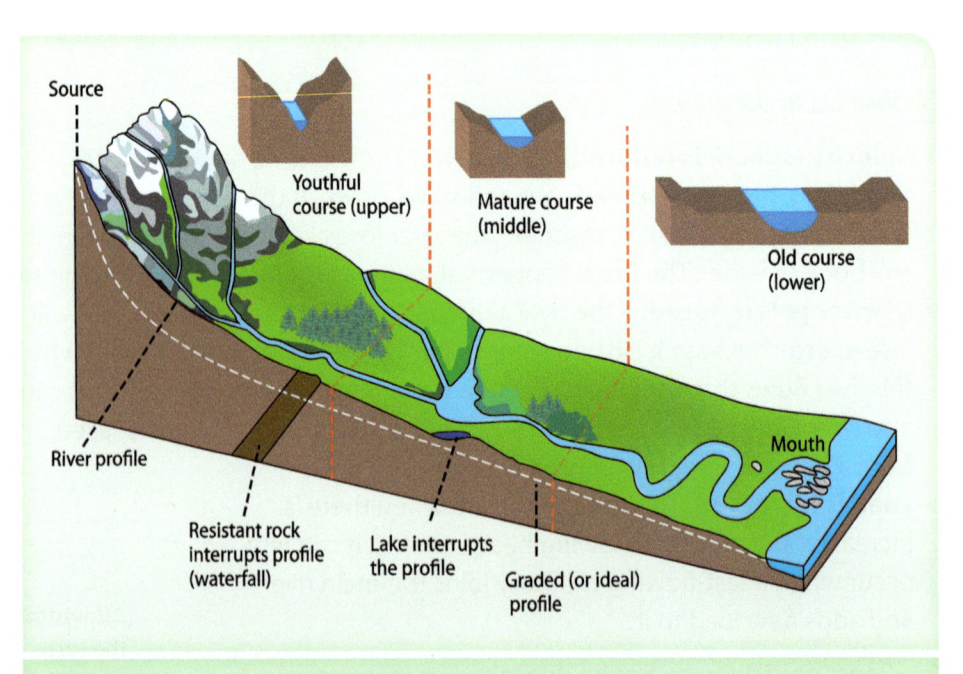

Figure 11.14 The long profile of the river and the cross-section of the valley vary over the course of the river

The river channel is now deep and wide. The river has widened its valley to the extent that it resembles a broad, almost flat plain. Although there is some lateral erosion, deposition is the dominant process.

Landforms of the youthful stage

The youthful stage of a river is also called its **mountain** or **torrent stage**. The discharge is small, the gradient is steep and the load is limited except in times of flood. Erosion is the main process.

The main landforms associated with the youthful course of a river are:

- V-shaped valleys
- Waterfalls.

V-shaped valleys

The valley cut by the young river is narrow, deep and steep sided. The river channel completely fills its base. **V-shaped valleys** are found in the upper stages of most rivers in Ireland, including the Slaney, Avoca, Moy and Blackwater.

When a river has more energy than it needs to transport its load, the excess energy is used in erosion. This results in the downcutting and deepening of the valley by **vertical erosion**.

As the river rushes down the mountainside, the fast-flowing water dislodges stones and sediment by hydraulic action. The swirling water creates air bubbles that collapse and weaken the banks by cavitation, loosening more material. All this material is hurled against the riverbanks and bed, resulting in further erosion by abrasion. This load is then gradually worn down and smoothed by attrition.

Processes
- Vertical erosion
- Hydraulic action
- Cavitation
- Abrasion
- Attrition
- Weathering
- Mass movement

ACTIVITY

Thinking

What processes are active in the youthful stage of a river?

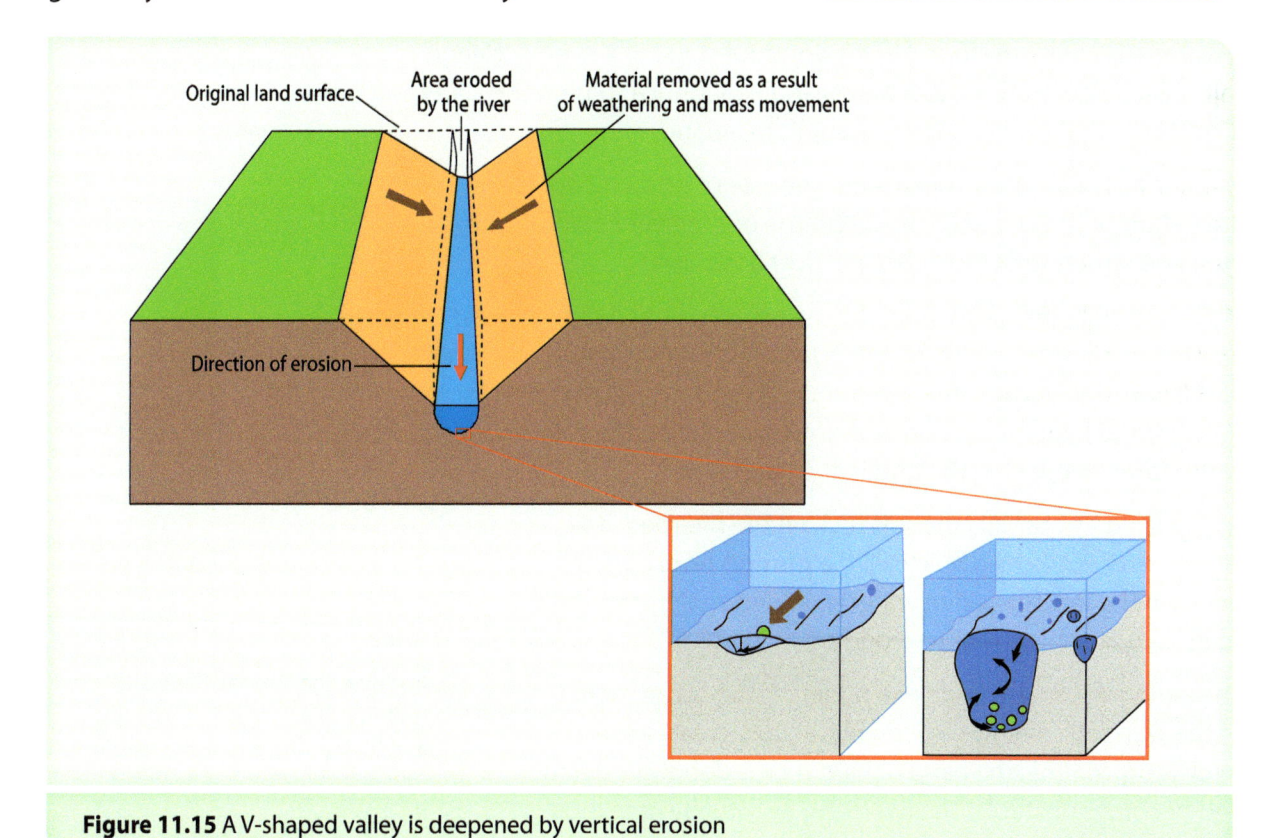

Figure 11.15 A V-shaped valley is deepened by vertical erosion

If the riverbed is uneven, the water swirls about in currents called eddies and becomes turbulent. With the aid of its load, it cuts hollows, called **potholes**, in the riverbed. As the potholes are deepened and enlarged, they eventually join up. This causes further deepening of the river channel.

The upper section of a river adopts a winding course as it tries to find the easiest route. As it cuts down, it flows around areas of resistant rock in its path. The result is that the river follows a zigzag course. The higher sections of land that remain jut out as **interlocking spurs**.

V-shaped valley and interlocking spurs in the youthful stage of a river

The sides of the valley are also shaped by weathering and mass movement. Weathering weakens the valley sides. Under the influence of gravity, the weakened material collapses into the river by mass movement. The river then removes the material as load. This gives the valley its characteristic V shape.

Waterfalls

A **waterfall** is a point where there is an interruption in the river profile and the water makes a vertical drop. It is a major interruption in the flow of a river.

A waterfall is normally found in the youthful stage of a river. Aasleagh Falls near Killary Harbour (Co. Mayo) and Pollaphuca Falls on the Liffey (Co. Wicklow) are well-known waterfalls in Ireland.

A waterfall is a landform of erosion. The rate of erosion depends on the height of the waterfall, the discharge of the river as well as the type and structure of rocks that the river flows over.

Most waterfalls develop where the river meets a band of softer, less resistant rock after flowing over harder, more resistant rock. As a result of **differential erosion**, the water quickly erodes the softer rock by the processes of hydraulic action and abrasion. It begins to cut down into the softer rock, steepening the gradient of the river.

As the falling water hits the soft rock on the riverbed, its energy cuts out a deep hole called a **plunge pool** directly beneath the fall. The falling water is unhindered by friction, so its velocity and power to erode are increased.

The falling water also begins to undercut the softer rock of the waterfall, mainly by hydraulic action, creating an **overhang**. In time, the band of hard rock is deeply undercut and becomes unstable. The overhang eventually breaks off and collapses into the plunge pool.

Processes
> Differential erosion
> Hydraulic action
> Abrasion
> Attrition
> Undercutting
> Retreat

ACTIVITY

Skills

Examine the OS map extract of Galtymore on page 417. Identify and locate with a four-figure grid reference any two landforms of fluvial erosion.

The processes of undercutting and collapse are repeated many times. As a result, the waterfall gradually retreats upstream in a process called **headward erosion**. This results in the formation of a valley with vertical sides, called a **gorge**. As Niagara Falls has retreated, it has cut a gorge that is more than 12 km long.

A waterfall is a temporary feature. Headward erosion will eventually undermine all the resistant rock, with the river flowing over a series of **rapids**. Eventually, the river will once again develop a regular profile.

GEOFACT

Waterfalls also develop where streams flow from a hanging valley down to the main glaciated valley and where a stream flows over a cliff and into the sea.

DEFINITION

Differential erosion: Different types of rock erode at different rates. Less resistant rocks are eroded far more quickly than more resistant rocks.

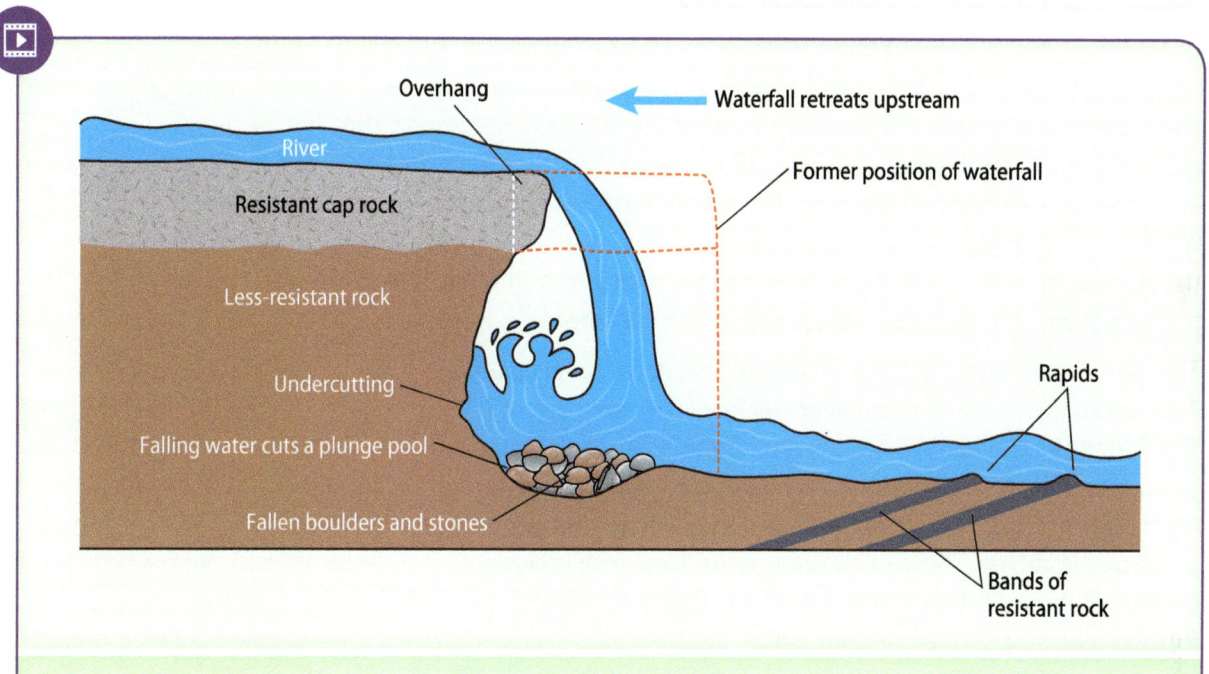

Figure 11.16 Undercutting the less resistant rock causes the waterfall to retreat upstream by headward erosion

The Iguazu Falls are on the border between Brazil and Argentina. Note the gorge that is developing as the waterfall retreats due to headward erosion.

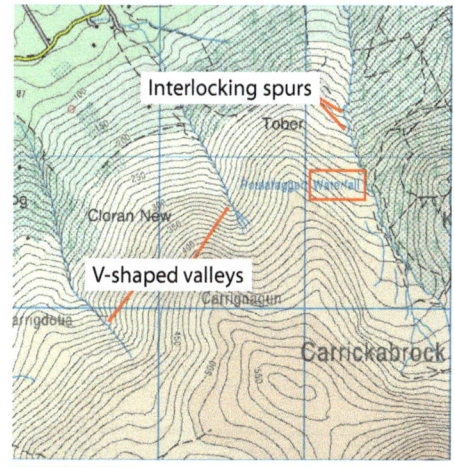

Figure 11.17 Characteristics of a youthful river on an OS map

CHAPTER 11 · RIVER PROCESSES 145

Landforms of the mature stage

The mature or middle course of a river has more energy and volume than in the youthful course as more tributaries join it. The channel has also become wider and deeper. The gradient is more gentle and the valley sides have become less steep.

The river has now begun to erode laterally and to deposit part of its load.

The main landforms associated with the mature course of a river are:

> Meanders
> Floodplains.

Meanders

Meanders are gently curving loops or bends that develop along the course of a river. They are the result of both erosion and deposition. Well-developed meanders are found on the rivers Liffey, Shannon and Moy.

When discharge is low, a river will deposit some sediment on its beds. The moving water then has to weave around these bars of sediment. This creates deeper pathways where most of the water flows, called **pools**, and shallow areas where less water flows, called **riffles**. This causes the water flow to swing from side to side in a snaking motion. It flows along the surface towards the outside bank and then returns along the riverbed towards the inside bank in a **corkscrew-like movement**.

The water that takes the longer route will need to travel faster. As a result, this section of the river will have the most energy. The water hits the bank and begins to erode it, creating a small bend on the river. The bend is then widened by lateral erosion. **Hydraulic action**, **cavitation** and **abrasion** are the main processes involved. The bank is undermined, especially during periods of high discharge. It eventually collapses or slumps to form a steep slope, called a **river cliff**.

After the surface flow of water hits the outer bank, it corkscrews and flows along the riverbed. In doing so, it transfers the eroded material sideways and forward towards the inner bank. Here the water is slow flowing and has less energy, so the material is **deposited.** These deposits of sand and gravel build up to form a gentle slope, called a **point bar**.

Processes
> Lateral erosion
> Hydraulic action
> Cavitation
> Abrasion
> Undercutting
> Slumping
> Deposition

GEOFACT

Meanders are also found in the lower course of a river, where the bends are even more pronounced.

ACTIVITY

Skills
Examine the OS map extract of Dungarvan on page 410. Identify and locate with a four-figure grid reference any two middle course landforms.

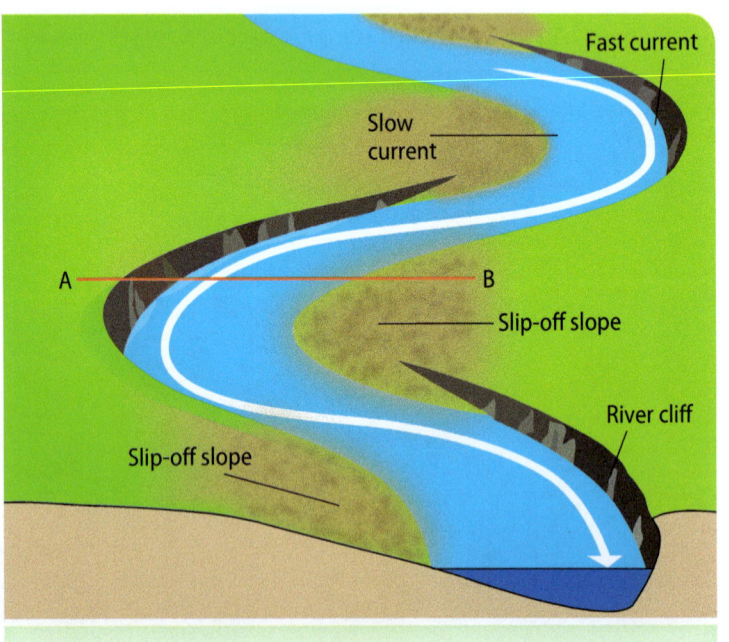

Figure 11.18 Meanders develop from a combination of erosion and deposition, with erosion taking place where the river flows fastest

As erosion on the outside (concave) bank and deposition on the inside (convex) bank continue, the meanders begin to migrate. They move from side to side across the valley floor and also migrate in a downstream direction. In this way, the river both widens and straightens the valley by removing the interlocking spurs. The widest that the meanders migrate to is marked by a prominent slope, called a **bluff line**. This represents the remnants of the interlocking spurs.

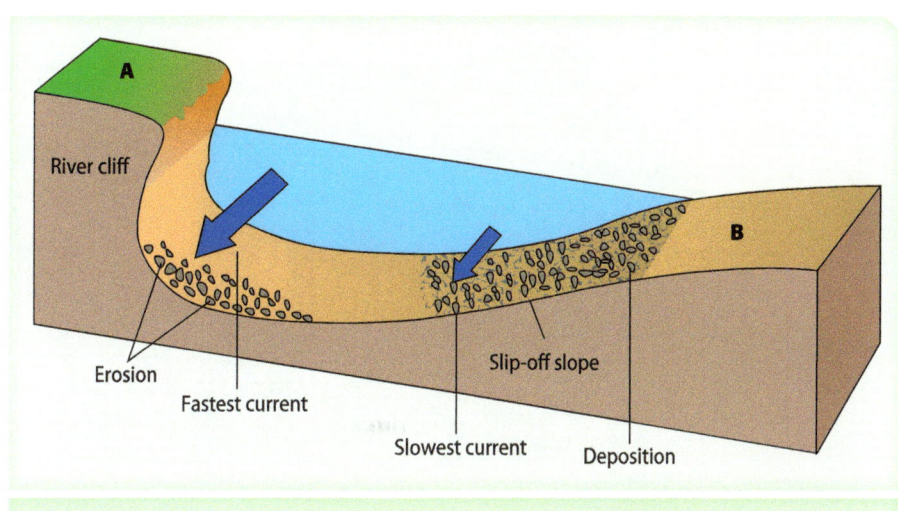

Figure 11.19 Cross-section of a river channel across a meander

Erosion is causing the outer (concave) bank of the meander to collapse, forming a river cliff. Deposition has led to the development of a point bar at the inner (convex) bend. Note the floodplain on both sides of the river.

Floodplains

This is the wide, flat floor of the river valley that the river floods over after periods of heavy rain. It lies between the bluff lines and has a very gentle gradient. **Floodplains** are found on the rivers Liffey, Suir and Shannon.

A floodplain is formed by a combination of erosion and deposition. It is linked to the formation of meanders. As the river channel migrates from side to side and downstream, it **erodes** the outside (or concave) bank to widen the valley floor. As the interlocking spurs are eroded, a steep, almost vertical slope, called a **bluff line**, marks the edge of the floodplain.

This eroded sediment is then transferred to the inside (or convex) of the meander. It is then **deposited** to create a series of point bars. The point bars gradually build up to form an area of flat land on either side of the river channel. This type of floodplain is called an **erosional floodplain**.

Following periods of heavy rain, the river is subject to much higher discharge and may overflow its banks. Large floods may cover the entire valley floor from bluff to bluff and the velocity

Processes
> Lateral erosion
> Hydraulic action
> Abrasion
> Flooding
> Loss of energy
> Deposition

GEOFACT

Floodplains are also found in the lower course of a river, where they are even wider. There is a link between the formation of floodplains and levees as well.

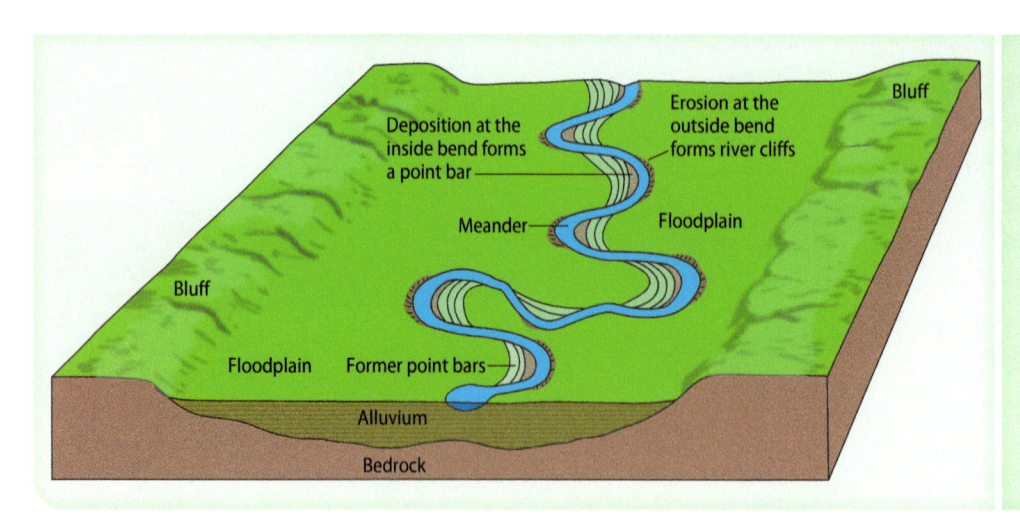

Figure 11.20 The floodplain developed as the meanders migrated both from side to side and forward. The remnants of the interlocking spurs stand out as bluffs.

of the water rapidly decreases. It is unable to support its load of suspended material and this is deposited in thin layers on the floodplain. Coarser material is deposited, while finer material is carried closer to the edge of the floodplain.

The deposited material, consisting mainly of sand and silt, is called **alluvium**. After each period of flooding, the depth of alluvium on the floodplain increases. This type of floodplain is called a **depositional floodplain**.

ACTIVITY

Discussion

Identify the differences between an erosional floodplain and a depositional floodplain.

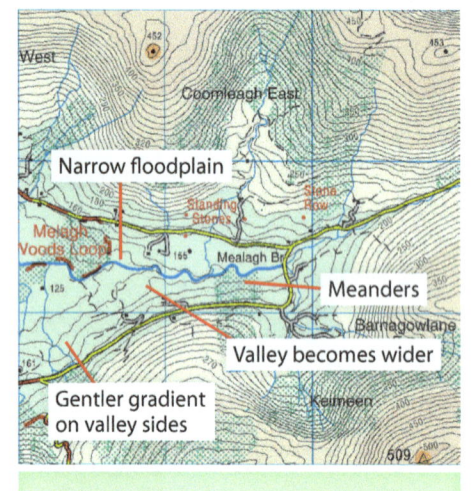

Figure 11.21 Characteristics of a mature river on an OS map

Landforms of the old course

In the old lower course of a river, erosion has practically ceased and **deposition** is the dominant process. The valley floor is very wide and flat. The valley sides have been lowered further by weathering and mass movement. The gradient of the river is very gentle.

The main landforms associated with the lower stage of a river are:

> Oxbow lakes
> Levees
> Deltas.

QUESTION

Why does a river deposit its load?

Oxbow lakes

An **oxbow lake** is a crescent-shaped lake that is found alongside a meandering river. It is formed when a meander is cut off from the river. Oxbow lakes are found along the lower course of the rivers Shannon, Moy (Co. Mayo) and Bride (Co. Waterford).

The formation of oxbow lakes follows the formation of meanders. Once meanders have formed, they are in a constant state of movement. By the lower stage of the river, the meanders have developed much larger loops and the course of the river is far more twisting.

Processes

> Lateral erosion
> Hydraulic action
> Cavitation
> Abrasion
> Deposition

Lateral erosion, by processes that include **hydraulic action** and **cavitation**, continues at the concave banks. This causes the loops to grow closer and the point bars to get bigger. Soon the neck of land between the meanders becomes very narrow. Eventually the river cuts through them. This is most likely when the river is in flood and has greater power to erode. The river then flows directly ahead along a straighter course and it abandons part of its original channel.

When the flood subsides, the river keeps this new course. The water flows fastest in the centre of the channel and slowest at the sides of the channel. As a result, **deposition** is most likely to occur here. Over time, sediments build up in the slow-moving water where the old meander was abandoned. The ends of the old meander are eventually sealed off from the main river. The cut-off loop is called an oxbow lake.

Oxbow lakes have a short life span. They do not have a stream feeding them, so they may dry up as a result of evaporation. Every time the nearby river bursts its banks, alluvium is deposited in the oxbow lake. It gradually silts up to form a marsh. The oxbow lake eventually dries up to leave a meander scar or **mort lake**.

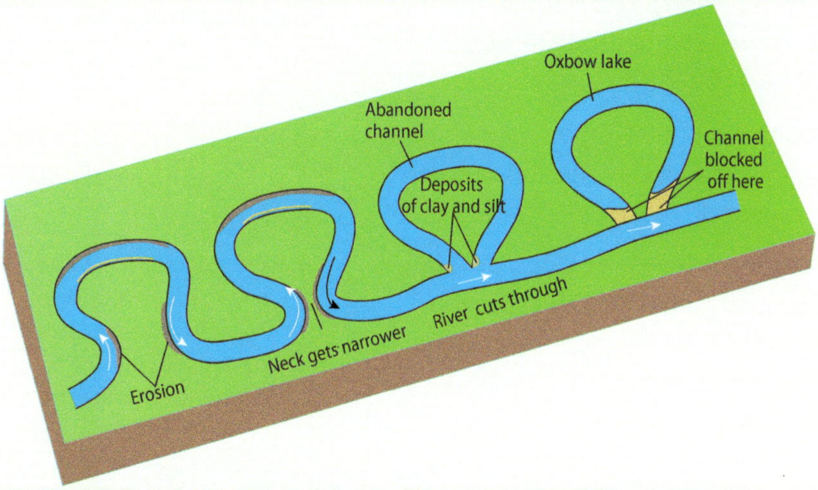

GEOFACT

The channel of the Rio Grande regularly changes course. This has led to several border disputes between Mexico and the USA in the past because the river forms part of the border between the countries.

Figure 11.22 How meanders develop to form an oxbow lake

Oxbow lakes along the old course of a river. Note how much of the course of the river is straight as a result of the meanders being cut off.

ACTIVITY

Skills

Examine the photograph on the left. List three pieces of evidence that suggest that the river is in its old stage.

Levees

These are natural **ridges** of **alluvium** that build up along the sides of a river channel in its old stage. They stand above the level of the floodplain and help to confine the river to its channel. They are steep on the side facing the stream channel and gently sloping on the other side.

Natural **levees** are built by successive floods over many years. When a river overflows its banks, the silt-laden water leaves its channel and spreads over the floodplain. As it does so, its velocity decreases and it loses much of its ability to transport material. The coarser portion of the suspended load, typically gravel and sand, is deposited first along a narrow strip close to the edge of the river channel. Over the years this deposition gradually builds up to form natural ridges or mounds.

As the flood water spreads further out along the floodplain, it loses more energy. Thus, a lesser amount of finer sediment is carried further from the river before being deposited.

During periods of low discharge, the river is confined within its channel and any deposition will take place on the channel bed. This gradually raises the level of the river. It also increases the risk of the river bursting its banks when it is in flood. Each time the river overflows its banks, more sediments are deposited and the levees are gradually built up.

Raising the levees and deposition on the riverbed may result in the river channel standing above the level of the surrounding floodplain as a **raised river channel**.

The floodplain that is furthest from the river consists of very fine-grained alluvium. This is poorly draining and is capable of holding the water on the surface. As the water cannot flow back into the river due to the levees, areas of marshy land, called **backswamps**, often develop.

Levees have developed along sections of the Moy River. The Mississippi River has more than 5,500 km of levees, most of them artificial.

Processes
> Flooding
> Loss of energy
> Deposition

GEOFACT

People often raise and strengthen levees to try to control flooding. These are known as artificial levees.

ACTIVITY

Research

Using Scoilnet maps, follow the course of the Moy River upstream from its mouth at Ballina and identify any five landforms listed in the text.

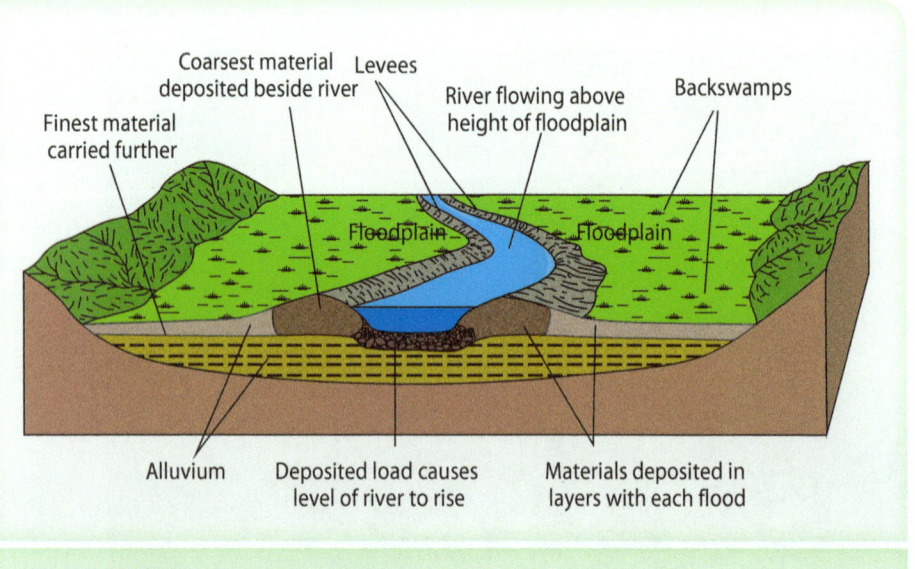

Figure 11.23 The formation of levees

Delta

A **delta** is a flat area formed of alluvium deposited by a river when it enters an area of slow-moving water or standing water, such as a lake (lacustrine delta) or a sea (marine delta).

For a delta to form, a river must have a large load of sediment. Even then, marine deltas grow only where the amount of sediment that is deposited by the river is greater than the amount that is removed by tides and currents.

Enclosed seas such as the Mediterranean have a small tidal range and the water is calmer, so deltas can form more readily. The Nile, Po and Rhône–Saône all have deltas at their mouths. In open seas and oceans, only very large rivers have deltas (Amazon, Mississippi, Ganges).

When a river enters a sea or lake, its velocity decreases. As a result, it loses its energy and begins to deposit its load of alluvium. As layer upon layer of these materials are deposited, platforms of alluvium are built up. These eventually rise above the water as a series of islands. As they do, the river breaks from a single channel into several smaller channels, called **distributaries**.

As the alluvial materials are deposited, they are sorted into three distinct groups:

> The **bottomset beds** are made up of horizontal layers of very fine clay and silt. These sediments are transported in suspension quite far out to sea because they are so fine. **Flocculation** occurs as the fresh water of the river mixes with seawater. In this process, tiny particles of clay and silt coagulate (stick together) as they react with the salt and become heavy enough to sink to the seabed.

> The **foreset beds** consist of thick layers of slightly coarser material and are deposited closer to the river mouth. They lie on top of the bottomset beds and slope steeply seawards. As more material is deposited, the delta advances.

> The **topset beds** consist of a mixture of materials that are deposited nearest to the land. The river channel becomes choked with sediment and the river is forced to divide into a number of separate channels, called **distributaries**. The delta now extends seawards as part of the river's floodplain.

Processes
› Flooding
› Loss of energy
› Deposition

ACTIVITY

Skills

Draw a simple labelled diagram of any landform of deposition.

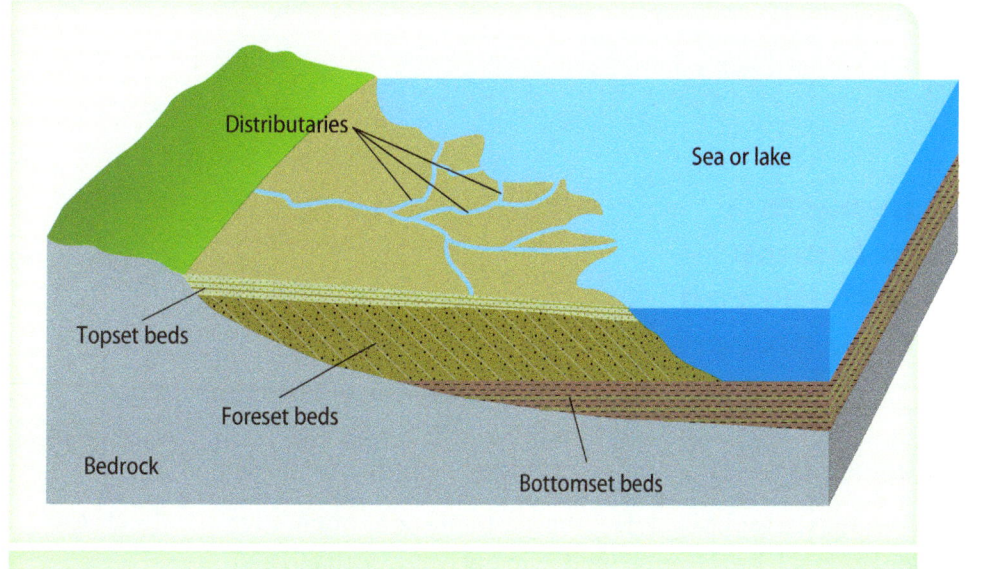

Figure 11.24 A cross-section through a delta

There are three main types of **marine delta**.

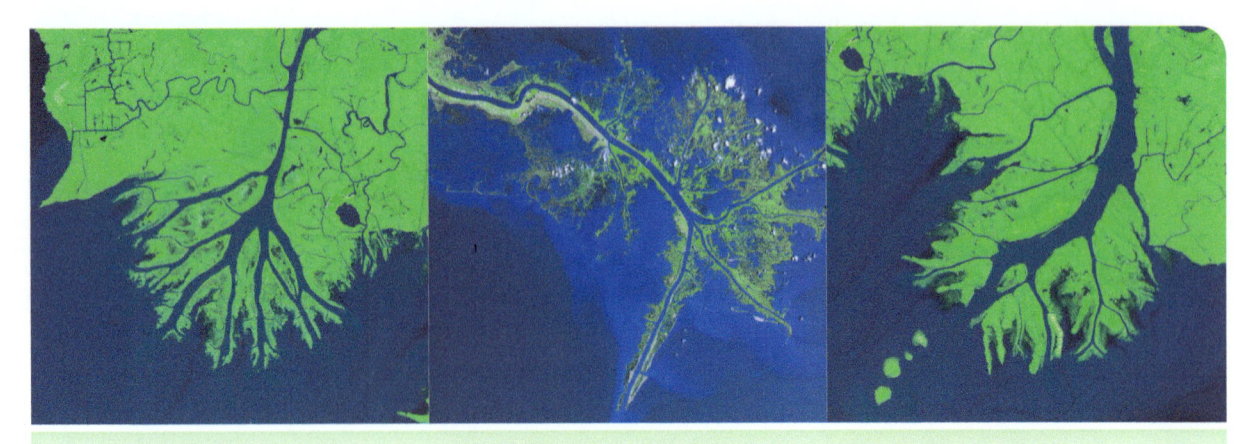

An **arcuate delta** is triangular. It consists of fairly coarse materials. It develops where sea currents are quite strong, keeping the outside edge of the delta straight. It has a large number of distributaries. The Nile Delta is an example of an arcuate delta.

A **bird's foot delta** has a relatively small number of distributaries. Each extends out into the sea like the claws of a bird's foot. It consists of very fine materials. Levees build up along the sides of the distributaries. The Mississippi Delta extends seawards by about 2 metres per year.

An **estuarine delta** has not yet extended beyond the coastline. It consists of sediments that have been deposited in the shallow water along the sides of the estuary. Estuarine deltas are found at the mouths of the rivers Rhine and Shannon.

A lacustrine delta may form where a stream flows into a lake, such as at Lough Tay in the Wicklow Mountains

LINK
See Chapter 14 for isostasy and fluvial adjustment to base level.

Impacts of human activities on river processes

A free-flowing river is defined as one that flows undisturbed from its source to its mouth. Very few large rivers are now free flowing. Most have been modified by human activities.

The **Mississippi** is one river that certainly does not fit this definition. It has been shaped in many ways, both big and small, to suit human needs.

Figure 11.25 Characteristics of an old river

CASE STUDY

The Mississippi River system

The Mississippi River and its tributaries have the third largest drainage basin in the world, exceeded in size only by the basins of the Amazon River and Congo River. They drain more than 3 million km² of the USA, including all or parts of thirty-one states and two Canadian provinces.

The Mississippi has forty-two tributary streams, including the Tennessee River, Arkansas River, Ohio River and Missouri River. The latter tributary is actually longer than the Mississippi itself.

Today, the Mississippi and its tributaries have a course that stays put. It has a minimum depth of 3 metres and a navigable length in excess of 25,000 km. It was not always so!

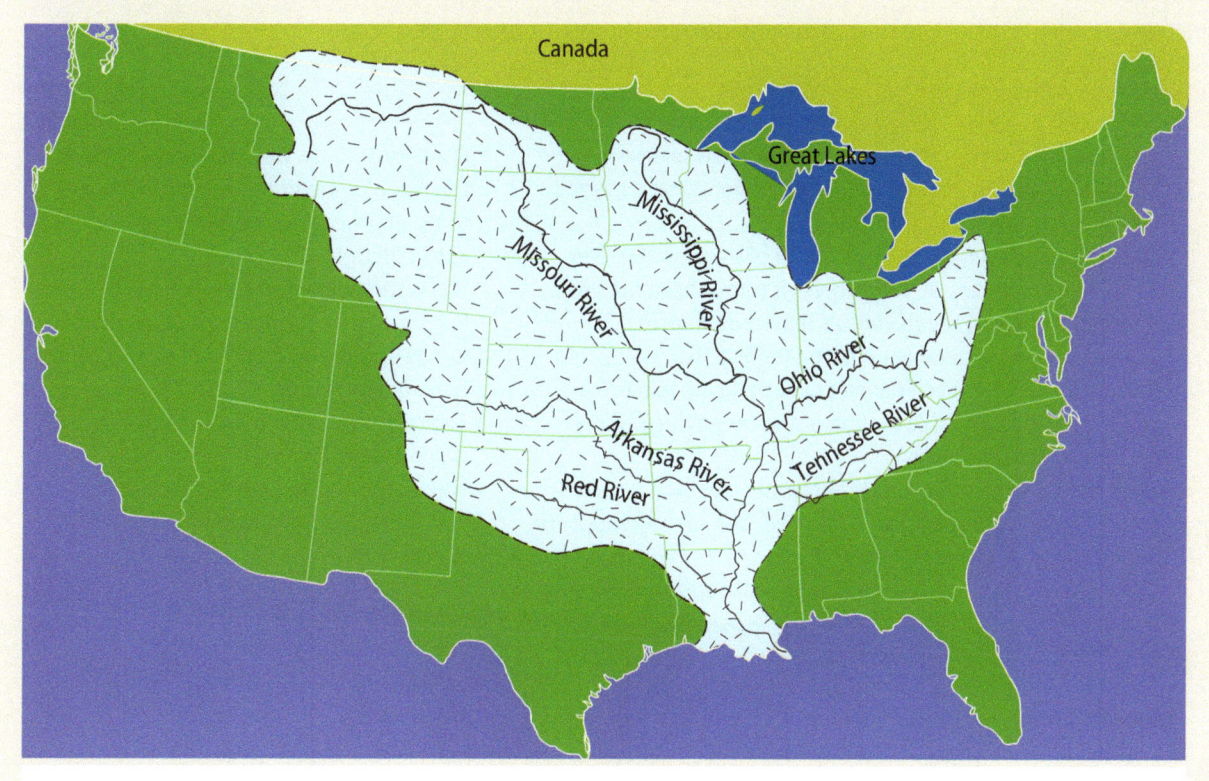

Figure 11.26 The drainage basin of the Mississippi River

Why was the river modified?

The modification of the river has been underway for over 200 years. It was undertaken in order to:

> Control flooding
> Improve navigation.

The discharge of the river system varied hugely depending on weather conditions. As a result, the river flooded regularly. On average, a major flood occurred every three years. This had a negative impact on farmland and urban settlements on the floodplains.

Rivers were once the principal transportation routes into the interior of the continent and remained so until the arrival of the railways. As the interior was developed, the scale of trade increased enormously. So did the number and size of the vessels using the river.

How was it modified?

The authorities undertook three main types of construction programme. They wanted to control both the flow and the course of the river. They tried to achieve this by:

- Building dams
- Building levees and walls
- Canalising the river.

Building dams: The impacts

A total of **seventy-five dams** were built on the Mississippi and its tributaries. Each dam includes a lock that allows shipping to move past it. The dams are used to control both the flow and the level of water.

However, there are no dams on the lower reaches of the Mississippi. Here, the gradient is very gentle, the river is very wide and the water is very deep.

POSITIVE IMPACTS	NEGATIVE IMPACTS
- The dams trap and store water. They can then release it in a controlled way. This can minimise the risk of flood, especially following heavy rain or snow melt. - The dams maintain a minimum depth of water in the river. This allows commercial traffic to use it throughout the year. The upper stage of the river has a minimum depth of 3 metres, making it suitable for barge traffic. - The locks built into each dam let river traffic travel far upstream. The navigable section of the Tennessee River is more than 800 km long. - Each dam also contains a series of turbines, which are used to generate hydro-electricity. This produces a ready supply of renewable energy for the region. - The reservoirs are used to maintain a water supply (domestic, industry and irrigation) for the region, especially in the summer months or periods of prolonged drought.	- Dams restrict the flow of alluvium, so the reservoir behind the dam will begin to silt up. This requires regular and costly dredging. - The water below the dam has now lost its load of sediments. As a result, it may use its energy to start eroding the landscape again. - Sediments are lost to areas further downstream. The delta is now shrinking by about 40 km^2 each year. - Nutrients are lost to the soil, so farmers now use more chemical fertilisers.

Table 11.1 Impacts of building dams

Dam and lock on the Tennessee River. A large reservoir has been created in the foreground.

Levees and walls: The impacts

The original **levees** on the Mississippi were formed naturally by the process of deposition. They were no more than 1 or 2 metres high. The river regularly overflowed them.

Now, artificial **levees** and **walls** run for almost 3,000 km along the main river and its tributaries. These are up to 15 metres high in places. As a result of these vast engineering works, the Mississippi has more or less been locked into an artificial channel for all of its lower course.

POSITIVE IMPACTS	NEGATIVE IMPACTS
› The levees have greatly reduced both the frequency and the severity of floods. › The levees help to maintain a deep channel in the river. The Mississippi continues to be an important navigation route for ships and barges. › When flooding was controlled, the backswamps could be drained, making the floodplains into some of the most fertile farmland in America. › Many of the walls have locks that lead to floodways. They can be opened if the water level gets very high.	› Since the river is unable to flood, it deposits some of its load on its bed, thus raising the level of the river well above that of the surrounding floodplain. › This means that the levees have to be raised again to prevent flooding. › The river is not allowed to follow a natural, winding course. As a result, its flow is faster. › This puts pressure on the levees. They may fail, leading to worse flooding. › The fast-flowing river is unable to deposit its remaining load on its floodplain. Instead, it transports it past its mouth and out to sea, where it is lost in deep water. › The levees and walls are now of such a scale that maintaining them has become costly and difficult.

Table 11.2 Impacts of building levees and walls

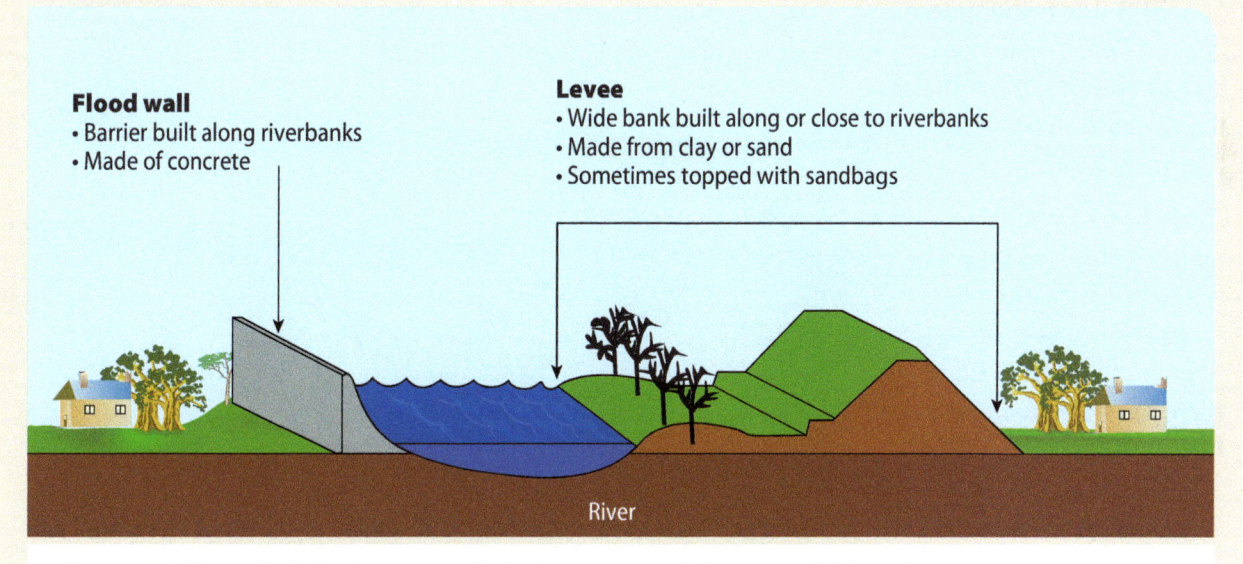

Flood wall
- Barrier built along riverbanks
- Made of concrete

Levee
- Wide bank built along or close to riverbanks
- Made from clay or sand
- Sometimes topped with sandbags

River

Figure 11.27 The Mississippi is hemmed in by levees and walls for over 3,000 km of its course

Canalisation: The impacts

The meandering course of the Mississippi has been modified by **canalisation**. Sections of the river now flow through manmade channels, similar to canals. In doing this, meanders have been by-passed and the course of the river has been straightened. Canalisation has also shortened the course of the river by more than 200 km.

POSITIVE IMPACTS	NEGATIVE IMPACTS
› The velocity of the water will increase. This will stop a backlog of water building up and should reduce the risk of flooding. › Without slip-off slopes, the new channel is much deeper, thus improving navigation.	› The faster flow of the water increases the potential for damage to levees, especially when the river is in flood. › Flooding becomes more likely downstream of a straightened section of a channel unless that channel is also straightened. › The fast-flowing water may cause erosion further downstream because the river has more energy.

Table 11.3 Impacts of canalisation

The current situation

By the 1970s, the US government felt that the Mississippi had been tamed and that all that would be needed was to maintain the structures that were in place.

Since then, there have been major floods in 1993, 2008 and 2011. The levee system around New Orleans was also unable to cope with the flood waters of Hurricane Katrina in 2005.

There has now been a major re-think on how to deal with the flooding issues. New levees have been built, set back from the river. This has created **floodway** areas. These are areas of farmland that water can be diverted onto in times of flood. This will lower the level of the river and reduce the risk of levees overflowing in urban areas.

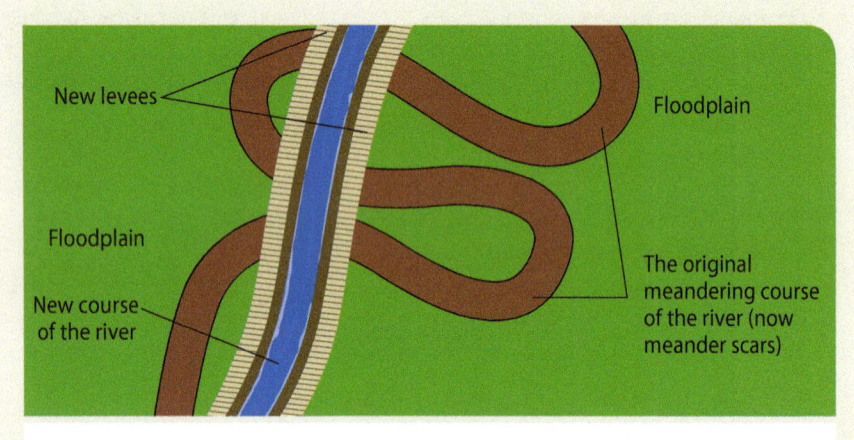

Figure 11.28 Canalising has straightened, deepened and shortened sections of the course of the Mississippi

Satellite image showing some of the changes that have been made to the course of the Mississippi

PowerPoint Summary

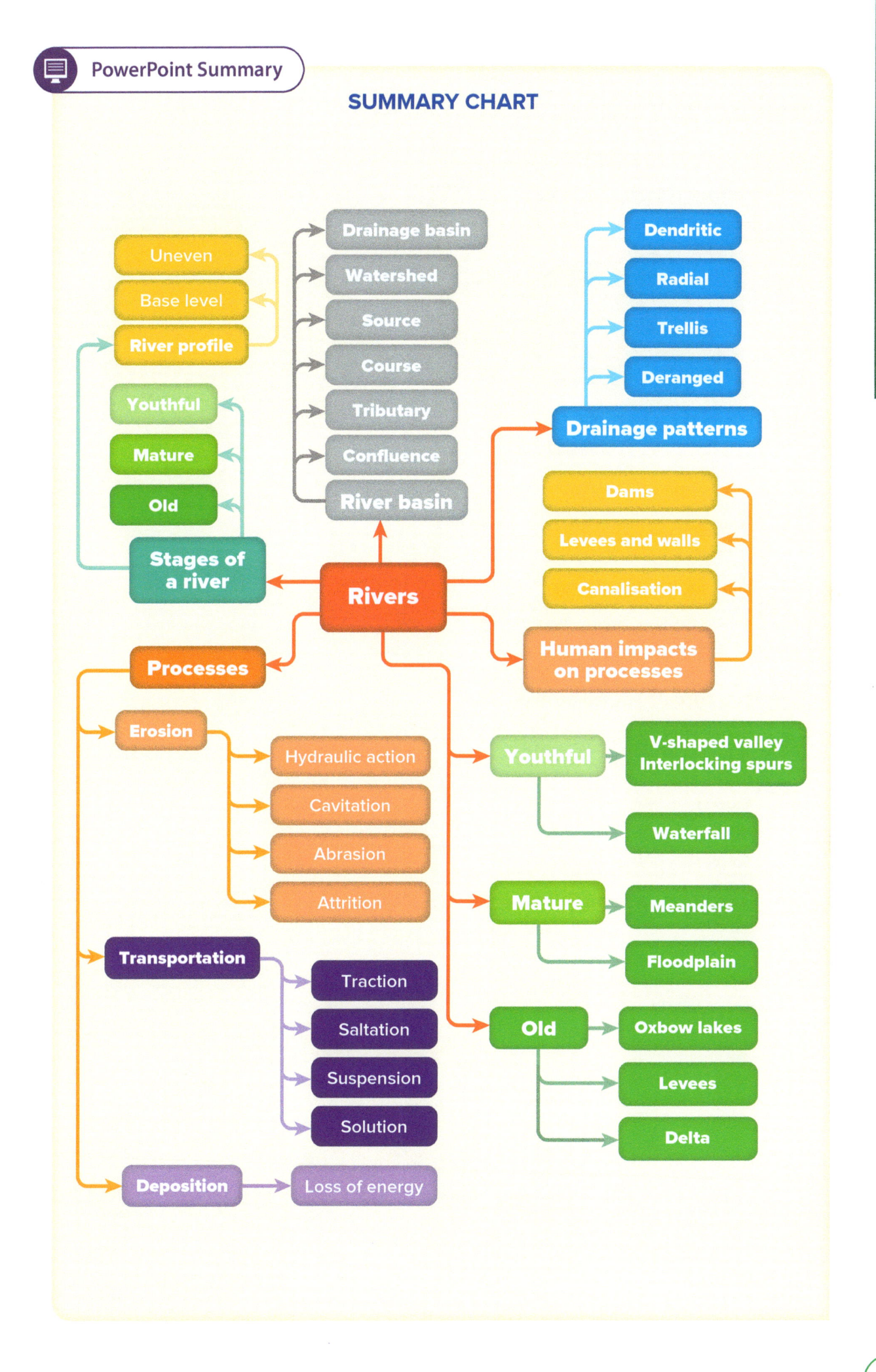

SUMMARY CHART

Rivers

- **River basin**
  - Drainage basin
  - Watershed
  - Source
  - Course
  - Tributary
  - Confluence

- **Stages of a river**
  - **River profile**
    - Uneven
    - Base level
  - Youthful
  - Mature
  - Old

- **Drainage patterns**
  - Dendritic
  - Radial
  - Trellis
  - Deranged

- **Human impacts on processes**
  - Dams
  - Levees and walls
  - Canalisation

- **Processes**
  - **Erosion**
    - Hydraulic action
    - Cavitation
    - Abrasion
    - Attrition
  - **Transportation**
    - Traction
    - Saltation
    - Suspension
    - Solution
  - **Deposition**
    - Loss of energy

- **Youthful**
  - V-shaped valley
  - Interlocking spurs
  - Waterfall

- **Mature**
  - Meanders
  - Floodplain

- **Old**
  - Oxbow lakes
  - Levees
  - Delta

UNIT 1 · PHYSICAL GEOGRAPHY

CHAPTER 11 · RIVER PROCESSES 157

Leaving Cert exam questions

HL SHORT QUESTIONS: HIGHER LEVEL

1 Drainage patterns (8 marks)

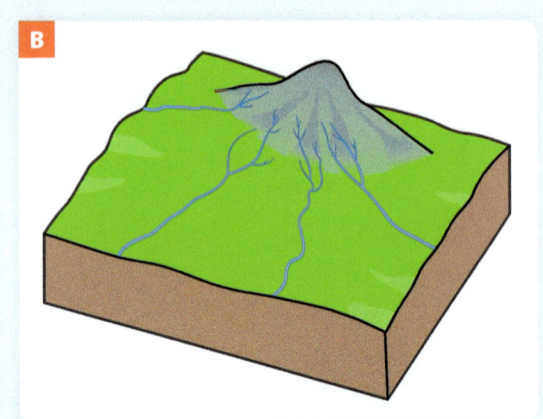

A

B

Name the drainage pattern shown in diagram **A**.	
Name the drainage pattern shown in diagram **B**.	
What is the name given to an area of high ground which separates two river basins?	
What is the name given to the point where a tributary joins a larger river?	

2 Transportation of sediment (8 marks)

Examine the diagram and link each process with its correct letter.

Process	Letter
Saltation	
Solution	
Suspension	
Traction	

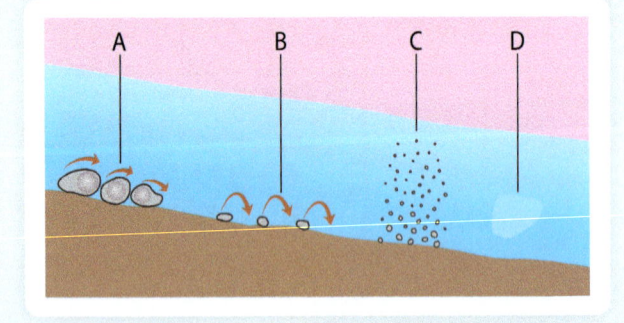

OL SHORT QUESTIONS: ORDINARY LEVEL

1 River landforms (10 marks)

(i) Examine the photographs and match each of the named landforms in the table with one of the letters on the photographs.

Landform	Letter
Waterfall	
Interlocking spur	
Meander	

OL (ii) State **one** reason why farming might be popular in the floodplain of a river valley.

(iii) State **one** reason why farming might not be popular in the floodplain of a river valley.

HL **LONG QUESTIONS: HIGHER LEVEL**

1 **River landforms** (20 marks)

Examine the diagram showing river landforms. Answer each of the following questions.

(i) Match each of the letters **A**, **B**, **C** and **D** with the landform that best matches it in the table below.

Landform	Letter
Levee	
Floodplain	
Meander	
Oxbow lake	

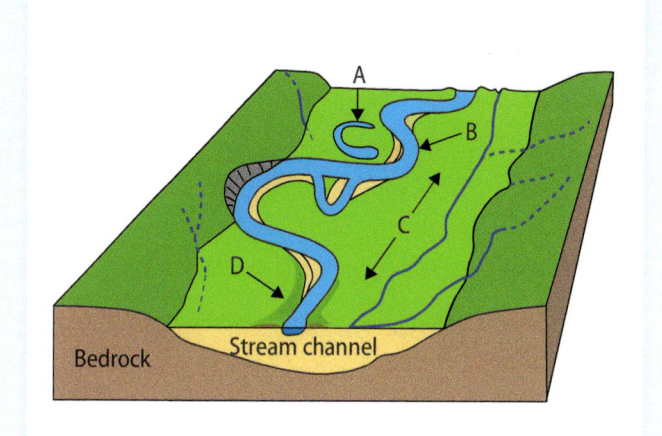

(ii) In which stage of a river, youthful or old, are the landforms referred to above associated?

2 **River terms** (20 marks)

(i) Examine the diagram and link each letter with its description.

Process	Letter
Source of the river	
Confluence	
Watershed	
Tributary	

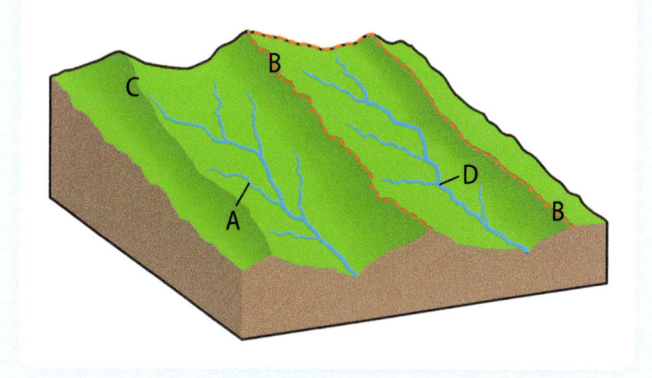

(ii) The area of land drained by a river (within the red lines in the diagram) is called its?

3 **Surface processes** (30 marks)

Examine the impact of the **processes of erosion** on the formation of **one** (Irish) fluvial landform that you have studied.

4 **Surface processes** (30 marks)

Examine the impact of the **processes of deposition** on the formation of **one** (Irish) fluvial landform that you have studied.

5 **Surface processes** (30 marks)

Examine the formation of **one** landform of erosion **and one** landform of deposition that you have studied.

HL

6 **Surface processes** (30 marks)

   Examine, with the aid of a labelled diagram, the formation of **one** landform of erosion that you have studied.

7 **Surface processes** (30 marks)

   Examine, with the aid of a labelled diagram, the formation of **one** landform of deposition that you have studied.

8 **Human interaction with surface processes** (30 marks)

   Examine, with reference to example(s) that you have studied, how human activities have impacted on fluvial (river) processes.

9 **Human interaction with surface processes** (30 marks)

   'Human activity impacts on surface processes.' Examine this statement with reference to the impact of dams on river processes.

10 **Human interaction with surface processes** (30 marks)

   With reference to example(s) that you have studied, describe and account for **one** way in which humans attempt to influence or control natural fluvial (river) processes.

OL

LONG QUESTIONS: ORDINARY LEVEL

1 **Surface processes** (40 marks)

   Explain, with the aid of diagram(s), the formation of any **two** fluvial (river) landforms.

2 **Human interaction with surface processes** (30 marks)

   Describe and explain how humans attempt to control river processes.

Chapter 12
Coastal Processes

KEYWORDS

- waves
- swash
- backwash
- fetch
- destructive waves
- constructive waves
- wave refraction
- hydraulic action
- compressed air
- abrasion
- attrition
- solution
- cliff
- wave-cut platform
- bay
- headlands
- cave
- arch
- stack
- stump
- blowhole
- geo
- longshore drift
- sandy beach
- storm beach
- sand dunes
- marram grass
- sandspit
- tombolo
- baymouth bar
- lagoon
- hard and soft coasts
- hard engineering
- soft engineering
- groynes
- rock armour
- beach nourishment

LEARNING OBJECTIVES

By the end of this chapter, you should be able to understand:

- The processes that are active along the coast
- How to describe and explain how coastal landforms develop
- How to identify coastal landforms on OS maps and aerial photographs
- How humans have impacted on the operation of coastal processes.

Introduction

The term **coastline** refers to the boundary between the coast and the ocean. The coastal zone is always changing as a result of erosion and deposition. It may be marked by a cliff line or a beach. All this change is brought about by the actions of **waves**.

DEFINITION

Shore: The area of the coast that is exposed between high tide and low tide.

Waves

Waves are caused by the wind as it blows over the sea. Energy is transferred from the wind to the surface of the water by friction. This causes small ripples that grow into waves. As a wave approaches the shore, the seabed becomes shallower. This creates friction with the bottom of the wave, slowing it down.

As a result, the wave topples forward and breaks. The water thrown forward by the breaking wave is called the **swash**. The water that drains back towards the sea is called the **backwash**.

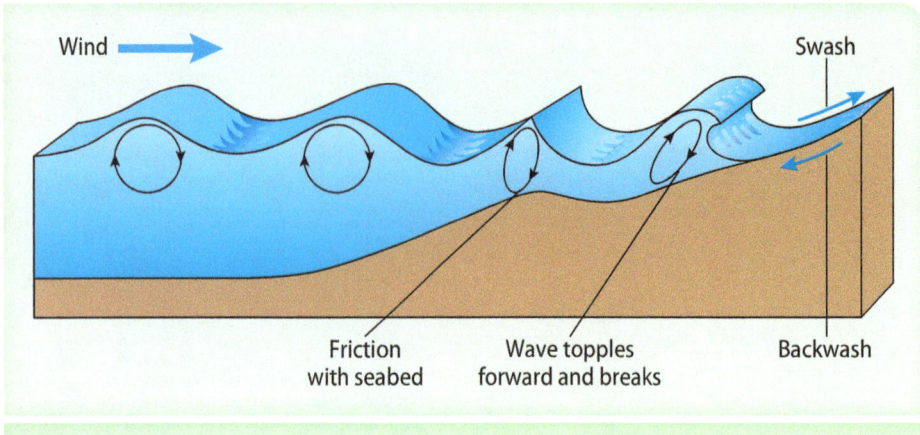

Figure 12.1 As the waves reach shallow water, they topple forward and break

The size and power of a wave depend on:
› The **strength of the wind**
› **How long it blows for**
› How far it travels (called the **fetch**).

The fetch is the length of open water over which the wind can blow unobstructed. The largest waves are produced where there is a long fetch accompanied by strong winds. Thus, Ireland's exposed Atlantic coast has stronger and more frequent waves than the east coast. This is because the east coast faces a smaller body of water in the Irish Sea.

Types of waves

There are two types of waves: **destructive waves** and **constructive waves**.

Destructive waves
› Are caused by local winds and storms
› Are high and steep
› Have a short wavelength
› Are high-frequency waves, with ten to twelve waves breaking every minute
› Break rapidly and **plunge** almost vertically towards the shore
› Are high-energy waves
› The backwash is more powerful than the swash, so the coastline loses material (**erosion**).

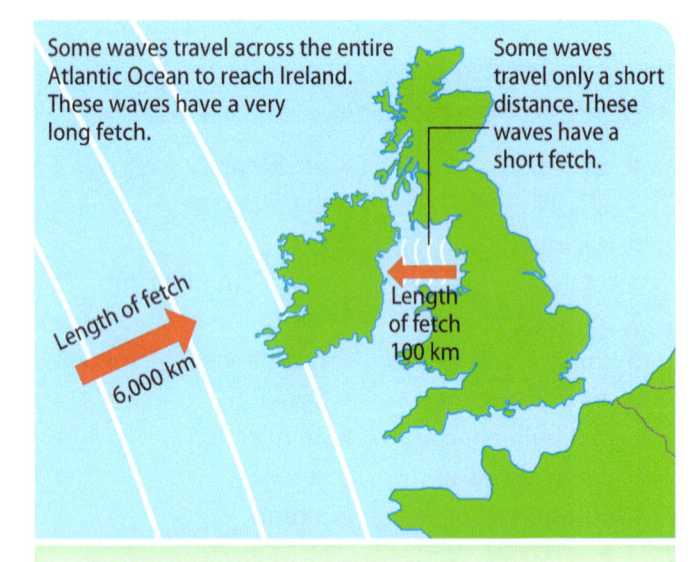

Figure 12.2 The large waves that regularly hit the south and west coasts of Ireland are caused by the prevailing south-westerly winds and a long fetch

ACTIVITY

Discussion
Why are the western and southern coasts of Ireland more indented than the east coast?

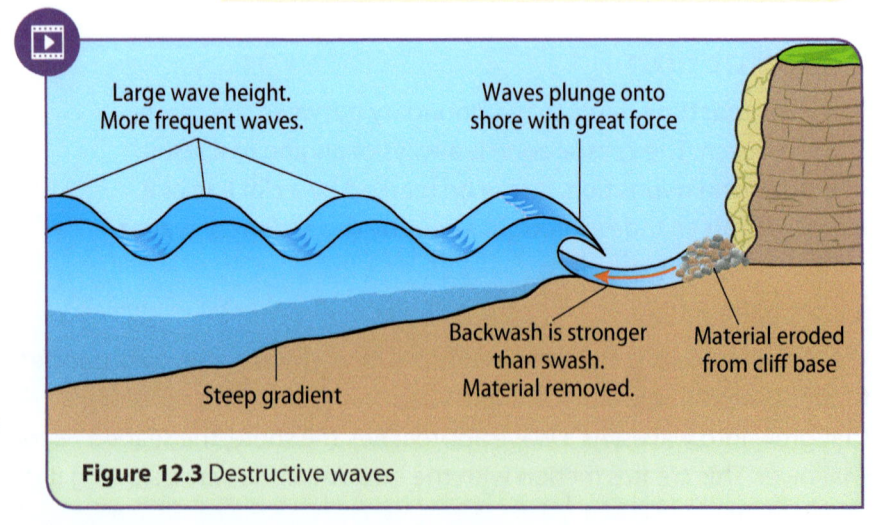

Figure 12.3 Destructive waves

Constructive waves

- Are caused by the swell from distant storms
- Are flat and low
- Have a long wavelength
- Have a low frequency of six to eight waves per minute
- Break gently and **spill** onto a shore with a gentle gradient
- Are low-energy waves
- The swash is more powerful than the backwash, so the coastline gains material (**deposition**).

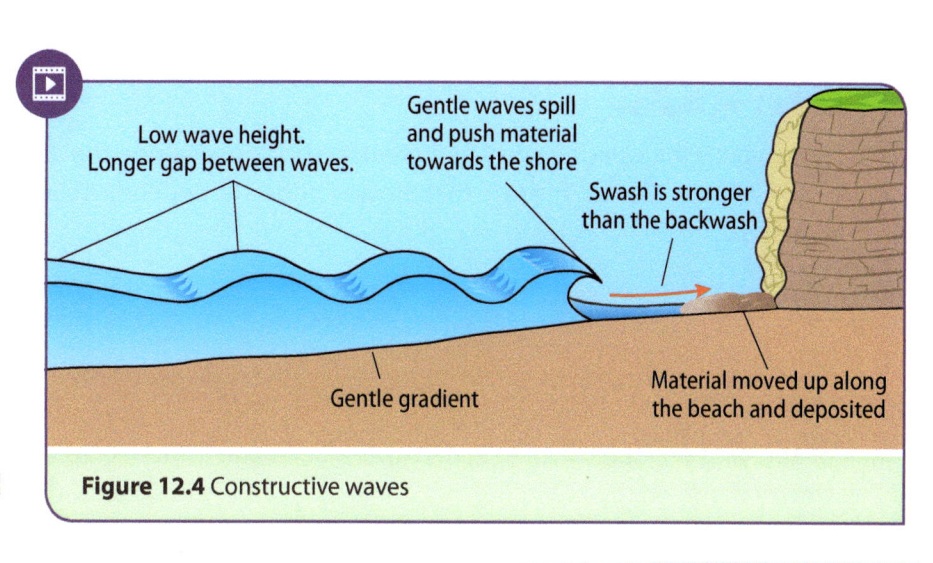

Figure 12.4 Constructive waves

Wave refraction

Wave refraction is the process by which waves bend and change direction as they approach the shore. Refraction is caused by different water depths. Friction with the seabed in shallow water causes waves to drag and slow down. The waves in deeper water continue to move forward. As a result, the waves become refracted (bent).

On a coastline of bays and headlands, the waves first meet shallow water in front of the headlands. The waves converge on the headland. They use up most of their energy there, resulting in erosion.

The opposite happens in a bay, where the waves spread out to a larger area and use up less energy. Deposition may take place, resulting in the formation of beaches.

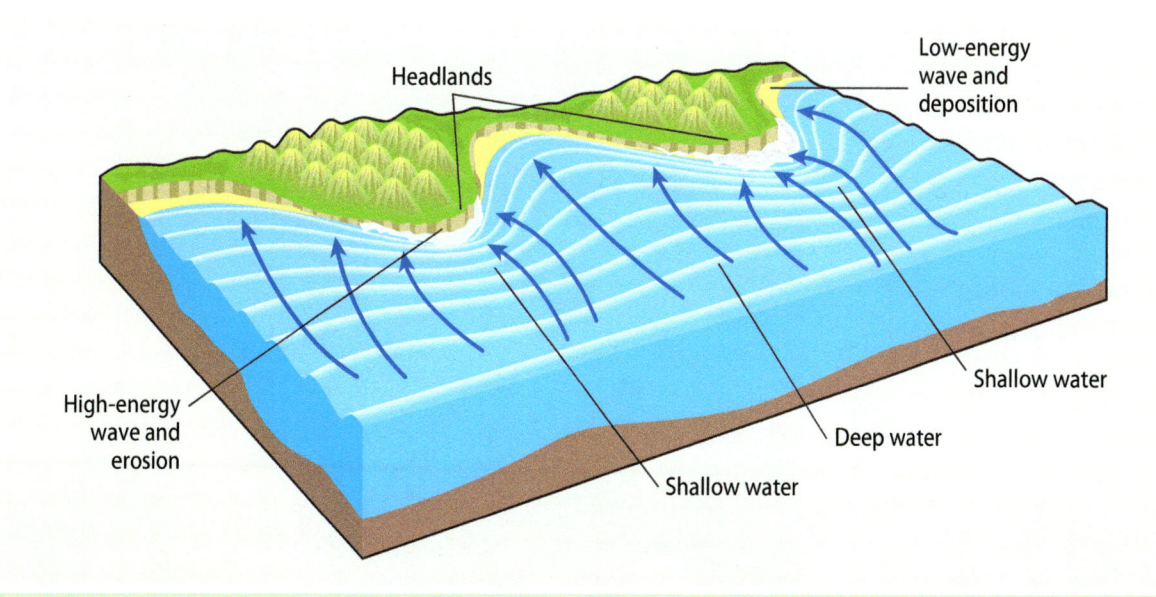

QUESTION

Explain three differences between constructive waves and destructive waves.

ACTIVITY

Research

Look up 'Storm Abigail' on the internet for images and videos.

Figure 12.5 Wave refraction causes wave energy to be concentrated on headlands, leading to erosion. Wave energy is weaker in bays, leading to deposition.

CHAPTER 12 · COASTAL PROCESSES

Coastal erosion

Coastal erosion is the wearing away and breaking up of rock along the coast by destructive waves. The rate that erosion occurs at depends on a number of factors.

Type of wave: Destructive waves have lots of energy. These waves are capable of applying pressure of up to 25 tons per square metre on the coastline.

Slope of the shore: On gently sloping shores, the waves break further offshore and lose much of their energy before they hit the coastline.

Shape of the coastline: On an irregular coastline, headlands are exposed to the full force of destructive waves. The headlands may in turn protect bays from erosion.

Structure of the rock: Rocks that are stratified, well jointed or faulted are more open to erosion, as these are points of weakness in the rock.

Rock type: Coastal erosion can be rapid in areas that consist of less resistant rock (e.g. shale) or soft material (e.g. boulder clay). Coastal erosion is much slower where the rock is more resistant (e.g. sandstone and limestone).

Factors that affect coastal erosion

Figure 12.6 The factors that influence the rate coastal erosion occurs at

Processes of coastal erosion

There are four main processes of coastal erosion:

- Hydraulic action
- Compressed air
- Abrasion
- Attrition.

Hydraulic action

Hydraulic action is the force of waves pounding on the coast. Waves carry out most of their erosive work during storms. Hydraulic action is most effective where the rock has bedding planes, joints and faults. Cracks are widened and loose material is broken away.

The rate of erosion of soft (non-rocky) coasts, such as the boulder clay coastline shown here, can be rapid and extensive

Compressed air

If air is trapped in bedding planes and cracks in the rocks, it is **compressed**. This puts increased pressure on the rocks. The sudden compression of air is followed by a sudden expansion of air as the waves retreat. This creates an explosive effect and weakens the rock. This makes it more open to other forms of erosion.

Abrasion

Sand, pebbles and boulders carried by waves are thrown against the base of a cliff, breaking off particles of rock and undercutting the cliff. **Abrasion** is probably the most effective method of coastal erosion, especially during storms, when the waves have a large load.

Attrition

All the eroded material is itself worn down. Wave action causes the particles to bump into each other. They are worn down into smaller, more rounded particles. These smaller particles of shingle and sand can then be removed by currents and tides.

Coastal erosion is also assisted by **weathering** and **mass movement**.

> Solution occurs when rocks contain minerals that can be dissolved by salts in the seawater. This is mainly true of limestone or chalk coasts, where the rocks are weathered by carbonation.
> Freeze-thaw widens cracks and weakens the rock, especially during winter.
> Waves deposit salt crystals in cracks. Over time the salt, like ice, puts pressure on the rocks.
> Slumping may occur when the base of a cliff is undermined by erosion. Slides may occur if heavy rainfall saturates soft (clay) cliffs.

ACTIVITY

Research

Look up 'video of four processes of coastal erosion' on the internet.

Landforms of erosion

The most common landforms that are formed as a result of coastal erosion are:

> Cliffs and wave-cut platforms
> Bays and headlands
> Sea caves, sea arches, sea stacks and stumps.

Other localised landforms are also formed. These include blowholes and geos.

Cliffs and wave-cut platforms

A **cliff** is a vertical or steep slope on the coastline. It is formed as a result of erosion, assisted by weathering. Spectacular cliffs are found at Slieve League in Co. Donegal and the Cliffs of Moher in Co. Clare. They are also found on the north coast of Mayo.

> Wave energy is at its greatest when high, steep waves break and plunge against a steep coastline. When these **destructive waves** crash against the land, they begin to break it down by **hydraulic action**. Waves can hit the cliff with a force of up to 25 tons per square metre.
> **Air compression** is most effective in rocks that have bedding planes and joints. It helps to enlarge openings and weaken rock.

Processes

> Hydraulic action
> Compressed air
> Abrasion
> Attrition
> Weathering

> Waves are now armed with boulders and pebbles. These are hurled against the rock, wearing it down. This process is known as **abrasion**.
> The slope is undercut just above the high water mark to form a wave-cut **notch**. As the notch is enlarged, the upper part of the slope is left unsupported. It is further weakened by **weathering**, wind and rain. Eventually it collapses and a steep rock face, called a **cliff**, is formed.
> As these processes are repeated, the cliff retreats or recedes inland and increases in height. Following each collapse, the debris at the base of the cliff is worn down by **attrition** and removed, allowing erosion of the cliff to begin again.
> Cliffs located in exposed areas are eroded more rapidly than those in sheltered areas. Erosion is also rapid where the coastline is soft and made of loose material such as boulder clay.
> As the cliff retreats inland, the rocks that were beneath it are exposed. They form a smooth surface that slopes gently seawards. This is known as a **wave-cut platform** and is uncovered at low tide. Much of the eroded material is deposited in deeper water at the edge of the wave-cut platform, where it forms a **wave-built terrace**.
> As the wave-cut platform becomes wider, the waves have to travel across a wide area of shallow water. They lose much of their energy as a result. The rate of erosion at the base of the cliff decreases and eventually ceases. The cliff is now said to be **inactive**. The slope of the cliff is gradually reduced by weathering and mass movement. Evidence that a cliff has become inactive includes slopes with vegetation cover and piles of debris gathered at its base.

Figure 12.7 Stages and processes in the development of coastal cliffs

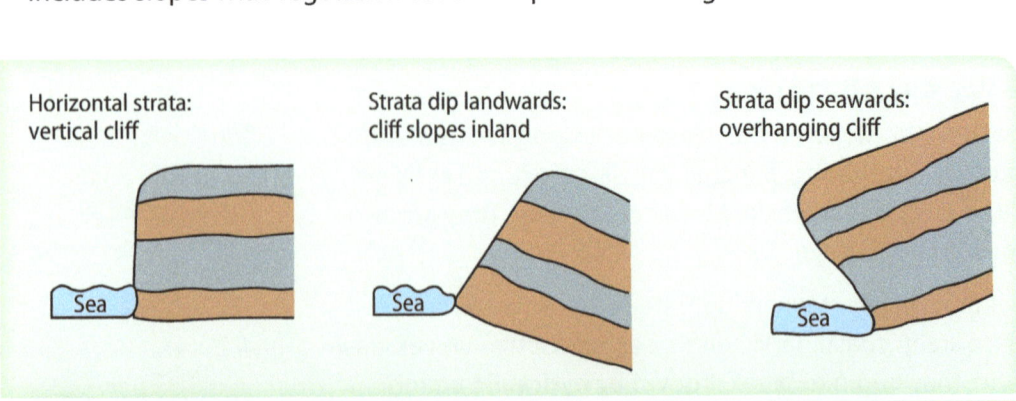

Figure 12.8 The shape of cliffs is linked to the rock structure. Vertical cliffs form in areas of uniform rock type or where the rock strata are horizontal. Sloping cliffs develop where the rock strata dip landwards or seawards.

> **ACTIVITY**
>
> **Skills**
>
> Identify two landforms of erosion in the photograph.

> **GEOFACTS**
>
> › The highest sea cliffs in Ireland (595 metres) are found at Slieve League in Co. Donegal.
> › The highest point of the Cliffs of Moher is 250 metres.

Coastal erosion at Muckross Point, Co. Donegal

Bays and headlands

Coasts are rarely worn back evenly by the sea. Some rocks are harder than others and are more resistant to erosion. Very resistant rocks such as quartzite and granite are eroded at a much slower rate than less resistant rocks such as shale and limestone. This is known as **differential erosion**.

> **Processes**
>
> › Differential erosion
> › Hydraulic action
> › Compressed air
> › Abrasion
> › Attrition
> › Wave refraction

› Headlands and bays are most likely to be found in areas where there are bands of less resistant and more resistant rocks next to one another.
› **Differential erosion** occurs since the rocks are eroded at different rates. The less resistant rocks undergo most erosion and retreat inland to form **bays**. The more resistant bands of rock stand out as **headlands**.
› Most erosion is caused by **hydraulic action**, where the force of waves pound the coast, especially during storms. It is most effective where the rocks have bedding planes, joints and faults. Air is trapped in the cracks and **compressed**. As the waves retreat, the air expands. This creates an explosive effect, weakening the rocks further. Cracks are widened and loose material is washed away.
› Sand, pebbles and boulders carried by waves are thrown against the coast, breaking off particles of rock and eroding by **abrasion**.
› Limestone coasts are worn back by **carbonation** as salts in the water dissolve the minerals in the rock. They are removed in solution.
› As the bays are cut back further, **wave refraction** occurs. The headlands receive the high-energy waves and become more open to erosion. The bays now receive low-energy waves and deposition may occur. As a result, sand may accumulate to form **bayhead beaches**.
› Examples of bays in Ireland include Galway Bay, Donegal Bay and Tramore Bay. The more impressive headlands include Bloody Foreland, Mizen Head and Wicklow Head.

> **ACTIVITY**
>
> **Skills**
>
> Examine the Ordnance Survey extract of part of the North Mayo coastline on page 170.
>
> Identify and locate (by six-figure grid reference) another example of any three of the landforms already identified on it.

CHAPTER 12 · COASTAL PROCESSES   167

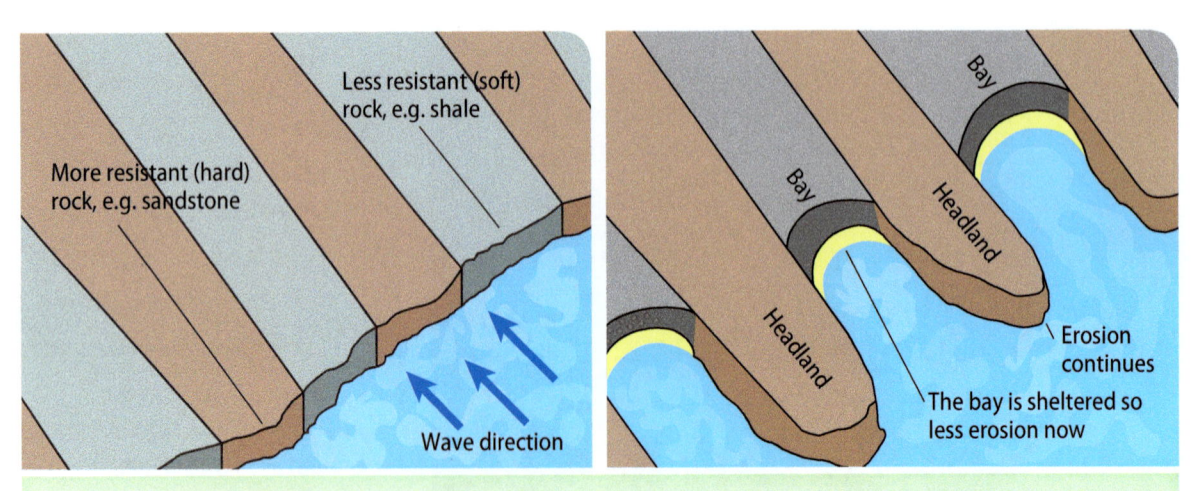

Figure 12.9a and 12.9b Headlands and bays form where there are alternate sections of rock with different resistance to erosion. The sea erodes the less resistant rock more rapidly than the more resistant rock.

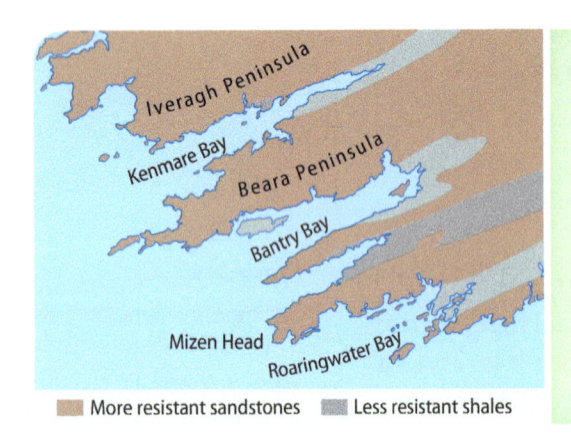

Figure 12.10 Wave erosion has been partly responsible for shaping the south-west coast of Ireland. The sandstone of the anticlines is more resistant to erosion than the shale and slate in the synclines. As a result, the sandstone stands out as headlands while the shale and slate have been eroded to form bays.

Sea caves, sea arches, sea stacks and stumps

Erosion is focused on headlands as a result of wave refraction. The wave action opens up points of weakness, such as joints, faults or bedding planes. If there is a local weakness in the rock, the processes of erosion combine to enlarge these cavities to form **sea caves**.

Processes
› Hydraulic action
› Compressed air
› Abrasion
› Weathering

QUESTION

Explain the term *differential erosion*.

› Most erosion is caused by **hydraulic action** as the force of the waves pounds onto the rocks, especially during storms. Air is trapped in cavities in the rocks and **compressed**. As the waves retreat, the air expands. This creates an explosive effect, weakening the rocks further.
› Cracks are widened and loose material is washed away. Soon a cavity or **cave** is cut into the base of the cliff. The cave is deepened further by **abrasion**, when pebbles and boulders carried by the waves are thrown against the coast.
› If the area of weakness cuts through a narrow headland, a cave may grow longer until it extends through to the other side to form a bridge-like feature called a **sea arch**. A sea arch may also form when two back-to-back caves form on opposite sides of the headland. Continuous erosion causes them to extend backwards until they meet.

- The sea arch is enlarged as the processes of erosion continue. The roof is also weakened by **weathering**. Eventually the roof becomes very wide or too heavy to support itself and it collapses. The seaward portion is cut off from the coastline and is left standing as a pillar of rock, called a **sea stack**.
- As erosion continues, the base of the sea stack is undercut by erosion and collapses. All that remains is a **stump** of rock that is usually low enough to be covered at high tide.
- These features can be seen on most rocky sections of the Irish coastline, including the Old Head of Kinsale, Kilkee and Hook Head.

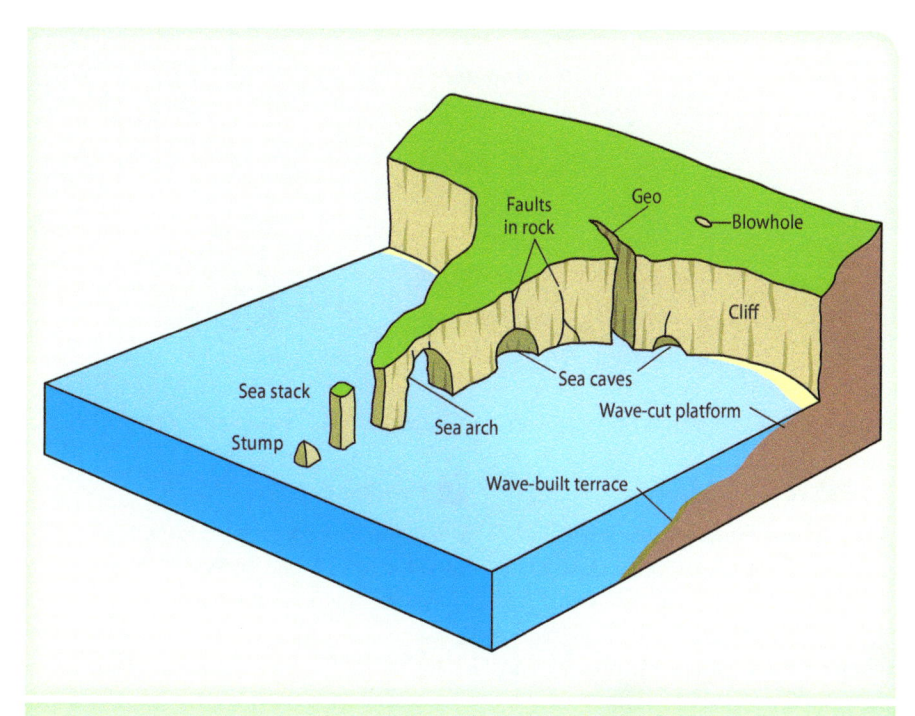

Figure 12.11 A number of landforms of erosion are associated with headlands

Cliffs, blowhole, sea caves, sea arch, sea stack and stumps off the coast of Scotland

DEFINITIONS

Blowhole: A passage linking the roof of a cave to the cliff top. It formed when the rock was shattered by air compression or by solution. Waves shoot through the blowhole during stormy weather.

Geo: A long, narrow, steep-sided inlet. It formed following the collapse of the roof of a cave that was linked to a blowhole or where waves eroded inland along a weakness in the rock.

GEOFACT

The Puffing Holes, the Two Pistols and McSwyne's Gun are blowholes in Co. Donegal. They get their names from the sound of compressed air being forced through the blowholes.

Figure 12.12 Landforms of coastal erosion shown on an OS map extract from Co. Mayo

A Sea cliffs
Sea cliffs are identified when the contour lines are extremely close to one another, indicating very steep slopes. They can also be identified when contours 'disappear' on reaching the coastline. The cliffs in this example are more than 200 metres high.

B Geo/inlet
Long, narrow inlets, called geos, are formed following the collapse of the roof of a cave that was linked to a blowhole or where waves eroded inland along a weakness in the rock.

C Headland
Headlands are sometimes identified by the names 'Head' or 'Point'. They may have a promontory fort.

D Sea stacks
Sea stacks appear on OS maps as small islands located very close to the coast.

E Bay
A bay is a large semicircular-shaped body of water, often bounded at its two sides by headlands.

F Blowhole
A blowhole is a passage that links a cave to the surface of the cliff above. A blowhole is identified on an OS map by being named or, if it is large enough, by a blue circle, as shown here.

G Cave
A cave cannot be identified on OS maps unless, as is the case here, it is named.

ACTIVITY
Research
Look up 'Horse Island, Mayo' on the internet using Scoilnet Maps, Google Maps or Bing Maps. Identify the landforms listed in the OS map extract above.

Processes of transportation

Transportation provides a link between erosion and deposition. It is necessary in order to move materials from one part of a coastline to a place of deposition elsewhere. The material that is transported is called **load**. The load comes from two sources: material eroded by destructive waves and material deposited at river mouths.

Waves and currents transport this material by suspension, traction and saltation, while dissolved minerals are carried in solution. (This is exactly how rivers transport materials. See Figure 11.13 on page 140.)

Up and down the beach
When waves break, the white foamy water that rushes up the beach is called the **swash**. The swash carries material up the beach.

The pull of gravity then causes the water to flow back down the beach towards the sea as **backwash**. The backwash will carry some material back to the sea.

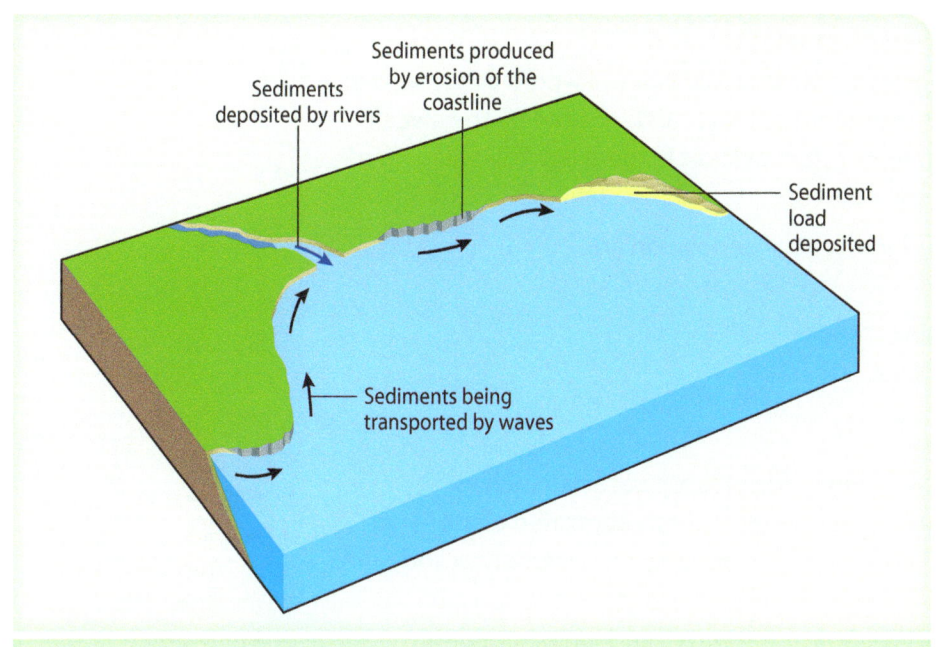

Figure 12.13 The load carried by waves comes from two sources: material produced by coastal erosion and sediments deposited by rivers when they reach the sea

ACTIVITY

Skills

Referring to Figures 12.13 and 12.14, explain the process of longshore drift.

Longshore drift

Longshore drift is the movement of material parallel to the coast.

It occurs when waves approach the shore at an **angle** rather than straight on. This angle is determined by the direction of the prevailing wind as it approaches the shore.

The waves break on the shore and their **swash** pushes beach material up the beach at the same angle. The **backwash** carries material back down the beach at a right angle (90°) as a result of gravity flow. It then meets the next incoming wave and the process is repeated. This produces a zigzag movement of sediment along the beach.

The overall result is that a large amount of sediment is moved along the coastline.

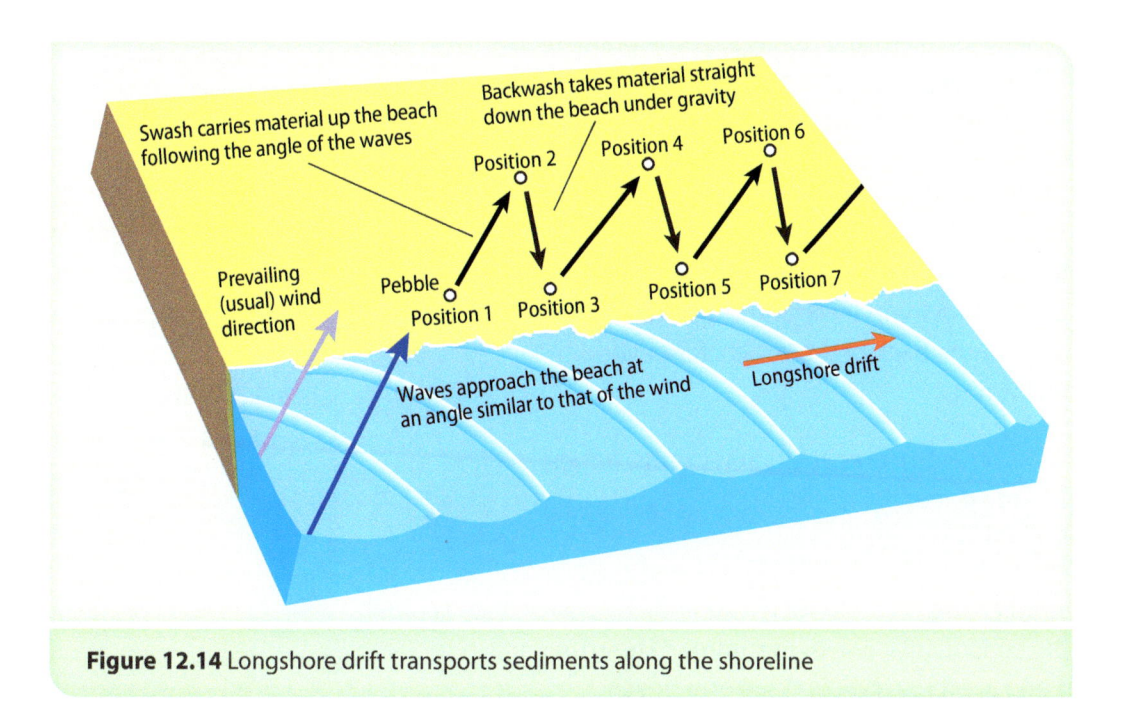

Figure 12.14 Longshore drift transports sediments along the shoreline

Landforms of deposition

Deposition occurs mainly along sheltered coastlines, where **constructive waves** are dominant. If the amount of material deposited by the **swash** is greater than that removed by the **backwash**, there is an overall gain of material and landforms can build up.

The most common features of coastal deposition are:

> Beaches
> Sandspits and tombolos
> Lagoons and salt marshes.

Beaches

A **beach** or strand is a formation made of loose particles such as rocks, pebbles, sand, mud, shingle or even shells deposited along the shoreline. Some of the material is formed by the weathering and erosion of the coastline. Other material is deposited at the coast by rivers. It is then transported onwards by waves and longshore drift.

Processes
> Deposition
> Constructive waves
> Longshore drift
> Storm waves

> Most beaches form on gently sloping shores between the low water mark and the highest point reached by storm waves. At coasts that are dominated by constructive waves, large, wide and flat beaches develop. These beaches may continue for kilometres over straight, relatively sheltered coastlines. **Bayhead beaches** develop at the head or innermost part of bays. These are the only sheltered places, with calm water, where materials can be deposited along exposed coastlines.
> Beach sediments are deposited by **constructive waves**. These waves have a powerful swash, which moves sediments up the beach. The backwash brings back only a little sediment and there is an overall gain of material on the beach.
> An ideal beach has two distinct parts. The upper beach is called the **backshore**. It has a steeper gradient and consists of coarse material such as **shingle** and broken shells. It is covered only by the highest tides or during storms. The lower section of the beach is called the **foreshore**. It has a gentle gradient and consists of sand, tiny shell particles and mud.
> The appearance of beaches varies from summer to winter. They may be wide and gently sloping in summer, but steep fronted and narrow in winter as they are stripped of sand by violent storm waves.
> **Storm beaches** consist of a steep ridge of large stones, shingle and gravel thrown up by strong storm waves. They are usually found at the back of the beach, far beyond the reach of normal waves.

DEFINITION

Shingle: Small or medium-sized rounded pebbles.

ACTIVITY

Discussion

Identify two differences between the following:

(i) Backshore and foreshore
(ii) Storm beach and bayhead beach.

Many beaches have other features, including berms, ridges, beach cusps and sand dunes.

Berms

Berms are ridges of coarse material such as shingle or gravel. They are built up on beaches by constructive waves in summer. They run parallel to the breaking waves and are found below the storm beach.

Ridges

Ridges of sand develop on the seaward edge of the foreshore and run parallel to the coastline. They develop as a result of constructive wave action near the point where the wave breaks. When a series of ridges develop, they are separated by depressions, called **runnels**.

Beach cusps

Beach cusps are a small feature of the beach profile. They are made up of various grades of sediment that form an arc pattern.

Sand dunes

Sand dunes or sand hills develop behind beaches and beyond the reach of the sea. They develop in areas where there is a plentiful supply of beach sand and the prevailing wind comes in from the sea. At low tide the sand dries out and wind transports it inland. The dunes develop when the sand is trapped by obstacles that include marshes, vegetation and fences.

Sand dunes are unstable and will migrate inland unless they are colonised by vegetation, normally by **marram grass**. Its deep roots stabilise the sand, while the plant itself helps trap more sand.

Sandy beaches backed by sand dunes are found at Curracloe, Rosses Point and Youghal. Bayhead beaches are found at Ventry and Dunmore East. Storm beaches are found at Achill and Annestown.

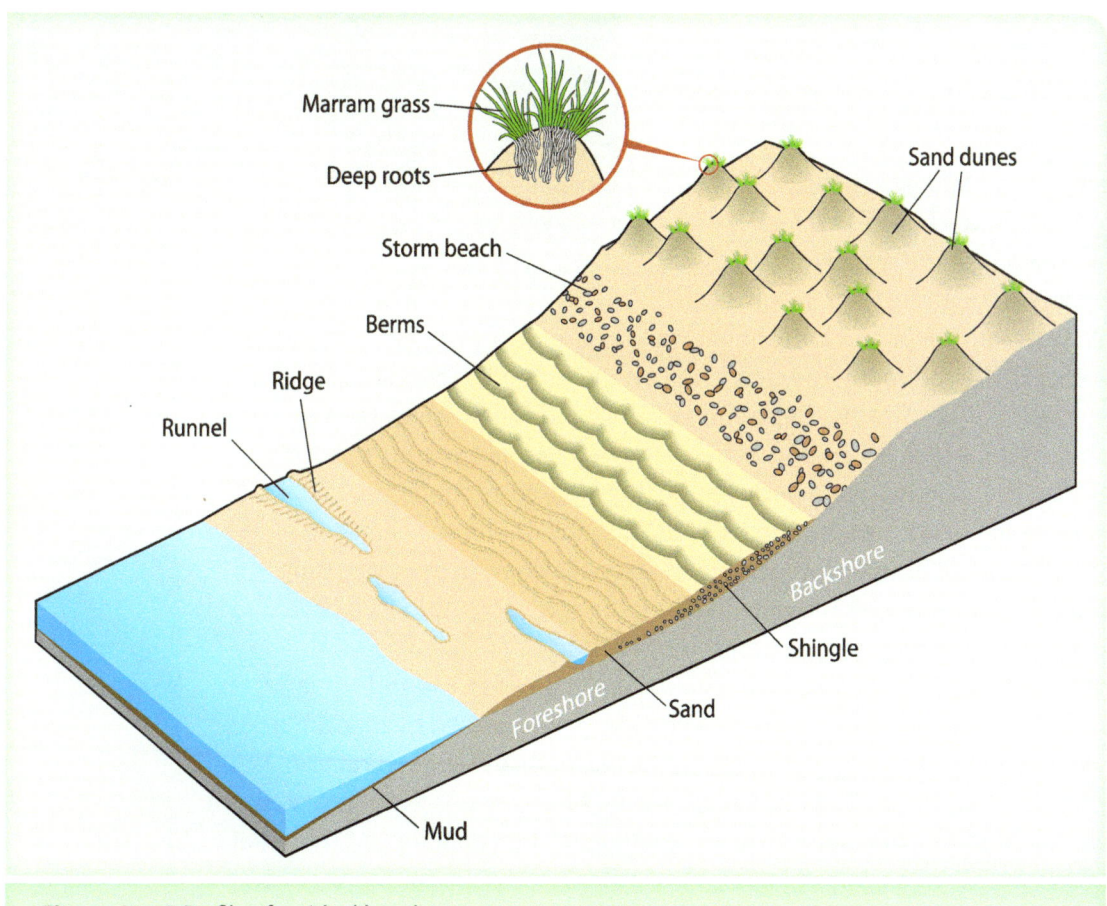

Figure 12.15 Profile of an ideal beach

Wide sandy beach backed by a storm beach and sand dunes

ACTIVITY

Skills

Examine the OS map extract of Strandhill on page 397. Identify and locate the following by a four-figure grid reference:

(i) Sandy beach
(ii) Sand dunes
(iii) Sand spit.

Sandspits and tombolos

Processes
> Longshore drift
> Deposition
> Constructive waves
> Wave refraction

A **sandspit** is a long, narrow ridge of sand or shingle that extends into the sea and is attached to land at one end. It is formed by constructive waves as longshore drift moves large amounts of sand along the coast.

Small beach cusps at Tramore beach

> It develops at a point where the coastline undergoes a sharp change of direction, possibly at a bay or the mouth of an estuary. The sediments are carried into an area of shallow, sheltered water and longshore drift is interrupted. The sediments are deposited on the seabed and build up to sea level to begin the spit. Further deposition extends its length across the bay.
> The spit continues to grow as long as the input of material by longshore drift is greater than the amount being removed by tides and currents.
> Constructive waves deposit sand to build up a **beach** on the seaward side of the spit. The result is that the spit becomes much wider. At the same time, longshore drift continues to move sand along the spit, increasing its length. At low tide, the sand may be exposed and start to dry.
> The lighter grains can then be blown towards land by winds. Mounds of sand, called **sand dunes**, soon build up on the spit and are stabilised by marram grass.
> If the wind changes direction occasionally, the waves also change direction. The end of the spit may be pushed inwards by wave refraction to form a **recurved** spit.
> The spit may stop growing across the body of water. This can happen if material is carried seawards by a powerful river, if the water is too deep for the sediments to build up or if currents and tides are too strong for deposition to occur.
> Sandspits have developed at Inch in Co. Kerry, Strandhill in Co. Sligo and Wexford Harbour.

> A **tombolo** is a type of spit that extends outwards from the coast to join with an offshore island. **Wave refraction** around the island causes longshore currents to converge and deposit sand in the sheltered water between the mainland and the island. Howth is linked to the mainland by the Sutton tombolo.

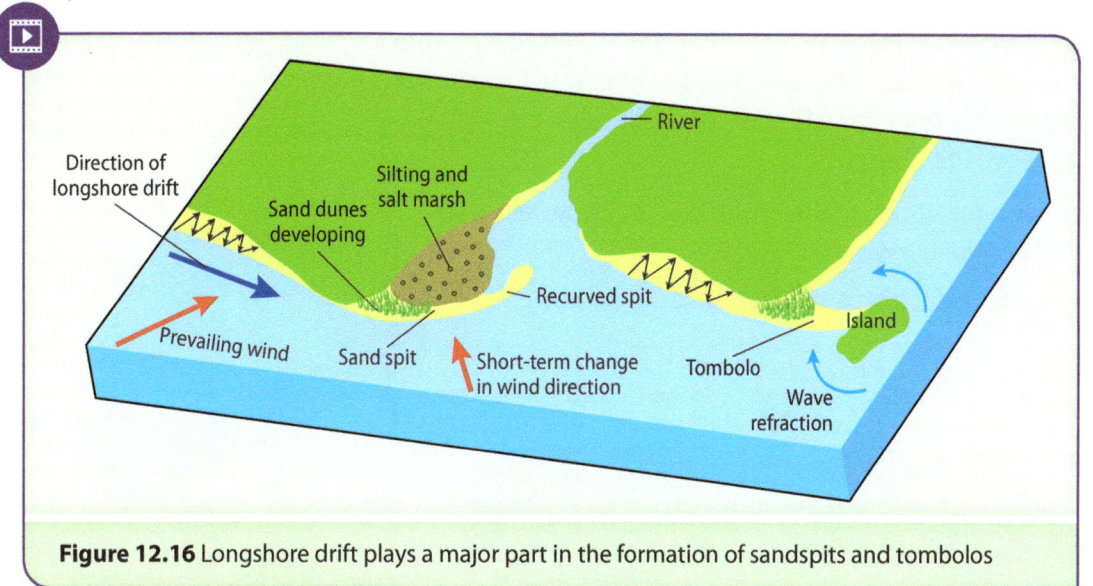

Figure 12.16 Longshore drift plays a major part in the formation of sandspits and tombolos

Lagoons and salt marshes

A **lagoon** is a shallow body of coastal water that has been cut off or almost cut off from the open sea by a sand barrier, called a **baymouth bar**.

A lagoon may form in two ways:
> When a sandspit extends fully across a bay
> When an offshore bar migrates onshore.

Processes
> Deposition
> Constructive waves
> Longshore drift
> Sedimentation

Sandspit

The **sandspit** is formed by constructive waves. Longshore drift moves large amounts of sand along the coast (see Figure 12.16 above). If the sand is deposited faster than it is removed by currents and tides, the spit continues to grow across the bay. It is now a **baymouth bar** and blocks off the bay to form a lagoon. Lagoons have developed in this way at Tramore, Co. Waterford, and Lough Murree, Co. Clare.

Offshore bar

An **offshore bar** is a ridge of sand that forms well out to sea. It lies parallel to the shoreline. It develops on very gently sloping coasts and is generally exposed only at low tide. Due to the shallow water, the waves break far from the coastline. When they break, they dig up the seabed and throw the loose material forward to form the bar. Once the bar is formed, it is increased in height by constructive waves and lengthened by longshore drift. At the same time, it may be pushed towards the shore by waves breaking over it. When it reaches the shore, it becomes a **baymouth bar** and blocks off the bay to form a lagoon. Lagoons have developed in this way at Tacumshane Lake and Our Lady's Island in Co. Wexford.

QUESTION

Describe the two ways by which a baymouth bar might form.

Salt marshes

Salt marshes often develop in lagoons or on the landward side of spits and bars. Mud and sand are deposited in these shallow, sheltered areas of water to form **mudflats**. Further infilling results from the deposition of alluvium carried by streams. As these deposits build up, the water becomes shallower and the sediments are exposed at low tide. Soon they are colonised by salt-loving plants and marsh vegetation. This increases the rate of sedimentation and the deposits are gradually built up to form salt marshes that are permanently above the normal tide.

Salt marshes have developed at the Backstrand in Tramore and Bull Island in Dublin Bay.

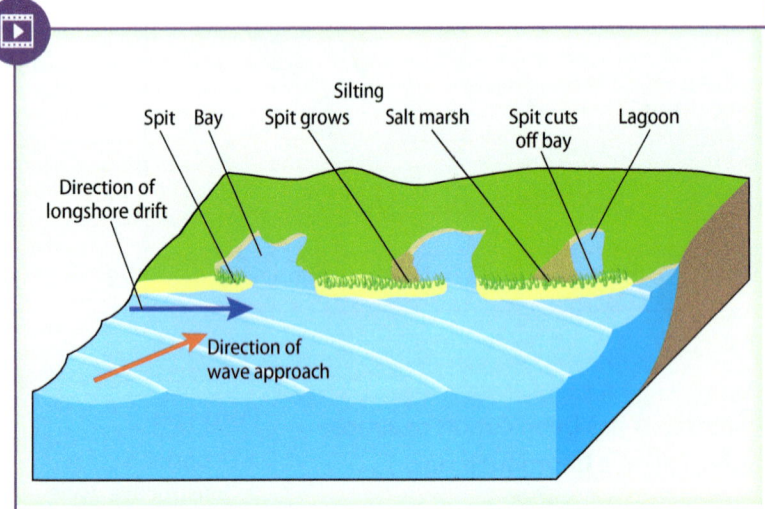

Figure 12.17a and 12.17b A lagoon is formed when a bay is cut off from the sea. This happens when a sandspit extends across the bay or when an offshore bar is pushed onshore.

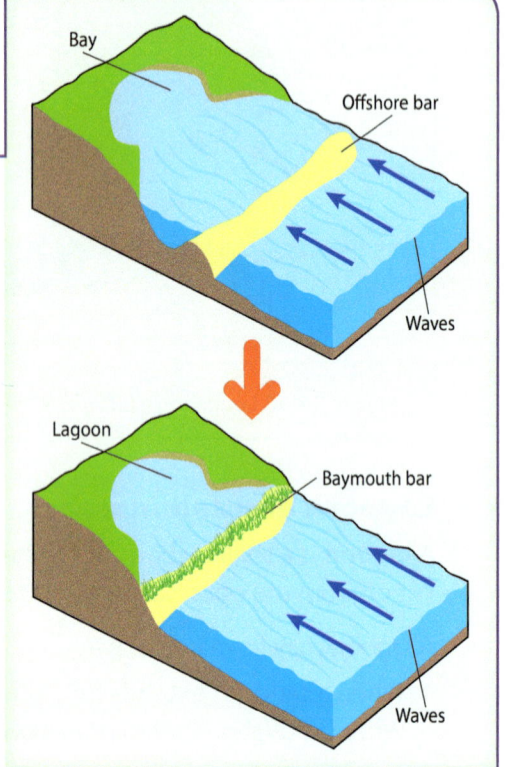

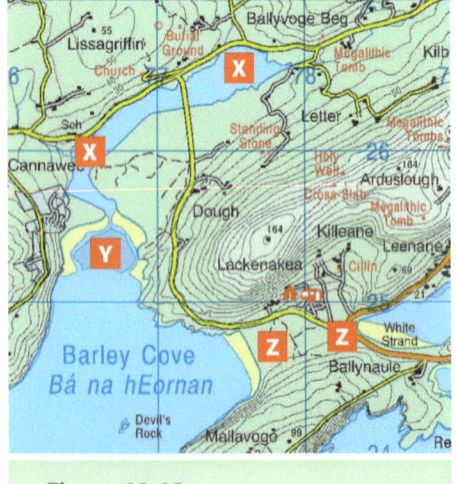

Figure 12.18

X: Lisagriffin Lough is a lagoon.

Y: Sandspit and beaches have developed across Barley Cove.

Z: A tombolo links a former island to the mainland.

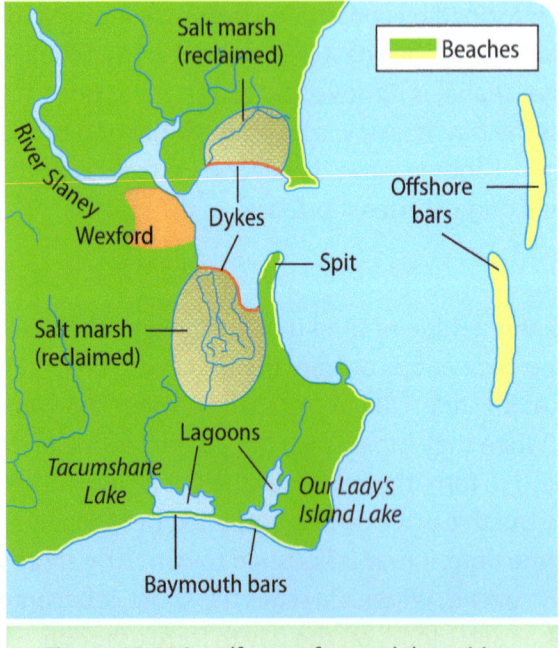

Figure 12.19 Landforms of coastal deposition along the south-east coast of Wexford

GEOGRAPHY TODAY

Ireland's fragile coastline

Coastal areas are of economic and environmental importance for:

> Tourism and recreation
> Nature habitat and nature reserves
> Transport, industry and energy.

Coastal areas are at constant risk from erosion. It is estimated that 1,500 km of the Irish coastline is at risk, with over 500 km in immediate danger. Soft coasts are at the greatest risk.

Coastal erosion is influenced by both **natural processes** and **human activities**.

LINK

See pages 164–5 for the natural processes of coastal erosion.

DEFINITIONS

Soft coast is made of unconsolidated (loose) material such as boulder clay, sand or shingle.

Hard coast is made of resistant rock that can be natural or put in place by humans.

The sandspit at Rossbeigh, Co. Kerry, has been badly affected by coastal erosion.

Photographs taken in 2008 (top), 2009 (centre) and 2016 (bottom) show how the spit has been breached and reduced in size.

CHAPTER 12 · COASTAL PROCESSES

CASE STUDY

Erosion resulting from human activities

More than three-quarters of the coastline of Co. Wexford is described as soft, consisting of boulder clay cliffs and long sandy beaches backed by sand dunes. It is severely affected by erosion.

Perhaps the most severely affected part is the stretch of coast between **Wexford Harbour** and **Rosslare Harbour**. Some areas here lose an average of 1 metre per year to the sea.

Human activities have accelerated this erosion by interfering with the natural movement of sediment in the area.

Land reclamation

› In the mid-1800s, more than 2,000 hectares of marshland in Wexford Harbour were reclaimed from the sea for farmland. Large dykes were built, creating polders, known locally as the Sloblands.
› The reclamation halved the tidal area of the harbour and changed the flow of the tides. The flow of sediment from the north was greatly reduced. The loss of sediment weakened the sandspit that stretched across the southern side of the harbour.
› Severe winter storms eventually cut through the weakened spit. Since then, over 3.5 km of sandspit has disappeared and with it a village, a fort and a lifeboat station.

> **GEOFACT**
>
> The Sloblands are bird sanctuaries of international importance. They are home to half the world's population of Greenland white-fronted geese.

Harbour construction

› The construction of Rosslare Harbour in the late 1860s interrupted the natural longshore movement of sediment from the south.
› The original pier was built offshore and connected to the mainland by a viaduct. The viaduct allowed sediment to pass through. However, the pier provided shelter, so sediment was deposited in the harbour. This required regular dredging. The dredged material was deposited offshore and lost to the coastal system.
› The expansion of the port in the 1980s and 1990s resulted in even greater interference with sediment flows. The viaduct was closed off to eliminate the need for dredging. The pier and sea wall were extended seawards. It now acted as a huge groyne, trapping large amounts of sediment. Some of this sediment built up to form a small beach to the south. However, the sea wall pushed the vast majority of the material offshore and into deeper water, where it was lost to the beach system.
› Now starved of sediment, the rate of erosion of the beach and dunes at Rosslare Strand was speeded up.

Recreational use

› Coastal areas, beaches and particularly sand dune systems are under pressure from human activity by both locals and tourists. Campsites, caravan parks and holiday homes have been built on or near dunes,

especially at Curracloe and Rosslare. The dunes are also used for recreational activities such as quad biking, horseriding, picnicking and rambling.
› Erosion of the sand dunes, either due to recreation in the dunes themselves or to using the dunes as an access route to the beach, is particularly serious where the marram grass cover has been damaged. This leads to blowouts and massive sand losses.

Coastal management

There are two types of measures to manage coastal erosion:

› Hard engineering
› Soft engineering.

Both types of engineering have been applied to stretches of the coastline between Wexford and Wexford Harbour to control or prevent further erosion.

Hard engineering

Hard engineering involves building structures such as sea walls, groynes, rock armour and breakwaters. Once built, these structures are rarely removed, only enlarged or renewed. Unfortunately, they may result in increased erosion further along the coast, thus requiring the construction of even more structures.

Groynes
› **Groynes** are artificial walls, generally constructed of wood, that are built at right angles to the waves. Their main purpose is to trap material that is transferred along the coast by longshore drift. In doing this, they help to build up beach deposits. They also help to break up the waves as they hit the coast. The negative aspect of groynes is that they starve areas further downshore of sand, thereby causing erosion.

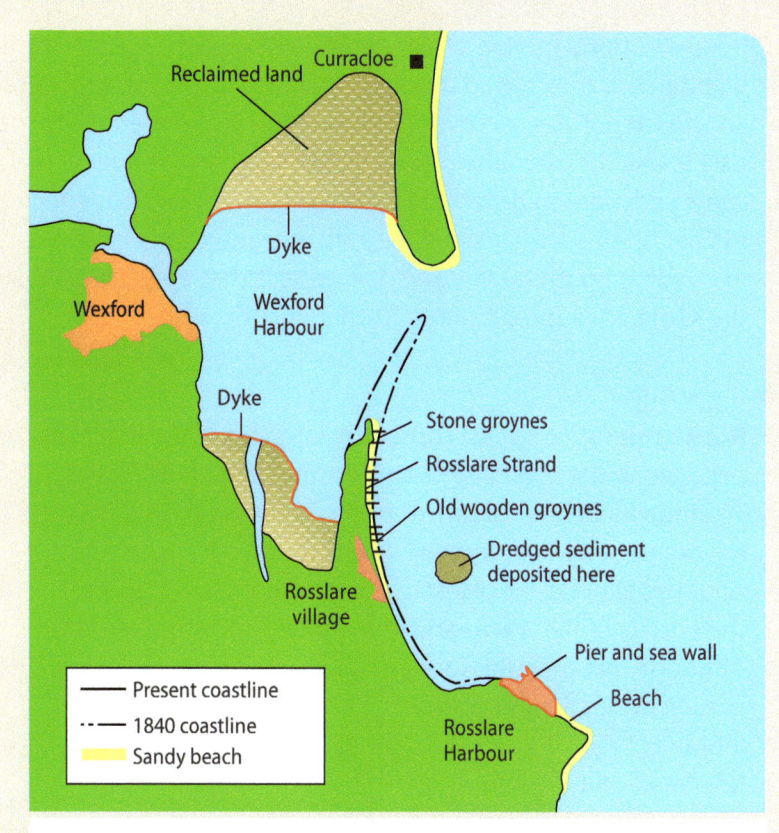

Figure 12.20 The changing coastline of Wexford. Human interference has interrupted the natural processes of erosion, transportation and deposition.

Breakwater and sea wall at Rosslare Harbour

ACTIVITY

Research

Look up 'Rosslare' on the internet using Scoilnet Maps, Google Maps or Bing Maps. Examine the maps alongside Figure 12.20.

CHAPTER 12 · COASTAL PROCESSES 179

- Rosslare Strand has long been protected by groynes. At first they were wooden but they rotted quickly. More recently, stone groynes have been constructed. These are over 100 metres long and are widely spaced.
- As a result, they have helped not only to widen the beach, but also to allow some sediment to pass them by. This in turn helped to reduce erosion further up the coast. Even if they are unsightly, they have been successful in building up the beach. The downside is that they have blocked most of the sediment supply to areas further north.

Rock armour

- **Rock armour** (or riprap) consists of large boulders that are piled along the shoreline to absorb the force of the waves. The individual boulders need to be very large so that they are not tossed about by the waves. The gaps between the boulders allow some water to pass through. This disperses the energy of the waves and reduces their power to erode.
- Although it is effective, rock armour is not a popular form of coastal protection because it is unsightly.
- Rosslare Golf Club had been losing strips of its links course to erosion for many years. To stop this, over 20,000 tons of rock armour were used. The boulders were placed for a distance of over 400 metres against the face of the sand dunes, protecting them from the worst effects of the waves.

Soft engineering

Soft engineering involves beach nourishment and sand dune protection. These can be expensive and may need regular renewal. Soft engineering is regarded as a more environmentally friendly method of coastal protection.

Stone groynes and rock armour. Note how the groynes have impeded longshore drift, enabling the beach in the right middle ground to become wider and deeper.

Beach nourishment

- Beach nourishment is the process of dumping or pumping sand from elsewhere onto an eroding shoreline, either to create a new beach or to widen an existing beach. The resulting beach provides some protection to the area behind it and is also a valuable recreational resource.
- In the case of Rosslare Strand, more than 160,000 m³ of sand was dredged from offshore bars and placed on the beach in the mid-1990s. Costing over €2 million, it is the largest beach nourishment scheme carried out in Ireland to date.

> **ACTIVITY**
>
> **Research**
>
> Use the internet to investigate the proposed use of sea walls at Doonbeg. You can also look up the use of gabions for coastal protection.

> **GEOFACT**
>
> Wexford County Council has introduced legislation to support coastal management by:
> - Prohibiting the removal of sand and gravel from beaches in the county
> - Prohibiting development, including new buildings, caravan parks and camping sites, within 50 metres of the shore.

- A dredger was used to suck material from sandbanks located about 6 km offshore. The sand was later pumped ashore via a floating pipeline. It was then spread into the required beach profile by a bulldozer. While some of the sand was lost to storms during the following winters, the overall width and depth of the beach have been increased as a result of the beach nourishment.
- A new nourishment scheme was put in place following severe storms in early 2014. The storms transported large amounts of sediment onto the shore and dumped it in the harbour area. Dredging was required to enable the harbour to operate fully.
- Studies of wave and tide patterns were undertaken ahead of the dredging. This identified a location where the dredged material could be dumped. As a result of this, during storm conditions from any direction, the deposited material would be transported towards the beach area of the shoreline, building it up (see Figure 12.20 on page 179).

Sand dune protection and restoration

- Vegetation encourages the growth of sand dunes by reducing wind speeds along the surface of the dune. It then traps and stabilises windblown sand. The most common type of vegetation planted on sand dunes is marram grass. It is salt resistant and has long roots. These help to bind the grains of sand and to get moisture from deep in the ground.
- In Rosslare Strand, the restoration also involved fencing off sections of the dunes temporarily. Access to the beach was confined to narrow pathways. Walkways were constructed to encourage visitors not to walk over the dunes. In some areas, sand was stabilised by the use of trap fencing (similar to fishing nets). These slowed the wind and trapped airborne sand. This helped to reduce wind erosion and build up the dunes. The sand has been anchored by the planting of salt-resistant shrubs and grasses.

ACTIVITY

Research
Look up images of coastal protection on the internet.

Pathway across sand dunes giving access to the beach. The dunes have been fenced off to protect the cover of marram grass from erosion.

PowerPoint Summary

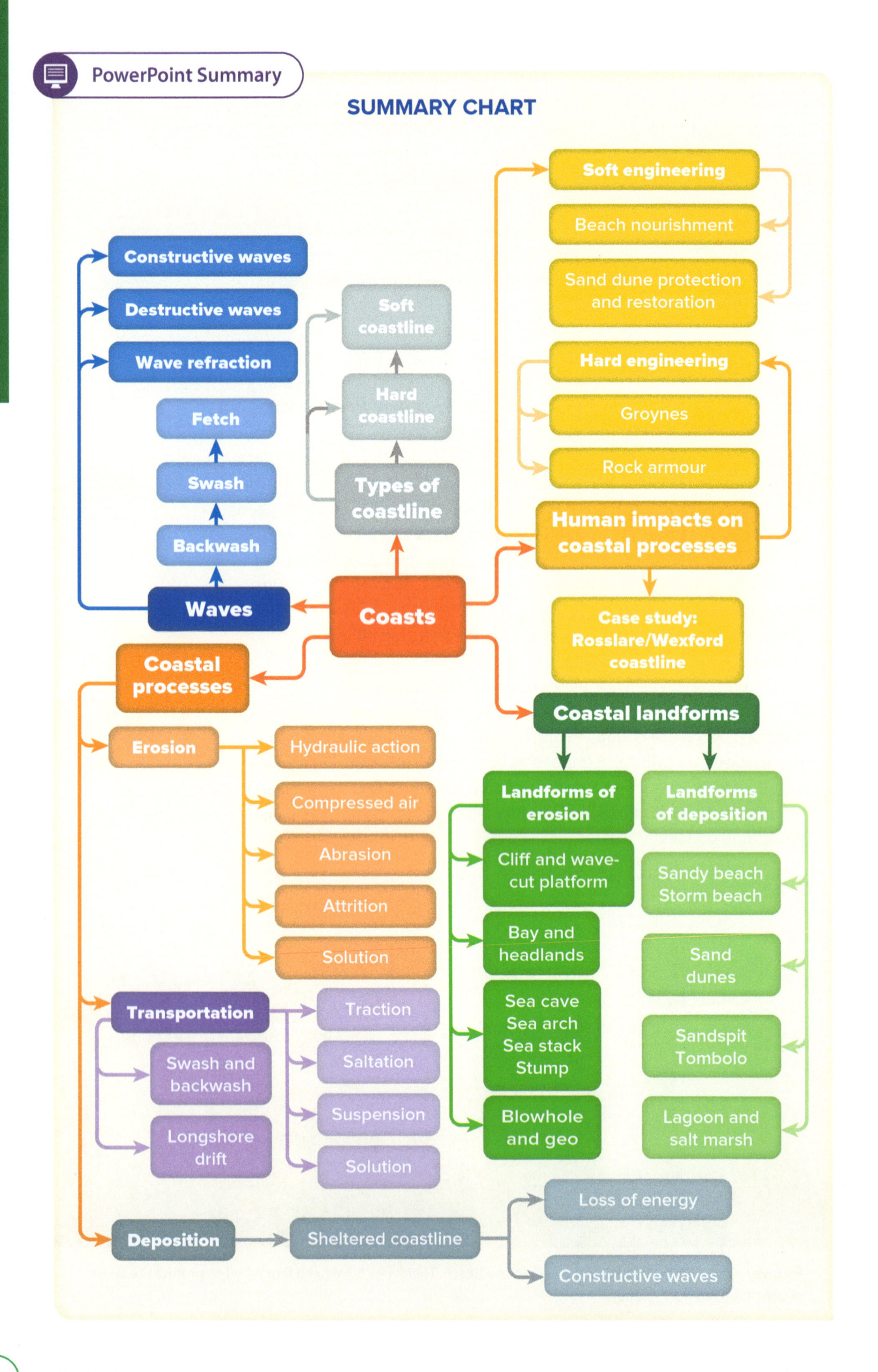

SUMMARY CHART

Coasts

- **Waves**
  - Constructive waves
  - Destructive waves
  - Wave refraction
  - Fetch
  - Swash
  - Backwash

- **Types of coastline**
  - Soft coastline
  - Hard coastline

- **Coastal processes**
  - Erosion
    - Hydraulic action
    - Compressed air
    - Abrasion
    - Attrition
    - Solution
  - Transportation
    - Traction
    - Saltation
    - Suspension
    - Solution
    - Swash and backwash
    - Longshore drift
  - Deposition
    - Sheltered coastline
      - Loss of energy
      - Constructive waves

- **Human impacts on coastal processes**
  - Soft engineering
    - Beach nourishment
    - Sand dune protection and restoration
  - Hard engineering
    - Groynes
    - Rock armour
  - Case study: Rosslare/Wexford coastline

- **Coastal landforms**
  - Landforms of erosion
    - Cliff and wave-cut platform
    - Bay and headlands
    - Sea cave, Sea arch, Sea stack, Stump
    - Blowhole and geo
  - Landforms of deposition
    - Sandy beach, Storm beach
    - Sand dunes
    - Sandspit, Tombolo
    - Lagoon and salt marsh

UNIT 1 • PHYSICAL GEOGRAPHY

Leaving Cert exam questions

SHORT QUESTIONS: HIGHER LEVEL

1 **Coastal landforms and rock structures** (8 marks)

Match each of the letters **A**, **B**, **C**, **D**, **E**, **F**, **G** and **H** with the coastal landform or rock structure that best matches it in the table below.

Landform/structure	Letter
Cave	
Sea stack	
Cliff	
Notch	
Fault	
Rock strata	
Stump	
Bayhead beach	

2 **Coastal features** (8 marks)

Examine the photograph and answer the following questions.

(i) Match each of the letters **A**, **B**, **C** and **D** with the feature that best matches it in the table.

(ii) Indicate whether each is a natural (**N**) or human feature (**H**) by ticking the correct box.

Feature	Letter	N	H
Beach			
Groyne			
Sea wall			
Rock armour			

3 **Coastal features** (8 marks)

(i) Match each of the letters **A**, **B**, **C**, **D**, **E** and **F** with the term that best matches it in the table below.

Landform	Letter
Headland	
Silting	
Tombolo	
Bay	
Beach	
Groynes	

(ii) What process does **B** interfere with?

SHORT QUESTIONS: ORDINARY LEVEL

1 Coastal landforms (10 marks)

Examine the diagram and link each landform of coastal erosion, labelled **A**, **B**, **C**, **D** and **E**, with its correct name in the table.

Landform	Letter
Sea cave	
Stump	
Sea arch	
Headland	
Sea stack	

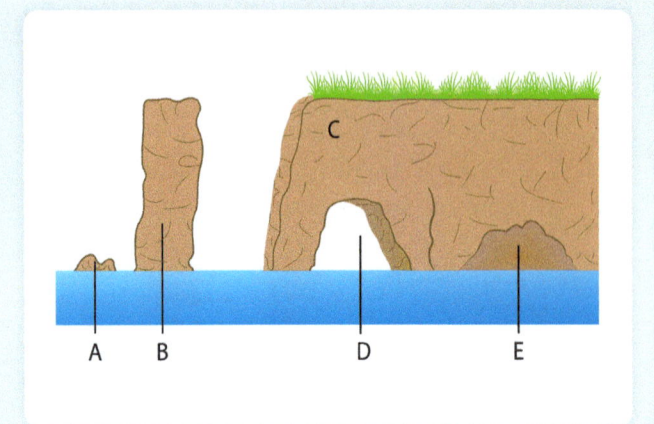

LONG QUESTIONS: HIGHER LEVEL

1 Landform development (30 marks)

Examine the role of the processes of erosion on the formation of any **one** coastal landform of **erosion** that you have studied.

2 Landform development (30 marks)

Examine the role of the processes of deposition on the formation of any **one** coastal landform of **deposition** that you have studied.

3 Landform development (30 marks)

Explain the formation of any **one** landform of **erosion** and **one** landform of **deposition** that you have studied.

4 Landform development (30 marks)

Explain, with the aid of a labelled diagram(s), the formation of **one** landform of coastal **erosion** or **deposition** that you have studied.

5 Human interaction with surface processes (30 marks)

'Human activity impacts on surface processes.'

Examine this statement with reference to the impact of coastal defence work on coastal processes.

6 Human interaction with surface processes (30 marks)

Examine, with reference to an example(s) you have studied, how human activities have impacted on the operation of coastal processes.

LONG QUESTIONS: ORDINARY LEVEL

1 Surface processes (40 marks)

Explain, with the aid of diagrams, the formation of any **two** coastal landforms.

2 Human interaction with surface processes (30 marks)

Describe and explain how humans attempt to control coastal processes.

Chapter 13
Glacial Processes

KEYWORDS

- ice age
- snow line
- zone of accumulation
- zone of ablation
- glacier
- ice sheet
- basal slip
- plastic flow
- vertical erosion
- lateral erosion
- plucking
- abrasion
- striae
- cirque
- bergschrund
- tarn
- arête
- pyramidal peak
- U-shaped valley
- hanging valley
- truncated spurs
- fiords
- paternoster lakes
- lateral moraines
- medial moraines
- terminal moraines
- drumlins
- glacial spillway
- esker
- outwash plain
- kettle holes
- nunataks
- Munsterian glaciation
- Midlandian glaciation

LEARNING OBJECTIVES

By the end of this chapter, you should be able to understand:

- How to describe the processes of glacial erosion, transportation and deposition
- How to identify glacial landforms on an OS map and on photographs
- How to describe and explain how glacial landforms are formed
- The impact of glaciation on the Irish landscape.

The Great Ice Age

Earth has experienced a number of periods of extreme cold in its history, when several continents were covered by ice sheets. These periods are known as ice ages.

The most recent of these, called the **Great Ice Age**, began about 2 million years ago. It only ended about 10,000 years ago. During that period, five major phases of glacial advance have been recognised. Each of these was separated by a warmer period called an **interglacial**.

GEOFACT

In the Northern Hemisphere, the snow line is lower on north-facing slopes because they get less heat from the sun than south-facing slopes.

At the peak of the ice age, about 30% of Earth's land surface was covered by ice. Today, we are in an interglacial and only about 10% of the land surface is covered by ice. These high latitude or high altitude areas include Antarctica, Greenland and the Himalayas.

Ice formation

When winters become colder and longer, precipitation takes the form of snow. As summers become shorter, there is less time for snow to melt. Upland areas soon have a permanent cover of snow. The lower edge of this cover is called the **snow line**. As the climate continues to become colder, the snow line moves further down the slope.

Snow falls as flakes. These have a loose, grainy consistency. As additional layers of snow build up, the lower, older layers are compressed and air is forced out. This partially compacted ice is called **firn**. As still more snow is added from new snowfall and avalanches, all the air is eventually forced out. The firn is compressed into solid **blue ice** – a process that can take between 20 and 100 years. This is the ice that eventually begins to flow as **glaciers**.

Types of glaciers

Glaciers can be classified into four main types:

> A **cirque glacier** is named for the bowl-like hollow, called a cirque, that it occupies. Cirque glaciers are quite small and are found high on mountains, such as in the Alps.
> If a cirque glacier increases in size and begins to flow down through the valley, it is then described as a **valley glacier**. The Aletsch Glacier is one of the best-known valley glaciers.
> When valley glaciers escape the confines of the valleys and reach the flat lowlands, they spread out. Several of these glaciers may join together to form a **piedmont glacier**. The Malaspina Glacier in Alaska is one such glacier.
> The largest type of glacier is the **continental glacier**. It is an enormous mass of ice that covers a vast area of land such as Antarctica and Greenland. It is also known as an **ice sheet**.

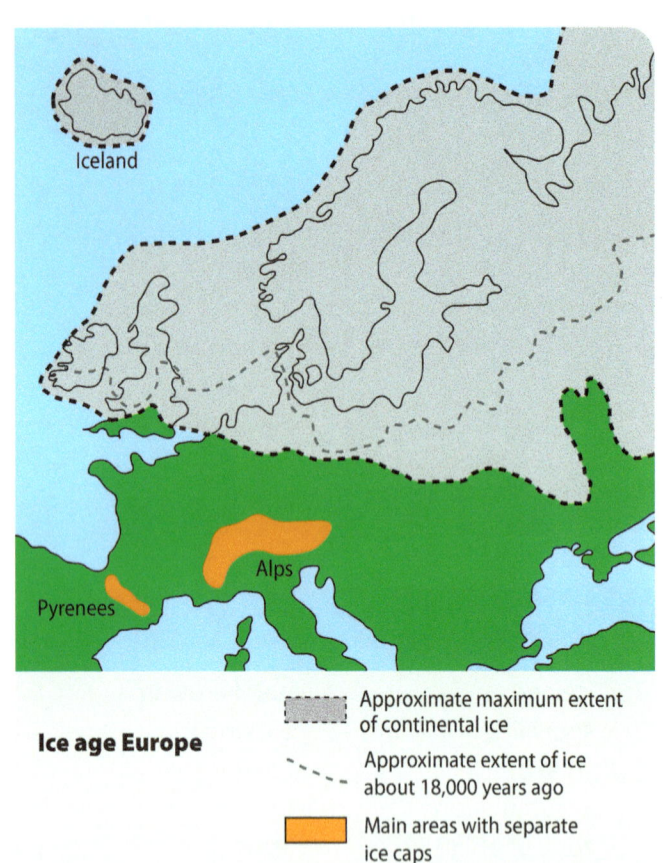

Figure 13.1 The maximum extent of the ice sheets over Europe during the last (great) ice age

QUESTION

Briefly explain how glaciers are formed.

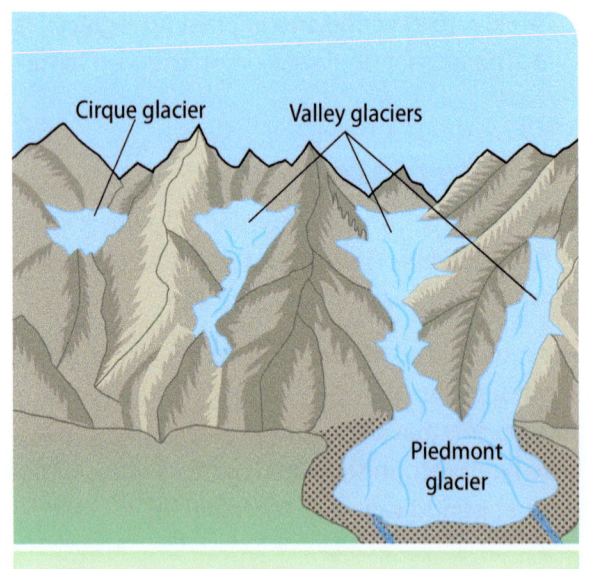

Figure 13.2 Three different types of glacier

Glacial advance and retreat

Glaciers grow because of accumulation. They shrink due to ablation.

› The **zone of accumulation** lies above the snow line. It is the area where snow can accumulate and it does not melt in the summer.
› The **zone of ablation** lies below the snow line and is found close to the snout or front of the glacier. It is the area where snow does melt during the summer.
› If accumulation exceeds ablation, the glacier grows and advances downslope.
› If ablation is greater than accumulation, then the glacier shrinks and retreats.

GEOFACT

If the Greenland ice sheet melted, it would cause sea levels to rise about 6 metres all around the world.

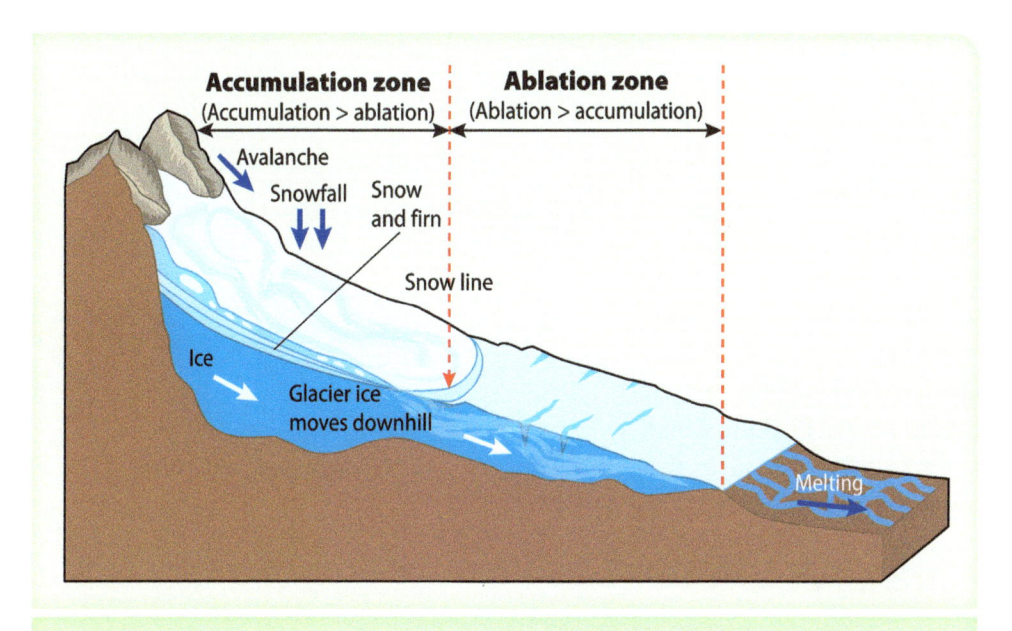

Figure 13.3 Accumulation takes place above the snow line. Ablation takes place below the snow line.

Movement of glacial ice

When a mass of compressed ice reaches a certain thickness, usually around 20 metres, it becomes so heavy that it begins to move. The pressure from the sheer bulk of the ice, along with the force of gravity, causes the glacier to move downhill very slowly. The ice moves in two ways:

› Basal slip
› Plastic flow.

DEFINITION

Climate change has led to an increase in the melting of glacial ice, especially since 1995.

GEOFACT

The average speed a glacier travels at is less than 1 metre per day.

Basal slip

Basal slip is where the glacier simply slides across the rock at its base.

› Glaciers can slide because ice melts when it is under extreme pressure.
› As the weight of a great depth of ice presses downwards, a thin layer of ice at the base of the glacier melts.
› The meltwater acts as a lubricant and reduces friction.

- This enables the glacier to slide downhill over the rock.
- This process is similar to the impact of the blade of a skate on an ice rink.

Plastic flow

Plastic flow allows the ice to bend and flow over the uneven rock surface beneath it.

- It only occurs where there is a great depth of ice.
- Deep within the glacier, the weight of the overlying ice causes the ice crystals to creep past one another.
- The central and upper portions of a glacier flow more quickly than those near the bottom and sides, where friction between the ice and valley walls slows down the flow.
- The process is similar to a deck of cards on which pressure is applied from above. Pushing down slowly on the deck at a small angle causes the upper cards to slide past the lower cards.

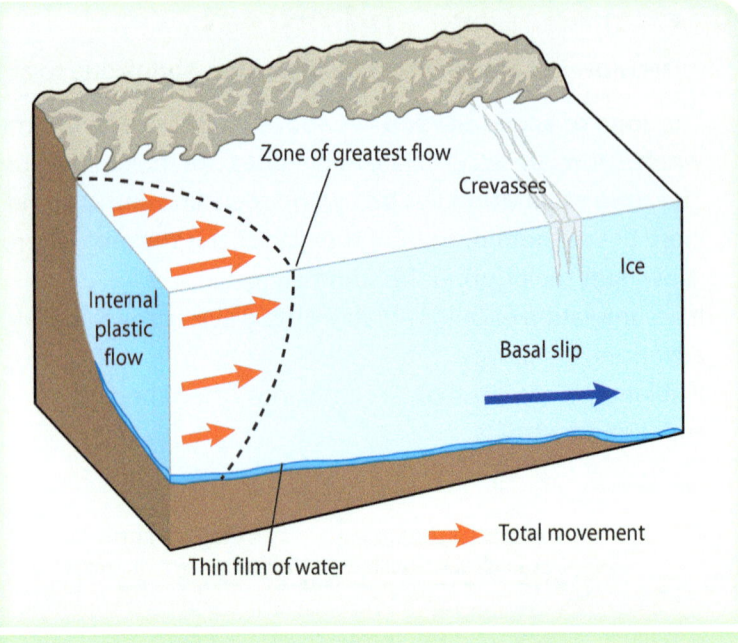

Figure 13.4 Glaciers move by plastic flow and basal slip

ACTIVITY

Discussion

Explain the differences between basal slip and plastic flow.

Processes of glacial erosion

Pure ice is softer than most rock and it moves very slowly. Yet ice is a powerful force, able to shape the landscape by the processes of erosion, transportation and deposition.

Glacial erosion tends to occur in upland regions. Stationary ice has limited ability to erode. But moving ice, especially if it has a **load** of debris, can drastically shape the landscape.

The two main processes by which glaciers erode are:

- Plucking
- Abrasion.

Plucking

Plucking is also called quarrying. It is the tearing away of blocks of rock that have become frozen onto the base and sides of a glacier. It is most effective in well-jointed rocks. The pressure of the overlying ice causes a slight thaw at the base and sides of the glacier. The meltwater seeps into cracks and joints in the rock. When the meltwater refreezes, it expands and weakens the rock while at the same time attaching itself to the glacier. As the glacier moves forward, it pulls away or **plucks** pieces of the loosened rock as its load. Plucking generally creates a rough, jagged surface.

Abrasion

Abrasion is the result of the friction between the ice and the material it contains against the bedrock. The rock surface at the base and sides of the glacier are eroded by the rock fragments (load) carried in the glacier as it moves forward. The ice and these rock fragments act like an enormous sheet of sandpaper.

Most of these fragments used in abrasion are the result of plucking. Others are **scree**, the result of freeze-thaw, which breaks off rock fragments from slopes above the ice. Carried as moraine, these fragments slip down into the ice through crevasses.

Larger rocks leave scratches called **striae** on the rock surfaces they scrape across. Some fragments are worn down into fine particles called **rock flour**. This helps to smooth and polish the rock surface that the glacier travels over.

> **QUESTION**
>
> Describe how plucking and abrasion operate beneath a glacier.

> **GEOFACT**
>
> Striae are important in indicating the direction in which the ice flowed.

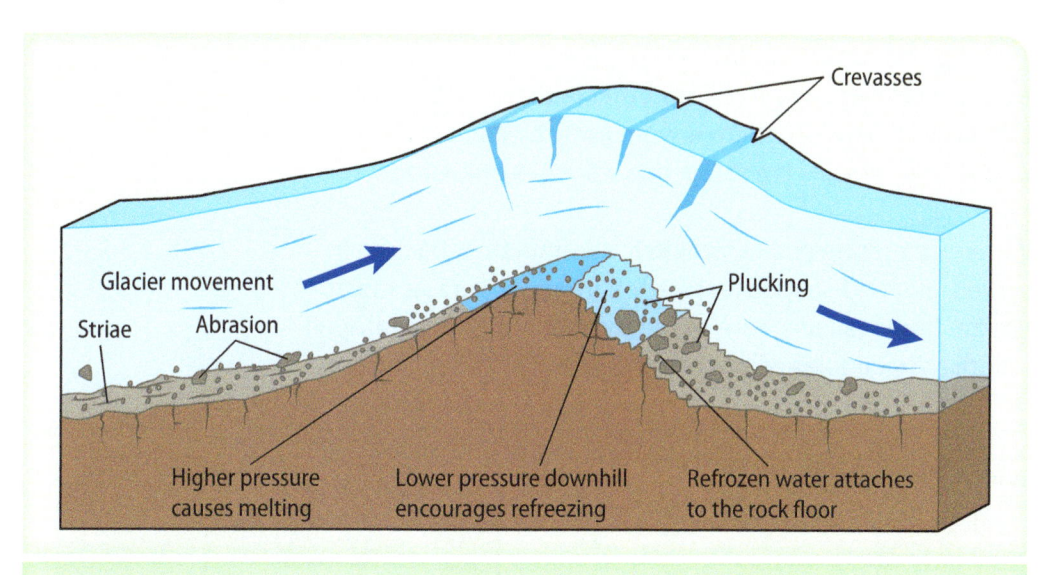

Figure 13.5 How rocks and the base and sides of a glacier are eroded by plucking and abrasion

Landforms of glacial erosion

Cirque and associated features

A cirque (also called coom or corrie) is an armchair-shaped hollow in an upland region.

> - Its back wall and sides are steep and cliff like. The side that faces down the valley is open, but may have a lip that holds in a small lake called a **tarn**.
> - Examples of cirques include Coumshingaun (Comeragh Mountains), the Devil's Punch Bowl (Mangerton Mountain, Killarney) and Lough Bray (Wicklow Mountains).
> - The formation of a cirque begins when snow accumulates in a sheltered hollow, mainly on slopes that face to the north or north-east. These slopes are protected from the sun's energy and sheltered from the prevailing wind.

Processes
> - Nivation
> - Freeze-thaw
> - Plucking
> - Abrasion
> - Rotational slide

> Freezing and thawing beneath the snow break up the rock and enlarge the hollow in a process called **nivation**. As the hollow is enlarged, more snow accumulates. As the layers of snow build up, the lower levels are compressed to form **firn** and, eventually, glacier ice.
> As the ice increases in depth, it begins to move downslope under the influence of gravity. It pulls rock from the back wall and base of the ice by **plucking**. As the glacier moves forward, some ice remains attached to the back wall, forming a deep crack or crevasse called a **bergschrund**.
> **Freeze-thaw** shatters rock on the back wall and scree falls into the bergschrund. This is picked up and carried forward by the ice. It is used to wear away more rock by **abrasion**.
> As the ice moves forward, it twists about a central point in a process called **rotational slide**. This is responsible for deepening the base of the hollow. Since the ice is now moving upwards, there is less erosion at the front of the cirque. This creates a lip at the mouth of the cirque.
> The over-deepened hollow may fill with water to form a lake, called a **tarn**, hemmed in by the lip and some moraine.
> When two cirques are formed close to one another (either side by side or back to back), the land between them is worn away by plucking and freeze-thaw until all that remains is a steep-sided, sharp-edged ridge. This is called an **arête**.
> When three or more cirques meet at a mountain summit, their back walls form a steep-walled, pyramid-shaped feature, where several arêtes radiate out from the centre. This is called a horn or **pyramidal peak**. Carrauntoohil and the Matterhorn are examples of pyramidal peaks.

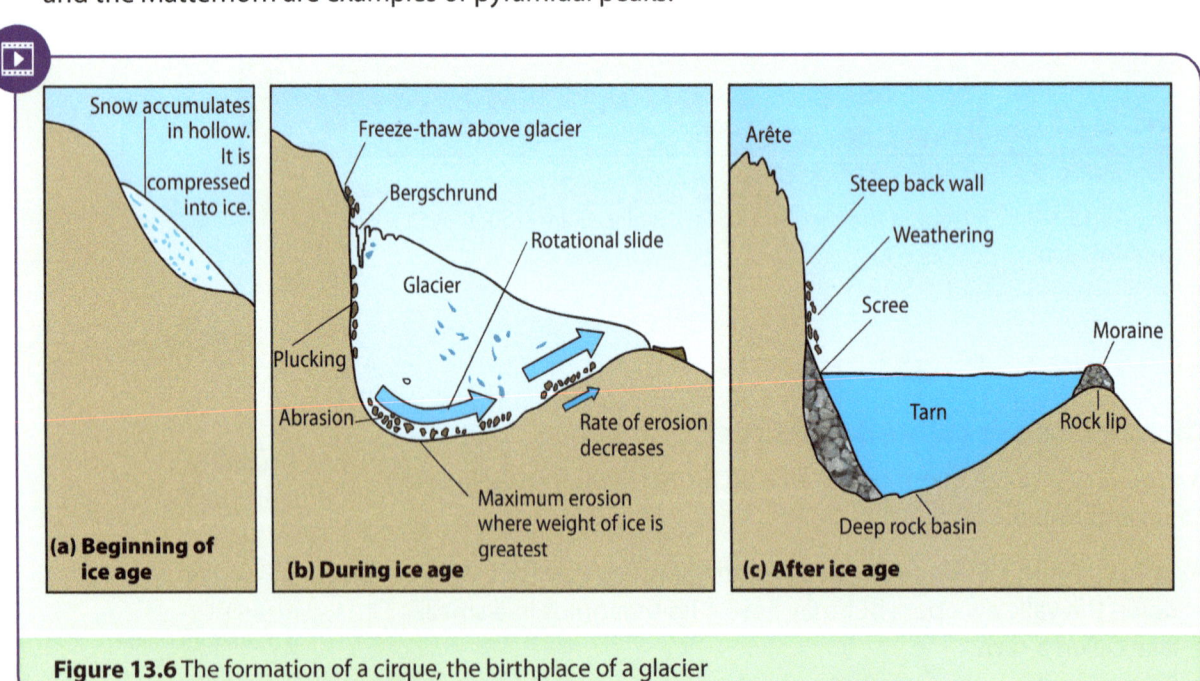

Figure 13.6 The formation of a cirque, the birthplace of a glacier

ACTIVITY

Research

Look up 'how glaciers shape landscape' on the internet.

QUESTION

List and explain the processes that help to shape a cirque and its associated landforms.

Aerial photograph showing cirques and associated features of glacial erosion

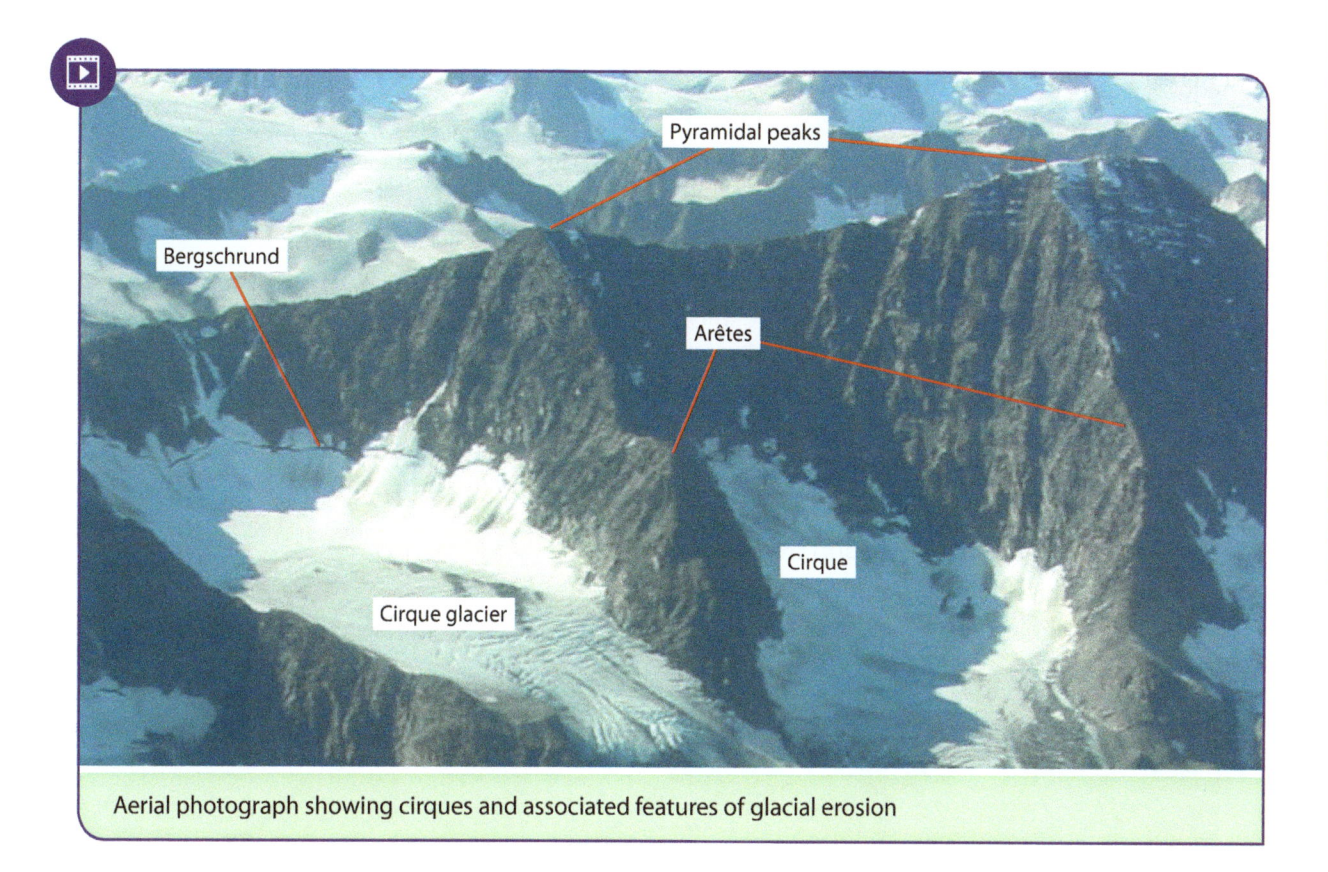

U-shaped valley

Well-developed glaciated valleys are known as **U-shaped valleys** or **glacial troughs**.

Processes
› Freeze-thaw
› Plucking
› Abrasion
› Differential erosion

› Irish examples of glaciated valleys include Glendalough and Glendasan (Wicklow Mountains), Glenveagh (Donegal) and the Gap of Dunloe (Kerry).
› When glaciers move out of the cirque, they take the easiest route downslope, following the course of pre-glacial, V-shaped river valleys. Unlike the river, which only occupied the channel on the valley floor, the glacier occupies the whole valley.
› As the glacier moves downslope it changes the slope of the original valley, deepening it by **vertical erosion** and widening it by **lateral erosion**. This gives the valley its U-shaped profile, with a broad, flat floor and steep sides. The depth of the ice is the dominant factor in the deepening process.
› The old valley is also straightened as the powerful glacier drives through it. Interlocking spurs are removed as the glacier cuts their heads off to form **truncated spurs**.
› **Freeze-thaw** breaks off scree from the upper slopes. Some of this falls into crevasses in the glacier. When meltwater freezes onto the floor and sides of the valley, the glacier pulls rock away in a process called **plucking**. The material embedded in the glacier is then used to erode the valley in a sandpapering effect called **abrasion**.
› Smaller tributary glaciers have much less erosional power than the main glacier does. Thus, it does not erode downwards to the same extent. When the glaciers melt, the tributary valleys are left as **hanging valleys**, high on the walls of the main glacial valley. Streams may form waterfalls as they flow from the hanging valleys to the main valley.

- The long profile of a glaciated valley is often quite irregular. The valley floor may descend in a series of sudden drops to form a **glacial stairway**. This can occur as tributary glaciers join the main glacier. This increases the volume of ice, which gives it more power to erode vertically. Glaciers are capable of eroding their valleys far below sea level.
- Less resistant sections of the valley floor may be over-deepened due to **differential erosion** of the bedrock. The resulting hollows fill with water to form **rock basins**. If they are linked by a stream that flows through the valley, they are known as **paternoster lakes** (for their imagined resemblance to rosary beads).
- A **fiord** is a steep-sided inlet that was formed when the sea flooded a glaciated valley. When it reached the sea, the glacier gradually melted and the sea occupied the deeper section of the valley. Killary Harbour is an example of a fiord in Ireland.

ACTIVITY

Skills

Draw a labelled diagram of a U-shaped valley.

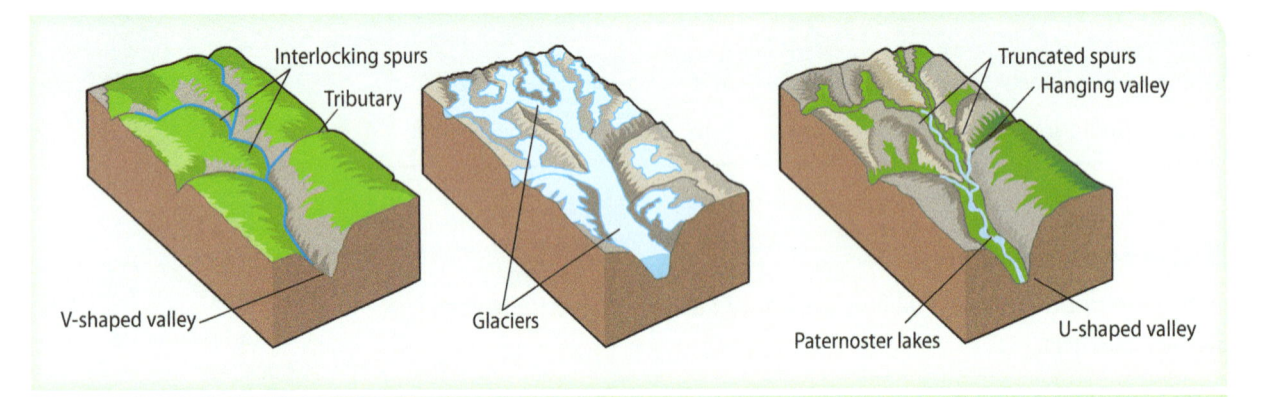

Figure 13.7 Landscape changes from a pre-glacial landscape (left) to a post-glacial landscape (right)

Glaciated U-shaped valley and paternoster lakes

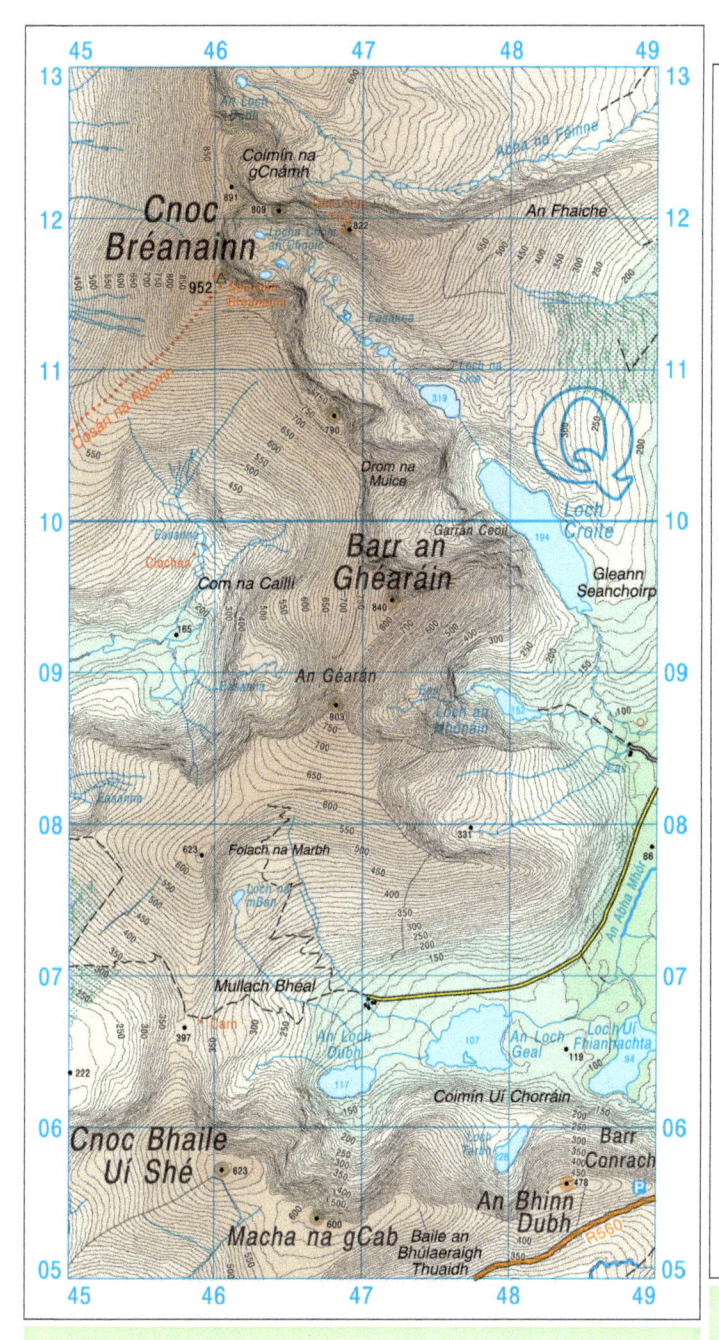

Figure 13.8 Ordnance Survey map showing the glaciated landscape at Mount Brandon in Kerry

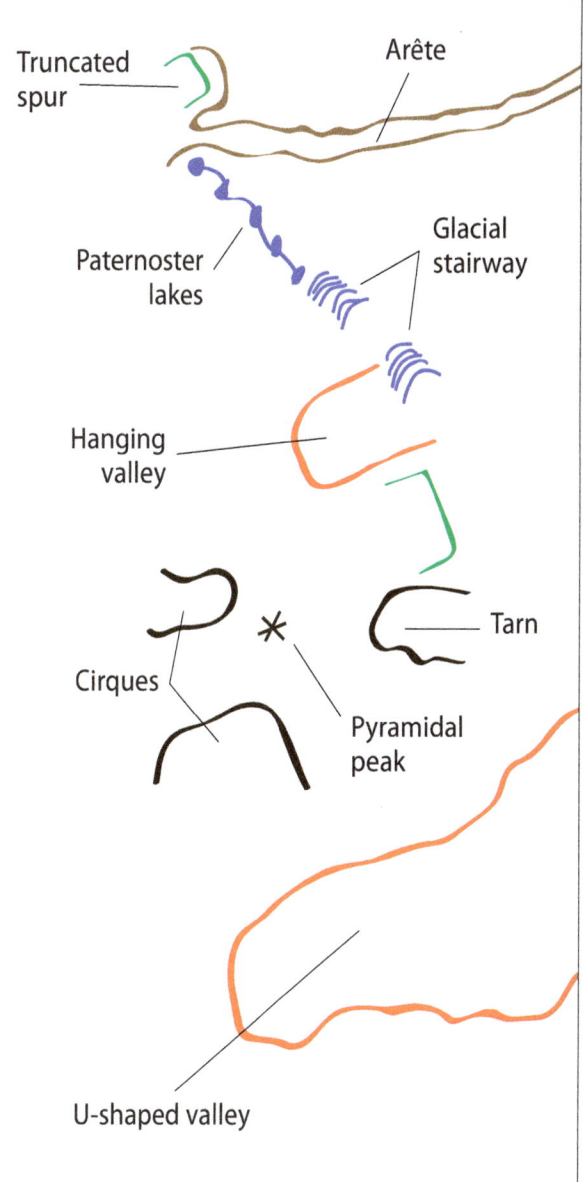

Figure 13.9 Sketch map showing the location of some of the glacial landforms identified on the map

ACTIVITY

Skills

Examine the Ordnance Survey map extract. Identify and give a four-figure grid reference for each of the following landforms:

(i) Cirque with tarn
(ii) Cirque without tarn
(iii) Arête
(iv) Pyramidal peak
(v) Rock basin/paternoster lake(s)
(vi) Glaciated valley
(vii) Hanging valley
(viii) Truncated spur
(ix) Glacial stairway.

ACTIVITY

Research

Locate Mount Brandon on Google Maps. Identify the landforms referred to above.
Hint: Use the 3-D mode.

Transportation by glaciers

Since glaciers are solid, they can transport all sizes of sediment, from huge house-sized boulders to fine-grained clay-sized material. Unlike other agents of erosion, glaciers transport their load without sorting it. All material transported by a glacier is called **moraine**.

There are many types of moraine, each named for its position with respect to the glacier that formed it.

- **Lateral moraines** are ridges of debris that were deposited at the sides of a valley glacier. They are usually found in a matching pair on either side of the glacier. They mostly consist of scree that was broken off the upper rock slopes by freeze-thaw and fell onto the glacier.
- A **medial moraine** is formed when two glaciers meet. Two lateral moraines from the different glaciers are pushed together. This material forms one line of rocks and debris in the middle of the new, bigger glacier.
- **Englacial moraines** consist of any material that is trapped and transported within the ice. It includes material that has fallen down crevasses and material from medial moraines that may have slipped into the body of the glacier.
- **Ground moraines** consist of material that is moved along at the base of the glacier. It consists mainly of material produced by plucking. This material varies in size from large boulders to finely crushed rock flour.
- **Push moraines** consist of assorted debris that is pushed along in front of the moving glacier or ice sheet in a bulldozing effect.

ACTIVITY

Research

Look up images of moraines on the internet.

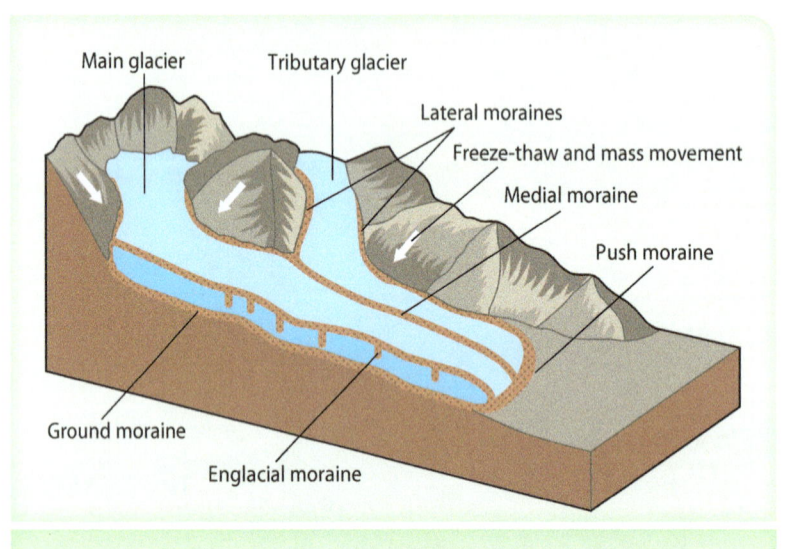

Figure 13.10 All material transported by a glacier is called moraine

ACTIVITY

Skills

Examine the photograph. Identify (i) three landforms of glacial erosion and (ii) two types of moraine.

Glaciers and moraines in Alaska

Landforms of deposition

A glacier deposits its load when it is in the process of melting because it has less energy to transport it. This occurs in the zone of ablation.

The glacier deposits whatever material was carried on its surface or was once frozen in the ice. It is usually a mixture of rocks and particles of all sizes, called **glacial till**. Till is also known as boulder clay. It is an unsorted and unstratified mixture of boulders, gravel, sand and clay.

The main landforms that result are:

› Moraines
› Drumlins.

Moraines

Lateral moraine

A **lateral moraine** is a well-defined ridge of unsorted debris built up along the side of a glaciated valley. Material from the valley walls was broken up by freeze-thaw and fell onto the ice surface because of mass movement. It was then carried along the sides of the glacier. When the ice melted, it formed a ridge of material along the valley side.

Medial moraine

A **medial moraine** was formed when two lateral moraines joined after a tributary glacier met up with the main glacier. The two lateral moraines merged in the middle of the glacier and formed a large ridge of material on the glacier's surface. When the ice melted, the ridge of unsorted material was deposited along the centre of the valley.

Processes
› Freeze-thaw
› Mass movement
› Melting (ablation)
› Deposition

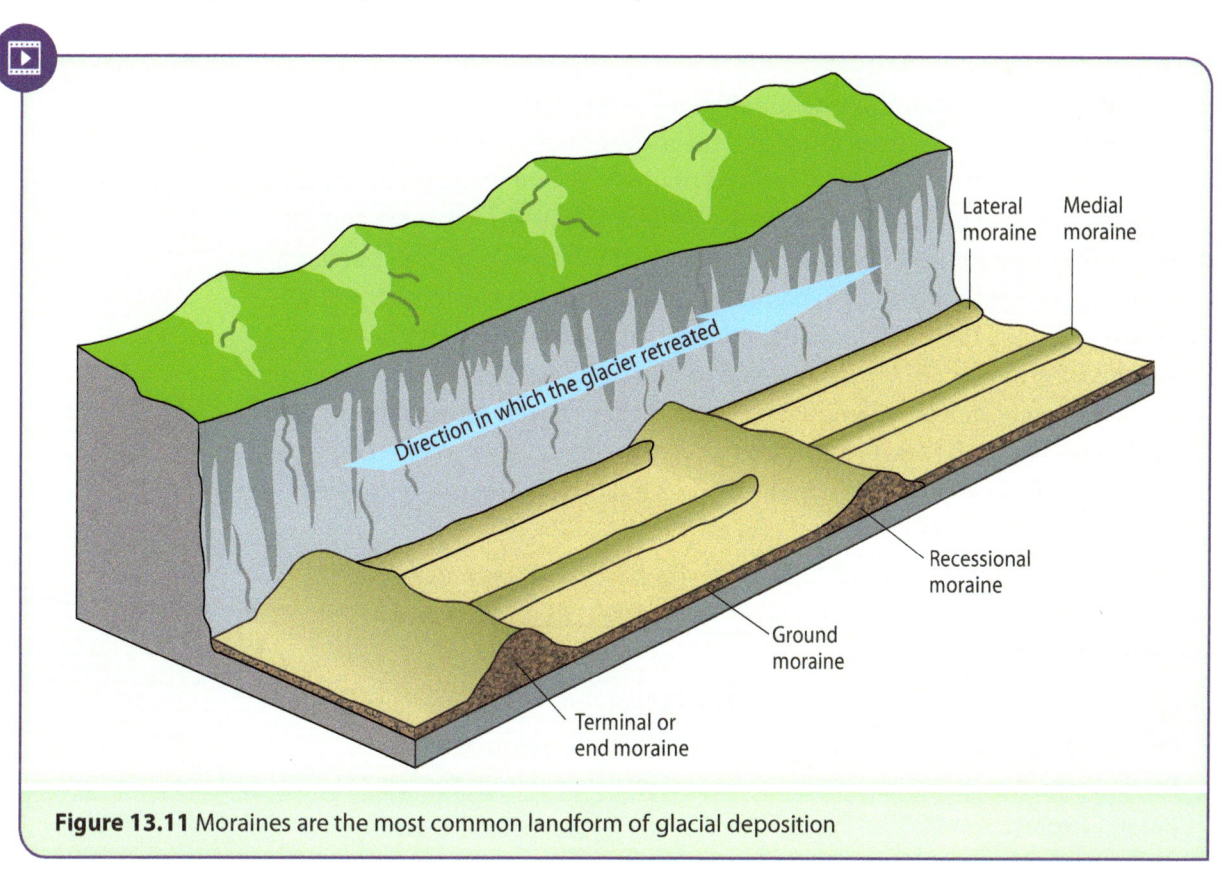

Figure 13.11 Moraines are the most common landform of glacial deposition

Ground moraine

A **ground moraine** consists of a thick, featureless layer of deposits of till (or boulder clay) that were deposited over the valley floor and adjacent lowlands. It was deposited as the ice rapidly retreated, not pausing long enough to build any other landforms. Today, till covers bedrock in many parts of the country and soils of varying levels of fertility have developed on it.

Terminal moraine

A **terminal moraine** marks the furthest extent of the ice advance. It forms across the valley floor. It is a rough, irregular series of low hills composed of till. It is the feature that marks the end of unsorted deposits and the start of material that is sorted by meltwater.

It forms when the rate at which a glacier advances is equal to the rate at which it melts (ablates). When this occurs, the snout of the glacier remains in the same position for years or even decades. The ice continues to advance and melt, depositing its load in the same way that a conveyor belt delivers material.

The terminal moraine ceases to grow when temperatures increase and the ice begins to retreat. This may lead to the formation of one or more **recessional moraines**. They develop across the valley floor in the same way as a terminal moraine. They occur where, due to a temporary drop in temperature, the retreating ice paused and remained stationary for enough time to produce a mound of material.

> **GEOFACT**
>
> Almost half of the landscape of Ireland is a boulder clay plain. It consists of ground moraine deposits up to 30 metres deep. It includes the Golden Vale and South-East Ireland.

Drumlins

Drumlins are small, oval-shaped, streamlined hills of **till** or boulder clay. This is an unsorted and unstratified mixture of sand, clay, gravel and boulders. However, the material has been shaped and moulded rather than dumped.

> One end of a drumlin is quite steep, while the other end tapers away gently to ground level. The steep or **stoss** end faces the direction from which the ice flowed. The gently sloping or **lee** end points in the direction that the ice was moving. The long axis of the drumlin lies parallel to the movement of the ice.
> Individual drumlins vary between 500 metres to 1 km in length and between 30 and 50 metres in height. It is common to find drumlins clustered together in **swarms**, all of them similarly shaped, sized and oriented. Landscapes with swarms of drumlins are sometimes said to have a **basket-of-eggs** topography.
> Glaciers transported large amounts of load as they moved across the landscape. When the temperatures began to rise, perhaps in an interglacial, the glacier began to melt (ablate) and retreat. As it did so, it deposited its load.

Processes
> Melting
> Friction
> Deposition

The formation of drumlins is not fully understood because they are formed beneath the ice sheet. However, there are many theories on their origin, including the following.

> The slow-moving ice became overloaded with debris. Unable to transport its load, the glacier deposited some of it. As the ice continued to move forward, the deposited material was shaped into drumlins as the ice passed over it.

- A covering of boulder clay was deposited on a ground moraine as the ice sheet melted and retreated. The ice sheet later advanced again and shaped the boulder clay into drumlins as it passed over it.
- The ice sheet deposited till in irregularly shaped piles when it became overloaded. These mounds were later shaped into drumlins, either by the ice as it continued to flow over the mounds or by the action of meltwater.
- As it advanced, the ice encountered a large, resistant rock and was subjected to increased friction. Thus, it deposited some of its load around the obstacle. It then shaped the deposits as it passed over them.

However, these theories do not explain why drumlins occur in swarms. Nor do they explain why drumlins are found only in some parts of the country.

- Ireland has some of the most extensive drumlin deposits in the world. The majority occur in the so-called **Drumlin Belt** that stretches from Sligo through counties Fermanagh, Monaghan, Cavan, Armagh and Down. Smaller drumlin swarms are found in parts of Co. Clare and in West Mayo. Here, some of the drumlins (called drowned drumlins) have been partly submerged by a post-glacial rise in sea level and now appear as the islands of Clew Bay.

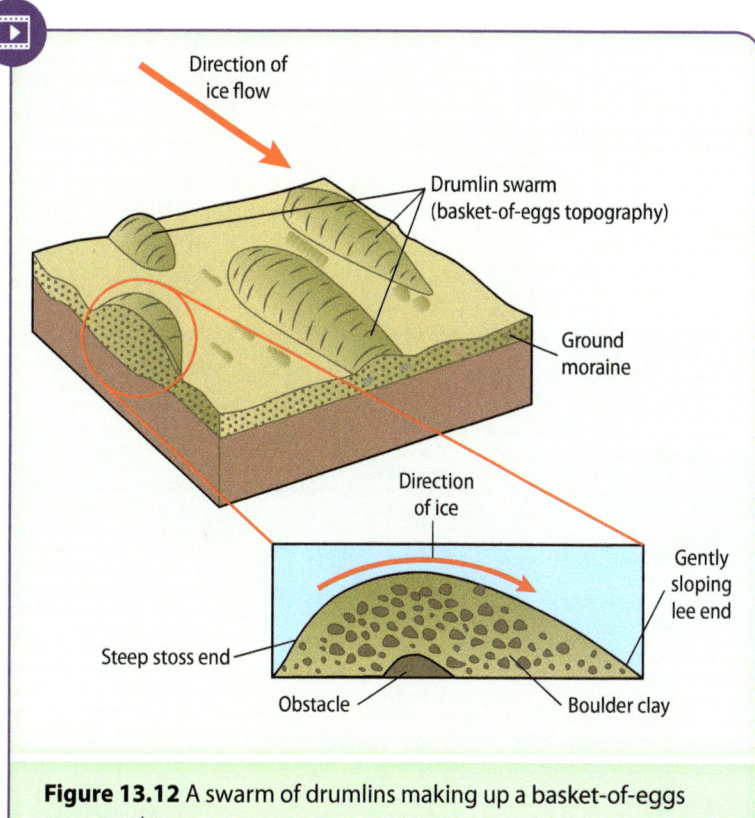

Figure 13.12 A swarm of drumlins making up a basket-of-eggs topography

Drumlin landscape at Strangford Lough in Co. Down. Some of the drowned drumlins have been reshaped by coastal processes.

LINK

See the OS map of Westport on page 434.

ACTIVITY

Discussion

Why is so little known for certain about the formation of drumlins?

CHAPTER 13 · GLACIAL PROCESSES

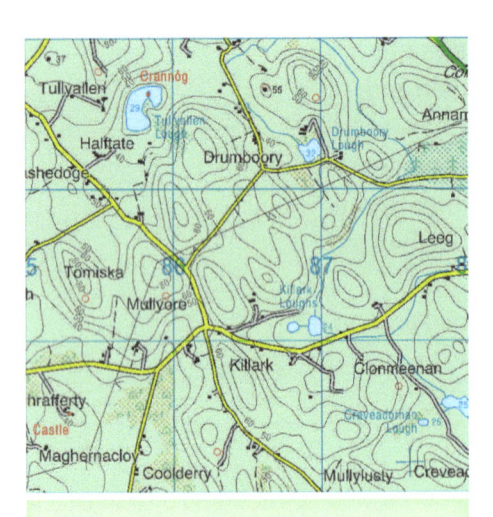

Figure 13.13 Drumlin landscape in Co. Cavan. Lakes often occupy the poorly drained areas between the drumlins.

QUESTION

Examine the map extract. List two pieces of evidence that confirm that this is a drumlin landscape.

Erratics are boulders that have been picked up by glacial ice and transported from their place of origin. They are then deposited in an area where the bedrock is different. Erratics are a good indicator of the direction and distance of ice movement. The Cloughmore Stone (below) weighs over 50 tons. It is a granite boulder that was transported from Scotland to Ireland during the last ice age and then deposited on a sedimentary landscape.

Fluvio-glacial landforms

Fluvio-glacial landforms are those that are formed by the work of meltwater streams in front of a retreating glacier. Glaciers release huge amounts of water when they begin to melt and retreat. These meltwater streams have enormous discharge and can transport huge volumes of material. This enables them to carry out large amounts of erosion. The streams then deposit their load when they lose their energy.

DEFINITION

Fluvio-glacial: A term that describes the processes and effects of glacial meltwater.

Fluvio-glacial erosion

Meltwater streams erode rock in the same way as surface rivers today. Glacial meltwater is a very effective form of erosion. This is due to a high volume of water that is flowing rapidly.

Glacial spillway

A **glacial spillway** (or glacial overflow channel) is a landform of fluvio-glacial erosion that was formed by glacial meltwater.

Processes
> Glacial melting
> Hydraulic action
> Abrasion

› Water from melting glaciers has great erosive powers because of its huge volume and the large load of debris that it carries. Stream load is great due to the plentiful supply of loose material following glacial erosion. Thus, glacial spillways tend to be straight and deep. They take the classic V-shape profile of a young river valley.

› Irish examples of glacial spillways include the Scalp (Co. Dublin), the Pass of Keimaneigh (Co. Cork) and the Glen of the Downs (Co. Wicklow). The Glen of the Downs is up to 100 metres deep and about 2 km long.

› During glacial retreat, vast amounts of meltwater were released from the ice sheet. Sometimes this water was trapped between the retreating glacier and a nearby upland region. With the glacier acting as a dam, it built up to form a **pro-glacial lake**.

› As the melting continued the water level in the lake built up, but only to the level of the lowest point of the nearby upland region. Eventually the lake overflowed and vast amounts of water spilled out through this low point under great pressure. The water began to erode vertically into the landscape.

› The main processes were **hydraulic action** (due to the huge volume of fast-flowing water) and **abrasion** (due to the large load of debris carried by the river). The result was a deep, V-shaped gash that showed many of the characteristics of a young river valley.

› When the ice sheet finally melted, the pro-glacial lake disappeared. Today, many spillways are dry. Some, like the Glen of the Downs, have a small stream flowing along their base. These small streams, flowing through deep channels, are known as misfit streams.

GEOFACT

Other glacial overflow channels include the Scalp (Co. Dublin) and the Pass of Keimaneigh (Co. Cork).

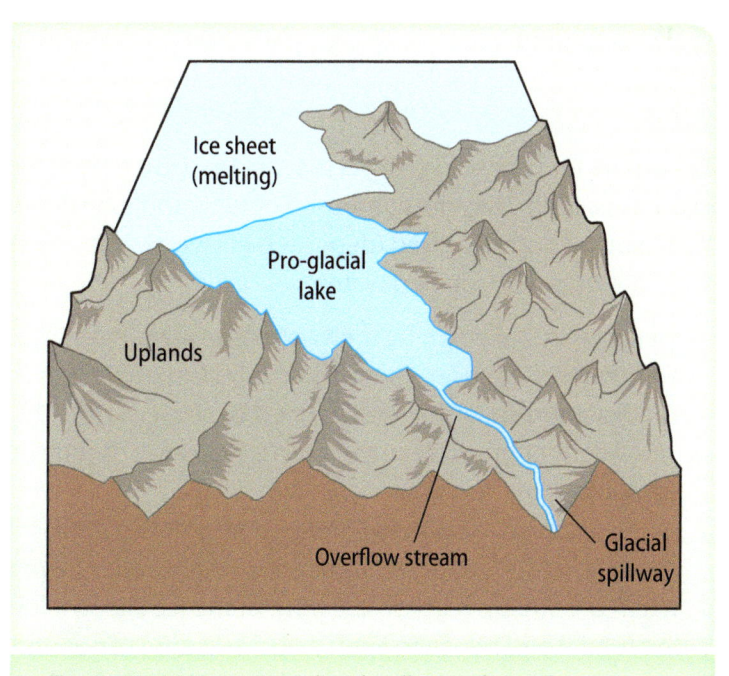

Figure 13.14 How a pro-glacial spillway is formed

The Glen of the Downs in Co. Wicklow is a glacial spillway. It was cut by a fast-flowing stream from a former pro-glacial lake to the north.

Figure 13.15 The Glen of the Downs is a straight, deep, steep-sided glacial spillway. Today it enables access through the adjacent upland area.

ACTIVITY

Skills

Examine the aerial photograph and OS map extract. What direction is the camera pointing?

ACTIVITY

Discussion

Identify two differences between *glaciation* and *fluvio-glaciation*.

Fluvio-glacial deposition

When the volume of meltwater discharge decreased, the energy to transport material was reduced. This resulted in deposition and the formation of fluvio-glacial landforms beyond the point reached by the ice.

As with all water deposition, the heavier particles will be dropped first, resulting in sorting of the material. Deposits may also be found in layers (**stratified**) because of seasonal variations in the meltwater flow.

Eskers

Eskers are long, winding ridges that are up to 30 metres high and several kilometres long. They are composed of sand and gravel deposits that have been **sorted** and **stratified** (deposited in layers). This indicates that they were deposited by running water.

> Eskers were laid down by **meltwater streams** that flowed in tunnels beneath the ice sheet. During glacial retreat, there was a lot of meltwater. The resulting streams were confined by the ice walls. Thus, the streams flowed under great pressure and were capable of transporting large amounts of material.
> When the load became too great, some of it was deposited on the bed of the river. This raised the level of the river channel and the process continued.
> When the stream reached the front of the ice sheet, it left the confines of the tunnel and began to spread out. As it spread out and lost its energy, the meltwater stream deposited the remainder of its load. In both cases, heavier material is deposited first, leading to sorting.

Processes
> Melting
> Transportation
> Sorting
> Deposition

- In spring and summer, ice melt was rapid and the meltwater streams were large. They transported large loads of coarse particles before eventually depositing them in layers of coarse material.
- In autumn and winter melting was slow, so the meltwater streams transported smaller loads of finer materials before depositing them in thin layers.
- When all the ice finally melted, the deposits stood out above the flat landscape as **esker ridges**. Over time, their slopes have become more gentle because of weathering and mass movement.
- The best-developed eskers in Ireland are found in the Central Plain. The Eiscir Riada extends almost continuously from Galway to Dublin. Eskers are also found at Clonmacnoise, Athlone and Shannonbridge.

ACTIVITY

Research

Look up three facts about the Eiscir Riada on the internet.

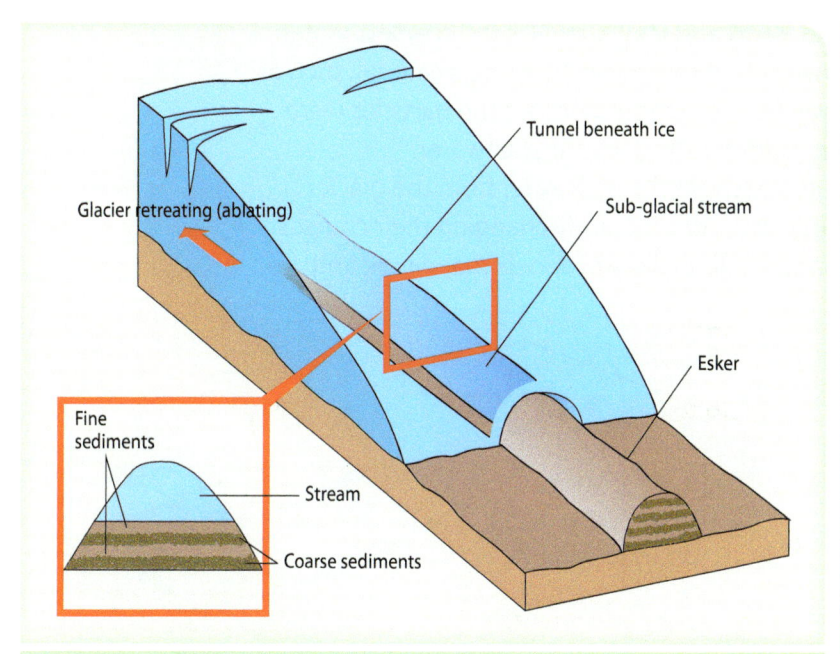

Figure 13.16 An esker is formed from sediments that were deposited beneath a sub-glacial stream and at the mouth of the sub-glacial tunnel

Aerial view of an esker ridge winding its way through a plain

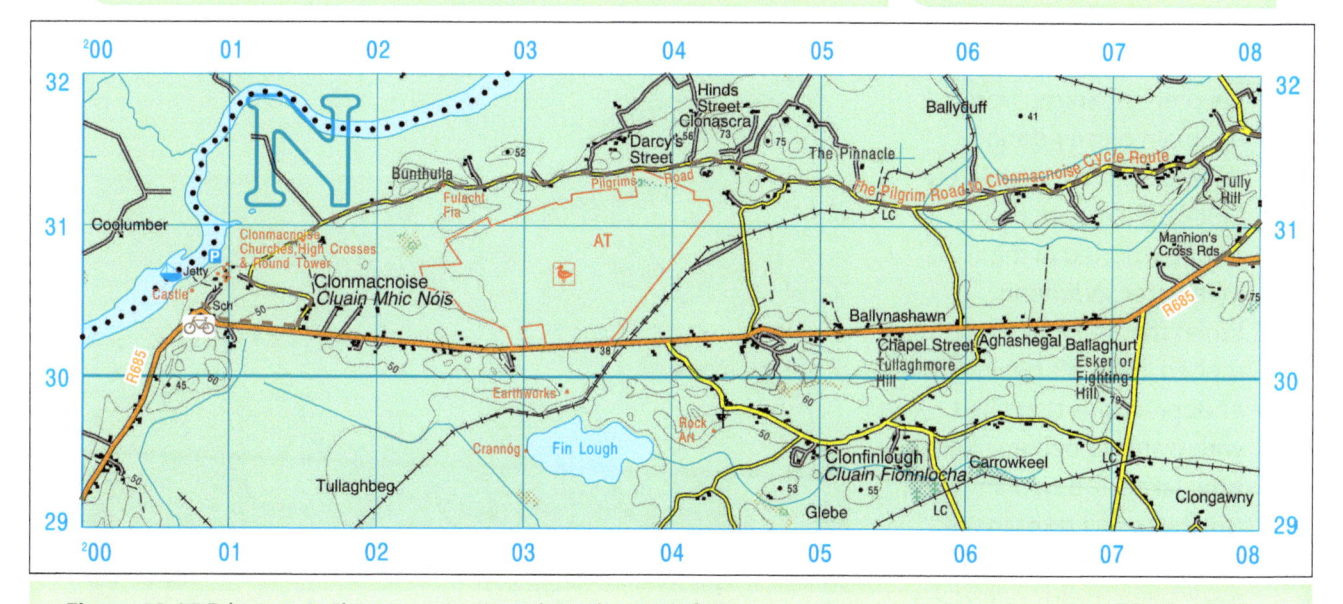

Figure 13.17 Eskers near Clonmacnoise. Note how the roads follow the eskers that rise above the floodplain (callows) of the Shannon River, which are prone to flooding. Most settlement is on or near the esker, also to avoid flooding. This is an example of dry point settlement.

Outwash plains

Outwash plains are low-lying, gently sloping and featureless areas of land that were formed from materials deposited by glacial meltwater. They are found beyond the line of the terminal moraine. If there are recessional moraines, there may be more areas of outwash plain.

Processes
› Melting
› Transportation
› Sorting
› Deposition

› The best examples of outwash plains in Ireland are the Curragh of Kildare and the Great Heath of Portlaoise. Here, the well-drained sands and gravels are almost 70 metres deep.
› Outwash plains consist of materials that had originally been transported by the ice. Then, as the ice melted, the material was picked up by the meltwater. It was transported, sorted and finally deposited by the meltwater. Deposition occurred as the meltwater began to spread out and lose some of its energy.
› Outwash plains consist of **gravel**, **sand** and **clay**. Gravel is the coarsest material and was deposited closest to the front of the glacier. The finer material, such as clay, was deposited furthest away from the snout because the particles were smaller and lighter, so they were carried further by the meltwater.
› Outwash plains cover a broad area because the meltwater from the glacier took the form of **braided streams** that are constantly changing their courses. A braided stream consists of many small, shallow channels that divide and merge numerous times. As the streams deposited more sediment on their beds, each channel was separated into several smaller channels, creating a braided appearance.
› Outwash plains are layered (like eskers). This is due to the varying levels of meltwater throughout the year, with the greatest melting taking place in the warmer summer months.
› Blocks of ice may have become separated from the main glacier during the melting. These isolated blocks of ice were then partially buried in the meltwater sediments.
› When the ice blocks eventually melted, they left behind holes or depressions that filled with water to become **kettle hole** lakes. Today, many form isolated small lakes in the outwash plains. Others have been infilled with sediments, especially peat.

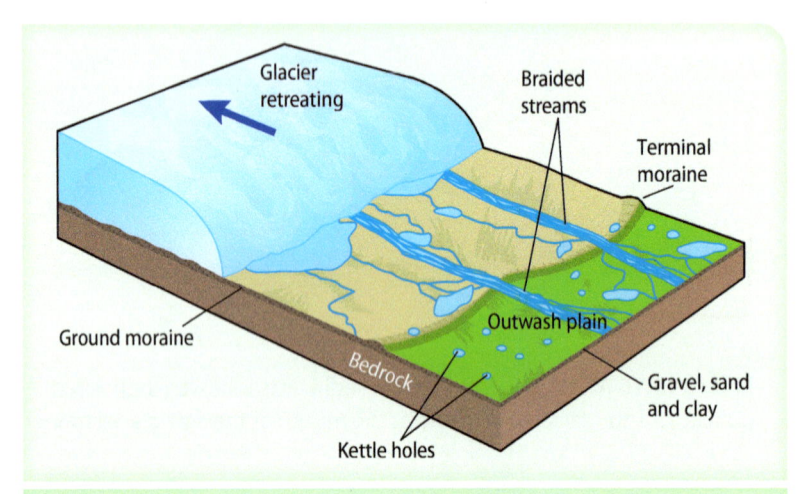

Figure 13.18 Outwash plains are laid down in a broad zone beyond the terminal moraine

Outwash plain with braided streams and kettle holes. This example is currently being laid down by meltwater from a glacier in Iceland.

CASE STUDY

The glaciation of Ireland

The Great Ice Age

The Great Ice Age began over 2 million years ago and ended only about 10,000 years ago. During this ice age, there were at least five cold phases that led to ice advances. These were separated by warmer interglacials, when the ice retreated. We are now in another **interglacial**.

The whole of Ireland was covered by an ice sheet. Only the highest mountains peaks stuck up above the ice as **nunataks**. The nunataks were then shaped by freeze-thaw.

Ireland may have been affected by several of these glacial advances, but the more recent advances would have destroyed all evidence of them.

Nunataks in the Alaska ice sheet today. This is how the highest peaks of Munster might have looked during the Munsterian glaciation.

GEOFACT

The names of some glacial landforms have Gaelic origins. **Esker** comes from a Gaelic word for *ridge*. **Corrie** comes from a Gaelic word for *saucepan*. **Drumlin** comes from a Gaelic word for *rounded hill*.

The Great Ice Age in Ireland

The Irish landscape shows evidence of two periods of glacial advance with a warmer interglacial period between them. Each is named after the area where the best evidence for it is found.

These two advances are known as the:

› Munsterian glaciation
› Midlandian glaciation.

Legend:
- Unglaciated areas (nunataks)
- Munsterian glaciation
- Midlandian glaciation
- Drumlins
- Eskers
- Terminal moraines
- Recessional moraines

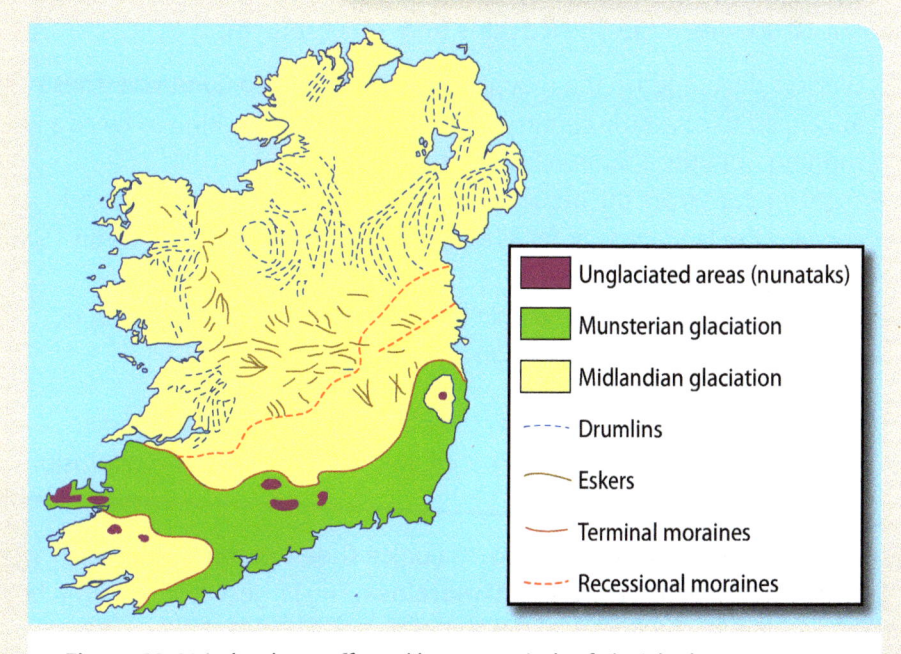

Figure 13.19 Ireland was affected by two periods of glacial advance. This map indicates the extent of each advance.

Munsterian glaciation

The **Munsterian glaciation** began about 175,000 years ago and lasted for about 20,000 years. The whole of Ireland, with a few exceptions, was covered by a sheet of ice that was up to 300 metres thick. The exceptions were the highest mountain peaks, which rose above the ice as **nunataks**. The ice came from two sources:

> Native ice formed in the mountainous regions to the west and south of the country and moved down through valleys to cover much of the country.
> Scottish ice moved across the North Channel to cover the north-eastern part of the country and meet up with the native ice.

ACTIVITY

Research

Look up 'animating Irish ice sheet video' on the internet.

Evidence of the direction of ice movement is provided by **erratics**. These are rocks that are of a different type to the surrounding rock. They are believed to have been transported from their original location by glaciers and then deposited as the ice melted. Connemara marble erratics have been found in North Cork and South Kilkenny. Erratics of Scottish granite are found as far south as Dublin.

As the ice retreated, it deposited a thick mantle of glacial and fluvio-glacial deposits over the lowlands. Many of these deposits were destroyed by the actions of the later Midlandian glaciation.

Boulder clay plains and eroded uplands of a landscape shaped during the Munsterian glaciation

Midlandian glaciation

The **Midlandian glaciation** began about 70,000 years ago and lasted until about 10,000 years ago. The ice came from three sources:

> Glaciers developed in the mountains of Donegal and Connacht. These advanced to cover the country with an ice sheet stretching as far as a line running from the Shannon Estuary to Wicklow.
> Local ice caps from the mountains of Cork and Kerry spread out and covered the landscape as far as Killarney to the north and to within 15 km of Cork to the east.
> A small ice cap also developed in the Wicklow Mountains. This cut out valleys that include Glendalough and Glenmalure.

The Midlandian ice bulldozed over the glacial landforms of the earlier Munsterian glaciation. In so doing, it created its own landforms of erosion and deposition.

The limit of the advance of the two major ice sheets of the Midlandian glaciation are marked by **terminal moraines**. The largest of these stretches from Wicklow to the mouth of the Shannon.

Once again, as the ice retreated it covered the landscape with a thick mantle of glacial and fluvio-glacial deposits. These are best seen in the Midlands.

PowerPoint Summary

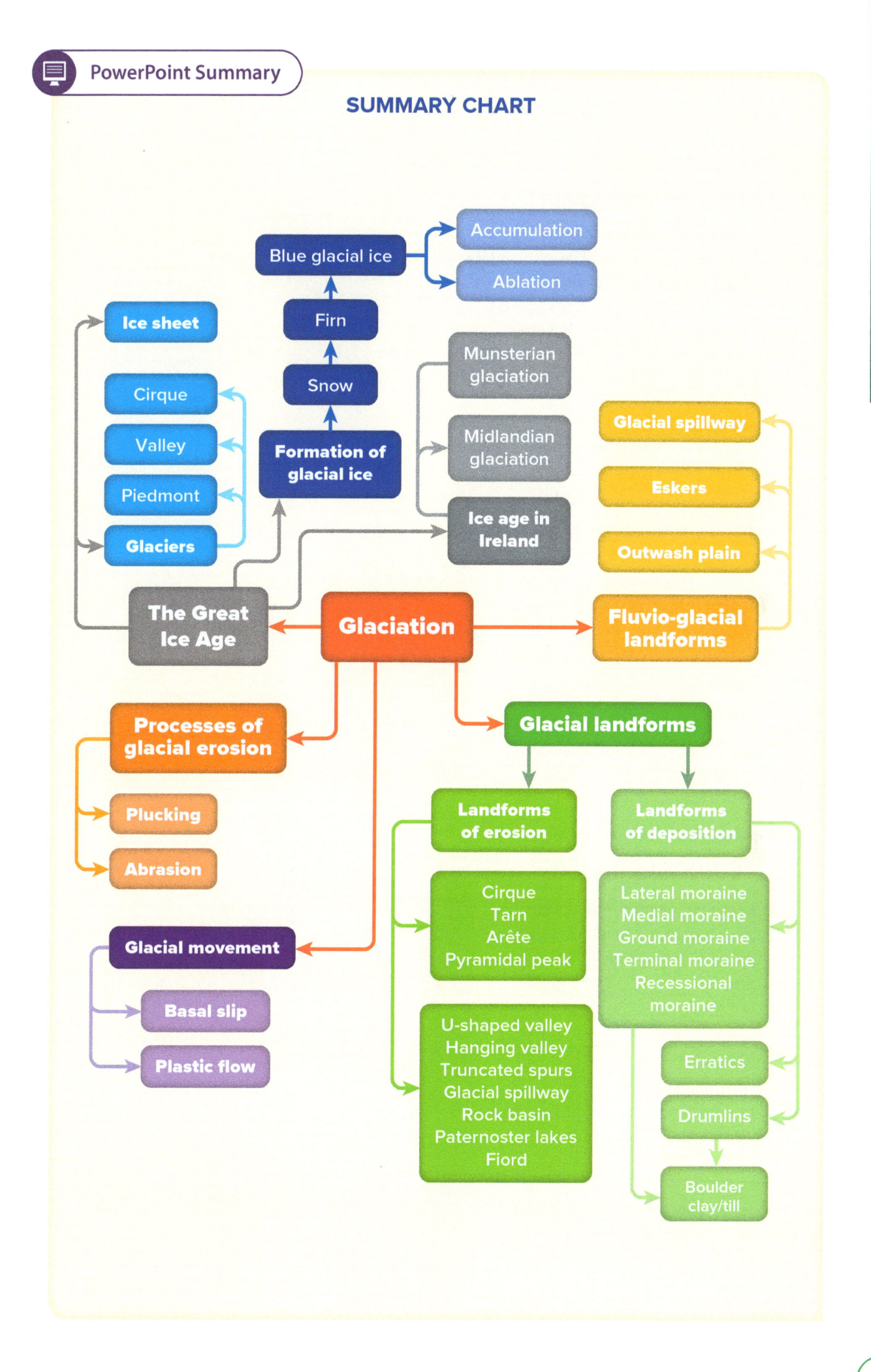

SUMMARY CHART

```
                          Accumulation
         Blue glacial ice
                          Ablation
              ↑
            Firn
              ↑
Ice sheet   Snow        Munsterian
              ↑          glaciation       Glacial spillway
Cirque    Formation of
          glacial ice   Midlandian
Valley                   glaciation       Eskers
Piedmont
                        Ice age in        Outwash plain
Glaciers                 Ireland

  The Great          Glaciation          Fluvio-glacial
   Ice Age                                 landforms


Processes of                        Glacial landforms
glacial erosion
                                Landforms        Landforms
Plucking                        of erosion       of deposition

Abrasion                        Cirque           Lateral moraine
                                Tarn             Medial moraine
                                Arête            Ground moraine
Glacial movement                Pyramidal peak   Terminal moraine
                                                 Recessional
Basal slip                                       moraine

Plastic flow                    U-shaped valley
                                Hanging valley   Erratics
                                Truncated spurs
                                Glacial spillway
                                Rock basin      Drumlins
                                Paternoster lakes
                                Fiord           Boulder
                                                clay/till
```

UNIT 1 · PHYSICAL GEOGRAPHY

CHAPTER 13 · GLACIAL PROCESSES   205

Leaving Cert exam questions

SHORT QUESTIONS: HIGHER LEVEL

1 Glacial landforms (8 marks)

Examine the OS map extract. Link each of the glacial landforms labelled **A**, **B**, **C** and **D** with its title in the table.

Landform	Letter
Arête	
Truncated spur	
Tarn lake	
Rock basin/finger lake	

2 Glacial landforms (8 marks)

Examine the aerial photograph of a glaciated landscape. Link each of the glacial landforms labelled **A**, **B**, **C** and **D** with its title in the table.

Landform	Letter
Arête	
Cirque	
Medial moraine	
U-shaped valley	

SHORT QUESTIONS: ORDINARY LEVEL

1 Glacial landforms (8 marks)

(i) Examine the photographs and match each of the letters and photograph with one of the landforms named in the table.

Landform	Letter
U-shaped valley	
Pyramidal peak	
Erratic	
Corrie lake	

(ii) Name **one** way in which glacial landscapes benefit the economy in areas in which they are found.

OL

2 Glacial landforms (8 marks)

Examine the diagram and correctly match each of the descriptions with one of the appropriate letters.

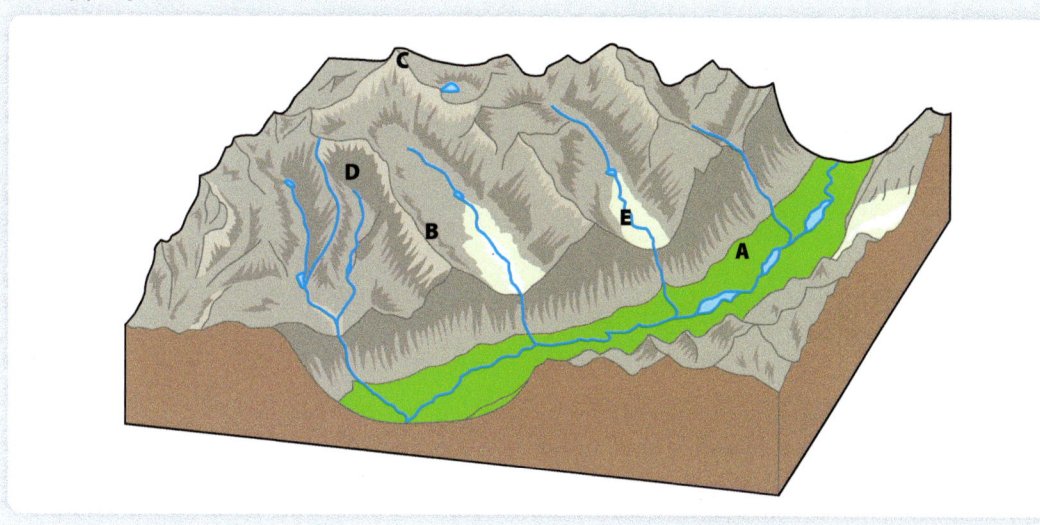

Landform description	Letter
A deep hollow called a **corrie**	
A tributary valley called a **hanging valley**	
A knife-edged ridge called an **arête**	
A **pyramidal peak** caused by erosion	
A deep trough called a **U-shaped valley**	

HL **LONG QUESTIONS: HIGHER LEVEL**

1 **Landform development** (30 marks)

Examine the role of the processes of erosion on the formation of any **one** glacial landform of **erosion** that you have studied.

2 **Landform development** (30 marks)

Examine the role of the processes of deposition on the formation of any **one** glacial landform of **deposition** that you have studied.

3 **Landform development** (30 marks)

Explain the formation of any **one** landform of glacial **erosion** and **one** landform of glacial **deposition** that you have studied.

4 **Landform development** (30 marks)

Explain, with the aid of a labelled diagram(s), the formation of **one** landform of glacial **erosion** that you have studied.

OL **LONG QUESTIONS: ORDINARY LEVEL**

1 **Surface processes** (40 marks)

Explain, with the aid of diagrams, the formation of any **two** glacial landforms.

2 **Surface processes** (40 marks)

Explain, with the aid of diagrams, the formation of any **one** Irish landform resulting from glacial action.

UNIT 1 · PHYSICAL GEOGRAPHY

HIGHER LEVEL STUDENTS ONLY

Chapter 14
Landscape Cycle and Isostasy

KEYWORDS

- endogenic forces
- exogenic forces
- landscape cycle
- uplift
- peneplain
- base level
- rejuvenation
- isostasy
- knickpoints
- incised meanders
- paired terraces
- coastline of emergence
- raised beach
- raised cliff
- raised platform
- coastline of submergence
- ria
- consequent stream
- superimposed drainage
- subsequent stream
- river capture
- elbow of capture
- misfit stream
- wind gap

LEARNING OBJECTIVES

By the end of this chapter, you should be able to understand:

- The landscape cycle
- Isostasy
- The impact of isostasy on fluvial and coastal landscapes
- Peneplain development
- The development of the drainage pattern of Munster.

Exogenic (external) forces
- Destructive forces
- Reduce the relief of the land surface
- Level off surfaces.

Endogenic and exogenic forces

We have seen in previous chapters that the Earth's crust is in a constant state of change. This change is the result of two forces:

- Endogenic forces
- Exogenic forces.

Endogenic (internal) forces
- Constructive forces
- Increase the relief of the land surfaces
- Make these surfaces uneven.

EXOGENIC (EXTERNAL) FORCES
Weathering
Mass movement
Erosion
Deposition

Earth's surface

Folding
Faulting
Earthquakes
Volcanic activity
Plate tectonics

ENDOGENIC (INTERNAL) FORCES

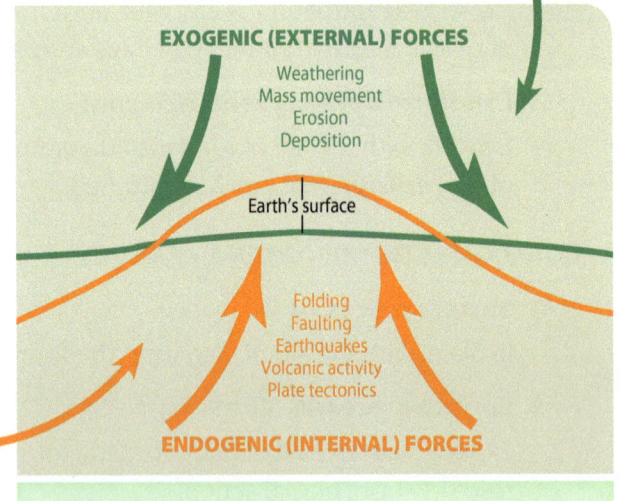

Figure 14.1 The forces that have shaped the Earth

208 GEOGRAPHY TODAY

All these forces work as part of a grand idea, called the geographic cycle or the **landscape cycle**.

The landscape cycle

The landscape cycle suggests that landforms change over time. They go from a youthful stage to a mature stage and finally to an old stage. It could take hundreds of millions of years to go through the cycle.

Each stage of the cycle has its specific characteristics. (In this example, we concentrate on the impact of rivers, even though weathering and glacial activity also play their part.)

> **QUESTION**
>
> List two differences between endogenic forces and exogenic forces.

> **DEFINITION**
>
> **Uplift** is where the level of the Earth's surface is raised by natural causes, such as tectonic activity.

The initial stage
The cycle begins with **uplift**. The landscape is generally flat and featureless. Streams begin to flow on the surface, following whatever slope is in the landscape.

The youthful stage
Rivers and streams begin to cut V-shaped valleys into the landscape. This is the stage where the landscape is steepest and most irregular, with deep, narrow valleys, sharp ridges and mountains.

The mature stage
The rivers carve wider valleys and begin to meander. The valley floors are levelled out and slopes become more gentle.

The old stage
The relief is almost flat and level, creating a surface called a **peneplain**. The only exceptions are some gently rolling hills of resistant rock. The landscape is at the lowest elevation, close to sea level. This is called the **base level** of erosion and it completes the cycle.

Rejuvenation
The real world is not quite as orderly as the theory states. The cycle could be interrupted by tectonic uplift during any stage and thus returned to the youthful stage. This is called **rejuvenation**. When it occurs, the landscape cycle starts again.

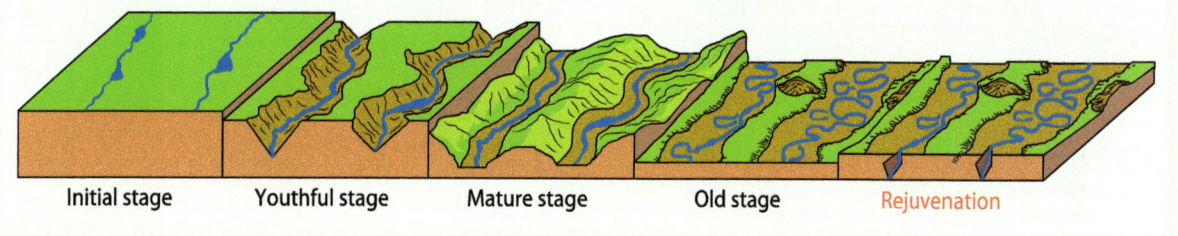

Figure 14.2 The landscape cycle

Base level of erosion

Base level is the lowest level to which erosion by rivers can occur. If the river enters the sea, its absolute base level is sea level. However, a river may also have a local base level if it flows into a lake.

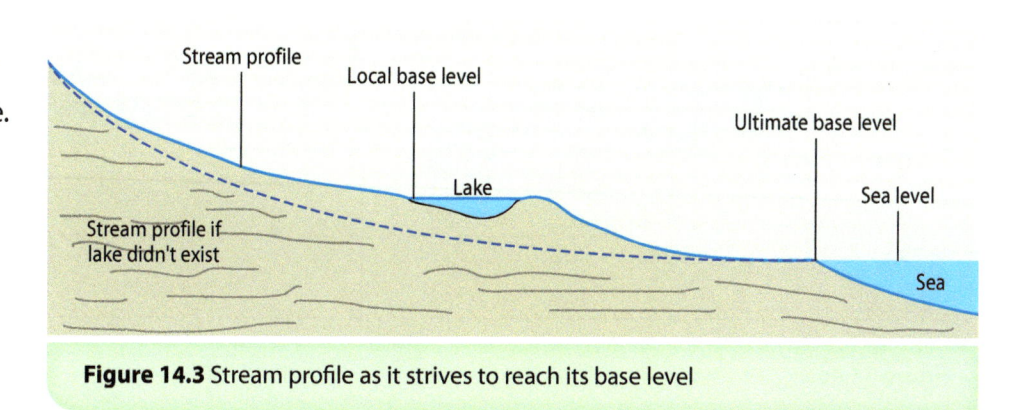

Figure 14.3 Stream profile as it strives to reach its base level

The balance between land and sea

The Earth's crust is not perfectly rigid. It can sink or rise in response to changing loads on it. When weight is put on the Earth's crust, it sinks. When that weight is removed, the crust rises or rebounds. In both cases, the boundary between land and sea is altered relative to one another. This change in the balance between land and sea levels is primarily caused by **isostatic change**.

Most isostatic change in the Irish landscape is influenced by the sequence of events during and following the last glaciation.

DEFINITION

Isostasy refers to the vertical movement (up or down) of the Earth's crust.

GEOFACT

Isostatic change also occurs when land is uplifted by tectonic forces such as faulting and folding.

As the ice age began

At the beginning of the ice age, the temperature fell. Large volumes of water were stored on the land as glaciers and snow. Since that water was not returning to the sea, the sea level began to fall.

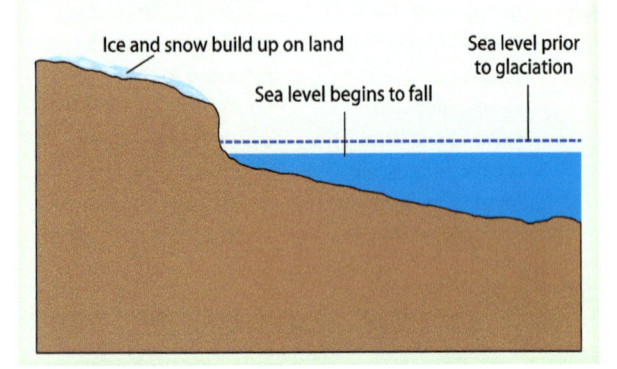

Figure 14.4a

During the ice age

The weight of the ice on the land surface compressed the rock and slowly pushed it down into the mantle. It is estimated that a cap of 600 metres of ice could depress the crust by about 200 metres. Sea level fell rapidly as the water cycle was no longer in operation.

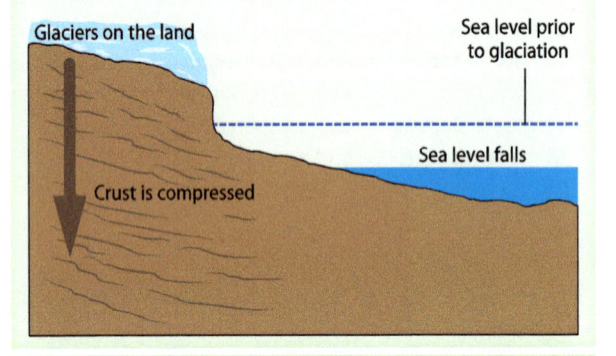

Figure 14.4b

As the weather began to warm up

When the climate began to get warmer, the ice sheets started to melt. Water previously held in storage as ice began to return to the oceans. The warmer water also expanded. This caused a rapid rise in sea level.

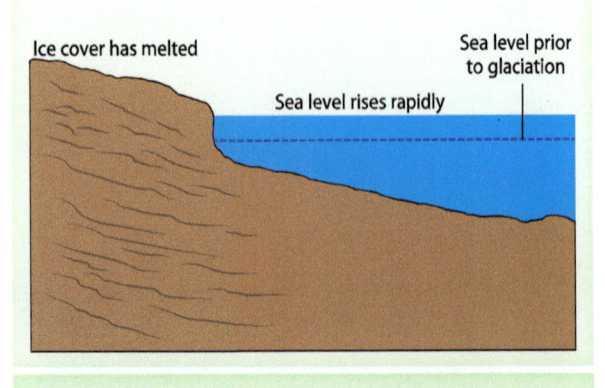

Figure 14.4c

Thousands of years later

However, after the weight of the ice was removed from the crust, it began to slowly rebound to its original level. As a result, there was a local uplift of the land relative to the level of the sea.

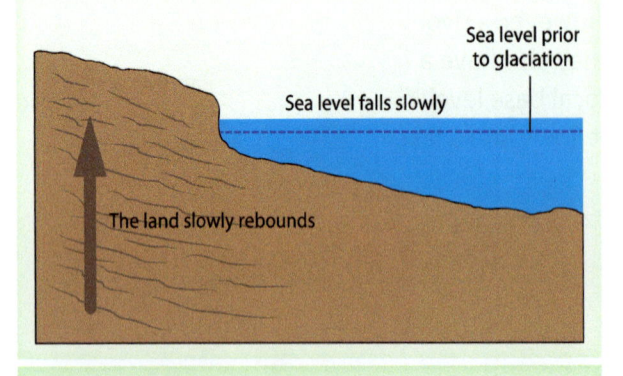

Figure 14.4d

Isostatic change in the Irish landscape

The effects of isostatic change can be seen on both **fluvial** and **coastal** features around Ireland.

Fluvial landforms of isostasy

A river aims to achieve a generally smooth long profile over time (see Figure 14.3 on page 209) as it moves towards achieving ultimate base level. There is a delicate balance between erosion and deposition.

When the crust rebounds (upwards) after an ice age, the sea level is lower relative to the land. The river finds itself flowing down a steep slope into the sea, increasing the gradient of the long profile. It cuts down into the landscape, trying to reach a new base level. This moves the river from its old stage to a young stage once again. This is called **rejuvenation**.

Rejuvenation starts at the lower stage of the river and gradually moves upstream by headward erosion. The rivers Nore and Barrow show evidence of several periods of rejuvenation. Evidence for this rejuvenation includes:

- Knickpoints
- Incised meanders
- Paired terraces.

Knickpoints

- A **knickpoint** is a sudden break or change in the gradient of a river. It marks the point at which the new (young) river profile meets the original (old) river profile.
- If there is a sharp change in the gradient, the knickpoint is marked by a waterfall or rapids.
- If a river has undergone rejuvenation on a few occasions, it may have several knickpoints, each separated by a gentle section of long profile. As a knickpoint advances upstream by headward erosion, it removes all traces of the earlier profile.

Rapids on a river mark a knickpoint

> **ACTIVITY**
>
> **Research**
> Look up a video called 'From glaciation to global warming: A story of sea level change' on YouTube.

> **QUESTION**
> What are rapids?

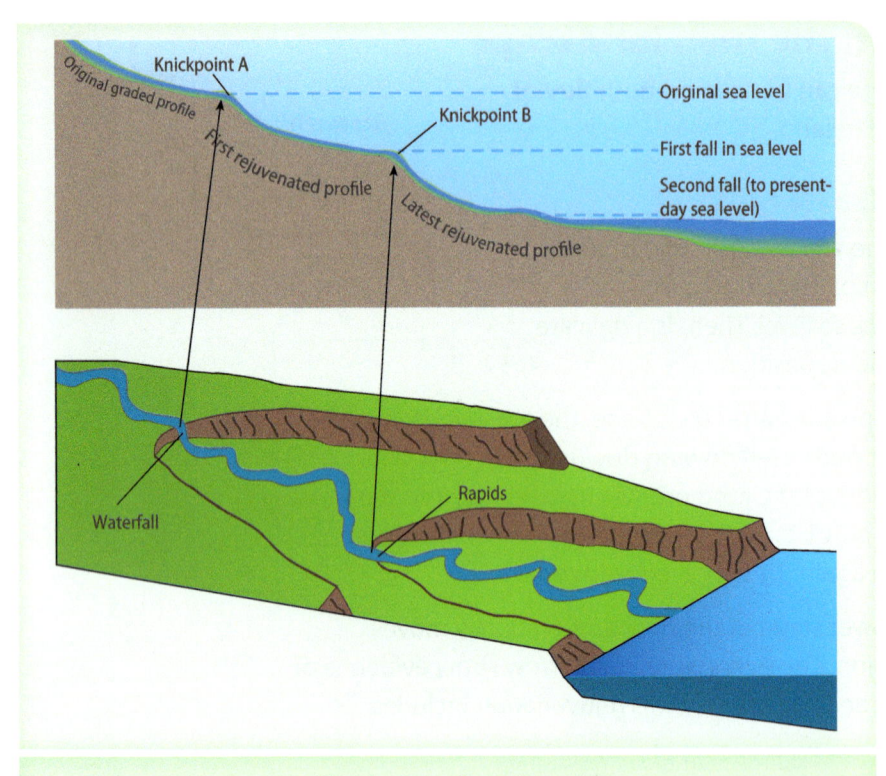

Figure 14.5 The long profile of a river after rejuvenation

Incised meanders

› Usually, rivers in a floodplain are meandering. When a meandering river is rejuvenated, the river has renewed energy.
› Vertical erosion begins to dominate over lateral erosion and the river begins to cut down into the floodplain.
› If this vertical erosion is rapid, the river will cut quite deeply into the valley floor while keeping its meandering course.
› In this way, the river forms **incised meanders** with symmetrical valley sides. The sides of the new valley are steep and the former floodplain lies far above the new level of the river.

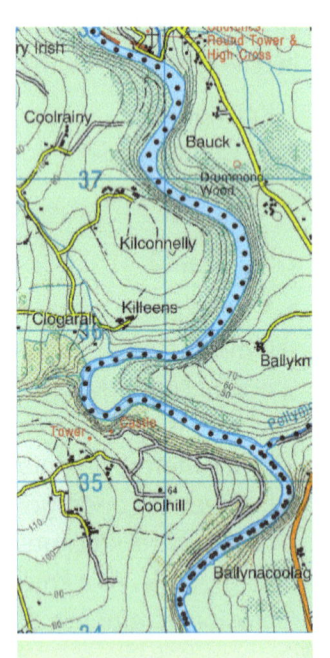

Figure 14.6 Incised meanders on the Barrow River, just below St Mullins. The closely packed contours indicate the steep sides of the new valley.

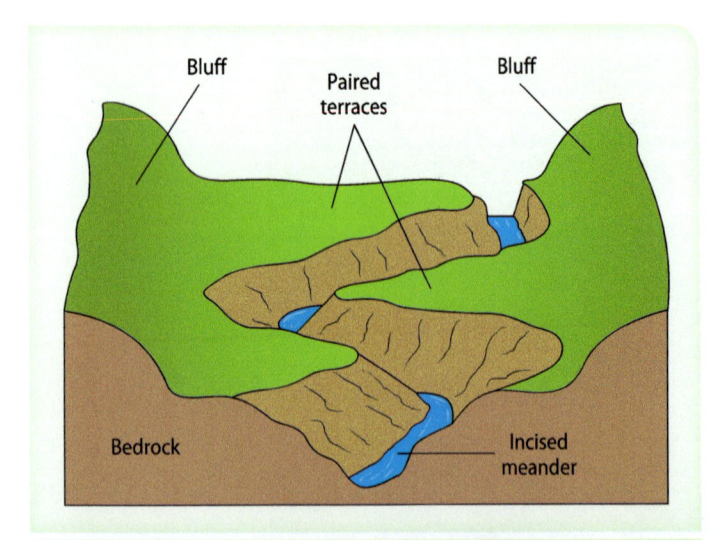

Figure 14.7 Incised meanders have cut deeply into the floodplain. They are the result of vertical erosion following rejuvenation.

ACTIVITY

Discussion

Look at the OS map. Identify and describe two pieces of evidence that show that this section of the river has undergone rejuvenation.

Paired terraces

> River terraces are remnants of former floodplains that have been left high and dry above the present floodplain.
> After rejuvenation, the river begins to slowly cut into the original floodplain by vertical erosion, creating a new valley at a lower level.
> The new valley is eventually widened by lateral erosion and a new floodplain forms. The remnants of the original floodplain are then left as **paired terraces**.
> They are called paired terraces because the height of the terrace on one side of the river corresponds with the height of the terrace on the other side. A valley may have several paired terraces, depending on how often rejuvenation has occurred.

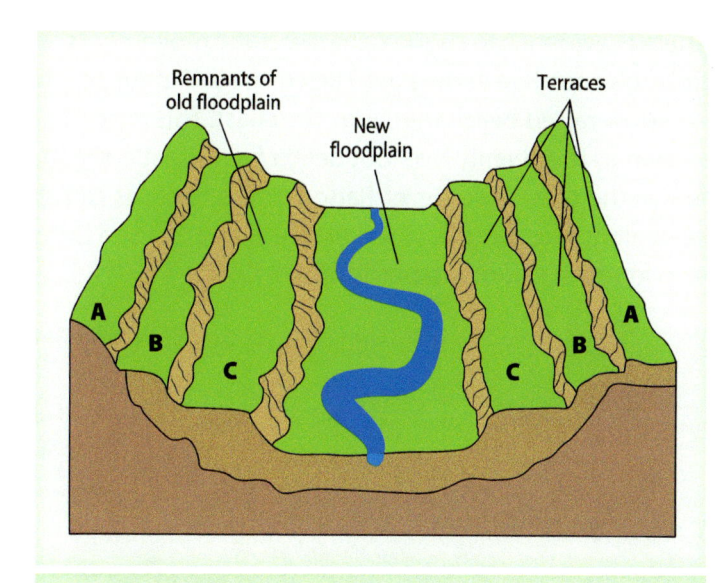

Figure 14.8 Three sets of paired terraces formed by both vertical and lateral erosion

Succession of river terraces on one bank of the river. Most of these terraces are not paired because lateral erosion has removed those on one side of the river.

Coastal landforms of isostasy

A coastline whose level has risen relative to the level of the sea is called a **coastline of emergence**. Evidence of emergence includes **raised beaches**, **raised cliffs** and **raised platforms**. They were formed by erosion or deposition by wave action. However, uplift of the land following ice melt has put them beyond the water's reach. Today, they are found at a level that is too high to be reached by the sea. The present sea level is marked by a new series of similar landforms at a much lower level than the raised landforms.

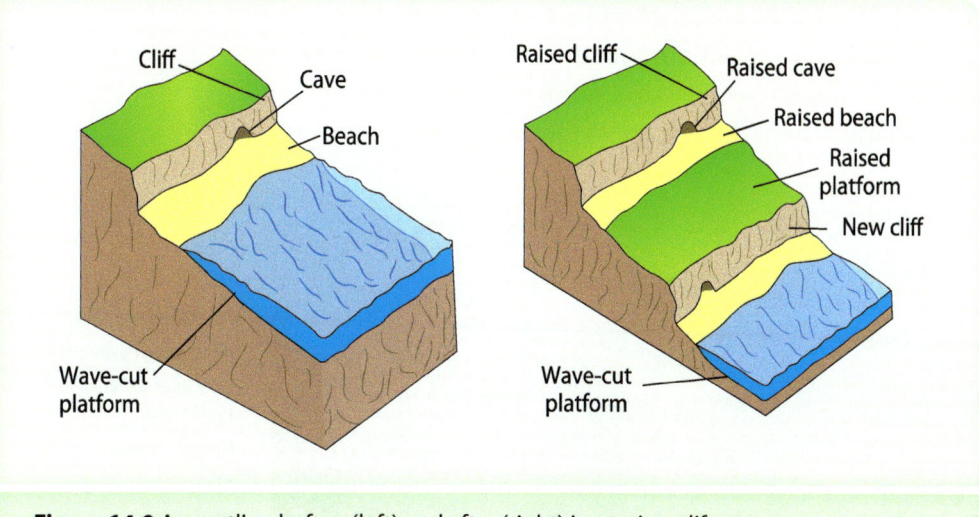

Figure 14.9 A coastline before (left) and after (right) isostatic uplift

There is evidence to suggest that isostatic movements affected Ireland's coastline in the past. The coast road in Antrim follows a narrow raised beach that hugs the coast. This raised beach is known as the 'twenty-five foot beach' because it is that height above the present sea level. Raised cliffs and caves can also be seen along the route. A raised platform and a raised beach are also found at Courtmacsherry in West Cork.

> **ACTIVITY**
>
> **Research**
>
> Look up images of 'raised beaches in Ireland' on the internet.

Raised cliffs, raised platform and raised beach

> **ACTIVITY**
>
> **Research**
>
> Look up Courtmacsherry on Google Maps. **Hint:** Use the 3-D and rotate widgets to get a good view of the raised beach the village is built on.

The South Ireland Peneplain

The **South Ireland Peneplain** covers hundreds of square kilometres in counties Cork and Waterford. The best example is found in the Knockmealdown Mountains. The height of the peneplain varies between 180 metres and 240 metres above today's sea level.

It is formed on the sandstones that were uplifted during the Armorican period and consists of a reasonably flat landscape broken by individual hills. The uplifted sandstone was worn down to a peneplain by an ancient river system (see Figure 14.2 on page 209).

The peneplain was later submerged beneath the sea. A covering of chalk and limestone was laid over it. Later uplift brought the land above sea level once again. The new surface sloped gently to the south. This led to the development of the drainage system that we see in Munster today.

> **GEOFACT**
>
> Sometimes sea level rises relative to the level of the land, creating a **coastline of submergence**.
>
> When this occurs, the sections of old river valleys that are closest to the coast are partially flooded or drowned. This forms long narrow inlets called **rias**. Examples include Bantry Bay and Kenmare Bay (see Figure 12.10 on page 168).

The surface of the South Ireland Peneplain can be seen on the flank of the Knockmealdown Mountains in the background

The drainage system of South Munster

> At one stage, Ireland lay beneath a shallow sea and a chalk surface was laid down on top of the older folded sandstones.
> When this surface was uplifted about 60 million years ago, it was gently tilted to the south.
> This was the initial stage of the landscape cycle.

Figure 14.10a Streams flow in a southerly direction on a newly uplifted and gently sloping landscape

> The rivers followed the slope of the land and flowed in a southerly direction.
> These are said to be **consequent streams** because their direction is as a result (consequence) of the natural slope of the land.

> The rivers began to cut down into the chalk landscape and soon met the more resistant sandstone anticlines. The rivers began to cut narrow valleys into the anticlines and continue their original course.
> This meant that the rivers now flowed against the direction of the anticlines. This is called **superimposed drainage** (because it was formed on a higher surface).

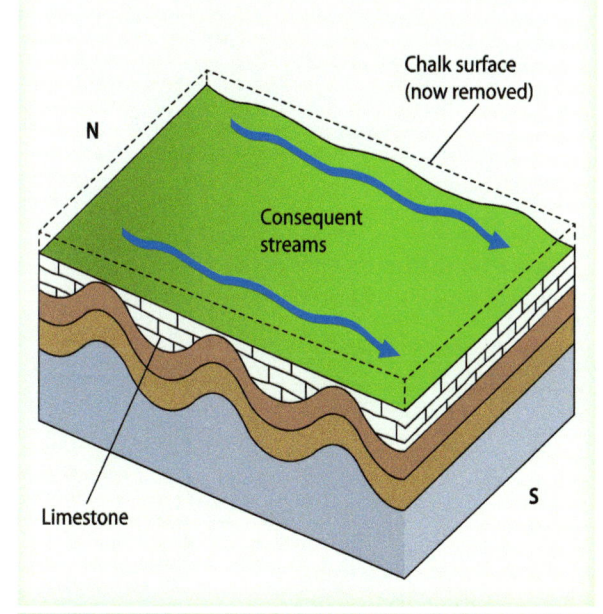

Figure 14.10b These southerly-flowing streams are called consequent streams

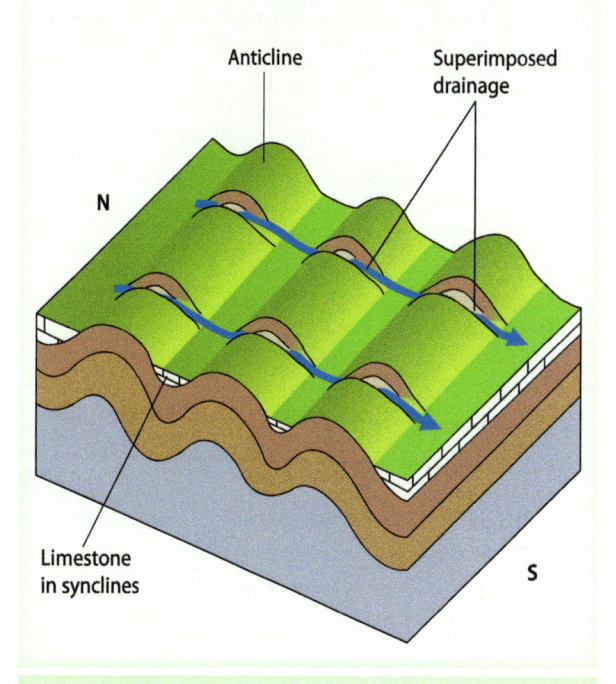

Figure 14.10c As the chalk is removed, the rivers cut down into the sandstone anticlines

CHAPTER 14 · LANDSCAPE CYCLE AND ISOSTASY

- The east–west synclines consisted of chalk and limestone. These were more easily weathered and eroded than the sandstone.
- The tributaries of the consequent rivers began to erode these bands of less resistant rocks, growing in length by headward erosion.
- Since these tributaries made their appearance long after the main rivers, they are called **subsequent streams**.

- These subsequent rivers continued to erode headwards until they intercepted the consequent (south-flowing) rivers. These rivers were diverted to follow the course of the subsequent rivers.
- This process is known as **river capture**. The right-angled bend where the river capture took place is called the **elbow of capture**.
- By now the captured river had lost most of its volume and became too small for the valley that it occupied. Because of this, it is called a **misfit stream**. The dry part of the valley between the elbow of capture and the misfit stream is called a **wind gap**.

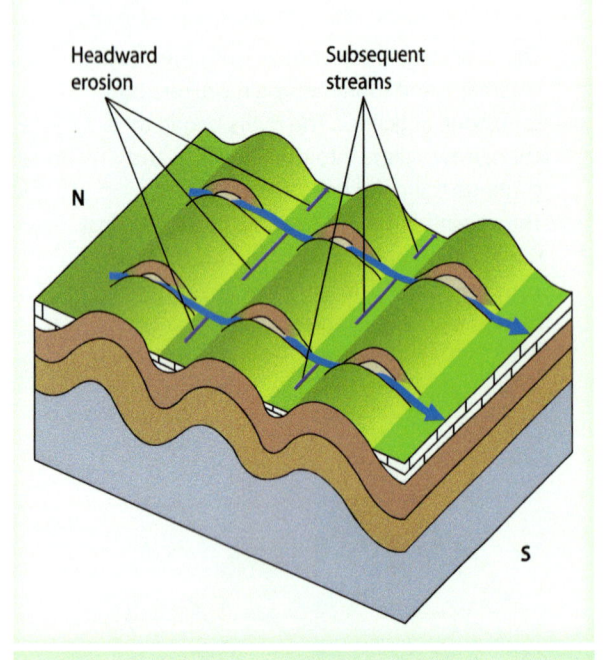

Figure 14.10d Tributaries develop in the anticlines at a later (subsequent) stage

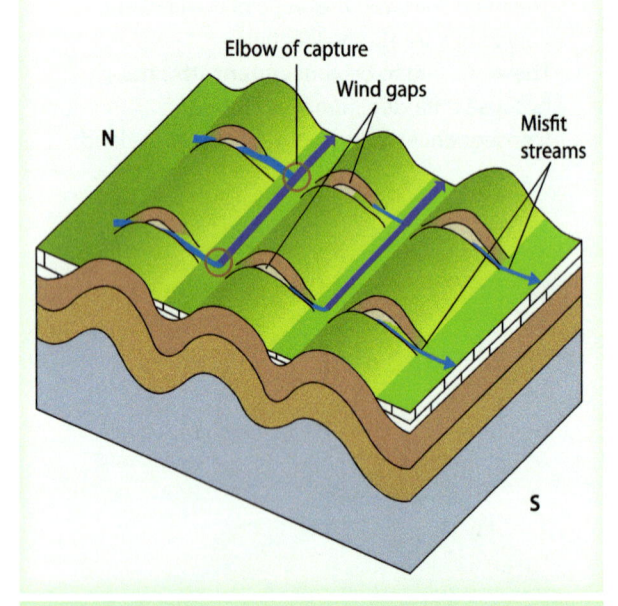

Figure 14.10e The tributaries grow and capture the waters of the older consequent streams

Rivers of South Munster today:

- The Suir River enters the sea at Waterford Harbour.
- The Blackwater River now enters the sea at Youghal.

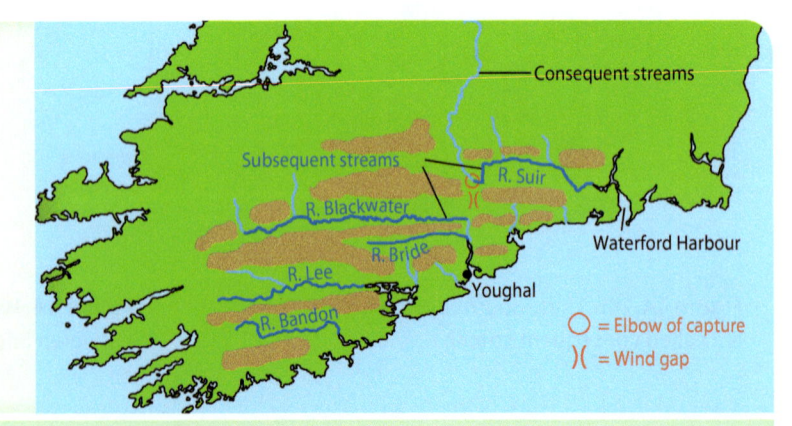

Figure 14.10f The drainage pattern of the South of Ireland is a mixture of consequent streams and subsequent streams

PowerPoint Summary

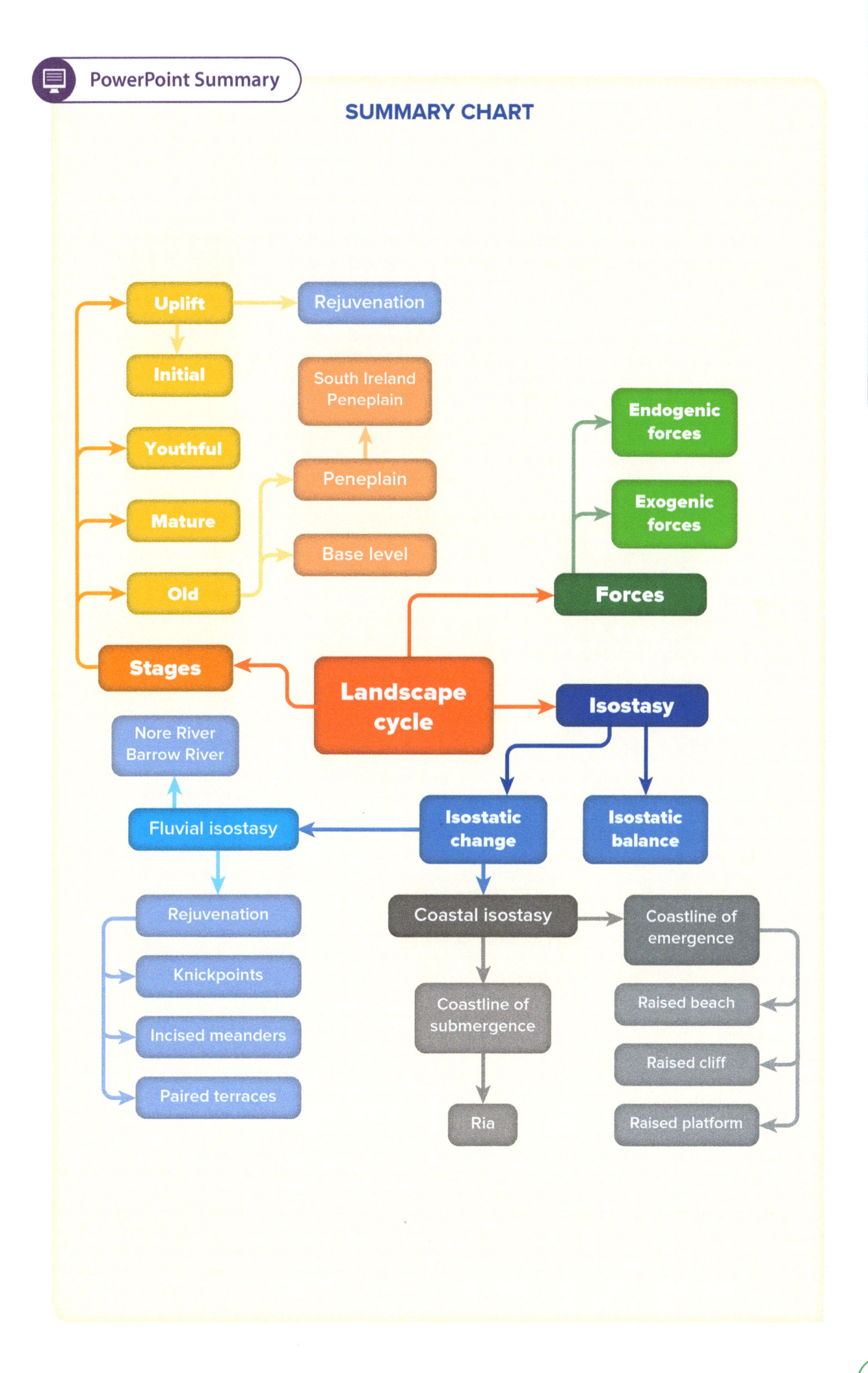

SUMMARY CHART

```
Uplift ──→ Rejuvenation
  ↓
Initial          South Ireland
                 Peneplain
                      ↑
Youthful         Peneplain
                      
Mature           Base level
                              
Old
  ↓
Stages ←─── Landscape cycle ───→ Forces ──→ Endogenic forces
                │                         ──→ Exogenic forces
                ↓
             Isostasy ──→ Isostatic balance
                ↓
             Isostatic change
                ↓
  Nore River / Barrow River
        ↑
  Fluvial isostasy ←─── 
        ↓
  Rejuvenation
    ├─ Knickpoints
    ├─ Incised meanders
    └─ Paired terraces

Coastal isostasy ──→ Coastline of emergence
        ↓                ├─ Raised beach
  Coastline of           ├─ Raised cliff
  submergence            └─ Raised platform
        ↓
       Ria
```

CHAPTER 14 · LANDSCAPE CYCLE AND ISOSTASY

UNIT 1 · PHYSICAL GEOGRAPHY

Leaving Cert exam questions

LONG QUESTIONS: HIGHER LEVEL

1. **Landform development** (20 marks)

   Examine the diagram, which shows the stages in the cyclical development of a fluvial landscape, and answer each of the following questions.

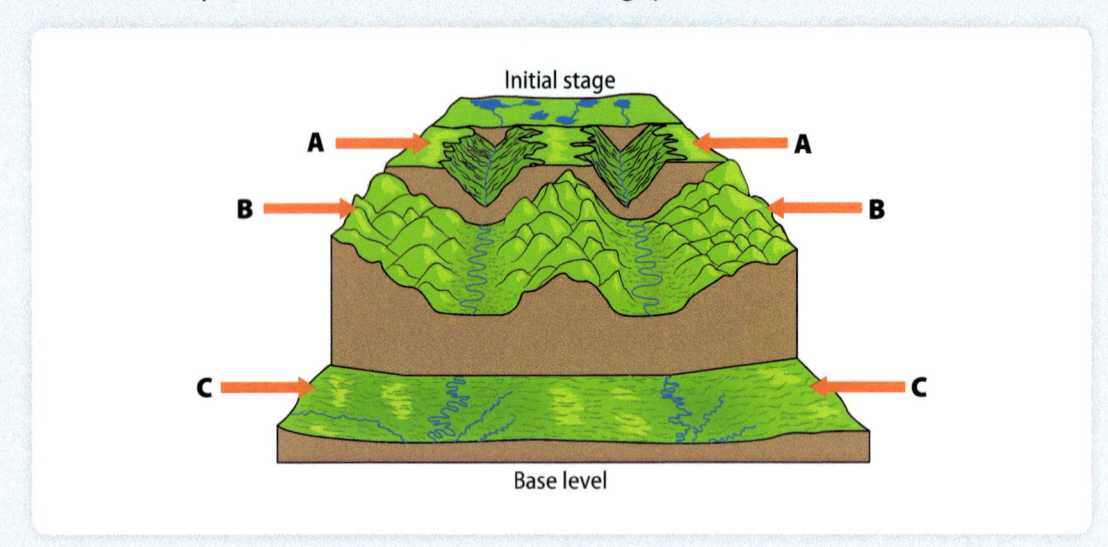

   (i) Name each of the stages **A**, **B** and **C**.
   (ii) Name **one** fluvial landform from each of the stages **A**, **B** and **C**.
   (iii) Explain briefly what is meant by *peneplain*.
   (iv) Explain briefly what is meant by *base level*.

2. **Fluvial adjustment** (30 marks)

   Examine how changes in base level impact on geomorphic processes and landforms in a fluvial environment.

3. **Isostacy** (30 marks)

   Examine how isostacy has impacted on the Irish landscape.

4. **Fluvial adjustment** (30 marks)

   Explain how rivers adjust to a change in base level, using example(s) that you have studied.

5. **Isostatic changes** (30 marks)

   Explain how isostatic changes have impacted on the Irish landscape, using examples that you have studied.

6. **Landform development** (30 marks)

   Isostatic processes involve adjustments to the balance between land and sea. Discuss how these processes have shaped the Irish landscape over time.

CORE UNIT 2
REGIONAL GEOGRAPHY

Chapter 15	**The Concept of a Region**	220
Chapter 16	**The Dynamics of Regions 1**	251
Chapter 17	**The Dynamics of Regions 2**	295
Chapter 18	**The Dynamics of Regions 3**	341
Chapter 19	**The Complexity of Regions**	372

Chapter 15
The Concept of a Region

KEYWORDS

- region
- geomorphological
- North European Plain
- cool temperate oceanic climate
- administrative regions
- French communes
- French *départements*
- French regions
- the Gaeltacht
- Flanders/Wallonia
- Flemish/French
- Islam
- Unionist/Nationalist
- socio-economic regions
- core regions
- peripheral regions
- industrial decline

LEARNING OBJECTIVES

By the end of this chapter, you should be able to understand:

- The concept of a region
- The physical characteristics of the North European Plain
- The main features of the climate of North-West Europe
- The administrative regions of France
- The language regions in Ireland and Belgium
- The regions that are defined by religion
- The socio-economic regions: core, peripheral and regions of industrial decline.

What is a region?

A region is an area that has one or more characteristics that distinguish it from neighbouring regions. These characteristics can be **physical**, **cultural** or **socio-economic**.

Regions can be small or large. For example, the Burren – a physical region – occupies a small area of Co. Clare. On the other hand, the Islamic region – a cultural region – extends from Morocco through North Africa and the Middle East into Pakistan and beyond.

In this chapter we will look at five types of regions:

- Physical
- Administrative
- Cultural
- Socio-economic
- Urban.

REGIONS		
TYPES OF REGIONS	**EXAMPLES**	
1 Physical	Geomorphological	› The Burren limestone region › North European Plain
	Climatic	› Cool temperate oceanic climate found in Ireland and North-West Europe
2 Administrative	Local authorities	› Irish county councils
	Regional authorities	› The Northern and Western Region
3 Cultural	Language	› Gaeltacht › Wallonia and Flanders in Belgium
	Religion	› Northern Ireland › Islamic region
4 Socio-economic	Core	› Dublin region › Paris Basin
	Peripheral	› Western region in Ireland › Mezzogiorno in Italy
	Industrial decline	› Nord in Northern France
5 Urban/nodal/city		› Dublin, Paris and Naples

Table 15.1 The major types of regions

PHYSICAL REGIONS

Geomorphological regions

A geomorphic region is a physical region that is defined by its landscape and the forces that have shaped it.

HINT

A geomorphological region can also be called a geomorphic region.

You have already examined two geomorphic regions in Ireland:

› The Munster ridge and valley region (a landscape of fold mountains, page 27)
› The Burren (a limestone landscape shaped by weathering, page 110).

We will now examine another geomorphic region: the North European Plain.

The city of Wolfsburg in North Germany with the Volkswagen car plant. The Mittelland Canal runs beside the plant. The North European Plain is very densely populated.

CASE STUDY

The North European Plain

Geomorphology

The North European Plain is an extensive region of lowland that extends almost 4,000 km from France to Russia. It includes the Paris Basin, the Low Countries, Northern Germany, Denmark, Poland and East-Central Europe. It also includes South-East England and the extreme south of Sweden.

In the past, the plain slipped beneath the sea. Sedimentary rocks built up on the sea floor. As the region was uplifted, these sedimentary rock strata were bent and warped, but were not sharply reshaped by faulting and folding. Therefore, the region has remained flat and undulating.

> **DEFINITION**
>
> **The Low Countries:** The Netherlands, Belgium and Luxembourg.

Figure 15.1 The North European Plain is a major physical region in Northern Europe

> **ACTIVITY**
>
> **Research**
>
> Examine Figure 15.1.
>
> (i) Find out the names of three countries that are part of the North European Plain.
>
> (ii) Name one sea that is surrounded by parts of the North European Plain.

Shaping the landscape

The landscape of the plain has been shaped by rivers, wind and glacial action.

Glacial action

During the last ice age, large sheets of continental ice covered much of the plain. As this ice retreated north, it left behind glacial and fluvio-glacial deposits. Terminal moraines, boulder clay and outwash plains are found in Denmark.

Wind action

At the end of the last ice age, finer materials were blown south by northerly winds. These materials, known as **limon**, were deposited in the Paris Basin, Belgium and parts of North Germany. Limon has weathered into fertile soils.

Fluvial action

The North European Plain is drained by several rivers. These include the **Seine** in France and the **Rhine**, which flows through Germany and the Low Countries. Parts of the river basins are covered by rich alluvial soils.

Along the North Sea coast, the landscape of the plain is low-lying in East Anglia in England, the Netherlands and North Germany. The Dutch have reclaimed much of the land that lies under sea level. These areas are known as **polders**.

Longshore drift and coastal deposition have shaped and straightened much of the coast, especially along the North Sea coast of Europe.

> **GEOFACT**
> The average height of Denmark above sea level is only 31 metres.

Part of the North European Plain in North Germany. The region is a productive area agriculturally.

Economy

Agriculture

The North European Plain is a region of great agricultural importance because of its fertile soils and flat landscape. Much of the region has become the **bread basket** of the EU. Agriculture is highly mechanised and agricultural productivity is among the highest in the world.

The climate of the plain is suitable for growing wheat and barley. Precipitation is well distributed throughout the year. Summer temperatures are suitable for the ripening of cereals.

Manufacturing

Coal deposits were mined in the Franco-Belgian coalfields, the Ruhr in Germany and in Poland. Coal and deposits of iron ore have helped the region to become a major manufacturing zone.

For these reasons, the North European Plain is one of the most densely populated regions in Europe. The region contains Western Europe's largest cities, including London, Paris and Berlin.

> **ACTIVITY**
> **Thinking**
> Why does a high population density develop in many regions that are rich in mineral resources?

> **DEFINITION**
> **Bread basket:** A region where cereals, such as wheat, are grown. Cereals are used in the production of bread and flour.

Climatic regions

There are six broad climatic regions in the world:

› Tropical
› Temperate
› Polar
› Dry
› Continental
› Mountain.

Climatic regions can be further divided into categories based on temperature and precipitation. For example, in the mid-latitudes, e.g. latitudes between 40° and 60°, **two mild climates** are found:

› Warm temperate oceanic, also known as the Mediterranean climate
› Cool temperate oceanic, also known as the Western European climate.

LINK

The Mediterranean climate will be examined in Chapter 17 in the study of the Mezzogiorno.

World climatic regions

- Tropical climates
- Dry climates
- Temperate climates
- Continental climates
- Polar climates
- Mountain climates

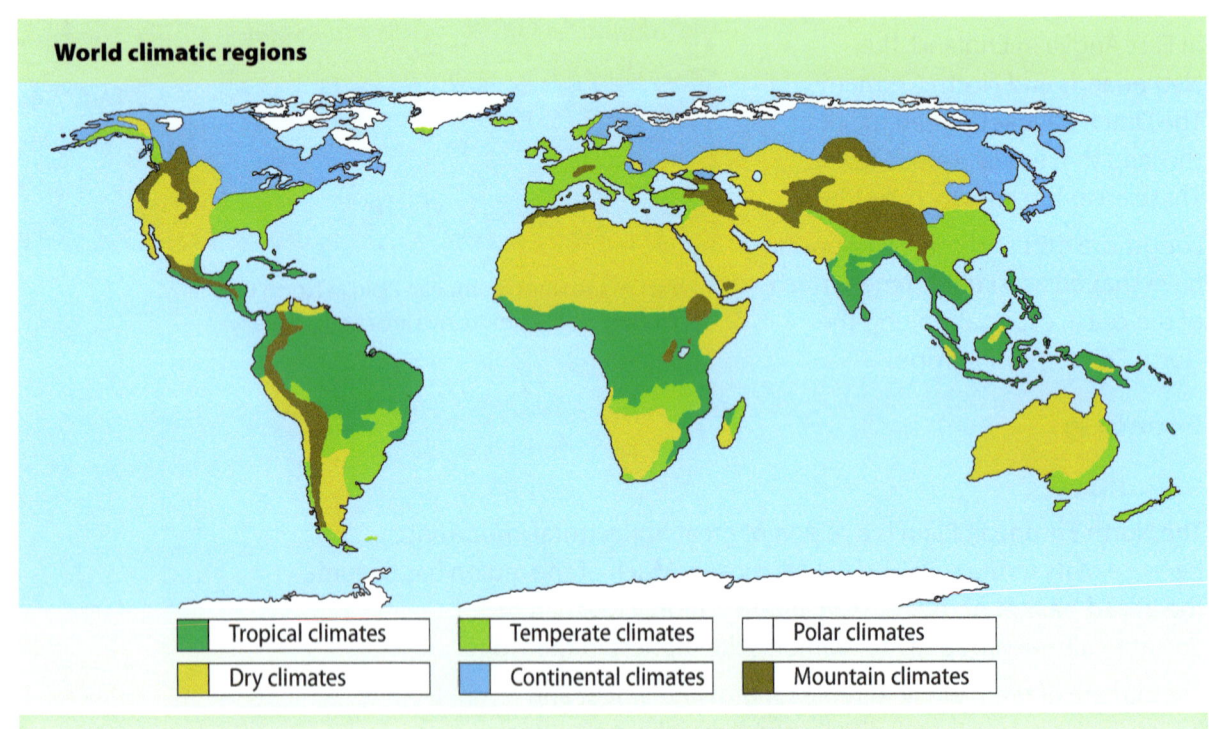

Figure 15.2 The six major climatic types according to the Koppen classification

ACTIVITY

Skills

Examine Figure 15.2.
  (i) Name two continents where continental climates are found.
  (ii) What are the main climates found in Western Europe?
  (iii) Name two climate types that are found in Brazil.
  (iv) Name two countries in North America where dry climates are found.
  (v) What is the most widespread climate type found in North Africa?

CASE STUDY

Cool temperate oceanic climate

This is a mid-latitude climate. It is found on the western margins of Europe. As its name suggests, it is a maritime climate and is strongly influenced by its proximity to the sea. This climate is found in all parts of Ireland.

Characteristics of Ireland's climate

Temperature

> Summers are moderately warm, with June/July average temperatures ranging from 15°C in the North-West to 17°C in the South-East.
> Winters are mild, with January temperatures averaging 4°C to 6°C.
> There is an annual temperature range of about 11°C.

Precipitation

> Precipitation is distributed throughout the year, but it rains the most in winter.
> Total annual precipitation varies from less than 800 mm in Dublin, Carlow and Louth to more than 2,800 mm in the Kerry mountains.
> Warm and cold fronts bring rain from the Atlantic throughout the year.

ACTIVITY

Numeracy

How to work out the average temperature

Daytime: 22°C
Night-time: + 10°C
32°C divided by 2 = 16°C
16°C is the average temperature

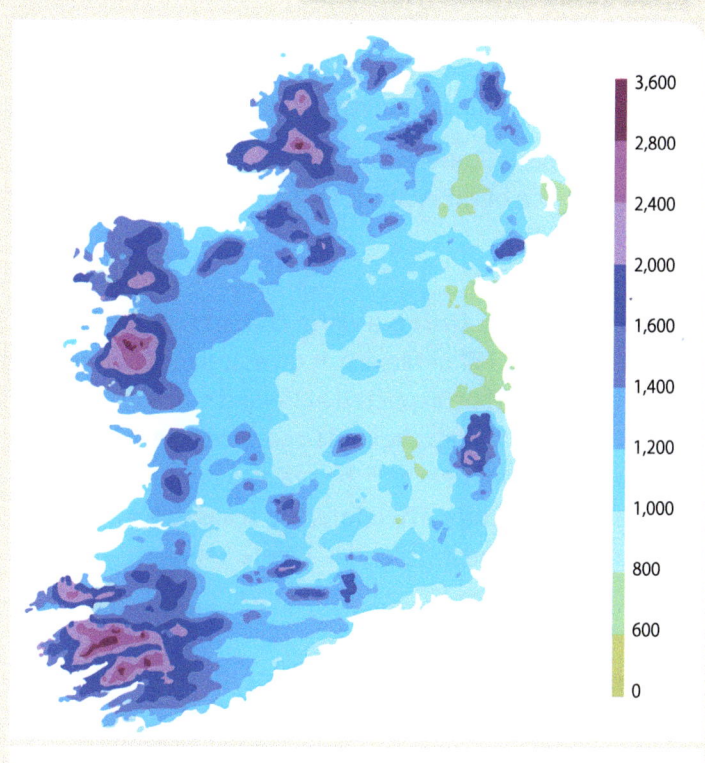

Figure 15.3 Mean annual rainfall (mm), 1981–2010

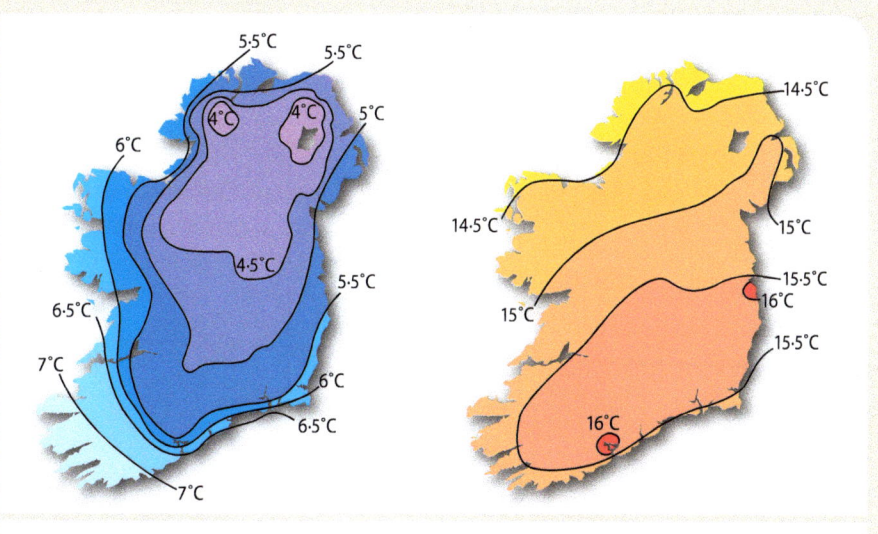

Figure 15.4 Average air temperatures in Ireland for January (left) and July (right)

ACTIVITY

Thinking

(i) Can you explain why Kerry and West Cork have the mildest temperatures in Ireland in January?

(ii) Can you explain why the north coast of Ireland has the coolest temperatures in summer?

Sunshine

- Ireland receives between 1,100 and 1,600 hours of sunshine each year. The sunniest months are May and June. During these months, sunshine averages between 5 and 6.5 hours per day over most of the country. The South-East gets the most sunshine, averaging over 7 hours a day in early summer.
- Cloud cover is a feature of Ireland's climate. December is the dullest month, with average daily sunshine ranging from about 1 hour in the north to almost 2 hours in the South-East. Over the year, most areas in Ireland get an average of between 3.25 and 3.75 hours of sunshine each day.

Factors that influence Ireland's climate

The main factors that influence Ireland's climate are:

- Ireland's mid-latitude location
- The influence of the Atlantic Ocean.

North Atlantic Drift

The **North Atlantic Drift** is a warm current that reaches Ireland from the Gulf of Mexico. It gives Ireland a much milder winter than would be expected at Ireland's latitude of 52–55° north. The current keeps Ireland's coast ice free in winter. The moderating influence of the sea also reduces Ireland's summer temperatures. Therefore, the sea is the reason why the **temperature range** in Ireland is a mere 11°C.

Prevailing winds

The **prevailing winds** are **south-westerly**. As they blow over the warm North Atlantic Drift, these winds absorb moisture. The result is that Ireland has a damp climate, as south-westerly winds bring precipitation over Ireland. The mountains of the West of Ireland are the wettest areas because of relief rain. Mild south-westerly winds also help to make Irish winters mild.

Frontal depressions

Ireland is located along the **polar front**. This is where warm air from the south clashes with cold air from the polar region. **Frontal depressions** form where warm and cold air meet. These rain-bearing fronts are blown over Ireland by south-westerly winds. Because of this, Ireland's weather is very changeable, as warm rain-bearing fronts are followed by cold fronts that bring bright spells and showers.

DEFINITION

The South-East (of Ireland): Counties Waterford, Wexford and southern parts of the adjoining counties of Kilkenny, Wicklow and Carlow.

GEOFACT

April is generally the driest month in Ireland.

GEOFACT

The North Atlantic Drift begins its life as the Gulf Stream.

ACTIVITY

Research
Look up the location of the Gulf of Mexico on the internet.

GEOFACT

The average number of wet days in Ireland (days with 1 mm or more of rain) ranges from about 150 days a year along the east and south-east coasts to about 225 days a year in parts of the West of Ireland.

ADMINISTRATIVE REGIONS

An administrative region is a geographic area with specific boundaries managed by an authority. Governments provide services for their citizens. Governments use councils at a local level to do this effectively.

CASE STUDY

Administrative regions in Ireland

County councils and city councils are elected bodies that have many local functions. For example, they provide:

> Planning permission
> Motor taxation
> Fire services
> Street lighting
> Upkeep of local roads.

Council meetings are reported in local newspapers. People ask for help from their local councillors for many reasons. For example, they might want to get street lights fixed or make road junctions safer to cross.

County and city councils draw up development plans for the economic and social improvement of their administrative areas every five years.

City and county councils

The Republic of Ireland has the following councils:

> **County councils:** Twenty-three counties have one council each, while Co. Dublin has three county councils. There are twenty-six county councils in all.
> **City and county councils:** Limerick city and county council; Waterford city and county council.
> **Three city councils:** Dublin, Cork and Galway city councils.

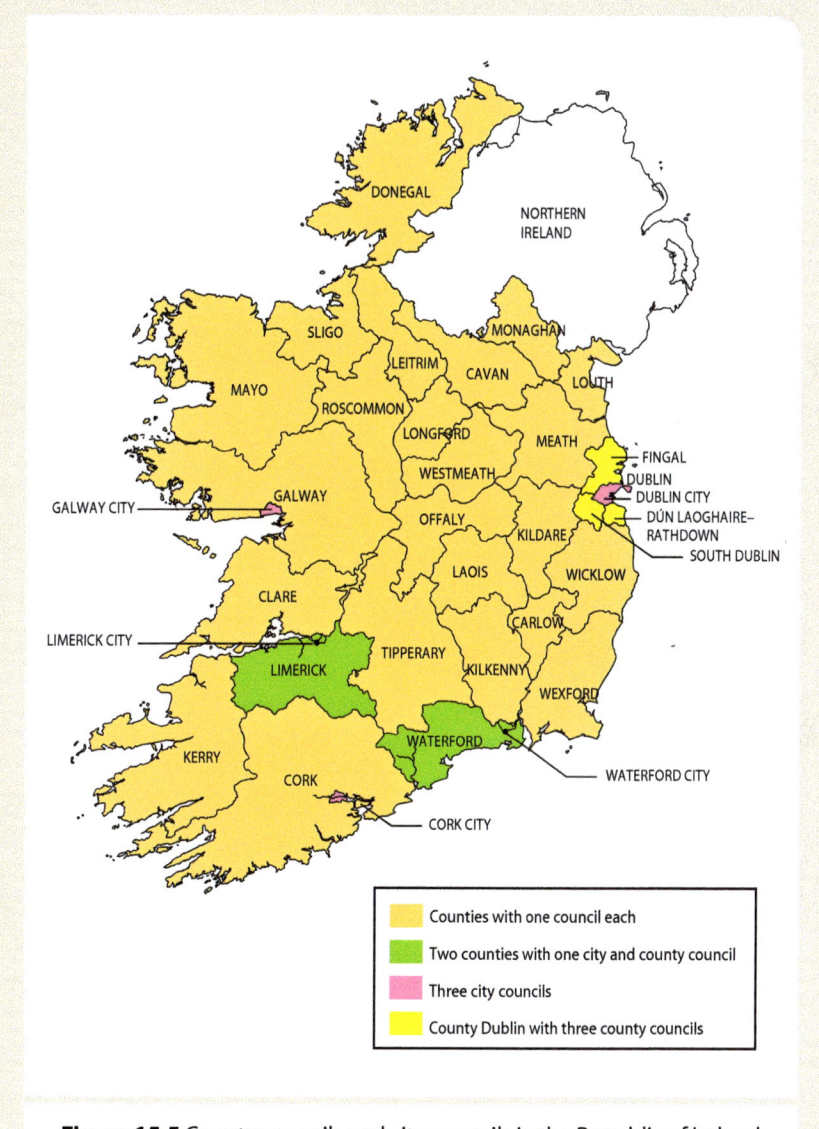

Figure 15.5 County councils and city councils in the Republic of Ireland

Legend:
- Counties with one council each
- Two counties with one city and county council
- Three city councils
- County Dublin with three county councils

ACTIVITY

Skills

Examine Figure 15.5. Name three cities that have city councils.

UNIT 2 · REGIONAL GEOGRAPHY

CHAPTER 15 · THE CONCEPT OF A REGION 227

Regional assemblies

Ireland has three regional assemblies. These have replaced the two assemblies of the BMW and the Southern and Western region.

- The **Northern and Western Regional Assembly** meets in Ballaghadereen, Co. Roscommon.
- The **Southern Regional Assembly** meets in Waterford.
- The **Eastern and Midland Regional Assembly** meets in Ballymun, Dublin.

The functions of the assemblies are to:

- Co-ordinate, promote or support strategic planning and sustainable development
- Promote effective local government and public services
- Manage EU regional funds.

Figure 15.6 Regional assemblies in Ireland

CASE STUDY

Administrative regions in France

France has three levels of local government:

- Communes
- *Départements*
- Regions.

Communes

There are 36,682 communes in France. Some rural communes have very few people. Commune authorities register births, marriages and deaths. They look after the local water supply and the sewage system. They collect local taxes and domestic and commercial rates. Some communes run campsites for tourists.

Départements

There are 95 *départements* in mainland France and two in Corsica. The *préfet* is the chief administrator in the *département* and is a powerful figure. *Départements* are more important than Irish county councils.

They have important functions in schools. They recruit and pay non-teaching staff in secondary schools. They maintain school buildings and pay the running costs, such as heating and electricity. They provide subsidised school meals in state-run secondary schools.

Départements also provide social services, such as child protection and foster homes for children at risk. They build and manage social housing. They provide pensions for disabled people.

Regions

Until the end of 2015, France had 22 administrative regions. From January 2016, France reduced that number to 13 regions, including one in Corsica. Each region includes several *départements*.

Regional authorities provide many public services. They are responsible for the maintenance and running costs of senior secondary schools, known as *lycées*. They also draw up plans for the economic, tourist and transport development of their regions.

The local government is a big employer in France. Because of the many layers of local government in France, even the French sometimes get confused as to who does what.

GEOFACT

In addition to 13 regions in mainland France and Corsica, the French also have five overseas regions in the Caribbean, such as Martinique and Guadeloupe.

GEOFACT

The number of the *département* where people's cars are registered appears on the number plate of the car in France.

ACTIVITY

Research

Look up where Martinique and Guadeloupe are located on the internet.

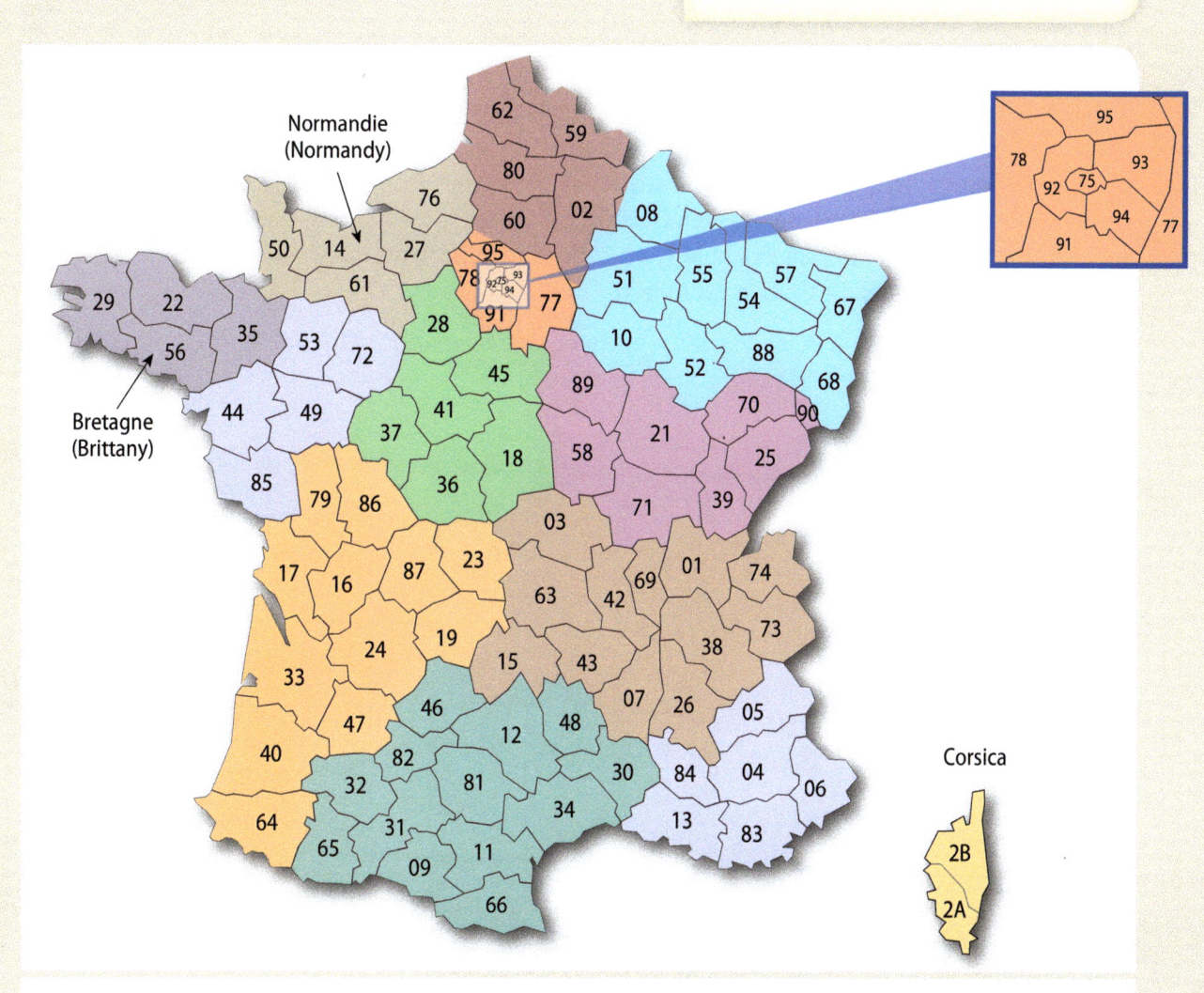

Figure 15.7 The *départements* of France. Also included are the 13 regions, which are colour coded, e.g. Bretagne, Normandie and Corsica. Regions have several *départements*.

CULTURAL REGIONS

Regions can be distinguished from each other by **cultural characteristics**, such as language and religion. When people speak the same language or practise the same religion, they have a **shared sense of identity**. They have a **sense of belonging** because of shared beliefs and values.

Language regions

The EU is a 'patchwork quilt' of language regions, with 24 official languages. People from countries such as England, Germany, France, Italy and Poland have their own languages. Many smaller cultural groups, such as the Swedes, Greeks, Estonians and Czechs, also have their own languages. Language is a **unifying force** among people who share the same language.

CASE STUDY

The Gaeltacht

Irish is a Celtic language. It is spoken as the everyday language by most of the people in the Gaeltacht. The Gaeltacht areas are in widely dispersed parts of Ireland. They are mainly on the western seaboard in counties Donegal, Galway and Kerry. Irish is spoken in several islands off the west coast. There are also small pockets of the Gaeltacht in West Cork, Ring in Co. Waterford and in Ráth Chairn and Baile Ghib in Co. Meath.

Irish survived in the West of Ireland because the area was less exposed to the English language when Ireland was a colony up to 1922.

Scoil Éinne is a school located in An Spidéal

ACTIVITY

Research
Look up a list of other Celtic languages on the internet.

DEFINITION

Dialect: A local variety of a language that is spoken in one area.

QUESTION

What Gaeltacht county is An Spidéal located in?

Both the Irish language and the boundaries of the Gaeltacht have been declining for generations. Two million people spoke Irish before the Great Famine of the 1840s. However, according to the 2011 census, only 66,238 people out of the 96,000 Irish living in the Gaeltacht could speak Irish. The great reduction in the numbers of Irish speakers in Gealtacht areas since the 1840s is partly due to outward migration.

A recent study was conducted on everyday spoken Irish in the Gaeltacht. There are 155 electoral divisions in the Gaeltacht. Within these divisions, there were only 21 communities where Irish is spoken on an everyday basis by 67% or more of the population. The **tipping point for language survival** is regarded as 67%.

Irish as the **language of play** among children, a sure measure of the future of the language, is no longer as strong in the Gaeltacht as it once was.

The change in boundaries of the Gaeltacht region over time

> **DEFINITION**
>
> **Language of play:** The spontaneous, unprompted language that children use among themselves in their interactions with each other.

> **QUESTION**
>
> What do you think the phrase *tipping point for language survival* means?

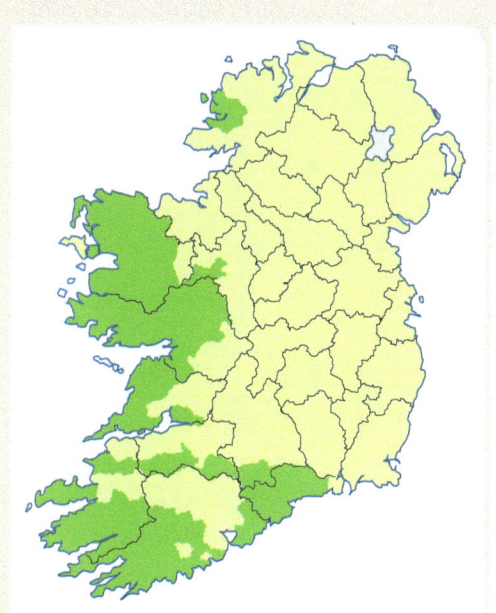

Figure 15.8a Regions where more than 50% of the people spoke Irish in 1851

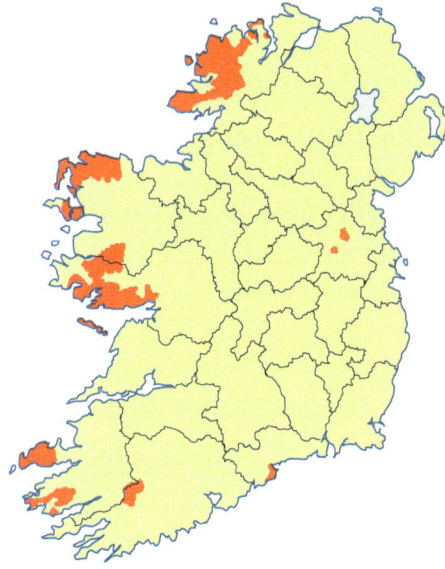

Figure 15.8b Gaeltacht regions today are located mainly along the west coast. There are some small Gaeltacht areas in counties Cork, Waterford and Meath.

> **ACTIVITY**
>
> **Skills**
>
> Examine Figure 15.8b. Name three counties in Munster that have Gaeltacht areas.

> **ACTIVITY**
>
> **Research**
>
> Examine Figure 15.8b. Find out the name of the Gaeltacht in Co. Waterford.

Since the Great Famine of the 1840s, the Gaeltacht has retreated west. Gaeltacht areas are no longer **contiguous** (beside each other). There are English-speaking areas in between them, a fact that further weakens Gaeltacht areas.

The Irish language is also declining in the islands. For instance, the last inhabitants of the Great Blasket Islands left for the mainland in 1953.

The following factors account for the **retreat west** of the boundaries of the Gaeltacht region:

- Emigration greatly reduced the population of Irish speakers.
- As far back as the 1850s, parents encouraged their children to learn English to help them in the USA and Britain when they emigrated.
- English was the **language of rule**. It was used in law courts, local administration and politics.
- English was the language used by teachers in primary schools after these schools were established in 1831.
- English was the language of newspapers, with one or two exceptions, such as *An Claidheamh Soluis*, edited by Pádraig Mac Piarais.
- The Irish Free State government required primary school teachers to teach children the Irish language. They also had to teach through the medium of Irish. This strategy was not successful.

The Meath Gaeltacht

Despite the decline in the boundaries of the Gaeltacht, one new Gaeltacht took root in the twentieth century in Co. Meath.

Fianna Fáil actively supported the restoration of the Irish language, especially during the era of Éamon de Valera. In the 1930s, Fianna Fáil established a Gaeltacht in **Ráth Chairn** and in **Baile Ghib** in Co. Meath, where Irish-speaking small farmers and their families from Connemara were given farms on former Anglo-Irish estates. This Gaeltacht has survived to this day.

Government support for the Gaeltacht

The Irish government has provided several supports to the Gaeltacht over the years.

- **Irish is the first official language** of the Republic of Ireland. It is also an official language of the EU.
- **Údarás na Gaeltachta** is responsible for the economic, social and cultural development of the Gaeltacht.
- To conserve existing Irish-speaking regions, planning laws now require that people who apply for planning permission in certain Gaeltacht areas may have to prove that they are fluent in Irish.
- **Radió na Gaeltachta** and **TG4** were established to counterbalance the influence of English-medium radio and television. These Irish-medium stations have given the Irish language a greater public profile and have helped many people to take pride in a language that is one of Europe's oldest living languages.

Aran Islands population decline

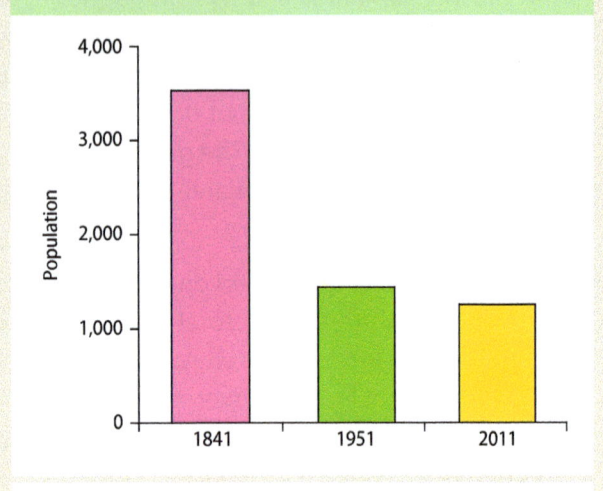

Figure 15.9 Population decline in the Aran Islands over time

GEOFACT

In the early 1800s, 40% of the population of Ireland spoke Irish.

Eoghan McDermott, a television personality, is a fluent Irish speaker

ACTIVITY

Research

Find out when Radío na Gaeltachta and TG4 were established.

GEOFACT

Students who answer certain Junior Cert and Leaving Cert examinations through Irish receive an additional 5–10%.

CASE STUDY

Belgian language regions: Where language divisions exist

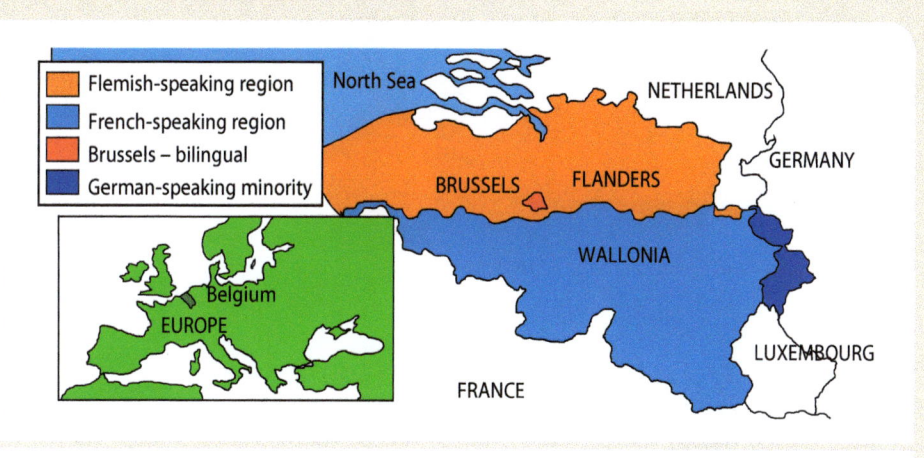

Figure 15.10 The language regions of Belgium

When two or more languages are spoken by different groups in the same state, great tension between speakers of those languages can develop. This has happened in Belgium.

Belgium, which is only a little bigger than Munster, has been an independent kingdom since 1830. The country has three languages:

- **Flemish** in Flanders
- **French** in Wallonia
- **German** in a small area in East Belgium.

Brussels is officially a bilingual city where French and Flemish have equal status, but most people in the capital speak French.

Each language community in Belgium guards its traditions fiercely. This is evident along the **border** that divides the language regions, where villagers from each side frequently clash and deface signposts that use the other's language.

As urban expansion of Brussels occurs into Flemish-speaking villages outside the city, French-speaking housing estates invade Flemish-speaking villages. This leads to great tension. In some primary schools in the outer suburbs of Brussels, children of the same age but from different language groups are taught in separate classes.

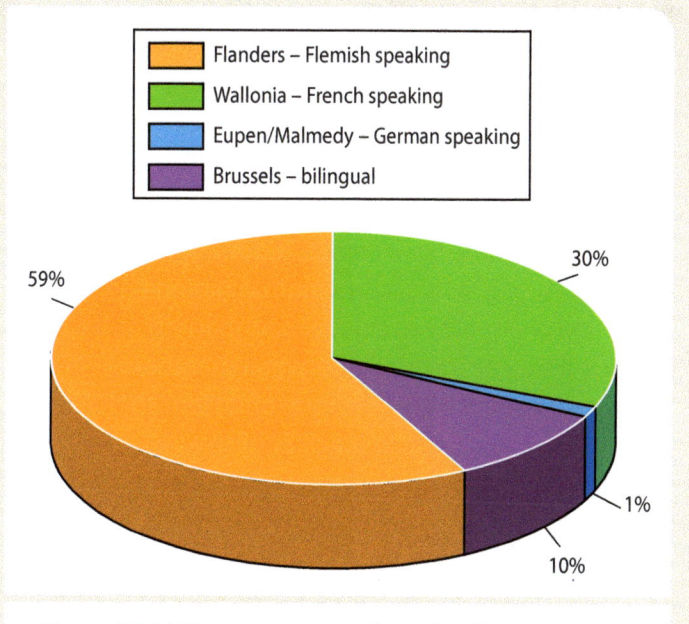

Figure 15.11 The percentages of people who speak the languages of Belgium

- Flanders – Flemish speaking: 59%
- Wallonia – French speaking: 30%
- Eupen/Malmedy – German speaking: 1%
- Brussels – bilingual: 10%

GEOFACT

Flemish is closely related to the Dutch language.

A signpost in Brussels with both French and Flemish place names

GEOFACTS

- By law, all advertisements in supermarkets in Brussels must be in both languages.
- One of the few things that unites Belgians is sport, e.g. the Belgian soccer team.

Flemish and French

Language tensions are heightened by economic differences. Wallonia is an **area of industrial decline** because the coal, steel and textile industries have weakened. High unemployment and outward migration have followed. On the other hand, Flanders has modern growth industries, such as healthcare, electronics, oil refining and petrochemicals. Flanders also has only half the unemployment rate of Wallonia.

Belgium lacks the unifying forces that create a national identity. For instance, it does not have a common school curriculum, a national television channel or a national newspaper. There is little intermarriage between members of the two communities. Walloon and Flemish schools are more likely to teach English as a second language than the language of the other community.

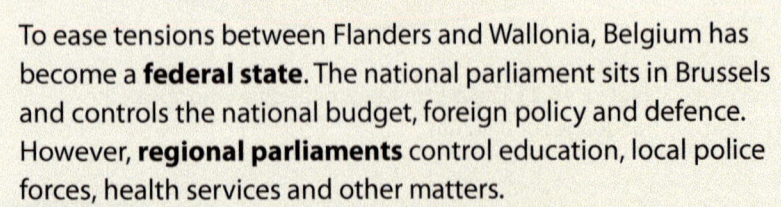

To ease tensions between Flanders and Wallonia, Belgium has become a **federal state**. The national parliament sits in Brussels and controls the national budget, foreign policy and defence. However, **regional parliaments** control education, local police forces, health services and other matters.

Flemish politicians are becoming increasingly separatist in their demands. However, the Flemings and the Walloons may be stuck together because of the high cost of breaking apart.

Unemployment map for Belgium

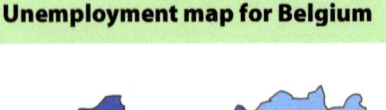

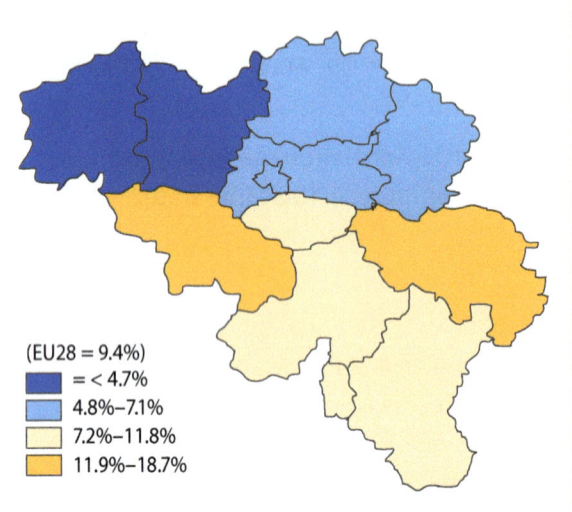

(EU28 = 9.4%)
- = < 4.7%
- 4.8%–7.1%
- 7.2%–11.8%
- 11.9%–18.7%

Figure 15.12 Unemployment in the south of Belgium (Wallonia) is considerably higher than it is in the north of Belgium (Flanders)

DEFINITIONS

Federal state: A federal state is a union of self-governing states or regions under a central national government. The USA has a federal system.

Separatists: People who want their region to become politically independent.

Religious regions

Regions defined by religion

Religion is a powerful cultural force. Sharing a common religion may give people **a strong sense of identity** and **a sense of belonging**. People of the same religion hold the same religious beliefs. They share many rituals, ceremonies and attitudes.

Religions can also **divide people**. When different religions are practised in the same region by different communities, hostility can develop between them.

ACTIVITY

Thinking

Examine Figure 15.13. Can you explain why Catholicism is strong in Latin America?

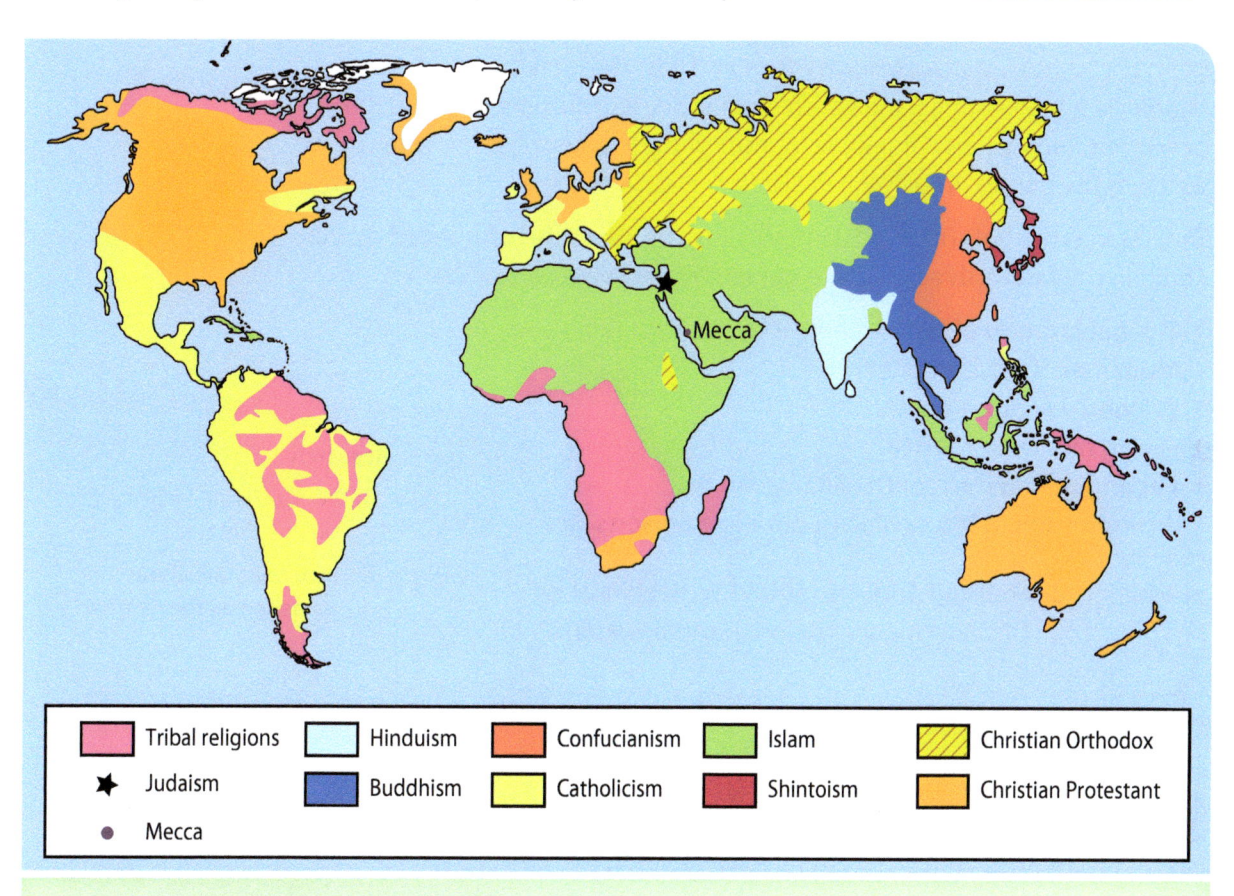

Tribal religions	Hinduism	Confucianism
Judaism	Buddhism	Catholicism
Mecca		Shintoism
		Islam
		Christian Orthodox
		Christian Protestant

Figure 15.13 Religious regions of the world

Pope Francis being greeted in St Peter's Square, Rome. Religion is a powerful cultural force.

CHAPTER 15 · THE CONCEPT OF A REGION   235

CASE STUDY

The Islamic region

The word **Islam** means 'submission to the will of God'. People who are members of Islam are called **Muslims**. Islam is one of the world's largest religions, with about 1.6 billion followers.

The cultural hearth of Islam is **Mecca** in Saudi Arabia, where Islam was founded in the seventh century with Mohammed. Islam stretches west across North Africa and east through the Middle East to Pakistan, Bangladesh and Indonesia. Muslims make up the overwhelming majority of people in most of these countries. For instance, 96.3% of the people who live in Pakistan are Muslims.

The Koran is the holy book of Islam. Muslims are **strongly influenced** by the Koran in their **daily lives**. They are guided by the five pillars of Islam:

> The **declaration of faith** – 'there is no God but Allah and Mohammed is his prophet'
> **Praying** five times a day
> Giving money to **charity**
> **Fasting** during the month of Ramadan
> A **pilgrimage** to Mecca at least once in a person's life.

In addition, alcohol and pork are forbidden. Beef must be slaughtered in the halal manner before it can be eaten.

GEOFACT
About 98% of the people who live in Turkey are Muslims.

ACTIVITY

Research

(i) Look up what halal meat is on the internet.

(ii) Find out more about Ramadan on the internet.

Pilgrims at prayer in Mecca, the holy city of Islam

Islam has two major sects: Muslims are either **Sunni** or **Shia**. Members of the two sects share many fundamental beliefs and practices. They differ in doctrine, ritual, law, theology and religious organisation. Sunnis account for around 85% of all Muslims and are in the majority in most Islamic countries. However, Shias are in the majority in **Iran**, **Iraq**, **Bahrain** and **Azerbaijan**. The division between Sunnis and Shias has caused much tension and strife in some Islamic areas of the Middle East.

The importance of the family in Islam

The unity of the family is very important in Islam. Muslims see the stability of the family as vital to society. A stable family is also necessary for spiritual growth. Adult children would usually not put their ageing parents in a home for the elderly. Traditionally, marriages are arranged.

Women are covered when they appear outside the home in many Islamic countries for reasons of modesty and privacy, amongst other things.

GEOFACTS

- According to the 2011 census, 49,204 Muslims are living in the Republic of Ireland. (Source: CSO)
- The Islamic Cultural Centre of Ireland is in Clonskeagh, Dublin.

Islamic minorities in Europe

Millions of Muslims now live as religious minorities in many countries in Europe, the USA and Canada because of migration. Great numbers of Islamic refugees have fled war-torn Syria to Europe in recent times.

The presence of large numbers of Muslims in European cities has led to cultural divisions. For instance, the wearing of the facial veil (the niqab) has sparked some debate. The facial veil was banned in France in 2011 even though it was worn by a mere 2,000 Muslim women in France.

DEFINITION

Caliphate: In a caliphate, a state is governed in accordance with Islamic or Sharia law.

LINK

See page 314 for more on Islam in the chapter on the Paris Basin.

Extremism in the Islamic region

The overwhelming majority of Muslims live peaceful lives. However, a very small number of Muslims are members of extremist militant groups. The activities of so-called Islamic State are widely known. The aim of Islamic State is to establish a caliphate in Iraq and Syria. Islamic State has pursued its aims with much violence.

The existence of extremist Islamic groups has created tensions both within the Islamic world and abroad because of acts of terrorism. Examples include the attacks in Paris in 2015 and in Brussels in 2016.

Girls studying the Koran in Iran

CASE STUDY

Northern Ireland

Generations of hostilities in Northern Ireland have created conflicts in a society that is divided on religious grounds. When the Southern Irish state was established in 1921, six counties in Northern Ireland opted out of a united Ireland and remained part of the UK. Most of the people in those six counties were **Protestants** and **Unionists**. They wanted to maintain **the union** with Britain.

Discrimination against the Nationalist community

The Unionist community established 'a Protestant parliament for a Protestant people' in Northern Ireland in the years after 1921. The Unionist government, with a large political majority in Stormont, **discriminated** against the Nationalist minority in jobs, housing and policing.

In urban centres in Northern Ireland today, many people live in **segregated communities**. Most pupils attend segregated schools and have little contact with each other across the religious divide. GAA games are popular among Nationalists but not Unionists.

> Protestants migrated to Ulster in 1609 from Scotland and England. They were given land as part of the Ulster Plantation. The new settlers prospered. Their descendants are known as **Unionists** because they want to maintain **the union** with Britain and the British Crown.

> The native Catholic Irish were hostile to the Protestant settlers who now owned their land. Most of today's descendants of the native Irish are **Nationalist** in their politics. They want to break the link with Britain and become part of an independent and **united Ireland**.

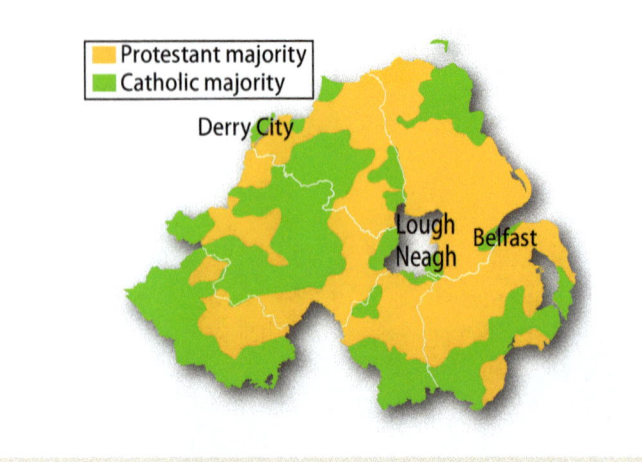

Figure 15.14 The distribution of religious groups in Northern Ireland

QUESTIONS

1. Name the six counties of Northern Ireland.
2. Why are Unionists so called?

ACTIVITY

Numeracy

How many centuries ago did Protestant settlers come to Ireland?

ACTIVITY

Skills

Examine Figure 15.14.

(i) Name the only county in Northern Ireland that is not adjoining Lough Neagh.

(ii) In which county is the city of Belfast located?

An Orange March in Rathfriland, Co. Down

Civil strife and power-sharing

After more than forty years of discrimination, Nationalists launched a civil rights campaign in the late 1960s. Almost thirty years of conflict between the two communities followed, called the Troubles, in which more than 3,000 people died. Today, following the **Good Friday Agreement** of 1998, power is shared between the two communities.

However, almost twenty years after the Good Friday Agreement, segregated communities still exist in Northern Ireland. Education is still largely segregated. Peter Robinson, former First Minister of Northern Ireland, has described the education system as a 'benign form of apartheid, which is fundamentally damaging to our society'.

Some integrated schools have been established where a small percentage of pupils from each community attend. It is hoped that these schools will help to build bridges across the divide in the future.

ACTIVITY

Research
Find out what the Orange Order commemorates on 12 July each year.

DEFINITION

Apartheid: Segregation of a group of people on the grounds of race or cultural differences.

QUESTION

What do you think *a benign form of apartheid* means?

GEOFACT

According to the Northern Education Department, 493 schools in the 2011–2012 school year educated almost exclusively pupils of just one religion, compared to 827 schools in 1997–1998.

CHAPTER 15 · THE CONCEPT OF A REGION

SOCIO-ECONOMIC REGIONS

Some regions are **more economically developed** than others. Reasons include fertile soils, favourable climates and natural resources such as minerals, fish and forests.

Socio-economic regions can be classified as follows:

> Core economic regions
> Peripheral regions
> Regions of industrial decline.

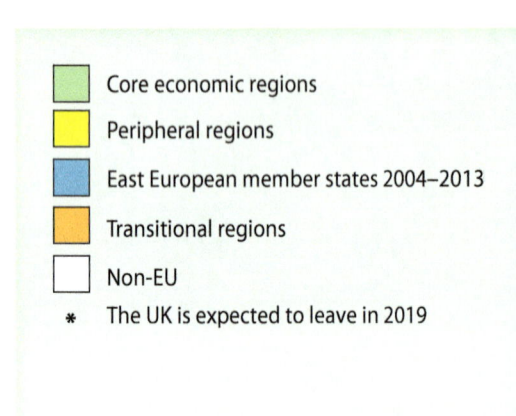

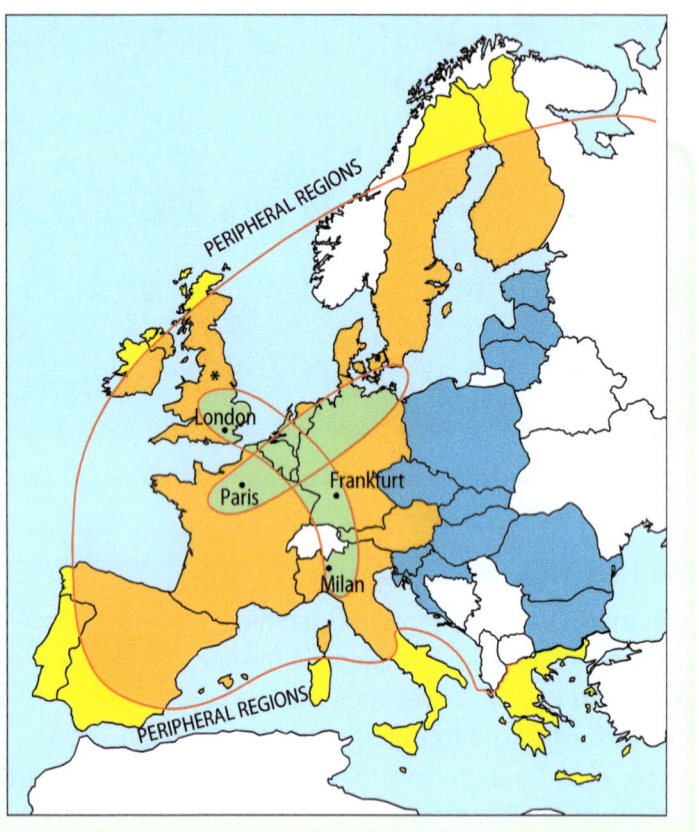

Legend:
- Core economic regions
- Peripheral regions
- East European member states 2004–2013
- Transitional regions
- Non-EU
- * The UK is expected to leave in 2019

Figure 15.15 A simplified map of the economic regions of the EU

Frankfurt's CBD is located in the EU economic core and is the location of the European Central Bank

Core regions

Core regions exist at both national and EU level. Dublin is Ireland's core region. Barcelona and Madrid are core regions in Spain. At the time of writing in the spring of 2017, the EU core region stretches from London to Milan and from Paris to Hamburg.

Characteristics of core regions

Good natural resources (soils, level terrain, favourable climate)
- Intensive agriculture with high output per hectare

Excellent communications
- Motorways that link the core region to distant markets
- Rail links converging on the core region
- International airports that provide the business community with connections to destinations abroad

High inward investment in manufacturing and service industries
- Advanced technologies in modern manufacturing, such as healthcare, pharmaceuticals, luxury goods and aerospace

Human resources
- Highly skilled and well-educated labour force
- Inward migration of young adults from surrounding regions and abroad
- A younger age profile in the population

High population density with a large local market
- Highly urbanised society, with more than 80% living in urban centres

Up to 80% of workers are in the tertiary sector
- Large numbers of office workers in banking, insurance and company headquarters
- Large media and advertising industries
- Highly educated researchers in new product development in the food industry, healthcare and computer technology

Figure 15.16 The physical, social and economic characteristics of economic core regions

Core regions are the **engines** that drive the economy of a country or indeed a region as large as the EU.

- The inhabitants of more developed regions have higher incomes than people in less developed regions.
- Core regions are more recession proof than peripheral regions.
- Unemployment is lower during recessions in core regions than in peripheral regions.
- Core regions recover from recessions more quickly than peripheral regions.

LINK

We will examine two core regions in depth: the **Dublin region** in Chapter 16 and the **Paris Basin** in Chapter 17.

Peripheral regions

Peripheral regions are located far from core regions. In Europe, they are found on the edges of the continent. Peripheral regions in the EU include the West of Ireland, the Highlands of Scotland, Northern Sweden and Northern Finland, the Mezzogiorno in Italy and Greece.

> **DEFINITION**
>
> **Peripheral regions:** These are regions that are located far from core economic regions. They are economically less developed than core regions.

A view of the Greek countryside, where productivity is low because of summer drought

Characteristics of peripheral regions

- Physical landscapes that have mountainous and difficult terrain make communication networks, such as road and rail, more difficult to build and maintain.
- Soils are often thin and infertile. Soils in mountainous areas may be eroded.
- The climate in peripheral regions is challenging. There are very long, cold winters in Northern Sweden. There is high rainfall and much cloud cover in the West of Ireland. There are summer droughts in Southern Spain, the Mezzogiorno and Greece.
- A high percentage of the workforce is found in the primary sector, such as farming, forestry and fishing.
- Peripheral regions have much less inward investment than core regions. Factory plants tend to be smaller than in core regions.
- During a recession, peripheral regions are more likely to see factory closures, as they are far from lucrative markets in the core regions.
- This leads to higher unemployment. Peripheral regions recover more slowly after a recession than core regions.
- Population densities are low, especially in rural areas. Outward migration of well-educated and ambitious young people causes a brain drain.

> **DEFINITION**
>
> **Brain drain:** The term used to describe the outward migration of young, well-educated and ambitious young people from an area because of the lack of opportunity there.

In the next two chapters, we will study **two peripheral regions** in detail:

› The Western region in Ireland (counties Mayo, Galway and Roscommon)
› The Mezzogiorno in Italy.

Eastern European regions

The Eastern European countries that have joined the EU since 2004 were Communist economies until 1991. They are located on the eastern periphery of the EU. Their economies are less developed than those of Western European countries.

The economies of these countries share many characteristics of peripheral regions of Western Europe. They have low personal incomes, high unemployment, high outward migration and a higher percentage of people in the primary sector, especially agriculture. They are also major recipients of EU funds.

Regions of industrial decline

The Industrial Revolution began around 1760. Factories quickly became anchored to the coalfield regions of Europe. Coal was the energy source that powered the steel mills. In addition, coal was used to power the steam engines that provided energy for the textile factories.

From that time until about 1960, these regions experienced an economic boom. Coal production, steel making and textiles were the **three pillars** of these regions. The First World War and Second World War fought in Europe and elsewhere in the first half of the twentieth century led to increased demand for the products of these regions.

ACTIVITY

Skills

Examine Figure 15.18. What country is Lorraine in?

LINK

See Figure 19.2 on page 378 for the names of the EU member states.

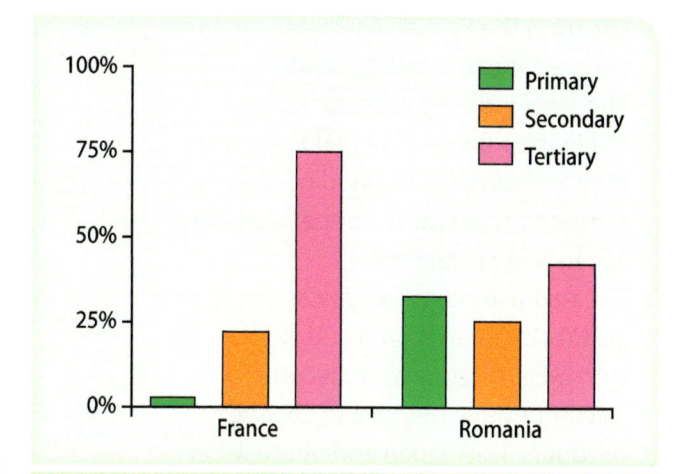

Figure 15.17 Economic sectors in France, one of the EU's wealthiest countries, and Romania, the EU's poorest country in terms of income per head

ACTIVITY

Numeracy

Examine Figure 15.17.

(i) What percentage of French workers are in the tertiary sector?
(ii) What percentage of Romanian workers are in the secondary sector?

Figure 15.18 The great industrial centres of the nineteenth and early twentieth centuries have experienced industrial decline in recent decades. These regions, such as the heavy industry triangle of Europe, have faced many plant closures and redundancies.

CHAPTER 15 · THE CONCEPT OF A REGION 243

Industrial decline

By 1960, the economic prime of these regions was over due to the following factors:

> The best coal seams in these regions were exhausted. Steel producers in Britain and the heavy industrial triangle of Europe began to buy cheaper coal from Poland and the USA. Oil and natural gas from the Persian Gulf were beginning to replace coal as a cheaper, cleaner energy source.
> The steel industry in South Wales, the Franco-Belgian coalfields and the Ruhr in Germany declined because of outdated plants and competition from Japan and South Korea.
> The textile industry in Lancashire and Yorkshire in Britain and Nord in North-East France were becoming uncompetitive because of cheaper products from Japan and South Korea.

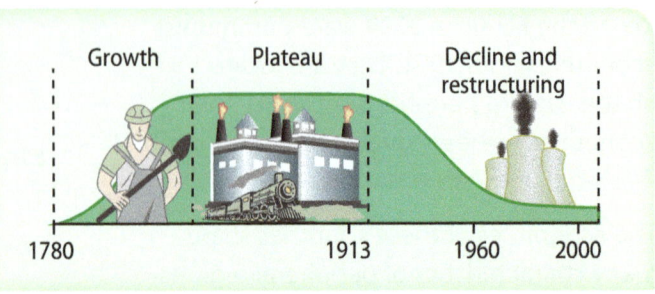

Figure 15.19 The fortunes of the coal industry over time in Europe

These rapid changes had many consequences in these regions.

> Hundreds of thousands of workers lost their jobs in Britain and in the heavy industrial triangle of Europe.
> The steel industry moved to the coast of Europe. This was a lower-cost location for the importation of coal and iron ore from abroad.

An abandoned steel mill in Dortmund, the Ruhr, Germany. Can you explain why sites such as this are often referred to as a rust belt?

ACTIVITY

Numeracy

Examine Figure 15.19. The plateau phase of the coal industry in Europe spanned what entire century?

DEFINITION

Microcosm: The literal meaning is 'small world'. Microcosm means a smaller representation of something.

GEOFACT

Industrial decline occurred in Cork city with the departure of Ford and Dunlop during the recession of the 1980s.

Recovery

In recent decades, these regions have begun to recover from the aftershocks of industrial decline. Government and EU aid have improved communications and modernised their economies.

Nord in North-East France is a microcosm of the economic redevelopment of these regions.

CASE STUDY

Industrial decline in Nord

Nord is located in North-East France. It has a population of more than 4.5 million people. Its economy was based on its coalfields, steel mills and textile factories. From 1960 onwards, the industrial economy of Nord was in decline because its coalfields were almost exhausted. Its steel and textile mills in Lille were also declining because of competition from countries in the Far East, such as Japan.

Consequences of decline

> By 1998, unemployment was as high as 16%.
> Outward migration had robbed the region of its young adults.
> The region became a rust belt, with slag heaps from the coalfields and decaying steel mills and factories scarring the landscape.

DEFINITION

Rust belt: A region that is experiencing industrial decline, with unattractive rusting plants and machinery scarring the landscape.

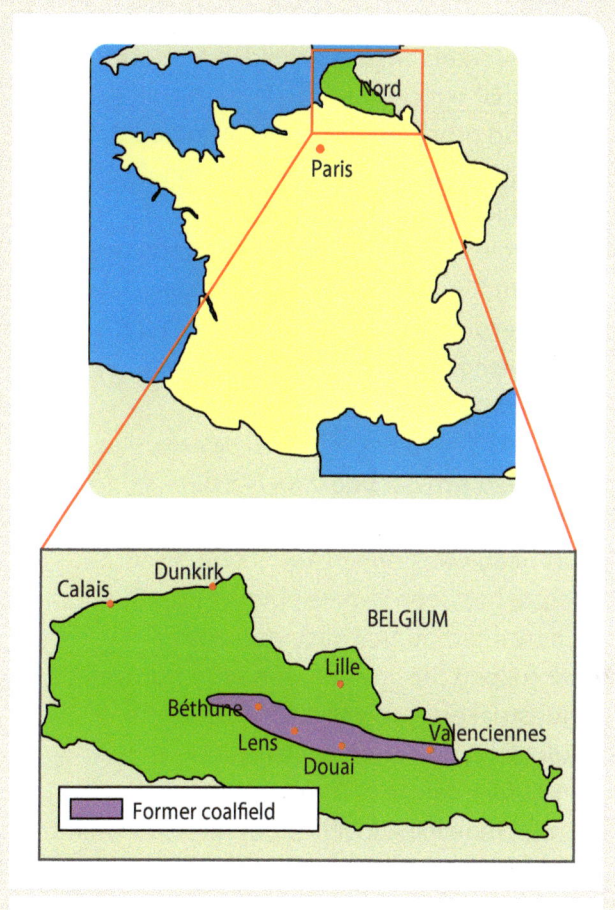

Figure 15.20 Nord's economy grew in the nineteenth century because of its coal resources

These large slag heaps in Nord are residues from the region's coalmining past

CHAPTER 15 · THE CONCEPT OF A REGION   245

The redevelopment of Nord

The French government has responded vigorously to the decline of the Nord economy in the following ways:

- Many workers were retrained in modern industrial skills.
- Lille and other urban centres attracted modern healthcare and information technology industries.
- The region was connected by motorway to Paris and Brussels.
- Lille became a **railway hub** for the **TGV** (high-speed train). The city is centrally located between London, Paris and Brussels. The Channel Tunnel has also provided a major boost for Nord.
- Lille, the major urban centre of the region, has been transformed and modernised. Its centre has been redeveloped as **Euralille**, a new international business centre. This has helped the city to move away from an industrial economy to a services centre. Euralille is now the third largest business and office centre in France.
- Urban renewal and redevelopment are taking place in other cities too. For instance, **the city** of **Arras** has also been transformed. Because of the decline in its textile industries, it was known as '**the sleeping beauty**' up until 1990. Today, thanks to the motorway and the TGV, it is an important tourist centre with many British tourists coming through the Channel Tunnel to admire its **outstanding medieval centre** and enjoy some shopping.

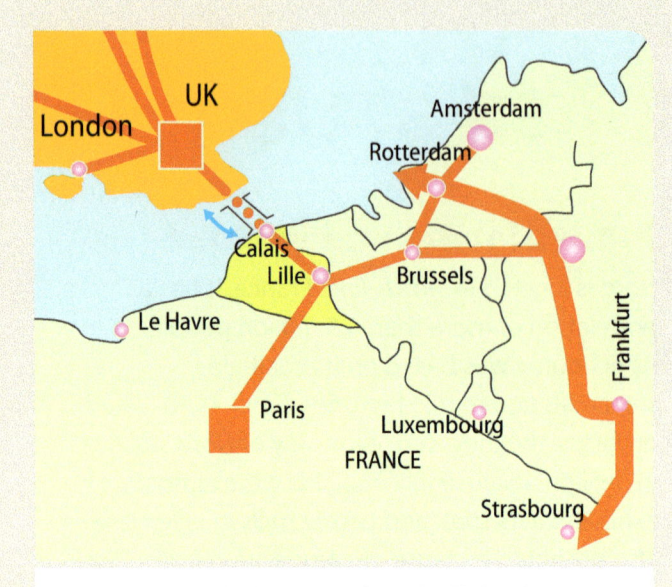

Figure 15.21 The location of Nord. Lille has become an intercity rail hub between London, Paris, Brussels and the Rhineland cities.

ACTIVITY

Thinking

Examine Figure 15.21. How has Lille taken advantage of its geographic location?

ACTIVITY

Research

Look up why tourists are drawn to the city of Arras on the internet.

Euralille, a major urban redevelopment programme, has transformed the city centre of Lille

URBAN REGIONS

Urban regions are important areas today because most people in Europe and elsewhere live in cities. Over the next three chapters, we will study the urban regions of **Dublin**, **Paris**, **Naples** in Southern Italy and **São Paulo** in Brazil.

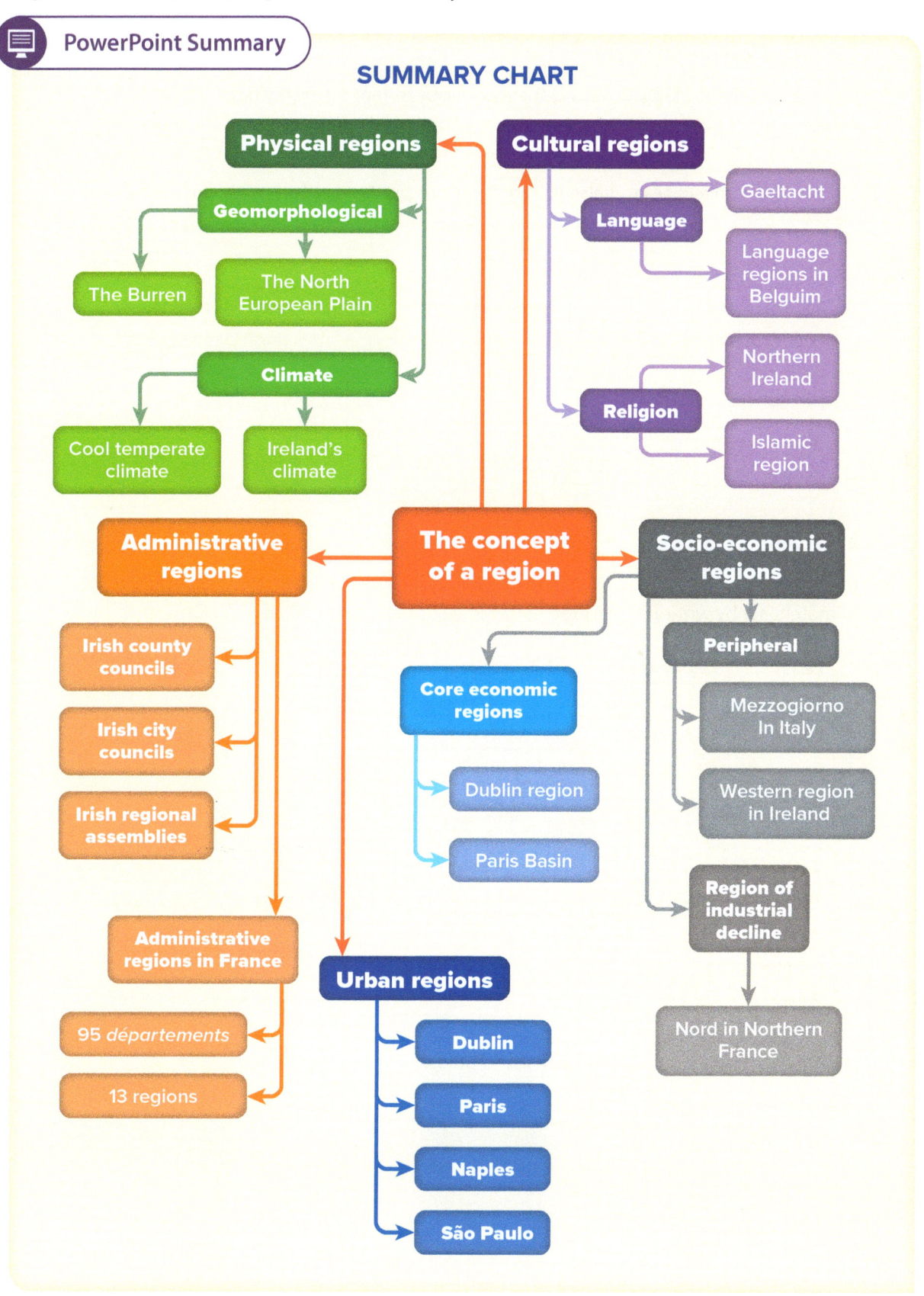

PowerPoint Summary

SUMMARY CHART

The concept of a region

- **Physical regions**
  - Geomorphological
    - The Burren
    - The North European Plain
  - Climate
    - Cool temperate climate
    - Ireland's climate

- **Cultural regions**
  - Language
    - Gaeltacht
    - Language regions in Belgium
  - Religion
    - Northern Ireland
    - Islamic region

- **Administrative regions**
  - Irish county councils
  - Irish city councils
  - Irish regional assemblies
  - Administrative regions in France
    - 95 départements
    - 13 regions

- **Core economic regions**
  - Dublin region
  - Paris Basin

- **Socio-economic regions**
  - Peripheral
    - Mezzogiorno In Italy
    - Western region in Ireland
  - Region of industrial decline
    - Nord in Northern France

- **Urban regions**
  - Dublin
  - Paris
  - Naples
  - São Paulo

UNIT 2 · REGIONAL GEOGRAPHY

CHAPTER 15 · THE CONCEPT OF A REGION 247

Leaving Cert exam questions

SHORT QUESTIONS: HIGHER LEVEL

1 Regions (8 marks)

The table below contains information on regions regarding their type, specific example and general location.

Complete the table by inserting the most appropriate terms from the list below in their correct position in the table. One row of the table is completed for you.

> Mediterranean   Ireland   ~~Paris Basin~~   Basque Lands   Berlin   Northern Spain
> Southern Europe   ~~North European Plain~~   Germany   County Meath

Type of region	Specific example	General location
Geomorphological	Paris Basin	North European Plain
Urban		
Climate		
Administrative		
Cultural		

2 Regions (8 marks)

(i) Examine the table below. Match the region type with the example in Europe that best matches it by writing the correct letter in each case in the space provided.

Letter	Region type
A	Climatic region
B	Urban capital
C	Geomorphological region
D	Language region

Example in Europe	Letter
The Central Plain of Ireland	
Wallonia	
Mediterranean	
Berlin	

(ii) Briefly define each type of region listed below:

(a) Peripheral region

(b) Administrative region

SHORT QUESTIONS: ORDINARY LEVEL

1 Regions (10 marks)

Match the description of a region with the example of the region most associated with it by writing the correct letter in each case in the table below.

Letter	Description of region
A	A climatic region
B	A region defined by language
C	A core region
D	A peripheral region
E	A region defined by religion

Example of region	Letter
The Gaeltacht	
Mezzogiorno, Southern Italy	
Islamic world	
Greater Dublin area	
Cool temperate oceanic	

2 Regions (10 marks)

Match the description of a region with the example most associated with it by writing the correct letter in each case in the table below.

Letter	Description of region
A	Region of industrial decline
B	Peripheral region
C	Climatic region
D	Administrative region in Ireland
E	Urban region

Example of region	Letter
Fingal County Council	
Paris	
Sambre Meuse	
Mezzogiorno, Southern Italy	
The Mediterranean	

3 Weather statistics (10 marks)

Mean monthly temperature and monthly rainfall at Shannon Airport, 2014

	Jan	Feb	Mar	Apr	May	June	July	Aug	Sept	Oct	Nov	Dec
Mean temp (°C)	6.0	6.1	7.7	10.9	12.1	15.2	17.1	14.9	15.2	11.8	8.1	6.7
Rainfall (mm)	176	195	87	38	90	41	36	90	72	105	129	110

(i) What was the highest mean monthly temperature (°C) at Shannon Airport in 2014?

(ii) In how many months were the mean temperatures greater than 10°C?

(iii) What was the annual mean temperature (°C) at Shannon Airport in 2014?

(iv) In which month was the highest level of rainfall?

(v) What was the total rainfall (mm) for June, July and August combined?

LONG QUESTIONS: HIGHER LEVEL

1 Concept of a region (30 marks)

'A region is an area on the Earth's surface which can be defined by one or more criteria.' Explain this statement with reference to example(s) that you have studied.

2 Concept of a region (30 marks)

Examine how culture **or** the physical landscape can be used to define regions, with reference to examples that you have studied.

3 Industrial decline (30 marks)

Examine the causes and impacts of industrial decline with reference to any region(s) that you have studied.

4 Concept of a region (30 marks)

Examine how socio-economic factors can be used to define regions, with reference to examples that you have studied.

LONG QUESTIONS: ORDINARY LEVEL

1 Types of regions (40 marks)

There are many types of regions on the Earth's surface. These include:

- Climatic regions
- Peripheral regions
- Core regions
- Urban regions.

(i) Give a named example of any **two** of the regions listed above.

(ii) Select any **one** of the regions above and explain **one** problem faced by that region. Clearly state the name of the region in your answer.

2 Regions and culture (30 marks)

The culture of a region can often be determined by religion, language, music and games. Describe and explain the importance of culture in any region that you have studied.

Chapter 16
The Dynamics of Regions 1

UNIT 2 · REGIONAL GEOGRAPHY

KEYWORDS

- tillage farming
- pastoral farming
- market gardening
- rough grazing
- aquaculture
- modern growth industries
- medical devices
- life sciences
- resource materials
- roll-on roll-off ferries
- tariff-free access
- public transport
- financial services
- IFSC
- Atlantic Corridor
- Western Railway Corridor
- Wild Atlantic Way
- human processes
- population dynamics
- inward migration
- nodal point
- urban regeneration

LEARNING OBJECTIVES

By the end of this chapter, you should be able to understand:

- How to locate two contrasting Irish regions
- How to identify the physical characteristics of each region
- How to discuss the primary, secondary and tertiary economic activities of each region
- How to examine some of the human processes of the region, such as population dynamics and urban development.

The Dublin and Western regions

The study of regions shows how physical, economic and human processes interact in a particular region.

In this chapter, two contrasting regions are examined: the Dublin region (a core region) and the Western region (a peripheral region).

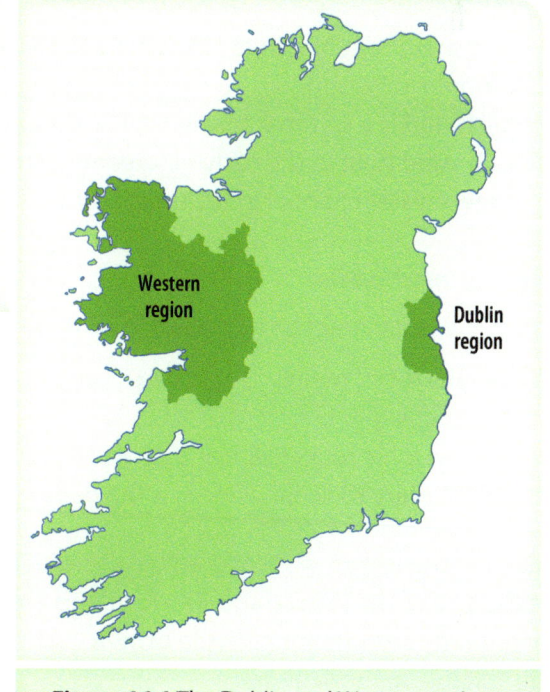

Figure 16.1 The Dublin and Western regions

CHAPTER 16 · THE DYNAMICS OF REGIONS 1   251

THE DUBLIN REGION: A CORE IRISH REGION

For our purposes, the Dublin region is the area within Co. Dublin. It is largely an urban region.

According to the preliminary 2016 census results, the Dublin region accounts for 28.3% of the population but only 1.3% of the area of the Republic. Dublin is the economic engine of the economy of the Republic and the political and administrative capital of Ireland. The region has many strengths, but it also faces several challenges.

Physical processes

North of the Dublin Mountains, the relief of the Dublin region is made up of lowlands. The area is drained by the rivers Liffey, Tolka and Dodder.

The coast experiences some erosion, for instance at Howth Head and the Dalkey area. However, deposition is more important in shaping the coast. Many features of deposition are found on the coast, including beaches, a tombolo, spits and bars.

Longshore drift is operating along the coast.

> Longshore drift has linked Howth Head to the coast by a tombolo at Sutton.
> Bull Island is a spit that formed in Dublin Bay after the bull walls were built in the early nineteenth century to maintain a deep-water channel into Dublin Port.

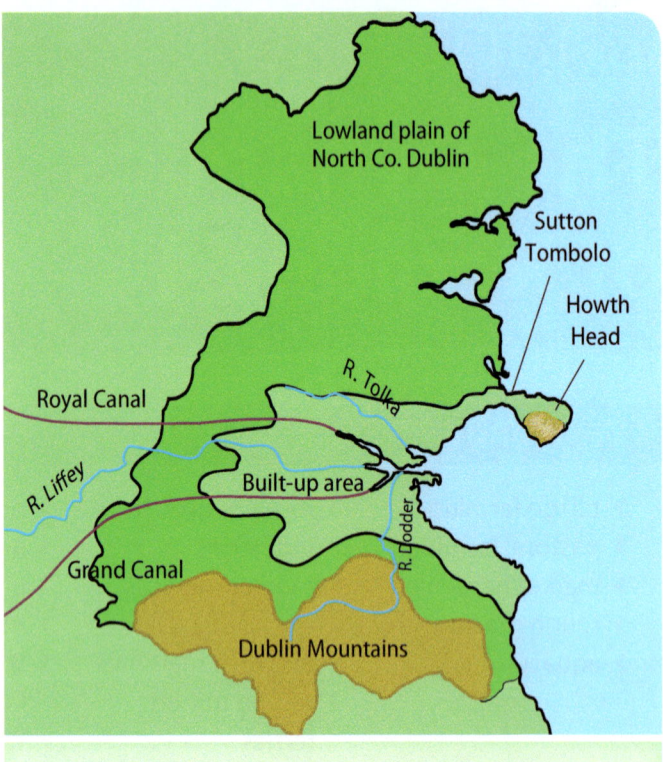

Figure 16.2 Physical features of the Dublin region

ACTIVITY

Skills

Examine Figure 16.2. Name one example of marine deposition on the coast.

Rocks and soils

There are three main rock types in the Dublin region.

> Igneous rocks, mainly granite, are found in the Dublin Mountains.
> Metamorphic rocks (slate and quartzite) are found in Howth.
> Sedimentary rock (limestone) is the bedrock of the lowlands.

Much of the region was covered by glacial deposition at the end of the last ice age. The lowlands are covered by free-draining, fertile **brown earths** that are suitable for agriculture.

GEOFACTS

> Brown earths developed under deciduous tree cover over a long period.
> The Dublin region experiences almost 1,500 hours of sunshine per year.

Climate

The climate of the region is cool temperate oceanic. However, apart from the Dublin Mountains, which attract relief rain, the region is the driest in Ireland, with 733 mm of rainfall per year. This is because the region is on Ireland's east coast. Atlantic depressions have lost much of their moisture by the time they reach the east coast. Dublin is also sunnier than the west coast. Average temperatures range from 5°C in January to 15.1°C in July.

MONTHLY PRECIPITATION AND TEMPERATURES FOR DUBLIN AIRPORT													
	Jan	Feb	Mar	Apr	May	June	July	Aug	Sept	Oct	Nov	Dec	Total
Precipitation (mm)	70	50	54	51	55	56	50	71	66	70	64	76	733
Temperature (°C)	5.0	5.0	6.3	7.9	10.5	13.4	15.1	14.9	13.1	10.6	7.0	5.9	–

Table 16.1 Climatic chart for Dublin Airport (74 metres above sea level)

Primary economic activities

Agriculture

While many farms have been lost to the expansion of urban areas in Dublin in recent decades, farming is nevertheless still important in Co. Dublin today. Co. Dublin's farms are the biggest in the country, with an average size of 47.6 hectares. This is twice the size of the typical farm in counties Mayo and Monaghan.

Tillage farming

Co. Dublin farms are very productive. A high proportion of the land is devoted to tillage crops, such as wheat, barley and potatoes. In fact, 11% of the wheat crop and 15% of the potato crop of the Republic are grown in Co. Dublin.

The flat, undulating landscape that is found west and north of the capital makes the land suitable for machinery. The **brown earth soils** are ideal for tillage. As the region has the lowest rainfall in Ireland, cereal crops ripen in late summer.

Pastoral farming

More than one-third of the farmland of Co. Dublin is under pasture. The pastoral farms of Co. Dublin support 8,000 cattle and 19,000 sheep.

DEFINITION

Pastoral farming involves the production of livestock, such as cattle and sheep, rather than growing crops.

ACTIVITY

Numeracy

Examine Table 16.1.

(i) Name the driest months in Dublin.

(ii) What is the difference between the temperature of January and July?

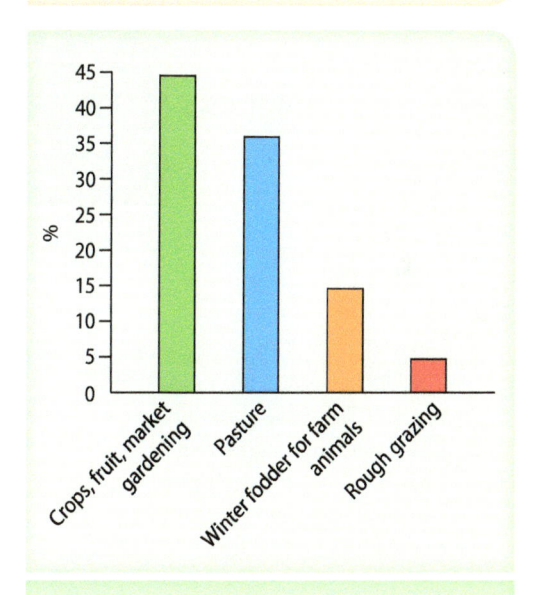

Figure 16.3 Agricultural land use in the Dublin region

ACTIVITY

Numeracy

Examine Figure 16.3. What percentage of the agricultural land in the Dublin region is used for pasture and rough grazing combined?

A high proportion of the cattle are dairy cows. Their milk is bottled for the daily needs of the capital. Cattle graze outdoors during the summer months. They are taken off the land in late autumn and fed indoors on silage and other cattle feeds during the winter.

Sheep are fattened for the mutton needs of the nearby urban market. Rough grazing of mountain sheep is confined to the Dublin Mountains in the south.

Market gardening

North Co. Dublin has the highest concentration of market gardening in the state. **Specialist farms** with potato, fruit, vegetable and flower production are found here. Many early vegetables such as lettuce, spring onions and cucumbers are grown under glass or tunnels. These are high-yielding and high-value crops. Market gardens are labour intensive. Many farmers work in the area.

Market gardening is an example of an economic activity where physical, economic and human processes combine to create a profitable activity.

> **ACTIVITY**
>
> **Thinking**
>
> Can you explain why the agricultural land use of the Dublin Mountains is rough grazing?

> **DEFINITION**
>
> **Market gardening**, also known as horticulture, is defined as the science of growing fruits, vegetables and flowers.

Fresh lettuce in a greenhouse in the horticultural area

- The Dublin region has longer hours of sunshine and much lower rainfall than the West of Ireland. This creates better growing conditions and reduces the risk of potato blight.

- North Dublin farmers have a tradition of market gardening. They have the skills and knowledge to pursue this specialist farming activity.

- The cost of farmland close to the capital is very high. Farming is therefore intensive, with high yields and high costs per hectare.

- Dublin's growing market of 1,345,402 people is located close to the market gardening area. Perishable vegetables and cut flowers are in the shops within a short time.

- The trading areas for market gardening produce from North Dublin have expanded into the provinces. Motorways, such as the M50, have brought urban centres in the provinces within easy reach.

Market gardening in North Dublin

Figure 16.4 Factors that encourage market gardening in North Dublin

Fishing

The sea fishing industry has a long tradition in the communities of North Dublin, such as Balbriggan, Skerries, Rush and Howth.

The conditions necessary for a successful fishing industry exist off Dublin's coast.

> The Irish Sea is part of the continental shelf. Plankton, the beginning of the fish food chain, is found there. This encourages the presence of fish.
> The large urban population of Dublin provides a market for fish, which are landed in Howth and Skerries.

The catch is mainly composed of demersal fish, such as cod, whiting, hake and plaice. Shellfish, such as prawns and shrimp, are also caught.

However, the fishing industry in the Dublin region is in decline. The fishing economy in the Dublin area boomed in the 1970s and early 1980s. This was because of the lucrative **herring fishing industry** in the Celtic Sea, off the south-east coast of Ireland. But the boom is over. There are no boats in the Irish Sea operating from Skerries or Howth fishing for herring. They are now confined to fishing for white fish and prawns, many of which are also overfished and subject to quotas.

Overfishing has long been a problem and is a threat to future stocks. EU laws have imposed restrictions on the industry in the Irish Sea and elsewhere in order to conserve stocks.

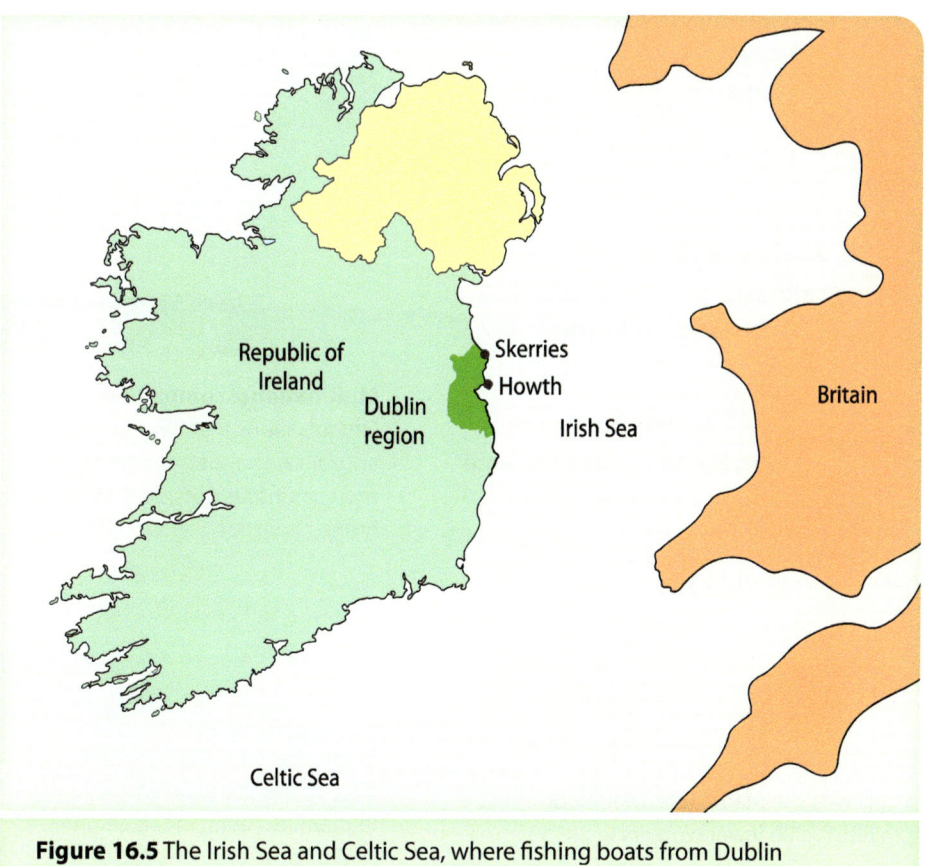

Figure 16.5 The Irish Sea and Celtic Sea, where fishing boats from Dublin can be found

Secondary economic activities

Manufacturing

The Dublin region is the largest single manufacturing centre in the Republic. **One-quarter** of all the manufacturing plants in the country are in this region.

Types of manufacturing in the Dublin region

Consumer industries

Food processing, baking and confectionery, beverages, printing and clothing are important because of the requirements of the large local market.

Food processing and beverages provide many jobs in the Dublin manufacturing sector today. For instance, the brewing of Guinness takes place in St James's Gate in the centre of Dublin. The **Irish Distillers Pernod Ricard** bottling plant is in Clondalkin. Many famous whiskey brands, including Jameson, Powers and Paddy, are bottled here. **Baileys Irish Cream** is manufactured in Clondalkin and employs 235 people.

Light industries

Many light industry companies are involved in the production of:

- Sports and fitness equipment
- Clothing and fashion
- Plastics
- Metal fabrication
- Health monitoring and testing equipment
- Water softening and filtering systems
- Household goods.

Modern growth industries

In recent times, the best performers in terms of employment and exports are healthcare, pharmaceuticals, information and communication technology (ICT) and electronic engineering industries.

The Industrial Development Authority (IDA) has been very successful in encouraging **multinational companies** to come to Ireland. The Dublin region is home to many multinationals, such as Pfizer (Clondalkin) in the pharmaceutical sector and IBM (Mulhuddart) in the computer industry.

> **DEFINITION**
>
> **Multinational companies:** Organisations that have plants and/or sales outlets in one or more countries outside their home countries.

> **ACTIVITY**
>
> **Thinking**
> Can you suggest two reasons why the manufacturing sector in the Dublin region employed 10,000 fewer workers in 2016 than in 2007?

> **GEOFACT**
>
> In the second quarter of 2016, **53,700 people** were employed in manufacturing in the Dublin region, down from 63,000 in the first quarter of 2007. (Source: CSO)

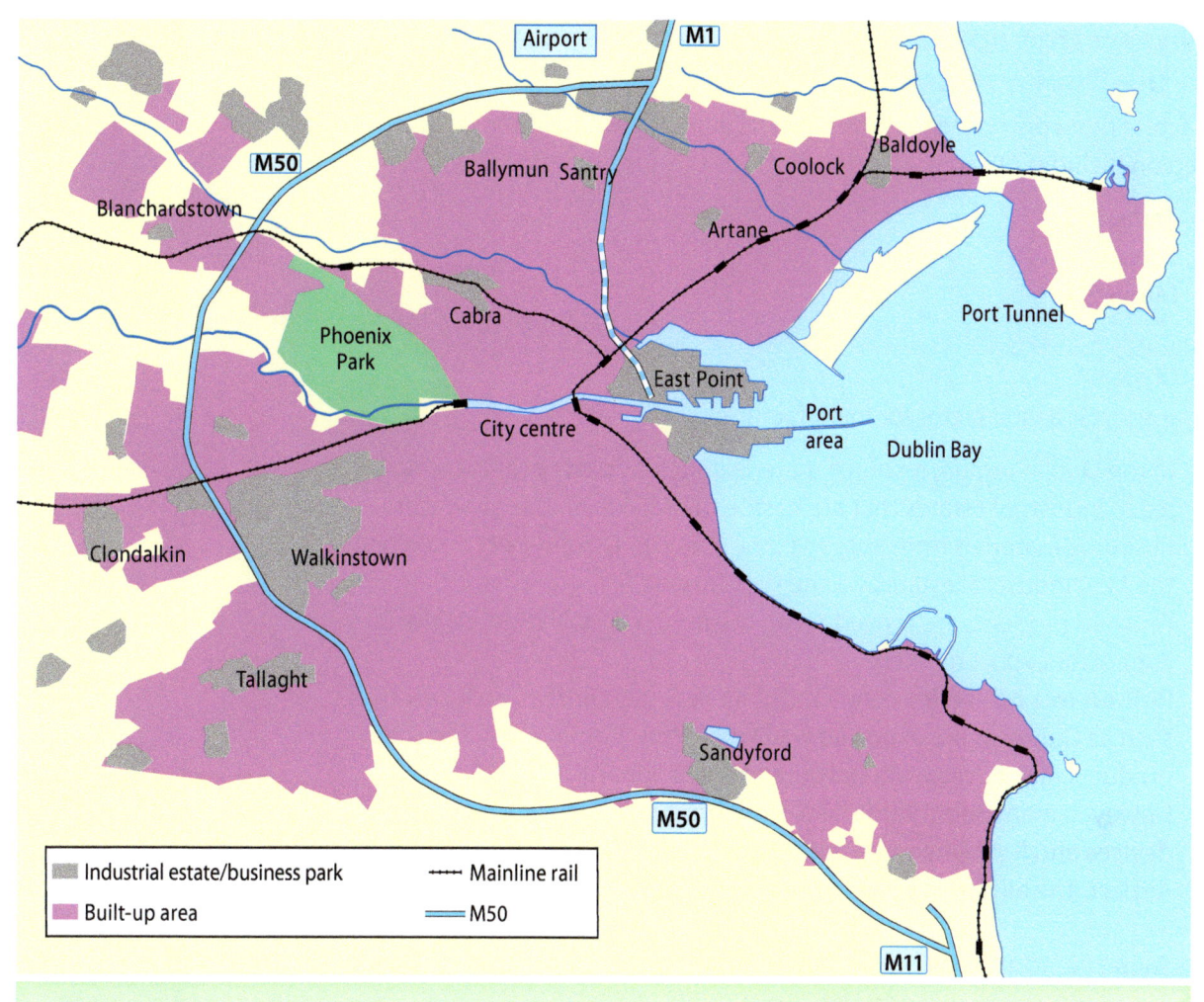

Figure 16.6 The distribution of manufacturing in the Dublin region. The M50 has become a magnet for manufacturing.

Distribution of manufacturing plants

In the past, manufacturing plants such as brewing and biscuit making were located within the city of Dublin, close to where the workers lived.

In recent decades, development agencies such as the IDA and Enterprise Ireland established industrial estates and business parks on the perimeter of the city. These locations offer several advantages to industrialists:

› Land is cheaper here and sites are bigger than in the city.
› Workers live in nearby suburbs and new towns.
› Transport networks are far less congested than in city centre sites.

These industrial estates have attracted many Irish and foreign companies over the years.

ACTIVITY

Skills

Examine Figure 16.6.

(i) Name the ring road that is located on the perimeter of the city of Dublin.

(ii) Can you identify two advantages that proximity to this ring road provides for manufacturers?

ACTIVITY

Skills

Find the location of Walkinstown and Clondalkin in Figure 16.6.

Factors that account for the success of manufacturing in the Dublin region

Factors that contribute to the success of manufacturing in the Dublin region include:

> Transport
> Labour
> Markets.

Transport

Transport is a vital factor for manufacturers.

> In the Dublin region, resource materials such as **barley** for brewing reach industrial estates that are beside the M50 from the provinces. Resource materials from abroad come through **Dublin Port** and reach the M50 industrial estates via the Port Tunnel.
> Finished products are moved along the M50 to Dublin Port via the Port Tunnel for export markets.
> **Roll-on roll-off ferries** connect Dublin Port with Britain. Bulky products such as Guinness are exported via Dublin Port. Containers of finished products reach Britain via Holyhead and Fishguard.
> However, many **high-value**, **low-bulk** products, such as medical devices and light pharmaceuticals, are exported by air from Dublin Airport. The airport is also next to to the M50 in North Dublin.

Labour

A **large labour pool** exists in Dublin for the following reasons:

> Dublin has always been the recipient of inward migrants from the provinces of Ireland because of the opportunities that the city offers.
> The population structure has a greater percentage of people in their twenties and thirties than other Irish regions because of inward migration of young adults.
> Many highly skilled migrants came from the UK, EU and South Asia to fill job requirements in the Dublin economy. After the EU eastwards expansion in 2004, many young Eastern Europeans also came to Dublin.

An industrial estate in Walkinstown with a large number of manufacturing companies. The site here is flat and spacious. Land is cheaper here than in the city centre.

GEOFACT

Pfizer employs 3,300 people across seven sites in Cork, Dublin, Kildare and Sligo.

Pfizer Biotechnology in Clondalkin is located on a greenfield site. It is one of the largest plants in the Dublin region.

The quality of labour in the Dublin region is also high. Ireland has the highest proportion of young people who have successfully completed third-level education in the EU, according to Eurostat. In Ireland, **51.1% of 30–34-year-olds** have completed third level, closely followed by Cyprus, Luxembourg and Lithuania. In addition, Ireland has now gone **below the 10% rate for early school leavers**.

Universities and other third-level colleges in the Dublin region, including Trinity, UCD, DCU, DIT and NCAD, offer a wide variety of courses that prepare young people for the workplace.

DEFINITIONS

Eurostat: Eurostat is the statistical office of the EU and is based in Luxembourg. Eurostat provides statistics on a great number of economic and social sectors of the EU.

Life sciences: The science concerned with the study of living organisms in areas such as biology, microbiology and biochemistry.

Research and development (R&D) consists of investigative activities that a business pursues to develop new products or procedures.

Factors that contribute to the success of manufacturing in the Dublin region

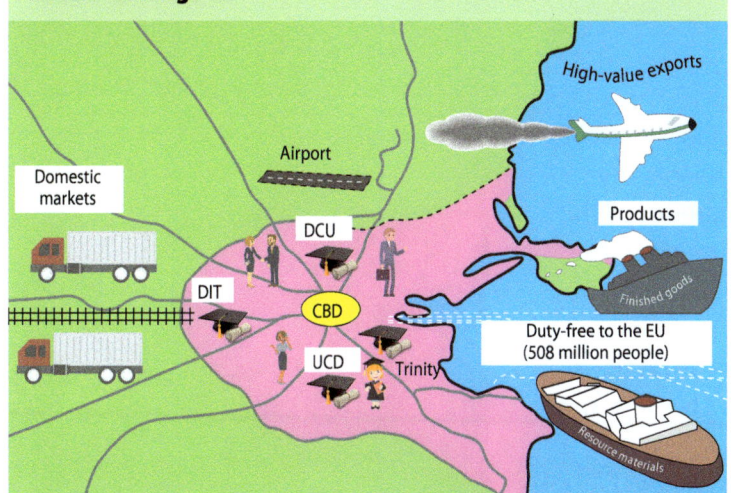

Figure 16.7 Transport, an educated labour force and EU markets are important factors in the success of manufacturing in the Dublin region

CHAPTER 16 · THE DYNAMICS OF REGIONS 1

UNIT 2 · REGIONAL GEOGRAPHY

Markets

- Dublin's manufacturers have good access to markets. The motorway network gives Dublin manufacturers access to provincial urban centres in Ireland.
- However, the Irish market, while significant, is less than 5 million people, which is **less than 1% of the EU market**. Dublin-based manufacturers who want to expand must target the export market.
- Ireland, as an EU member, has **tariff-free access** to the EU, one of the world's largest and wealthiest markets. The EU had a population of **508 million people** in 2016, including 65 million people in the UK. Along with a low corporation tax rate of 12.5%, tariff-free access to EU markets is one of the main reasons why multinationals choose Ireland as a manufacturing base.
- EU markets, especially those in the core regions of the EU, are among the wealthiest markets in the world. High-value products from the Dublin region, such as liqueurs and healthcare products, are in demand in those regions.
- Over many decades, Dublin manufacturers have established links with buyers in Britain and the EU. In this way, manufacturers build up **brand loyalty** among their customers.
- Dublin's food processing, clothing, chemical and engineering companies export goods to the EU either through Britain or directly via Rosslare to France and onwards to EU destinations.

Tertiary economic activities

The tertiary sector is very important in the Dublin region because four out of every five workers are employed in this sector. All branches of the tertiary sector are evident in the Dublin region. We will examine three of these:

- Tourist services
- Transport services
- Financial services.

Tourism

Tourism is a crucial sector of Dublin's economy, as over 7% of the workforce is employed in the hospitality sector. Dublin has the highest tourist figures of all the Irish regions by far, with 60% of tourist arrivals to the Republic from overseas – more than 5 million people – spending at least one night in Dublin. The great majority of Ireland's most popular tourist attractions are in Dublin. Only the Cliffs of Moher in Co. Clare and Doneraile Wildlife Park in Co. Cork rival Dublin's top attractions.

> **ACTIVITY**
>
> **Thinking**
>
> Can you explain the meaning of the term *brand loyalty*?

> **HINT**
>
> Three examples of tertiary activities are examined: tourism, transport and financial services. You should be familiar with **two** of these.

> **QUESTION**
>
> The Cliffs of Moher are located in which Irish county?

O'Connell Street, Dublin, with the GPO, the Spire and a statue of James Larkin, the trade union leader

The top five fee-charging attractions in 2015

Attraction	Visitors (Thousands)	% change from 2014
Guinness Storehouse	~1,450	+18%
Cliffs of Moher Visitor Experience	~1,250	+16%
Dublin Zoo	~1,100	+2.6%
National Aquatic Centre	~1,000	−6.5%
Book of Kells	~750	+18%

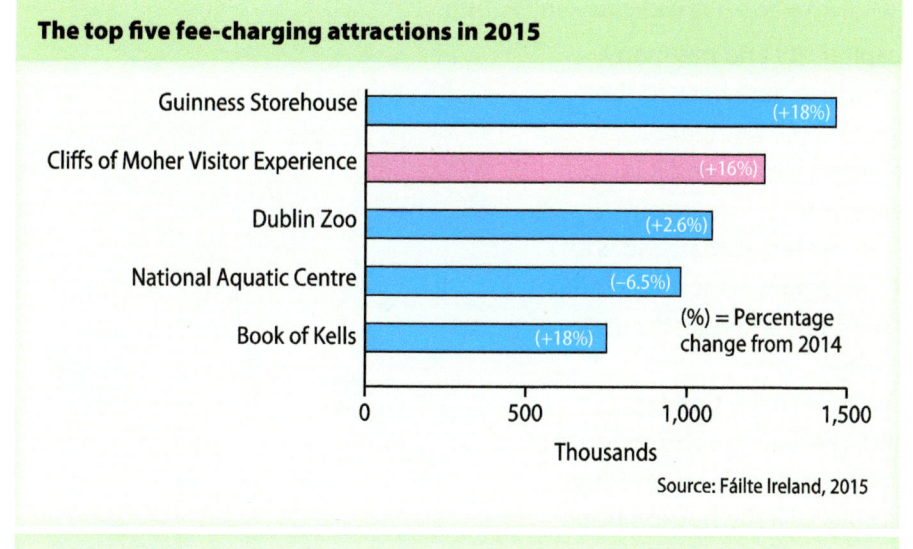

(%) = Percentage change from 2014

Source: Fáilte Ireland, 2015

Figure 16.8 Dublin was home to four of the top five fee-charging tourist attractions in 2015

ACTIVITY

Research

(i) Look up what is in the National Gallery of Ireland on the internet.

(ii) Look up where the National Botanic Gardens are located on the internet.

The top five free attractions in 2015

Attraction	Visitors (Thousands)	% change from 2014
The National Gallery of Ireland	~725	+21%
National Botanic Gardens	~550	+2%
Irish Museum of Modern Art	~475	+58%
National Museum of Ireland (Archaeology, Kildare St)	~460	+2%
Doneraile Wildlife Park, Cork	~440	−6%

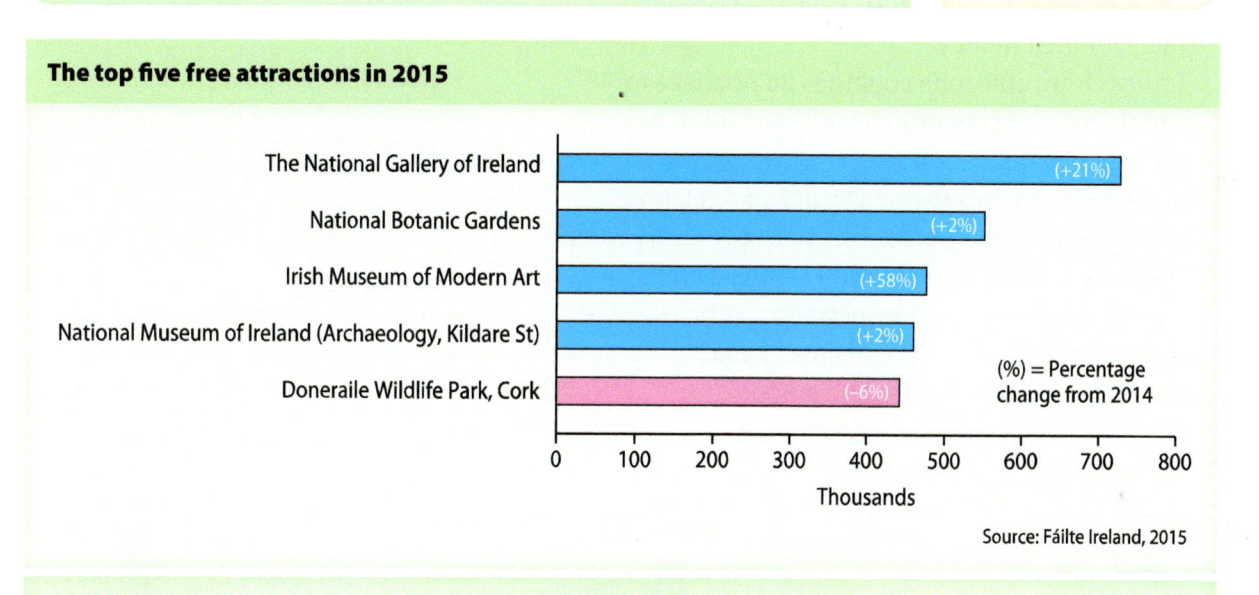

(%) = Percentage change from 2014

Source: Fáilte Ireland, 2015

Figure 16.9 Dublin was home to four of the top five free tourist attractions in 2015

Grafton Street in Dublin's city centre is one of the most important shopping streets in Ireland

GEOFACT

In 2016, 112 cruise liners, carrying tens of thousands of passengers, were booked to visit Dublin Port. (Source: Dublin Port Company)

CHAPTER 16 · THE DYNAMICS OF REGIONS 1

Factors that encourage a strong tourist industry in Dublin

- Dublin is the Republic's capital city and has many historic buildings, some of which date back to the Middle Ages, such as Christ Church Cathedral.
- Dublin has the country's largest airport and it is relatively close to the city centre.
- The city is extremely well-marketed abroad and is an accessible city for tourists who want a short city break.
- Dublin has a wide range of hotels and guesthouses that cater for every price range.
- Most tourist attractions, such as Trinity College (home to the Book of Kells), the Guinness Storehouse and the National Museum, are in or close to the city centre. They are easily accessed via the hop-on hop-off buses that tour the city many times every day.
- The strength of the US dollar against the euro since 2009 has given tourists from the USA good value for their money.
- Tourists from eurozone countries do not have to pay charges for currency conversions when they come to Ireland.
- Budget airlines, including Ryanair and Aer Lingus, bring great numbers of tourists to Dublin every week.
- Dublin is an important sporting centre, with international rugby and association football matches taking place several times a year.
- Dublin is a popular destination among domestic tourists who come to Dublin for shopping, sightseeing, family visits to Dublin Zoo and sporting fixtures, including GAA games in Croke Park.

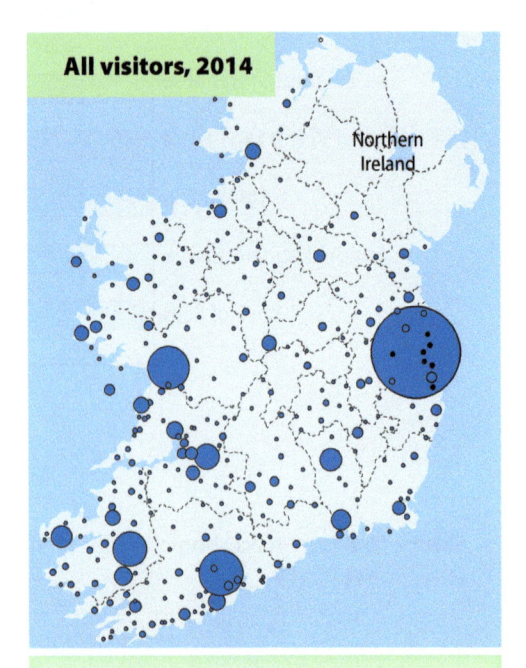

Figure 16.10 Dublin was by far the most popular destination for tourists who visited Ireland in 2014

ACTIVITY

Thinking
Examine Figure 16.10. Can you explain three reasons why far fewer incoming tourists visit centres outside Dublin?

Transport in the Dublin region

Street trams were the most important mode of transport in the years **before and after 1916**, when Dublin was a poor city. Dublin had around 106 km of electric tramlines at that time that provided an excellent service. They extended from the city centre to Howth in the north and Dalkey in the south.

The **rise of bus services** in the city brought about the end of the tramlines. Buses were more mobile and could travel to streets that were some distance away from tram stops. Dublin's first bus route opened in 1925 and the last tram ceased operations in 1959 – a decision that proved to be short-sighted.

Trams in Dublin's Sackville Steet (now O'Connell Street) in the early years of the twentieth century

QUESTION

Why did the decision to cease tram operations in 1959 prove to be short-sighted?

The M50 is a major commuter artery on the perimeter of Dublin city

The rise of car transport

The motor car became the most popular mode of transport in Dublin in the last fifty years. This was largely due to the following reasons:

- The rise in the standard of living that began in the Lemass era
- Cheap fuel
- Cheap car parking.

The car began as a novelty and became a habit over the years, so that by the beginning of this century, rush hour traffic in Dublin was a nightmare. Daily traffic speeds in the city became very slow.

Recent trends

Since 2006, when some 77,000 people used a car to enter the city centre every morning for work, the number of people using the car has declined by 15%. Several thousand people have switched to more **sustainable** modes of transport, such as **walking**, **cycling** and **public transport**. Public transport networks have also improved a great deal.

> **DEFINITION**
>
> **The Lemass era:** The years from 1959 to 1966, when Seán Lemass presided over the first major economic expansion in the Republic of Ireland.

> **GEOFACTS**
>
> - The average speed travelled by cars in Dublin is 27.7 km/hr.
> - In 2016, almost 11,000 people cycled into the city centre of Dublin each day.

> **ACTIVITY**
>
> **Thinking**
> Can you explain the term *sustainable modes of transport*?

IN 2015

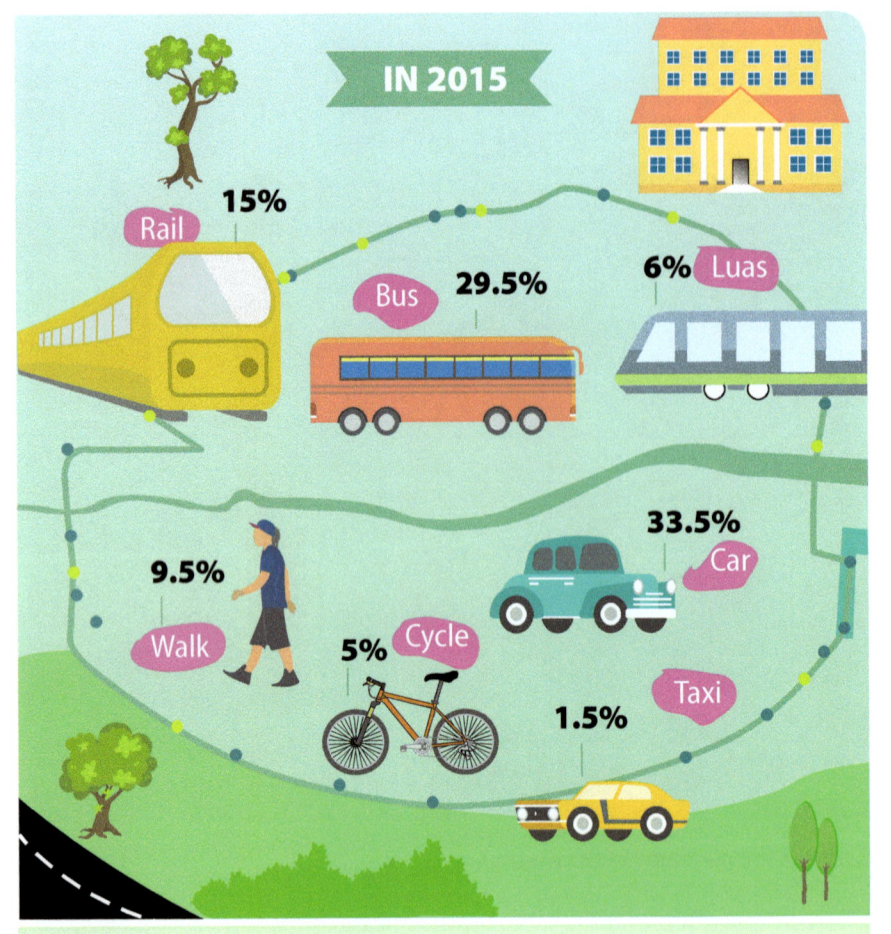

- Rail 15%
- Bus 29.5%
- Luas 6%
- Walk 9.5%
- Cycle 5%
- Car 33.5%
- Taxi 1.5%

Figure 16.11 The modes of transport used by commuters into Dublin's city centre on 11 November 2015

ACTIVITY

Numeracy

Examine Figure 16.11. Calculate the total percentage of commuters who did not use the car to get to work in Dublin on 11 November 2015.

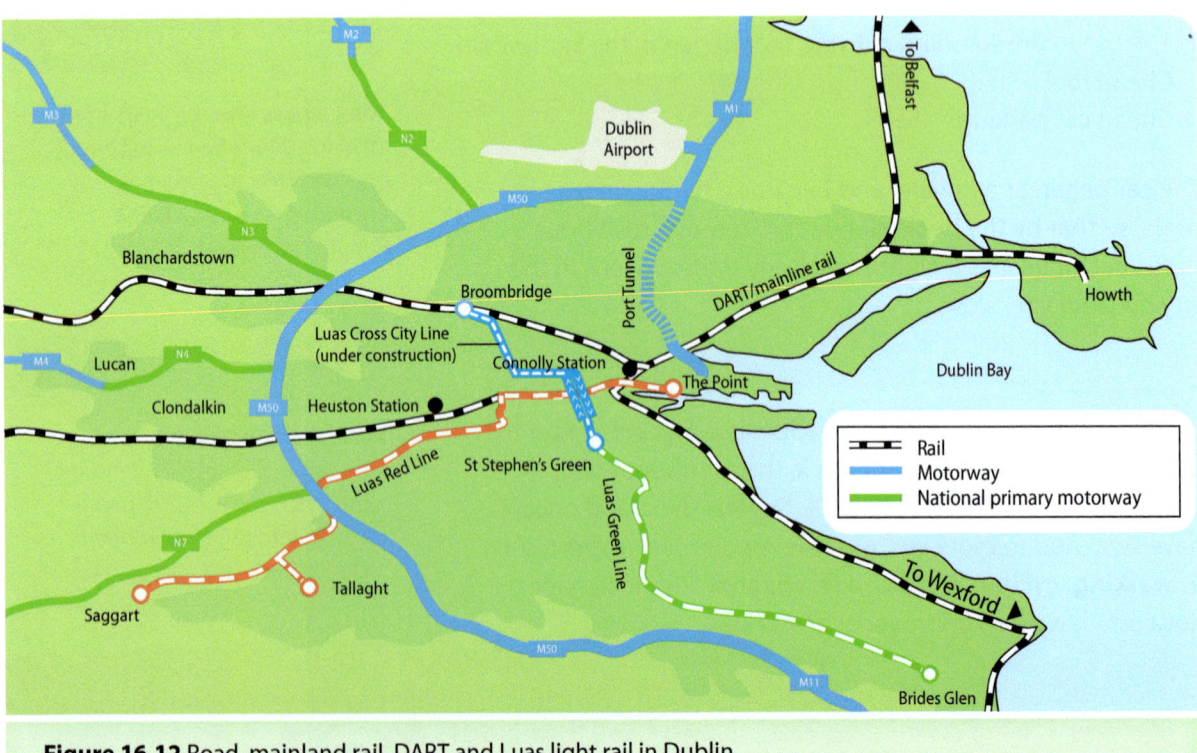

Figure 16.12 Road, mainland rail, DART and Luas light rail in Dublin

Legend:
- Rail
- Motorway
- National primary motorway

The Luas stop at the Red Cow station with park and ride facilities

Public transport in Dublin

- Dublin Bus is the workhorse of Dublin's public transport system. The company carried 122 million passengers in 2015. More than 3,400 people from 68 different countries work for Dublin Bus. QBCs (quality bus corridors) have improved bus journey times.
- The DART (Dublin Area Rapid Transport) is a commuter rail line running along the coast from Malahide and Howth in the north to Greystones in the south. It has expanded its services for commuters from coastal communities with more carriages, more frequent trains and longer platforms. The DART carried 55,000 passengers a day on weekdays in 2015.
- Two Luas lines connect Tallaght and Brides Glen to the city centre by light rail. Both lines carried a total of 34.6 million passengers in 2015. The Luas has been in operation since 2004 and is one of the city's success stories.
- A third Luas line is under construction. The new line, known as Luas Cross City, will see the two existing Luas lines joined in the city centre. Luas Cross City will connect Broombridge Station in Cabra to St Stephen's Green. It is expected that 10 million passengers will use the Luas Cross City line each year.
- Many commuters from outside the Dublin region use mainline rail to get to Dublin's rail terminals in Connolly Station and Heuston Station.
- In addition to public transport, there are 12,000 taxis that can use the QBCs.
- Bicycles in designated cycle lanes have become more popular with commuters in recent years. The Dublin bike rental scheme is also very popular.

Dublin Airport

Dublin Airport is vital to the economy of the city for business and tourism. It is served by 34 airlines and the airport provides flights to 180 destinations. It is a major European airport, with 25 million passengers in 2015. It is a vital part of Dublin's transport system. Dublin Bus provides an express connection to Dublin city centre for passengers on the appropriately named 747 bus.

Dublin Port

Dublin Port is by far the country's largest port. It is the deepest port on Ireland's east coast. The greater part of the port is on the north side of the Liffey at East Wall and North Wall. The port provides passenger and freight services. Ferries connect Dublin to Holyhead, Liverpool, the Isle of Man and Cherbourg.

Financial services

Dublin has many banks, including the Central Bank of Ireland, mortgage companies and insurance companies. The city is also an important player in internationally traded services because of the presence of the International Financial Services Centre (IFSC). The IFSC is located north of the Liffey in part of the old Docklands. It is a prime example of **land use change** in Dublin.

> **DEFINITION**
>
> **Internationaly traded services:** These are traded services that take place between producers and consumers who are based in different countries.

The recession of the 1980s led to high unemployment in Ireland: The IFSC was established in 1987 to create jobs for graduates and to launch a world-class financial services centre in the heart of Dublin.

The IFSC is one of the most successful projects ever undertaken in this country. The centre is host to more than 500 companies. These include half of the world's top fifty banks and half of the top twenty insurance companies. Merrill Lynch, Sumitomo Bank, ABN Amro, Commerzbank and BNP Paribas are all present in the IFSC.

Land use change in Dublin's Docklands with the Convention Centre and many more modern buildings

The IFSC:

› Employed over 38,000 people in 2016 (employment in 2015 alone grew by 7.4%)
› Accounts for more than 10% of multinational employment in Ireland
› Contributes 7.4% to Ireland's GDP (gross domestic product)
› Contributes €2.1 billion to the Irish Exchequer in corporation tax and income tax.

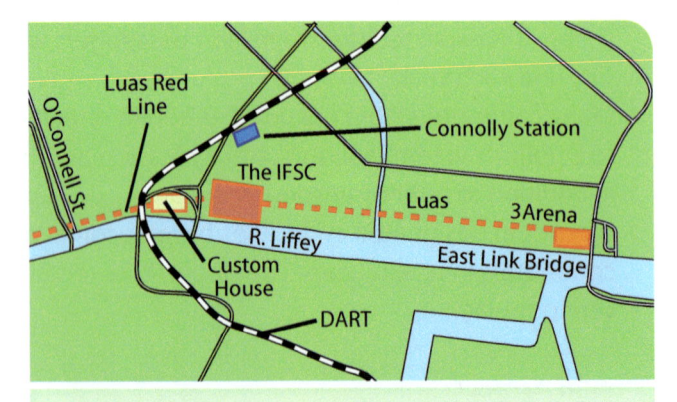

Figure 16.13 The location of the IFSC in Dublin's city centre

The IFSC has excellent broadband communications with Asian, European and North American financial services. This gives companies instant contact with customers across the financial world.

The IDA has played a key role in attracting global financial companies to the IFSC.

Ireland has a large pool of young graduates in business, accounting, finance, languages and computer sciences.

Why has the IFSC been successful?

The IFSC is easy to reach by public transport. It is beside Connolly Station and DART services. The IFSC is also served by a Luas red line stop.

The low corporation tax rate of 12.5% is very important to companies that trade in the IFSC.

Figure 16.14 Factors that have favoured the success of the IFSC

Human processes

Population dynamics

Population dynamics includes the study of population change over time, population structure and migration patterns.

Population change over time

The population of the Dublin region was **1,345,402** in 2016, according to the 2016 preliminary census results. That was an increase of **5.7% since 2011** and is considerably higher than the overall increase of **3.7%** for the Republic of Ireland. In addition, **28.3%** of the population of the Republic lives in the Dublin region. The population of each administrative county of the Dublin region has increased, as the figures in Table 16.2 show. There are two reasons for this increase:

> **Natural increase**, e.g. higher birth rates over death rates
> **Inward migration** from the provinces and from abroad.

ACTIVITY

Thinking

What third-level qualification do you think would be useful for young people who hope to work in the IFSC?

Population change: Dublin city and county, 1946–2016

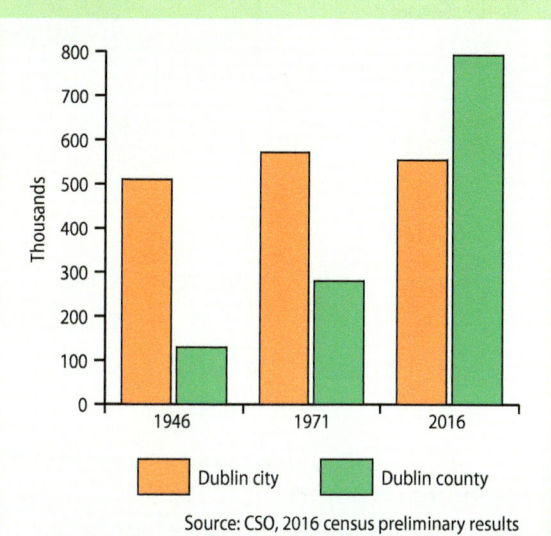

Source: CSO, 2016 census preliminary results

Figure 16.15 The increase in the population of the Dublin region has taken place in Dublin county

ACTIVITY

Numeracy

Examine Figure 16.15. What was the approximate population of Dublin county in 2016?

POPULATION CHANGE IN THE DUBLIN REGION				
	2011	2016	Change in population 2011–2016	
County	No. of people	No. of people	Actual	Percentage
Dublin city	527,612	553,165	25,553	4.8
Dún Laoghaire-Rathdown	206,261	217,274	11,013	5.3
Fingal	273,991	296,214	22,223	8.1
South Dublin	265,205	278,749	13,544	5.1
Total	1,273,068	1,345,402	72,333	5.7

Table 16.2 Population of administrative counties of the Dublin region, 2011 (census results) and 2016 (preliminary census results) (Source: CSO)

All areas of the Dublin region have had population increases since 2011. The population of **Fingal** grew by **8.1%** in five years. In Fingal, the urban centres of Blanchardstown, Balbriggan, Swords and Malahide have grown rapidly. The population of Blanchardstown, for instance, is now greater than Limerick city.

Because of continued strong population growth, the population density of the Dublin region has increased. It now stands at **1,461 people** per km². This is much greater than the national average population density of **67.7 people** per km² in 2016.

ACTIVITY

Numeracy

Examine Table 16.2 above.

(i) What was the percentage change in population in Fingal between 2011 and 2016?

(ii) What was the actual increase in the Dublin region between 2011 and 2016?

(iii) In which part of the Dublin region did the lowest percentage increase take place between 2011 and 2016?

GEOFACT

The populations of counties Meath, Louth, Kildare and Wicklow have grown rapidly. This is because people who work in Dublin have bought cheaper homes in those counties.

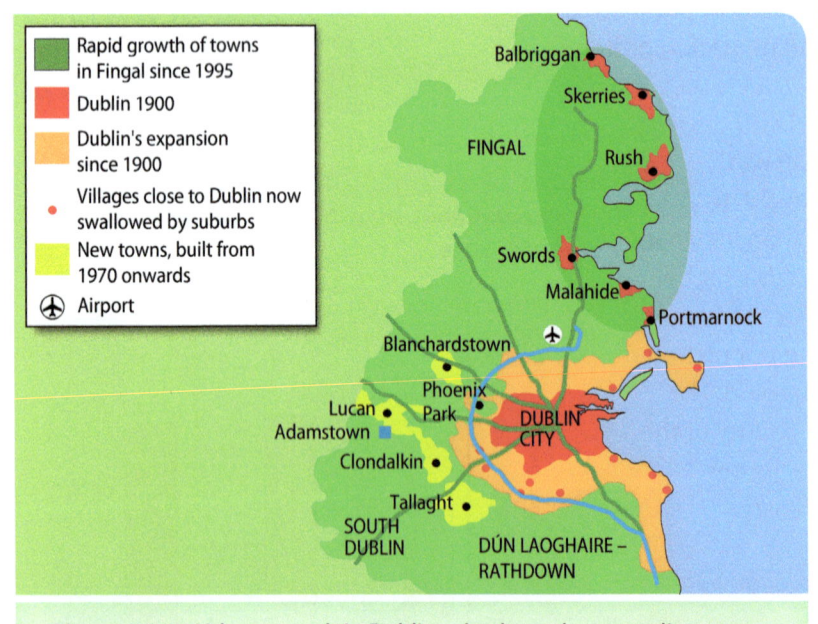

Figure 16.16 Urban growth in Dublin suburbs and surrounding towns

Population structure

The population structure of the Dublin region reflects the **inward migration** of third-level students and of job seekers to the region. As the economic engine of the state, the region has large numbers of young adults. This is clearly visible in the population pyramid of Fingal.

Population structure of the Dublin region

The percentage of elderly people in Fingal is very low. These are older residents who are outnumbered by the large influx of young adults who have moved to Fingal in recent years.

The large number of children shows that birth rates rose sharply in Fingal in the previous decade. The high number of people in their thirties (the peak childbearing years for women in Ireland) is the reason for the surge in the birth rate in recent years. This places great pressure on schools.

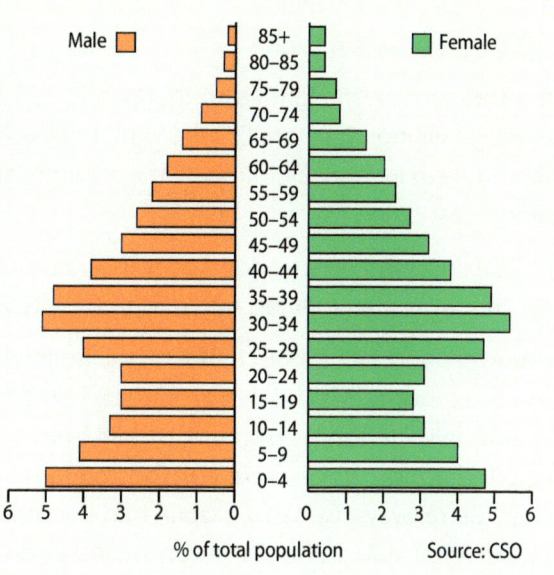

Women have a higher life expectancy than men in Ireland. This is evident in the over-75 age groups.

The pyramid is at its widest in the 25–44 age groups. This is an economically active age group. This suggests that many young adults live in the growing towns of Fingal and commute to work daily in Dublin city.

Figure 16.17 Fingal's population structure. Fingal has the youngest population in the country.

Inward migration

Dublin has been a magnet for migrants from other regions in Ireland for generations. Dublin's growing population has provided work in teaching, nursing and the civil service for young, well-educated migrants from around the country. The IFSC has attracted many highly skilled graduates in recent years.

Dublin also has many migrants from overseas. As the economy expanded rapidly after 1995, thousands of people with language and IT skills were required from abroad to fill the job vacancies that arose. In 2004, when the EU expanded into Eastern Europe with ten new member states, migrants from Poland and other new member states migrated to Ireland. Dublin also became home to many asylum seekers who were granted refugee status.

In 2011, the Dublin region had 249,479 people who were born outside Ireland. This was close to 20% of the population of the region in that year. Many live in Dublin's inner city. Their presence is reflected in classrooms, in ethnic restaurants and shops and in the number of languages spoken in the city.

The Dublin region began to recover earlier than other regions in the Republic from the effects of the economic recession of 2008. By 2012–2013, economic recovery was beginning to show in Dublin. This brought an increase of inward migrants. The 2016 census showed that the **net inward migration** of people into the Dublin region in the previous five years was almost **8,000**, easily the highest in the country.

Urban development of the Dublin region

Dublin is a primate city in the Republic of Ireland. Urban development has been taking place in Dublin up to the present day.

> **ACTIVITY**
>
> **Skills**
>
> Examine Figure 16.17. What percentage of the population in Fingal is aged 14 years and under?

CASE STUDY

Dublin's urban development

The Vikings established a settlement on the Liffey's south bank in 795 AD. Since then, Dublin has grown through Viking, Norman, Elizabethan and Georgian times. As the centre of British rule in Ireland, Dublin became an **administrative centre**, operated from Dublin Castle.

The GPO, Four Courts and Custom House were added over the years. Dublin became the centre of road and rail routes that led outward to the provinces.

Apart from the Guinness brewery and Jacob's biscuit factory, Dublin was not a manufacturing city. Dublin's economic life centred around the port, where thousands of men loaded and unloaded ships by hand. Dublin became a distribution centre for imported goods, which were transported to the provinces through the canals and later the railways. By 1916, Dublin had become a multifunctional city with port, retail, educational and cultural functions.

Urban sprawl

Dublin became the capital of the Irish state after independence in 1921–1922. The city continued to grow, especially after the 1960s. The central business district (CBD) expanded in the city centre. Manufacturing expanded as industrial estates were built on the perimeter of the city.

The rapid rise in population in recent decades has led to urban sprawl as suburbs with low-density semi-detached homes expanded into the countryside. Population densities have remained low by the standards of European cities. The car became the most popular mode of transport for commuters.

In an attempt to control urban sprawl, new towns such as Tallaght were developed to the west of the city in the late 1960s. In recent times, public transport has expanded with the Luas system and QBCs. These developments have reduced the importance of car transport.

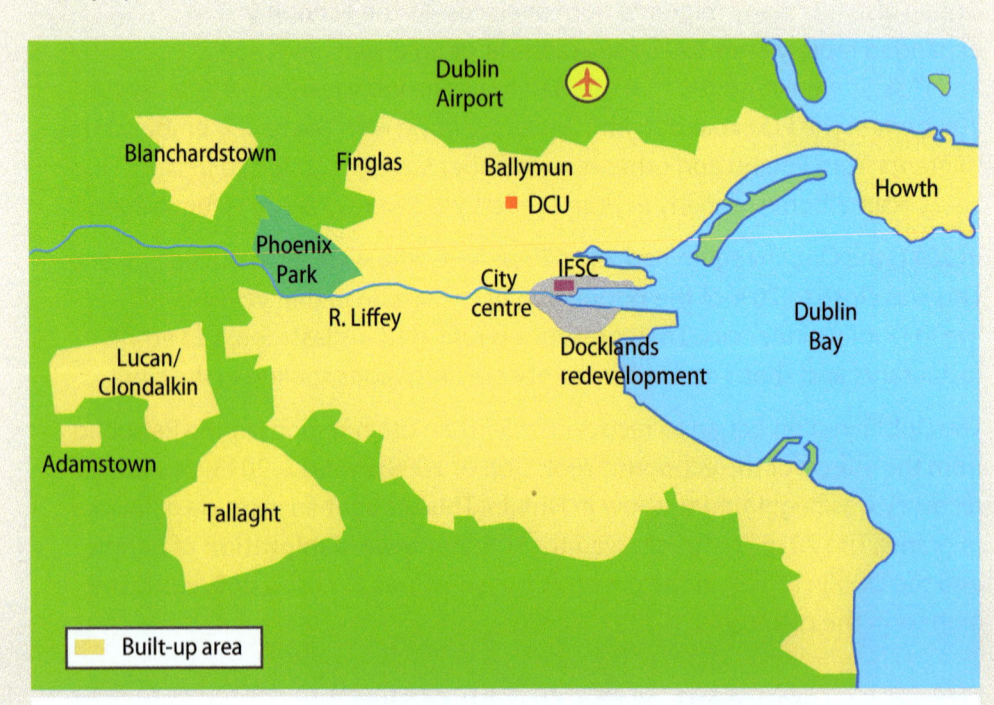

Figure 16.18 Three new towns were built west of Dublin over recent decades. Another new town, Adamstown, was launched in 2005 south of Lucan. The location of features such as DCU that are mentioned in the text are also shown.

Inner-city decline

Port developments such as the use of shipping containers and roll-on roll-off ferries led to a major decline in Dublin's port employment in the 1960s. For that reason, the area experienced inner-city decline. At the same time, many areas in the inner city saw a rapid rise in drug use and crime.

Housing quality in the port area was poor. City authorities built a high-rise suburb in Ballymun where many inner-city residents were housed. However, Ballymun was not a success. Young families were far away from their extended families in the inner city. The community facilities were poor and early school leaving became a problem.

Urban redevelopment in Dublin

Urban redevelopment has revitalised the port area. The Docklands have been transformed in recent decades. The IFSC, the Convention Centre and the 3Arena have changed the urban landscape north of the Liffey. South of the Liffey, the Grand Canal Dock area has been transformed with the Bord Gáis Energy Theatre. Office blocks are home to internet-related technology companies, such as Google. Many new apartment blocks have brought residents back to the Docklands.

Ballymun has also benefited from recent urban redevelopment. Tower blocks have been pulled down and replaced with modern homes. Community centres, sports facilities and retail outlets have been added.

The Northside is also the location of the modern Dublin City University.

The economic downturn after 2008 brought building in the Dublin region to a halt. As the economy in the Dublin region began to pick up again in 2012–2013, inward migration into the capital led to a great demand for housing. This led to an acute housing shortage in the capital by 2016.

Part of Grand Canal Dock in the redeveloped Docklands in Dublin's city centre

Low-density housing in Dublin's southern suburbs

THE WESTERN REGION: A PERIPHERAL REGION

The Western region is made up of counties Galway, Mayo and Roscommon. The region has a wide variety of physical landscapes and a rugged Atlantic coastline. The region has **21.4%** of the area of the state but only **9.5%** of the population.

As a peripheral region, the region has a higher dependence on primary activities than core regions. The region has experienced outward migration for generations. Apart from Galway city, it is a region of small towns and low population densities.

QUESTIONS

Examine Figure 16.19.
1. Name two rivers in the Western region.
2. What river runs along the eastern boundary of the Western region?

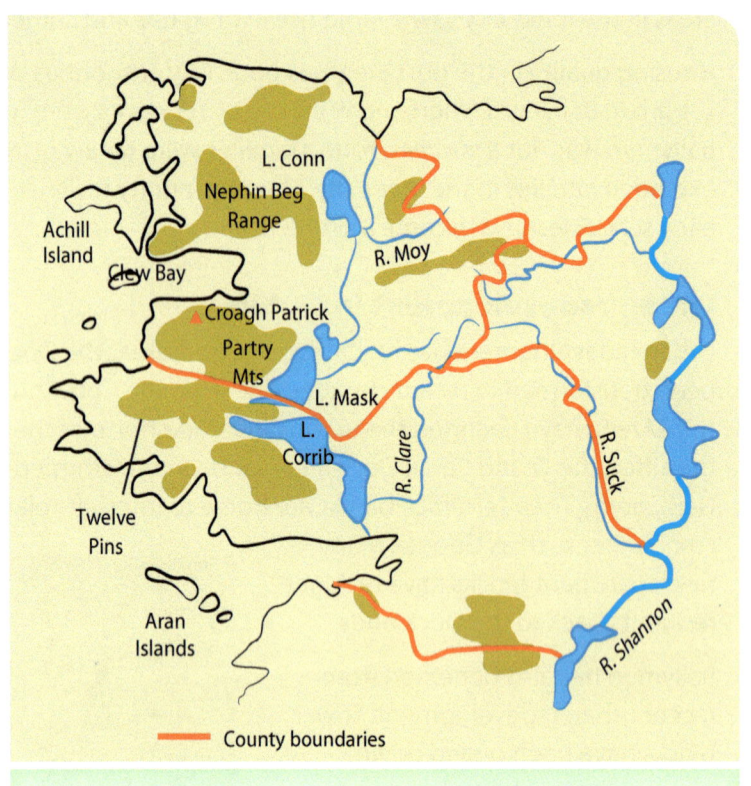

Figure 16.19 The physical features of the Western region

Figure 16.20 The Western region, counties and towns

ACTIVITY

Skills

Draw a sketch map of the Western region. Mark and name the following on it:
- (i) Two mountains
- (ii) Two rivers
- (iii) Two lakes
- (iv) Two urban centres.

ACTIVITY

Skills

Draw a sketch map of Ireland. Mark in and name the following:
- (i) The outline of two named contrasting regions
- (ii) One urban centre in each region
- (iii) One physical feature in each region.

Physical processes

Relief

The Western region has a varied physical landscape:

> The mountains of Connemara and West Mayo include the Twelve Bens or Pins and Nephin Beg. The shape of the mountains and valleys was scarred by glaciers during the ice age.
> East Galway, East Mayo and Roscommon have lowland relief.
> The lowlands that extend inland from Clew Bay have a basket-of-eggs topography and are covered by drumlins. Drumlins are features of glacial deposition.
> Rising sea levels after the ice age have shaped the coast. Killary Harbour is a fiord that was a U-shaped valley or glacial trough before submergence. The islands of Clew Bay are drumlins that were covered by submergence.

LINK

See *Drumlins*, pages 196–7.

Rocks and soils

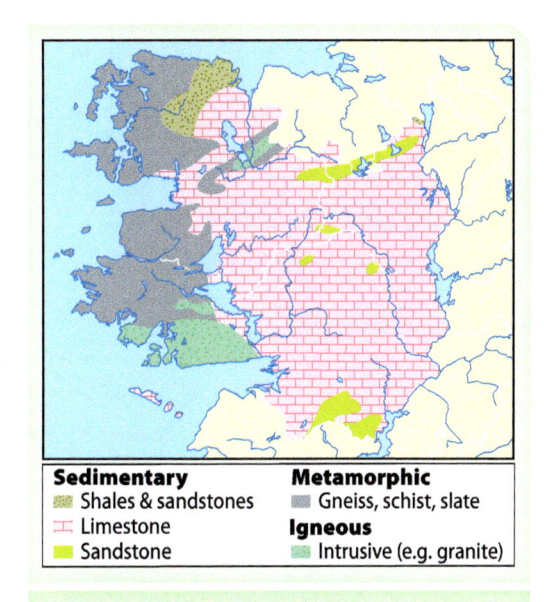

Sedimentary
- Shales & sandstones
- Limestone
- Sandstone

Metamorphic
- Gneiss, schist, slate

Igneous
- Intrusive (e.g. granite)

Figure 16.21 Rock types of the Western region

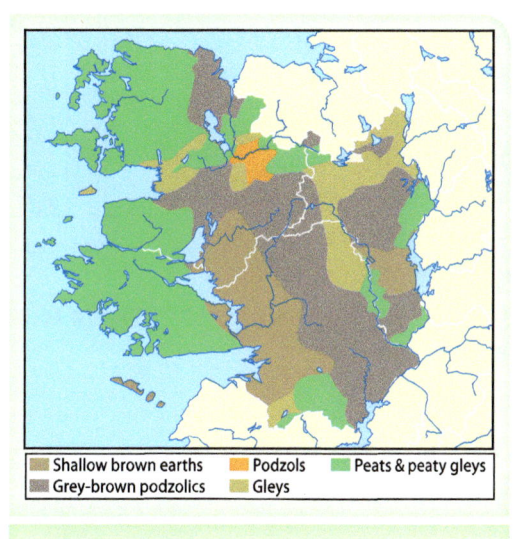

- Shallow brown earths
- Grey-brown podzolics
- Podzols
- Gleys
- Peats & peaty gleys

Figure 16.22 The soils of the Western region

ACTIVITY

Skills

Examine Figure 16.21. Name the type of rock that is found along the west coast of the region.

ACTIVITY

Skills

Examine Figure 16.22. What is the soil type of North-West Mayo?

Peat soils

Peat soils cover Connemara and West Mayo. Peat developed in cold upland areas that have a lot of rainfall. Peat soils are waterlogged because they retain water. They are infertile and have limited agricultural potential, such as rough grazing for mountain sheep.

Gley soils

Gley soils cover the drumlin lowlands east of Clew Bay. This soil has a high clay content that impedes free drainage and becomes easily waterlogged. Gley soils can support summer pasture.

Brown earths

Much of the lowlands of East Galway, East Mayo and Roscommon are covered by **brown earths**, which developed under deciduous tree cover. The parent material of the East Galway lowlands is limestone. These thin soils can dry out in summer, but they are suitable for sheep farming.

Alluvial soils

Alluvial soils are found in East Roscommon along the floodplain of the Shannon River. These are fertile soils but are liable to flooding.

Climate

The climate of the region is cool temperate oceanic. Precipitation occurs in each month of the year with an autumn/winter maximum. The climate is mild, with no extremes. The region has cool summers and mild winters. Average temperatures range from about 5°C in January to about 15°C in summer.

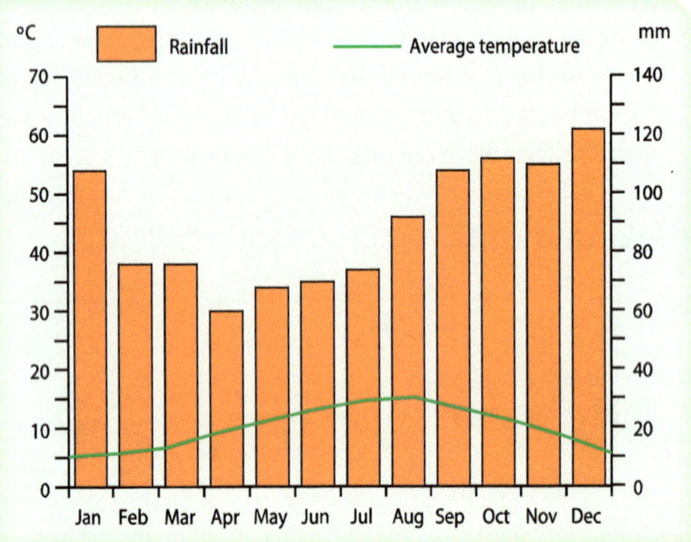

Figure 16.23 The climate of Galway city

Primary economic activities

Agriculture

Pastoral farming

The region has a damp climate and heavy soils that are prone to waterlogging. In many areas, it is unsuitable for tillage and the production of cereal crops. Therefore, pastoral farming is the main agricultural land use.

Farmers fertilise their land in spring and graze their cattle from April to October. Silage is harvested in summer as a winter feed. Most cattle farmers raise herds for beef. Farmers sell their cattle in local marts for fattening in Leinster farms.

North-East Mayo has many **dairy farms**. Lowland sheep production is concentrated in East Galway and South Roscommon.

ACTIVITY

Skills

Examine Figure 16.23.
  (i) Which month has the highest temperature?
  (ii) In which month does the lowest rainfall occur?
  (iii) What is the rainfall in mm during the wettest month?

DEFINITIONS

Pastoral farming is aimed at producing livestock rather than growing crops. Examples include dairy farming, beef cattle and sheep.

Tillage is the growing of crops in ploughed land.

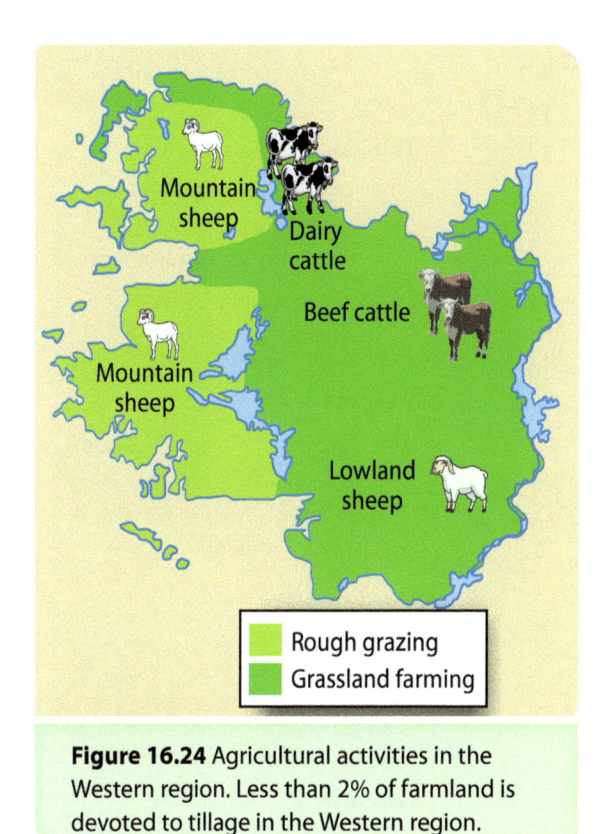

Figure 16.24 Agricultural activities in the Western region. Less than 2% of farmland is devoted to tillage in the Western region.

A sheep market in Maam Cross, Connemara

Rough grazing

Mountain sheep graze in the rough grazing lands of the hills and mountains in Connemara and West Mayo. The ratio of sheep per hectare is low because of the peaty soils and challenging climate in uplands.

Farm income in the Western region

Farm income is much lower in the Western region than it is nationally. In the three counties of the Western region, average farm income is less than €13,000 per year. This is below the average national farming income of over €23,000.

There are many reasons for the low income of the Western region, including physical and socio-economic factors.

Physical factors

> The climate is damp, cool and cloudy. The growing season is shorter and cooler than in the sunny South-East of Ireland.
> Terrain in Connemara and West Mayo is hilly and mountainous. Soil in these areas is thin, peaty or absent.
> Soils are leached and waterlogged in many areas.

Socio-economic factors

> Farms are smaller than the national average. The average farm size in the Western region is just below **22.4 hectares**. This is below the national average of **32.7 hectares**.
> Cattle farming is important over much of the lowlands. The average cattle herd size is small, at **33 cattle per farm**. In contrast, Kilkenny and Waterford, with larger farms, have an average herd size of **105 cattle per farm**.

QUESTION

Explain the term *leached*.

- Cattle farmers frequently experience fluctuating prices for their cattle while their costs continue to rise.
- Farmers in the Western region are older than the national average – a large percentage is over 65 years of age. Older farmers are sometimes more reluctant to invest in new machinery and equipment. This further reduces farm income.
- Most younger farmers have **off-farm jobs** and are therefore part-time farmers. In many instances, their partners are in full-time employment. Many farmers also use some of their land for forestry to supplement their income.
- The EU's Common Agricultural Policy (CAP) is a lifeline for farmers. The CAP provides direct cash payments to farmers. Many farmers would find it difficult to make a living without the payment. Keeping farmers on the land is vital to the fabric of rural life.

> **ACTIVITY**
>
> **Thinking**
> (i) Why are older farmers reluctant to invest in new machinery and equipment?
> (ii) Can you explain why keeping farmers on the land is vital to the fabric of rural life?
> (iii) Can you explain two reasons why the CAP payments are a lifeline for farmers in the Western region?

Fishing

The fishing industry is very important along the coast of the Western region because of the following factors:

- The coastline is very indented and provides many suitable harbours.
- Agricultural land along the coast and in the islands is very poor. Therefore, coastal communities have traditionally turned to the sea for a living.
- The continental shelf off the coast has always contained fish. Plankton, the beginning of the fish food chain, thrive in the unpolluted waters of the Atlantic coast.

> **ACTIVITY**
>
> **Research**
> Look up plankton on the internet to find out more.

The fishing industry in the Western region presently employs 2,000 people. Fish landings include **mackerel**, **sole** and **cod**. Shellfish such as **lobster** and **crab** are also caught. Fishermen experienced great losses of lobster and crab pots in the nine winter storms of January/February 2016 that battered the west coast. In volume terms, catches are low because fishermen have small trawlers that are confined to inshore fishing.

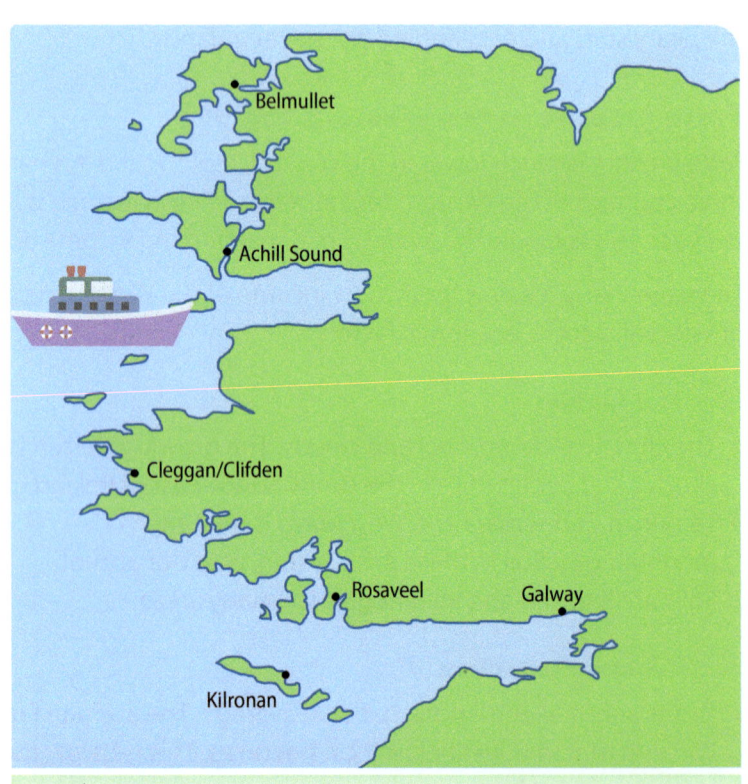

Figure 16.25 Fishing ports in the Western region

The role of the EU

Since 1983, one of the costs of Ireland's membership in the EU was opening Irish waters to foreign trawlers. This has led to overfishing in Irish waters and to an urgent need to conserve stocks. At the time of writing, quotas on annual catches and other restrictions are imposed on fishermen in the Western region and elsewhere in EU waters. For this reason, investment has begun to take place in aquaculture (fish farming).

Aquaculture

Fish farms are located in Galway Bay, Clew Bay and Killary Harbour. Shellfish farms produce oysters, mussels and clams. Salmon farms are also found on the coast. Catches are sold locally and on the European mainland.

Fish farming along the west coast has caused controversy and some opposition. Concerns have been raised that fish farming seems to lead to the decline of the natural population of wild salmon. This is because of the antibiotics used in the farms, as well as fish lice and waste from the fish farms.

In December 2015, Bord Iascaigh Mhara withdrew a proposal to construct a large salmon farm in Galway Bay. The proposal was opposed by local communities because of environmental concerns.

Fish farms in Killary Harbour

ACTIVITY

Research

Look up the location of Killary Harbour on the internet.

Natural gas

Natural gas was discovered 80 km off the Mayo coast in 1996. However, locals objected to the building of a gas pipeline to an inland refinery at Bellanaboy because of its proximity to homes. They wanted the refinery to be built offshore. Finding a solution led to many delays. Gas finally came ashore at the end of 2015.

The field will have the capacity to initially provide about 60% of Ireland's peak winter gas requirements. That figure will decrease within a few years as gas extraction declines. Most of the gas will be used by Bord Gáis.

The natural gas refinery in Bellanaboy in North-West Mayo

The Corrib gas field is expected to contribute an estimated €4.4 billion to Ireland's economy over its twenty-year lifetime. More than 6,000 people worked on the project at various times during its construction. It is reported that the project will continue to provide 175 jobs in North-West Mayo.

LINK

For more on the Corrib gas field, see pages 83–85.

ACTIVITY

Discussion

Examine two ways in which the Corrib gas field will help the economy of Ireland.

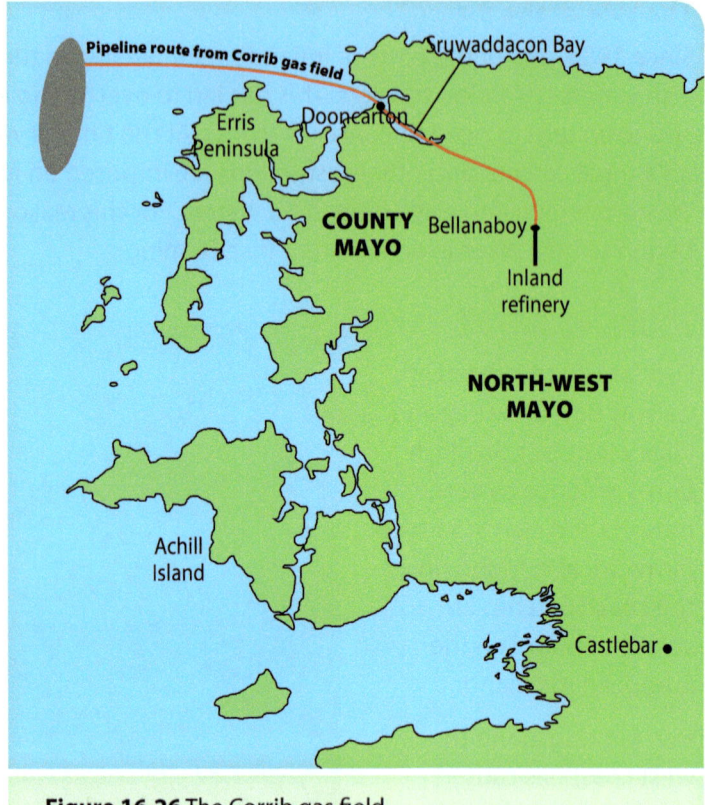

Figure 16.26 The Corrib gas field

Secondary economic activities

Manufacturing

Manufacturing is an important economic activity in the Western region. However, manufacturing in the region is hindered by a number of factors:

- The region is **peripheral** – it is at the western extremity of Ireland. During the recession that began in 2008, many jobs were lost in the region and growth in jobs since 2012 has been minimal. Peripheral regions decline much more than core regions during a recession.
- It is far from markets in Ireland. This increases the transport costs of raw materials and finished products. The region also has a small local market.
- Galway city is the only urban centre of significant size in the region. Other urban centres, such as Castlebar and Ballina, are medium-sized towns. Therefore, the labour supply is relatively small.

LINK

Do you remember the definition of peripheral regions from Chapter 15?

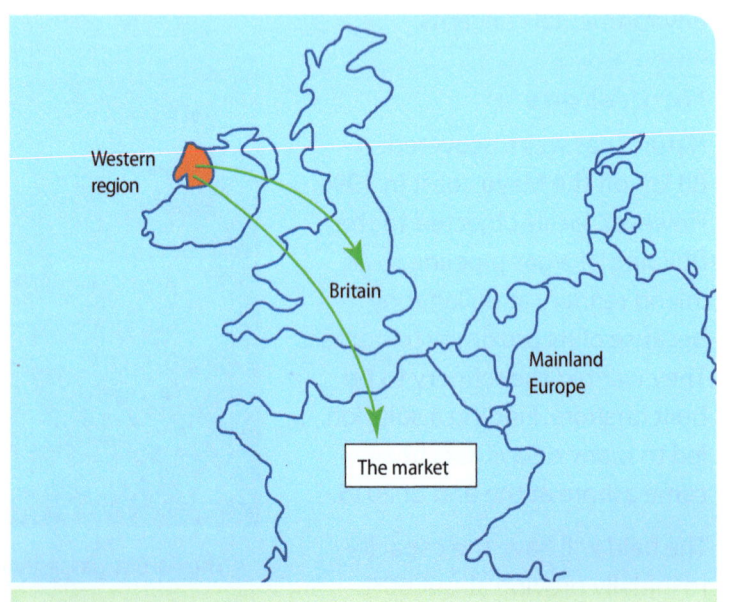

Figure 16.27 The Western region is on an island (Ireland) off an island (UK) off the coast of Europe. What impact does that have on the transport of export goods?

- Outside the urban centres, there are gaps in the **broadband network**, a vital form of communication for businesses today.
- Infrastructure is not as developed as it is in other areas of the country. For instance, Mayo does not have a single kilometre of motorway. Therefore, **transport links** are an issue for manufacturers.

Despite these challenges, the region has many successful manufacturing companies. This is partly because the **IDA** has targeted multinational companies that specialise in **high-value, low-bulk products**. **Medical devices** in the Galway city area are the classic example.

ACTIVITY

Thinking

Can you explain one reason why peripheral regions experience greater economic decline than core regions during a recession?

GEOFACT

There were 30,200 people working in manufacturing in the Western region in the second quarter of 2016. (Source: CSO)

Types of manufacturing in the Western region

Resource-based industries

These include meat processing plants using local beef in Ballinasloe, Gort and Ballaghaderreen. Údarás na Gaeltachta has helped to locate fish plants in the Gaeltacht areas.

Consumer industries

Consumer industries include bakeries and confectionery. Local family bakeries face strong competition from supermarkets, some of which produce their own bread in-house for their customers.

Light industries

Light industries are in the many **industrial estates** in the towns of the region, including Westport, Castlebar, Ballina, Tuam and Ballinasloe. Products include plastics, electronics, precision engineering and printing. Many of the plants are owned by local entrepreneurs who saw an opening in the market for their products.

Figure 16.28 Some leading manufacturers in the Western region. Elan's Athlone plant is in Co. Roscommon.

Multinational plants

Seventy multinational companies employ 16,000 workers in the region. The Western region has a globally recognised cluster of MNCs (multinational corporations) involved in **life science products and medical devices**. These include Baxter, Allergan and Hollister. Products include heart stents, optical equipment and pharmaceuticals, which are exported to a global market. Allergan, located in Westport, employs more than 850 people and produces pharmaceuticals. Its products include Botox. Allergan also has an important R&D sector in Westport.

ACTIVITY

Skills

Examine Figure 16.28.
(i) Westport is in which county?
(ii) Name a major plant in Ballina.

One of the world's largest brands also has a base in Mayo. Ballina Beverages, part of the **Coca-Cola** company, manufactures the concentrates used to make fizzy drinks such as Coca-Cola, Fanta and Sprite. These are sold to bottlers on four continents, which in turn manufacture the final product for customers all over the world. One of the main attractions of Ballina was the **purity of the water supply** in the area.

A highly skilled worker in the Elan pharmaceutical plant

The Galway medical devices cluster

The largest cluster of companies involved in medical devices is in **Galway city**. These include Boston Scientific and Medtronic. The factors that favoured the growth of this cluster include the following:

- As the largest urban centre in the region, Galway has a large labour pool. This includes 8,000 graduates a year from NUIG and GMIT.
- The city environs have a high-voltage electricity supply that can power large plants.
- The Galway city area has much better telecommunications links (broadband) than the average elsewhere in the West of Ireland.
- Galway has excellent infrastructure, such as the M6 motorway to Dublin and a rail terminal. Shannon Airport is only an hour away and will be fully connected by motorway by 2018.

Tertiary economic activities

Tertiary economic activities are important in the Western region, as about two-thirds of workers are employed in the tertiary sector. **Tourism** and **transport** are examined here.

Tourism

As a peripheral region, tourism in the Western region faces several challenges.

- The decline in the number of transatlantic flights to Shannon Airport has reduced the number of North American visitors to the Western region.
- The Western region is far away from Dublin Airport. Dublin is the favourite point of entry for tourists into Ireland.
- The trend towards more frequent, shorter holidays and city breaks may have contributed to a decline in the Western region's share of tourism.

ACTIVITY

Research

Look up the uses of Botox on the internet.

QUESTION

Explain the term *medical devices cluster*.

In spite of these factors, the Western region is visited by many overseas and domestic tourists each year and tourism is an important source of employment. Tourist facilities such as hotels, guesthouses and leisure services are well developed. However, **Galway city and county** receive many more visitors each year than counties Mayo or Roscommon.

GEOFACT

There were 125,600 people working in services in the Western region in the second quarter of 2016. (Source: CSO)

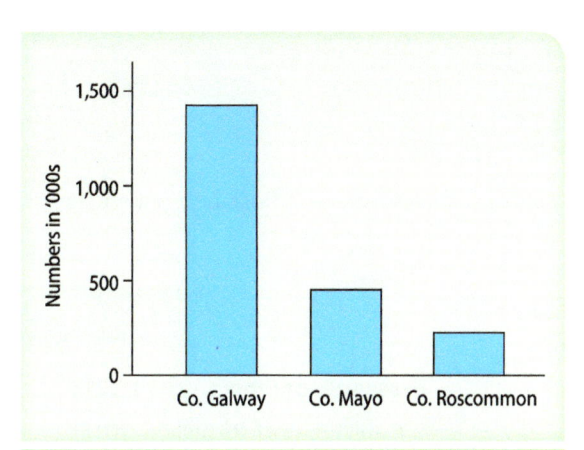

Figure 16.29 Overseas visitors to Western counties, 2015

ACTIVITY

Research

Examine Figure 16.30. Use the internet to find out more about:

(i) Lough Key Forest Park
(ii) The Céide Fields.

Figure 16.30 Tourist attractions of the Western region

LINK

Look at Figure 16.10 on page 262 to examine important tourist centres in the Western region.

Tourist attractions of the Western region

Natural amenities

The outstanding natural beauty of the Western region attracts many visitors. Attractions include:

> Boating facilities on the Shannon River, which forms Co. Roscommon's eastern boundary
> Angling rivers such as the Moy River, known to anglers from Western Europe
> Many coastal golf links
> Hill walking and cycling routes, including the Great Western Greenway
> The unspoiled natural landscape of Connemara National Park
> The cliffs of Achill Island, which can be reached on the **Wild Atlantic Way** (a popular tourist route).

Kylemore Abbey is located in a beautiful setting in Connemara

Cultural attractions

- The Western region is home to many heritage towns, including Westport, Clifden and Strokestown (the Irish National Famine Museum is in Strokestown).
- The Céide Fields in North Mayo contain a Stone Age archaeological site and an interpretative centre.
- The Gaeltacht in the Aran Islands and Connemara provides Irish language courses for students from all over the country. This is an important source of income for families during the summer school holidays.
- Pádraig Mac Piarais's cottage is in Rosmuc in the heart of the Connemara Gaeltacht. It was here that he wrote many of his poems and stories while he perfected his knowledge of Irish.

Pádraig Mac Piarais's cottage in Rosmuc, Connemara

Religious tourism

The Western region has a rich religious heritage that attracts many visitors and includes:

- Croagh Patrick, Ireland's religious mountain
- Ballintubber Abbey, near Castlebar, established in 1216
- Knock, a major Marian shrine (a shrine to the Virgin Mary).

The future of tourism in the Western region

- The Western region has some of the most unspoiled areas in Europe. This is a major selling point that can be further exploited.
- **Niche holidays** such as angling, heritage tourism, outdoor pursuits, both on the coast and the mountains, and health and fitness centres offer great opportunities for growth.
- Budget airlines must be lobbied to expand flights from Europe to Knock Airport and Shannon Airport.
- Attractive holiday packages need to be devised to attract tourists, both domestic and overseas, to the region.
- Cruise companies, already docking in Mutton Island in Galway Bay, are likely to dock more frequently in Galway when the new port comes on stream.

GEOFACT

Passenger numbers – 2014/2015
- Dublin Airport: 25 million (2015)
- Shannon Airport: 1.7 million (2015)
- Knock Airport: 703,324 (2014)

ACTIVITY

Research

Look up Ballintubber Abbey on the internet to find out more.

QUESTION

Can you explain the meaning of the term *niche holiday*?

The Galway Races in Ballybrit, Galway. The Galway Races are a major tourist attraction every year.

Transport and communications

Roads

Good communications are vital to the Western region in order to improve its links with other regions of Ireland. Several road improvements have taken place in recent years.

- Since 2009, Galway has been connected to Dublin by a toll motorway – the M6. It now takes little more than two hours to drive from the outskirts of Galway to the outskirts of Dublin, which makes the Western region less peripheral. It is likely that the M6 will encourage inward investment along its route. For instance, Apple has plans to develop a data centre in Athenry to serve its customer base.
- The building of the Gort/Tuam motorway got underway in 2015 and is expected to be complete by 2018. This motorway will connect the Galway area with Shannon Airport and Limerick. It will bypass many villages along the way.
- The Gort/Tuam motorway is part of the Atlantic Corridor in the West of Ireland. The continued upgrading of the **Atlantic Corridor** will make urban centres in the Western region more attractive for inward investment. The Atlantic Corridor will help to create a **counter pole** in the West of Ireland that will reduce the dominance of the Dublin region in the Irish economy.
- Westport and Castlebar are connected to Dublin by the N5. Some towns on this route, such as Charlestown, have been bypassed. Bypasses have greatly reduced traffic and pollution along the streets of those towns.

Rail

Daily passenger trains from Ballina, Westport and Galway link the Western region with Leinster and Dublin.

The north–south **Western Railway Corridor** closed many years ago. The **West on Track** community-based campaign has continued to lobby for its reopening. Already, the Galway to Limerick line via Athenry has been reopened since 2010. However, the reopening of the Athenry to Sligo railway line is unlikely in the near future because of the large investment that this would require.

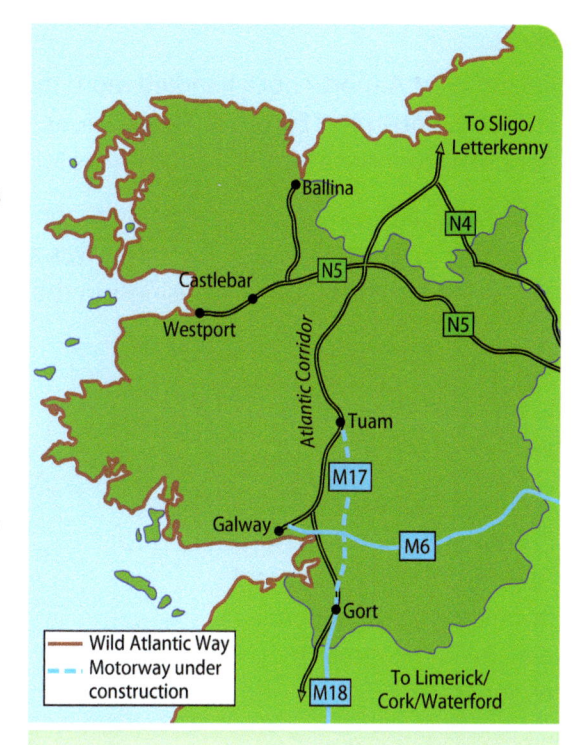

Figure 16.31 Roads in the Western region: the N4, N5, M6, the Atlantic Corridor and the new M18/M17 (opening in 2018 from Gort to Tuam)

DEFINITION

The Atlantic Corridor: A road project in Ireland that, when complete, will upgrade the route from Waterford via Cork to Letterkenny to dual carriageway or motorway standard.

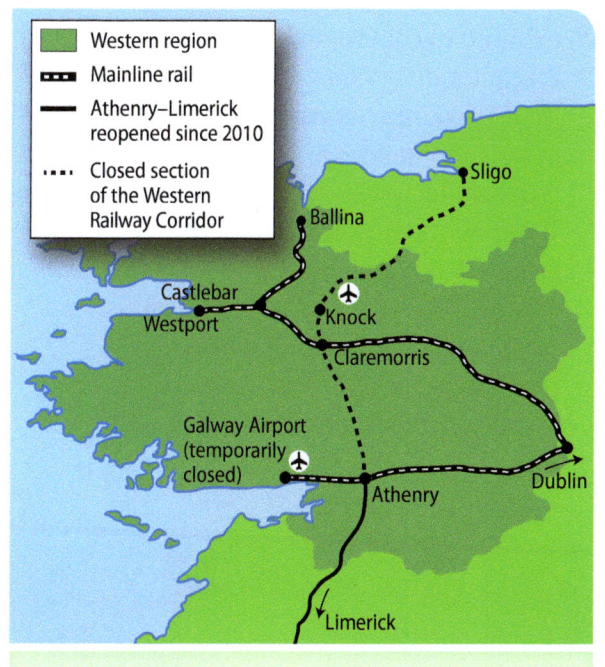

Figure 16.32 Railways and airports in the Western region

Airports

Ireland West Airport Knock handled more than 703,324 passengers in 2014 to and from British and European destinations. The airport is very important for the people of counties Mayo and Sligo and is located near the Marian shrine at Knock.

However, Galway Airport was a victim of the economic recession and ceased commercial flights in recent years. This was a major loss to the business community in the area. It may reopen for business in the future as the economy grows.

Human processes

Population dynamics

The population of the region is **unevenly distributed**. Apart from Galway city and its environs, population density in the Western region is low.

The mountainous areas of West Galway and Mayo have little or no settlement. Mountains **repel settlement**. The factors that are responsible for low population densities in the mountainous areas include the following:

- The mountains have lower temperatures than the lowlands and are exposed to cold winds.
- Precipitation of more than 1,600 mm per year in the mountains is a repellent factor.
- The mountains were largely denuded of soil during the last ice age. Therefore, farming is not an option, apart from rough grazing of mountain sheep, an economic activity that supports the few farmers who live in the valleys.

QUESTION

Explain the term *repellent factor*.

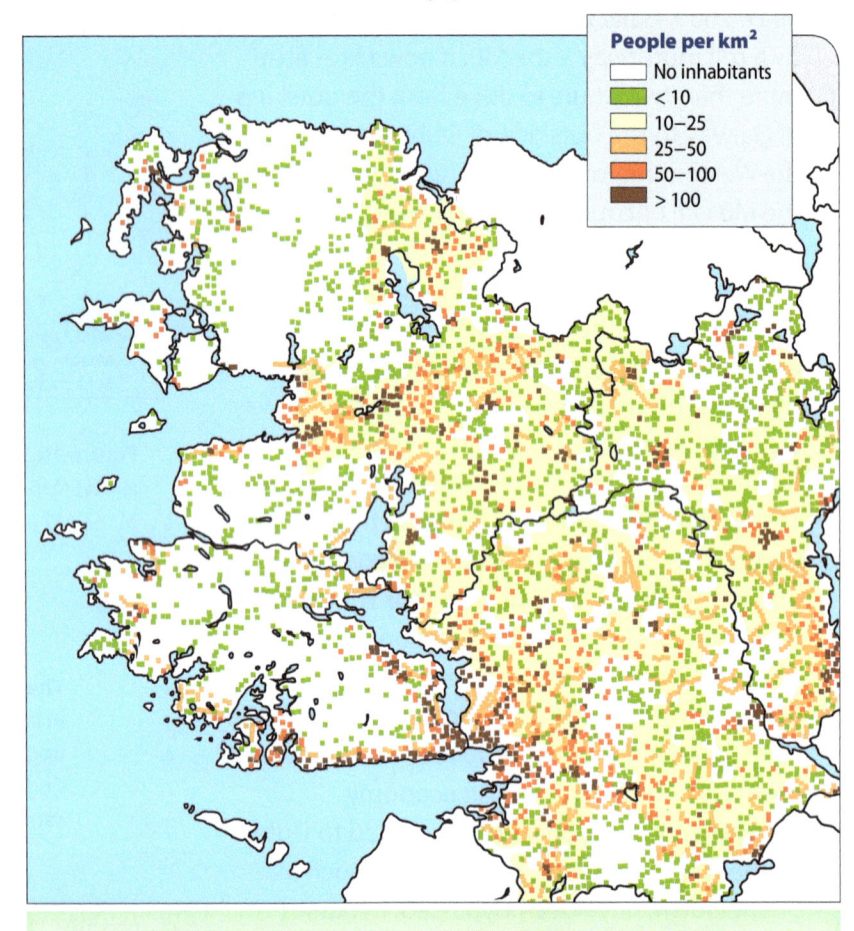

Figure 16.33 Population density per km^2 in the Western region (Source: CSO)

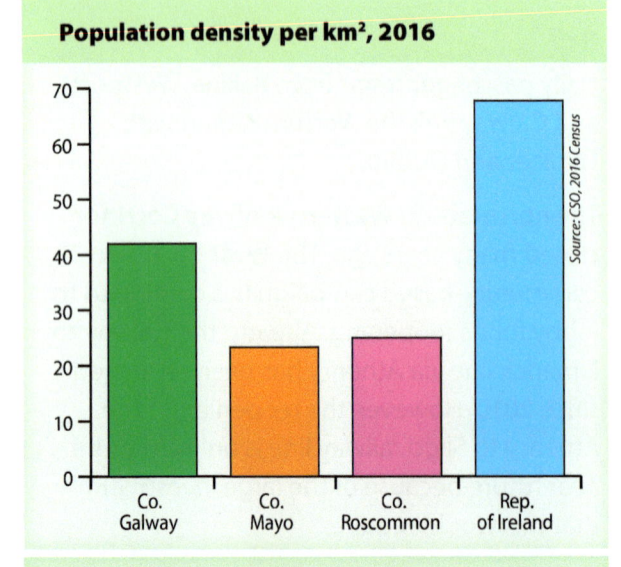

Figure 16.34 Population density in the counties of the Western region and in the Republic, 2016

Many of the coastal areas have low population densities. However, some parts of Achill Island and parts of the Mullet Peninsula in North-West Mayo have slightly higher densities where people are engaged in fishing and summer tourism.

Fish farming is important in Clew Bay and in Killary Harbour. It supports the higher coastal densities in these areas. Some coastal communities in the Connemara Gaeltacht support themselves through summer language schools and in Údarás na Gaeltachta factories.

> **GEOFACT**
>
> The function of Údarás na Gaeltachta is to develop the Gaeltacht economy. They want to preserve and secure the future of the Irish language as the daily language of its people.

> **ACTIVITY**
>
> **Skills**
>
> Examine the photograph of the rural community in Achill. What evidence suggests that the land is agriculturally unproductive here?

A rural community in Achill Island, Co. Mayo. Population density is very low here.

Rural depopulation has reduced the population of many rural areas as young people **migrate** to urban centres in the Western region and to other parts of Ireland and overseas.

Most of the lowlands of East Galway, East Mayo and Roscommon have higher densities than the mountainous areas of the west. This is because the land is better quality here and cattle and sheep farmers work on relatively small farms.

Higher population densities are found along an axis stretching from Ballina to Galway city. Within that axis, urban centres and their environs, such as **Ballina**, **Castlebar**, **Westport** and **Galway city**, have the highest population densities in the Western region.

> **GEOFACTS**
>
> › The average population density in the Western region was **31.7 per km²** in 2016, well below the national average of 67.7 per km².
> › Co. Roscommon is one of the most rural counties in Ireland, with some 74% of the population living in rural areas.

While most urban centres in the Western region are small, Galway city has now grown to become the third largest city in the Republic after Dublin and Cork, with a population of 79,504 people according to the 2016 census preliminary results. Galway city has grown to be a **multifunctional city** with two third-level colleges, medical device manufacturing businesses, several large hospitals, a large CBD and tourist activities. These all support thousands of jobs in the city.

The area around Galway city has the largest cluster of relatively high population densities. Many small towns and villages, such as **Oranmore**, **Athenry**, **Moycullen**, **Barna** and **An Spidéal***, have grown rapidly in recent decades. This is because many people choose to live in these smaller settlements and commute to their work in the city every day. The coastal lowlands west of Galway city have high population densities because many people like to live in an area that has a view of the sea.

Figure 16.35 The hinterland of Galway city is home to many villages and small towns

HINT

Logainmneacha Gaelacha

Tá an dá bhaile seo ins an nGaeltacht.

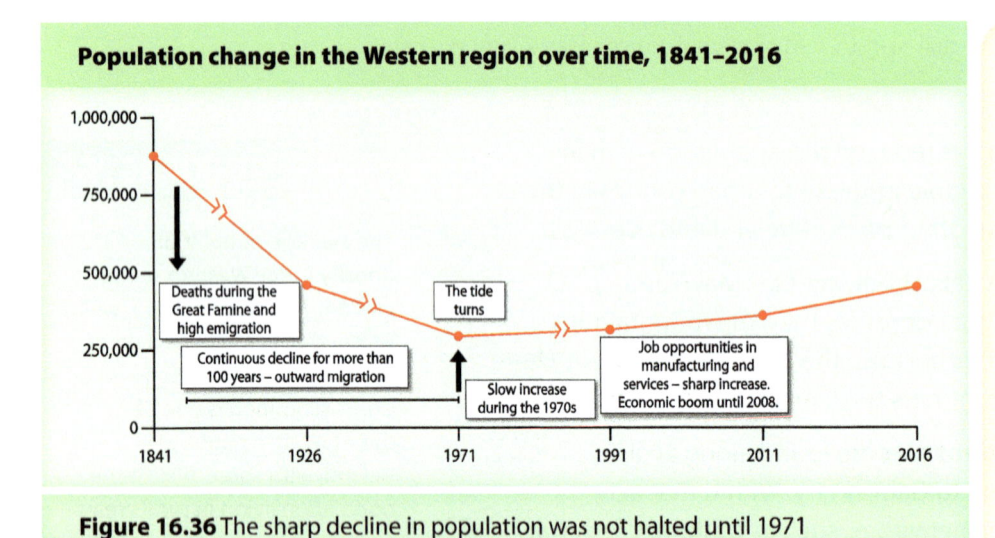

Population change over time in the Western region

The population of the three counties of the Western region has changed over time. In 1841, the population of the counties of the Western region had reached **850,000**.

The Great Famine of the 1840s led to a sharp decline in the population of the Western region. Outward migration over later generations reduced the population to a low of **312,000** by 1971.

Population change in the Western region over time, 1841–2016

- Deaths during the Great Famine and high emigration
- Continuous decline for more than 100 years – outward migration
- The tide turns
- Slow increase during the 1970s
- Job opportunities in manufacturing and services – sharp increase. Economic boom until 2008.

Figure 16.36 The sharp decline in population was not halted until 1971

ACTIVITY

Numeracy

Examine Figure 16.36.

(i) What was the approximate number of people in the Western region in 1841?

(ii) In what year did the popualtion of the Western region reach its lowest point?

However, economic developments since the early 1970s have helped the population of the Western region to increase. Ireland's **entry into the EEC/EU** in 1973 helped the economy to grow and to reduce outward migration from the Western region. A robust birth rate also helped the population to increase from the low point of 1971.

The **Celtic Tiger years** that began in 1995 brought a surge in economic development. This led to inward migration into the Western region. The population continued to expand.

DEFINITION

Celtic Tiger: The name given to the Irish economy during the period of rapid economic growth during the years 1995 to 2008.

POPULATION CHANGE IN THE WESTERN REGION				
County	2011	2016	Actual change	Percentage change
Galway city	75,529	79,504	3,975	5.3%
Galway county	175,124	179,048	3,924	2.2%
Mayo	130,638	130,425	−213	−0.2%
Roscommon	64,065	64,436	371	0.6%
Total	441,991	453,413	11,422	2.5%

Table 16.3 The change in the population of the Western region, 2011–2016 (preliminary census results, 2016) (Source: CSO)

However, the economic downturn of 2008 onwards slowed the strong population growth of the Celtic Tiger years. As you can see from Table 16.3, the population of Co. Mayo declined slightly in the years 2011 to 2016. Roscommon registered a small increase. Galway city, on the other hand, grew by some 4,000 people in the same period. This growth in Galway city was due to both natural increase and inward migration.

Population structure

Much of the population of the Western region lives in rural areas. This is reflected in the population structure of the region. The population of Co. Mayo is typical of rural counties in the West of Ireland from Kerry to Donegal.

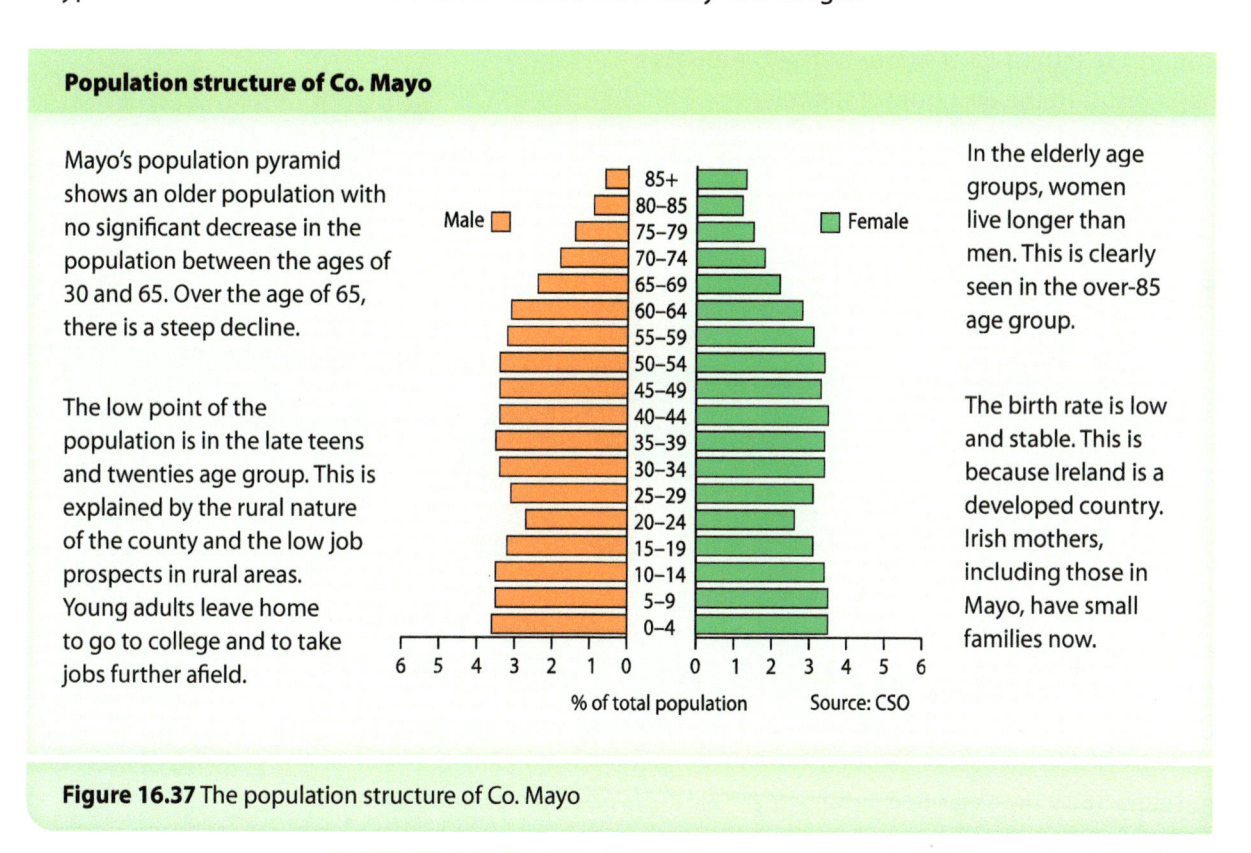

Population structure of Co. Mayo

Mayo's population pyramid shows an older population with no significant decrease in the population between the ages of 30 and 65. Over the age of 65, there is a steep decline.

The low point of the population is in the late teens and twenties age group. This is explained by the rural nature of the county and the low job prospects in rural areas. Young adults leave home to go to college and to take jobs further afield.

In the elderly age groups, women live longer than men. This is clearly seen in the over-85 age group.

The birth rate is low and stable. This is because Ireland is a developed country. Irish mothers, including those in Mayo, have small families now.

Figure 16.37 The population structure of Co. Mayo

ACTIVITY

Numeracy

Calculate the percentage of the population aged 9 years and under in Co. Mayo.

Urban development in the Western region

Apart from Galway city, urban centres in the region are small. Only two towns, Castlebar and Ballina, exceed 10,000 people. Castlebar is the county town of Mayo and provides many services, such as local authority administration, financial and commercial services.

Towns in the region provide market services for the people of their hinterlands. Some towns have specific functions. Westport has an important tourist function, while the village of Knock has a religious function.

As we have seen, several towns have an important manufacturing function, where multinational companies have a major impact on the economy of a town. These include Castlebar, Ballina and Tuam.

Castlebar also has an important educational function. The town is the location of the Mayo campus of the Galway Mayo Institute of Technology (GMIT). The campus has been in operation since 1994 and has around 1,000 third-level students. The campus is a major boost to the economy of the town.

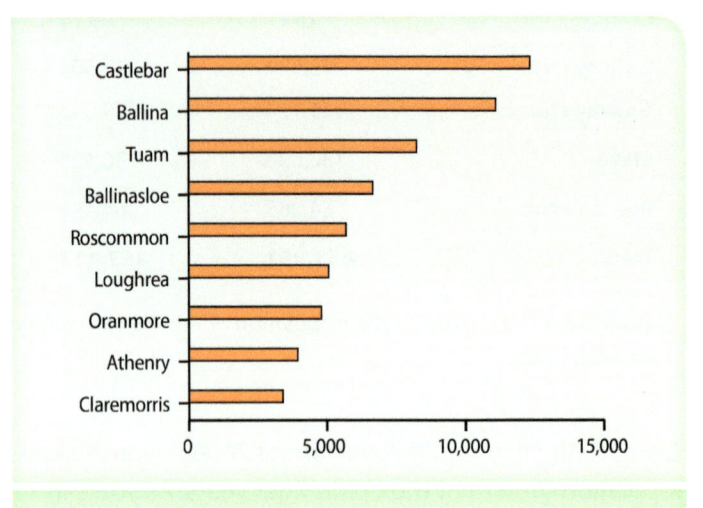

Figure 16.38 Population of selected urban centres in the Western region (excluding Galway)

ACTIVITY

Skills

Examine Figure 16.38.

What is the approximate population of the following urban centres?
  (i) Castlebar
  (ii) Tuam
  (iii) Athenry

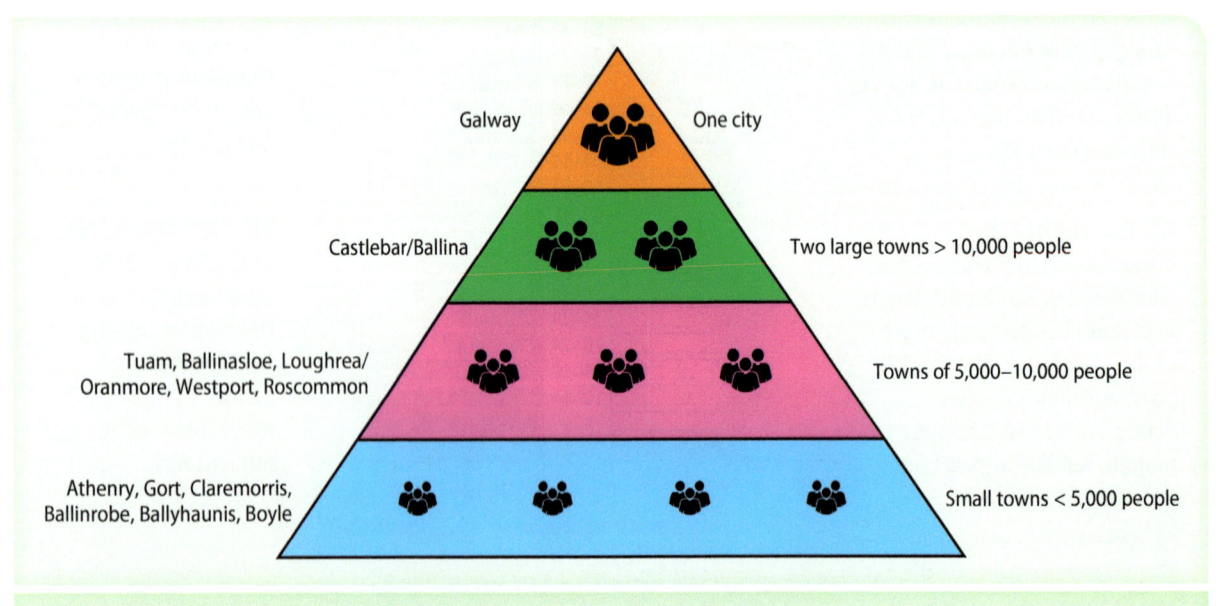

Figure 16.39 The hierarchy of urban settlements in the Western region

- Galway — One city
- Castlebar/Ballina — Two large towns > 10,000 people
- Tuam, Ballinasloe, Loughrea/Oranmore, Westport, Roscommon — Towns of 5,000–10,000 people
- Athenry, Gort, Claremorris, Ballinrobe, Ballyhaunis, Boyle — Small towns < 5,000 people

CASE STUDY

The development of one urban centre in the Western region

Galway city is located in a sheltered harbour in Galway Bay. Many of its functions are visible here.

Galway city is by far the most important urban centre in the Western region. In 2016, the population of Galway city and suburbs had grown to 79,504 people. It is a multifunctional city with a university, several large hospitals and a strong business life. The city owes its development to several factors, including its location, transport factors and human factors. We will examine two factors in its development: **location** and **transport**.

Location
- Galway city is located on the north coast of Galway Bay. The city is built on a flat and gently undulating lowland at the mouth of the Corrib River. This is a short river that drains Lough Corrib to the north.
- Galway began as a settlement in the year 1240 AD when a Norman lord, Richard de Burgo, built a castle there. Over time, the city grew around a **bridge point** on the Corrib River.
- Because the city's location is at the head of a relatively sheltered bay, Galway was an ideal harbour for ships. Therefore, the city acquired a **port function** early on in its history.
- Ships developed trading links from Galway with France and Spain and Galway became a **merchant city**. The merchant life of the city was controlled by fourteen families, such as the Joyce, Morris and Ffrench families. Galway became known as the '**city of the tribes**'.

- Large warehouses, used to store goods for import and export, were built beside the port.
- In the nineteenth century, ships left Galway with impoverished emigrants for North America before and after the Great Famine.
- Because of its **coastal location**, Galway became a small fishing port too.

Transport

- The city became an important **railway terminal** with the opening of the railway from Dublin in the nineteenth century. Trains brought many goods to the city, which became a **distribution centre** for its hinterland. The city became more important because of this.
- As the **only crossing point** on the Corrib River, Galway became a **nodal point** and a **market centre**. This helped the area to grow.
- Roads brought people into the city from Connemara and from Tuam, Athenry and Gort. As a route focus, Galway acquired many additional functions, such as retail, educational, legal and banking functions.
- In recent years the city has become a major manufacturing city with a large cluster of multinational medical device companies. However, the quality of the labour force in addition to good transport factors were important in attracting these companies. Many of these companies, such as Boston Scientific, are located beside the N6, which acts as a ring road on the eastern perimeter of the city.
- The completion of the M6 motorway to Galway in 2009 has brought much faster connections to Dublin and will further add to Galway's growth. The M17/M18 will connect Tuam to Limerick. This will make Galway even more accessible. A major bypass of the city from east to west is also proposed.
- Because of its position as a route focus, Galway markets itself as the **gateway to the West**. For that reason, it has an important tourist function. The Wild Atlantic Way also passes through Galway city, which is another boost for the city.
- As we have seen, Galway Airport was still closed at the time of writing in the spring of 2017. This is a loss to the business community of the city and to tourism.

> **DEFINITION**
>
> A **nodal point** is a route focus where routes, such as roads and/or railroads, meet.

Eyre Square in Galway city centre, where people take time out to relax

> **ACTIVITY**
>
> **Discussion**
> (i) How does the Wild Atlantic Way provide a boost for Galway city?
> (ii) Explain the term 'gateway to the West' in reference to Galway.

PowerPoint Summary

SUMMARY CHART

Two contrasting Irish regions

The Dublin region: A core region

- Primary economic activities
  - Agriculture
    - Tillage
    - Market gardening
  - Fishing
- Physical processes
  - Climate
  - Relief/drainage
  - Rocks
  - Soil
- Secondary economic activities
  - Key factors
    - Labour
    - Transport
    - Markets
- Tertiary economic activities
  - Transport
  - Tourism
  - Finance
- Human processes
  - Population change
    - Population structure
  - Migration
  - Urban development
    - Inner-city decline
    - Sprawl
    - New towns

The Western region: A peripheral region

- Physical processes
  - Climate
  - Relief/drainage
  - Rocks
  - Soil
- Primary economic activities
  - Agriculture
    - Grassland farming
    - Rough grazing
  - Fishing
    - Offshore gas
- Secondary economics activities
  - The challenges of a peripheral location
  - MNCs
  - The Galway cluster
- Human processes
  - Population distribution and density
  - Population change over time
  - Urban development
    - Galway city
- Tertiary activities
  - Transport
  - Tourism

CHAPTER 16 · THE DYNAMICS OF REGIONS 1

291

Leaving Cert exam questions

LONG QUESTIONS: HIGHER LEVEL

1. **Map skills** (20 marks)

   Draw an outline map of Ireland. On it, show and name different examples of each of the following:
   - The outline of a named geomorphological region
   - A named urban centre in a peripheral region
   - The outline of a named cultural region
   - The outline of a named core region.

2. **Agriculture in Ireland** (30 marks)

   Account for the development of agriculture in an **Irish** region that you have studied, with reference to any **two** of the following factors:
   - Relief
   - Climate
   - Markets.

3. **Agriculture in Ireland** (30 marks)

   Contrast the development of agriculture in **two Irish** regions that you have studied.

4. **Secondary economic activity** (30 marks)

   Examine the development of secondary economic activity in an **Irish** region that you have studied, with reference to any **two** of the following factors:
   - Raw materials
   - Transport
   - Labour
   - Markets.

5. **Secondary economic activity in Ireland** (30 marks)

   Examine the factors that influence the development of secondary economic activities in an **Irish** region that you have studied.

6. **Manufacturing industry** (30 marks)

   Describe and explain the development of manufacturing industry in an **Irish** region that you have studied.

7. **Tertiary activity in Ireland** (30 marks)

   Account for the development of transport **or** tourism in an **Irish** region that you have studied.

8. **Tertiary activities** (30 marks)

   Examine the development of tertiary economic activities in an **Irish** region that you have studied.

HL

9 Socio-economic regions (30 marks)

'Economic activities in core regions differ from those in peripheral regions.' Examine this statement with reference to examples that you have studied.

10 Population in Ireland (30 marks)

Account for the distribution of population throughout an **Irish** region that you have studied.

11 Irish regions (30 marks)

Irish regions can be defined by many factors, including:

> Physical
> Economic
> Human.

Examine how any **one** of the above factors has defined an **Irish** region that you have studied.

12 Urban development (30 marks)

Examine how **two** of the following factors have influenced the development of any **urban** region that you have studied:

> Transport
> Location
> Primary economic activities.

OL

LONG QUESTIONS: ORDINARY LEVEL

1 Irish region (30 marks)

Draw a sketch map of Ireland. On it, show and name each of the following:

> One region studied by you
> One named town or city in this region
> One named river in this region
> One named area of relief (upland or lowland) in this region.

2 Agriculture in Ireland (40 marks)

(i) Name **two** types of farming in Ireland.

(ii) Explain how any **two** types of the following factors influence the development of agriculture in an **Irish** region that you have studied.

> Relief and soils
> Markets
> Climate.

3 Agriculture in an Irish region (40 marks)

Name **one Irish** region that you have studied and answer each of the following questions:

(i) Name **two** types of agriculture practised in this region.
(ii) Explain the advantages that this region has for the development of agriculture.
(iii) Describe the challenges faced by agriculture in this region.

4 Economic activity in an Irish region (40 marks)

Explain any **two** of the following with reference to an **Irish** region that you have studied:

> The role of tourism in the economy of the region
> The reasons for the development of industry in the region
> The problems facing agriculture in the region.

5 Secondary economic activities – Irish region (40 marks)

Discuss how any **two** of the following factors influence the development of manufacturing industry in an **Irish** region that you have studied:

> Availability of transport networks
> Access to raw materials
> Markets
> Government and European Union policies.

6 Tourism in an Irish region (40 marks)

Name **one Irish** region that you have studied and answer each of the following questions:

(i) Name **two** tourist attractions in this region.
(ii) Explain the positive impacts of tourism in this region.
(iii) Explain the negative impacts of tourism in this region.

7 Regional problems (30 marks)

Describe **two** problems faced by any region that you have studied.

8 Urban growth (30 marks)

Explain the reasons for the growth of any urban region that you have studied.

Chapter 17
The Dynamics of Regions 2

UNIT 2 · REGIONAL GEOGRAPHY

KEYWORDS

- Paris Basin
- downwarp
- côtes
- granary
- Champagne
- Falaise d'Île-de-France
- deindustrialisation
- agri-resource biotech industry
- Cosmetic Valley
- theme park
- SNCF
- TGV
- primate city
- Mezzogiorno
- Sirocco
- Campania
- Apulia
- the Cassa
- Autostrada del Sole
- *latifundia*
- growth poles
- Taranto
- Etna Valley
- Gioia Tauro
- brain drain

LEARNING OBJECTIVES

By the end of this chapter, you should be able to understand:

- How to locate two contrasting Europeans regions
- How to identify the physical characteristics of each region
- How to discuss the primary, secondary and tertiary economic activities of each region
- How to examine some of the human processes of the region, such as population change and urban developments.

The dynamics of regions

This chapter examines physical, economic and human processes in **two contrasting European regions**: one from Western Europe and one from the Mediterranean. We will examine the Paris Basin (a core region) and the Mezzogiorno in Italy (a peripheral region).

Figure 17.1 The Paris Basin (a core region) and the Mezzogiorno (a peripheral region)

ACTIVITY

Skills

Examine Figure 17.1.

(i) What is the name of the sea between Europe and Africa?

(ii) Can you name the sea between the UK and France?

THE PARIS BASIN: A CORE EUROPEAN REGION

The Paris Basin is the most important economic region in France. The region has excellent soils and one of the most productive agricultural industries in the world. The manufacturing sector is very strong. However, the great majority of workers are in the tertiary sector.

One-third of the population of France lives in the Paris Basin. Greater Paris plays a dominant role in the economic and cultural life of France.

Physical processes

Relief

ACTIVITY

Research

Look up the meaning of the term *scarp* on the internet.

ACTIVITY

Skills

Examine Figure 17.2.

(i) What is the largest river in the Paris Basin?

(ii) What is the highest point in Normandy?

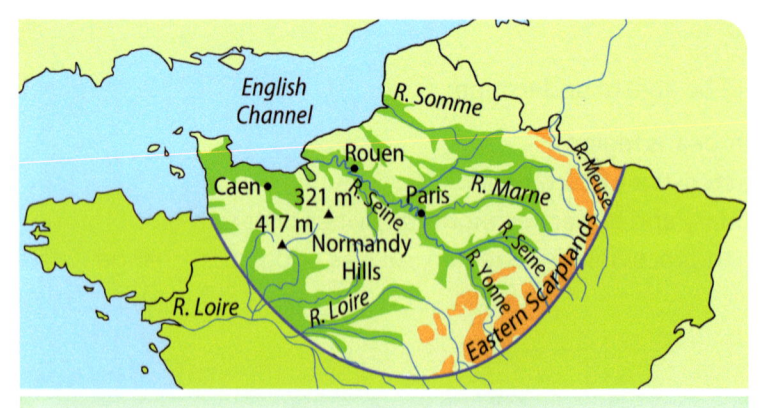

Figure 17.2 The Paris Basin showing relief, drainage and major cities

The Paris Basin is called a basin because it a great **downwarp** or **syncline** in the Earth's crust. Layers of bedrock shaped like saucers of decreasing size rest inside each other. The central layer is known as **Île-de-France**.

Travelling outwards from Île-de-France, lower layers appear. The lower layers of rock rise sharply around the outer limits of the basin, especially towards the south-east. These layers create distinctive areas known in France as *pays*. The relief in the south-eastern rim is composed of **scarps**, called *côtes* in French, such as the Côtes de Meuse.

GEOFACT

Examples of *pays* in the Paris Basin are Beauce, Brie and Champagne.

Drainage

The Paris Basin is well drained. Sedimentary rocks such as chalk, limestone and sandstone form the bedrock of much of the basin. These allow surface water to percolate downwards. The Seine River and its tributaries drain most of the basin. To the west, the Loire River and its tributaries flow into the Bay of Biscay.

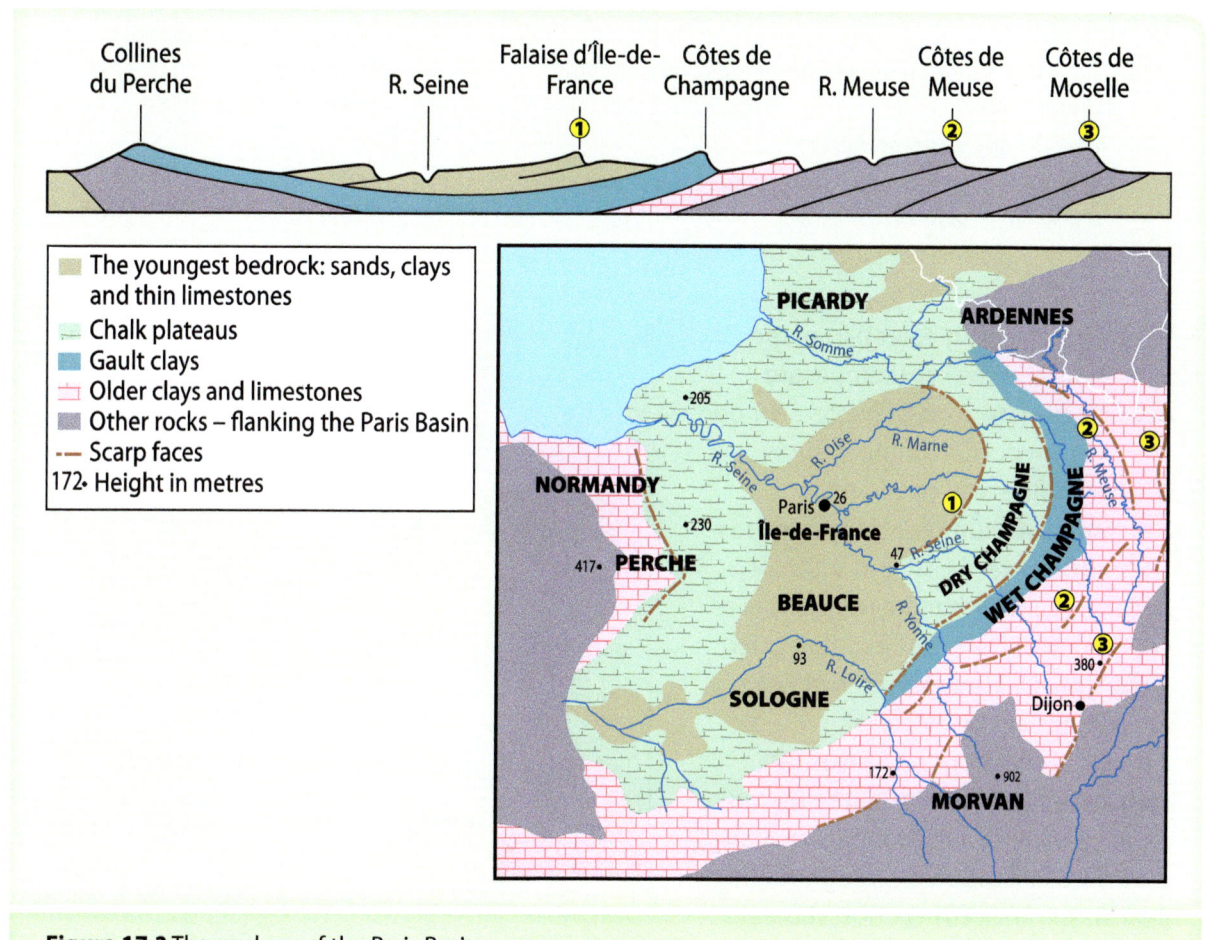

Figure 17.3 The geology of the Paris Basin

ACTIVITY

Skills

Examine Figure 17.3.

(i) What is the underlying rock in Picardy?

(ii) Name the area in the centre of the basin.

Climate

THE CLIMATE OF ÎLE-DE-FRANCE	Jan	Feb	Mar	Apr	May	Jun	Jul	Aug	Sept	Oct	Nov	Dec
Average temperature (°C)	5	5.5	8.5	10.5	15	18	20	20	16	13	8	5.5
Precipitation (mm)	46	39	41	44	56	57	57	55	53	56	54	49

Table 17.1 The climate of Île-de-France in the Paris Basin

ACTIVITY

Numeracy

Examine Table 17.1.
  (i) Calculate the total amount of precipitation per annum in Île-de-France.
  (ii) Name the two warmest months.
  (iii) For how many months does the average temperature drop to 8°C or below?

ACTIVITY

Skills

Using graph paper, draw a graph of the temperature in degrees Celsius of the Paris Basin.

- The climate of the greater part of the Paris Basin is in the **cool temperate oceanic climate zone** of Western Europe.
- The western portion of the basin is strongly influenced by the Atlantic. It has **moderate summer temperatures** and **mild winters**. East and south of Paris, the climate is more transitional as continental influences become evident. Here, summers are warmer and winters are colder than further west.
- Atlantic depressions bring **frontal rain** across the Paris Basin. The region receives more than 600 mm of rainfall that is well distributed throughout the year. In summer, **convection showers** occur during some afternoons.

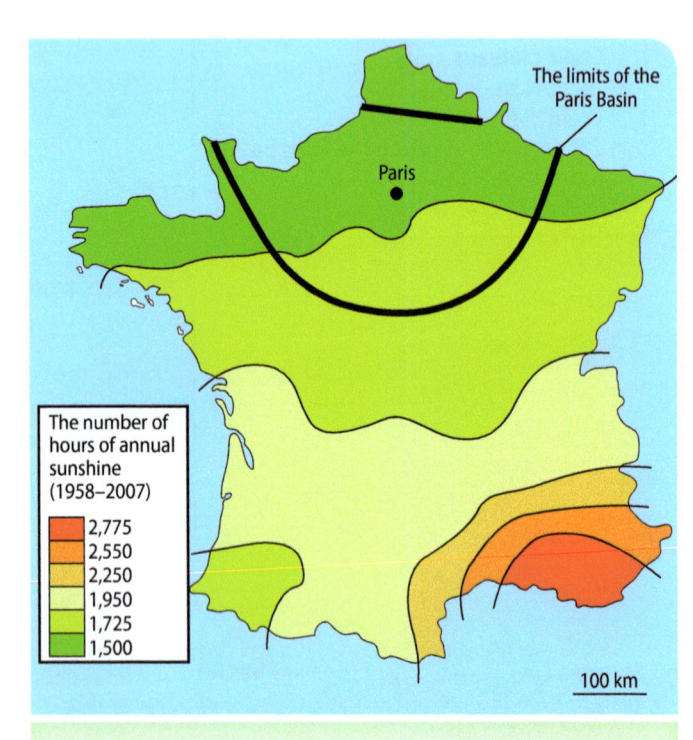

Figure 17.4 The number of hours of sunshine in France, with the Paris Basin outlined

Primary economic activities

Agriculture

The Paris Basin has a modern and highly mechanised agricultural sector that employs about 4% of the workforce. The region is one of the most important wheat producers in the EU.

Four distinct farming areas of the region are surveyed in Figure 17.5: Normandy, Beauce, Brie and Champagne.

HINT

Exam watch: The examiner is likely to ask for **two or three** factors that influence agriculture in a region of your choice.

Farming areas of the Paris Basin

Normandy

Normandy has a **maritime climate** because of its proximity to the sea. This suits grassland farming. Therefore, **dairy farming** is important here. Dairy processing companies process the milk into cheese and yogurt.

Normandy also specialises in **apple production** and the cider industry. The limestone bedrock encourages the existence of the bloodstock industry, where horses develop strong bone structure because the soil is rich in calcium.

> **DEFINITION**
>
> **Granary:** A region that produces grain, such as wheat and other cereals, or a storage area for grain in a farm.

Legend:
- Cereals
- Cereals and grazing of cattle
- Cattle, sheep
- Vine cultivation
- Market gardening

Beauce

Beauce, one of the great **granaries** of the EU, is devoted to cereal production of crops such as wheat and barley on rich limon soils. The farms are among the largest in Western Europe – most are more than 100 hectares each. This is industrial farming on a grand scale.

Farming methods are highly mechanised and output per hectare is among the highest in the EU. Agricultural contractors use light aircraft to dust the crops with fungicides and pesticides. **Rotation crops** such as maize and sunflowers are also grown. Farmers are progressive and embrace new technologies readily.

> **DEFINITION**
>
> **Rotation crops:** Under this system, crops such as wheat, maize, barley and sunflowers are rotated in successive years in farmland to avoid soil exhaustion.

> **LINK**
>
> Look back at the map of the administrative regions of France on page 229 with particular reference to the area occupied by the Paris Basin.

Brie

Brie, east of Paris, has **heavier soils** with a higher clay content because of some shale bedrock. These soils make ideal **grassland** for cattle grazing. Brie specialises in dairy farming and supplies Greater Paris with its fresh milk. Dairy herds are scientifically managed with feed concentrates and have high milk yields. The famous Brie cheese, butter and yogurt are processed in milk processing plants.

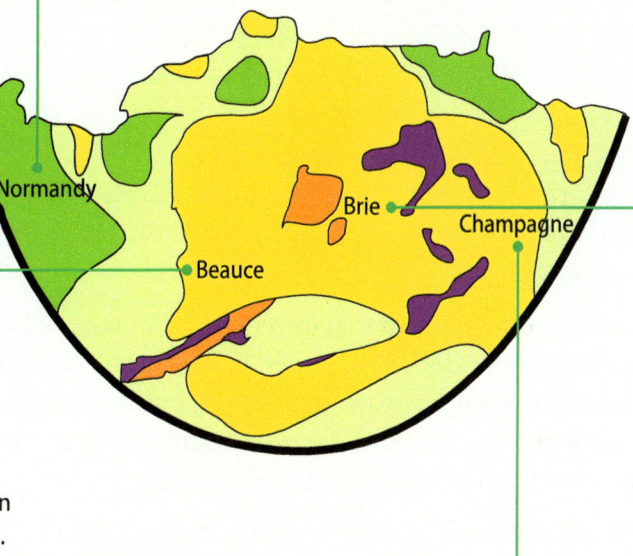

Champagne

Champagne wine is the most famous product of the Paris Basin. The grapes for this wine are grown on the **south-facing scarps** in the Champagne district, east of Paris. One such scarp is the Falaise d'Île-de-France (see Figure 17.3 on page 297 for its location).

The formula for this wine was developed by Benedictine monks in the eighteenth century and is one of the best-kept secrets in France. Champagne has been copied in other parts of the world. Champagne wine is a protected product and only wine produced in this region can be called Champagne.

The wine is aged in underground cellars that have been carved out of the soft chalk rock. The city of **Reims** is the market centre where new vintages of Champagne are launched.

Figure 17.5 Agriculture in the Paris Basin

Factors that influence agriculture in the Paris Basin

Relief

The relief of the Paris Basin is generally flat or undulating. This relief is ideal for using heavy farm machinery for tillage, planting and harvesting. The flat landscape also prevents soil erosion because runoff of rainwater is largely absent. Steep scarps in the south-east are wooded.

Climate

The climate has a positive influence on the agriculture of the Paris Basin (see details on page 298).

- The Paris Basin has a long growing season of about eight months.
- Winter frosts break up the ploughed soil in preparation for spring sowing of crops.
- The western and coastal areas of the Paris Basin have an early spring because of the influence of the sea, allowing for the early planting and germination of cereal seeds. Seeds begin to germinate when average temperatures reach 6°C. This happens around the end of March or early April.
- Summer temperatures, which exceed 20°C by day, are perfect for ripening cereals such as wheat, oats, barley and hybrid maize.
- Sunny weather in late July and August is ideal for harvesting cereals.

Soils

The soils of the Paris Basin are fertile. The basin is covered with a thick layer of **limon**. Limon is composed of light material that was blown south to the Basin following the last ice age. Limon has weathered into a fertile and stoneless soil.

The soil is a **brown earth** that developed from the original natural vegetation of deciduous tree cover. The minerals are not leached because of the moderate rainfall. The soil is a free-draining mix of silt, sand and clay. This makes it a **loam soil**. It is ideal for ploughing and for the rapid germination of cereal seeds.

> **GEOFACT**
> Loam soils have about 40% silt, 40% sand and 20% clay.

Fertile **alluvial soils** are found close to the rivers Seine, Loire and their tributaries. These support a wide variety of crops, such as vines and vegetables.

The variety of bedrock explains the presence of different minerals in each area.

Markets

The Paris Basin has a large market. With 22 million people in the Basin, there is a high demand for agricultural products such as fresh vegetables. These are grown in the market gardening belt around Paris. Many perishable and delicate vegetables are grown under glass, including lettuce, tomatoes and cucumbers.

The transport network of the Basin is radial and is focused on Paris. Farm produce such as milk from Brie is rapidly transported by truck to the Greater Paris **market** of some 12 million people.

The Paris Basin, a core economic region, is **centrally situated** in North-West Europe. This area has a population of at least 120 million people. The market is easy to reach, as one of the best rail and road transport networks in the world exists here. **Centrality** works in favour of the farm producers of the Paris Basin. Champagne, the most famous agricultural export of France, enjoys a global market.

Figure 17.6a The percentage of Champagne exports, both by volume and by value, in the total wine exports of France

Exports by volume: 89% Other wines, 7% Champagne, 4% Other sparkling wines

Exports by value: 68% Other wines, 29% Champagne, 3% Other sparkling wines

ACTIVITY

Numeracy

Examine Figure 17.6a.

(i) Champagne accounts for what percentage of French wine exports by volume?

(ii) Champagne accounts for what percentage of French wine exports by value?

(iii) What conclusion can you draw from that?

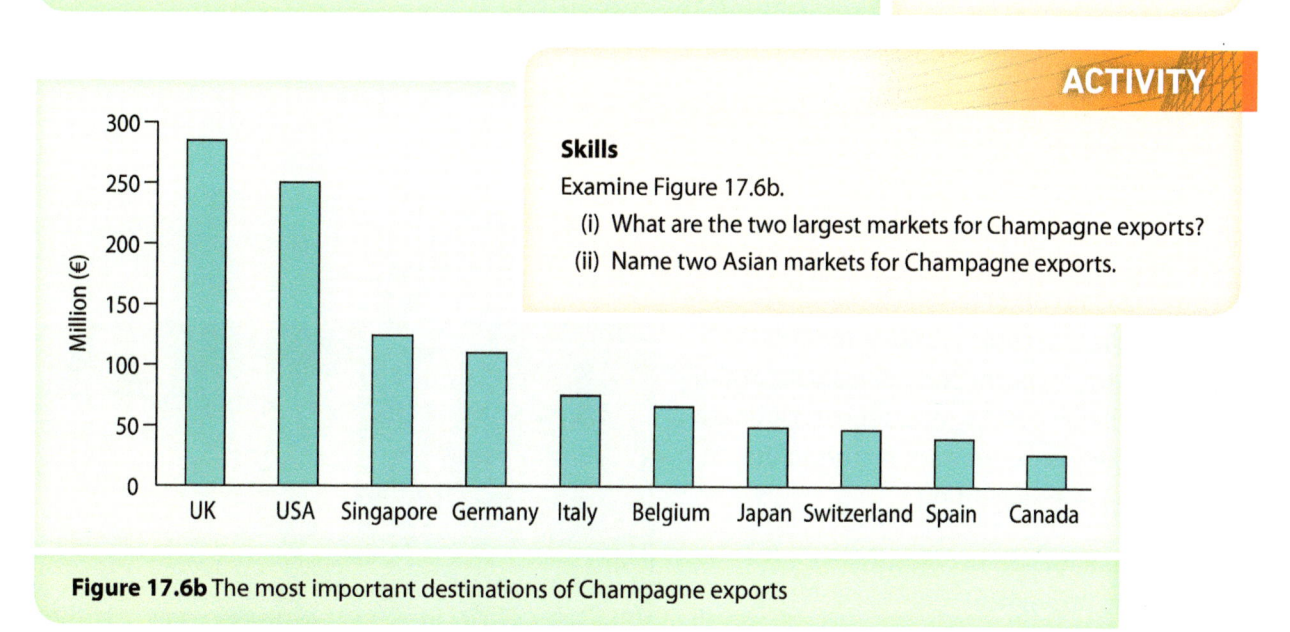

Figure 17.6b The most important destinations of Champagne exports

ACTIVITY

Skills

Examine Figure 17.6b.

(i) What are the two largest markets for Champagne exports?

(ii) Name two Asian markets for Champagne exports.

Fishing

The Paris Basin has a long coastline facing the English Channel. Fish is a central feature of French cuisine, as can be seen in supermarkets and fish shops in France.

Large fishing fleets dock in the sheltered ports of Cherbourg, Le Havre and Dieppe. Coastal and deep-sea trawlers land their fish in those ports. Fleets travel as far afield as the Bay of Biscay and the waters around Ireland. Demersal, pelagic and shellfish species are caught by French fleets. Trawlers are modern, with strong purse seine nets, heavy lifting gear and electronic technology.

Figure 17.7 Fishing ports on the coast of the Paris Basin

The French are governed by EU fishing restrictions, just like every other fleet in EU waters. Quotas are placed on annual catches as part of sustainable fishing policies so that fish will be available for the next generations.

Aquaculture is also practised in inlets and bays of the Channel coast, with a concentration on shellfish, such as oysters and mussels.

Fishing trawlers in Le Havre

Secondary economic activities

Manufacturing

France is the **sixth largest economy** in the world and is a major manufacturing economy. Manufacturing is very strong in the Greater Paris area and other urban centres in the Paris Basin. It accounts for one-fifth of the manufacturing production of France. Labour factors, the availability of resource materials and markets are important factors in the success of manufacturing.

Industries where the quality of labour is important

The fashion industry

Paris is a global leader in the fashion and luxury goods industry. This industry began when kings ruled in France long before the French Revolution of 1789.

Today, fashion workshops are in the city centre along the banks of the Seine. This location gives the industry access to the media for publicity and fashion shows. Fashion houses include Chanel, Céline, Chloé, Dior and Pierre Cardin. **Cartier** (jewellery and watches) and **Louis Vuitton** (a luxury goods manufacturer) are also in Paris.

Fashion and luxury goods enjoy a huge export trade, especially to China in recent decades.

A model wearing a dress designed by the French designer Jean Paul Gaultier at a Paris fashion show

In the fashion industry, a **skilled labour force** is very important. Apprentices are trained for several years in the delicate work that dressmaking and tailoring requires. The fashion industry in Paris has a long tradition and many parents pass on their skills to their children in small family businesses. **Designers** in high fashion houses possess exceptional artistic flair and are drawn from all over the world.

The cosmetics industry

France and especially Paris have been associated with perfumes for many centuries. However, much of the cosmetics industry has moved to cities in Centre such as Chartres, Orléans and Tours, where sites are cheaper and more spacious than in Paris. This move out of Paris is an example of the **decentralisation** of manufacturing.

The area where this **cluster** of cosmetics manufacturers is located has become known as **Cosmetic Valley**. A wide range of toiletries, perfumes and soaps are produced here. Hermès, Nina Ricci, Lierac, Paco Rabanne, L'Oréal and Guerlain are located here.

The most important person in the *parfumerie* is **the nose** (*le nez*). The nose is a highly trained specialist with an exceptional sense of smell who blends new perfumes.

ACTIVITY

Thinking

(i) Explain why the French fashion industry is based in Paris. Give two reasons.

(ii) The fashion industry in Paris gives the city a global influence. Explain that statement.

Figure 17.8 Cities with cosmetics industries in Centre

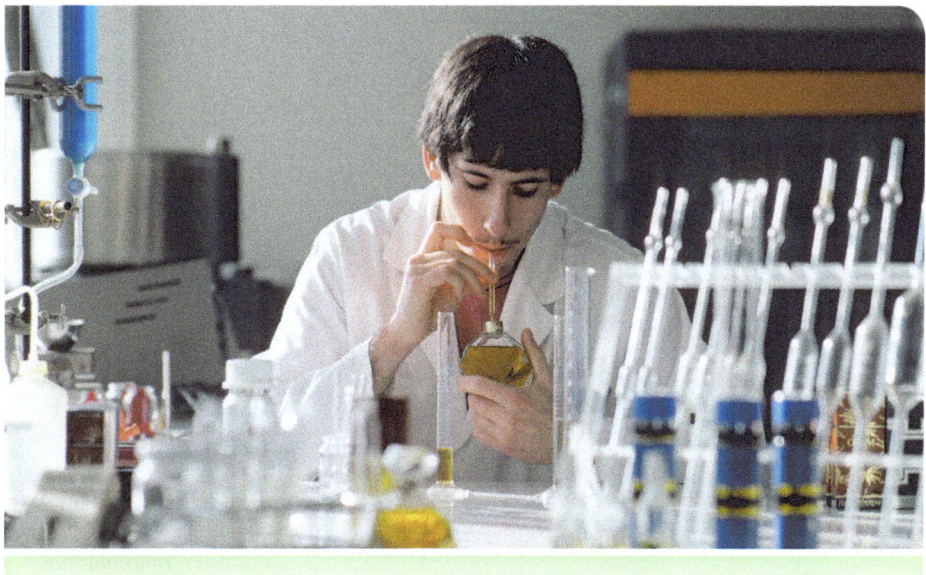

A scientist, known as *le nez*, in a Guerlain laboratory preparing a new perfume

Modern fields of manufacturing

Modern industrial processes such as healthcare, pharmaceuticals, defence and aerospace also require highly skilled workers. These manufacturers are located in **technological parks** in the new satellite towns around Paris. France is a world leader in **missile systems** and in guidance systems for aircraft.

Paris has seventeen universities and other third-level regional colleges that produce thousands of graduates in management, the sciences and engineering. These include the **Pantheon-Sorbonne University**, one of Europe's oldest universities, and the **École Polytechnique (ParisTech)**, one of the world's foremost engineering universities.

Manufacturers use the **skills of research workers** in scientific organisations in Paris to design new products at the cutting edge of science. These include the biomedical area, aerospace and pharmaceuticals.

> **GEOFACT**
>
> France is a major arms producer.

> **DEFINITION**
>
> A **technological park** is an area, often beside a university, where companies involved in scientific research and producing new technologies are based.

A French Exocet missile, manufactured in the Greater Paris area

Industries where resource-based materials are important

The Paris Basin provides a wide variety of **resource materials** for manufacturing. Agricultural raw materials are first on the list:

- **Wheat** is processed into flour in Caen, Amiens and Rouen.
- **Flour** is used in the bakery and confectionery industry, found in many urban centres.
- **Milk** from Brie and Normandy is used for dairy processing in Paris, Caen and Rouen.
- **Grapes** from Champagne and the Loire Valley are pressed into grape juice and wine in Reims and Orléans.
- **Apples** are used in Normandy to produce cider, apple juice and calvados (an apple liqueur).
- **Sunflowers oils** are processed into cooking oils and spreads used on bread.
- **Cereals and vegetable oils** are refined for the biotech industries in Picardy.

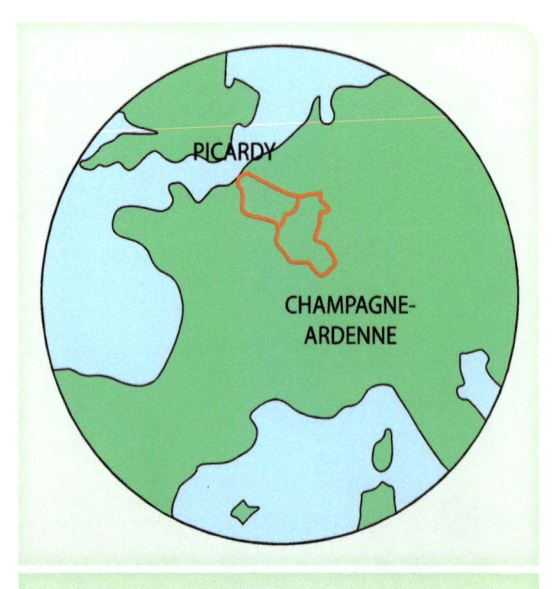

Figure 17.9 The Picardy and Champagne district, where agricultural raw materials are used to create new biotech products

Innovation in biotech industries

Since 2005, many developments have taken place in **biotech industries** in the areas of Picardy and Champagne. These are based on agricultural raw materials. In association with the University of Reims Champagne-Ardenne and public/private laboratories, **cereals**, **sunflowers**, **hemp** and **wood** have been processed to make new **industrial products**. **Scientists** working in laboratories have refined and extracted materials from these agricultural resources to manufacture a wide variety of biologically based products. These include insulation materials, paints, ethanol fuel, washing powders, natural dyes and nail polish.

This biotech manufacturing is a new field of modern industry where France is becoming a **world leader**. Manufacturing plants are located in Amiens, Laon and Reims.

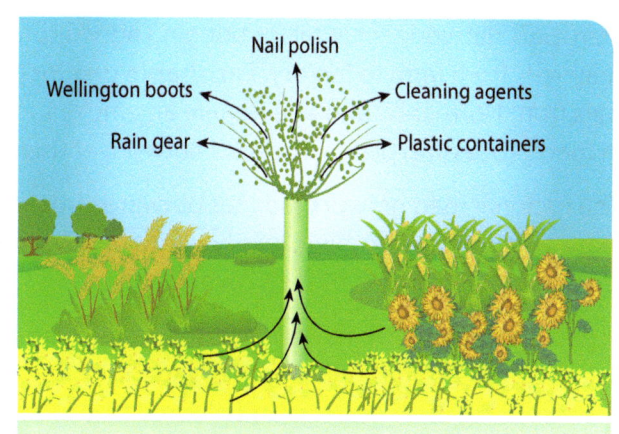

Figure 17.10 Industrial biotech products processed from agricultural raw materials in the Paris Basin

Figure 17.11 Manufacturing centres in the Paris Basin (excluding Paris)

The importance of transport in manufacturing in the Paris Basin

Transport factors are important to the success of manufacturing in the Paris Basin. The ports of **Le Havre** and **Rouen** are important for the import of industrial raw materials, such as crude oil for oil refineries. Ores and semi-finished products are transferred to barges for transport along the **Seine River**, which is navigable as far as Paris.

GEOFACT

Paris has a large inland port.

These barges enter the Canal Saint-Denis in northern Paris. There are many factories and foundries on its banks. The factories use steel for manufacturing heavy machinery, such as boilers and girders.

Transport networks are vital for bringing agricultural raw materials from farm to factory. **Perishable products** such as milk from Normandy and Brie require an efficient road network for processing in food processing plants. The road network of the Basin is excellent.

The national road network radiates outwards from Paris to the provinces of France. This brings clothing, luxury goods and healthcare products from the Greater Paris area to markets all over France.

A great network of motorways and railways connects the Paris Basin to urban centres in the Low Countries and the Rhineland, where French processed foods, wines, cars and pharmaceuticals find a market. The location of the Paris Basin in the economic core of the EU gives it an advantage over more distant regions.

> **LINK**
>
> See the transport map (Figure 17.15) on page 309.

Deindustrialisation in the Greater Paris area

Greater Paris has experienced some **deindustrialisation** of manufacturing because of small sites and the high cost of land and labour in the city. An example is car assembly. Renault closed its cramped assembly plant in Billancourt in Paris and moved to Yvelines, 40 km outside the city. Citroën-Peugeot decamped to Rennes in Brittany many years ago.

> **DEFINITION**
>
> **Deindustrialisation:** The decline of manufacturing in an area (both in the number of plants and the number of workers).

Tertiary economic activities

About 70% of the population of the Paris Basin works in the tertiary sector across a wide range of economic activities. This figure is increasing. We will examine two tertiary economic activities:

- Tourism
- Transport.

Tourism

Tourism is very important in the urban centres of the Paris Basin. There are several factors responsible for its development.

Historic attractions

Most cities of the Paris Basin date from the Middle Ages. **Historic centres** have been pedestrianised, which makes them more pleasant for tourists. Historic attractions are well signposted. The cities of the Paris Basin have some of the finest **Gothic cathedrals** in Europe, which have free entry. Tourist guides are available to help tourists deepen

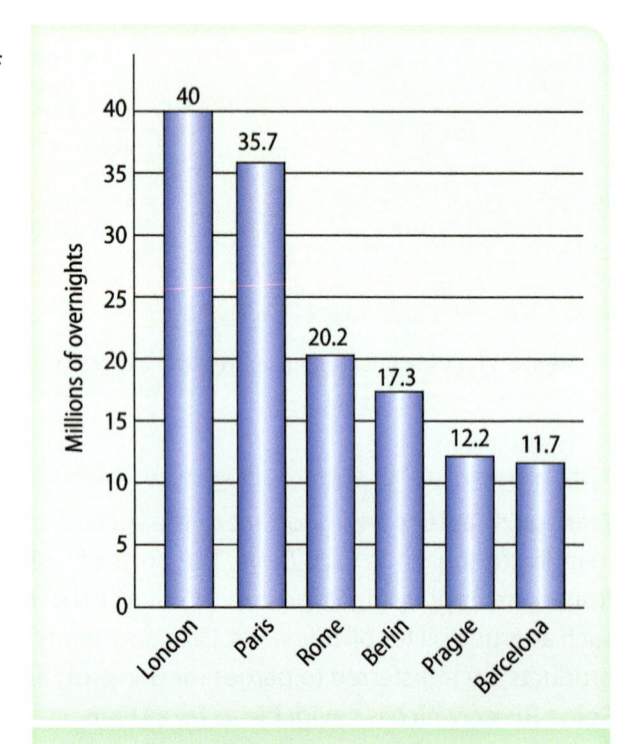

Figure 17.12 The number of overnights per annum spent by tourists in Europe's most popular urban tourist centres

City	Millions of overnights
London	40
Paris	35.7
Rome	20.2
Berlin	17.3
Prague	12.2
Barcelona	11.7

their understanding of these magnificent structures. Gothic cathedrals are found in Chartres, Reims and Rouen.

There are many interesting chateaux or **castles** in the region. Foremost among them is **Versailles**, built in the seventeenth century by Louis XIV and home to the royal family before the French Revolution. The chateau in **Fontainebleau**, south of Paris, was built by the kings as a hunting lodge. The chateau, its woodlands and grounds are now open to visitors.

The **beaches of Normandy** saw the Allied invasion of Nazi-occupied Europe in 1944. This coast and the Allied graveyards now attract many British and American visitors.

> ### ACTIVITY
>
> **Research**
>
> Look up images of the Gothic cathedrals of Reims and Chartres on the internet.

The entrance to the Chateau of Versailles outside Paris

Theme parks

There are two theme parks close to Paris:

› Disneyland Paris is in Marne-la Vallée, east of the capital. It is near Charles de Gaulle Airport and is well served by the TGV and motorways.
› Parc Astérix is also close to Paris and is very French in character.

> ### GEOFACTS
>
> › The Chateau of Versailles receives some 7.5 million visitors each year.
> › Disneyland Paris hosted 14.8 million visitors in 2015.

Figure 17.13 Tourist attractions of the Paris Basin

The attractions of Paris

Paris is the second most visited city in Europe after London. The tourist industry in Paris supports 240,000 jobs. Paris is a world city, so many businesspeople spend time there.

The city has one of the world's most famous streets: the **Champs-Élysées**. The art galleries and museums such as the Louvre and the Palais-Royal are among the world's greatest.

Other outstanding attractions include:

- The Eiffel Tower
- Notre Dame Cathedral
- The Arc de Triomphe
- The artists' quarter in Montmartre
- Napoleon's tomb at *les Invalides*.

DEFINITION

World city: A city with a global influence. Paris is a world city because of its fashion industry, which attracts customers from all over the world.

ACTIVITY

Research

Use the internet to find out more about the attractions of Paris that are mentioned in the text.

The artists' quarter in Montmartre, Paris attracts many tourists

The infrastructure of tourism

The Paris region is well suited to visitors. The region has several **airports**, including Charles de Gaulle, Orly and Beauvais. Tourists can use the excellent **transport networks** both in the region and in Greater Paris to get to their favourite attractions.

Hotels range from basic to sophisticated. The Bois de Boulogne, a green area in the centre of Paris, has a campsite and caravan park.

Restaurants cater for every taste. In recent years, it has become fashionable for the French to make an effort to speak **English** to tourists. This is partly because most EU visitors learn English as a second language.

Café culture is alive and well on the pavements of Paris

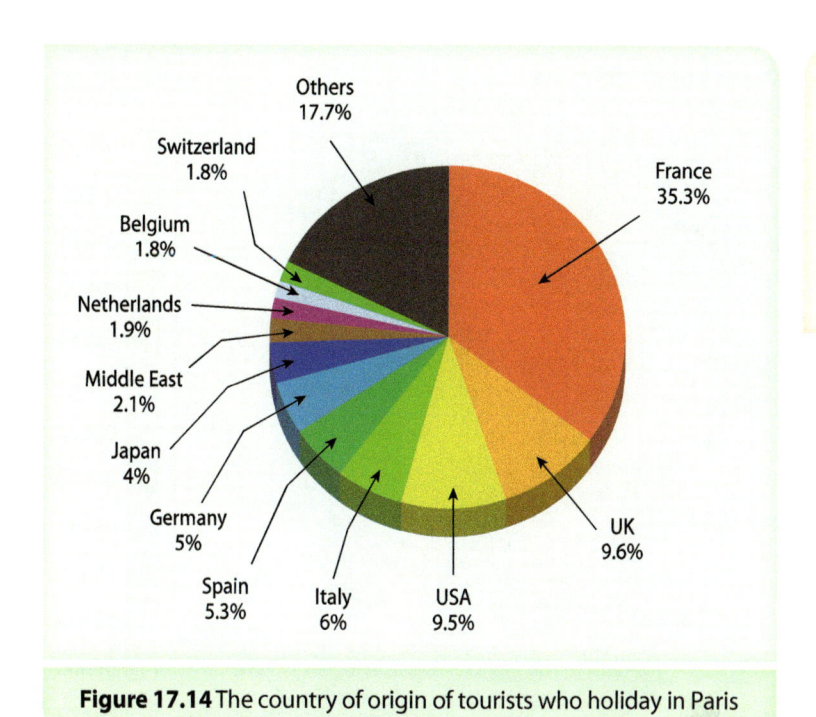

Figure 17.14 The country of origin of tourists who holiday in Paris

ACTIVITY

Numeracy

Examine Figure 17.14. What percentage of visitors to Paris come from Germany, Spain and Italy combined?

Transport

Since the Paris Basin is one of the core economic regions of the EU, its transport networks are highly advanced. As Paris is the **economic engine** of the region, routeways in the Basin are **radial**, e.g. road and rail networks radiate outwards across France from Paris.

Road networks

Motorways connect Paris with all the other regions of France. These are toll roads and are well maintained. The flat, undulating landscape has made motorway construction cheaper. Paris itself is surrounded by the Boulevard Périphérique, a great ring motorway. All of the major cities of the region have bypasses.

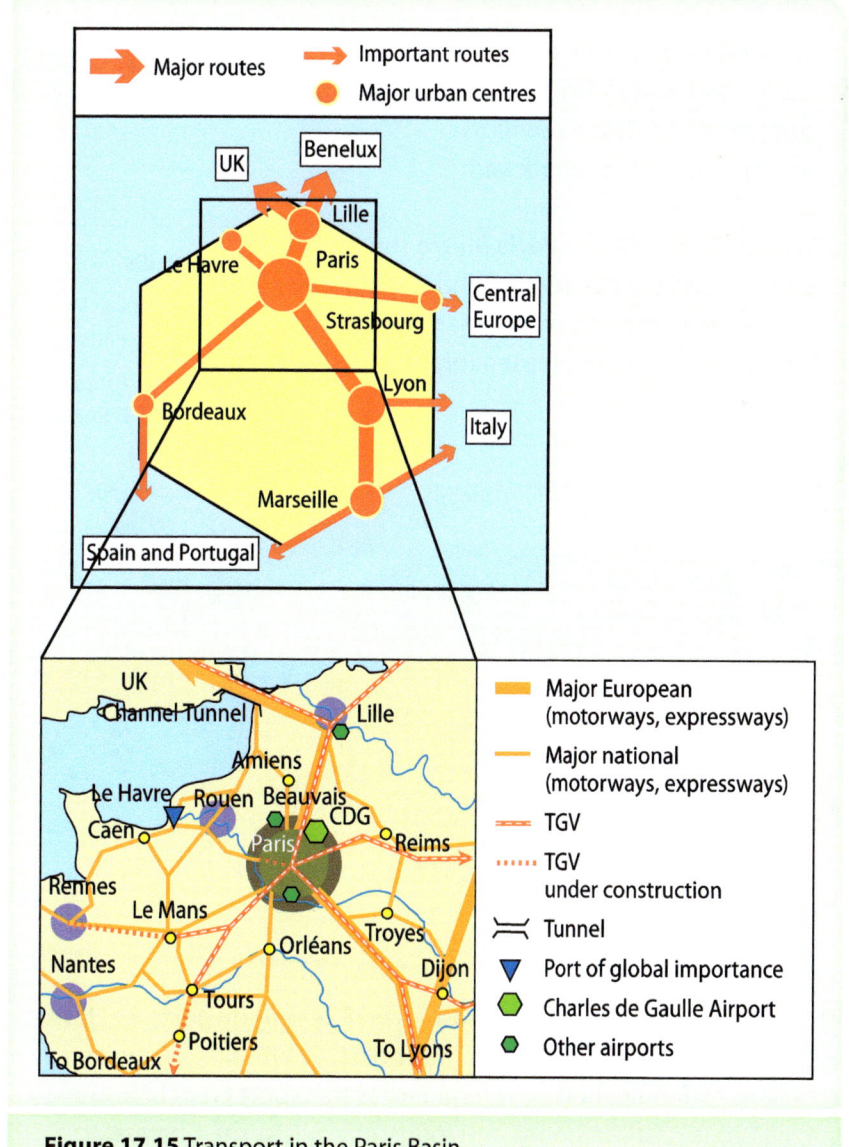

Figure 17.15 Transport in the Paris Basin

CHAPTER 17 · THE DYNAMICS OF REGIONS 2   309

Rail

The national rail company is called the SNCF. The rail network travels outwards from Paris. The pride of the rail network is the TGV, which run on special tracks and regularly reach speeds of 320 km/hr. TGV trains connect Paris to the provinces of France. TGV trains also connect Paris to Cologne, Brussels, Amsterdam and London via the Channel Tunnel. This high-speed transport has greatly reduced the use of internal air transport in France.

Many passengers commute to work in Paris from the Île-de-France every day. Suburban and urban rail services in Paris include:

> The **RER** rapid transit system brings commuters from the suburbs and satellite towns to the city. The RER has park and ride facilities outside Paris.
> Within Paris itself, the **Paris Metro** runs underground. It has 16 lines and 303 stations. The Metro carries 4.5 million passengers a day. It is fast, efficient and reasonably cheap.

Departures from Paris

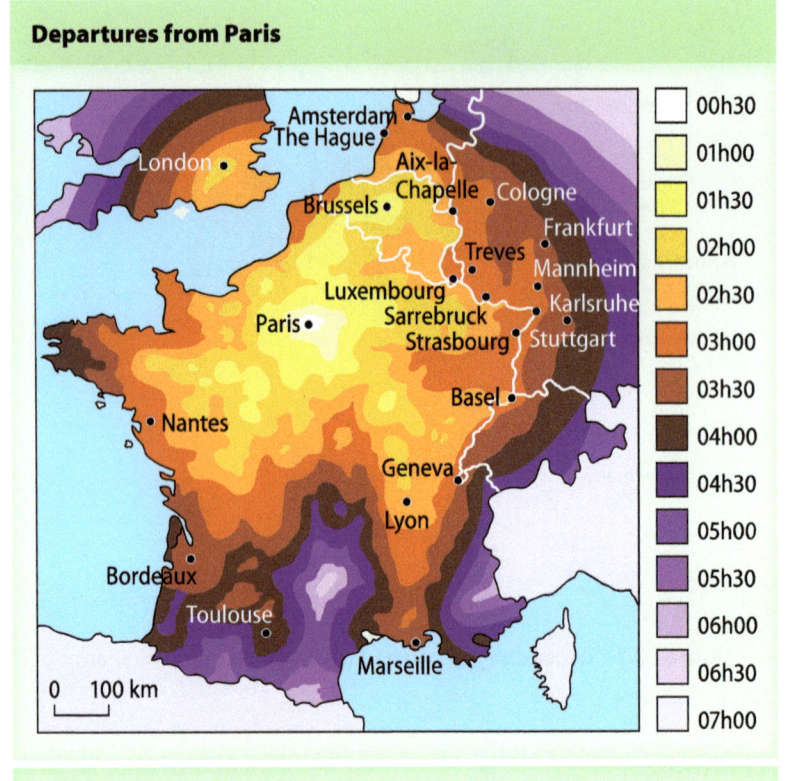

Figure 17.16 The journey times for passengers using rapid rail transport from Paris

ACTIVITY

Skills

Examine Figure 17.16. How long does the journey from Paris to the following destinations take?

(i) Amsterdam
(ii) Frankfurt
(iii) Lyon
(iv) Marseille

TGVs ready to depart from Paris-Gare de Lyon

Ports

The Channel coast of the Paris Basin is well served by ports. Le Havre is one of Europe's busiest ports. The English Channel has many ferry crossings to Britain. Roll-on roll-off ferries transport French produce such as wine, fashion goods and foodstuffs across the Channel to Britain. The Seine River is navigable as far as Paris.

Airports

Charles de Gaulle Airport (CDG), also known as Roissy Airport, was opened in 1974. It is the sixth busiest airport in the world. It is also home to **Air France–KLM**, one of the world's largest airlines. The airport has 80,000 employees who provide the services required by an average of 200,000 passengers a day.

Several modes of transport exist in this vast airport complex to facilitate passenger journeys to and from the airport and to the departure gates within the airport.

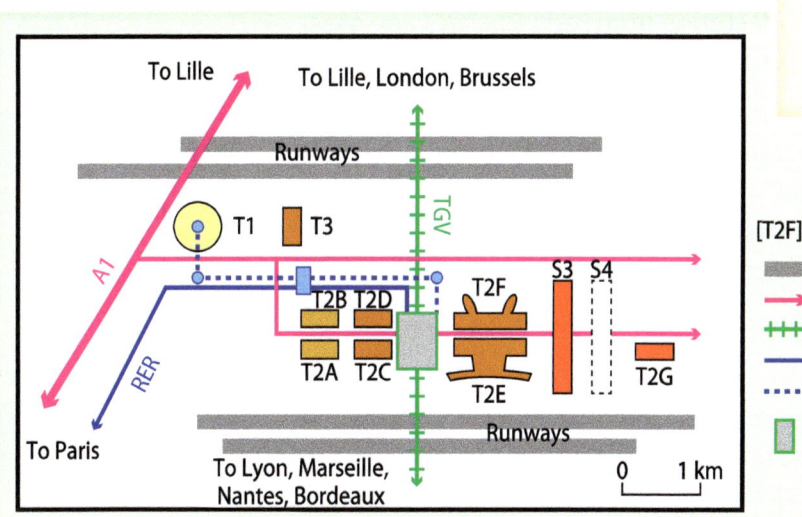

> **GEOFACT**
>
> Charles de Gaulle Airport carried 64 million passengers in 2015.

> **ACTIVITY**
>
> **Discussion**
>
> Examine Figure 17.17. Passengers who travel to and from the CDG Airport are well served by public transport. Explain that statement.

Figure 17.17 Charles de Gaulle Airport. The airport is served by many modes of transport.

Human processes

Population density and distribution

The Paris Basin, with some 22 million people, contains one-third of the population of France. The population is unevenly distributed within the basin.

Île-de-France, which includes Greater Paris, had slightly more than **12.2 million people** in 2016 and has very high densities. Why is this?

› There are many economic opportunities in the Greater Paris area.
› Paris is the seat of government and is supported by many public service workers.

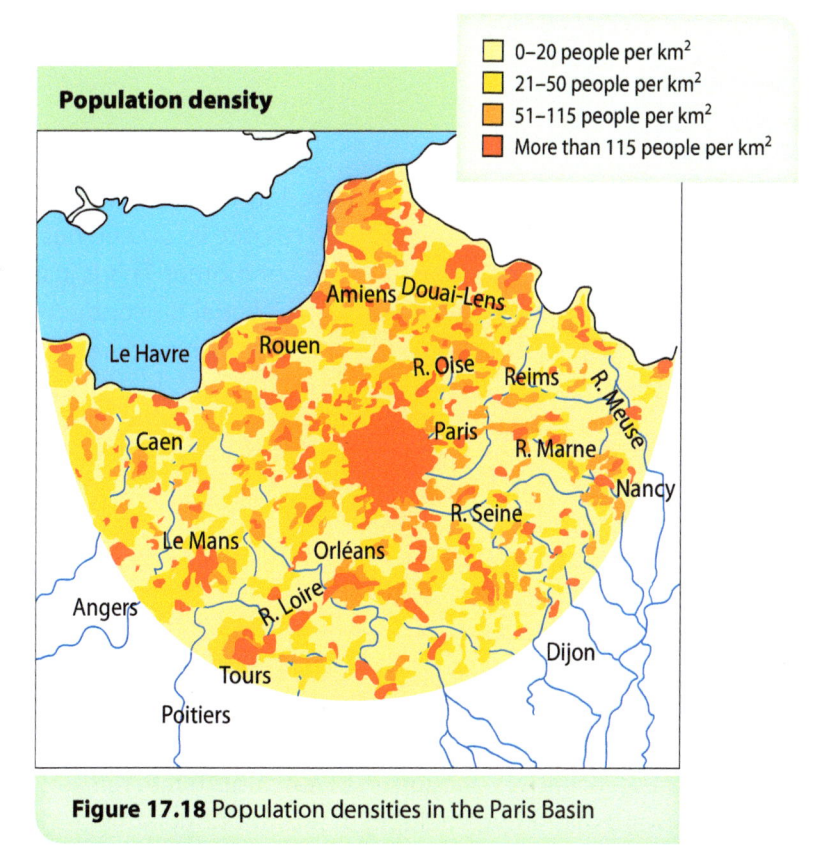

Figure 17.18 Population densities in the Paris Basin

- The banking, commercial, cultural, entertainment and tourist sectors are huge. The manufacturing sector is still strong.
- Greater Paris has received vast numbers of inward migrants from the provinces of France and from further afield. This is adding to its population.

High densities also exist along the lower valley of the Seine River between Paris and Le Havre. **Rouen** is the next largest city in the Paris Basin after Paris, with 466,000 people. Rouen supports major manufacturing and tertiary activities.

Chartres and **Orléans** have seen their populations increase in recent decades due to the decentralisation of manufacturing from Paris. Chartres and other cities in the region form part of Cosmetic Valley (see page 303).

The population density in the Paris Basin outside the Île-de-France is quite low. While these areas have urban centres, such as Amiens and Rouen, they are predominantly rural in character. The flight from the countryside has left a **low rural density** of people, in many cases fewer than 20 per km^2.

The flight from the countryside during the last hundred years has been due to:

- The mechanisation of agriculture and the decline in the demand for farm workers
- The decline of small rural towns and villages due to the decline of the rural economy
- The increase in educational levels among the young, who aspire to jobs that are only available in towns and cities
- The pull of Paris in terms of jobs, culture and lifestyle has proved irresistible for young people from the countryside.

GEOFACT

Rural areas of the Paris Basin have very low densities. These are close to the rural densities of the Western region in Ireland.

Population change

Birth rates

France, including the Paris Basin, is at stage 4 (the low fluctuating stage) of the demographic cycle. Therefore, the birth rate is low and has been for decades. The fertility rate is 2.0 children per mother. This is just below the replacement level. The French government is conducting a campaign to raise the birth rate with the following incentives:

- France offers a means-tested birth/adoption grant.
- France has a generous maternity leave policy. Women on maternity leave receive their full salary for 16 weeks (26 weeks if it is their third child). Fathers are entitled to 11 consecutive days of paternity leave with no loss of pay.
- France provides subsidised crèche fees for working mothers related to their means.
- France also provides high children's allowances, especially for a third child.

ACTIVITY

Numeracy

If the birth rate is 2.0 per mother on average, how many babies do twenty mothers have between them?

Even with these incentives, though, the French birth rate remains low. However, inward migration is helping to prevent population decline.

Death rates

As a very advanced country, death rates in France are low. This is because **life expectancy** is high. **Infant mortality rates** are among the lowest in the world.

Because birth rates and death rates in the Paris Basin are very low, there is only a small natural increase. However, inward migration of young adults has caused a small increase in population.

LIFE EXPECTANCY AND INFANT MORTALITY IN FRANCE, 2015	
Males	78.5 years
Females	84.9 years
Infant mortality per 1,000 live births	4

Table 17.2 In France, women outlive men. The infant mortality rate is one of the lowest in the world.

ACTIVITY

Discussion

Examine Table 17.2. Can you suggest two reasons why women's life expectancy is more than 6.5 years longer than that of men?

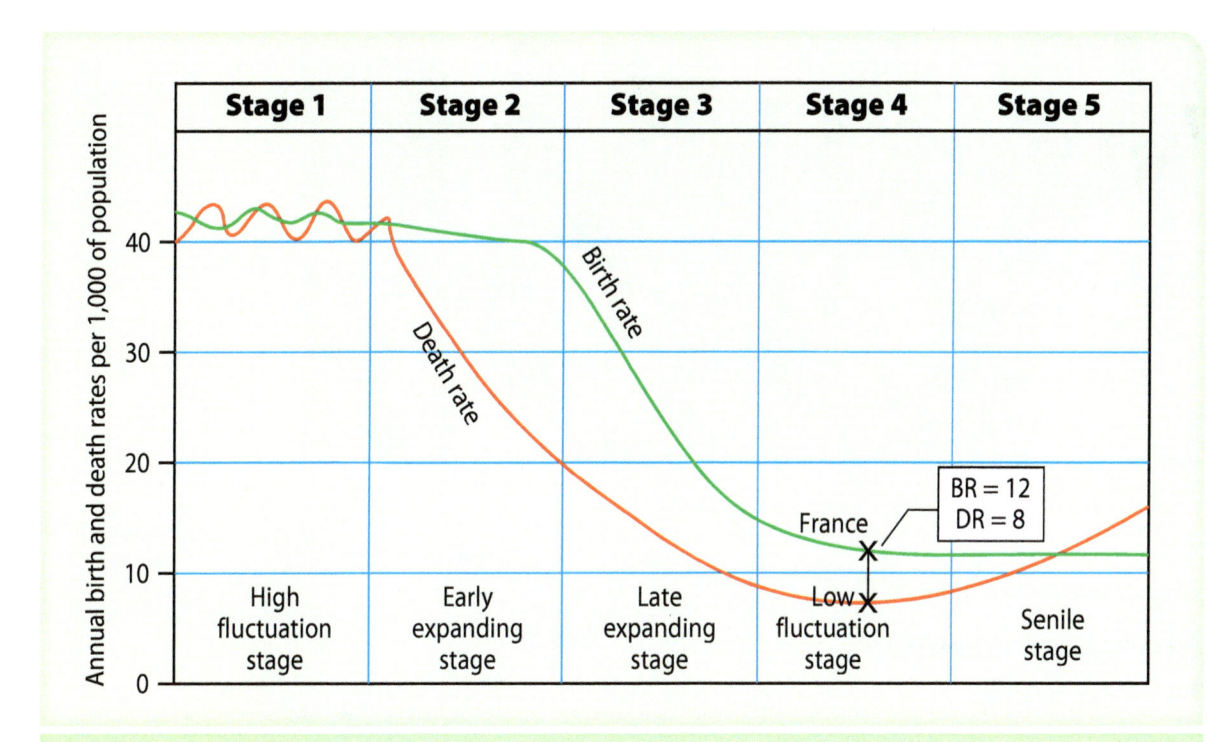

Figure 17.19 The population of France is at stage 4 of the population transition model

ACTIVITY

Skills

Examine Figure 17.19. Is there a natural increase or decrease in the French population at present? Explain your answer.

Inward migration

The Greater Paris area has **300,000 foreign nationals**. Many refugees from Eastern Europe, Russia and Poland made their homes here in the early twentieth century and their descendants have assimilated well.

In the second half of the twentieth century there was a labour shortage in France because of the low birth rate and the rapid expansion in the 1950s and 1960s. Workers from **North and West Africa**, which had been part of the French overseas empire, migrated to France for work.

Many of these migrants have not fared as well as Eastern Europeans. Traditionally, a large number have worked in menial jobs and have experienced discrimination in job applications and housing. Many remain in relative poverty. They were among the first to lose their jobs in the recession that began in 2008. A large percentage are Islamic in their religious beliefs (see page 236).

Muslims at prayer in a Parisian street outside a mosque

Urban development in the Paris Basin

Urbanisation has been a feature of the Paris Basin since the Middle Ages. Each sub-region has an important urban centre with its own economic life.

Cities such as **Rouen**, **Amiens**, **Reims**, **Caen** and **Orléans** are significant cities. However, Paris outranks them all in size, influence and hinterland.

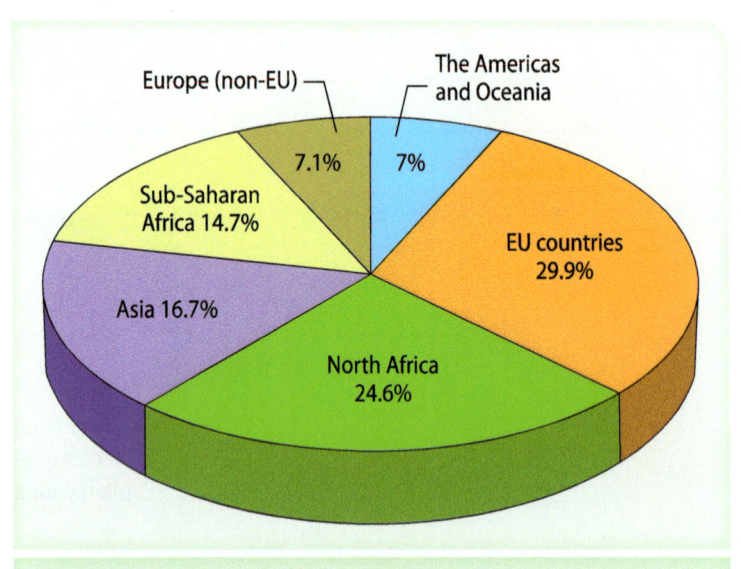

Figure 17.20 The regions of origin of foreign nationals in Greater Paris

- The Americas and Oceania 7%
- EU countries 29.9%
- North Africa 24.6%
- Asia 16.7%
- Sub-Saharan Africa 14.7%
- Europe (non-EU) 7.1%

CASE STUDY

Greater Paris: Urban development

Greater Paris rivals London as the most important city in Europe. It has the largest urban economy in the European mainland by far, **with a GDP that is larger than that of Switzerland or Belgium**. In fact, its GDP is more than three times that of the Republic of Ireland.

How did Paris achieve this position in its development? There are several factors, including its **location**, **transport networks** and **its global influence**.

Location

Paris occupies a **core location** in the Paris Basin. Because of its relatively central position in France, Paris became the capital of France during the Middle Ages. French monarchs spread French, the language of Île-de-France, outwards towards the borders of France and beyond. Monarchs centralised their power in Paris and later in Versailles, just outside the city. This gave the capital power and prestige. It became a **primate city**.

> **DEFINITIONS**
>
> **GDP (gross domestic product):** This is the total value of goods and services that are produced in a country. GDP figures also include the value of goods and services produced in that country by foreign-owned companies.
>
> **Primate city:** This is a city that is at least twice as big as the next largest city in the same state.

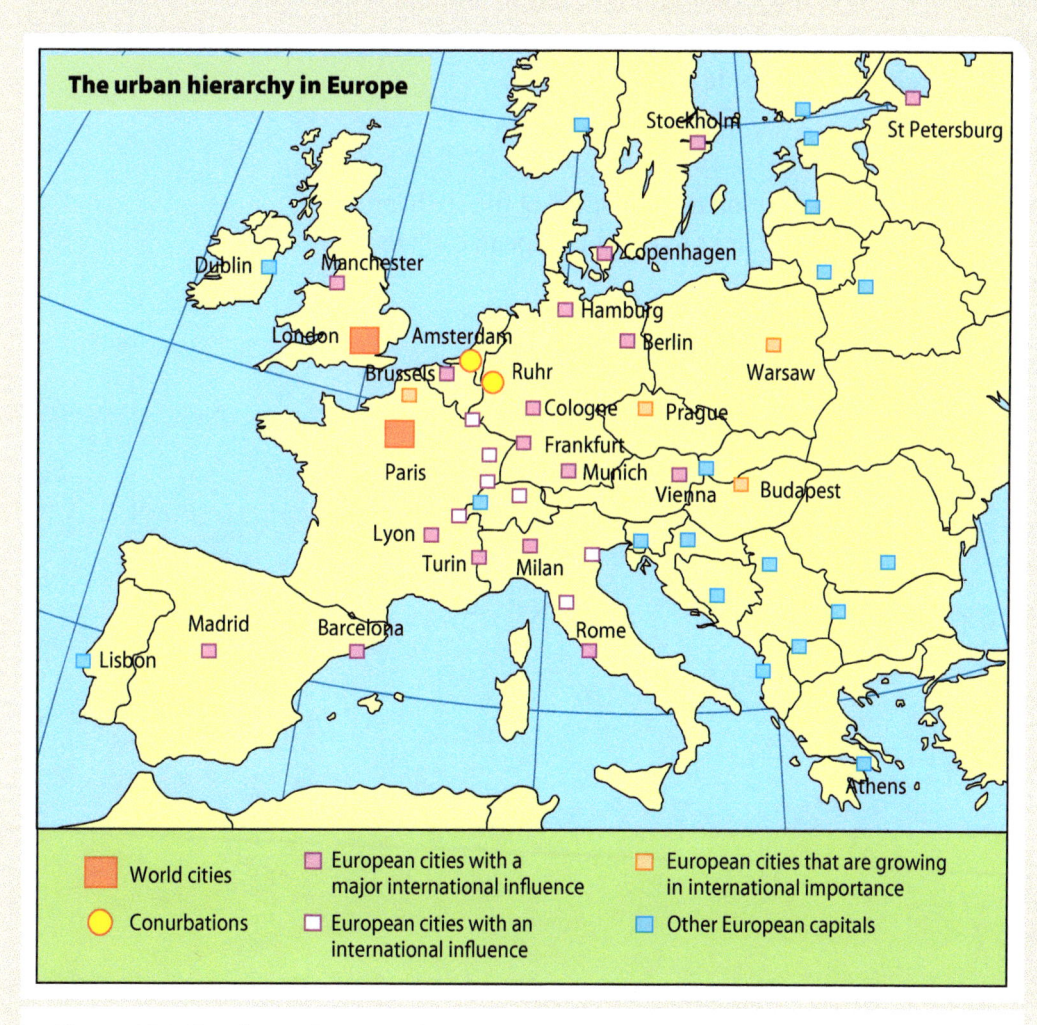

Figure 17.21 London and Paris are far ahead of other European cities in wealth and influence

Paris benefits from the great agricultural wealth of the Basin and is an important food processing centre. Because of its centrality, Paris has grown to become a **multifunctional city**.

The great majority of the workforce is engaged in tertiary activities. These include political, administrative, retail, educational, research and cultural activities. Paris is also an important tourist and artistic centre, with some of the greatest art galleries in the world, such as the Louvre.

On a European scale, Paris is part of the **economic core** of the EU and rivals London in wealth and influence. Greater Paris continues to attract young ambitious migrants from all over the world.

Transport

French rulers built roads that radiated outwards to all the corners of France as part of their centralising policy. In that way, Paris became the focus of transport routes (see Figure 17.15 on page 309). The flat relief of the Paris Basin provided no obstacles to the building of roads and railways. As all routes led to Paris, the city became an important manufacturing centre because resource materials could be brought together in Paris for processing or assembly.

On a wider scale, Paris became a **railway hub** for North-West Europe and is within a few hours' reach of London, Amsterdam, Brussels, Lyon and Frankfurt. Charles de Gaulle Airport is one of the most important **airports** in the world. Paris itself has an **inland port** on the Seine River, which helped in the establishment of heavy industry in riverside districts of Paris.

The global influence of Paris

Because of its large population, its position as the capital of the sixth largest economy in the world and its transport links to other European capitals, Paris has acquired a global influence.

A view of Paris with the Eiffel Tower and the towers of La Défense, the financial district, in the background

- Paris is the second urban destination in the EU (after London) for foreign direct investment (FDI).
- It has 9,000 foreign companies – 40% of the total in all of France.
- Its stock exchange is one of the largest in the European mainland and is tracked across the financial world.
- Paris is a European leader in convention centres, international exhibitions and trade fairs.
- The Paris fashion industry is possibly the most prestigious in the world and enjoys a global market.
- Paris is home to Disneyland Paris, which is Europe's most visited tourist destination.
- Paris is home to the headquarters of several international organisations, such as UNESCO, OECD and the International Energy Agency.
- Paris hosts the Paris Motor Show every two years. It is one of the world's largest and most prestigious motor show events.
- Paris has the second largest airport complex in Europe after London.

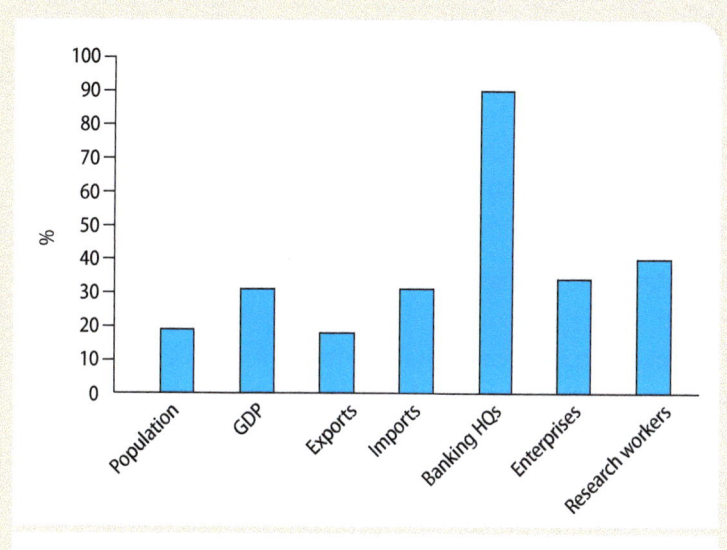

Figure 17.22 The role of Paris in the economy of France

ACTIVITY

Research

(i) Look up the Paris Motor Show on the internet.

(ii) Look up the Latin Quarter on the internet.

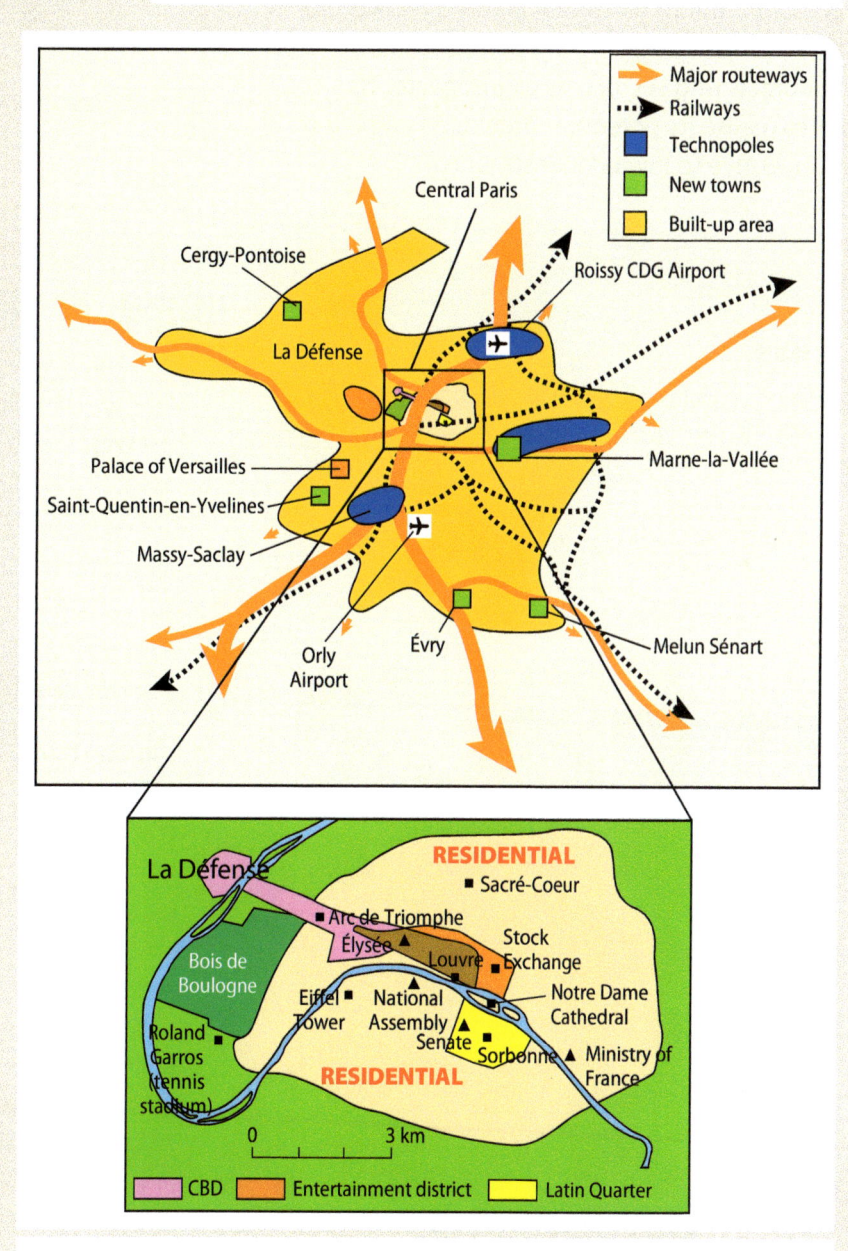

Figure 17.23 Paris is a road, rail and airport hub. Central Paris with the CBD and other important features are also included.

CHAPTER 17 · THE DYNAMICS OF REGIONS 2   317

THE MEZZOGIORNO

The Mezzogiorno is the name that Italians give to Southern Italy together with the islands of Sardinia and Sicily. The region is mountainous and hilly.

The Mezzogiorno has some 22 million people, roughly one-third of the population of Italy. It is much less advanced economically than Central and Northern Italy. It is a **peripheral region** with the characteristics of peripherality (see page 242). These include a challenging physical landscape, a long summer drought, low inward investment and high outward migration of young adults.

The Mezzogiorno was badly hit by the economic recession that began in 2008 and is recovering slowly. It has struggling agricultural and manufacturing sectors. Its tourist sector has yet to realise its potential. Organised crime is a disincentive to inward investment.

> **DEFINITION**
>
> **Mezzogiorno** translates as 'the land of the midday (sun)'.

> **GEOFACT**
>
> The Paris Basin and the Mezzogiorno have the same number of people: about 22 million each.

ACTIVITY

Skills

Examine Figure 17.24. What is the name of the province that occupies the toe of Italy?

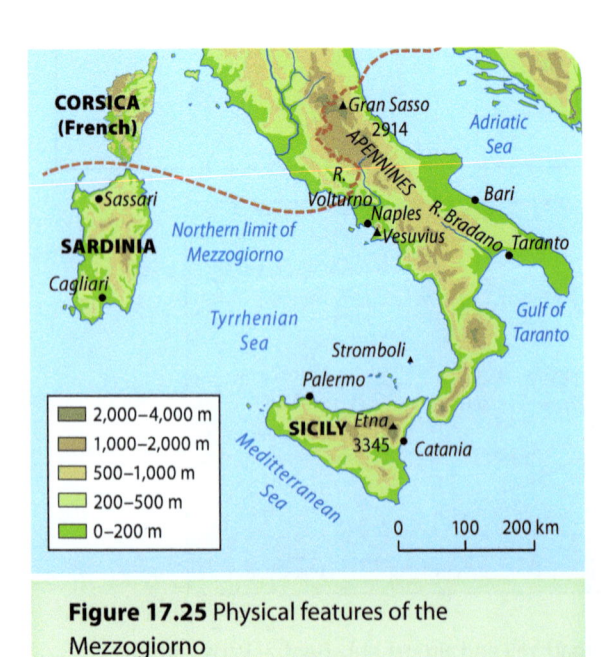

Figure 17.24 Sub-regions of the Mezzogiorno

Figure 17.25 Physical features of the Mezzogiorno

ACTIVITY

Skills

Examine Figure 17.25.

(i) What is the altitude of Mount Etna in Sicily in metres?

(ii) What is the name of the sea between Sardinia and the South Italian mainland?

(iii) Find the following rivers in the Southern Italian mainland: the Volturno and the Bradano.

Physical processes

Climate

The Mezzogiorno has hot, dry summers and mild, damp winters.

> In summer, **high pressure** brings mostly cloudless days with little or no rainfall. Daytime temperatures are about 12°C in winter and rise to more than 30°C in summer.
> In winter, **low pressure systems** are blown inwards from the Atlantic. Frontal and relief rain, which Irish people are familiar with, is a feature of the winter in the Mezzogiorno.
> Much of the Mezzogiorno is affected by a local wind, called the **Sirocco**, which blows northwards from the Sahara.
> The Apennines influence the climate. Mountain temperatures are cooler than those of the coastal lowlands. The mountains also attract relief rain in winter. The east coast of the Italian peninsula is drier than the west coast because of the **rain shadow**.

GEOFACT

Catania in Sicily, with 2,492 hours of sunshine per year, gets more hours of sunshine than any other city in Italy.

THE CLIMATE OF NAPLES	Jan	Feb	Mar	Apr	May	Jun	Jul	Aug	Sept	Oct	Nov	Dec
Daytime temperature (°C)	12	13	15	18	22	26	29	29	26	22	17	14
Precipitation (mm)	116	85	73	62	44	31	19	32	64	107	147	135
Daily sunshine hours	4	4	5	7	8	9	10	10	8	6	4	3

Table 17.3 Climatic conditions in Naples

ACTIVITY

Numeracy

Examine Table 17.3.
(i) What are the hottest two months of the year?
(ii) What is the temperature in January?
(iii) What is the wettest month?

ACTIVITY

Skills

Use the information in Table 17.3 to draw a bar graph of the daytime temperatures in Naples from January to December.

Relief

The Mezzogiorno has narrow coastal plains. The interior is either hilly or mountainous. In fact, hilly and mountainous land accounts for 85% of the total land area. The Apennines run along the spine of the Italian Peninsula from north to south. In several areas, hilly land runs into the sea.

However, the coastal plains are quite extensive in Campania (the Neapolitan Lowlands) and along the east coast in Apulia.

The Mezzogiorno has an unstable geology because the African Plate is pushing north into Italy. There are several volcanic mountains, including Mount Vesuvius and Mount Etna. Earthquakes are a regular occurrence and cause extensive damage to buildings, roads and bridges.

LINK

See *Plate boundaries*, page 11.

The hilly, relatively parched landscape of Sicily in summer

ACTIVITY

Discussion

Examine the photograph of the landscape in Sicily. Explain how summer drought severely reduces agricultural output in Sicily.

Soils

In general, soils over much of the Mezzogiorno are thin and poor. Deforestation and heavy winter rains have led to severe soil erosion on slopes since Ancient Roman times.

Eroded soils have accumulated along river channels, causing rivers to overflow onto the floodplains. This led to the formation of swamps in the lower course of rivers. These became a breeding ground for malaria-carrying mosquitoes into the twentieth century, but the swamps have been drained for many decades.

The landscape of Campania is dominated by Mount Vesuvius. Its frequent eruptions have covered the plain with volcanic dust. This parent material weathers into fertile soils over time.

GEOFACTS

- Hilly land is about 200–400 metres in height, whereas mountainous land is above 400 metres.
- Some **60%** of the oranges and tangerines and **90%** of the lemons produced in Italy come from Sicily.

ACTIVITY

Discussion

Examine the photograph of soil erosion in Basilicata. Explain why this region has little or no agricultural potential.

ACTIVITY

Skills

Find the location of Basilicata in Figure 17.24 on page 318.

A severely eroded mountainous landscape in Basilicata

Primary economic activities

Agriculture

Agriculture is limited by **climate**, **relief**, **soils** and **the system of land ownership**. In addition, many farms are too small for farmers to be able to afford machinery.

Three products dominate agriculture: **wheat**, **olives** and **vines**. Tree crops such as lemons, limes and olives are suited to the Mezzogiorno because their fruits require high summer temperatures to ripen. These trees put down deep roots to reach scarce ground water during the summer drought. The vines also bind the soil on slopes together.

Winter wheat is also a response to the climate. Wheat is sown in late autumn and germinates and grows during the damp, mild winter months. It ripens in early summer when rainfall is low.

Animals such as **sheep** and **goats** are also reared on the upland farms of the Mezzogiorno. These can survive on poor pasture. Very few cattle are found in the Mezzogiorno because summer drought limits grass growth.

By far the most productive area is that of **Campania**, the area around Naples. The volcanic soils here are among the most fertile in Europe. Campania grows a wide variety of cereals, including wheat and maize; fruit crops, such as pears, plums, peaches and grapes as well as olives; and salad crops, such as tomatoes, lettuce and cucumbers under irrigation. However, **seasonal overproduction** is a problem in late summer and prices can collapse.

A family taking a break in Sicily during the lemon harvest

Plastic tunnels in Sicily where tomatoes are grown with the assistance of irrigation

HINT

Reminder: Apulia is located on the heel of Italy.

DEFINITIONS

Latifundia: Large estates in Southern Italy that have been owned and underused by absentee landlords for generations.

Cassa per il Mezzogiorno means 'the fund for the South'.

The modernisation of agriculture in the Mezzogiorno

Since 1950, some efforts have been made to modernise agriculture. The **Cassa per il Mezzogiorno** (a government agency) poured funds into the South. This was invested in breaking up the *latifundia* into smallholdings, draining swamps, spraying mosquitoes and agricultural training.

The Cassa was wound up in 1984. Since then, EU and Italian central funds from Rome have continued to support agriculture in the Mezzogiorno. There have been several improvements:

> Thousands of farm labourers have been given small farms from the former large estates. This increases their incentives to increase crop production.
> Irrigation and horticultural tunnels have increased the production of salad crops for the local population and the tourist trade.
> The **Apulian Aqueduct** is the largest irrigation scheme in Southern Italy and has greatly boosted crop production in Apulia. It takes water from the Sele River in the west through tunnels in the mountains eastwards to the heel of Italy. It was completed in 1939.
> The **Autostrada del Sole** is a motorway that connects the South with Northern Italy. It allows for the transport of fruit and salad crops to distant markets in the North of Italy.
> Farmers have formed co-ops to keep control of their output and to market their products.

However, *latifundia* still dominate many areas in the uplands of the Apennines and in Sicily. As a result, large swathes of land are underused by absentee owners or left unfarmed.

DEFINITION

Autostrada del Sole translates as 'the motorway of the sun'.

LINK

The Autostrada del Sole is the A1 motorway in Figure 17.30 on page 329.

ACTIVITY

Research

Look up the location of the Sele River in Southern Italy on the internet.

Part of the Autostrada del Sole, along which fresh produce from the Mezzogiorno is transported to the North of Italy

Fishing

Fishing is important for many reasons:

> The region is surrounded by sea on all sides.
> The hilly and mountainous terrain has always pushed the population towards the seas for a living.
> The region has a tradition of fishing. The coastal fishing communities are highly skilled in it.
> Population density is high along the coast.
> The region has many sheltered harbours.

- The Mediterranean is a shallow sea and is essentially a continental shelf where fish are found.
- Runoff from streams in the rainy winter months provides the nutrients for the growth of plankton (the beginning of the fish food chain).
- Hake, marlin, bream, swordfish, anchovy, squid and tuna are fished in the Mediterranean.
- Cities such as Palermo, Messina, Bari, Brindisi and Naples are fishing ports in addition to their other functions.
- The sea also supports many small coastal communities who supply the local shops.

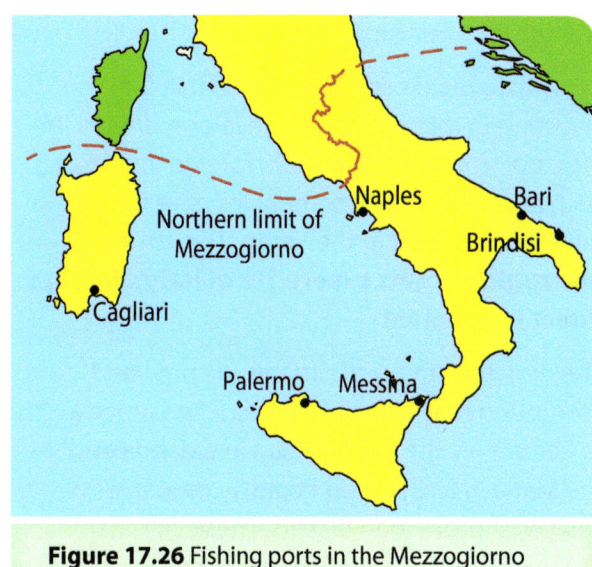

Figure 17.26 Fishing ports in the Mezzogiorno

Overfishing

Fish stocks have declined in the Mediterranean, as they have all along the EU coast. **Overfishing** is the main cause.

- There are too many trawlers chasing too few fish.
- The Mediterranean has a limited supply of fish, as it is small and almost completely enclosed.
- Modern fishing technology, including electronic detection instruments, unbreakable nets and hydraulic winches, can land large catches and empty the seas of fish.
- Italy's fishing fleet has been subject to EU fishing restrictions. These include annual quotas, recording landings and reduced fishing seasons. Thus, fish farming of shellfish such as oysters, mussels and clams has become important. These are harvested in coastal lagoons where longshore drift has created spits.

Secondary economic activities

Manufacturing

Manufacturing is a weak sector of the economy of the Mezzogiorno due to several factors.

A lack of resources

The **region was bypassed by the Industrial Revolution** of the nineteenth century because the South had no coal resources. Neither does it have hydro-electricity because the rocks of the Apennines are mainly composed of limestone, a jointed rock that is unsuitable for reservoirs. Therefore, a **tradition of manufacturing did not exist**. However, small natural gas reserves came on stream in recent decades.

GEOFACT

The five provinces in the grip of organised crime – Sicily, Campania, Calabria, Apulia and Basilicata – are also the poorest in Italy.

ACTIVITY

Research

Look up *omertà* on the internet. This is the tight-lipped silence of communities who live in fear of the Mafia.

A negative image

Very little local capital was available for investing in manufacturing developments in the Mezzogiorno. For this reason, foreign investors such as multinational companies have been reluctant to invest in the South. The **entire Mezzogiorno gets a mere 1% of Italy's foreign direct investment**.

The negative image of organised crime and corruption may account for this. The Camorra in Campania, the 'Ndrangheta in Calabria and the Mafia in Sicily bleed healthy companies of cash with protection rackets. These criminal organisations have now expanded their influence into Basilicata and Apulia. The murder rate is four per 100,000 people every year, which is four times the murder rate in Central and Northern Italy. What company would wish to invest in this environment? The result is that Italian state companies have had to become major investors in the South. Some of that investment is siphoned off by corrupt politicians and by kickbacks to local organised crime bosses.

The peripherality of the Mezzogiorno

The Mezzogiorno is a peripheral region. It is far away from the markets of Northern Italy and the core of the EU. As a peripheral region, the Mezzogiorno suffers from much **outward migration** to Northern Italy and other EU countries. This has become a **brain drain** as many young, educated Southern Italians leave for Northern Italy. This is happening more often since the recession that began in 2008. Net migration from South to North between 2001 and 2015 was more than **750,000 people**, 70% of whom were aged between 15 and 34 and **more than a quarter were graduates**. Getra, a Neapolitan manufacturer of electric transformers, claims that **finding engineers in Naples**, or engineers willing to move there, is becoming ever harder.

Figure 17.27 Unemployment in Italy in 2015. The unemployment rate in the Mezzogiorno is one of the highest in the EU and is a lot higher than in Northern Italy.

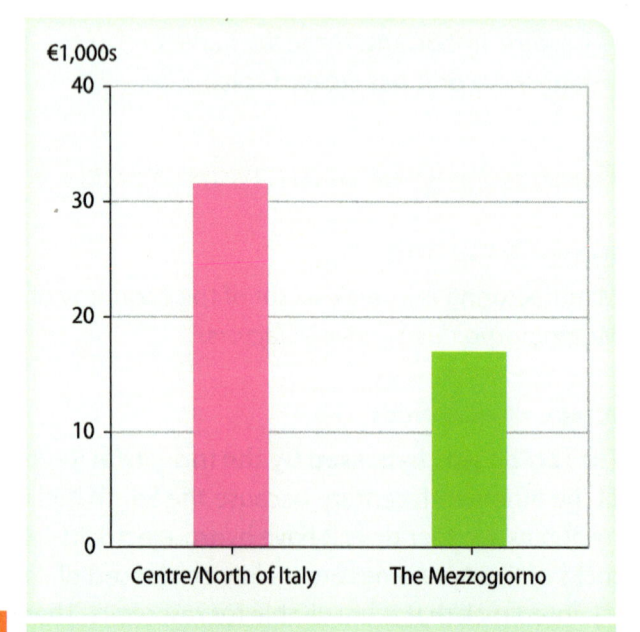

Figure 17.28 Per capita income in Italy in 2015. The Mezzogiorno is far behind Central and Northern Italy in per capita income.

ACTIVITY

Thinking

The purchasing power of Southern Italians is low. What evidence for that statement is on this page?

Infrastructural services

Because of its peripherality, infrastructural services such as **transport** and **broadband** are less developed than in Northern Italy.

As a result of its weak manufacturing sector, the entire Mezzogiorno, with 36% of the population of Italy, accounts for a mere 11% of Italy's total exports.

The role of the state in manufacturing in the South

In the absence of private investment, the Cassa began to invest in manufacturing in the Mezzogiorno fifty years ago. Cassa developed **growth poles** in the large urban centres. The **Bari–Brindisi–Taranto industrial triangle** is an example of growth poles. Motorways and ports were developed to assist growth.

Figure 17.29 Growth poles in the Mezzogiorno and the Bari–Brindisi–Taranto industrial triangle

> **DEFINITION**
>
> **Growth pole:** An urban area chosen by the government as a centre of economic activity and investment in manufacturing and services.

An oil refinery in Siracusa, Sicily

Large state companies

Large state companies in the steel sectors, the oil refining and petrochemical industries were obliged by the state to invest in the Mezzogiorno. Large refineries and steel plants were built on the coast. However, not all have been successful. These plants were capital intensive and employed relatively few workers. Some came at a high environmental cost too.

> **GEOFACT**
>
> Many large plants such as steel mills and oil refineries that employ relatively few workers are called *cathedrals in the desert*.

In 1965, **Taranto** became the location of the **largest steel plant** in all of Europe. It produces 40% of Italy's steel. The plant was a Cassa initiative. However, the plant has been dogged by environmental emission and corruption scandals. In 2005, the plant was responsible for 83% of all the **dioxin emissions** in Italy. A report from the local prosecutor's office stated that dust emissions caused 90 deaths a year in the Taranto area. Dust emissions also led to 650 further hospitalisations for cardiovascular and respiratory diseases annually. The plant is in a coastal area that would otherwise have great tourist potential.

ACTIVITY

Research

Look up the nature of dioxin on the internet.

A protest against the health hazard caused by emissions outside the Taranto steel plant in 2012

Private companies

Private Italian companies such as Fiat and Alfa Romeo were also encouraged to invest in the South through financial incentives. Fiat has a car production plant in Melfi with a workforce of 8,000 people. Fiat, with Chrysler, has now entered the lucrative SUV market and produces the Fiat 500X and the Jeep Renegade in the Melfi plant. Of these, 60% are exported to the USA. This is a major boost for Melfi.

ACTIVITY

Skills

Find the location of Melfi in Figure 17.29 on page 325.

A new direction for manufacturing in the Mezzogiorno

In recent years, manufacturing activities that use **local resources and/or are labour intensive** have been encouraged. For example, the fruit canning industry has expanded. Products include canned fruit, olive oil, fruit juices and processed vegetables.

Traditional industries such as leather goods and jewellery are growing. In addition, modern growth industries, such as the **high-tech industry**, are also developing. We will now examine two different and successful manufacturing projects.

The Tari project in Naples

Naples is a traditional centre for jewellery manufacturing. In the late 1980s, the shops in the historic centre of the city had become too cramped for manufacturing. EU funding was provided so that land could be purchased outside the city for workshops. A training centre and exhibition space were created. The centre attracted gold and silversmiths, jewellers and gem cutters.

The site has good road, air and rail links. It is now a state-of-the-art jewellery centre where the number of jobs has increased to 1,500 highly skilled people.

The Etna Valley high-tech development

EU funds and other incentives have led to the development of an important **high-tech cluster** in Catania in Sicily, known as **Etna Valley**. There are several reasons for the development:

> Strong science and technology departments in the University of Catania
> A close link between the universities and the manufacturers' R&D departments in Etna Valley
> A well-educated young workforce, as high unemployment has meant that many young people have stayed on to study further at third level
> Up to 75% grant assistance for companies' R&D
> Up to 80% grant assistance for upskilling workers.

GEOFACT
Because of the success of Etna Valley, Catania is being called the Milan of the South.

Etna Valley is possibly Sicily's greatest economic success story. The most important manufacturer in Etna Valley, **STMicroelectronics**, employs over 4,000 people and more than 200 other firms have moved into the area. Many firms in Etna Valley are involved in biotechnology and pharmaceuticals. These are modern growth industries.

ACTIVITY

Research

Look up STMicroelectronics on the internet to find out more.

Catania, with the port in the foreground and Mount Etna in the background

Tertiary economic activities

Tertiary economic activities are important in the Mezzogiorno, as the great majority of people now work in services. We will now examine two tertiary economic activities:

> Tourism
> Transport.

Tourism

Southern Italy has many attractions for tourists:

> The landscape of Southern Italy is very attractive. The Amalfi coast is one of the most famous coastlines in Europe and has spectacular views. The resorts of Sorrento and Positano are very popular. The Bay of Naples, overlooked by Mount Vesuvius, is one of the most beautiful in the world.

- The Isle of Capri in the Bay of Naples, with the Villa San Michele, is very popular.
- The climate is Mediterranean, with long summer days of endless sunshine and high temperatures. This is attractive for tourists from North-West Europe who are sometimes starved of sunlight.
- The region is a treasure trove of historic sites. The ruins of Greek temples from classical times are found in Sicily. Ruins of the Roman Empire are everywhere. Pompeii and Herculaneum, dating from the first century AD, have been excavated. Theses sites reveal evidence of daily life in Roman times. Remnants of the Appian Way and ancient aqueducts are visible in many places.
- Motorways extend all the way to the toe of Italy. Tourists from Central Europe can reach Southern Italy in two days by car. However, diesel and petrol are expensive in Italy and motorway users pay a toll.
- Airports are now used by budget airlines such as Ryanair.
- The South has excellent Italian cuisine. The people of Naples claim that pizza was invented there. The region has a wide variety of fresh fruit and vegetables.
- Tourist infrastructure such as hotels, caravan parks, restaurants and campsites is expanding to cater for more tourists.

> **LINK**
>
> You will find the location of the Isle of Capri in Figure 17.35 on page 335.

Tourists strolling through Pompeii, with Mount Vesuvius in the background

However, the Mezzogiorno is a jewel waiting to be discovered. Instead of being a thriving industry, tourism in the Mezzogiorno is an example of a **missed opportunity**. Why is this the case?

- **Only 13% of foreign tourists** who come to Italy travel to the Mezzogiorno. The rest remain in Central and Northern Italy. Furthermore, in one week in the summer of 2016, **223 flights** left German airports for the Balearic Islands in the Mediterranean but **only 17 flights** travelled to the Mezzogiorno. That clearly indicates that most Germans are not as interested in the Mezzogiorno.
- **Poor marketing** is another problem. The Italian Tourist Board spends most of its budget on staff salaries and offices, with only 2% left to promote the country's attractions. In the 1970s, Italy was the number one destination for international tourists. Now it is **fifth**, behind France, the USA, China and Spain. That may be because of the poor promotion of Italy abroad.

> **ACTIVITY**
>
> **Research**
>
> Look up the following on the internet:
> (i) Villa San Michele on the Isle of Capri in the Bay of Naples
> (ii) The Amalfi coast.

> **Infrastructure** in the Mezzogiorno is another issue. Italy has yet to build a bridge to Sicily, home to one in twelve Italians. A bridge to Sicily from the toe of Italy would bring many motoring tourists to Sicily.
> There is **little co-ordination** between the provinces of the Mezzogiorno when it comes to attracting tourists. For instance, trains and scheduled flights into Calabria (the toe of Italy) are not co-ordinated with ferry schedules to Sicily because Calabrians want tourists to stay longer in Calabria.
> Tourists are spoiled for choice in Northern and Central Italy with the treasures of Venice, Florence and Rome.
> The **negative image** of the Mezzogiorno due to organised crime does not encourage tourism.

Positano on the Amalfi coast is one of the jewels of the coast of Southern Italy

Transport

Transport is a challenge in much of the Mezzogiorno because of **relief**. The spine of the Apennines runs along the peninsula. Coastal plains are narrow and in some cases the hills run into the sea. This requires tunnelling for road and rail networks.

Roads

Road transport has improved a great deal in recent decades. This was largely because of funding from the Cassa and EU regional funding. Motorways such as the Autostrada del Sole have reduced the peripherality of the Mezzogiorno and have made the region much more accessible. They also speed up economic activity between the urban centres of the South. The absence of a bridge to Sicily from the mainland has already been mentioned. In addition, **landslides** onto roads caused by earthquakes continue to be a problem from time to time.

ACTIVITY

Research
Look up the location of Positano on the internet.

GEOFACT

The distance from Milan to the toe of Southern Italy is 1,251 km.

Figure 17.30 The motorway network of Italy. Southern Italy is well connected to markets in the North. The A1 is the Autostrada del Sole.

CHAPTER 17 · THE DYNAMICS OF REGIONS 2   329

In 2015 in Sicily, a column supporting a viaduct on the main road connecting Palermo and Catania collapsed following a landslide, cutting off one of the island's main transport routes. Travellers between Sicily's two biggest cities had to either follow the coast or take smaller local roads, adding hours to the journey. The repair was likely to take two years to complete. Observers have suggested that reduced public spending during the recent recession along with poor management and corruption have caused a decline in the quality of infrastructure in the Mezzogiorno.

GEOFACT

The Sicilian viaduct collapse is an example of the challenges that **relief** causes in the Mezzogiorno economy.

A viaduct in Sicily. The terrain in Sicily makes building roads very challenging and expensive.

Rail

The Mezzogiorno has had rail transport since 1839. There is a marked emphasis on **coastal routes** because all the large urban centres are on the coast. However, high-speed rail has yet to reach much of the South. Some lines are very slow. For instance, it takes six hours to cross Sicily from east to west. However, rail travel is relatively cheap in Italy.

Ports

Most coastal urban centres in the Mezzogiorno have port activities. This is because the sea is vital to the economy of the peninsula and the islands. The Mediterranean is at the centre of sea routes that cross the Mediterranean. The Cassa and EU funding have helped to upgrade the port infrastructure. However, the economic recession of 2008, which hit Italy severely, has seen a decline in port infrastructure. The port of Naples needs further investment to modernise its facilities.

There are some **positive developments in port activities**. **Gioia Tauro** in Calabria is now the busiest container port in the Mediterranean. Gioia Tauro has been operating since 1995 and is a container hub. Large container ships from South-East Asia dock there. The containers are then distributed in smaller vessels to more than sixty ports across the Mediterranean and Black Sea. Gioia Tauro is located on the **Suez Canal–Gibraltar shipping route**, one of the busiest shipping lanes in the world. The port has provided employment for more than 1,000 workers. Cagliari in Sardinia also has a successful container port.

HINT

Gioia is pronounced *Joe-ya*.

ACTIVITY

Skills

For the location of Gioia Tauro, see Figure 17.29 on page 325.

The container port of Gioia Tauro

> **HINT**
>
> Climate and relief are significant in the economic development of the Mezzogiorno. They are useful ways in which to address key factors such as **agriculture**, **transport** and **tourism** in the development of the Mezzogiorno.

Human processes

The genetic pool of the people of the Mezzogiorno is very wide. Because of its central position in the Mediterranean, the region has been invaded by Greeks, Romans, Arabs, Catalans and Normans. The people of the Mezzogiorno tend to have sallow complexions and dark hair.

Population distribution and density

The population is unevenly distributed. The Apennine Mountains **repel people** because of poor soils, difficult terrain and poor communications. Coastal areas have far higher densities of people. Farming is not profitable in the hills and inward investment in hill towns is negligible. In addition, temperatures in the mountains are colder in winter.

Campania, the area around Naples, has high population densities. It is home to 5.9 million people, more than a quarter of the population of the entire Mezzogiorno. The rich volcanic soils support a high agricultural population. Naples is the third largest city in Italy, where many people find work.

The cities of Bari and Brindisi are located in **Apulia**, on the heel of Italy. These cities are part of an industrial triangle with Taranto. These areas support jobs and help to maintain the population in the heel of Italy. The agriculture of the coastal lowlands of Apulia is thriving because of irrigation. Irrigated farms specialise in vegetable crops and cut flowers, which are labour intensive.

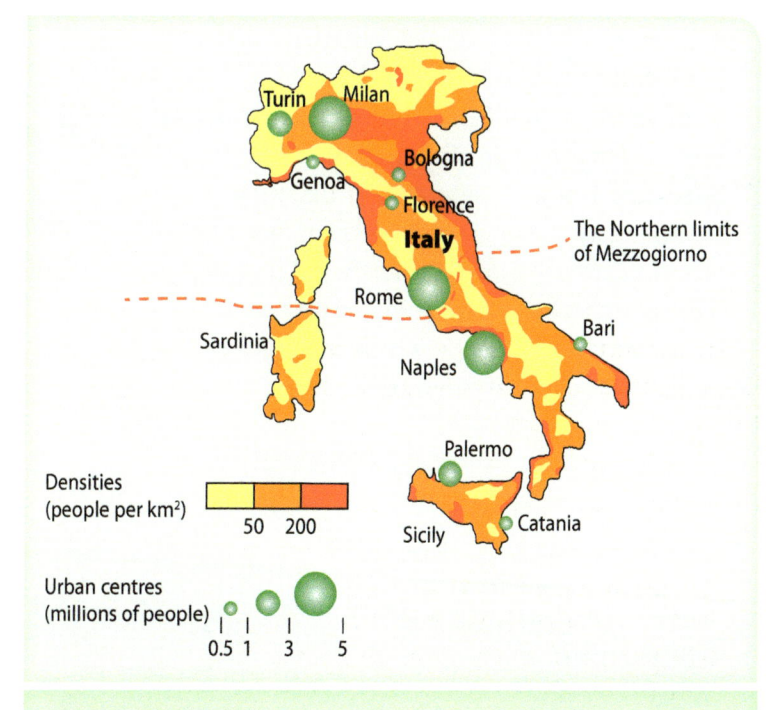

Figure 17.31 Population density in Italy. In general, population densities in the South are far higher along the coast than inland.

On the other hand, Basilicata has low population densities. This is the poorest area in the Mezzogiorno, with a rugged, hilly, soil-eroded landscape and a long history of outward migration.

Sicily has a population of 5.1 million people and has high coastal densities. Tourism is an important industry in the coastal cities. As we have seen, Etna Valley in Catania is a thriving area of modern manufacturing and has been a growth centre since the time of Cassa.

Where is the Mezzogiorno on the demographic transition model?

The Mezzogiorno is at stage 5 (the senile stage) of the model. Birth rates are lower than death rates. Without inward migration, the population will decline. The average number of babies per mother in the Mezzogiorno is now 1.4, lower than Northern Italy, where birth rates are 1.5 per mother.

The low birth rate is due to the following factors:

> Higher educational levels among mothers in Italy than in the past
> The declining influence of the Catholic Church regarding artificial means of birth control and abortion
> Increasing levels of urbanisation, as raising children in cities is expensive.

Life expectancy in Italy is very high at more than 82 years. This is the second highest in the world and is a tribute to Italy. Many factors help to account for this:

> High government spending on public health.
> A good standard of living.
> Italians eat a wide variety of food that provides them with a balanced diet.
> Another important factor is the **Mediterranean diet**, which is high in olive oil, almonds, hazelnuts, walnuts, vegetables, fruit and a moderate intake of wine. Italians eat fewer animal fats than are consumed in Northern Europe. This diet seems to be connected to lower levels of stroke and heart disease, which are major causes of death among the elderly elsewhere.

GEOFACTS

> 1.4 babies per mother means that 10 mothers have 14 babies between them.
> There were 174,000 births in the Mezzogiorno in 2015, the lowest since 1862!

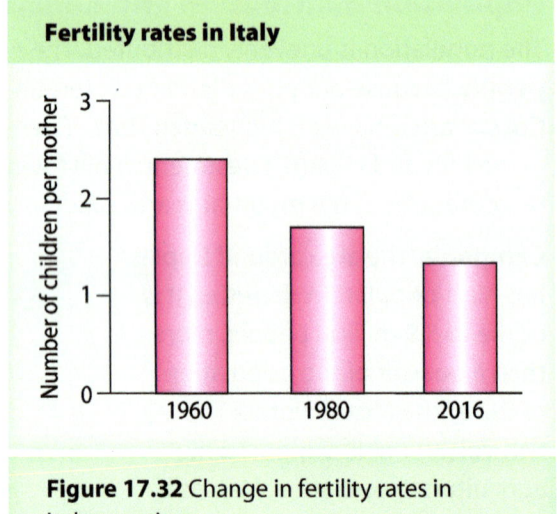

Fertility rates in Italy

Figure 17.32 Change in fertility rates in Italy over time

QUESTION

On average, there are 151 Italians over 65 years for every 100 young people under 15. What challenges does this present to Italy?

ACTIVITY

Discussion

Can you explain how increasing urbanisation may lead to lower birth rates?

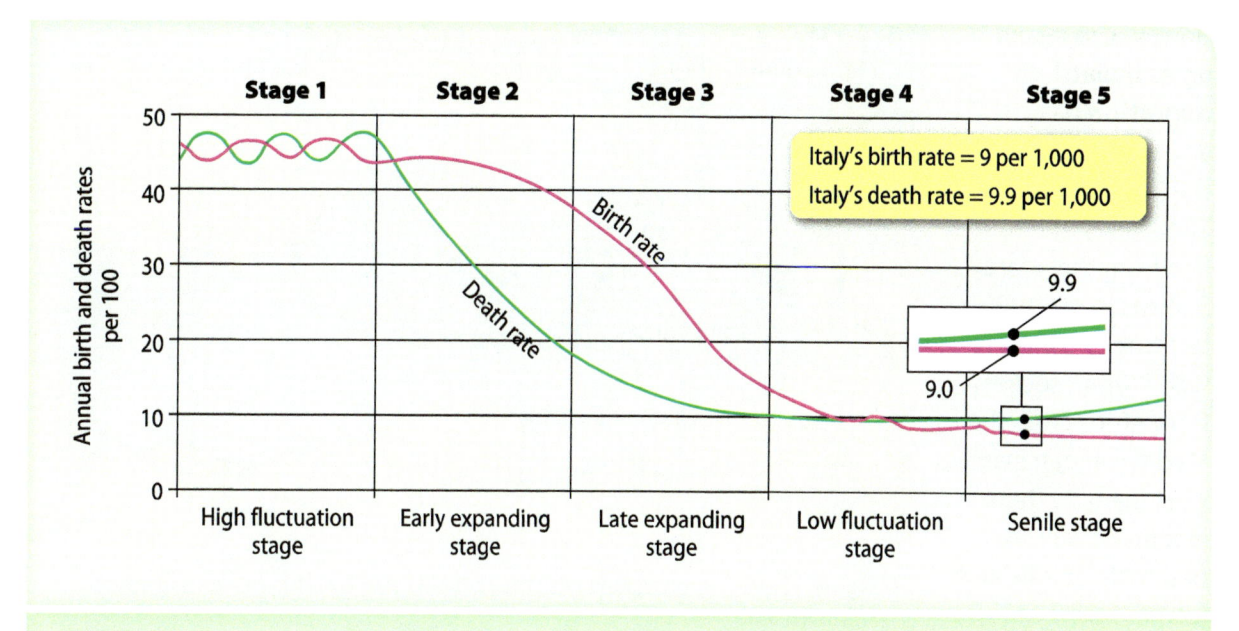

Figure 17.33 The population transition model. Italy's birth rates and death rates are now at stage 5, the senile stage.

Migration patterns

Outward migration has been a feature of life in the Mezzogiorno for generations. The push of poverty at home and the pull of jobs elsewhere have encouraged young people to migrate. Economic migrants from the Mezzogiorno have migrated to Northern Italy and to other parts of Europe. Many also emigrated to the USA, Australia and Brazil.

The recession of 2008 onwards had a major impact on migration in the Mezzogiorno. The Mezzogiorno lost **650,000 jobs** during the years 2008 to 2014. The economy of the region **declined by 13%** in the same period. That led to massive out-migration from the Mezzogiorno of **526,000 people** in those six years alone, almost all of them young adults. This is a loss of the best and brightest of the people of the Mezzogiorno.

ACTIVITY

Discussion

How may a good standard of living lead to higher life expectancy?

Eritrean migrants rescued from the sea near the Italian island of Lampedusa pray for friends who were lost at sea

However, in recent times **inward migration** has also occurred in the Mezzogiorno. Thousands of refugees fled from the nearby Balkans in the 1990s because of a bloody war. Asylum seekers from Africa cross the Mediterranean every year, many of them in flimsy crafts, for a better life in Italy and further north. Many refugees have died on the crossings to Italy because of overcrowding on boats that are not fit for purpose. More than 111,000 refugees entered Italy in 2015.

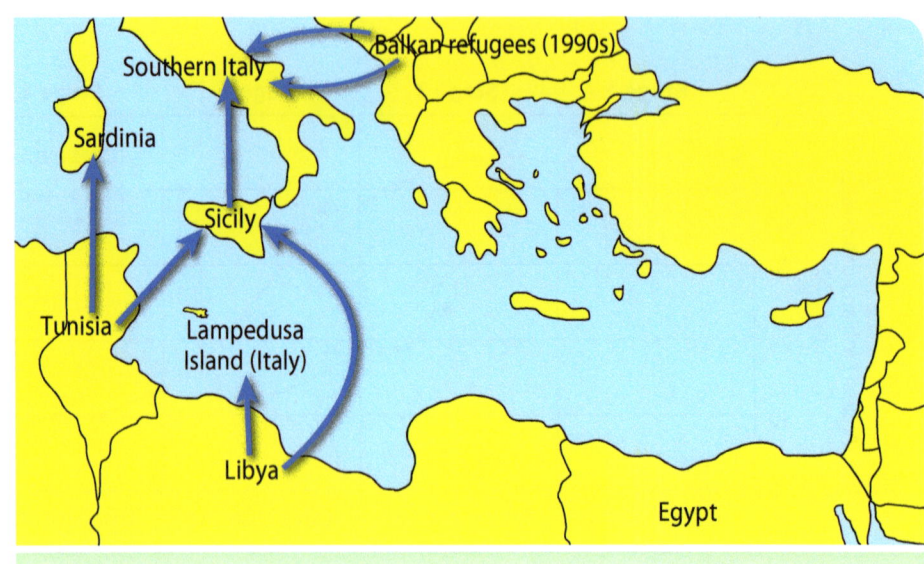

Figure 17.34 The routes taken (at the present time) by refugees from Africa to Southern Italy

The result of the refugee influx is that the population of the Mezzogiorno is changing, with many diverse **ethnic and cultural groups** now living there. More than 2% of the people of the Mezzogiorno are now of foreign origin.

> **DEFINITION**
>
> **Ethnic group:** A group of people sharing a common and distinct culture, language, religion and history.

Urban developments in the Mezzogiorno

The Mezzogiorno has had urban centres since the time of the Roman Empire. Ancient Pompeii is estimated to have had a population of 20,000 people. Today, 68% of the population of Italy lives in towns and cities. The largest urban centres of the Mezzogiorno are on the coast. This can be explained by the difficult relief of the interior and the economic activities on the coast that provide jobs.

Hilltop towns

Much of the Mezzogiorno had a violent past and many people settled in hilltop towns in the Appenines and in Sicily. These towns were easier to defend from hostile invaders. However, these towns are losing population today because of their isolation.

The hilltop town of Castelmezzano in Basilicata

CASE STUDY

Naples: Urban development

Naples, the largest city in the Mezzogiorno, was founded by the Greeks around 600 BC. It is almost as old as Rome. The original Greek street pattern still exists in the city, which is a UNESCO World Heritage Site. The city is situated on a beautiful bay overlooked by Mount Vesuvius. However, the area is geologically unstable and suffers from regular earth tremors.

While the city itself has 1 million people, the total urban population of the Bay of Naples is more than 3 million. Naples has had a violent past and was occupied by many foreign invaders, including Catalans, Spaniards and French. To this day, the city is resentful of outside authority.

Factors that have influenced the development of Naples

Location

Naples is surrounded by the plain of Campania, the most fertile and productive agricultural area on the Italian Peninsula. Vast quantities of fruit, vegetables, tree crops and wheat are grown in the plain. Naples became and remains a market and distribution centre for agricultural produce from Campania.

The city is located in the magnificent and beautiful Bay of Naples. The bay is an excellent and sheltered harbour because of the headlands that lie to the north and south. For that reason, the city has become one of the most important ports in the Mediterranean.

The port has influenced the development of Naples since ancient times. Naples occupies a core position in the Mediterranean and is close to one of the busiest shipping lanes in the world, between the Suez Canal and the Strait of Gibraltar. Therefore, much of the commercial activity of Naples is centred around the port. The port employs thousands of workers. Ferry services run from Naples to Sardinia, Sicily and nearby islands such as Capri. The docks were extensively damaged during the Second World War but were rebuilt afterwards. At this time, upgrading is required to maintain the importance of the port of Naples. The floor of the bay is slowly rising because of **seismic uplift**, which has damaged port structures.

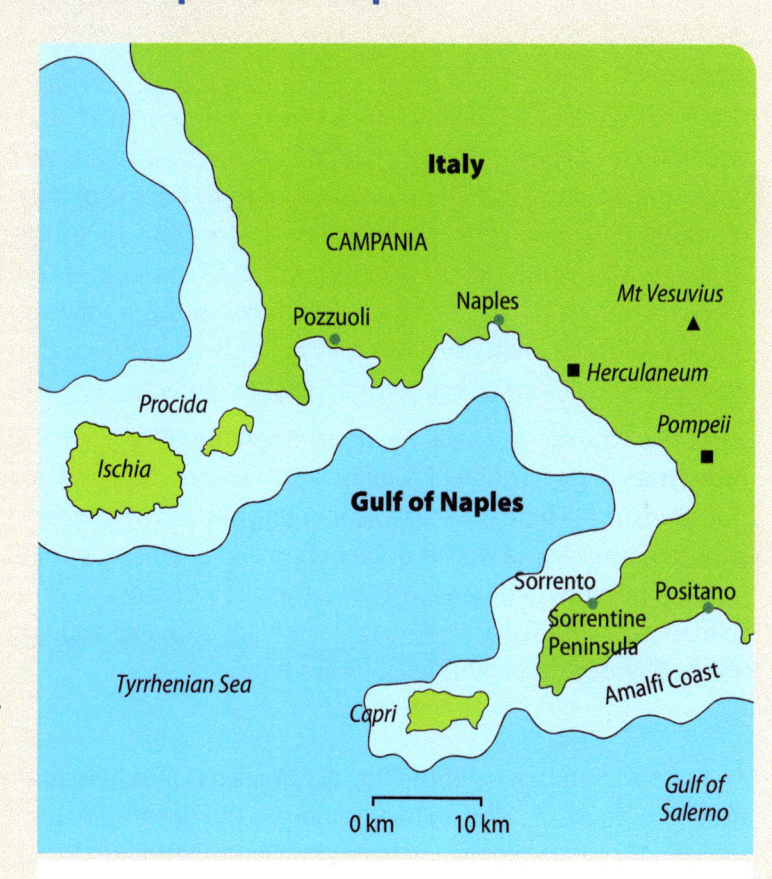

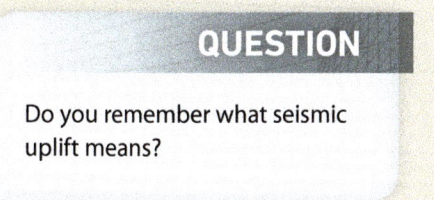

Figure 17.35 The Bay of Naples

QUESTION

Do you remember what seismic uplift means?

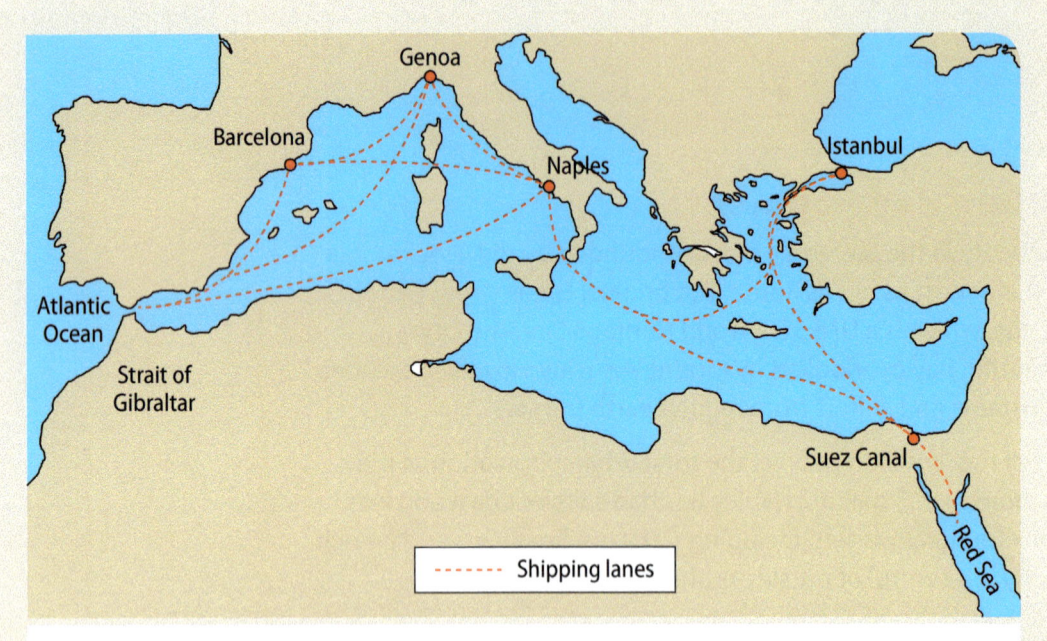

Figure 17.36 Naples occupies a central position in the Mediterranean Sea lanes

Transport

Good transport networks are vital to the development of any city and this is equally true of Naples. The city has been connected to Rome from ancient times and is on the main coastal route south to the toe of Italy. Today, thanks to Cassa investment in the years before 1984, the Autostrada del Sole connects Milan with Naples. A network of dual carriageway and motorway roads surrounds Naples. Rail connections to Northern Italy are also good. Because of its location, excellent harbour and modernised transport, the city was chosen by Cassa as a growth pole for manufacturing.

Since the time of the Cassa, the government has located many **heavy industries** in the vicinity of Naples, which are served by road, rail and port transport. There is a steel plant in **Bagnoli**, an industrial suburb of the city, as well as engineering and chemical works. Modern rail and road transport as well as the port are important to manufacturers for accessing raw materials and dispatching finished goods to markets in Northern Italy.

> **LINK**
> See Figure 17.30 on page 329 for the motorway map of Italy.

Tourism

The astounding beauty of the Bay of Naples has also helped the growth of tourism. Tourism has influenced the development of the city. The city is a gateway to nearby Mount Vesuvius. Many thousands of tourists arrive by cruise ships into the port of Naples. Tourists also arrive by air at Naples Airport from Northern Europe.

> **DEFINITION**
> The adjective for Naples is **Neapolitan**. The Italian for Naples is **Napoli**.

Tourism is an important sector in the economy and supports much employment in the hospitality industry. Tourists also enjoy the cuisine of the city. Neapolitans claim that they invented pizza.

- Naples is a gateway to Pompeii and Herculaneum.
- The National Archaeological Museum in Naples is one of the world's greatest museums of artefacts from Roman times. It is a magnet for tourists who are interested in classical times.
- The Teatro di San Carlo is one of Europe's greatest opera houses.

Naples in the foreground, with Mount Vesuvius in the background

The city's image: A negative influence on its development

In spite of many positive factors that have helped its development, Naples has been described as *la città perduta* – '**the lost city**'. The influence of the Camorra, the local mafia, is strong. Criminal gangs operate protection rackets. The Camorra controls the illegal drugs trade. High youth unemployment has brought many recruits into drug gangs. Murder rates are high between feuding criminal gangs.

Corruption has long been a problem among the city's politicians and has slowed development. The collection of refuse waste is a challenge, much of which is illegally dumped and burned. The city is regularly affected by rotting waste. This is partly because the Camorra is involved in many of the waste disposal contracts handed out by the city council.

However, recent reforming mayors have made great efforts to improve politics in the city. They have enacted some changes that have given the city a makeover. These include:

› The pedestrianisation of key streets in the city centre
› An annual arts festival
› The building of attractive new metro stations
› A new commercial and leisure centre at Nola in the suburbs.

The recession that began in 2008 was hard on Naples, as tourism dried up and services were starved of funds. When this is added to the inefficiency and slowness of public services, many people in Naples believe that they have been abandoned by the national government in Rome.

PowerPoint Summary

SUMMARY CHART

Two contrasting European regions

The Paris Basin: A core region

- **Primary economic activities**
  - Agriculture
  - Fishing
  - Influencing factors
    - Climate
    - Relief
    - Soils
    - Market
- **Physical processes**
  - Climate
  - Drainage
  - Relief
- **Secondary economic activities** — Manufacturing
  - Resource-based industries
    - Food processing
    - Wine production
  - Skills-based industries
    - Biotech industries
    - Fashion
    - Cosmetics
    - Modern growth industries
- **Tertiary economic activities**
  - Tourism
  - Transport
- **Population dynamics**
  - Population distribution and density
  - Population change
    - Birth rate
    - Death rate
    - Migration
  - Urban development
    - Paris

The Mezzogiorno: A peripheral region

- **Physical processes**
  - Climate
  - Relief
  - Soils
- **Primary economic activities**
  - Fishing
  - Agriculture
    - Vines, olives, wheat
    - Challenges
      - Climate
      - Relief
      - Peripherality
    - Modernisation
      - Cassa
      - Irrigation
      - Improved access to markets
- **Secondary economic activities**
  - Poorly developed manufacturing
    - Role of Cassa: Growth poles
    - State enterprises: Taranto steel
    - Private investment: Fiat – Melfi
    - Tari project
    - Etna Valley
- **Tertiary economic activities**
  - Tourism
  - Transport
- **Population dynamics**
  - Distribution and density
  - Birth rates, death rates, migration
  - Urban development
    - Naples

Leaving Cert exam questions

LONG QUESTIONS: HIGHER LEVEL

1 **Unemployment** (20 marks)

| | Unemployment as % of total population ||| Youth unemployment as % of active population (15 to 24 years) ||||
Country	2008	2014	2008	2012	2013	2014
Germany	7.4	5.3	10.4	8.0	7.8	7.7
Ireland	6.4	11.3	13.3	30.4	26.8	23.9
Greece	7.8	26.5	21.9	55.3	58.3	52.4
France	7.4	10.3	19.0	24.4	24.8	24.0

Examine the table above showing unemployment as a percentage of total population and youth unemployment as a percentage of active population, in selected countries, and answer each of the following questions.

(i) Which two countries had the same percentage of total population unemployed in 2008?

(ii) What was the trend in the percentage of total population unemployed in Ireland between 2008 and 2014?

(iii) Explain briefly one reason for this trend.

(iv) Which country's youth unemployment, as a percentage of active population, decreased between 2008 and 2014?

(v) Which country had the greatest increase in its youth unemployment, as a percentage of active population, between 2008 and 2014?

(vi) What has been the trend in Ireland's youth unemployment, as a percentage of active population, from 2012 to 2014 inclusive? State one reason for this trend.

2 **Agriculture in Europe** (30 marks)

Account for the development of agriculture in a **European** region (not in Ireland) that you have studied, with reference to any **two** of the following:

> Relief   > Markets   > Climate.

3 **Manufacturing in a European region** (30 marks)

Account for the development of manufacturing in a **European** region (not in Ireland) that you have studied.

4 **Economic activities** (30 marks)

Examine the factors that influence the development of **one** tertiary activity in a **European** region (not in Ireland) of your choice.

5 **Socio-economic regions** (30 marks)

'Economic activities in core regions differ from those in peripheral regions.' Examine this statement with reference to examples that you have studied.

6 **Dynamics of regions – climate** (30 marks)

Examine the importance of climate to the economic development of any **two contrasting European regions** (not in Ireland) that you have studied.

7 **European regions** (30 marks)

Examine the importance of relief to the economic development of any **two contrasting European regions** (not in Ireland) that you have studied.

HL

8 Population in a European region (30 marks)

Examine the distribution of population throughout a **European** region (not in Ireland) that you have studied.

9 Urban development (30 marks)

Examine how **two** of the following factors have influenced the development of any **urban** region that you have studied:

- Transport
- Location
- Primary economic activities.

10 Urban regions (30 marks)

Discuss the factors that influenced the development of **one** urban area in a **European** region (not in Ireland) that you have studied.

OL

LONG QUESTIONS: ORDINARY LEVEL

1 European region (30 marks)

Draw a sketch map of a **European** region (not in Ireland) that you have studied. On it, show and name each of the following:

- **Two** named towns or cities
- **One** named river
- **One** named area of relief (upland or lowland).

2 Primary economic activity in a European region (40 marks)

Answer each of the following questions with reference to a **European** region (not in Ireland) that you have studied.

(i) Name **one** primary economic activity that contributes to the economy of this region.
(ii) Explain the advantages that this region has for the development of the primary economic activities named in part (i) above.
(iii) Describe **one** challenge faced by this primary economic activity in this region.

3 Economic activity in a European region (40 marks)

Name a **European** region (not in Ireland) that you have studied and explain any **two** of the following:

- The importance of transport in this region
- The reasons why tourists are attracted to this region
- The type of farming practised in this region
- The reasons for the development of industry in this region.

4 Tourism in a European region (40 marks)

Name a **European** region (not in Ireland) that you have studied and answer each of the following questions.

(i) Name **two** tourist attractions in this region.
(ii) Explain the reasons why tourists are attracted to this region.
(iii) Describe **one** problem associated with tourism in this region.

5 Regional problems (30 marks)

Describe **two** problems faced by any region that you have studied.

6 European urban growth (30 marks)

Name **one** urban area in a **European** region (not in Ireland) that you have studied. Explain **two** reasons for the growth of this urban area.

Chapter 18
The Dynamics of Regions 3

UNIT 2 · REGIONAL GEOGRAPHY

KEYWORDS

- quickly developing country
- Central Plateau
- Great Escarpment
- arid North-East
- savanna grasslands
- Minais Gerais
- ethanol
- soya
- Embrapa
- terra rossa soils
- frontier forest
- biomes
- biodiversity
- slash and burn
- ecotourism
- the IMF
- Mercosul
- Itaipu Dam
- Carnaval
- samba schools
- bossa nova
- *favela*

LEARNING OBJECTIVES

By the end of this chapter, you should be able to understand:

- How to identify the major physical regions of Brazil
- How to describe the climates, soils and vegetation of Brazil
- How to discuss the primary, secondary and tertiary activities of Brazil
- How to identify the races that make up the population of Brazil
- How to examine some of the human processes of the region, such as population dynamics and urban development
- How to discuss the cultural characteristics that are unique to Brazil.

BRAZIL: A SUB-CONTINENTAL REGION

This chapter examines physical, economic and human processes in **one sub-continental region: Brazil**.

Introduction

- Brazil, the fifth largest country in the world, is 8.5 million km² in size. It has the largest area of tropical rainforest in the world, the Amazon Basin.
- Brazil became a colony of Portugal in the sixteenth century. It has been independent since 1822. Brasilia is its capital city.

- Brazilians speak Portuguese and the majority of the population are baptised Catholics. People of multiracial origin make up a sizeable proportion of the country.
- Brazil has exciting carnivals and distinctive music. Brazilians also tend to be passionate about soccer.
- Economically, Brazil is a quickly developing country. It is no longer a mainly agricultural economy. It now exports cars, aircraft and chemicals. However, there is a huge income gap between rich and poor.

GEOFACT

The name Brazil comes from brazilwood, a tree that grows in the country.

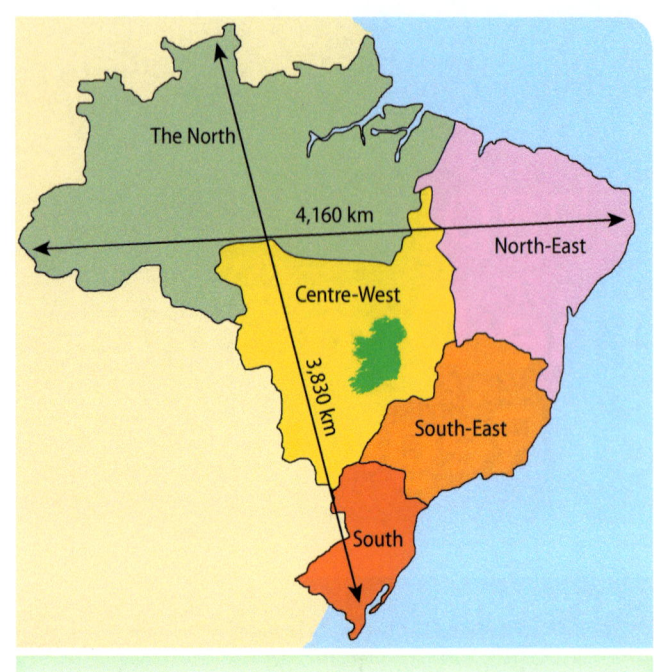

Figure 18.1 Brazil's regions

Physical processes

Relief

The **Brazilian Highlands** reach to about 1,200 metres above sea level. They cover most of the central, eastern and southern parts of the country. They are home to a wide variety of fauna and flora. The highest point in Brazil is Pico de Neblina at 2,994 metres.

Parallel to the eastern coastline, the **Great Escarpment** can be found. This gives those looking at the shore from the sea the impression of looking at a huge, imposing wall.

The enormous **Central Plateau** is west of the Eastern Highlands. It is approximately 1,000 metres above sea level.

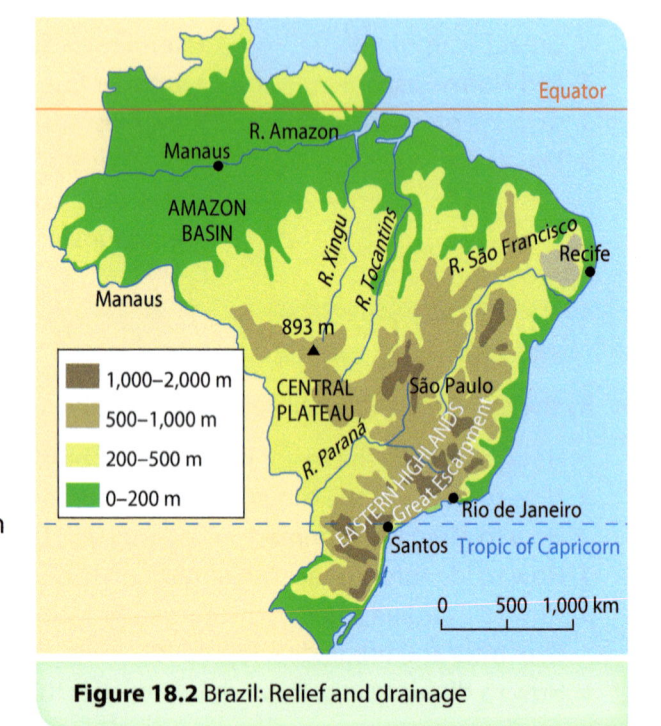

Figure 18.2 Brazil: Relief and drainage

Drainage

The Amazon Basin is one of the world's greatest rivers. The Amazon River carries more water into the sea than any other river does. This river flows for more than 3,200 km within the country and holds about one-fifth of the world's fresh water. Even at its narrowest point in Brazil, the river is 1.6 km wide. At its widest, it is 48 km wide during the wet season. The Amazon and its tributaries drain about two-thirds of the country's area.

Brazil is particularly abundant in rivers and has many more drainage basins, such as the Paraná Basin in the South and the São Francisco in the North-East.

GEOFACT

Rio de Janeiro has a latitude of 23 degrees south, close to the Tropic of Capricorn.

Climate

MONTHLY PRECIPITATION AND TEMPERATURES FOR RIO DE JANEIRO

	Jan	Feb	Mar	Apr	May	Jun	Jul	Aug	Sept	Oct	Nov	Dec	Total
Precipitation (mm)	114	105	103	137	85	80	56	50	87	88	95	169	1,169
Temperature (°C)	26	27	26	25	24	23	22	22	22	23	24	25	

Table 18.1 Rio de Janeiro has a tropical oceanic climate

Most of the country has tropical and sub-tropical climates. In general, this means hot, humid conditions. The Amazon Basin has average temperatures of more than 26°C all year round, with high rainfall and humidity.

However, the North-East is arid, with 500 mm or less of rainfall annually. This area can even experience occasional droughts because of the high evaporation.

In the South, average temperatures fall below sub-tropical levels. Here, winters are cool, with some frost and snow showers in the uplands.

ACTIVITY

Numeracy

Examine Table 18.1.
(i) What is the total rainfall for June, July and August?
(ii) For how many months of the year does rainfall exceed 100 mm per month?
(iii) What is the hottest month? Can you explain your answer?

Natural vegetation

Until recently, rainforests cover or have covered almost 60% of the entire area of Brazil, with just under 3 million km². Brazil is home to one-third of the world's rainforests. These rainforests provide the ideal habitat for one-third of all the world's animal species.

GEOFACT

Almost two-thirds of the Amazon rainforest is located in Brazil.

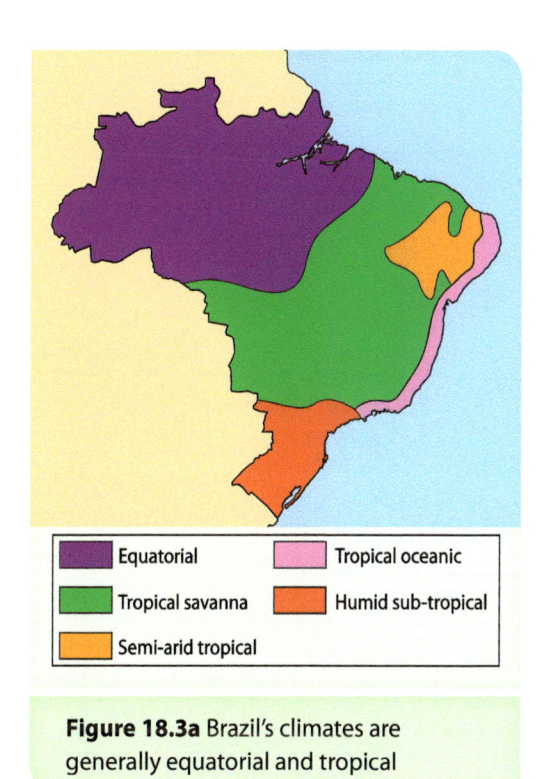

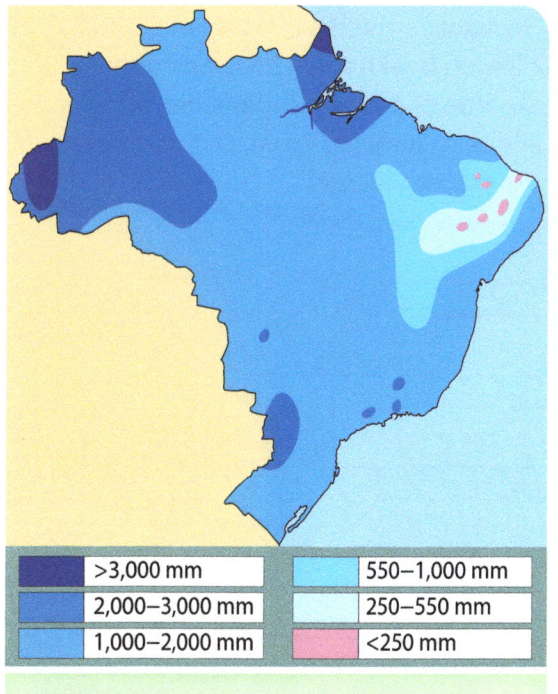

Figure 18.3a Brazil's climates are generally equatorial and tropical

Legend:
- Equatorial
- Tropical savanna
- Semi-arid tropical
- Tropical oceanic
- Humid sub-tropical

Figure 18.3b Apart from the arid North-East, Brazil receives high levels of rainfall. Low pressure in the Amazon Basin pulls in rain-bearing winds from the Atlantic.

Legend:
- >3,000 mm
- 2,000–3,000 mm
- 1,000–2,000 mm
- 550–1,000 mm
- 250–550 mm
- <250 mm

To date, approximately 56,000 species of plants, 1,700 bird species, 700 amphibian species, 580 mammal species and 650 reptile species have been identified. The rainforest is a treasure chest of **biodiversity**.

In Central Brazil, rainfall is more seasonal than in the Amazon Basin. Here, rainforests give way to tropical savanna grasslands with trees along the river floodplains. The arid North-East has scrubland and cacti. The sub-tropical region of the east coast gives way to temperate grasslands in the extreme south.

Figure 18.3c Brazil's natural vegetation

DEFINITION

Savanna grasslands are found in tropical regions that are not wet enough to support continuous forest. Shrubs and isolated trees are scattered among the grasslands.

DEFINITION

Biodiversity: The term given to the variety of life on Earth.

Primary economic activities

Agriculture

Agriculture is very important in the Brazilian economy and accounts for more than one-fifth of its GDP. Brazil has made extraordinary strides in agriculture in the last thirty to forty years.

This tropical country is now a **food giant** and is competing with the USA, Canada and the EU for markets abroad. It has the second largest **beef herd** in the world after India and is a leading exporter of **poultry**, **sugar cane**, ethanol and **soya beans**. In addition, Brazil has spare land that can still be brought into food production.

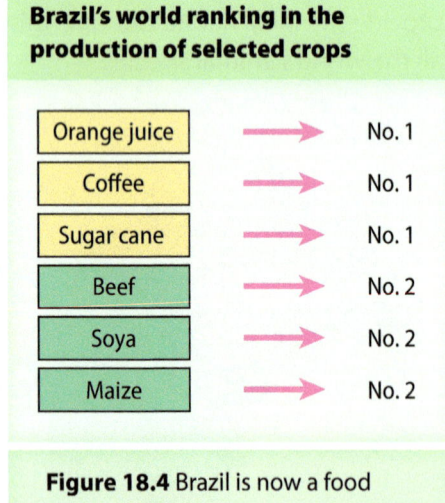

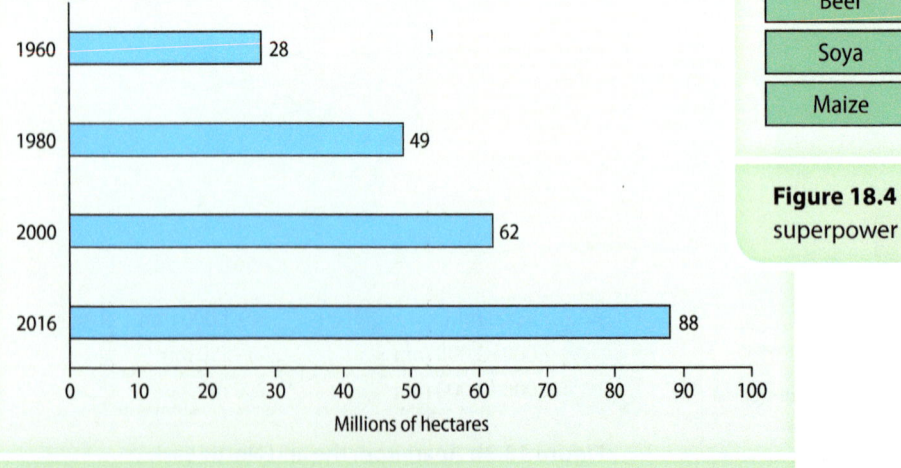

Brazil's world ranking in the production of selected crops

Orange juice	No. 1
Coffee	No. 1
Sugar cane	No. 1
Beef	No. 2
Soya	No. 2
Maize	No. 2

Figure 18.4 Brazil is now a food superpower

Year	Millions of hectares
1960	28
1980	49
2000	62
2016	88

Figure 18.5 The extension of the cultivated land (cropland) since 1960 in Brazil. Sixty million additional hectares were deforested and cleared for cropland during the years 1960 to 2015.

Beef

Brazil's savanna grassland in the Central Plateau is called the **Cerrado** by Brazilians. Large ranches are devoted to cattle grazing using extensive methods of farming. While output per hectare is still low by EU standards, the enormous areas involved lead to high beef output.

High-yielding grasses have been introduced from Africa by **Embrapa**, the state-owned agricultural research corporation. These grasses are much more productive and nutritious than the native Cerrado grasses. New land is continuously being brought into production as tropical rainforest is cleared. This change to the environment has provoked great controversy both at home and abroad.

Cattle are also reared in the temperate grasslands of Southern Brazil.

> **DEFINITION**
>
> **Cerrado:** The name given to the vast tropical savanna grassland region of the Central Plateau in Brazil.

Coffee

Coffee is a major plantation crop in the state of São Paulo. Plantations are called *fazendas*. Coffee grows best on sloping ground at altitudes of 1,000 metres and thrives on the fertile terra rossa soils of the region. Coffee is a labour-intensive crop at the harvesting stage. At one time coffee accounted for 69% of Brazil's exports, but this figure is now down to 2%.

> **GEOFACT**
>
> Brazil had 219 million cattle in 2016, while the EU had 88 million.

> **ACTIVITY**
>
> **Discussion**
>
> Can you explain why the clearing of tropical rainforest provokes much controversy in Brazil and around the world?

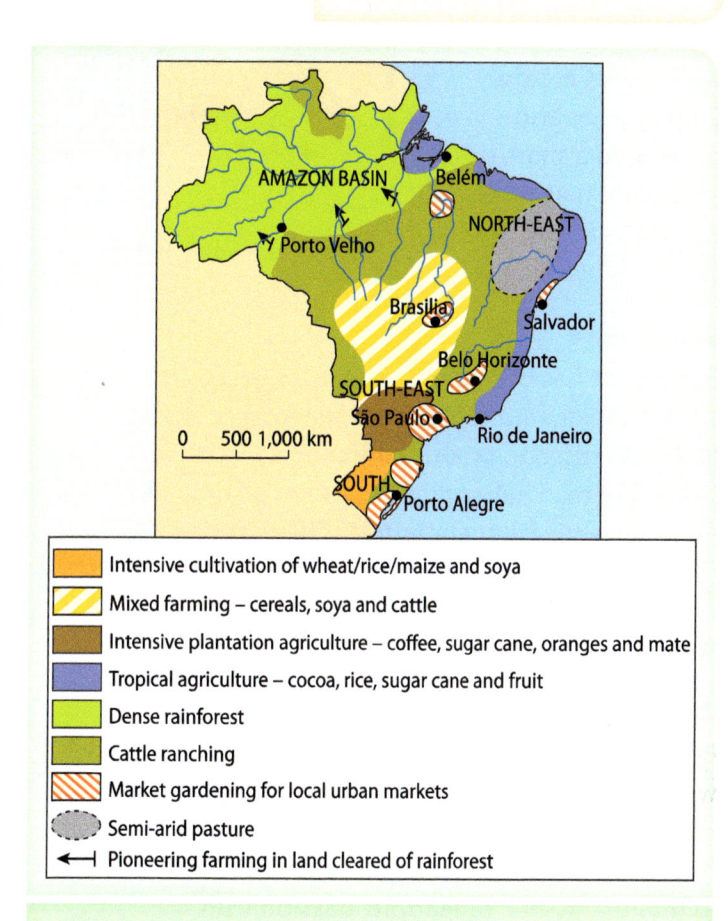

Figure 18.6 Agricultural land use in Brazil

Map legend:
- Intensive cultivation of wheat/rice/maize and soya
- Mixed farming – cereals, soya and cattle
- Intensive plantation agriculture – coffee, sugar cane, oranges and mate
- Tropical agriculture – cocoa, rice, sugar cane and fruit
- Dense rainforest
- Cattle ranching
- Market gardening for local urban markets
- Semi-arid pasture
- Pioneering farming in land cleared of rainforest

A coffee plantation in the state of São Paulo, Brazil

Soya

The production of soya in the Cerrado has vastly increased in the last few decades. More than 6% of Brazil's arable land is now under soya production. Soya is a major export.

Soya production is highly mechanised in large farms owned by agri-companies. Soya's success in Brazil is largely due to the pioneering work done by Embrapa. Embrapa has developed hybrid seeds that grow well in the Cerrado. Embrapa has also developed a short-cycle soya plant that allows for two crops a year. This has doubled soya output.

ACTIVITY

Research

Look up more about the work of Embrapa on the internet.

Soya beans are stored in these secure silos awaiting export to global markets

Sugar cane

Sugar cane has been grown on Brazil's east coast since the sixteenth century. It is still a major export and is also used to produce **ethanol**, a biofuel for cars. More than half of Brazil's cars run on biofuel. The crop is still labour intensive at harvest time.

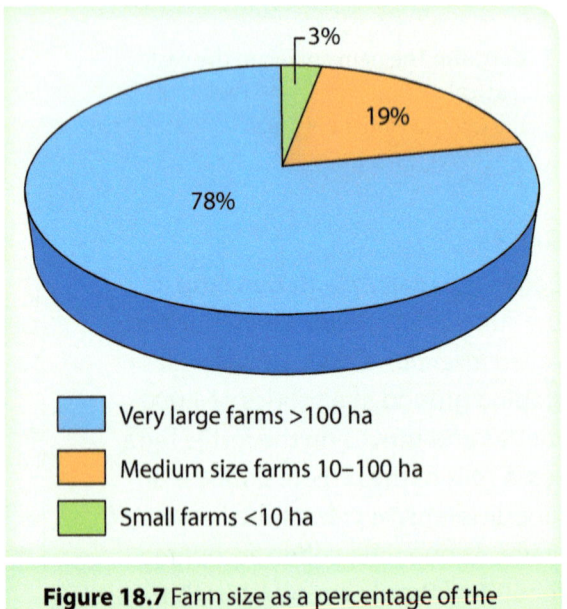

Factors that affect the development of agriculture in Brazil

Climate

Because of the high temperatures and rainfall, a wide variety of tropical crops such as **coffee**, **sugar cane**, **cocoa** and **rice** can be grown. The climate is also suitable for producing tropical fruits such as **mango**, **guava**, **pineapple**, **passion fruit**, **oranges** and **bananas**.

- Very large farms >100 ha — 78%
- Medium size farms 10–100 ha — 19%
- Small farms <10 ha — 3%

Figure 18.7 Farm size as a percentage of the total area farmed in Brazil

A fruit market in Rio de Janeiro. Brazil grows a wide variety of tropical fruits.

ACTIVITY

Research

Look up guava on the internet to find out what it is.

Coffee, for example, is a demanding crop in terms of climate. It requires:

› A total absence of night frost – even one hour of frost will kill every coffee plant
› An average temperature of at least 21°C all year round
› Plentiful supplies of rainfall of at least 1,000 mm annually with high humidity
› Altitudes of more than 300 metres.

These conditions are found in many parts of Eastern Brazil. They are especially abundant in São Paulo state along the Tropic of Capricorn. Coffee cannot grow in the extreme south of Brazil because of the occasional frost.

Soils

Tropical red soils of the Amazon Basin support luxurious rainforest vegetation because of the humus layer that is derived from fallen leaves. However, these soils have limited agricultural potential due to heavy leaching. To produce crops in forest clearances, native tribes have traditionally practised **slash and burn subsistence farming**.

This involves clearing a small area of trees and burning the timber. This produces a layer of ash, which provides a natural fertiliser that lasts for three to four years. After that, the soil is exhausted because of leaching. The tribe moves on and does not return to that area for about thirty years.

The **terra rossa soil** of the state of São Paulo in South-East Brazil is very fertile. It has a dark colour, is rich in iron, is free draining and has high levels of humus. It is ideal for coffee bushes, which have thrived in this region since they were introduced in 1727. Brazil produces one-third of the world's coffee, largely because of its terra rossa soils and climatic conditions.

The soils of the Cerrado – **the Central Plateau** – are not particularly fertile. Here, the soil is **acidic** with a low pH. This has traditionally supported coarse tropical grasses for cattle grazing. However, Embrapa has encouraged farming enterprises to apply high applications of **crushed lime** at the rate of **five tons per hectare** per year as necessary. This, along with fertiliser, has turned the Cerrado into a major producer of crops such as **soya**, **maize** and **cotton**. For good measure, soya thrives in soil that is somewhat acidic.

Along the river floodplains of the Paraná and the São Francisco River, rich alluvial soils develop where annual flooding occurs. These are very productive and have many uses.

> **GEOFACT**
>
> Brazil has been the largest exporter of coffee beans for 150 years.

> **DEFINITION**
>
> The term *terra rossa soils* translates as *red soils*.

> **QUESTION**
>
> Can you explain why soils that have been cleared of forest in the Amazon Basin quickly become exhausted?

Harvest time on a soya farm in Brazil

Markets

Brazil has a large internal market of 210 million people and it is increasing by 2 million people a year. This is a huge market that consumes great quantities of cereals, meat and vegetables. As Brazilians' standard of living increases, domestic **meat consumption** is growing.

However, the export market has also driven Brazil's ambition to become a global food superpower. Brazilian **meat**, **soya**, **sugar cane** and **coffee** are exported all over the world. Some of Brazil's meat products are used in the beef burger trade in North America. Soya is fed to pigs and poultry in Brazil, the EU, China and the USA.

Brazil is also the single biggest exporter of agricultural products into the EU and is seeking to increase its meat exports to the EU through trade agreements. Irish beef farmers are unhappy with this development.

Brazilian marketing teams have targeted the huge and growing Chinese market as standards of living in China have grown in recent years. Brazil's exports of foodstuffs to China have grown by 500% since the year 2000.

Finally, the global population is expected to grow from more than 7 billion to 9 billion before 2050. Brazil's spare farmland is poised to feed many of those additional people in the decades ahead.

Mineral exploitation

Brazil is a major producer and exporter of minerals, with almost 50% of the total value produced in the state of Minas Gerais and another quarter produced in the Carajás area. Brazil is rich in iron ore, gold, copper, lead, zinc, tin and nickel as well as offshore oil and natural gas.

Oil

Brazil's investment in offshore oil exploration in the 1970s has been very successful. The country has considerable offshore reserves of oil. The **Campos Basin** oil field is the largest. While the country was self-sufficient in oil supplies for many years, increased demand has led to the resumption of imports. Nevertheless, the country was 66% self-sufficient in 2015. Natural gas is also found offshore.

A large beef herd in land that has been cleared of rainforest in Brazil

GEOFACT

Brazil produces more than 90% of the world's **niobium**, an alloy that is used to produce heat-resistant steel.

DEFINITION

Minas Gerais translates as '(the state) of many minerals'.

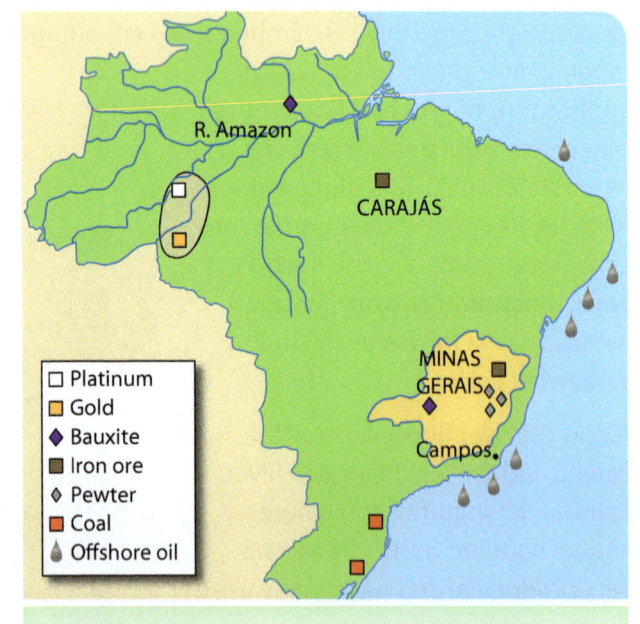

Figure 18.8 Brazil has a wide variety of minerals

Metal ores

Brazil has great quantities of metal ores. Iron ore is produced in the state of Minas Gerais and in Carajás, close to the Amazon Basin. Brazil exports iron ore to China, Japan and the USA. Bauxite found in the Amazon Basin is exported to many countries, including Ireland. **RUSAL's alumina refinery** in the Shannon Estuary imports ore from Brazil.

Gold

No discussion of mineral reserves in Brazil would be complete without reference to gold mining. Gold has been mined in Minas Gerais for generations. Today, important discoveries in the Amazon Basin have attracted the usual rush of migrants in search of the elusive metal. Serra Pelada was the top gold mine of the 1980s, while today, Eldorado do Juma is the centre of attention. A maths teacher in the nearest town posted the discovery of gold there on the internet, the first time that a gold discovery had been publicised in this way.

> **ACTIVITY**
>
> **Research**
>
> Look up Serra Pelada and Eldorado do Juma on the internet.

Thousands of people established a makeshift town in a very short time, despite the rain, humidity, excessive heat and malaria. The local town of Apuí has become the centre for buying and selling gold. It is an area where fortunes are made by some. Even cooks and cleaners are making six times the Brazilian minimum wage there.

The timber industry

The timber industry is very important in the Brazilian economy. Brazil is home to the third largest remaining **frontier forest**, after Russia and Canada, in the world. It has the greatest biodiversity of all the world's natural regions.

> **DEFINITION**
>
> **Frontier forest:** A large and undisturbed forest in an area of low population density.

Wildcat miners pan for gold in the Amazon rainforest in Novo Aripuanã, 80 km from the town of Apuí. More than 6,000 miners set up camp in the area after the discovery of gold deposits became public in December 2006.

Timber is harvested from both native forests and managed forests. The native forests of Brazil are mainly found in the Amazon Basin and comprise more than 98% of the country's forests. Managed forests are located south of Brazil. A small section of native forest is still being harvested in the dwindling Atlantic Forest on the east coast.

Forestry generates a lot of employment in Brazil and is an important export. The country is a leading exporter of **tropical hardwoods**, which are used to make windows, doors and beautiful furniture in the developed world.

A fleet of lorries transporting logged rainforest timber to ports for exports

DEFINITION

Atlantic Forest: The forest that is located along Brazil's east coast. Much of it has been cut down to make way for settlement and farmland.

GEOFACT

The Tijuca Forest beside Rio de Janeiro has been successfully reforested in recent decades.

ACTIVITY

Research

Look up the Tijuca Forest on the internet to find out more about it.

Legal harvesting of forests is permissible in the following ways:

› From managed forests in Southern Brazil with permission from the Brazilian Institute of Environment and Renewable Natural Resources
› From permitted land clearance for agriculture or legal mining in the interior and on the southern margins of the Amazon rainforest.

However, centuries of exploitation of this magnificent natural resource is placing enormous pressure on Brazil's forests. To date, **well over 570,000 km²** (an area the size of France and the Low Countries) of the Amazon forests have been deforested. Roads that are built into the Amazon Basin have seen great swathes of forest cleared for farmland and timber production. Much of the deforestation is illegal. There are many **illegal loggers**, who often go undetected because of the sheer size of the country.

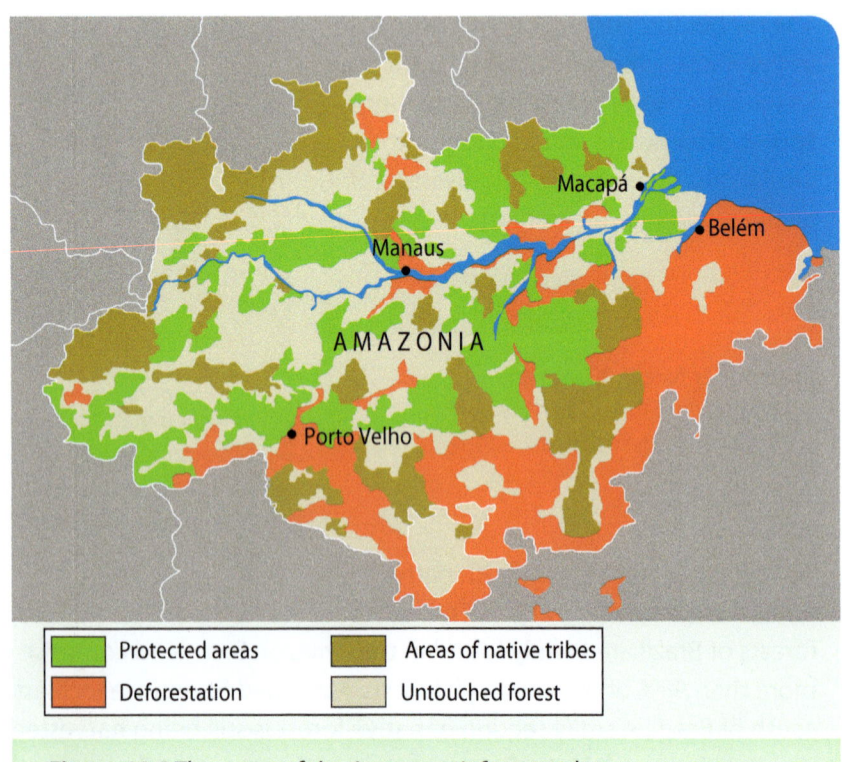

Figure 18.9 The status of the Amazon rainforest today

Deforestation has a devastating effect on the natural resources of Brazil and its biodiversity. It also reduces the capacity of the forest to absorb CO_2. Accidental fires destroy almost half of all the area that has been burned in the Amazon Basin.

However, there is hope. Average rates of deforestation in 2012–2015 are reported to have fallen significantly compared to the peak in 2004 for the following reasons:

- **Satellite surveillance** is helping the government to control illegal deforestation.
- Much of the rainforest of the Amazon Basin is now protected.
- Native peoples are speaking up for their traditional rights and voicing their objections on television.
- Customers in the construction industry seem to have a growing preference for certified, legitimate suppliers. Importers in the EU are increasingly demanding certified timber only from Brazil.
- The Brazil nut tree, native Brazilwood and Brazilian rosewood (or jacaranda) are protected species and may no longer be harvested.

Nevertheless, it is likely that the area under forest will continue to be reduced because of corruption, disrespect for the law, accidental fires and the demands of the agricultural industry to clear more land for soya.

ACTIVITY

Research

Look up how Amazon forest dwellers are opposing the destruction of the rainforest on the internet.

ACTIVITY

Discussion

Imagine that you were a native Amazon forest dweller. Compose a short speech outlining your objections to the cutting of the rainforest.

Secondary economic activities

In 1960 Brazil was a largely agricultural economy, with 80% of its exports coming from agriculture and mineral resources. Today, primary resources and manufactured goods each account for about half of Brazil's exports.

Manufacturing

Manufacturing took off in Brazil in the 1940s when world trade collapsed. Brazil was unable to import goods from abroad and had to develop its own manufacturing.

The steel industry was established with a major steel mill in Volta Redonda in Rio de Janeiro in the 1940s. Manufacturing growth has expanded ever since, but with periodic hiccups. This was because Brazil has had a turbulent political and economic history, including hyperinflation and a major debt crisis in the 1980s. This affected manufacturing output as domestic demand declined.

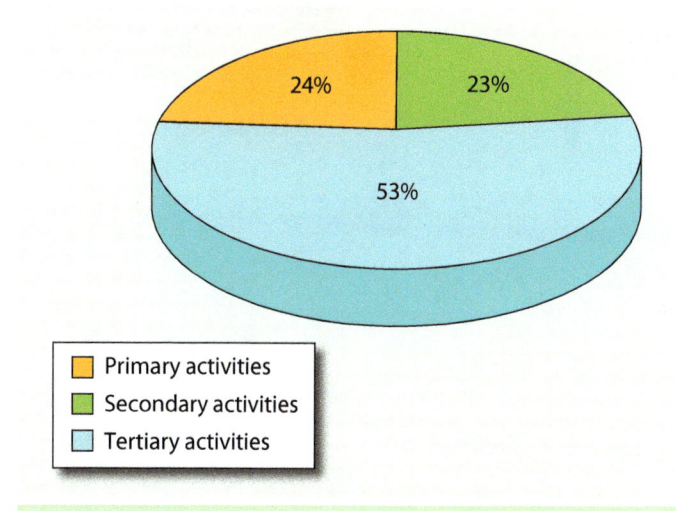

Figure 18.10 The employment structure in Brazil. This structure is typical of a quickly developing economy.

Pie chart:
- Primary activities: 24%
- Secondary activities: 23%
- Tertiary activities: 53%

DEFINITION

Hyperinflation: Where inflation reaches runaway figures. For instance, in 1990, inflation reached an annual rate of 30,777% in Brazil.

As part of economic restructuring, the **IMF** was called in to help Brazil to manage its economy. Because of this, the steel industry, which had been state owned until then, has been privatised.

Despite those upheavals, the range of manufactured goods in Brazil today is impressive. These include steel, cars, tractors, aircraft, chemicals, electronics, electrical and consumer goods. Brazil is also a world leader in the production of tropical medicines.

The role of foreign investment

Brazil is a developing economy. The country had a limited supply of capital, so from the 1960s onwards, governments encouraged multinational manufacturing companies to invest in Brazil. Volkswagen, Ford and General Motors have long-established assembly plants in the country. Renault and leading Japanese car makers came later.

Inward investment continues today. In recent times, BMW and Jaguar Land Rover have opened factories in the south and south-east of Brazil. China is now a major trading partner with Brazil. Chery International, the Chinese car maker, has opened a car assembly plant in Brazil.

> **GEOFACT**
>
> The International Monetary Fund promotes world trade, stable exchange rates and the correction of balance-of-payment problems.

A Fiat car assembly plant in Belo Horizonte, Brazil

Sugar cane awaits delivery to a cane ethanol plant in the São Paulo state, Brazil

> **ACTIVITY**
>
> **Thinking**
>
> Explain two reasons why Brazil has encouraged multinational companies to become established there.

Car assembly plants in Brazil produced 3.75 million cars in 2014. Many car engines are built to run on a mix of petrol and ethanol or on pure ethanol, derived from sugar cane.

Because of inward investment, Brazil has benefited from the transfer of technology from abroad and its workforce continues to learn modern mechanical and other manufacturing skills. These companies invested in the South and South-East – the economic core region of the country.

Mercosul

Mercosul is a common market between Brazil, Argentina, Paraguay, Uruguay and Venezuela. It was established in 1991. Mercosul allows the movement of goods and services between the member states free of import duties. Brazil's manufacturers have greatly benefited from the export opportunities in these emerging markets.

Most of the other countries of South America are associate members of Mercosul. Because of the great distances involved, goods from Brazil are exported through ports such as **Santos** and **Rio de Janeiro** to Argentina, one of Brazil's major markets. They then go on to South American countries on the Pacific coast such as Chile and Peru. Argentina imports **71%** of all Brazil's car exports.

Brazil itself imposes tariffs on imported goods from North America, the EU and Asia. This protects manufacturers in Brazil against foreign competition from these regions.

Figure 18.11 The members of Mercosul. Brazil is the largest economy in Mercosul.

Figure 18.12 South American shipping routes. Most of Brazil's exports to Mercosul trading partners and associate members are exported by sea.

ACTIVITY

Thinking

Explain two reasons why Brazil's exports to its Mercosul partners are transported by sea.

Geographic concentration of manufacturing

Manufacturing is concentrated in South-East Brazil, the economic core region of the country. The **industrial triangle** of São Paulo, Rio de Janeiro and Belo Horizonte produces the greater portion of Brazil's manufactured goods. Because of this, standards of living are far higher here than in the rest of the country.

The following factors favour manufacturing in South-East Brazil:

- The South-East is the location of many industrial raw materials. Iron and steel mills are concentrated in Minas Gerais because the state is rich in iron ore.
- In recent decades, the discovery of offshore oil and gas led to the development of a major refining and petrochemical industry in the region.
- Large ports such as Rio de Janeiro and Santos, the port that serves São Paulo, already existed in the South-East.
- Car assembly plants were attracted to the South-East because of plentiful supplies of labour in major cities such as São Paulo. São Paulo, with 20 million people, is the largest city in South America and is a huge market for consumer goods.
- The best communication infrastructure, such as road and rail, is in the South-East. Broadband facilities, an essential requirement for business, are also well developed in the region.
- The Itaipu Dam on the Paraná River – one of the largest dams in the world – provides hydro-electricity for much of the South-East.

Figure 18.13 Manufacturing cities in Brazil. Manufacturing is largely concentrated in the industrial triangle of the South-East.

GEOFACT

Some 63% of all foreign MNCs operating in Brazil are in the city of São Paulo.

ACTIVITY

Research

Look up images of the Itaipu Dam on the internet to see the scale of the project.

Tertiary economic activities

Brazil is a developing economy. Therefore, the tertiary sector is not as important as it is in Ireland, France or Italy. Nevertheless, it employs slightly more than half of the Brazilian workforce.

We will examine transport services and tourism.

Transport

Brazil is a very large country, which makes building national routeways challenging. In general, transport networks in the economic core of the South and South-East are dense. However, much of the interior has poor communications.

A spectacular motorway connects São Paulo (in the background) to the coast

Road transport

Road transport is the most important mode of transport in Brazil. Motorways or dual carriageways connect Brasilia, Rio de Janeiro, Belo Horizonte, São Paulo and Curitiba – the most important urban centres of the South and South-East.

Since Brasilia was built as the new capital, 1,000 km north of Rio de Janeiro, Brazilians have looked to the interior for future economic development. This has led to the development of road networks all the way to the Amazon. New roads, many of them still dirt tracks, cross Central Brazil and north to the Amazon Basin. These roads have cut through pristine rainforest to open new lands to miners, loggers and ranchers. Environmentalists fear that new highways will lead to faster destruction of the rainforest.

Manaus and Santarém on the Amazon are now connected by road to Central and Southern Brazil. Great distances lead to very long journeys. It takes 55 hours to drive from São Paulo to Manaus by truck or car on the BR 364 over a distance of 2,700 km.

Since the establishment of Mercosul, road connections to Brazil's Mercosul partners such as Uruguay and Argentina have been modernised.

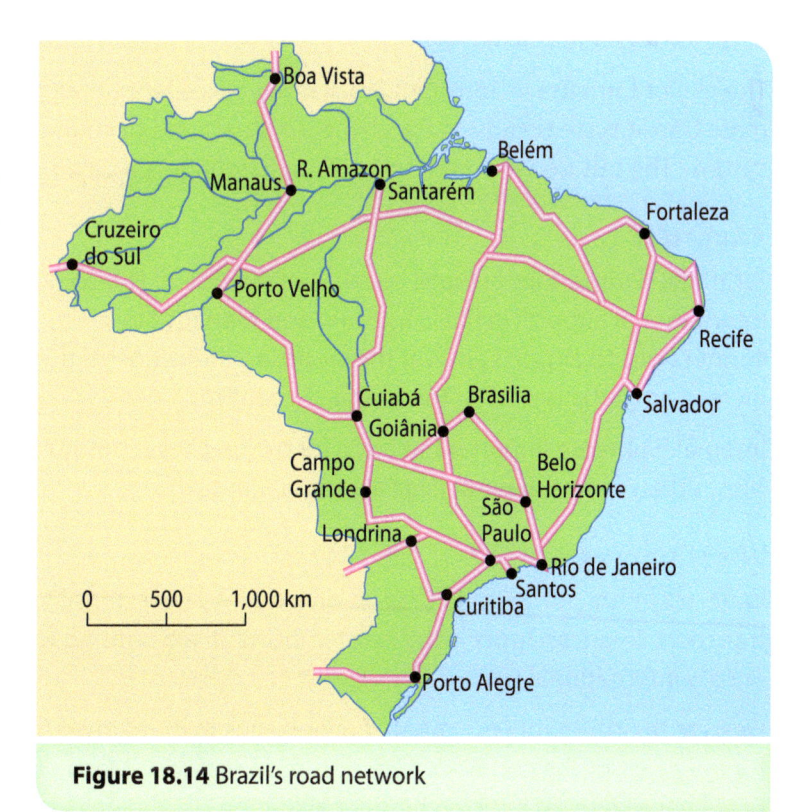

Figure 18.14 Brazil's road network

Rail transport

Most of the urban centres are found in Brazil's eastern regions. For that reason, the rail networks are in the same regions. The rail network is about 28,500 km in length, a surprisingly low figure for such a big country.

Railways are used mostly for freight. This is because railways were built to connect mineral deposits to the coast for export. For example, in the state of Minas Gerais, railways are ideal for the transport of large, bulky, non-perishable cargo such as minerals. The rail network is also important for the transport of some agricultural commodities, such as coffee beans, refined sugar and soya for export.

Although Brazil borders ten countries, it has international rail links with only three: Argentina, Uruguay and Bolivia.

Urban mass transit rail systems

There are metro systems in eight Brazilian cities. These include São Paulo, Rio de Janeiro, Brasilia and Belo Horizonte.

The São Paulo Metro is the largest metro system in Brazil and the second largest in South America. It has sixty-four stations and five rail lines. It operates and transports 4 million passengers from 4 a.m. every day of the week up to midnight and on Saturdays until 1 a.m.

The bus network in Curitiba. This network has attracted worldwide attention.

The city of **Curitiba** in Southern Brazil has an excellent urban bus mass transit system and a state-of-the-art smartcard ticketing system. The bus network carries 2 million passengers a day.

Airports

Air travel is important in Brazil because of the size of the country. International airports in Rio, São Paulo and Manaus have connections to airports all over the world, an indication of the increasing globalisation of the Brazilian economy.

Internal flights are important in Brazil for the business community. Most urban centres have at least a grass landing strip.

Water transport

Waterway transportation in Brazil is divided into river transport and sea transport. **Sea transport** is the most important, accounting for almost 75% of Brazil's international trade.

Despite the navigable potential of river basins in Brazil, river transport accounts for only 13% of the country's transportation network. Many plateau rivers in Brazil have waterfalls, which hinder navigation.

> **ACTIVITY**
>
> **Research**
>
> Look up the bus system in Curitiba on the internet.

> **GEOFACT**
>
> Brazil has the second highest number of airports in the world, after the USA.

The Amazon region depends almost exclusively on river transport where there are practically no roads. However, because of the low population density in the Amazon Basin, river traffic is light. The Amazon is navigable as far as Iquitos in Peru. River transport is important to residents of Manaus and Santarém. Belém is an important port at the mouth of the Amazon.

Tourism

Brazil is the most visited country in South America. There are many tourist attractions, but Brazil's tourism potential has yet to be realised. Barely **6 million** international tourists visit Brazil each year. This is partly due to the great distance of Brazil from North America, Europe and China. Nevertheless, Brazil has a great deal to offer tourists.

Partly to encourage tourists, tourist visa requirements have been waived for many countries. These include Greece, Italy, Hong Kong, New Zealand, Poland, South Africa, Turkey and many more.

ACTIVITY

Discussion

More international tourists come from Argentina to Brazil than from any other country. Why, do you think, is this so?

Figure 18.15 Brazil has a wide range of tourist attractions

The coast

Brazil's coast is almost 9,000 km in length. The tropical climate and long stretches of beach make the coast very attractive. Rio's Copacabana beach is known worldwide. The Green Coast, east of Rio, is also a great favourite with the wealthy from Rio and São Paulo. Paraty, a port on the coast dating from the colonial era, is an architectural jewel.

Ecotourism

This is a niche tourist sector where tourists can enjoy unique ecosystems and observe the fauna and flora of the country. Brazil has unrivalled ecotourism attractions that include the **Pantanal wetlands** and the Amazon rainforest.

Pantanal wetlands

These remote wetlands are situated in the interior of Brazil. They are more than twice the size of the island of Ireland. During the rainy season, they comprise the largest wetlands in the world and are a unique ecosystem of plants, birds and fish.

The **Pantanal biome** is home to approximately 3,500 known plant species. Species continue to be discovered and identified by scientists on a regular basis. Tourists can see crocodiles, anaconda snakes, monkeys and exotic birds. The wetlands can be reached from the Campo Grande Airport.

DEFINITIONS

Ecotourism: The promotion of tourism that does not harm the environment or its resources.

Biome: A large, naturally occurring community of flora and fauna occupying a major habitat, e.g. forest or wetlands.

ACTIVITY

Research

Look up the Pantanal wetlands on the internet to find out more.

The Amazon rainforest

This is a vast region. Tourists can study the region while it is still relatively unspoiled, but they are slow to do so for several reasons:

- The difficulty of getting there
- The lack of facilities in most of the Basin
- A hot, humid and very wet climate
- The necessity of taking medication against health risks such as yellow fever and malaria.

The best way to tour the Basin is by boat. Tourists can see rare animals, birds, insects and plants. Tourists can also do a treetop tour of life at the top of the forest canopy in some places. Manaus and Santarém each have several hotels and tour operators.

A pair of scarlet macaw parrots in the Amazon rainforest. The macaw is the national animal of Brazil.

Carnivals

Brazil specialises in carnivals. The largest festival is **Carnaval**, which takes place during the days before Ash Wednesday each year. During Carnaval, there is much excitement in large and small cities.

Rio's Carnaval is the wildest and most outrageous of them all. Rio has a specially constructed stadium called the **Sambadrome** for parades. Up to 200 samba schools give displays that involve samba dancing, lavish costumes, loud music and deafening percussion.

The samba dance, originating from the Bahia region with African rhythms, came to Rio de Janeiro around 1920. However, the noise, the crowds and the excitement of it all are not to everyone's taste. Many of Rio's wealthiest citizens take off to the Green Coast for the duration of Carnaval.

> **DEFINITION**
>
> **Samba schools:** Schools where people practise and perform samba, an African-Brazilian dance.

The Sambadrome in Rio de Janeiro, where dancing groups parade during Carnaval

Human processes

Population dynamics

The population of Brazil reached 210 million people in 2017. Brazil is the fifth most populous nation on Earth. The population of Brazil was a mere 17 million in the year 1900. It has grown rapidly since then due to inward migration and a birth rate that was high until relatively recently.

Fertility rates

The fertility rate in Brazil is now less than two babies per mother, a major decline in recent decades. Therefore, Brazil has reached **stage 4** of the population cycle. The decline in fertility is due to several reasons:

› High urbanisation, where children are an economic liability rather than an economic asset
› Economic development – fertility rates per mother decline as an economy develops
› A high literacy level (92%) among mothers – literate mothers are aware of family planning.

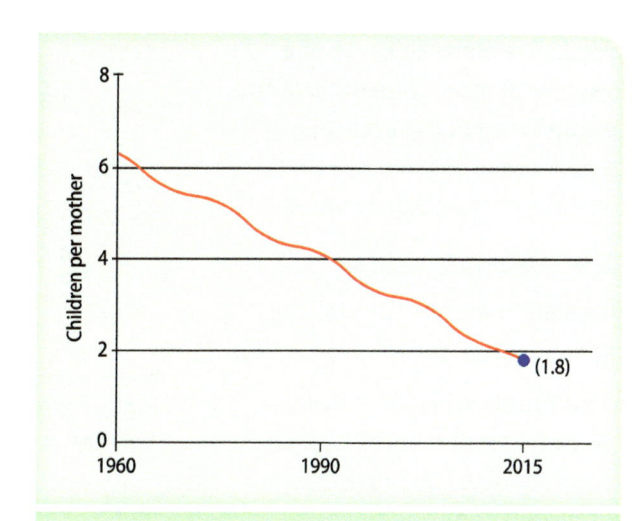

Figure 18.16 The fertility rate has declined rapidly over time in Brazil

However, Brazil has many young adults because of the higher birth rate of earlier years. Therefore, annual population growth is in the region of 1.1%.

Life expectancy

› Life expectancy in Brazil is typical of a middle-income country.
› Women's life expectancy is 77 years compared to 71 for men. The figure is below European standards.
› Infant mortality rates are 15 per 1,000, compared to 4 per 1,000 in France. Brazil has also been affected by the Zika virus in recent times, which has led to the death of some infants.

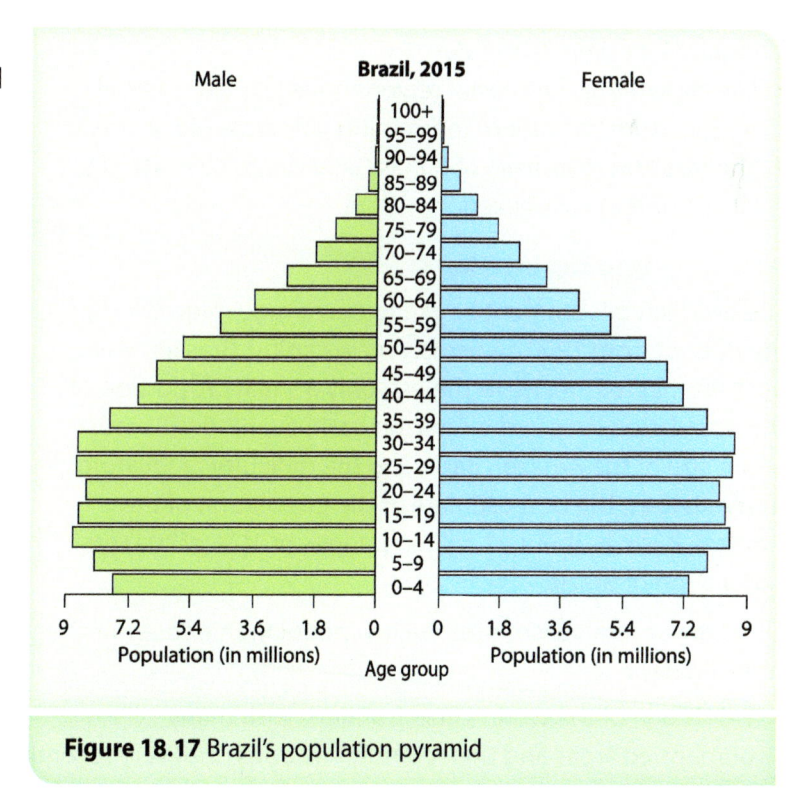

Figure 18.17 Brazil's population pyramid

Population distribution and density

By European standards, the average population density of 25 people per km² is low. However, population distribution is uneven in Brazil. The great majority of people live **close to or on the coast**, with more than **40%** of the people living in the South-East, an area that occupies less than one-fifth of the country's area.

High coastal densities

There are many reasons for the high coastal population densities:

- Emigrants who came from Europe settled in the coastal regions. Coastal ports that shipped commodities to Europe grew into **large cities** and absorbed new waves of migrants.
- With very few exceptions, the great cities of Brazil, such as Rio de Janeiro and São Paulo, are found on or close to the coast. These cities continue to grow as they absorb the annual population increase in Brazil's population.
- Poor inward migrants from Southern Europe found jobs as farm workers close to the coast on coffee, sugar cane, cocoa and coffee plantations. Indeed, the coffee *fazendas* of São Paulo state and other plantations still require labourers to this day.
- The climates of the coastal regions have less extremes of temperature because of the cooling influence of the ocean.
- The **mineral resources** of Minas Gerais state have attracted large numbers of workers.

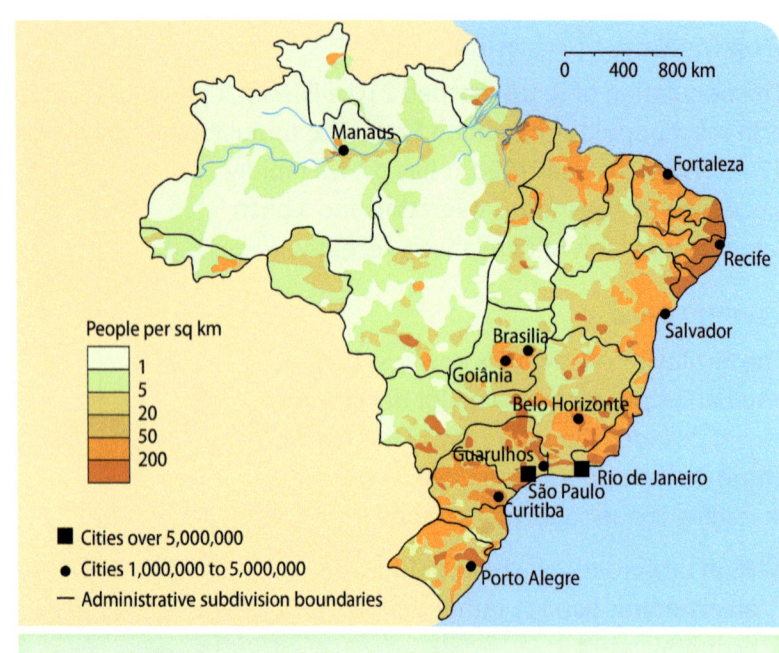

Figure 18.18 Population density in Brazil

Migration into the interior

The Brazilian government began to encourage migration into the interior from 1960 onwards. A new capital, Brasilia, was built for that reason. Nevertheless, only a small proportion of the population lives in the Amazon Basin even now. Because of the size of the Amazon Basin and the difficulty of locating **native tribes**, the best estimate of the population of the Amazon Basin is about 21 million people, or 10% of the total population of Brazil.

There are several reasons for the low population density of the Amazon Basin:

- This is one of the world's final frontiers, with many unmapped areas and poor communications until very recently.
- Water transport is still the most practical mode of transport. This has confined most settlements close to river banks in the Basin.
- The climate is extremely wet and humid. Many people find it very uncomfortable.

GEOFACTS

- Some 85% of Brazil's population lives in cities.
- Brazil is believed to have the biggest population of uncontacted peoples on Earth. The National Indian Foundation has reported that there are about 67 uncontacted tribes.

ACTIVITY

Thinking

Can you explain how it is possible that there are tribes in the Amazon Basin that have not yet been contacted?

- The dense rainforest of the Basin has made settlement difficult.
- Mineral resources, such as the iron ore that is exploited in Carajás, are highly mechanised and require relatively few workers.
- The soya farms that are now encroaching on the southern edge of the rainforest require very few workers because of mechanisation. Cattle farms also support few employees. A dozen farm workers on horseback and one helicopter can tend herds on farms the size of an Irish county.
- Many small farmers in the Basin, migrants from North-East Brazil, have given up and left farming because the soil loses its fertility in a very short time.
- The Brazilian government has faced great criticism abroad and increasingly in Brazil itself because of the destruction of the rainforest. This may have reduced the enthusiasm for using the rainforest.

Figure 18.19 Internal migration from the impoverished North-East and into the West has caused changes in population distribution and density. Densities in the South-East continue to increase.

Urban development in Brazil

The great majority of people in Brazil live in urban areas. The coast has a string of cities, while only a few are inland. Most of the large coastal cities were first settled by the Portuguese in the 1500s. These settlements became ports for the export to Europe of sugar and coffee. They also became capitals for the states that developed around them.

Inland cities developed as centres of food processing and manufacturing. For instance, **Curitiba** in the South is the capital of the state of Paraná and the commercial centre for a rich agricultural region. Its factories process agricultural products. As we have seen, it has become an example of a sustainable city with an excellent bus transit system.

Figure 18.20 Urban centres in Brazil

Manaus is the capital of the state of Amazonas. It is located at a great confluence in the Amazon River system. It became a wealthy city in the late nineteenth century as the centre of trade in the **rubber industry**. This trade ceased long ago. Today, it has a free trade zone where many factories have been built.

ACTIVITY

Research

Look up the rubber boom in the late nineteenth century in the Amazon Basin on the internet.

Rio de Janeiro is world famous for its magnificent harbour and beaches, such as Copacabana. The city's location between the sea and steep granite peaks makes it one of the world's most easily recognised cities. Its lifestyle and warm climate make it a magnet for tourists. Until 1960, it was the capital of Brazil.

In later decades, the city was misgoverned by politicians and fought over by drug gangs in the *favelas*, or shanty towns. A corrupt police force did not help the city's image. Rio became dangerous, with more than twice the murder rate of São Paulo. The exodus from the city gained pace as businesses and the rich fled, mostly for São Paulo. However, the city received a major boost as the location of the 2016 Olympics.

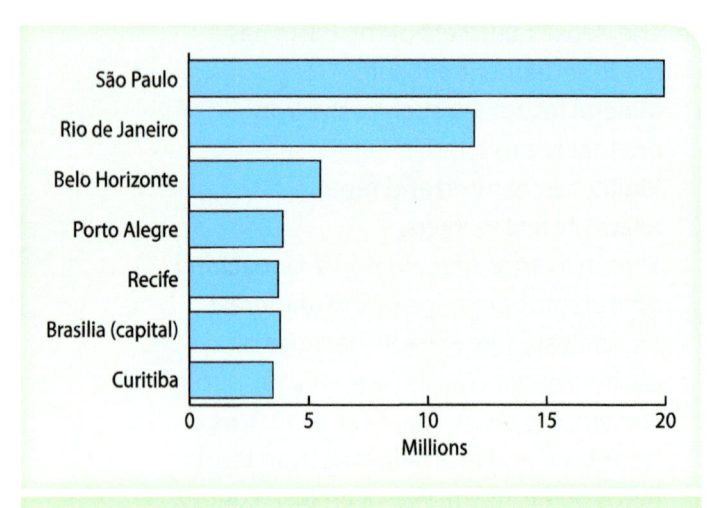

Figure 18.21 The population of the metropolitan areas of the largest Brazilian cities

GEOFACT
The cost of staging the 2016 Rio Olympics was about $11.5 billion.

Rio de Janeiro, situated in one of the world's most beautiful harbours

Brasilia is a specially designed capital city on an empty site in the interior and 1,000 metres above sea level. Its centre was built in the years 1957 to 1960. Much of its futuristic architecture was designed by Oscar Niemeyer. The location of the capital was symbolic of Brazil's wish to develop the resources of the interior. It is also a way of slowing the growth of São Paulo and Rio. Brasilia has close to 4 million people today.

And finally, **São Paulo**, one of the largest cities in the world, requires a case study.

ACTIVITY
Research
Look up the building of Brasilia on the internet.

CASE STUDY

São Paulo

São Paulo is the largest city in the Southern Hemisphere and the foremost industrial centre in all of Latin America. It was founded in the sixteenth century by the Jesuits. It grew in importance with the discovery of gold further inland. Its urban area has a population of some 21 million people. The city itself produces 10.7% of the GDP of Brazil.

Many factors are important in São Paulo's development, including the following.

GEOFACT
São Paulo is the largest city in the Southern Hemisphere.

Location

São Paulo is located 50 km inland from its port of Santos. It is also located on the Tropic of Capricorn, at an elevation of 769 metres above sea level. The city lies just west of the Great Escarpment. While the climate is tropical, the elevation reduces the temperature a little.

The city is located in the **core economic region** of South-East Brazil. For that reason, São Paulo has benefited from much foreign investment for decades.

With its core location, São Paulo also benefits from the inward migration from rural areas of Brazil, especially the impoverished North-East. These are young, energetic and ambitious people eager for work.

São Paulo is the most important economic player in Brazil's industrial triangle along with Rio de Janeiro and Belo Horizonte. São Paulo city is the capital of the state of São Paulo, which has a population of 44 million people. Therefore, there is a high demand for the goods and services that are produced in the city.

ACTIVITY

Thinking

Explain two reasons why the location of São Paulo city has helped its development.

Luxury apartments in São Paulo are located beside the poor housing found in Paraisópolis. Income inequality is stark in the city.

CHAPTER 18 · THE DYNAMICS OF REGIONS 3

UNIT 2 · REGIONAL GEOGRAPHY

A multifunctional city

São Paulo has had a strong agricultural hinterland for generations. Coffee, cotton and sugar cane became the most important agricultural products of the city's hinterland in the nineteenth century. *Fazenda* owners from the countryside built town houses in the city to supervise the selling of their agricultural products. São Paulo city became the **commercial centre** for the packing, marketing and export of these products. It became a **university city** and the **capital** of the state of São Paulo.

When slavery was abolished in 1888, many inward migrants from Portugal, Greece, Italy and Germany took the place of the slaves. The city of São Paulo boomed as industrialists in the city supplied the consumer needs (clothing, footwear and household goods) of a growing agricultural population in the countryside.

As a centre of the export trade, São Paulo became a city of **merchants**, **banks** and **a stock exchange**. Jewish and Japanese migrants increased the population of the city, bringing their skills and entrepreneurial drive with them.

In the second half of the twentieth century, the city became the location of choice of many foreign manufacturing MNCs.

São Paulo urban area population, 1990–2010: Core city and suburbs

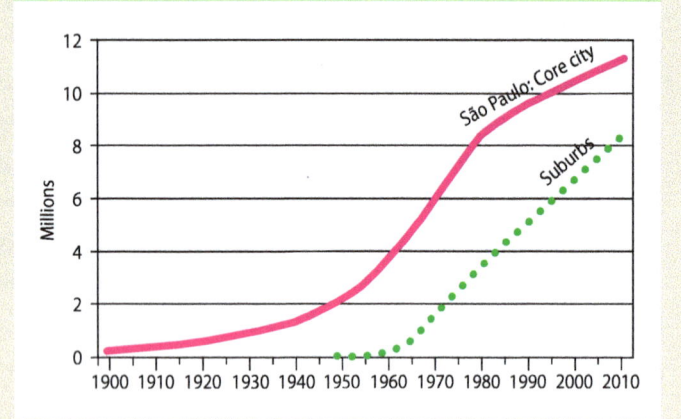

Figure 18.22 Population growth in São Paulo city and in its suburbs over time

> **GEOFACT**
>
> The people of São Paulo are known as Paulistas in Brazil.

Transport

São Paulo is the conduit for the movement of agricultural and manufactured goods to Santos, its port. A motorway and railroad connect São Paulo to Santos. Santos is a modern port with advanced loading and unloading equipment, used for the export of São Paulo's goods.

As the economic engine of Brazil, São Paulo has motorway connections to Belo Horizonte and to Rio. However, Brazil is a developing country and the transport networks are a work in progress. The railway network with other cities is underfunded.

> **GEOFACT**
>
> São Paulo's main airport catered for 39 million passengers in 2015.

São Paulo has suffered from appalling traffic jams partly because despite being the largest city in the Southern Hemisphere, it did not have a ring road until recently. Long-distance trucks had to drive through the city centre. The **Mario Covas Beltway** – the long-awaited ring road – was finally completed in 2016. This is already encouraging many industries to move from the city to the suburbs beside the Beltway. These will provide work for the poor migrants who live in appalling conditions in the many *favelas* of the city and suburbs.

São Paulo has **five underground metro lines**, which carry 4 million people every day. However, the city lags behind Curitiba in bus transport. Commuter journeys in the city remain a challenge for many people.

Brazilian culture

Brazilian culture is quite different in many ways from that of its neighbouring countries. This is reflected in its racial diversity, religions, languages, music and carnivals.

Race in Brazil

Brazil is a multiracial society. Originally the country was occupied by native peoples. Portuguese colonists arrived in the sixteenth century.

Brazil's native peoples are divided among about 200 cultural groups with 120 different languages. Most live in the Amazon Basin. Today, they may number 350,000, a mere fraction of the 2 to 6 million who lived there 500 years ago.

What caused such a terrible decline in their numbers? Contact with European diseases such as the common **cold**, **measles** and most of all, **smallpox** were the main reasons in addition to slavery and cruel treatment at the hands of Portuguese planters.

Even today, native peoples remain under threat from deforestation of the Amazon Basin. However, the Brazilian government is much more aware of its responsibilities than before. About 20% of the rainforest has been set aside for Brazil's native people.

Slaves were later brought from Africa to work on sugar cane and coffee plantations. Brazil eventually freed its slaves in 1888. It was the last country to do so.

Today, the North-East has the greatest concentration of African-Brazilians in the country. The city of Salvador is their cultural capital. Here, African food and dress are evident.

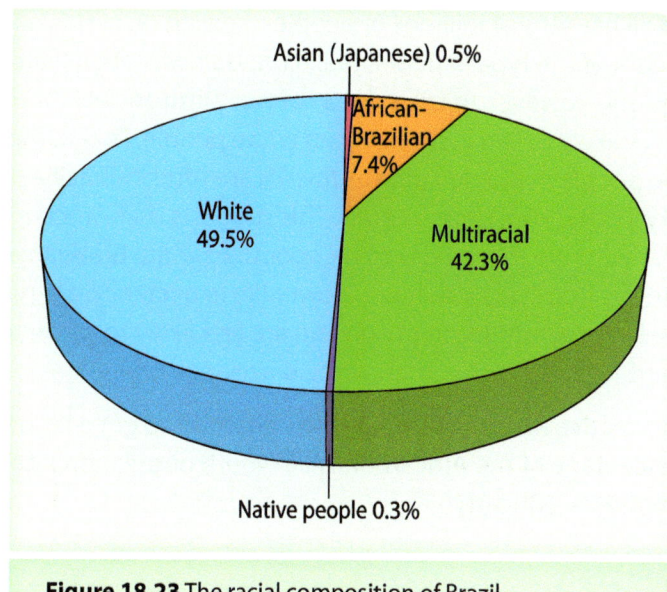

Figure 18.23 The racial composition of Brazil

- White 49.5%
- Multiracial 42.3%
- African-Brazilian 7.4%
- Asian (Japanese) 0.5%
- Native people 0.3%

GEOFACTS

› Some 4.9 million slaves were shipped to Brazil from Africa from the sixteenth to the nineteenth century.
› Brazil has the greatest concentration of people of Japanese descent outside Japan.

A group of Brazilian children with the national flag

Brazil has tens of millions of people of mixed race. This happened because racism of the type experienced in the USA was not a feature of Brazilian society. However, Brazil is not a **colour-blind** society. African-Brazilians are more likely to live in *favelas* than white people. For example, more than half the people in Rio de Janeiro's *favelas* are African-Brazilian. The figure in the city's richer districts is just 7%. This suggests that African-Brazilians are more likely to be poor than white Brazilians. African-Brazilians also have a lower life expectancy, are more likely to spend time in prison and are less likely to go on to third-level education than white Brazilians.

Affirmative action is now used in education to get a higher percentage of the African-Brazilian youth population into third-level education.

> **DEFINITION**
>
> **Affirmative action:** Action favouring those who tend to suffer from discrimination.

Religion

The Portuguese colonists brought the Catholic religion to the country. Today, most Brazilians are Catholics. There are more Catholics in Brazil than in any other country in the world. The Catholic religion is evident in church architecture and in religious festivals. European architectural styles such as **baroque** are evident in churches in towns and cities in Brazil.

> **DEFINITION**
>
> **Baroque:** A highly ornate and extravagantly detailed artistic style found in European art, music and architecture in the seventeenth and eighteenth centuries.

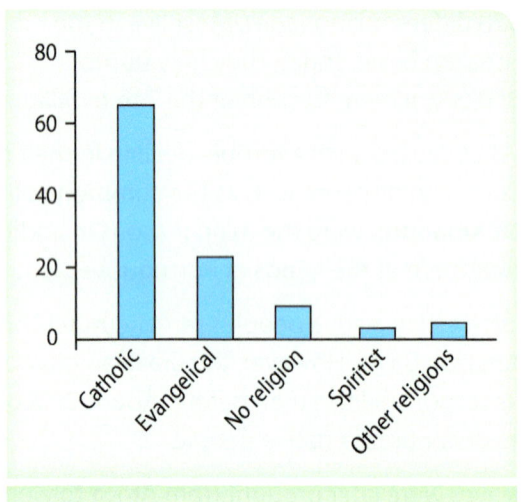

Figure 18.24 Religious groups in Brazil (%)

The cathedral in Salvador, Brazil is very Portuguese in style

The entrance to an Evangelical church in Brazil

Brazil's native peoples have their own **spiritist** or **animist** religions. In addition, African slaves brought their own African religions with them. Their masters forbade them from practising their religions in case this strengthened their **group identity**. Slaves responded by giving Christian names to their African gods and symbols. This helped them to preserve their religions and their beliefs. Over time, African and Christian beliefs fused to form religions such as Candomblé and Macumba, which still exist among people of African descent on Brazil's east coast.

While the Catholic Church was the religion of 92% of the people in 1970, that figure has declined to less than 65% today because of the growth of Evangelical churches in the slums of Brazilian cities.

Why are Evangelical churches winning many new members? Observers put forward several reasons.

> Many parents join these churches so that their teenage children might develop a moral compass in an environment of drugs and crime.
> A person with a basic knowledge of the Gospels can become a minister, whereas a Catholic priest must train for several years.
> **Tithes** (a portion of one's salary) that members pay to the churches are used to feed and clothe the poor.
> Evangelical churches also fund themselves and spread their message by producing hit songs with religious themes. They buy time on television stations to spread their message. Evangelical churches are continuing to spread.

DEFINITION

Spiritist/animist religions: The belief that natural things such as plants, animals and thunder have spirits and can influence human events.

Language

Portuguese is spoken by over **99%** of the country's population. It is the official language because until 1822, Brazil was a colony of Portugal. However, Brazilian Portuguese has drifted away from the original Portuguese. Language is an important expression of **Brazilian national unity** and **identity**.

Spellings in both Portugal and Brazil are generally the same, but Brazilian pronunciations, vocabularies and the meanings of words have changed a lot from the original Portuguese. This is because many borrowed words have modified Brazilian Portuguese to give the national language in Brazil its own identity.

Brazilian Portuguese has borrowed words and expressions from Italian-, German-, Japanese- and Spanish-speaking migrants who have settled in Brazil. For example, everyone uses the word **tchau**, copied from the Italian *ciao*. Foreign everyday products and technologies have also added several English words in recent years.

Brazilian Portuguese has also borrowed many words and expressions from African languages that were used by African slaves in the nineteenth century. Many of these words are from music, emotions, food and the natural world. Some words have also been borrowed from native tribes.

Written Brazilian Portuguese varies a lot from the spoken language. As a result, many immigrants in Brazil who can speak Portuguese well may still have difficulty writing it.

Music

Music is an important characteristic of Brazilian culture. Brazilian music is distinctive because as different groups of migrants settled in Brazil, each brought their music with them and developed their own unique style of song and music. Over time, these musical traditions blended to create sounds and rhythms unique to Brazil.

Samba

Brazil has given samba music to the world. Samba is based on African rhythms brought to Brazil by slaves in the eighteenth and nineteenth centuries. Samba is dance music and is heard repeatedly during Carnaval. Samba is practised in the samba schools and can be heard in Rio's Sambadrome. Since the 1930s, when samba became widely known due to radio and records, samba has evolved into many styles.

Bossa nova

In the 1960s, bossa nova (new wave music) emerged. This is slower and more melodic than samba. Bossa nova was influenced by American jazz. It was first heard in Rio and became popular among educated Brazilians. The style became known worldwide with the hit song '**Garota de Ipanema**', which is translated into English as 'The Girl from Ipanema'. The English version has been recorded by Frank Sinatra, Cher, Madonna and many more artists.

LINK

Carnaval (page 358) is a central part of Brazilian culture.

ACTIVITY

Research

Look up samba and bossa nova on the internet.

PowerPoint Summary

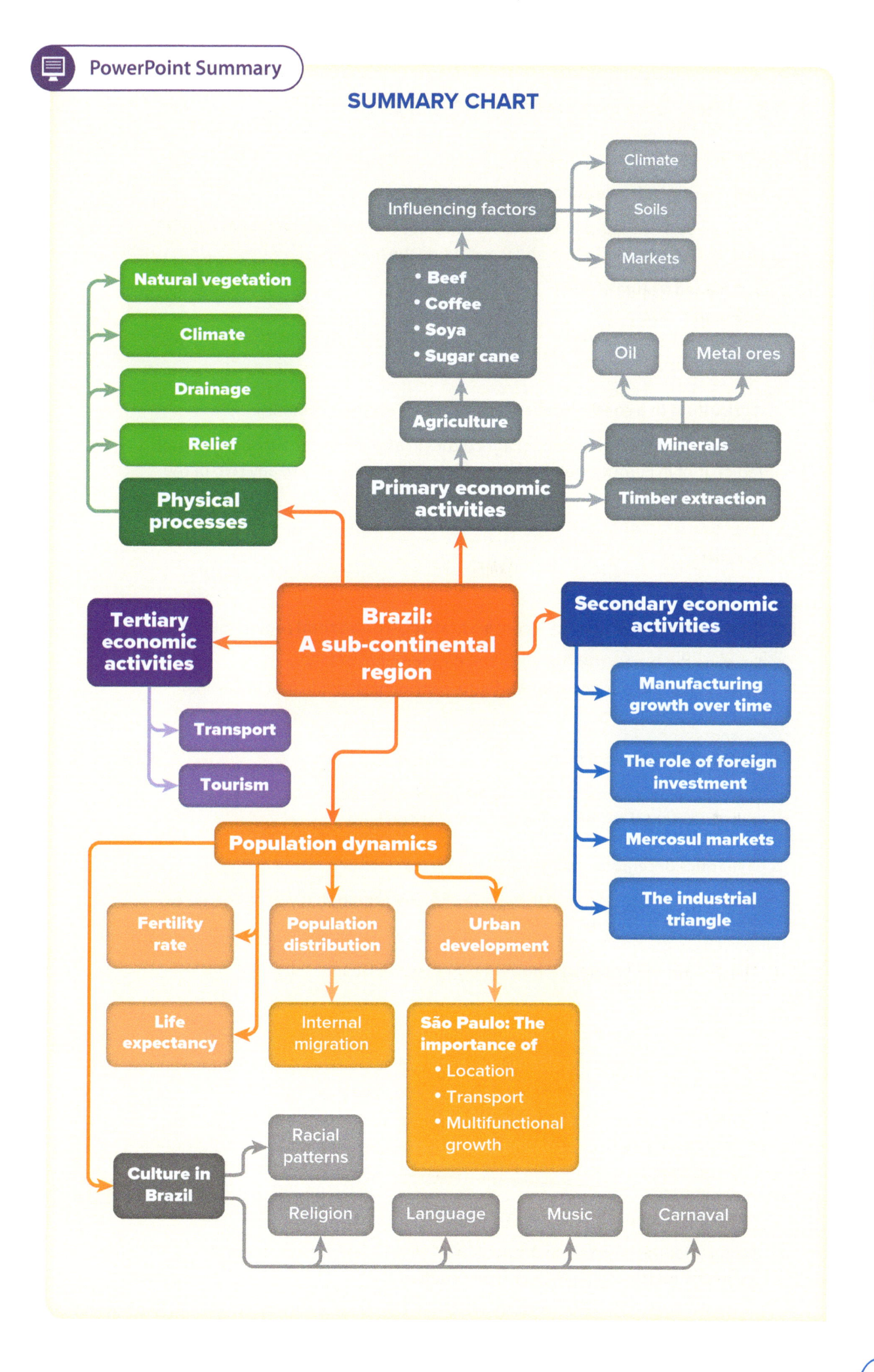

SUMMARY CHART

Brazil: A sub-continental region

- **Physical processes**
  - Natural vegetation
  - Climate
  - Drainage
  - Relief

- **Primary economic activities**
  - Agriculture
    - Beef
    - Coffee
    - Soya
    - Sugar cane
    - Influencing factors
      - Climate
      - Soils
      - Markets
  - Minerals
    - Oil
    - Metal ores
  - Timber extraction

- **Secondary economic activities**
  - Manufacturing growth over time
  - The role of foreign investment
  - Mercosul markets
  - The industrial triangle

- **Tertiary economic activities**
  - Transport
  - Tourism

- **Population dynamics**
  - Fertility rate
  - Life expectancy
  - Population distribution
  - Internal migration
  - Urban development
  - São Paulo: The importance of
    - Location
    - Transport
    - Multifunctional growth

- **Culture in Brazil**
  - Racial patterns
  - Religion
  - Language
  - Music
  - Carnaval

CHAPTER 18 · THE DYNAMICS OF REGIONS 3

Leaving Cert exam questions

LONG QUESTIONS: HIGHER LEVEL

1. **Continental/sub-continental region** (20 marks)

   Draw an outline map of a **continental/sub-continental** region (not in Europe) that you have studied. On it, show and name the following:
   - A named feature of relief
   - A named river
   - A named urban centre
   - A major road or rail link.

2. **Agriculture in a continental/sub-continental region** (30 marks)

   Account for the development of agriculture in a **continental/sub-continental** region (not in Europe) that you have studied, with reference to any **two** of the following factors:
   - Soil
   - Relief
   - Climate.

3. **Primary economic activity – continental/sub-continental region** (30 marks)

   Examine the factors that influence the development of **one** primary economic activity in a **continental/sub-continental** region (not in Europe) that you have studied.

4. **Economic activity** (30 marks)

   Discuss the development of secondary economic activity in a **continental/sub-continental** region (not in Europe) that you have studied.

5. **Dynamics of regions – climate** (30 marks)

   Describe and explain the challenges facing **any region** that you have studied as a result of its climate.

6. **The dynamics of regions – human processes** (30 marks)

   > Population dynamics · Language · Religion
   > Urban development · Rural development

   Examine the influence of any **two** of the human processes in the box above on the development of a **continental/sub-continental** region (not in Europe) that you have studied.

7. **Population dynamics** (30 marks)

   Account for the growth and distribution of population in a **continental/sub-continental** region that you have studied.

8 Urban development in a continental/sub-continental region (30 marks)

With reference to **one** urban area in a **continental/sub-continental** region (not in Europe) that you have studied, explain why this urban area developed at its present location.

9 Urban development (30 marks)

Examine how **two** of the following factors have influenced the development of any **urban** region that you have studied:

> Transport
> Location
> Primary economic activities.

LONG QUESTIONS: ORDINARY LEVEL

1 Agriculture in a continental/sub-continental region (30 marks)

Explain how any **two** of the following influence the development of agriculture in a **continental/sub-continental** region that you have studied:

> Relief and soils
> Climate
> Markets.

2 Primary economic activity in a continental/sub-continental region (40 marks)

Name a **continental/sub-continental** region (not in Europe) that you have studied and answer each of the following questions.

(i) Name **one** primary economic activity that contributes to the economy of this region.

(ii) Explain the advantages that this region has for the development of the primary economic activity named in part (i) above.

(iii) Describe **one** problem faced by this primary economic activity in this region.

3 Manufacturing in a continental/sub-continental region (30 marks)

Describe and explain the development of manufacturing in a **continental/sub-continental** region (not in Europe) that you have studied.

4 Economic activities in a continental/sub-continental region (40 marks)

Name a **continental/sub-continental** region (not in Europe) that you have studied and explain any **two** of the following with regard to this region:

> The type of farming practised in this region
> The reasons for the development of industry in this region
> The reasons why tourists are attracted to this region.

5 Regional problems (30 marks)

Describe **two** problems faced by any region that you have studied.

Chapter 19
The Complexity of Regions

KEYWORDS

- interaction
- sectarianism
- power-sharing
- economic dividend
- Titanic Quarter
- PSNI
- integration
- interdependence
- extreme nationalism
- remittances
- Brexit
- sovereignty
- eurozone
- austerity

LEARNING OBJECTIVES

By the end of this chapter, you should be able to understand:

- The interaction between economic, political and cultural activities within Northern Ireland
- The interaction between Northern Ireland and the Republic
- The development and expansion of the EEC/EU
- The economic and cultural impact of EU enlargement on Ireland
- The economic, political and sovereignty issues that are facing the EU
- How boundaries of regions can change over time.

POLITICAL, ECONOMIC AND CULTURAL INTERACTIONS WITHIN A REGION

The interaction between **political**, **economic** and **cultural** activities is very important within regions. A stable and publicly supported political system, where a government addresses the economic and social needs of the people, is vital to the economic and social well-being of a region.

CASE STUDY

Northern Ireland

Northern Ireland experienced thirty years of civil strife during the years 1969 to 1998. More than 3,000 lives were lost and the negative images of bombings, of lives lost and of sectarianism were seen on television all over the world.

The Good Friday Agreement

All of that changed with the Good Friday Agreement of 1998. Unionist and Nationalist MPs agreed to a new political accord. With the mediation of political leaders from London and Dublin, Northern politicians agreed to **power-sharing** between the two communities.

The new police force, the PSNI, replaced the RUC, which had never had the confidence of most Nationalists. Sinn Féin accepted the legitimacy of the PSNI and encouraged Nationalists to join it and to co-operate with the force in helping to resolve crime.

A new air of confidence breathed life into Northern Ireland. While there have been many political hiccups in Stormont since 1998, the North has moved into a new era of peace and reconciliation.

> **DEFINITIONS**
>
> **PSNI:** Police Service of Northern Ireland.
> **RUC:** Royal Ulster Constabulatory.
> **Stormont:** The seat of parliament in Northern Ireland.

The impact of the new political landscape on economic developments

In 1998, the North was the poorest region in the UK. It had little inward investment, high unemployment at 17%, outward migration and very little tourism. Long-term unemployment was almost double that of the UK. The public sector, e.g. the part of the economy that provides government services, accounted for 30% of all jobs – a very high dependence. The educational and health services were heavily dependent on financial subsidies from London.

The economic benefits of peace

The new political landscape did not transform the Northern Ireland economy. Nevertheless, many economic developments took place. Inward investment, with more than 700 international companies employing 75,000 people, became established in Northern Ireland. This helped to reduce unemployment to 5.9% by 2016. While many companies were in the manufacturing sector, most were in the tertiary sector, such as insurance, banking and R&D.

Caterpillar, a US multinational, has a strong presence in Northern Ireland

The following factors are likely to encourage further inward investment in Northern Ireland:

- The North has the same corporation tax rate as that of the UK at 20%. This figure is likely to fall further in the years ahead.
- Salaries in Belfast are 30% lower than in London, Dublin and Paris.
- The North is the first region in the entire EU to achieve 100% broadband rollout over its territory.

Tourist and cultural developments

Economic planners in the North have targeted tourism as an important growth area. Access for tourists to the North is very easy by road from the Republic and by air and sea from Britain and Europe. The region has three international airports, where facilities have been upgraded to meet future demand.

Tourists can enjoy outstanding **cultural experiences**. These include:

- A magnificent coast, including the Giant's Causeway, which now has an interpretative centre, the Giant's Causeway Visitor Experience
- Medieval castles such as Dunluce and Carrickfergus
- Cultural features such as the Ulster Folk and Transport Museum, the Walls of Derry and the Ulster American Folk Park
- The Titanic Quarter in Belfast.

> **GEOFACT**
>
> The Giant's Causeway is Northern Ireland's only UNESCO World Heritage Site.

The Titanic Quarter

The Titanic Quarter in Belfast is one of the world's largest waterfront urban regeneration projects. The area is a centre of commercial, tourist, residential and retail space. More than 18,000 people now live, work or study in the area.

The Titanic Quarter celebrates the industrial heritage of shipbuilding in Belfast. The Science Park in the Quarter has recently been rebranded as Catalyst Inc. and is home to 160 companies, many of which do R&D in the IT sector.

The Titanic Quarter in Belfast

> **ACTIVITY**
>
> **Research**
>
> Look up the Titanic Quarter on the internet.

> **ACTIVITY**
>
> **Thinking**
>
> Can you suggest a reason why the Science Park has been rebranded as Catalyst Inc?

POLITICAL, ECONOMIC AND CULTURAL INTERACTION BETWEEN REGIONS

CASE STUDY

Northern Ireland and the Republic of Ireland

Regions that are located close to each other do not always interact peacefully. A 'cold war' existed between Northern Ireland and the Republic of Ireland for many decades after 1920. However, political, economic and social interactions between the two states have now improved. The relationship between the two states is better now than it has been since 1920.

Economic interaction

Much economic interaction takes place between the North and South. The M1 is now one of Ireland's busiest roads. The Enterprise train from Dublin to Belfast is operated jointly between both states.

Since both Ireland and Britain joined the EU in 1973, trade between the Republic and the North has grown rapidly. The customs posts were dismantled after the **Single European Act (SEA)** of 1987. Since then, both states have enjoyed full free trade with each other.

› Citizens from both states travel north and south on tourist trips.
› People from the North and South shop across the political boundary, depending on the relative value of both the euro and sterling.

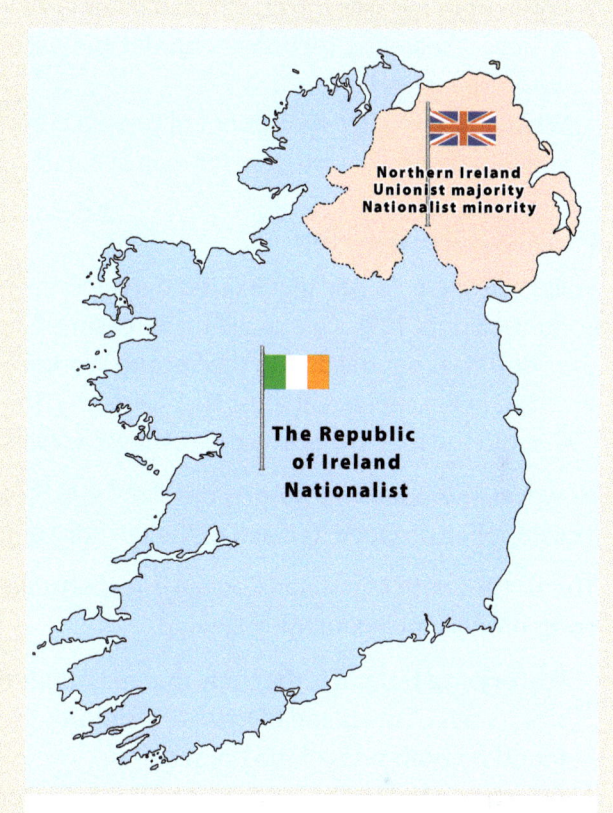

Figure 19.1 There are two states on the island of Ireland

The motorway that connects Dublin and Belfast. Travellers have enjoyed unrestricted access across the border for decades.

DEFINITION

The **Single European Act of 1987** eliminated all the hidden barriers to trade between members of the EU.

CHAPTER 19 · THE COMPLEXITY OF REGIONS

375

- Many people from Northern Ireland use Dublin Airport for foreign travel because of the greater choice of destinations from that airport.
- An electricity interconnector in Co. Louth links ESB supplies with the electricity network of the North.

However, the Brexit referendum of June 2016 has serious implications for economic and social interactions between the North and South. The **issues** that will be worked out in discussions in Brussels in the coming years include the following:

- When Britain leaves the EU Single Market in 2019, how will the promises to have a 'seamless, frictionless border' between the North and South work in practice?
- What about the free movement of people between North and South, which has been unrestricted for many years?

Political interaction

Politically, the 'cold war' that existed between the North and South after 1920 continued until 1998. One of the main reasons for this 'cold war' was that the South was neutral during the Second World War and the North was fully involved in Britain's war against Nazi Germany. The Troubles that lasted from 1969 until the mid-1990s also drove the two states apart.

However, the Good Friday Agreement of 1998 brought peace to the North. The Republic dropped its claim to the territory of the North.

The North-South Ministerial Council is responsible for several areas of co-operation, including the following.

- **Waterways Ireland** is the body that maintains the navigable inland waterways of the island of Ireland, including the Ulster Canal that is found on both sides of the border.
- **Intertrade Ireland** co-ordinates trade and e-commerce between the North and South.
- **The Food Safety Promotion Board** is responsible for food safety through common campaigns in both states.

However, Brexit has implications here too. The peace process of Northern Ireland is fragile and the maintenance of good relations between Belfast, London and Dublin is vital to its future.

Cultural interaction

Cultural interaction is relatively limited between the North and South. Sport illustrates both division and co-operation.

- **Each state has its own soccer team.** However, a soccer team composed of players from the North and South lined out against Brazil in Dublin in 1973.
- **Athletics are divided.** Track and field athletes from Northern Ireland may choose to compete for either Britain or Ireland at the Olympics.

ACTIVITY

Research
Find out who won the All-Ireland soccer game against Brazil on the internet.

- However, the **Irish Rugby Football Union (IRFU)** is All-Ireland. Pooling talent from the North and South may help to explain the successes of the Irish rugby team.
- **Boxing** is also All-Ireland. Boxers from the North have won medals representing Ireland.
- The **Gaelic Athletic Association (GAA)** promotes Irish games and has a strong presence in Northern Ireland. Teams from the North are often seen in Croke Park and Northern teams have won the Sam Maguire Cup numerous times. In 2001, the GAA lifted its ban on members of the British security forces from playing Irish games. After that, Nationalists who were members of the GAA could join the PSNI without being expelled from the GAA.

ACTIVITY

Research

Look up the words of the song 'Ireland's Call' on the internet. How does it reflect the All-Ireland nature of the IRFU?

The Irish rugby team draws on members from the four provinces of Ireland

INTERACTION BETWEEN PEOPLE ON A EUROPEAN SCALE

EU development and expansion

In the first half of the twentieth century, much of Europe experienced the First and Second World Wars. Millions of lives were lost. The main reason for these wars was the hostility between France and Germany. By 1950, it was clear that hostilities between these two countries had to be eliminated. Extreme nationalism had to be contained within a more **integrated Europe**.

How could this be done? Robert Schumann and Jean Monnet, both French, believed that economic interaction, e.g. increased trade, between these two old enemies could create **interdependence** and heal past hostilities.

GEOFACT

'The EU is the greatest example of conflict resolution in the history of the world.' – John Hume, former politician from Derry and a recipient of the Nobel Peace prize

DEFINITION

Extreme nationalism: An excessive love of one's country that can quickly turn into hostility with neighbouring states.

Figure 19.2 The formation and expansion of the EU

The EEC

The European Economic Community was established in 1957 with six member states under the Treaty of Rome. Brussels became the capital of the EEC. The EEC became a **customs union**, e.g. tariffs placed on the import of agricultural and manufactured goods were eliminated between the members.

Trade between the member states immediately grew. German cars and chemicals were sold free of import tariffs in France. French wine, food products and fashion goods found their way into German homes. It was a **win–win situation** for EEC states. The standard of living rose among the members.

Enlargement of the EEC/EU

Over the years, other countries joined the EEC. Britain, Ireland and Denmark joined in 1973. Throughout the 1980s and 1990s, **Greece**, **Spain**, **Portugal**, **Austria**, **Finland** and **Sweden** became members. By **1995**, the EU had **fifteen members**.

> **HINT**
>
> You must know the order and the dates in which members joined the EEC/EU.

Expansion into Eastern Europe

The collapse of Communism led to many former Eastern bloc countries applying to join the EU. This led to the entry of ten new members in 2004. Two new members joined in 2007. This brought the number of members in the EU to 27. Croatia became the twenty-eighth member in 2013.

Summary of enlargement

- 1957: West Germany, France, Italy, Netherlands, Belgium, Luxembourg = 6 members
- 1973: United Kingdom, Ireland, Denmark = 9 members
- 1981: Greece = 10 members
- 1986: Spain and Portugal = 12 members
- 1990: East Germany (after the unification of Germany)
- 1995: Sweden, Finland, Austria = 15 members
- 2004: Estonia, Latvia, Lithuania, Poland, Czech Republic, Slovakia, Hungary, Slovenia, Malta, Cyprus = 25 members
- 2007: Romania, Bulgaria = 27 members
- 2013: Croatia = 28 members
- 2016: The British people voted to leave the EU = 27 members by 2019

Future enlargement

It is likely that the EU will accept more members in the future. There are currently five candidate countries for EU accession: **Albania**, **FYR Macedonia**, **Montenegro**, **Serbia** and **Turkey**. Negotiations will take many years and the candidates must satisfy strict economic and social criteria before they are allowed to join.

Impact of EU enlargement on existing member states

By far the most important enlargement of the EU in recent times took place in the years 2004 (ten new members) and 2007 (two new members). These countries added some 130 million people to the EU, bringing the total population of the EU to more than 500 million people.

Enlargement had important impacts for existing members, as you can see in the case study of Ireland.

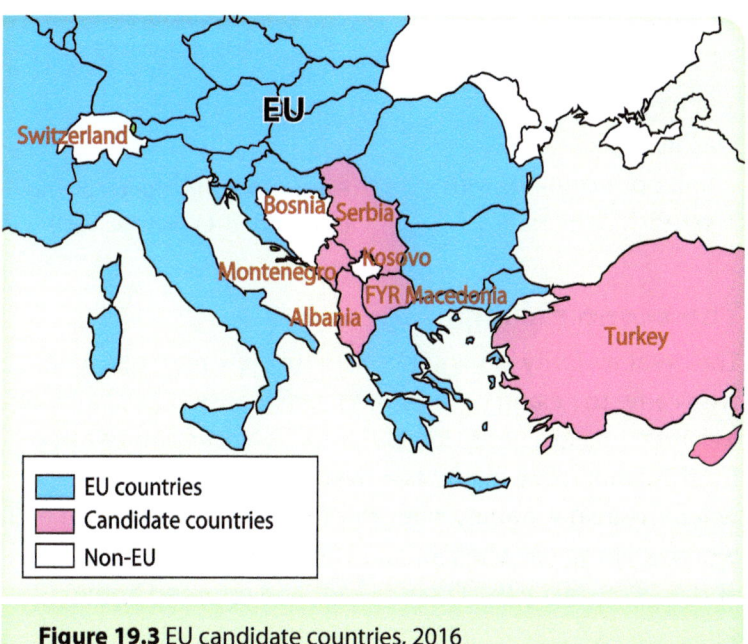

Figure 19.3 EU candidate countries, 2016

DEFINITION

FYR Macedonia is the former Yugoslav Republic of Macedonia.

CASE STUDY

Impact of EU enlargement on Ireland

As the boundaries of the EU economic region expanded eastwards, migrants from Eastern Europe moved to the economies of Western Europe in search of a better life. These migrants came from Eastern European cultures and had an impact on the countries they migrated to.

Many people from Eastern Europe came to live and work in Ireland after 2004. The push factors were:

> A low standard of living in Eastern Europe
> Higher unemployment in Eastern Europe.

The pull factors in Ireland and other Western European countries were:

> A higher standard of living
> Job opportunities with much higher wages.

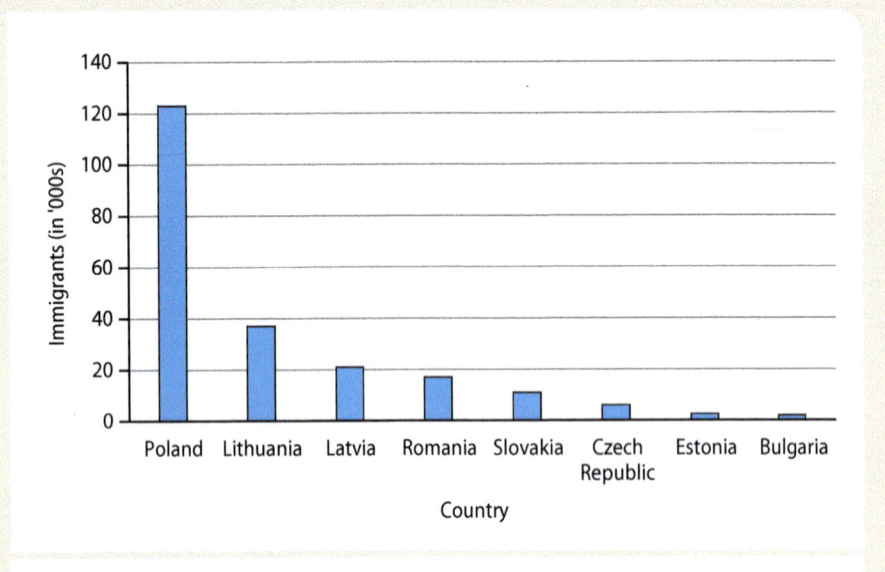

Figure 19.4 The country of origin of migrants from EU countries living in Ireland, 2011 (Source: CSO)

The economic impact

The great majority of migrants from the new member states who came to Ireland were economic migrants – they came to Ireland to make a better life. By far the largest number came from Poland. These migrants arrived in Ireland in the years when the Irish economy was growing rapidly and needed extra workers. However, when Ireland's economic boom came to an end in 2008, many Polish people left and returned home.

Eastern Europeans helped to fill jobs during the Irish economic boom in areas such as construction, the hospitality industry, manufacturing, retail services, crèches and car servicing. However, many Eastern Europeans who have third-level educational qualifications have worked in jobs that are well below their qualifications because in many cases these were the only jobs they could get.

Eastern Europeans living in Ireland continue to help the Irish economy and the Irish population to grow. They buy cars, homes and goods in Ireland. Migrants pay taxes and VAT on their purchases in Irish shops.

ACTIVITY

Skills

Examine Figure 19.4. Name two Baltic countries in the graph.

GEOFACT

In 1980, there were fewer than 100 Polish people living in Ireland.

Remittances

The cost of living in Eastern Europe is much lower than it is in Ireland. Some Eastern Europeans send home savings to their families. This money, called remittances, provides support to ageing family members at home. According to the CSO, immigrants living in Ireland sent home remittances of €776 million in 2013 alone. This is an important lifeline for family members in their home country.

The cultural impact

The Republic of Ireland was a **monolithic culture** before 2004. That means that one culture existed here. Today, Irish society is much **more diverse**, with many minority cultures living here. Polish and other shops provide foods and other goods for migrants in many urban centres. Masses conducted in Polish in many Irish towns and cities have helped migrants to get to know one another. Students in secondary schools can use their home language as one subject in the Leaving Cert examinations.

A Polish shop on Talbot Street, Dublin

Inward migrants have also been changed culturally by the experience of living in Ireland. The teenage children of many inward migrants are **second-generation migrants** and have **assimilated** well. They are fluent in English. They have Irish friends and their own social networks. Some teenagers of Eastern European parents regard the 'home country' as a foreign country to which they have little sense of belonging.

> **DEFINITION**
>
> **Monolithic culture:** One culture where most people share the same past and the same values, traditions and language.

The challenge of the language

Learning English was a challenge for many adult migrants from Eastern Europe. This partly explains why some migrants were exploited by employers. Migrants' children pick up English much more easily.

However, children had to adjust to new schools where teachers taught through the medium of English. Learning maths, science and other subjects through English was challenging. However, after several years in Ireland, most Eastern Europeans become fluent in English.

> **GEOFACT**
>
> Latvian, Lithuanian, Romanian, Modern Greek, Finnish, Polish, Estonian, Slovakian, Swedish, Czech, Bulgarian, Hungarian, Portuguese, Danish, Dutch and Croatian are among the languages examined in the Leaving Cert.

A bilingual pedestrian walkway sign in English and Polish in Belfast city centre

Issues facing the EU in the future

Thanks to the free movement of capital, goods and people within the EU, it has become the world's largest trading bloc. However, the EU still faces many challenges, especially in regards to **economics**, **political union** and **the sovereignty of member states**.

Economic union

The EEC was established in 1957 as a free trade zone. That process was completed in 1987 with the Single European Act, when all of the **hidden barriers** to trade between the members were eliminated.

ACTIVITY

Skills

Examine Figure 19.5.

(i) Name two Scandinavian countries that do not use the euro.

(ii) Name two island members in the eurozone that are located in the Mediterranean.

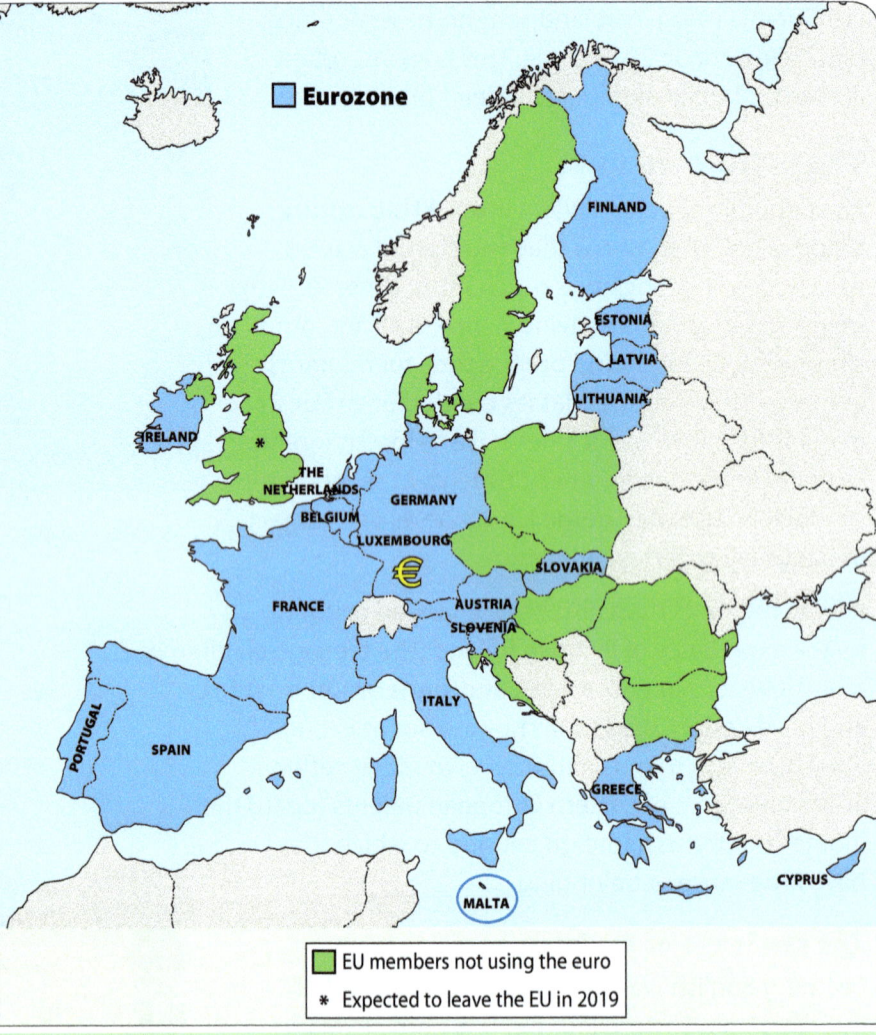

Figure 19.5 The 19 countries that used the euro as their currency in 2016

The common currency

A common currency, **the euro**, was adopted in 2002. Today, the euro is the common currency of 19 of the 28 member states with a total population of 338.6 million people.

Of the **member states** that do not use the currency, **Sweden**, **Denmark** and **Britain** have retained their own currencies. Six other relatively recent members – Bulgaria, Croatia, the Czech Republic, Hungary, Poland and Romania – are not members but may choose to become members of the eurozone in the future when they meet the conditions of entry. All members that use the euro surrendered their power to decide interest rates within their states. This represents a major loss of sovereignty.

Problems in the eurozone

The euro was severely affected by the financial crisis that accompanied the economic crash after 2008. Portugal, Italy, Spain, Ireland and Greece, all peripheral countries, ran up large budget deficits and their economies flatlined or decreased. This put pressure on the stability of the euro.

Over the following years, the **troika** of the EU, the European Central Bank and the IMF had to provide bailouts for Greece, Spain, Cyprus, Ireland and Portugal. The troika forced all the bailout countries to adopt **austerity programmes** – cutbacks in government spending in education, social welfare and public sector salaries. This led to great hardship among less well-off people in these countries. On several occasions, the future of the euro was uncertain.

However, the euro has survived thanks to the support of Angela Merkel, the German chancellor. It is likely to continue to survive in the future if for no other reason than that EU leaders now have more experience in how to get the currency through several crises.

The euro has weakened against some currencies, such as the US dollar, over time. However, that is a help to eurozone exports such as German cars and French wine.

The Greek debt crisis was not over as of 2017 and will continue to focus the minds of EU leaders for some time to come.

Angela Merkel, the German chancellor

Political union and national sovereignty

The ideal of the EU is that member states would strive towards '**ever closer union**' between its members. The issue that prevents greater political integration is the issue of national sovereignty. People who are concerned about **national sovereignty** want to know how much power member states are willing to hand over to Brussels. This issue was at the heart of the Brexit referendum in 2016.

Brexit

The Brexit debate in the UK centred on the issues of national sovereignty, economic matters and **inward migration**. **Eurosceptics** in the UK pointed to the ways in which members have surrendered national sovereignty to the EU. For instance, a House of Commons Library study in London estimated that 14–17% of UK laws were derived from EU membership. People in the UK saw the EU as a **remote**, **unelected** and **bureaucratic elite**.

> **DEFINITIONS**
>
> **Troika:** A group of three people or organisations.
>
> The **Greek debt crisis** refers to the instability caused by the huge national debt that exists in Greece.
>
> **National sovereignty** is the idea that an independent nation has a right to exist without any interference from outside.
>
> **Brexit** is an abbreviation of the words 'British exit'. It refers to Britain's decision to leave the EU after a narrow majority of the British people voted to leave in a referendum in 2016.
>
> **Eurosceptics** are people, especially in Britain, who oppose greater co-operation and integration with the EU.

A leave leaflet in the UK during the Brexit debate before the referendum

ACTIVITY

Discussion

Examine the photograph. What do you think the words *and take back control* refer to?

GEOFACT

The result of the British referendum on EU membership on 23 June 2016:

Leave: 52%

Stay: 48%

Regions of industrial decline such as North-East England, Yorkshire and the English Midlands voted strongly to leave the EU.

The referendum result in the UK was a profound shock to the EU. For the first time, a member state – Britain, the fifth largest economy in the world and the second largest in the EU – will cease to be a member in the coming years.

Britain's exit negotiations with Brussels

Britain and the EU will negotiate a trade agreement because it is in the interests of both sides to do so. The negotiations will be very challenging and are likely to take a long time. The EU will want to show other member states that leaving the EU comes at a cost. However, the bottom line is that both Britain and the EU must remain good neighbours.

Brexit's impact on the Republic of Ireland

Britain's exit will have important consequences for Ireland because Britain is one of Ireland's most important trading partners.

› It is vital that the Republic of Ireland continues to have full access to the British market for Irish exports.

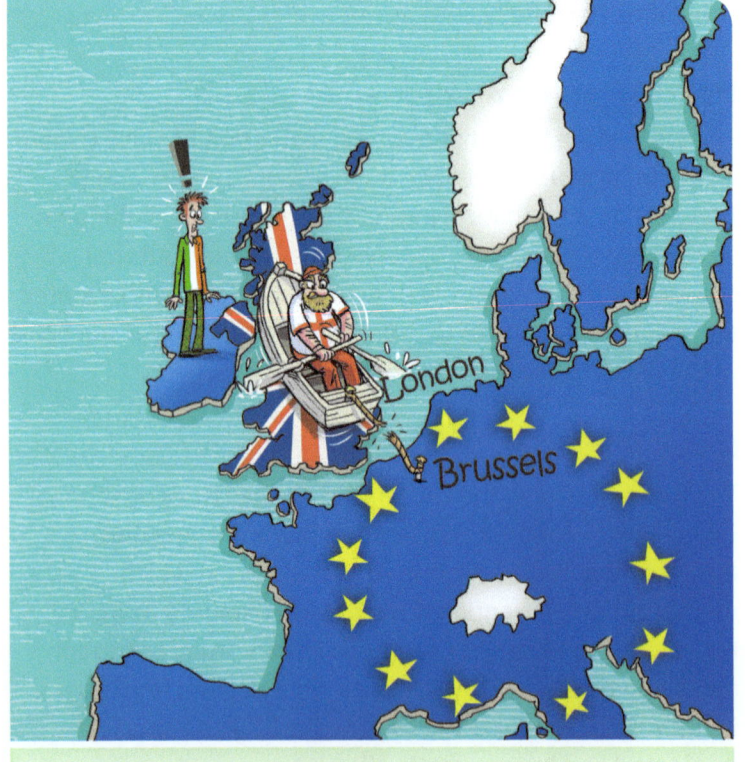

Brexit's impact on the Irish economy in the coming years is difficult to predict

- The free movement of people between Britain and the Republic of Ireland, which has been in existence since Irish independence in 1922, must continue.
- We have already seen that close relations between London, Belfast and Dublin are vital to the continued success of the peace process in Northern Ireland.

> **GEOFACT**
>
> Some 56% of the people of Northern Ireland voted to remain in the EU in the Brexit vote of 2016.

Impact of Brexit on other regions

Britain's exit will have ripple effects elsewhere. As 62% of the population of Scotland voted to remain in the EU in the Brexit referendum, it is possible that the Scottish National Party (SNP) will seek another referendum on Scottish independence with a view to joining the EU.

Anti-EU parties in other member states in the EU, such as the French National Front and the Dutch Party for Freedom, have been encouraged by the UK exit vote. These parties are likely to demand a referendum on the future of their respective countries' membership of the EU.

The EU will face challenges in the years ahead as the UK leaves. It is difficult to predict whether the 27 members will move towards greater integration in the future absence of Britain. The priority for the EU in the short term may be to steady the ship.

CHANGES IN THE BOUNDARIES OF REGIONS

The boundaries of regions may change over time.

Boundary changes in language regions

We have already seen that the boundaries of the **Gaeltacht region** have been greatly reduced over time (see pages 231–232).

Urban growth and the expansion of city regions

We know that urban areas have grown over time. For example, at the time of the French Revolution in 1789, Paris was a small city. In recent years, the population of Greater Paris reached 12 million. Planners tried to control and direct the expansion of Paris. For that reason, new towns were developed outside Paris. Therefore, the area of Greater Paris has vastly expanded over time.

> **LINK**
>
> See page 315 for more on the expansion of Paris.

The growth of Dublin

Similarly, Dublin was a small city in 1916. Most of it was contained between the canals. However, the population continued to grow over time. Suburbs grew outwards, showing evidence of sprawl. New towns such as Tallaght were established in order to contain sprawl.

The spill-over into neighbouring counties

Many young couples were forced by the rise in house prices to purchase homes beyond the Dublin region. They faced a long commute every day. The result is that the population in counties Meath, Kildare, Laois and Wicklow has increased sharply in recent years.

New councils in the Dublin region

Because the population had grown so much, the city and county were divided into four administrative regions in 1994. There are four elected councils in the Dublin region. The area that each council represents is small. This gives the people a sense of closer access to the offices of the councils and to county councillors.

Figure 19.6 Local authorities in Dublin city and county, including the location of the council offices

Changes in political boundaries

Extraordinary changes occurred in Eastern Europe in recent decades as the Soviet bloc collapsed and Eastern European countries joined the EU.

The Iron Curtain that divided Europe during the Cold War

CASE STUDY

Boundary changes in Eastern Europe

During the Cold War, the Baltic republics, Poland, East Germany and many other states had Communist governments and were controlled by Moscow. They were behind the **Iron Curtain**, a heavily guarded line that stretched from the Baltics to the Black Sea and divided Europe. The Iron Curtain effectively cut off the people of Eastern Europe from Western Europe.

With the end of the Cold War and the fall of Communism in the Soviet bloc, the Iron Curtain boundary disappeared. Former Eastern bloc countries such as Poland saw their future in the West. These countries applied to Brussels to join the EU. Ten former Soviet bloc countries joined the EU between 2004 and 2007.

This pushed the boundaries of the EU much further east. Thus, the political landscape of Eastern Europe was transformed in less than two decades. After more than forty years of Communism, Eastern Europe had thrown off the oppressive hand of Moscow.

On the other hand, the western boundaries of the EU will change when the UK leaves the EU. When Brexit comes into force, the Republic of Ireland will share a land border with a non-member of the EU.

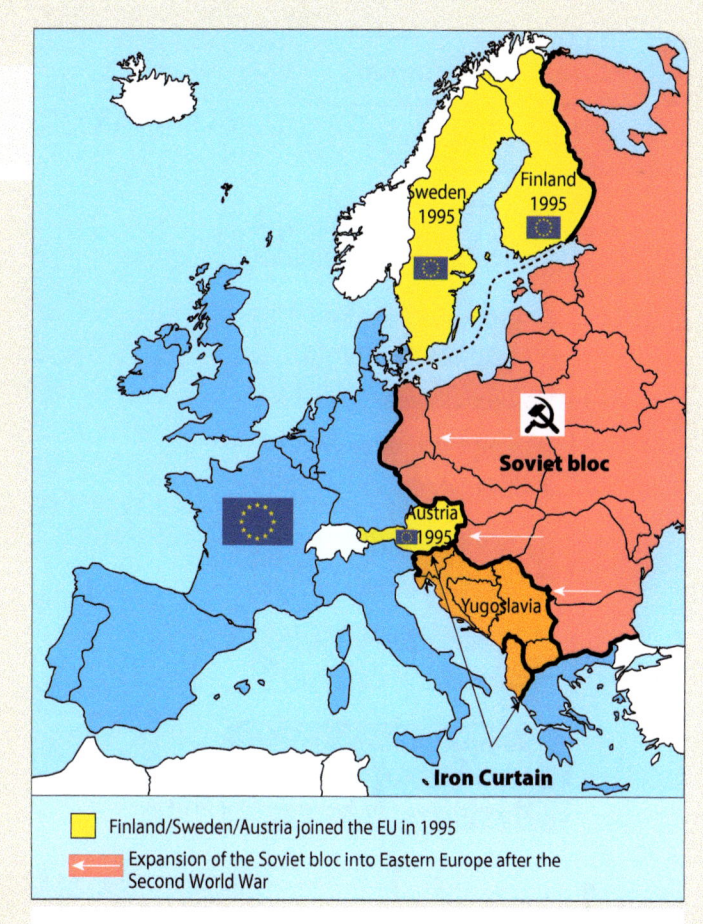

Figure 19.7 The EEC (EU) boundaries in 1989 at the end of the Cold War

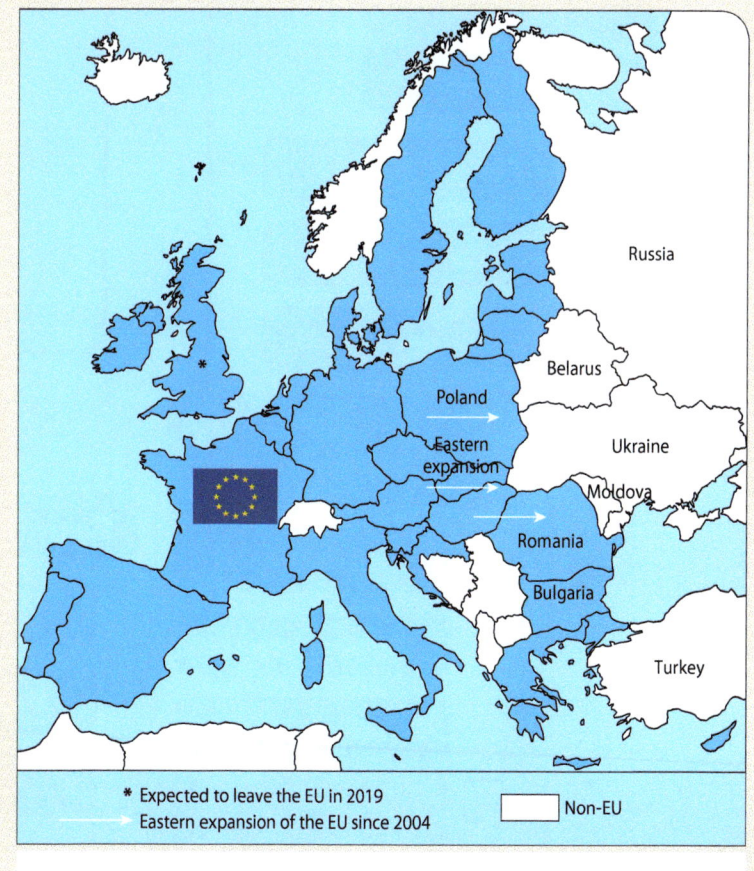

Figure 19.8 The eastern expansion of the EU in the years after 2004 led to changes in the eastern boundaries of the EU

ACTIVITY

Discussion

Examine Figures 19.7 and 19.8. Explain how the international boundaries in Central and Eastern Europe have changed dramatically in recent decades.

PowerPoint Summary

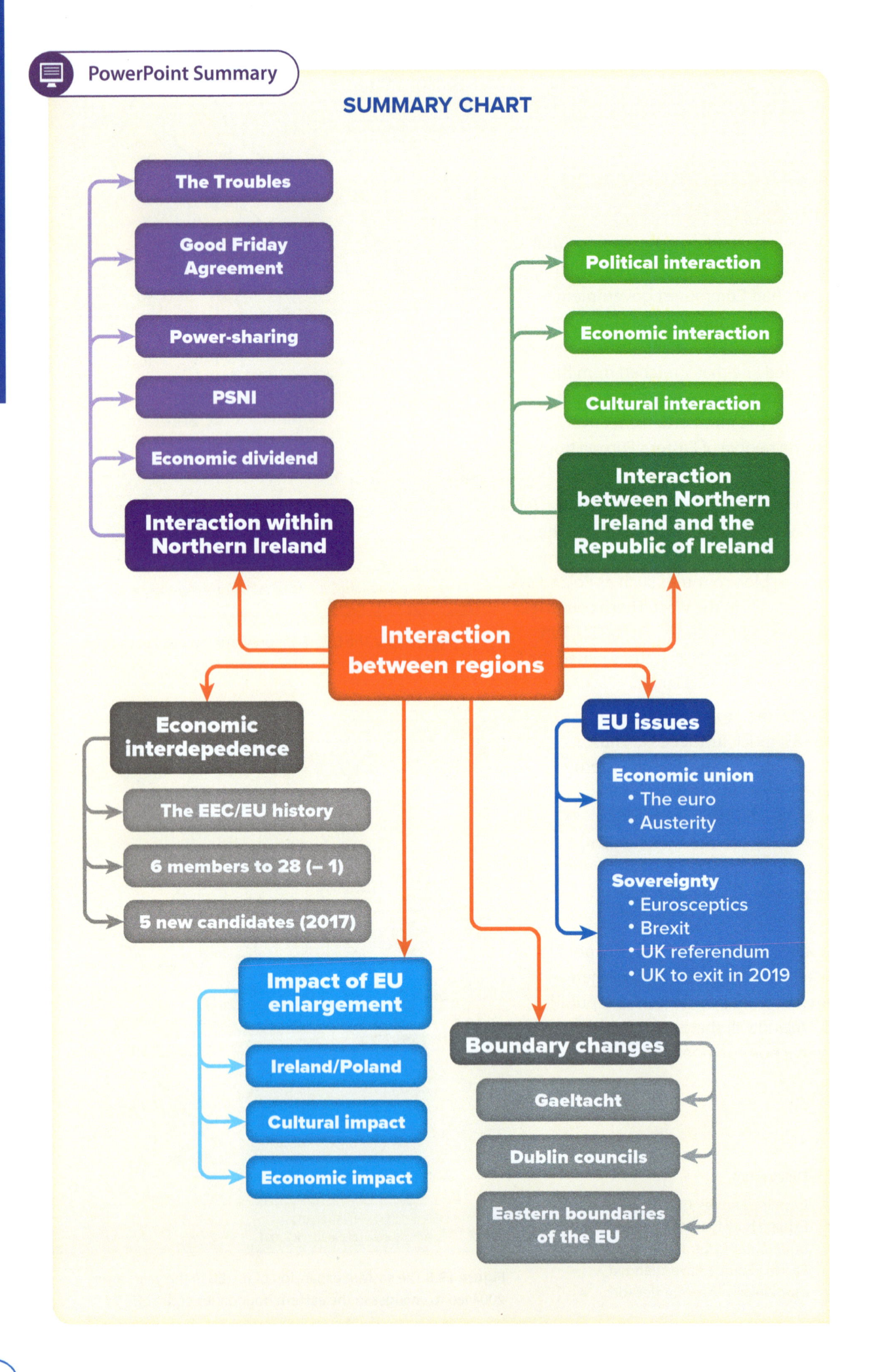

SUMMARY CHART

Interaction between regions

Interaction within Northern Ireland
- The Troubles
- Good Friday Agreement
- Power-sharing
- PSNI
- Economic dividend

Interaction between Northern Ireland and the Republic of Ireland
- Political interaction
- Economic interaction
- Cultural interaction

Economic interdependence
- The EEC/EU history
- 6 members to 28 (– 1)
- 5 new candidates (2017)

Impact of EU enlargement
- Ireland/Poland
- Cultural impact
- Economic impact

EU issues
- **Economic union**
  - The euro
  - Austerity
- **Sovereignty**
  - Eurosceptics
  - Brexit
  - UK referendum
  - UK to exit in 2019

Boundary changes
- Gaeltacht
- Dublin councils
- Eastern boundaries of the EU

UNIT 2 · REGIONAL GEOGRAPHY

388 GEOGRAPHY TODAY

Leaving Cert exam questions

LONG QUESTIONS: HIGHER LEVEL

1 **European Union** (20 marks)

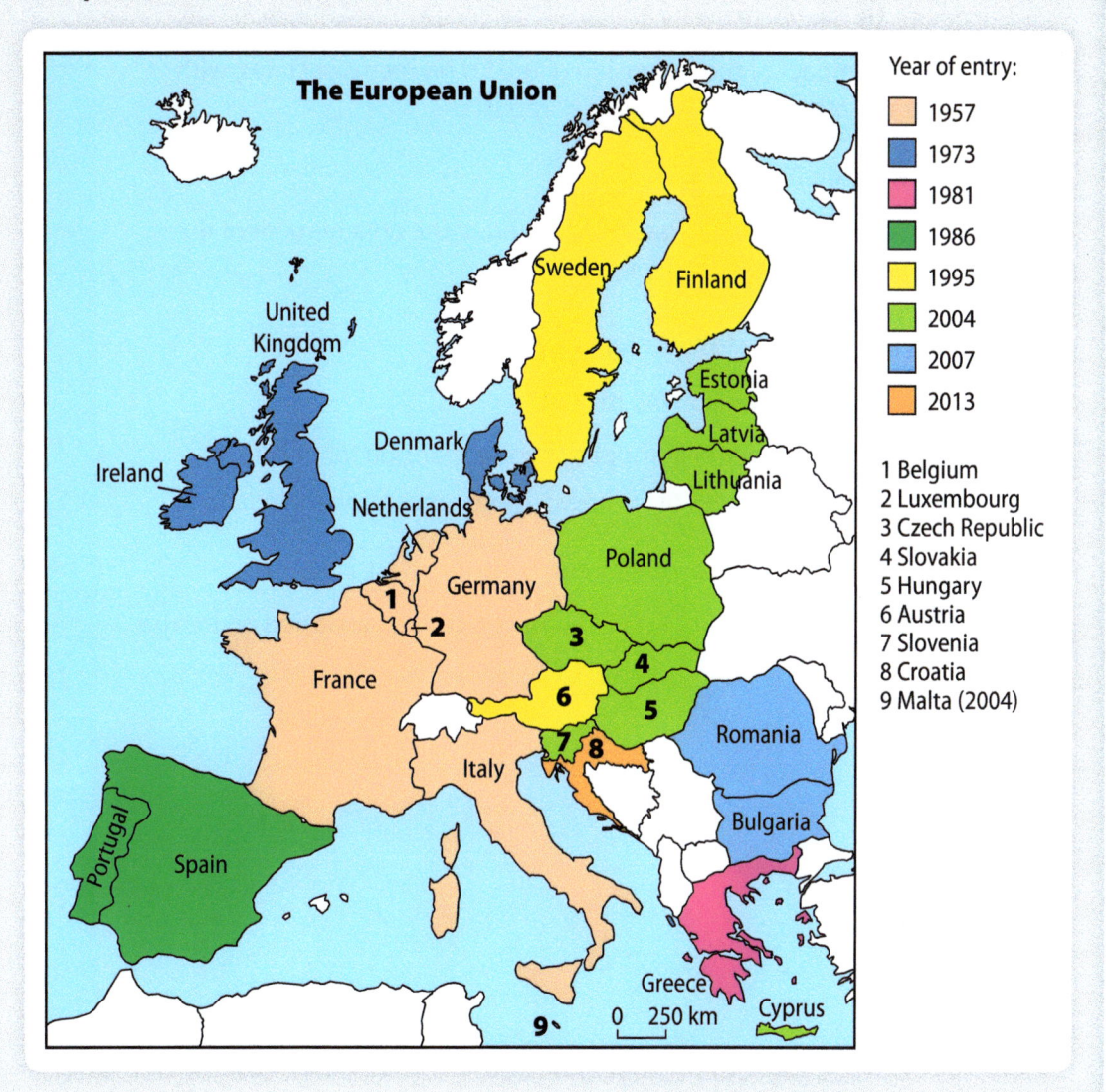

Examine the map of Europe above showing the member states of the European Union and indicate whether each of the following statements is true or false.

(i) Only six countries joined the European Union in 2004.
(ii) Belgium joined the European Union in the same year as the Netherlands.
(iii) Denmark joined the European Union in 1971.
(iv) Slovakia joined the European Union in 2013.

HL

2 Economic, political and cultural activities (30 marks)

Examine the interaction between economic, political and/or cultural activities in any region that you have studied.

3 European Union (30 marks)

Examine the impact of the expansion of the EU on member states, with reference to both economic and social impacts.

4 European Union (30 marks)

Describe and explain **two** impacts on Ireland of the enlargement of the European Union.

OL

LONG QUESTIONS: ORDINARY LEVEL

1 European Union expansion (40 marks)
 (i) Describe the advantages of European Union expansion for Ireland.
 (ii) Describe the disadvantages of European Union expansion for Ireland.

2 European Union expansion (30 marks)

Describe and explain the impacts of European Union expansion on Ireland.

CORE UNIT 3
GRAPH SKILLS & GEOGRAPHICAL INVESTIGATION

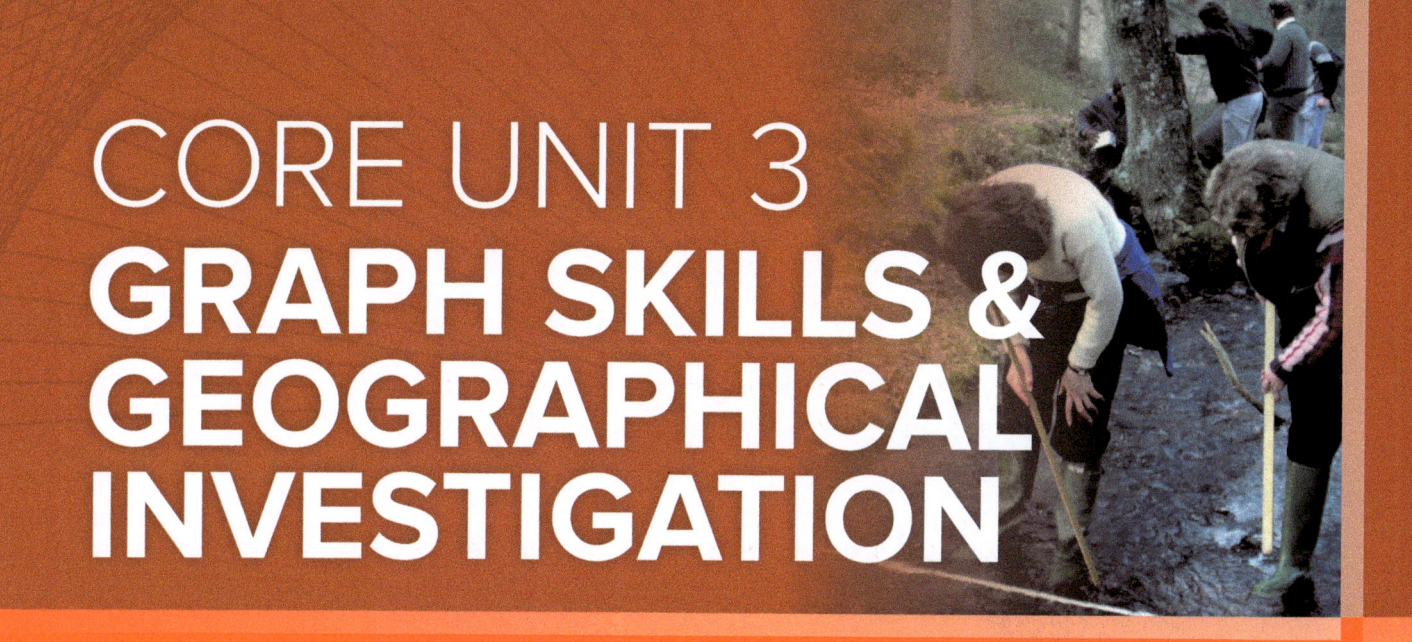

Chapter 20	**Ordnance Survey Maps**	392
Chapter 21	**Aerial Photographs**	419
Chapter 22	**Satellite Images**	438
Chapter 23	**Weather Charts**	454
Chapter 24	**Interpreting Graphs**	463
Chapter 25	**Geographical Investigation**	473

Chapter 20
Ordnance Survey Maps

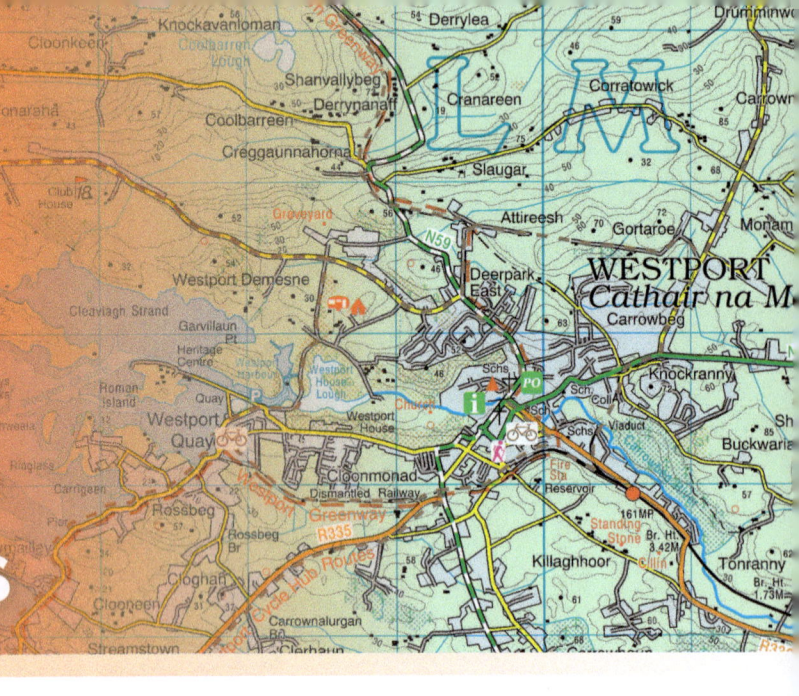

UNIT 3 • GRAPH SKILLS & GI

KEYWORDS

- scale
- straight-line distance
- curved-line distance
- National Grid
- sub-zone letter
- grid reference
- eastings
- northings
- cardinal points
- sketch map
- contour lines
- colour layers
- triangulation pillar
- spot height
- even slope
- convex slope
- concave slope
- stepped slope
- average gradient
- cross-section
- vertical exaggeration
- communications
- settlement
- land use
- relief
- altitude
- drainage
- aspect
- rural settlement
- historic settlement
- settlement patterns
- nucleated
- linear
- dispersed
- absence pattern
- urban settlement
- urban functions

LEARNING OBJECTIVES

By the end of this chapter, you should be able to understand:

- How to describe location and direction on OS maps
- How to use measuring and sketching skills
- How information is displayed on OS maps
- How to interpret the physical landscapes on OS maps
- How to interpret the human and economic landscapes on OS maps.

Ordnance Survey Ireland

Ordnance Survey Ireland (OSi) is the national mapping agency of the Republic of Ireland. It produces a wide range of urban, rural, tourist and leisure maps at a variety of scales.

The Discovery Series

The **Discovery Series** of maps consists of 75 sheets that cover the entire Republic of Ireland. They give a wealth of detail on both urban areas and the countryside. They are ideal for planning, touring and exploring the landscape.

Scale

Map **scale** refers to the relationship (or ratio) between the distance of two points on a map and the corresponding distance between these points on the ground.

The Discovery Series maps are drawn at a scale of 1:50,000. This means that 1 centimetre on the map represents 50,000 centimetres (500 metres) on the ground. In this way, 2 cm on the map represents 1 km on the ground. The side of each square on the OS map is therefore 1 km in length. This is a **large-scale** map as it gives a lot of detail over a small area of land.

The scale is shown or stated in three ways:

> By a representative fraction (RF)
> On a linear scale
> By a statement of scale.

> **GEOFACT**
>
> **Small-scale** maps, such as those of countries or continents, show large areas of land but have little detail.

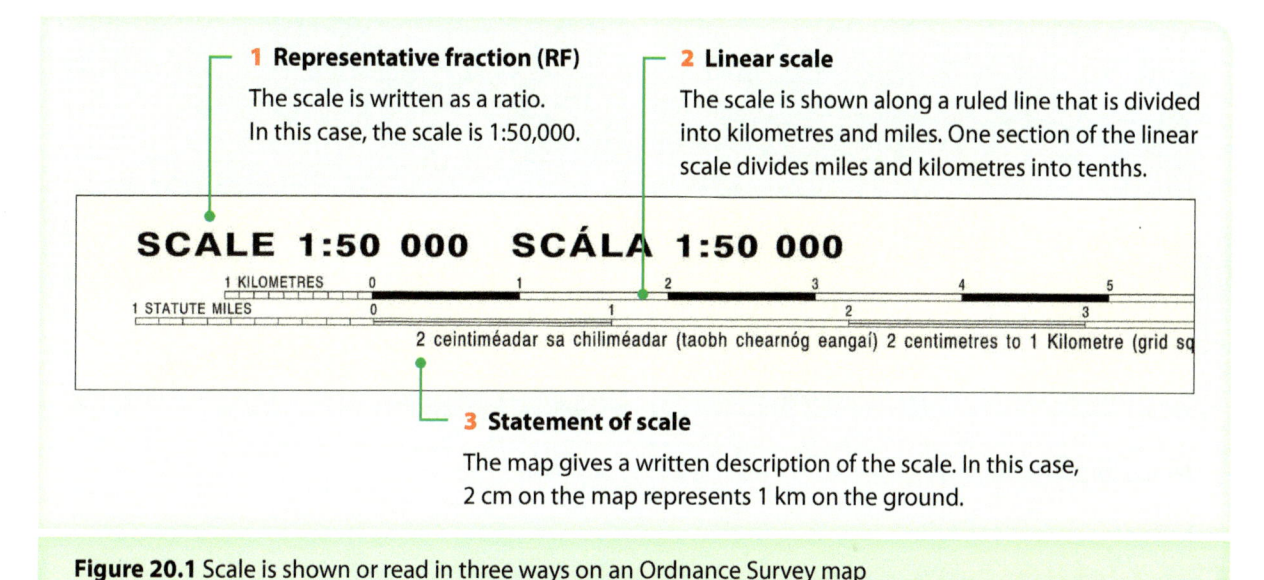

1 Representative fraction (RF)
The scale is written as a ratio. In this case, the scale is 1:50,000.

2 Linear scale
The scale is shown along a ruled line that is divided into kilometres and miles. One section of the linear scale divides miles and kilometres into tenths.

SCALE 1:50 000   SCÁLA 1:50 000

2 ceintiméadar sa chiliméadar (taobh chearnóg eangaí) 2 centimetres to 1 Kilometre (grid sq

3 Statement of scale
The map gives a written description of the scale. In this case, 2 cm on the map represents 1 km on the ground.

Figure 20.1 Scale is shown or read in three ways on an Ordnance Survey map

Measuring distance

To calculate distance, you need to measure the distance on the map and then convert it to the real-life distance on the ground. This can be done using a strip of paper and the linear scale of the map.

Straight-line distance

To measure a **straight-line distance**, 'as the crow flies', between two selected points on the map:

> Place a straight edge of paper on the map so that it passes through the two points.
> Mark the edge of the paper where it passes each of the points.
> Place the paper against the map's linear scale and read the distance in kilometres.

Figure 20.2 Measuring straight-line distance on a Discovery Series map

> **ACTIVITY**
>
> **Skills**
> Examine Figure 20.2. Calculate the straight-line distance in kilometres between the two points shown.

Distance along a curved line

When measuring distance along a **curved line**, such as a road or railway, remember that any curved distance is made up of several straight sections.

> Place a straight edge of paper along the first section. Mark the starting point.
> Mark off the first small straight section.
> Pivot the straight edge of the paper to follow the next straight section and mark its end point.
> Repeat this process until you have measured the required distance.
> Use the linear scale to read the distance in kilometres.

ACTIVITY

Skills

Examine Figure 20.2. Calculate the distance along the road between the two points shown on the map.

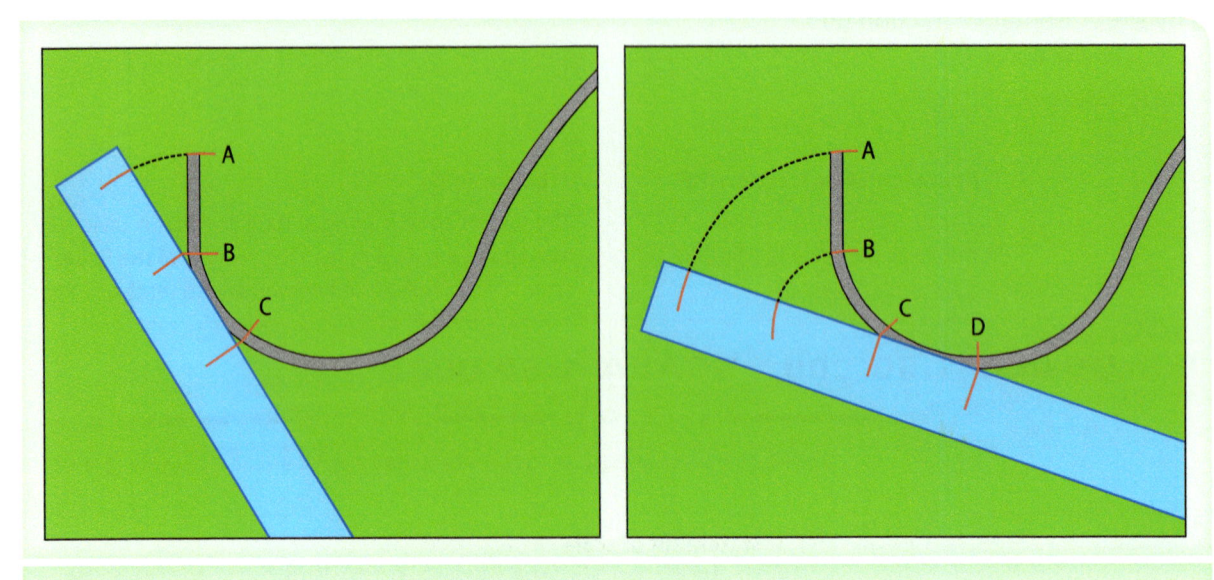

Figure 20.3 Measuring a curved distance, such as a road or a river

Calculating map area

Regular shapes

To calculate the area of a **regular shape**, for example all or part of the map, such as Figure 20.4:

> Count the number of grid squares along the base of the map.
> Count the number of grid squares along the vertical side of the map.
> Multiply the two totals.

Calculate the area of the map extract in Figure 20.4:

> 6 grid squares along the base ⇒ width of map = 6 km
> 5 squares up the side ⇒ length of map = 5 km
> Area of map extract = length × width = 30 km²

GEOFACT

The length of each side of a grid square is 1 km. This means that each grid square is 1 km² in area.

ACTIVITY

Skills

Examine Figure 20.2 on page 393. Calculate the area of the full map extract.

Irregular shapes

To calculate the area of an **irregular shape**, for example an island or a sea area:

> Count all the complete grid squares within the area to be measured (step 1).
> Count each grid square where more than half is included (step 2).

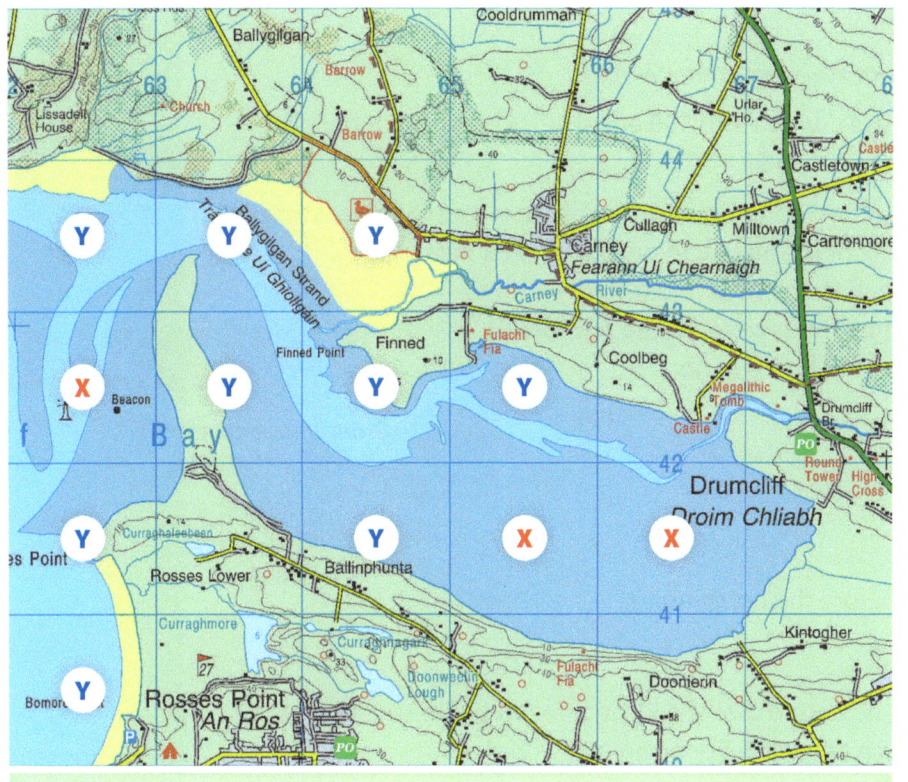

Figure 20.4 Calculating the area of an irregular shape on an OS map extract

ACTIVITY

Skills

Examine Figure 20.4. Calculate the land area in this extract.

› Ignore any grid squares where less than half is included.
› Add the totals from steps 1 and 2 to find the total area in square kilometres.

Examine the map extract of Rosses Point (Figure 20.4) and calculate the sea area shown:

› Number of complete squares (indicated by X) = 3
› Number of areas bigger than a half square (indicated by Y) = 9
› Area of island = 3 + 9 = 12 km²

The National Grid

The **National Grid** is a map reference system that is used on Ordnance Survey maps to indicate a location within the country.

› The area of Ireland is divided into 25 squares, or **sub-zones**.
› Each sub-zone measures 100 km in length by 100 km in width.
› Each sub-zone is identified by a single letter. Sub-zones are labelled from A to Z, with I being omitted.
› Some of the sub-zones do not actually cover any land.

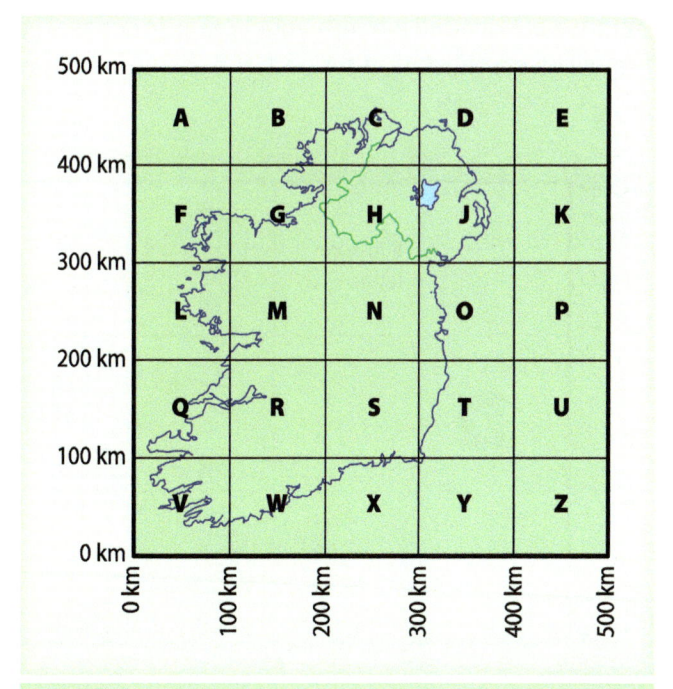

Figure 20.5 The National Grid consists of 25 sub-zones. Each is identified by a letter of the alphabet.

CHAPTER 20 · ORDNANCE SURVEY MAPS

Grid references

A **grid reference** is used to locate a feature on a map.

The sides of each sub-zone are divided into 100 equal parts by a grid of blue lines. These lines are numbered from 00 to 99.

> The vertical lines that run from left to right (or west to east) are called **eastings**. This is because the number of the line increases the further east you go.
> The horizontal lines that run from bottom to top (or south to north) are called **northings**. This is because the number of the line increases the further north you go.

A grid reference has three parts:
> Sub-zone letter (L)
> Easting (E)
> Northing (N).

The easting is always read before the northing.

> **HINT**
>
> Order is important in grid references. Think **LEN**:
> > **L:** sub-zone letter
> > **E:** easting
> > **N:** northing.

Four-figure grid reference

A four-figure grid reference is used to give the location of an entire square on the map or of a large feature such as a village or an area of woodland.

It consists of the following:

> **Sub-zone letter** (L)
> **Two-digit easting** that forms the left side of the square (E)
> **Two-digit number** that forms the base of the square (N).

Six-figure grid reference

A six-figure grid reference is used to give the precise location of a feature such as a church or hilltop on a map.

Imagine that the sides of the grid square that you identified in your four-figure grid reference are divided into ten equal parts. Imagine that these are numbered 0 to 9. This will give a **third digit** for both the easting and the northing.

Sample grid references

Four-figure grid references

Parking:	T 59 24
Built-up area:	T 61 25
Golf course:	T 63 25

Six-figure grid references

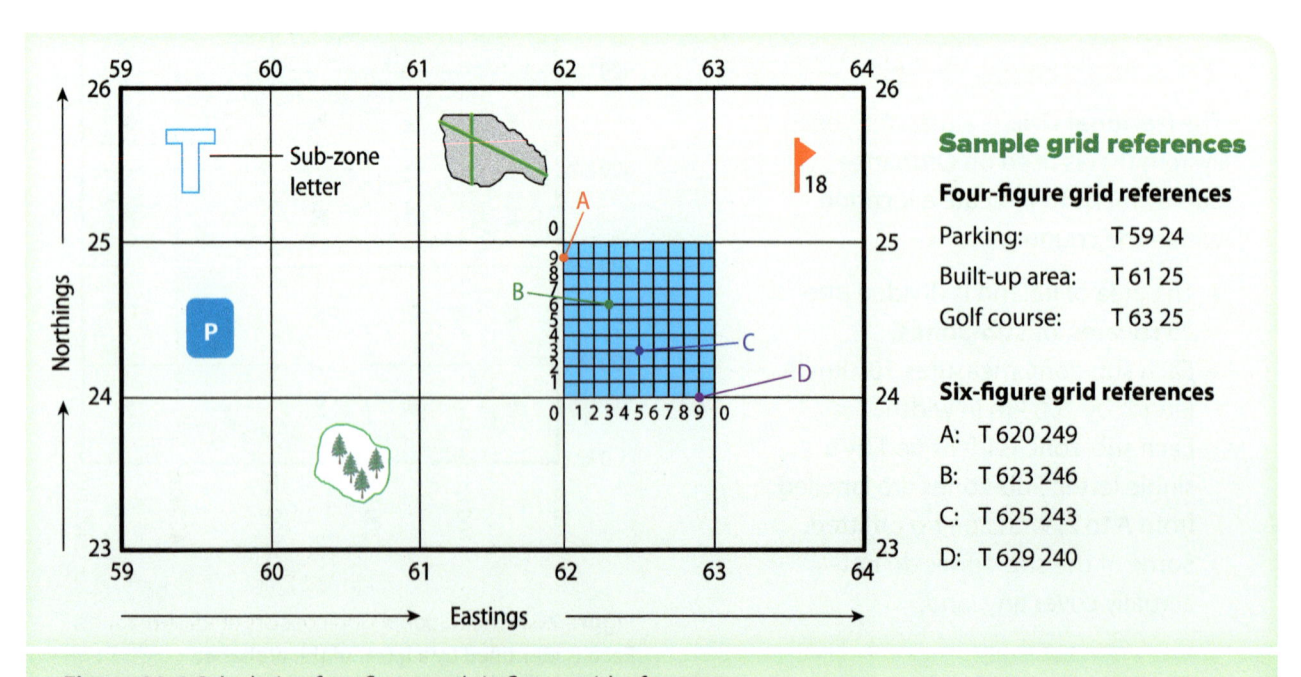

A:	T 620 249
B:	T 623 246
C:	T 625 243
D:	T 629 240

Figure 20.6 Calculating four-figure and six-figure grid references

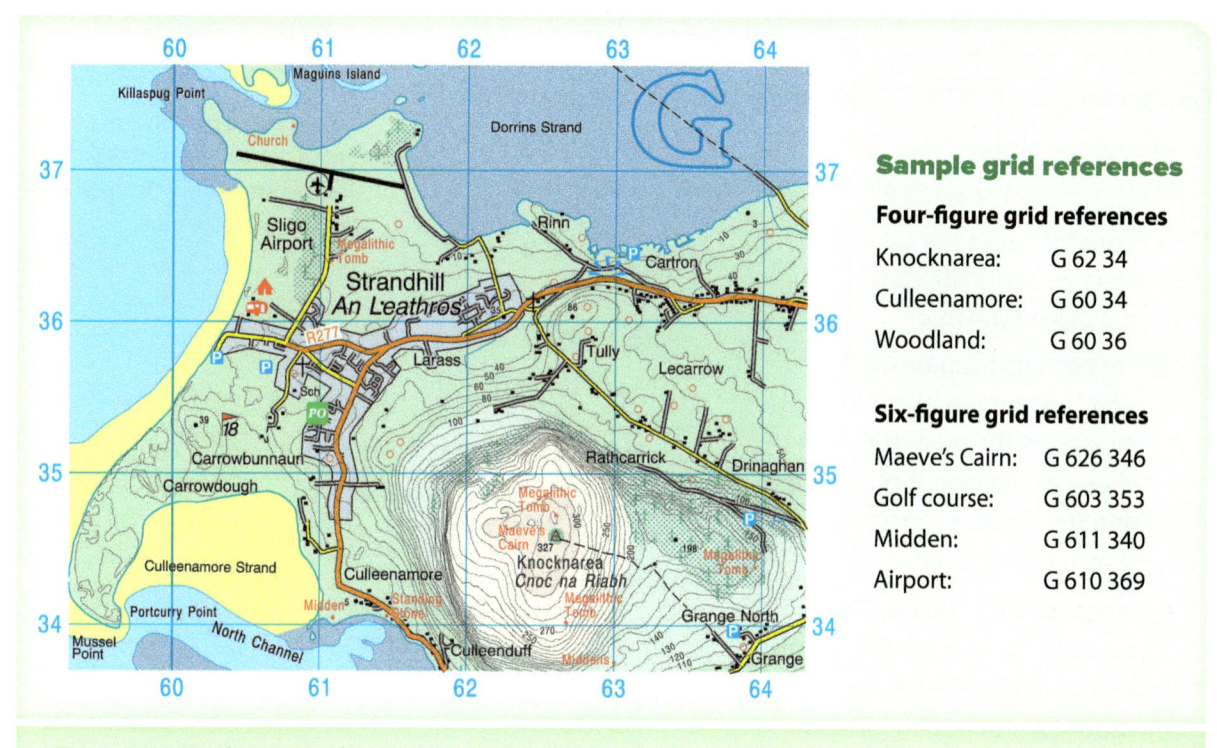

Figure 20.7 Reading grid references on an OS map

Sample grid references

Four-figure grid references
- Knocknarea: G 62 34
- Culleenamore: G 60 34
- Woodland: G 60 36

Six-figure grid references
- Maeve's Cairn: G 626 346
- Golf course: G 603 353
- Midden: G 611 340
- Airport: G 610 369

Direction on OS maps

Ordnance Survey maps are always printed so that when you read them, north is at the top of the sheet. Some map extracts may also have an arrow that points north.

> The four main points of the compass – north, east, west and south – are called the **cardinal points**.
> When the spaces between the cardinal points are divided, more directions can be described. In this way, we get 16 points with which to describe direction.

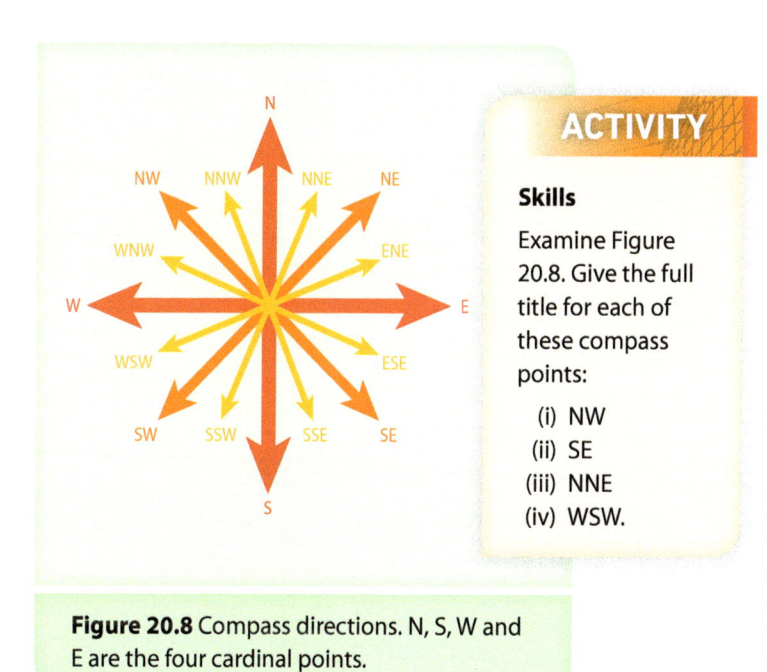

Figure 20.8 Compass directions. N, S, W and E are the four cardinal points.

ACTIVITY

Skills

Examine Figure 20.7.

1. Give a four-figure grid reference for each of the following:
   (i) Two adjacent car parks
   (ii) A sandspit
   (iii) A large area of woodland.

2. Give a six-figure grid reference for each of the following:
   (i) A caravan park
   (ii) Killaspug Point
   (iii) Post office.

3. Identify the feature at each of the following grid references:
   (i) G 609 357
   (ii) G 606 362
   (iii) G 597 340.

ACTIVITY

Skills

Examine Figure 20.8. Give the full title for each of these compass points:
(i) NW
(ii) SE
(iii) NNE
(iv) WSW.

ACTIVITY

Skills

Examine Figure 20.7. Identify the following directions from the airport building to:
(i) The post office
(ii) Killaspug Point
(iii) The summit of Knocknarea
(iv) Portcurry Point.

CHAPTER 20 · ORDNANCE SURVEY MAPS

Sketch maps

Sketch maps should be carefully drawn using these guidelines:

> Always use graph paper.
> Draw a frame to **half-scale** on graph paper. To do this:

  1 Count the number of grid squares along the base and up the side of the map.
  2 Let each half square on the graph paper represent a full grid square on the map. Thus, the shape of the map is maintained and the sketch map frame is drawn at half-scale.

> Give the sketch map a title and insert a direction arrow (N).
> Insert the required features, showing the boundary or outline of each.

  1 Draw features in the correct proportion. The squares on the graph paper and the grid squares on the map should act as a guide to inserting features.
  2 Always start with major features such as the coastline, roads or rivers, if they are asked for. This will help you to locate other features more easily.

> Identify each feature by name or by key.
> Show only those features that have been asked for.

HINTS

> **Always use a pencil.** It makes it easier to correct mistakes.
> **Use colour wisely.** Overuse of colour can waste time.

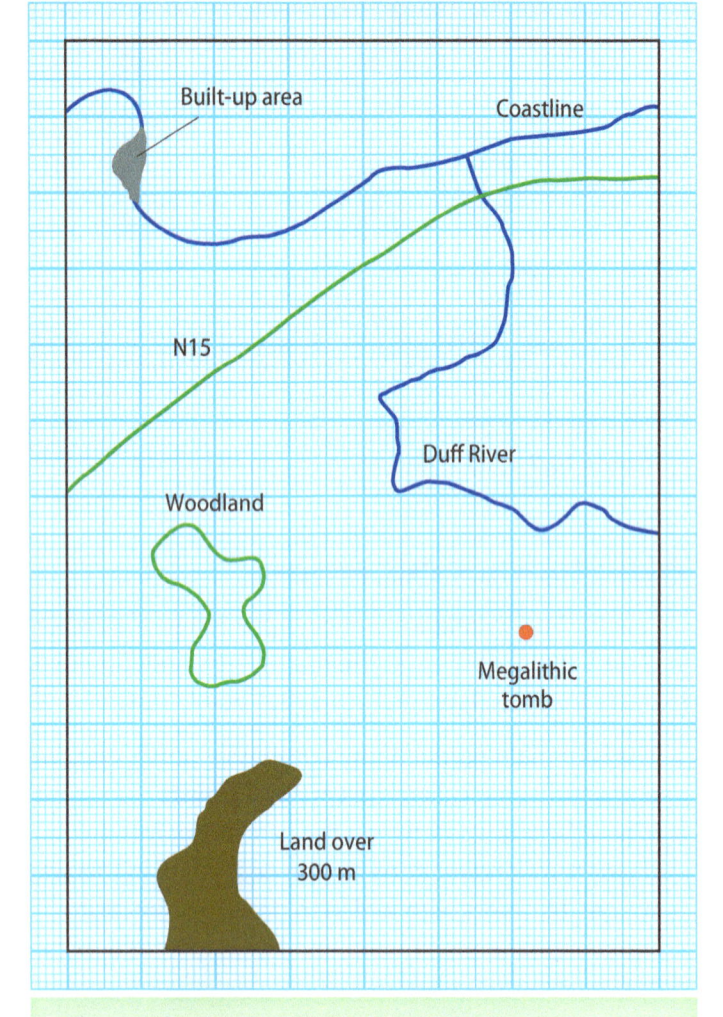

Figure 20.9 Sketch map drawn at half-scale

ACTIVITY

Skills

Examine Figure 20.10. On a sketch map of the region drawn to half-scale, show and name the following:

(i) The coastline
(ii) The R729
(iii) A county boundary
(iv) The highest point on the map
(v) A named beach
(vi) A car park
(vii) A caravan park.

Worked example

Examine Figure 20.10. On a sketch map of the region drawn to half-scale (Figure 20.9), show and name the following:

(i) The coastline
(ii) The N15
(iii) The Duff River
(iv) An area of woodland
(v) An area over 300 metres in height
(vi) A built-up area
(vii) A named antiquity.

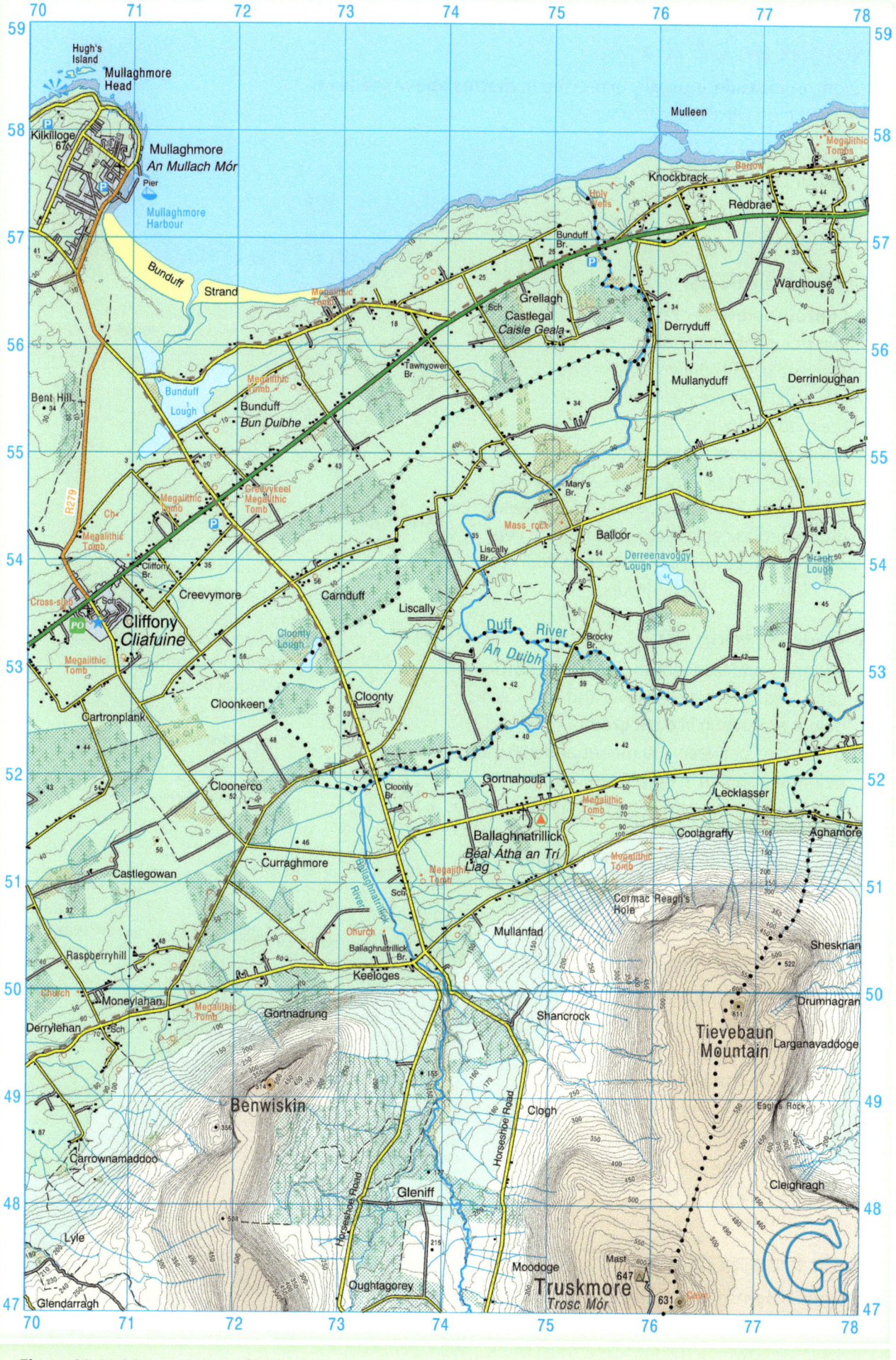

Figure 20.10 OS map extract of Mullaghmore and its surrounding area

Height on OS maps

Height, or **altitude**, is usually expressed in **metres above sea level**. It is shown on OS maps in four ways:

› Contour lines
› Colour layering
› Triangulation pillars
› Spot heights.

Contour lines (A)

› **Contours** are lines drawn on a map that join points of equal height above sea level.
› They are usually drawn at 10-metre intervals. They are numbered if space on the map allows it.
› **Index contours** represent contours at 50-metre intervals (50 metres, 100 metres, 150 metres, 200 metres, etc.) and are always numbered, except where contours are very close together. They are thicker and darker in colour than other contours.

Figure 20.11 Altitude on an OS map

Colour layering (B)

› Sea areas and lakes are shown in **light blue**.
› Land areas between sea level and 100 metres in height are shown in **dark green**.
› Land areas between 100 metres and 200 metres in height are shown in **light green**.
› Land areas between 200 metres and 300 metres in height are shown in **cream**.
› Land areas above 300 metres in height are shown in brown. The **brown** becomes darker as altitude increases.

GEOFACT

Additional colour-coded information is also provided on individual peaks.

- Above 600m
- 599m - 400m
- Below 400m

Triangulation pillars (C)

› **Triangulation pillars** are points on the tops of hills and mountains for which the exact altitude has been measured.
› Each is indicated on the map by a small black triangle with the altitude written beside it.
› The pillars were part of a network of surveying stations that OSi used for mapping.

Spot heights (D)

› **Spot heights** indicate the exact altitude of the point where it is marked.
› Each is shown on the map by a small black dot with the altitude written beside it.

Triangulation pillar at the summit of Nephin, Co. Mayo

Slope on OS maps

Different types of **slope** can be identified by contour patterns. Widely spaced contours indicate a very gentle slope. The closer the contours are to one another, the steeper the slope.

There are four basic slope types:

> Even
> Convex
> Concave
> Stepped.

HINT

See *Gradient*, page 402.

Even slopes, also called regular slopes, have an evenly spaced contour pattern.

Convex slopes are steep at the base (closely packed contours) but slope gently at the top (widely spaced contours).

Concave slopes have a gentle slope at the base (widely spaced contours) but become steep at the top (closely packed contours).

Stepped slopes are made up of alternating steep and gentle slope sections (a repeated pattern of closely packed and widely spaced contours).

Figure 20.12 Different types of slope

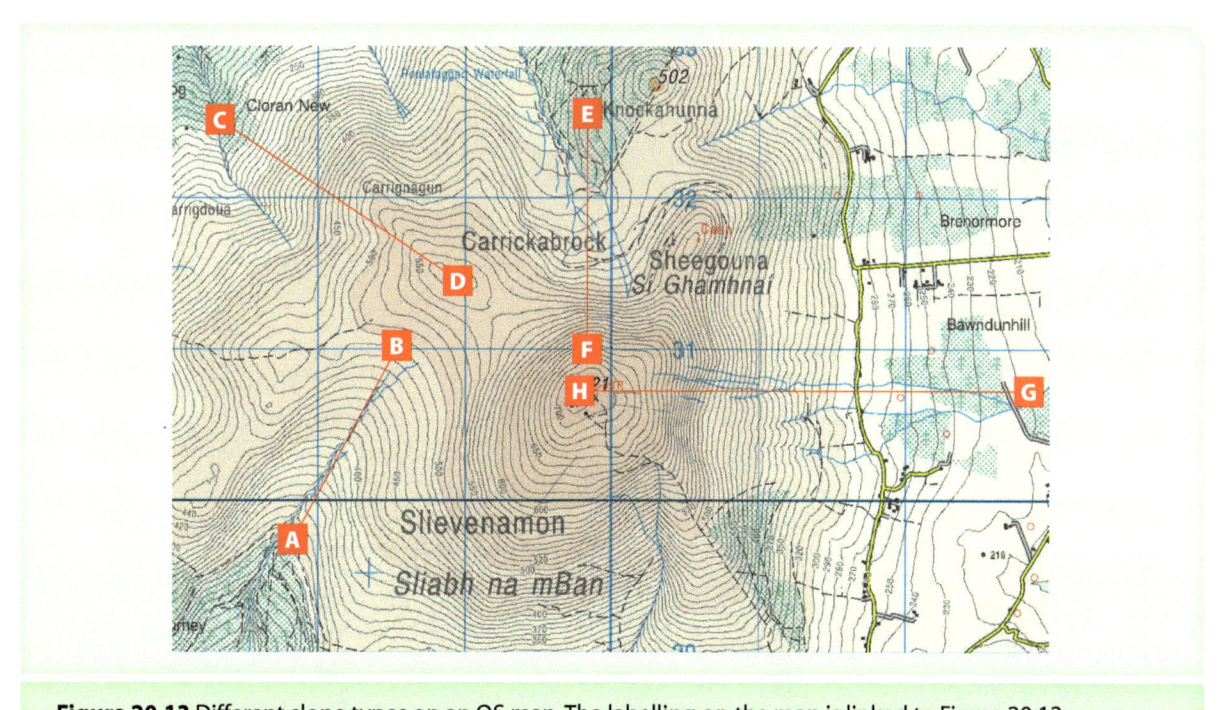

Figure 20.13 Different slope types on an OS map. The labelling on the map is linked to Figure 20.12.

CHAPTER 20 · ORDNANCE SURVEY MAPS

Calculating average gradient

Gradient refers to the degree of incline or rise of a slope. We can use general terms such as 'steep' or 'gentle' to describe it.

Average gradient can also be calculated accurately. It is expressed as a **ratio** of 1:x. For example, a gradient of 1:8 means that on average, for every 8 metres you travel horizontally, you climb 1 metre in altitude.

To calculate the average gradient, you need to do two calculations:

> Find the **vertical interval** (VI). This is the difference in height in metres between the two points (think *rise* in maths).
> Measure the **horizontal equivalent** (HE). This is the horizontal distance in metres between the two points (think *run* in maths).

The formula that is used to calculate average gradient is:

$$\text{Average gradient (AG)} = \frac{\text{Vertical interval (VI)}}{\text{Horizontal equivalent (HE)}}$$

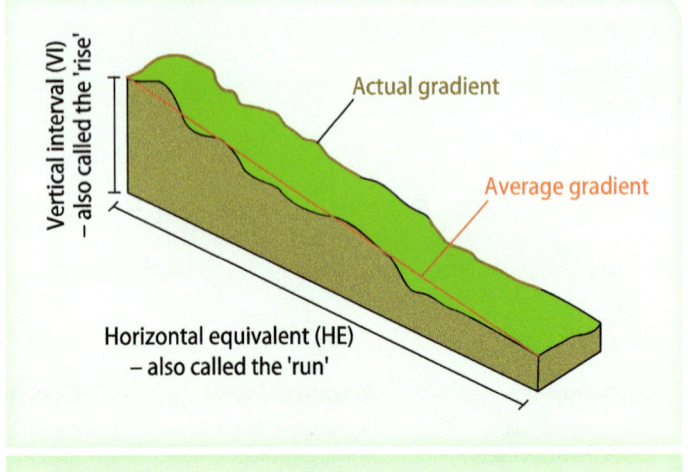

Figure 20.14 Note the difference between the actual gradient (which varies) and the average gradient

Figure 20.15 OS map showing Mount Leinster with its triangulation pillar and three mountaintops marked by spot heights

Example

Calculate the average gradient between the triangulation pillar at Mount Leinster and the spot height at Black Rock Mountain.

Vertical interval (rise) = 795 metres – 599 metres = 196 metres
Horizontal equivalent (run) = 3.3 km = 3,300 metres

$$AG = \frac{196}{3,300} = \frac{1}{16.9}$$

Average gradient is 1:16.9 (or 1 in 16.9).

ACTIVITY

Numeracy

Examine Figure 20.15. Calculate the average gradient (AG) between:

(i) The triangulation pillar at Mount Leinster and the spot height .647
(ii) The spot height .654 and the spot height .599 at Black Rock Mountain.

Cross-sections

A **cross-section** shows relief along a line. It can be compared to taking a side view or 'slice' through the landscape.

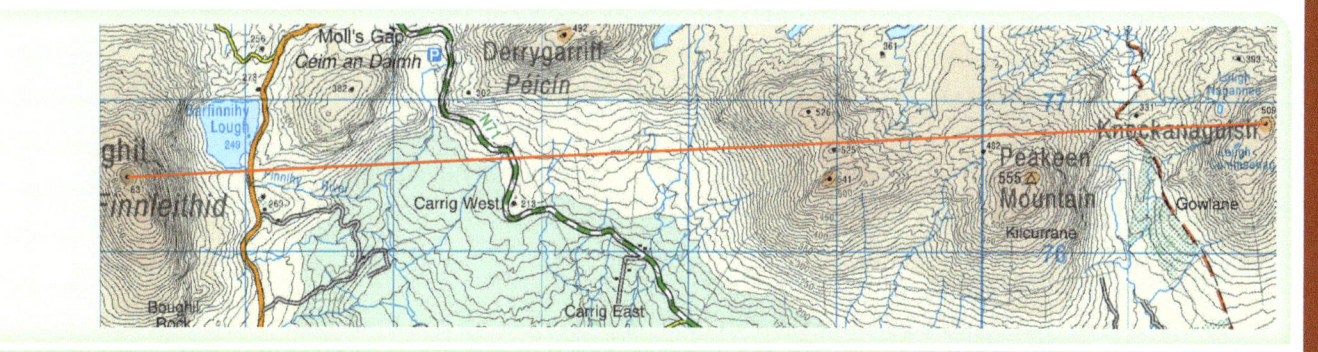

Figure 20.16 Constructing a cross-section from the summit of Finnleithid to the summit of Knockanaguish

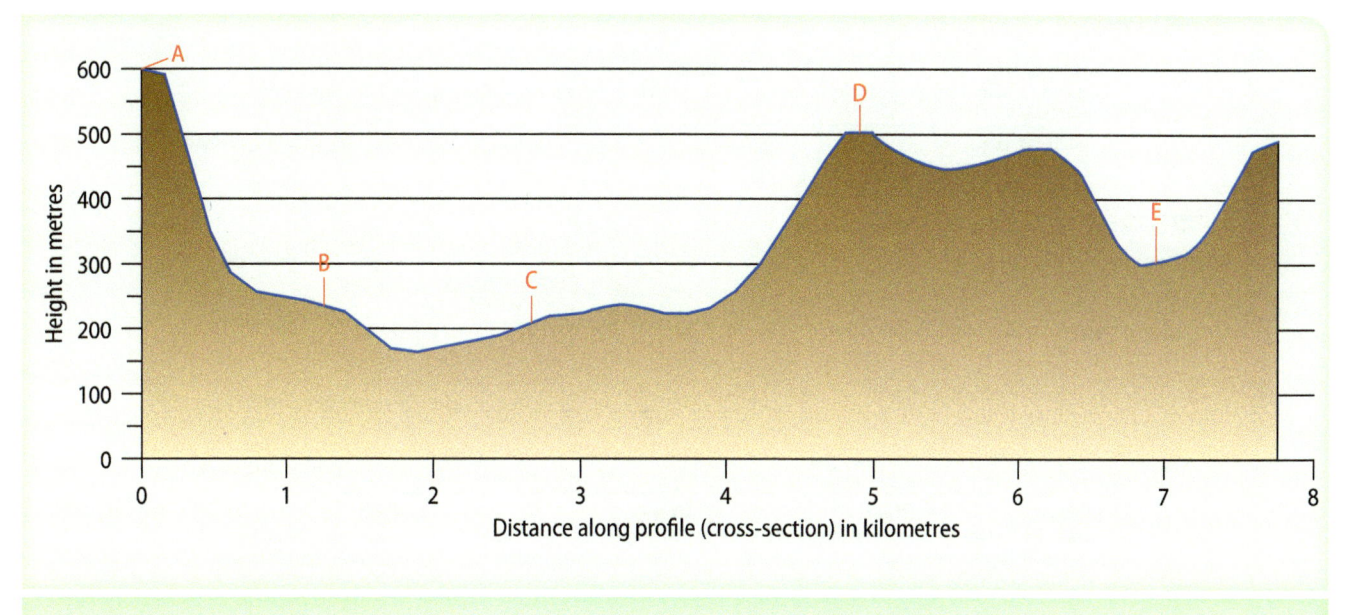

Figure 20.17 Cross-section from the summit of Finnleithid to the summit of Knockanaguish

Vertical exaggeration

When you examine a cross-section, you might notice that the height and gradient of features on the cross-section may be distorted. It can appear much steeper and higher than it is in real life. This is because the vertical scale is exaggerated when compared to the horizontal scale.

In Figure 20.17:

> The horizontal scale is 2 cm per km (1,000 metres).
> The vertical scale is 2 cm per 200 metres.
> The **vertical exaggeration** is 1,000 ÷ 200 = 5.

ACTIVITY

Skills

Examine Figure 20.16 and Figure 20.17.

(i) What is the name of the mountain peak at A?

(ii) What is the name of the lake at B?

(iii) What is the road type at C?

(iv) What is the spot height at D?

(v) What is the tourist/leisure attraction at E?

The physical landscape

In studying the **physical landscape**, we deal with the following:

- **Topography (or relief):** This refers to the height and shape of the land surface and the physical features and landforms it consists of. These include mountains, valleys, lowlands, slopes, etc.
- **Drainage:** This refers to all the water elements of the map. It includes rivers, lakes, bogs, etc.
- **Landforms:** These refer to features on the Earth's surface that have been shaped by weathering, erosion and deposition.

Contour patterns

We have seen that contours are lines drawn on a map connecting points of equal height above sea level. They are also useful because they illustrate the shape of the land surface (topography) on a map. They allow us to imagine a three-dimensional landscape on a two-dimensional map surface.

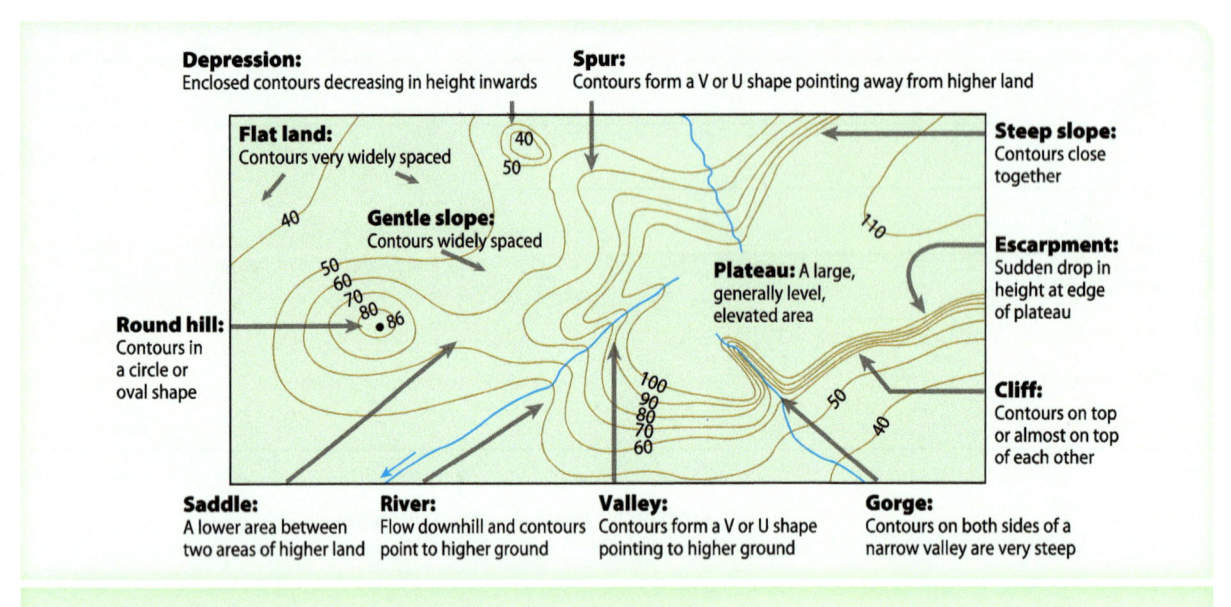

Depression: Enclosed contours decreasing in height inwards

Spur: Contours form a V or U shape pointing away from higher land

Flat land: Contours very widely spaced

Steep slope: Contours close together

Gentle slope: Contours widely spaced

Plateau: A large, generally level, elevated area

Escarpment: Sudden drop in height at edge of plateau

Round hill: Contours in a circle or oval shape

Cliff: Contours on top or almost on top of each other

Saddle: A lower area between two areas of higher land

River: Flow downhill and contours point to higher ground

Valley: Contours form a V or U shape pointing to higher ground

Gorge: Contours on both sides of a narrow valley are very steep

Figure 20.18 Contour patterns and their associated topography

Landforms shaped by weathering, erosion and deposition

We have already examined landscapes that have been shaped by weathering, erosion and deposition. Labelled maps of these landscapes can be found at:

Chapter 9	› Surface landforms of a limestone (karst) landscape	› Page 112
Chapter 11	› Drainage patterns	› Pages 135–7
	› Landforms of a youthful river	› Page 145
	› Landforms of a mature river	› Page 148
	› Landforms of an old river	› Page 152
Chapter 12	› Landforms of coastal erosion	› Page 170
	› Landforms of coastal deposition	› Page 176
Chapter 13	› Landforms of glacial erosion	› Page 193
	› Landforms of glacial deposition	› Page 198
	› Landforms of fluvio-glacial erosion	› Page 200
	› Landforms of fluvio-glacial deposition	› Page 201
Chapter 14	› Landforms of rejuvenation and isostasy	› Page 212

Table 20.1

The human and economic landscape

In studying the **human** and **economic** landscape, we will deal with the following:

> Communications
> Settlement
> Land use
> Urban functions.

> **LINKS**
>
> > Topics on the economic landscape will be treated in greater depth in Book 2.
> > Topics on the human landscape will be treated in greater depth in Book 3.

Communications

Communications refer to all aspects of transport, including roads, rivers, railways, ports and airports.

The road network is by far the most important and widespread form of communications. The road system is made up of:

> Motorways (M)
> National primary and secondary routes (N)
> Regional roads (R)
> Third-class roads (yellow) and other roads (no colour).

FACTORS THAT INFLUENCE THE ROAD NETWORK	
Relief	> Roads are built to serve people, most of whom live in low-lying areas. > Most low-lying areas have gentle gradients, which makes construction easier. > Roads avoid upland areas with their steep gradient. > Where roads cut across uplands, they do so at the lowest point, called a gap.
Rivers	> Roads in river valleys are built well back from the river to avoid flooding. > Roads cross rivers at shallow or narrow locations called bridging points.

Table 20.2

Settlement

Settlement refers to where people live. It can range from an individual house to a large city. The study of settlement can be divided into:

> Historic settlement
> Rural settlement
> Urban settlement.

Historic settlement

> Most evidence for **historic settlement** is in the form of antiquities. Most of these are shown and named in red, while others are identified by a symbol, also in red.
> Other evidence, such as demesnes, is named but the historic aspect must be interpreted.
> Some aspects are also incorporated into place names, for example Lismore and Dundalk.

HISTORIC SETTLEMENT OF THE IRISH LANDSCAPE, BY PERIOD OF HISTORY AND FUNCTION		
PERIOD	FUNCTION	LISTED ON OS MAP EXTRACTS
Pre-Christian	Defence	› Dún, rath, lios, crannóg, promontory fort, enclosures (o)
	Domestic	› Fulacht fia, midden
	Worship	› Standing stone (gallaun), stone circle, stone row, bullaun stone
	Burial places	› Standing stone (gallaun), ogham stone, megalithic tomb, cairn, dolmen, barrow, mound, cist
Christian	Defence	› Round tower
	Worship	› Holy well, cill, church, abbey, monastery
	Burial	› High cross, cross base, graveyard, cillín
Norman and Plantation	Defence	› Castle, town wall, motte, moat, moated site
	Worship	› Friary, monastery, mass rock
	Residential	› House, demesne, place names ending in -town

Table 20.3

ACTIVITY

Skills

Examine the map extract of Dungarvan on page 410 and answer the following questions.

(i) Name **three different** phases (periods) of historical settlement evident on the Ordnance Survey map.

(ii) Name and locate, using six-figure grid references, examples of each of the **three** phases of historical settlement named above.

(iii) Explain briefly each of the **three** phases of historical settlement named above.

Rural settlement

› A **rural settlement** is a sparsely populated community that lives in the countryside, away from the more densely populated urban centres.

Factors that influence rural settlement

The location and density of rural settlement are influenced by several physical factors.

FACTORS THAT INFLUENCE RURAL SETTLEMENT	
Altitude	› Most people live on land that is below 200 metres in height, where the climate is favourable and land is mostly fertile. › People avoid upland areas, as soil is infertile and weather can be cold, wet and windy.
Slope	› Gentle gradients make it easier and cheaper to build houses and roads. It is also easier to use machinery on this type of land.
Drainage	› People prefer to settle in well-drained areas. They avoid boggy areas and areas that are prone to flooding. They may choose to build a dry-point settlement on a nearby area of higher ground.
Shelter	› Settlement avoids areas that feel the worst effects of winds. Many settlements are in valley floors or in the lee of an upland area.
Aspect	› Settlement prefers south-facing slopes to obtain the maximum amount of sunshine.

Table 20.4

Rural settlement patterns

Settlement pattern refers to the way or shape in which human settlements are distributed across the landscape. Four patterns of rural settlement can be identified on an OS map extract.

> **ACTIVITY**
>
> **Skills**
>
> Examine the map of Dungarvan on page 410. Identify and locate (by four-figure grid reference) one location where each of the factors in Table 20.5 has influenced settlement.

PATTERNS OF RURAL SETTLEMENT ON OS MAPS	
Nucleated	› Houses are clustered together in small groups. › This usually happens at a small village, where roads meet or at a bridging point.
Linear	› Houses are built in a line along a road. › The pattern also develops along the coast or at the foot of a mountain. › **Ribboned** settlement is a form of linear settlement that develops along a road or roads leading out from a town and into the countryside.
Dispersed	› Individual houses are dispersed around the countryside in a random fashion. › Many are farmhouses, each on its own farm and surrounded by outbuildings. › Others are one-off houses.
Absence	› Some sections of the countryside are completely devoid of settlement. › See the negative factors that influence settlement on page 406.

Table 20.5

Figure 20.19 Rural settlement patterns

> **ACTIVITY**
>
> **Skills**
>
> Examine the OS map of Dungarvan on page 410.
> (i) Identify and locate any **three** patterns of rural settlement.
> (ii) Briefly explain each pattern.

CHAPTER 20 · ORDNANCE SURVEY MAPS

Land use

Land use refers to the way in which people use the land.

Rural land use

Some **rural land use** simply means the ways in which the land is in fact used. Certain land uses can be read directly from the map. Others, such as agriculture, can only be inferred.

Examples of rural land use include:

- Settlement
- Agriculture
- Forestry
- Communications
- Industry
- Power generation
- Leisure/recreation
- Tourism
- Mining.

Tourism and leisure

A wide range of **tourist attractions** and **leisure** (recreation) facilities can be identified on OS maps. Many of them are identified on the legend by symbols. Others must be inferred.

Many of these attractions and facilities are also found in urban areas.

TOURISM, LEISURE ACTIVITIES AND ATTRACTIONS ON OS MAPS	
FEATURE	ACTIVITIES/ATTRACTION
Mountains	› Scenery, hill walking, rock climbing
Rivers and lakes	› Scenery, sailing, canoeing, fishing
Coast, beaches and harbours	› Scenery, swimming, fishing, windsurfing, sunbathing
Forests	› Nature trails, adventure trails, picnic sites, walking
Nature reserves and national parks	› Wildlife, scenery, flora
Antiquities and demesnes	› History, culture
Golf courses and racecourses	› Watching sport, playing sport
Caravan parks and camping grounds	› Accommodation
Youth hostels	› Budget accommodation

Table 20.6

Urban settlement

Urban settlement refers to cities, towns and large villages. These are built-up areas where buildings are closely grouped together.

Factors that influence urban settlement

The location and development of urban settlement is influenced by many factors.

ACTIVITY

Skills

Examine the OS map of Dungarvan on page 410. Identify and locate by grid reference any **five** different examples of rural land use.

ACTIVITY

Skills

Examine the OS map of Dungarvan on page 410. Identify, locate and describe any **three different** attractions that the area has for tourism.

FACTORS THAT INFLUENCE URBAN SETTLEMENT	
Relief	› Most towns are developed on low-lying areas that are flat or gently sloping. › A fertile hinterland could supply sufficient food.
Rivers	› In times past, rivers were used for water supply and transport as well as providing defence from attack. › Towns tended to develop at crossing (bridging) points on rivers.
Transport	› Good transport links enabled trade to develop. This was most likely if the town was built at a route focus. › Being on a rail route (station) or having a canal link (locks) was an advantage too.
Coast	› A coastal location enabled settlements to develop as ports (trade and fishing) as well as tourism destinations.

Table 20.7

Urban functions

Urban functions refer to the services that the town provides for the people who live or work there as well as in its hinterland.

Certain urban functions can be read directly from the map.

Urban functions include the following.

ACTIVITY

Skills

Examine the OS map of Dungarvan on page 410. Identify and describe any **three** factors that led to its development at that location.

URBAN FUNCTIONS	
Residential	› Residential suburbs, housing estates
Industrial	› Industrial estate
Transport	› Roads, railway and station, car parks
Port	› Harbour, pier, quay, lighthouse
Educational	› School, college, university, IOT
Religious	› Cathedral, church
Medical	› Hospital
Recreational	› Golf course, park, stadium
Tourist	› See Table 20.6.

Table 20.8

Other urban functions, such as **retail** (shops), **commercial** (offices) and **finance** (banks), can only be inferred.

Functions of an urban area can **change over time**. Some are now outdated while others have new uses.

ACTIVITY

Skills

Examine the OS map of Dungarvan on page 410.

(i) Identify and describe any **three present-day** functions that the town provides.

(ii) Identify and describe **one past** (historic) function of the town.

CHANGING FUNCTIONS OF AN URBAN AREA	
Defence	› Motte, castle, mound, town wall, town gate
Ecclesiastical	› Priory, abbey, round tower
Transport	› Canals are now used for tourism and leisure rather than for transporting goods. › Many railways have been dismantled. Some of these have been converted to greenways.

Table 20.9

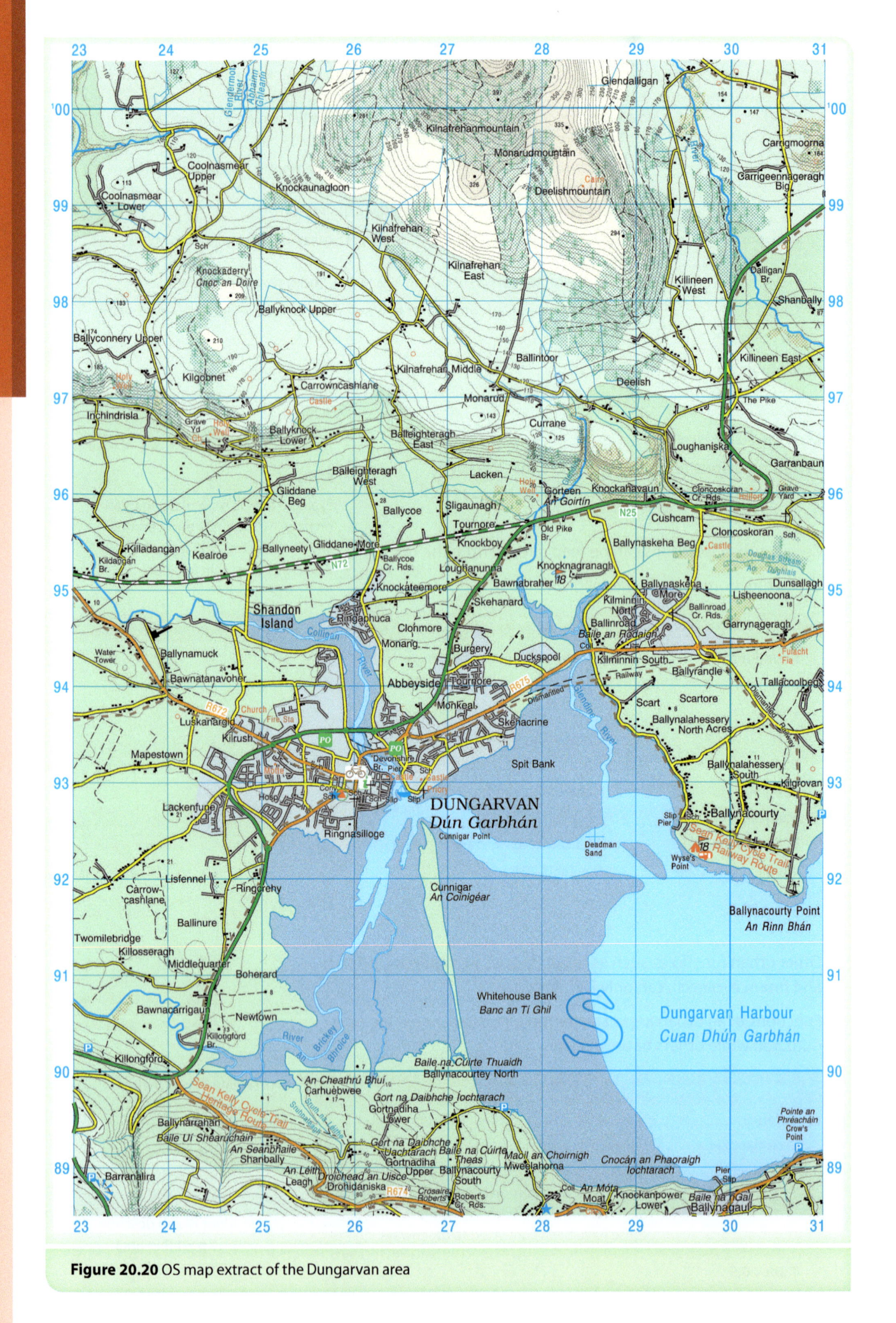

Figure 20.20 OS map extract of the Dungarvan area

Legend Eochair

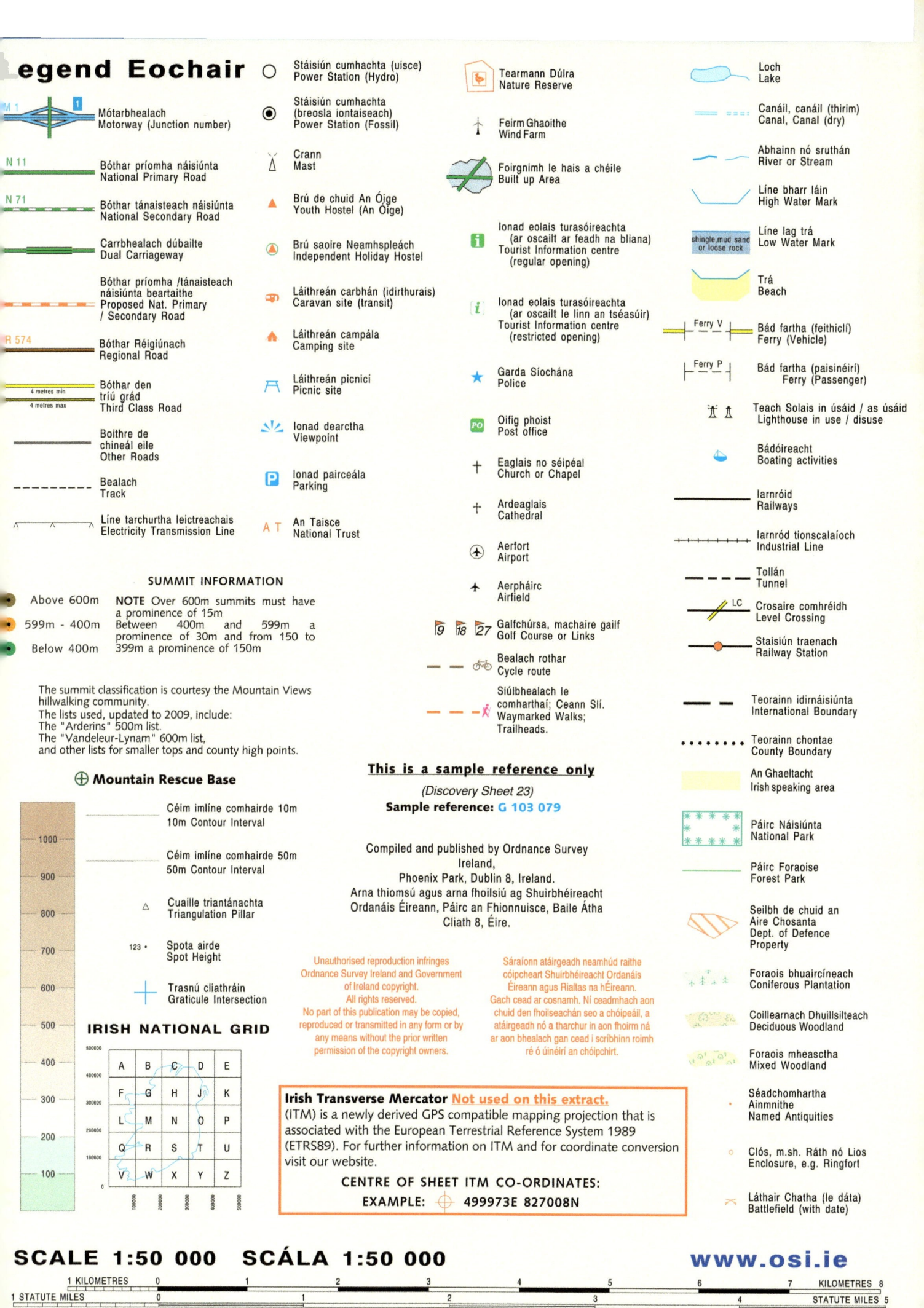

M 1 ①	Mótarbhealach	Motorway (Junction number)
N 11	Bóthar príomha náisiúnta	National Primary Road
N 71	Bóthar tánaisteach náisiúnta	National Secondary Road
	Carrbhealach dúbailte	Dual Carriageway
	Bóthar príomha /tánaisteach náisiúnta beartaithe	Proposed Nat. Primary / Secondary Road
R 574	Bóthar Réigiúnach	Regional Road
4 metres min / 4 metres max	Bóthar den tríú grád	Third Class Road
	Boithre de chineál eile	Other Roads
-------	Bealach	Track
	Líne tarchurtha leictreachais	Electricity Transmission Line

SUMMIT INFORMATION

Above 600m	**NOTE** Over 600m summits must have a prominence of 15m
599m - 400m	Between 400m and 599m a prominence of 30m and from 150 to
Below 400m	399m a prominence of 150m

The summit classification is courtesy the Mountain Views hillwalking community.
The lists used, updated to 2009, include:
The "Arderins" 500m list.
The "Vandeleur-Lynam" 600m list,
and other lists for smaller tops and county high points.

⊕ **Mountain Rescue Base**

	Céim imlíne comhairde 10m	10m Contour Interval
	Céim imlíne comhairde 50m	50m Contour Interval
△	Cuaille triantánachta	Triangulation Pillar
123 •	Spota airde	Spot Height
+	Trasnú cliathráin	Graticule Intersection

IRISH NATIONAL GRID

A	B	C	D	E
F	G	H	J	K
L	M	N	O	P
Q	R	S	T	U
V	W	X	Y	Z

○	Stáisiún cumhachta (uisce)	Power Station (Hydro)
⦿	Stáisiún cumhachta (breosla iontaiseach)	Power Station (Fossil)
	Crann	Mast
▲	Brú de chuid An Óige	Youth Hostel (An Óige)
	Brú saoire Neamhspleách	Independent Holiday Hostel
	Láithreán carbhán (idirthurais)	Caravan site (transit)
▲	Láithreán campála	Camping site
	Láithreán picnící	Picnic site
	Ionad dearctha	Viewpoint
P	Ionad pairceála	Parking
A T	An Taisce	National Trust

	Tearmann Dúlra	Nature Reserve
✈	Feirm Ghaoithe	Wind Farm
	Foirgnimh le hais a chéile	Built up Area
i	Ionad eolais turasóireachta (ar oscailt ar feadh na bliana)	Tourist Information centre (regular opening)
i	Ionad eolais turasóireachta (ar oscailt le linn an tséasúir)	Tourist Information centre (restricted opening)
★	Garda Síochána	Police
PO	Oifig phoist	Post office
†	Eaglais no séipéal	Church or Chapel
✚	Ardeaglais	Cathedral
✈	Aerfort	Airport
✈	Aerpháirc	Airfield
9 18 27	Galfchúrsa, machaire gailf	Golf Course or Links
	Bealach rothar	Cycle route
	Siúlbhealach le comharthaí; Ceann Slí. Waymarked Walks; Trailheads.	

This is a sample reference only
(Discovery Sheet 23)
Sample reference: G 103 079

Compiled and published by Ordnance Survey Ireland,
Phoenix Park, Dublin 8, Ireland.
Arna thiomsú agus arna fhoilsiú ag Shuirbhéireacht Ordanáis Éireann, Páirc an Fhionnuisce, Baile Átha Cliath 8, Éire.

Unauthorised reproduction infringes Ordnance Survey Ireland and Government of Ireland copyright.
All rights reserved.
No part of this publication may be copied, reproduced or transmitted in any form or by any means without the prior written permission of the copyright owners.

Sáraíonn atáirgeadh neamhúd raithe cóipcheart Shuirbhéireacht Ordanáis Éireann agus Rialtas na hÉireann. Gach cead ar cosnamh. Ní ceadmhach aon chuid den fhoilseachán seo a chóipeáil, a atáirgeadh nó a tharchur in aon fhoirm ná ar aon bhealach gan cead i scríbhinn roimh ré ó úinéirí an chóipchirt.

Irish Transverse Mercator Not used on this extract.
(ITM) is a newly derived GPS compatible mapping projection that is associated with the European Terrestrial Reference System 1989 (ETRS89). For further information on ITM and for coordinate conversion visit our website.

CENTRE OF SHEET ITM CO-ORDINATES:
EXAMPLE: ⊕ 499973E 827008N

	Loch	Lake
	Canáil, canáil (thirim)	Canal, Canal (dry)
	Abhainn nó sruthán	River or Stream
	Líne bharr láin	High Water Mark
shingle, mud sand or loose rock	Líne lag trá	Low Water Mark
	Trá	Beach
Ferry V	Bád fartha (feithiclí)	Ferry (Vehicle)
Ferry P	Bád fartha (paisinéirí)	Ferry (Passenger)
	Teach Solais in úsáid / as úsáid	Lighthouse in use / disuse
	Bádóireacht	Boating activities
	Iarnróid	Railways
	Iarnród tionscalaíoch	Industrial Line
	Tollán	Tunnel
LC	Crosaire comhréidh	Level Crossing
●	Staisiún traenach	Railway Station
	Teorainn idirnáisiúnta	International Boundary
....	Teorainn chontae	County Boundary
	An Ghaeltacht	Irish speaking area
	Páirc Náisiúnta	National Park
	Páirc Foraoise	Forest Park
	Seilbh de chuid an Aire Chosanta	Dept. of Defence Property
	Foraois bhuaircíneach	Coniferous Plantation
	Coillearnach Dhuillsilteach	Deciduous Woodland
	Foraois mheasctha	Mixed Woodland
	Séadchomhartha Ainmnithe	Named Antiquities
○	Clós, m.sh. Ráth nó Lios	Enclosure, e.g. Ringfort
✕	Láthair Chatha (le dáta)	Battlefield (with date)

SCALE 1:50 000 SCÁLA 1:50 000

www.osi.ie

2 ceintiméadar sa chiliméadar (taobh chearnóg eangaí) 2 centimetres to 1 Kilometre (grid square side)

PowerPoint Summary

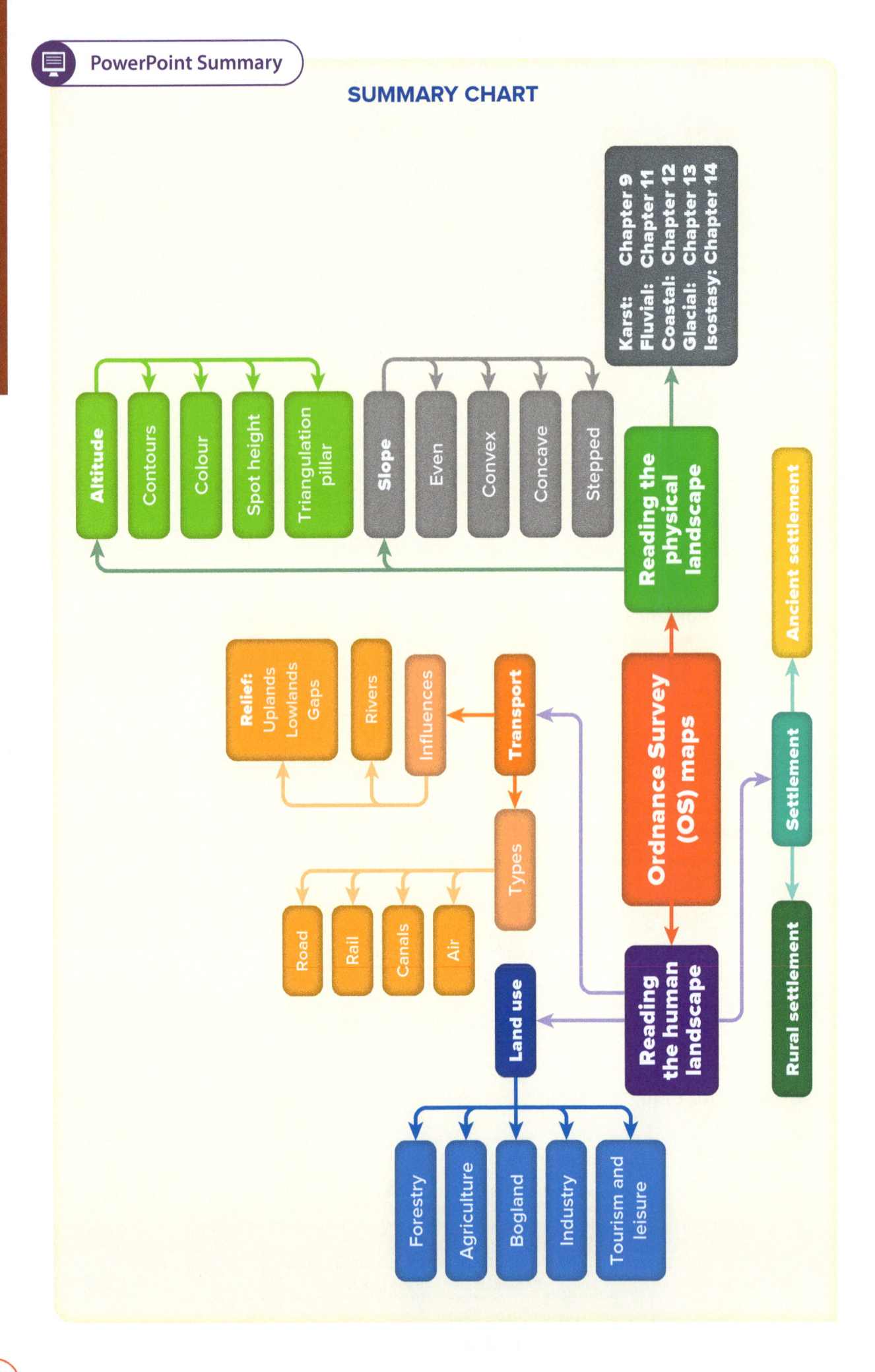

SUMMARY CHART

Ordnance Survey (OS) maps

- **Reading the physical landscape**
  - Altitude: Contours, Colour, Spot height, Triangulation pillar
  - Slope: Even, Convex, Concave, Stepped
  - Karst: Chapter 9
  - Fluvial: Chapter 11
  - Coastal: Chapter 12
  - Glacial: Chapter 13
  - Isostasy: Chapter 14

- **Reading the human landscape**
  - Transport
    - Influences: Relief (Uplands, Lowlands, Gaps), Rivers
    - Types: Road, Rail, Canals, Air
  - Land use: Forestry, Agriculture, Bogland, Industry, Tourism and leisure
  - Settlement: Ancient settlement, Rural settlement

Leaving Cert exam questions

Examine the OS map of Mullaghmore on page 415 to answer the questions on pages 413 and 414.

SHORT QUESTIONS: HIGHER LEVEL

1 Ordnance Survey map (8 marks)
 (i) Identify the settlement pattern at G 76 57.
 (ii) Calculate the area of the body of sea to the east of easting 70.
 (iii) Identify two landforms of coastal deposition at G 69 54.
 (iv) Identify the land use at G 750 550.

2 Ordnance Survey map (8 marks)
 (i) In what direction does one travel along the N15 going from Cliffony towards Tullaghan?
 (ii) Identify the antiquity at G 72 53.
 (iii) How is height shown at G 700 568?
 (iv) Identify the slope type at G 76 51.

SHORT QUESTIONS: ORDINARY LEVEL

1 Ordnance Survey map (10 marks)

Identify the feature that can be found at each of the following grid references:

 (i) Antiquity at G 703 535
 (ii) Settlement pattern at G 78 57
 (iii) Tourist facility at G 702 583
 (iv) How height is shown at G 690 535
 (v) Coastal landform at G 690 540.

2 Ordnance Survey map (10 marks)
 (i) What is the length, in kilometres, of the stretch of R279 shown on the map?
 (ii) Identify the direction when looking from Cliffony (G 70 54) towards Mullaghmore (G 70 57).
 (iii) True or false: All the land in the map extract is below 200 metres in height.
 (iv) Identify the type of woodland at G 76 53.
 (v) Is the landform at G 71 56 the result of coastal erosion or coastal deposition?

LONG QUESTIONS: HIGHER LEVEL

1 Tourism (20 marks)

With reference to the OS map, identify and explain **two** reasons why Mullaghmore and its surrounding area has developed a tourism industry.

2 Land use (30 marks)

With reference to the OS map, identify and describe any **three** land uses in the area shown on the map.

3 Urban functions (20 marks)

With reference to the OS map extract, identify and describe any **two** functions of the village of Mullaghmore.

4 Patterns of settlement (30 marks)

(i) Identify and locate, by four-figure grid reference, four patterns of rural settlement in the area shown on the map.

(ii) Explain the development of any **two** of those patterns in some detail.

LONG QUESTIONS: ORDINARY LEVEL

1 Sketch map (30 marks)

Draw a sketch map of the area shown on the map. On it, show and label each of the following:

(i) The coastline
(ii) The N15
(iii) A built-up area
(iv) Another named road
(v) A named lake
(vi) A church.

2 Economic development (40 marks)

Imagine you have been given the task of finding a suitable location for a new hotel.

(i) State clearly, by grid reference, where you would locate it.

(ii) Explain fully **two** reasons in favour of the location that you chose.

(iii) Explain fully **one** reason against this location.

3 Tourist attractions (40 marks)

(i) Name and give the location by grid reference of any **two** examples of tourist attractions on the map.

(ii) Write a brief description of each attraction and its location.

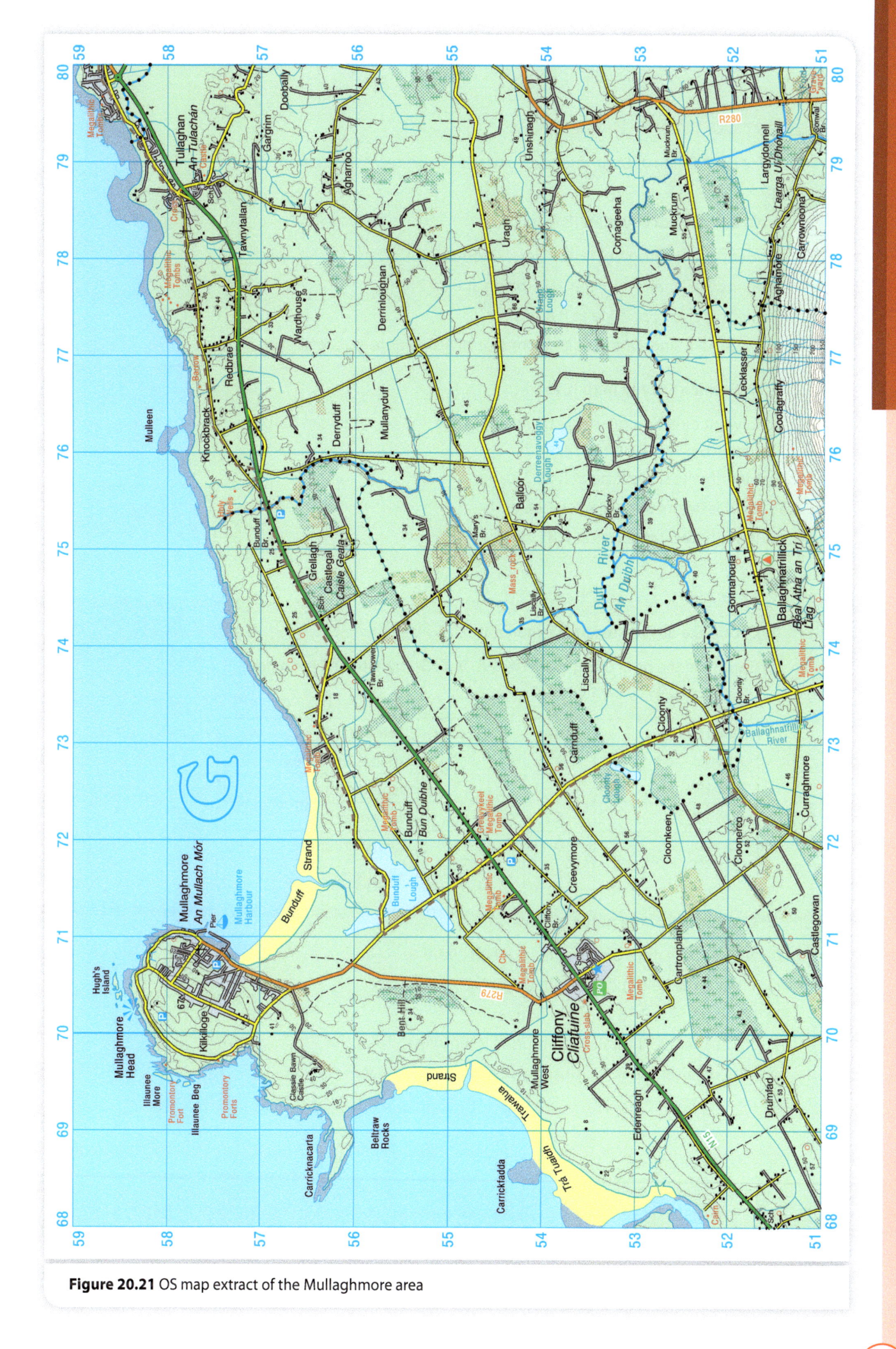

Figure 20.21 OS map extract of the Mullaghmore area

SHORT QUESTIONS: HIGHER LEVEL

Examine the OS map of Lisvarrinane on page 417 to answer the questions on pages 416 and 418.

1 Ordnance Survey map (8 marks)

(i) Identify a landform of fluvial deposition at R 90 30.
(ii) Identify a landform of glacial erosion at R 86 24.
(iii) Identify the slope type at R 84 25.
(iv) Locate a triangulation pillar by means of a six-figure grid reference.

2 Ordnance Survey map (8 marks)

(i) In what direction does one travel along the R663 going from Galbally towards Lisvarrihane?
(ii) Identify the slope type at R 85 25.
(iii) How is height shown at R 879 238?
(iv) Identify **two** land uses at R 85 29.

SHORT QUESTIONS: ORDINARY LEVEL

1 Ordnance Survey maps (10 marks)

Complete the grid, using the letters **A**, **B**, **C**, **D** and **E** to link each grid reference to its correct feature.

Grid reference	Letter
R 90 30	A
R 81 25	B
R 86 24	C
R 81 29	D
R 86 26	E

Letter	Feature
	V-shaped valley
	Isolated hill
	Meanders
	Lowland area
	Cirque/tarn

2 Ordnance Survey maps (10 marks)

(i) Name the feature of antiquity at R 808 299.
(ii) What is the height of the highest point on the map?
(iii) Is the slope at R 86 25 steep or gentle?
(iv) Name the river that flows through Lisvarrinane.
(v) True or false: The R663 runs in an east–west direction.

Figure 20.22 OS map extract of the Lisvarrinane area

CHAPTER 20 · ORDNANCE SURVEY MAPS

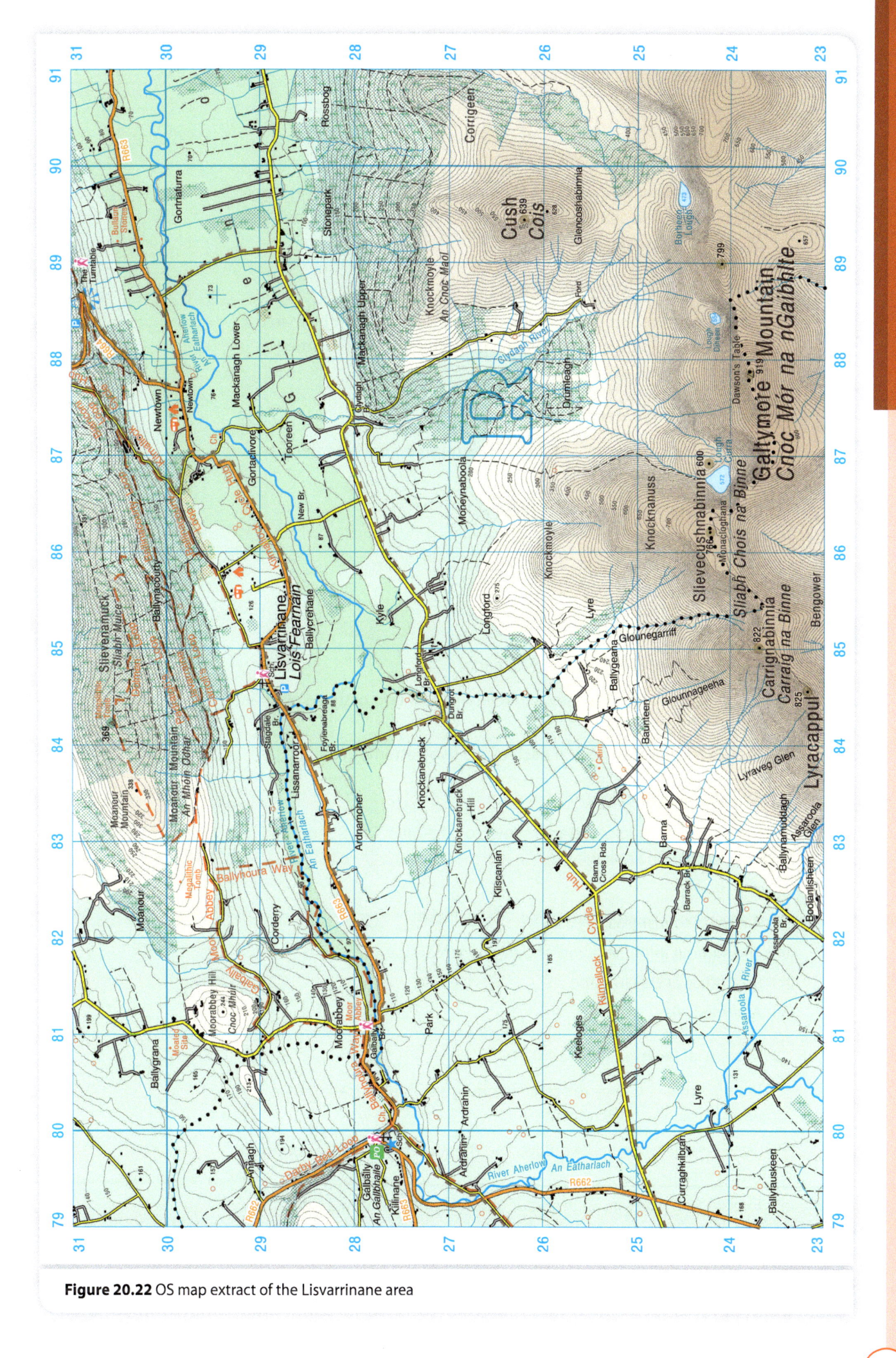

LONG QUESTIONS: HIGHER LEVEL

1 Location of economic activity (30 marks)

Explain **three** reasons why it may be difficult to attract large foreign companies to the area shown on the OS map. Use evidence from the OS map to support each reason.

2 Population distribution (20 marks)

Explain **two** reasons why the region to the south-east of the map is less attractive to human settlement. Use evidence from the map to support each answer.

3 Tertiary economic activity (30 marks)

Discuss the development of tourism in the area shown on the map under the following headings:

(i) Accessibility
(ii) Attractions
(iii) Services (other than transport).

LONG QUESTIONS: ORDINARY LEVEL

1 Patterns of rural settlement (40 marks)

(i) Name and give locations (by grid reference) for **two** patterns of rural settlement on the map.
(ii) Explain the development of **each** of the two patterns in detail.

2 Sketch map (20 marks)

Draw a sketch map of the area shown on the map. On it, show and label each of the following:

(i) The R663
(ii) A named tourist trail
(iii) The summit (highest point) of Galtymore Mountain
(iv) Post office at Lisvarrinane
(v) A named lake.

3 Industrial location (30 marks)

Imagine that you have the task of finding a suitable location for a wind turbine farm (windmills).

(i) State clearly where you would locate the wind farm using a **six-figure** grid reference.
(ii) Explain fully **one** reason in favour of this location and **one** against.

Chapter 21
Aerial Photographs

KEYWORDS

- vertical
- oblique
- background
- middle ground
- foreground
- line of sight
- sketch map
- function
- land use
- traffic management
- urban planning
- greenfield site
- brownfield site

LEARNING OBJECTIVES

By the end of this chapter, you should be able to understand:

- How to identify the different types of aerial photograph
- How to use location and sketching skills
- How to explore the physical, human and economic information contained in an aerial photograph
- The link between OS maps and aerial photographs.

Uses of aerial photographs

Most of the advances in aerial photography were originally developed for military uses. **Aerial photographs** have many other uses, including the following.

- **Map making:** Vertical aerial photographs, taken from various angles, are used in the construction of Ordnance Survey maps.
- **Recovering the hidden landscape:** The foundations of many historic buildings and field patterns are now buried beneath the ground. They can be seen on aerial photographs during dry summers as crop marks.
- **Land use:** Aerial photographs are used to identify various types of farming, e.g. arable, pastoral or forestry. The images are also used to check the accuracy of claims made by farmers for EU subsidies.
- **Planning:** Local authorities and the National Roads Authority (NRA) use aerial photographs for traffic management, land use and to lay out the routes of new roads.

Figure 21.1 Outline of foundations of a star-shaped fort dating from the 1640s

Types of aerial photographs

Aerial photographs are classified according to the angle at which the camera is pointing when they are taken. There are three types of aerial photographs:

> Low oblique
> Vertical
> High oblique.

GEOFACT
Many aerial photographs are now taken using drones rather than planes or helicopters.

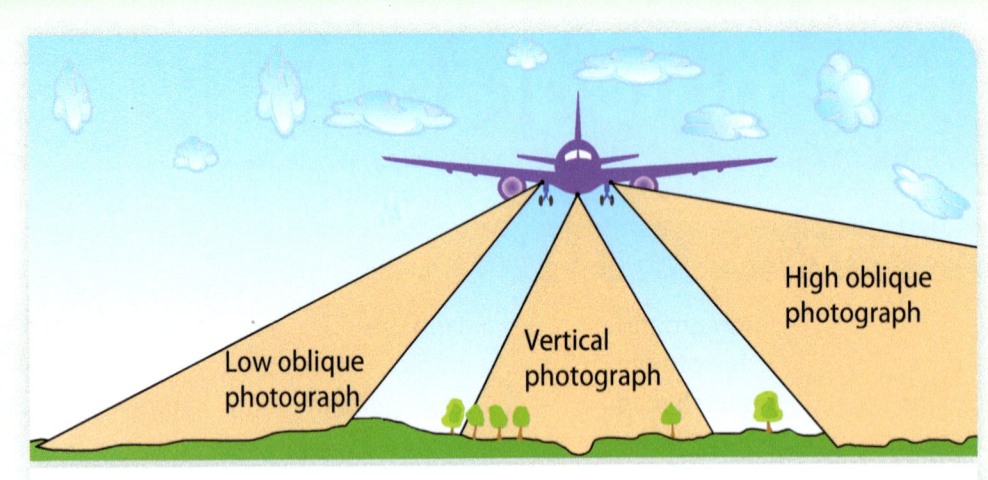

Figure 21.2 The angle that the camera points for each type of aerial photograph

Low oblique photo
> The camera is pointing at an angle of about 30° from the vertical.
> The horizon is never visible.
> Scale is not true. Features in the foreground appear larger than those in the background.
> Sides of buildings are visible.
> The view of features is familiar.

Vertical photo
> The camera is pointing directly down at the ground.
> The roofline of buildings dominates.
> Surface features (roads, etc.) are clearly seen.
> Scale is true throughout the whole photograph.
> The landscape always appears to be flat.
> Direction is as accurate as the map.

High oblique photo
> The camera is pointing at an angle of about 60° from the vertical.
> Some of the horizon is visible in the background.
> It covers a large area.
> Scale is not true. Features in the foreground appear much larger than those in the background.
> Relief may be detected.

Figure 21.3 Low oblique aerial photograph

Figure 21.4 Vertical aerial photograph

Figure 21.5 High oblique aerial photograph

Location on aerial photographs

Aerial photographs should be divided into nine equally sized sections. These can be named according to the type of photograph involved.

Vertical aerial photographs

Direction is true on **vertical aerial photographs**, so features are named according to compass points.

Figure 21.6 Compass points are used to locate features on a vertical aerial photograph

ACTIVITY

Skills

Examine the vertical aerial photograph (left) and describe the location of each of the following:

(i) The town centre
(ii) A motorway junction
(iii) Isolated trees in fields.

LINK

See Figure 20.8 on page 397 for compass directions.

Oblique aerial photographs

Since direction is not true on either **low oblique** or **high oblique** photographs, compass points cannot be used. Instead, the nine sections are named as shown in Figure 21.7.

	Left	Centre	Right
Background	LB	CB	RB
Middle ground	LM	CM	RM
Foreground	LF	CF	RF

Table 21.1 Locating features on oblique aerial photographs

Figure 21.7 Locating features on an oblique aerial photograph

ACTIVITY

Skills

Refer to the aerial photograph of Cavan (left). Give a location for each of the following:

(i) Lake
(ii) School
(iii) Sports ground
(iv) Church spire
(v) Car park.

Identifying camera direction

It is possible to identify the direction in which the camera was pointing when an oblique aerial photograph was taken. To do so, you need the OS map extract of the area shown in the photograph.

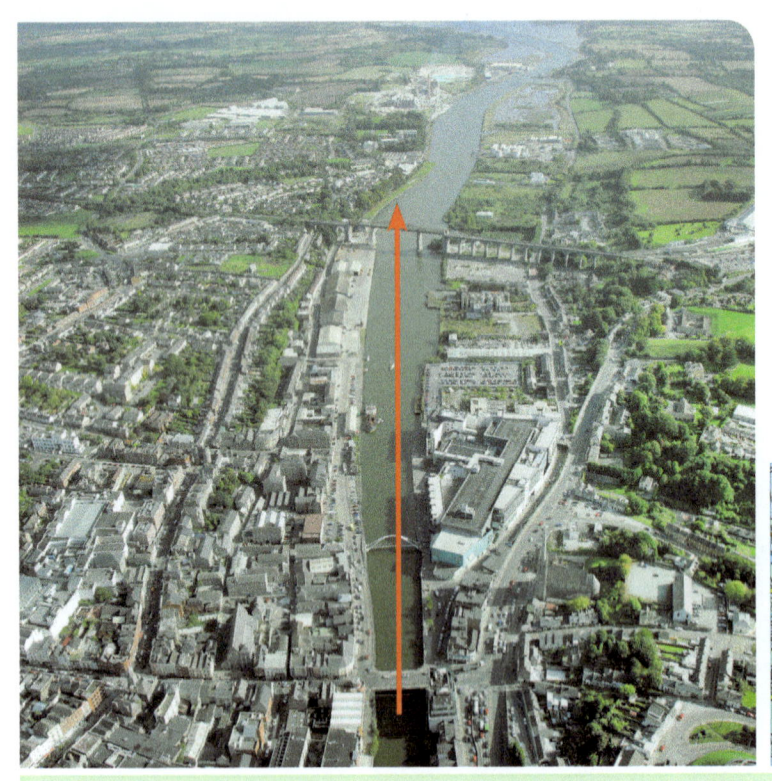

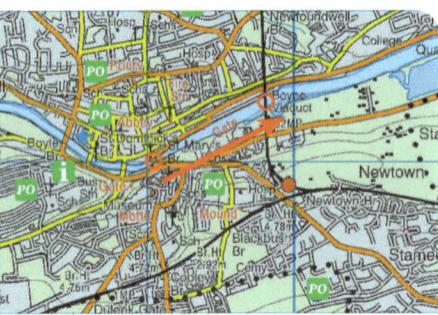

Figure 21.8   The camera was pointing in an ENE/north-easterly direction   **Figure 21.9**

1. Pick two distinctive features on the photograph (Figure 21.8) that follow the **line of sight** of the camera.

   One should be in the foreground and the other in the background.

   > In the above photograph, the two features are the railway viaduct (background) and the nearest road bridge to it (foreground).

2. Draw an arrowed line linking the two features.

3. Look at the OS map extract (Figure 21.9). Identify and mark the same two features (O). Draw an arrow through them (or parallel to them). Ensure that the arrow is pointing in the correct direction.

   > In the above example, the arrow points from the road bridge towards the railway viaduct.

4. Identify this direction with the aid of the compass in Figure 20.8 on page 397.

   > This is also the direction in which the camera was pointing (line of sight).

ACTIVITY

Skills

Examine the aerial photograph and OS map extract of Kenmare on page 433. What direction was the camera pointing when the photograph was taken? **Hint:** Use the main street and the two triangles of the street pattern.

Sketch map of an aerial photograph

Apply these rules when drawing a sketch map of an aerial photograph:

1. Draw a frame that is **half the scale** of the photograph (half the width and half the height). This will ensure that the photograph and sketch map are the same **shape** and have the same **orientation**.
2. Divide the photograph into **nine sections**, as shown below. Lightly mark in the nine sections on your sketch map too. Use the sections as a guide when locating features.
3. Draw in the **coastline** if it is shown.
4. Insert the required features, showing the boundary or **outline** of each.
5. **Identify** each feature by name or key and give the sketch a title.

Hints

- Use a pencil. It is easier to correct mistakes.
- Always start with roads or rivers if they are asked for. They will help you to locate other features.
- Avoid making features such as streets or roads too wide (keep them to scale).
- Show only the features that have been asked for.

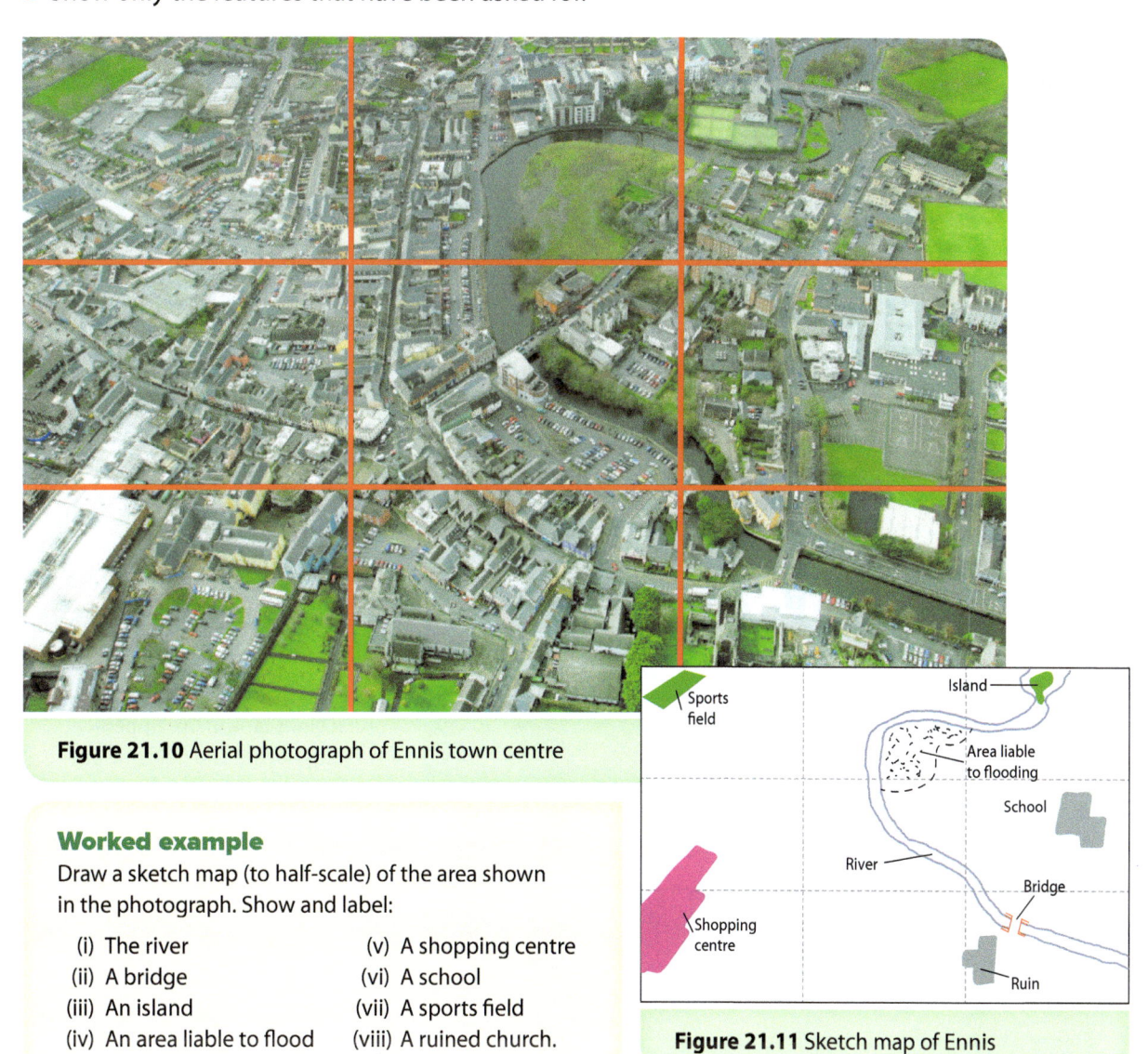

Figure 21.10 Aerial photograph of Ennis town centre

Worked example

Draw a sketch map (to half-scale) of the area shown in the photograph. Show and label:

(i) The river
(ii) A bridge
(iii) An island
(iv) An area liable to flood
(v) A shopping centre
(vi) A school
(vii) A sports field
(viii) A ruined church.

Figure 21.11 Sketch map of Ennis

Identifying the time of year

It is often possible to estimate the time of year (season) when a photograph was taken by recognising some of the following characteristics.

Spring	› Ploughed fields › Some signs of foliage on trees
Summer	› Deciduous trees have full foliage › Animals grazing in fields › Short shadows (high angle of sun) › Different colours in fields (pasture, ripening and harvested crops) › Bales of hay/silage in fields
Autumn	› Various shades of colour on deciduous trees › Longer shadows (lower sun)
Winter	› Deciduous trees have no foliage › Absence of animals in fields › Smoke rising from chimneys

Table 21.2 What to look for when identifying seasons on an aerial photograph

Rural functions and land uses

Rural functions (in bold) and land uses that can be identified on aerial photographs include the following.

Agriculture	› Pastoral farming (fields under grass, animals grazing in fields) › Arable farming (ploughed fields in brown, harvested fields in yellow)
Horticulture	› Market gardening (glasshouses or polytunnels – close to urban areas)
Forestry	› Coniferous plantations, deciduous or mixed woodland
Energy	› Wind farms (windmills), power stations (hydro or fossil fuel)
Tourism and leisure	› Mountains (walking), lakes and rivers (fishing, marinas and boating), caravan parks, golf courses, parks, trails
Residential	› One-off houses, houses, farmhouses

Table 21.3 What to look for when identifying rural land use on an aerial photograph

ACTIVITY

Skills

Examine the photograph below, showing a rural landscape in Co. Tipperary.

(i) Identify the season.
(ii) Give **two** reasons to explain your answer.

ACTIVITY

Skills

Examine the photograph of a rural landscape in Co. Tipperary. Identify, locate and describe any **three** rural land uses.

Figure 21.12 Rural landscape in Co. Tipperary

Factors that influence urban settlement

The location and development of urban settlement is influenced by factors that include the following.

Relief	› Most towns developed on low-lying areas that are flat or gently sloping. › A fertile hinterland could supply sufficient food.
Rivers	› In times past, rivers were used for water supply and transport as well as to provide defence from attack. › Towns tended to develop at crossing (bridging) points on rivers.
Transport	› Good transport links enabled trade to develop. This was most likely if the town was built at a route focus. › Being on a rail route (station) or having a canal link (locks) was an advantage too.
Coast	› A coastal location enabled settlements to develop as ports (trade and fishing) as well as tourism destinations.

Table 21.4 Influences on urban settlement

Urban functions and land uses

Urban functions (in bold) and land uses that can be identified on aerial photographs include the following:

› **Residential** (apartments, housing estates – detached, semi-detached, terraced, bungalows)
› **Transport** (roads, rail, car parks, canals, airports)
› **Port** (docks, piers, containers, cranes)
› **Retail** (shops, shopping streets, shopping centres)
› **Commercial** (office blocks)
› **Religious/ecclesiastical** (cathedrals, churches, abbeys, convents)
› **Industrial** (industrial estates, factories)
› **Education** (schools, colleges)
› **Recreation/leisure** (tennis courts, sports grounds, golf courses)
› **Tourist** (marinas, beaches, antiquities, golf courses, caravan parks).

It is also possible to identify some **former functions** of a town. These include:

› **Defensive** (castles, towers, town walls, mottes)
› **Industrial** (mill-races, weirs, old mill buildings)
› **Market** (market squares, warehouses near a river or canal)
› **Monastic** (abbeys).

QUESTION

Examine the photograph of Drogheda on page 422. Identify and describe **two** reasons why the town developed at that location.

ACTIVITY

Skills

Examine the photograph of Kilkenny town centre. Identify, locate and describe:

(i) Any **four present-day** urban functions or land uses
(ii) **One former** (historic) function.

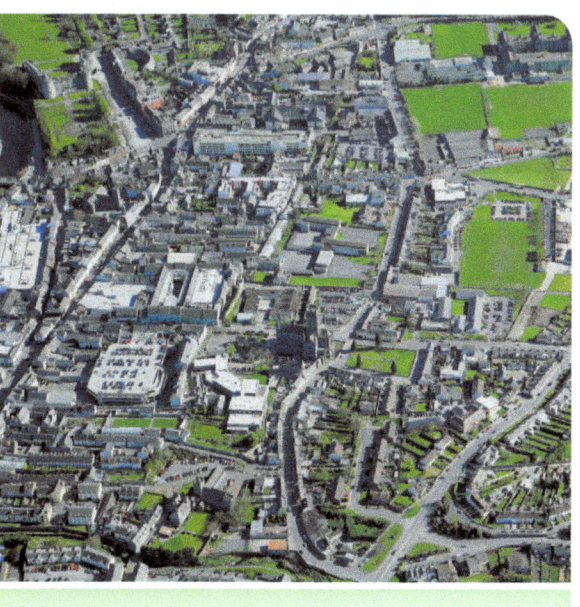

Figure 21.13 Kilkenny town centre

Traffic management

Traffic management involves organising traffic so that it uses the existing road and street system efficiently. Its main goal is to reduce or eliminate **traffic congestion**.

Traffic congestion is when vehicles travel at slower speeds because there are more vehicles than the roads can handle. This makes trip times longer and causes traffic jams. The places where traffic congestion is most likely to occur include:

> Main shopping streets and shopping centres
> Where several streets meet
> Narrow streets and bridges
> Where on-street parking occurs
> Roads close to schools.

Many of the measures that have been taken to **reduce traffic congestion** can be identified on aerial photographs. They include:

> Traffic lights to control traffic flow
> Filter lanes to allow traffic to turn in the direction of the arrow at a junction
> Yellow boxes at busy junctions to prevent traffic from blocking them
> Double yellow lines to prevent on-street parking
> Pedestrianised streets in the main shopping areas
> Roundabouts to reduce delays at junctions
> One-way streets to regulate traffic flow, especially in narrow streets
> Bypasses and ring roads to reduce the amount of traffic passing through towns
> Off-street parking and multi-storey car parks
> Bus lanes and cycle lanes.

ACTIVITY

Skills

Examine the aerial photograph of Eden Quay. Identify and describe **three** ways in which traffic is being managed.

Figure 21.14 Traffic management measures at Eden Quay, Dublin

Urban planning and development

Most urban expansion is accounted for by the growth in residential areas, industrial estates and services such as shopping centres, schools and hotels.

Development needs to be properly planned. The three key aspects to be considered are:

> Site
> Transport
> Environment.

Site

Site refers to the area of land where development takes place.

Greenfield sites have not previously been built on. These sites are found on the outskirts of towns and may include greenbelt land. These are usually easier and cheaper to develop. Larger parcels of land are also available.

> A large site is important for future expansion and storage as well as for providing parking facilities and playing fields.
> Overdevelopment may lead to urban sprawl. Traffic congestion may result as more people travel into urban areas from greenfield residential developments.

Brownfield sites consist of unused or derelict land and are found in urban areas. Many of these sites contain buildings that have become vacant.

> Building on these sites reduces urban sprawl. It also reduces the demand for car use.
> They may be expensive to develop because the site needs to be cleared. This is particularly true if it has been contaminated by former industrial use.

Transport

Transport requirements vary depending on the type of development. There may be conflict between differing demands.

> Efficient movement of goods (raw materials or finished products) requires easy access to motorways, main roads, a railway or port.
> Shopping centres and residential areas also require access to main roads. This is because the car is the most common form of transport and the availability of public transport may be limited.
> Schools should be located away from main roads due to traffic danger, noise and air pollution. They should also be close to residential areas to reduce the need for transport.

Environment

The proximity of industrial development to residential developments and schools needs to be considered. The main issues are noise levels, pollution and transport considerations.

Figure 21.15 Roscommon town

QUESTION

Examine the photograph of Roscommon town. It has been proposed that a supermarket will be built in the field in the right foreground. Identify and describe:

(i) **Two** advantages of the site for that purpose

(ii) **One** disadvantage of the site for that purpose.

Comparing OS maps and aerial photographs

The type of information and the way it is presented varies between maps and photographs. OS maps use symbols to show information, while aerial photographs show an actual image of the landscape.

ASPECT	OS MAP	AERIAL PHOTOGRAPH
Presentation	› Information is shown by symbols and colour.	› Photos show an image of the actual landscape.
Scale and distance	› Maps are true to scale. › Scale is stated on map.	› Vertical photographs are true to scale. › Oblique photographs are not true to scale.
Area	› Maps usually show a large area.	› Aerial photographs show smaller areas.
Direction	› Direction is stated and shown on a map by an arrow that points to the north.	› Direction is true on a vertical photograph. › Direction varies on oblique photographs.
Location	› Exact location by grid references.	› Location is given in general terms.
Altitude and gradient	› Clearly shown by contours, colour, etc. › Gradient can be calculated.	› Altitude can't be found. › Gradient is difficult to observe.
Transport	› Roads are identified by type and number. › Minor roads and some urban roads/streets are not shown.	› All roads are shown, but not by type or number. › Evidence of traffic management can be observed.
Functions and land use	› Some services and important public buildings are named. › Individual buildings in built-up areas are not shown. › Forestry and mining are named, but other rural land uses can only be inferred.	› Buildings are not named, but some uses and functions can be inferred. › Individual buildings and their shapes are shown. › The height of buildings (in storeys) can be seen on oblique photos. › Rural land use can be identified.

Table 21.5 Differences in how information is shown on OS maps and aerial photographs

📺 **PowerPoint Summary**

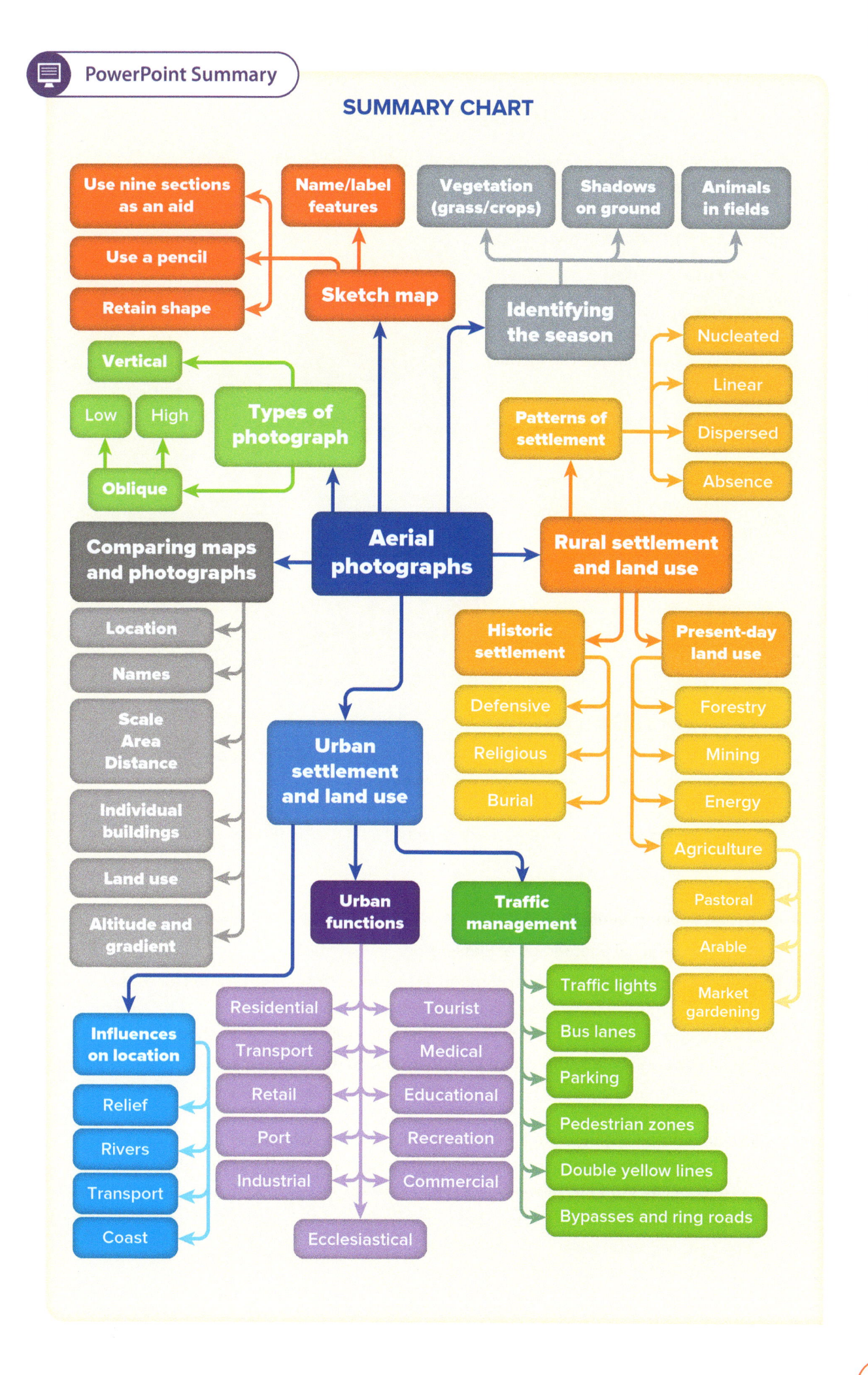

SUMMARY CHART

Aerial photographs

- **Sketch map**
  - Use nine sections as an aid
  - Use a pencil
  - Retain shape
  - Name/label features

- **Identifying the season**
  - Vegetation (grass/crops)
  - Shadows on ground
  - Animals in fields

- **Types of photograph**
  - Vertical
  - Oblique
    - Low
    - High

- **Rural settlement and land use**
  - **Patterns of settlement**
    - Nucleated
    - Linear
    - Dispersed
    - Absence
  - **Historic settlement**
    - Defensive
    - Religious
    - Burial
  - **Present-day land use**
    - Forestry
    - Mining
    - Energy
    - Agriculture
      - Pastoral
      - Arable
      - Market gardening

- **Comparing maps and photographs**
  - Location
  - Names
  - Scale / Area / Distance
  - Individual buildings
  - Land use
  - Altitude and gradient

- **Urban settlement and land use**
  - **Influences on location**
    - Relief
    - Rivers
    - Transport
    - Coast
  - **Urban functions**
    - Residential
    - Transport
    - Retail
    - Port
    - Industrial
    - Tourist
    - Medical
    - Educational
    - Recreation
    - Commercial
    - Ecclesiastical
  - **Traffic management**
    - Traffic lights
    - Bus lanes
    - Parking
    - Pedestrian zones
    - Double yellow lines
    - Bypasses and ring roads

UNIT 3 · GRAPH SKILLS & GI

CHAPTER 21 · AERIAL PHOTOGRAPHS

Leaving Cert exam questions

Examine the aerial photograph of Blessington on page 431 to answer the questions on pages 430 and 431.

SHORT QUESTIONS: HIGHER LEVEL

1 Land use (8 marks)

Examine the aerial photograph of Blessington. Identify and locate any **four** land uses that you can identify.

2 Location on an aerial photograph (8 marks)

Examine the aerial photograph of Blessington. Using accepted notation, write the correct location of each of the sections shown here from the aerial photograph.

SHORT QUESTIONS: ORDINARY LEVEL

1 Location on an aerial photograph (10 marks)

Examine the aerial photograph of Blessington. Using accepted notation, write the correct location of each of the following:

(i) A bridge
(ii) A roundabout
(iii) A quarry with a pile of gravel
(iv) A church
(v) Tennis courts.

LONG QUESTIONS: HIGHER LEVEL

1 Urban development (30 marks)

Examine the aerial photograph of Blessington.

(i) Using correct notation (right background, etc.), suggest a suitable location for a new shopping centre.
(ii) Explain **two** reasons why the location you chose is a suitable one for a shopping centre.
(iii) Explain **one** reason why there might be objections to the development.

2 Sketch map (20 marks)

Examine the aerial photograph of Blessington. Draw a sketch map of the area shown on the aerial photograph (half the length and half the breadth). On it, correctly show and label each of the following:

› The shoreline of the lake
› A Y-shaped street pattern
› Any **three** urban functions or land uses.

LONG QUESTIONS: ORDINARY LEVEL

1 **Aerial photograph** (30 marks)

Examine the aerial photograph of Blessington.

(i) Identify the season in which the photograph was taken. List **two** pieces of evidence that support your answer.

(ii) Identify and locate any **three** different residential types in the photograph.

2 **Aerial photograph** (30 marks)

Examine the aerial photograph of Blessington. Identify and locate, using correct notation (right background, etc.), **one** example of **each** of the following land uses:

(i) Religious
(ii) Residential
(iii) Industrial
(iv) Recreational
(v) Retail.

Figure 21.16 Oblique aerial photograph of Blessington

SHORT QUESTIONS: HIGHER LEVEL

Examine the aerial photograph and OS map of Kenmare on page 433 to answer the questions on pages 432 and 433.

1 Aerial photograph and OS map (8 marks)

Examine the aerial photograph **and** the OS map extract of Kenmare.

(i) Give a six-figure grid reference for the church located in the centre foreground of the aerial photograph.
(ii) In what direction was the camera pointing when the photograph was taken?
(iii) Name the main road that runs through the aerial photograph from the centre background to the centre foreground.
(iv) State **one** piece of evidence from the OS map or the aerial photograph that indicates that Kenmare is a plantation town.

2 Aerial photograph (8 marks)

Examine the aerial photograph of Kenmare.

(i) Identify **two** rural land uses.
(ii) Identify the season when the photograph was taken. Give **one** piece of evidence to support your choice.
(iii) Suggest a likely function (use) for the large building in the left background.
(iv) What type of aerial photograph is this?

SHORT QUESTIONS: ORDINARY LEVEL

1 Location on an aerial photograph (10 marks)

Examine the aerial photograph of Kenmare. Using the standard notation (centre background, etc.), describe the locations of each of the sections from the aerial photograph shown here. One has been completed for you.

LONG QUESTIONS: HIGHER LEVEL

1 Sketch map (20 marks)

Examine the aerial photograph. Draw a sketch map, half the length and half the breadth. On it, correctly show and label each of the following:

- A car park
- The triangular street network in the middle ground
- A large commercial/industrial building in the foreground
- An area of waste ground suitable for development.

HL   **2 Urban functions** (30 marks)

Examine the aerial photograph. Describe and explain **three** different functions of Kenmare, using evidence from the aerial photograph to support your answer.

OL   ### LONG QUESTIONS: ORDINARY LEVEL

1 Urban development (30 marks)

Examine the aerial photograph of Kenmare.

(i) Using correct notation (right background, etc.), suggest a suitable location for a new school.

(ii) Explain **three** reasons why the location you chose in part (i) would be a suitable location for a new school.

2 Development of towns (40 marks)

Using the aerial photograph **and** the OS map extract, explain **three** reasons why the town of Kenmare developed at its present location.

3 Traffic management (30 marks)

Examine the aerial photograph. Identify and describe any **three** ways by which the local authority has attempted to manage traffic flow in the town.

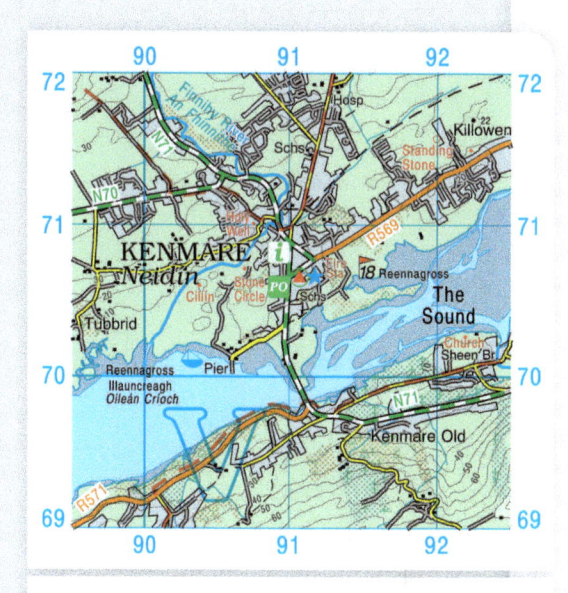

Figure 21.17 OS map extract of Kenmare

Figure 21.18 Oblique aerial photograph of Kenmare

CHAPTER 21 · AERIAL PHOTOGRAPHS   433

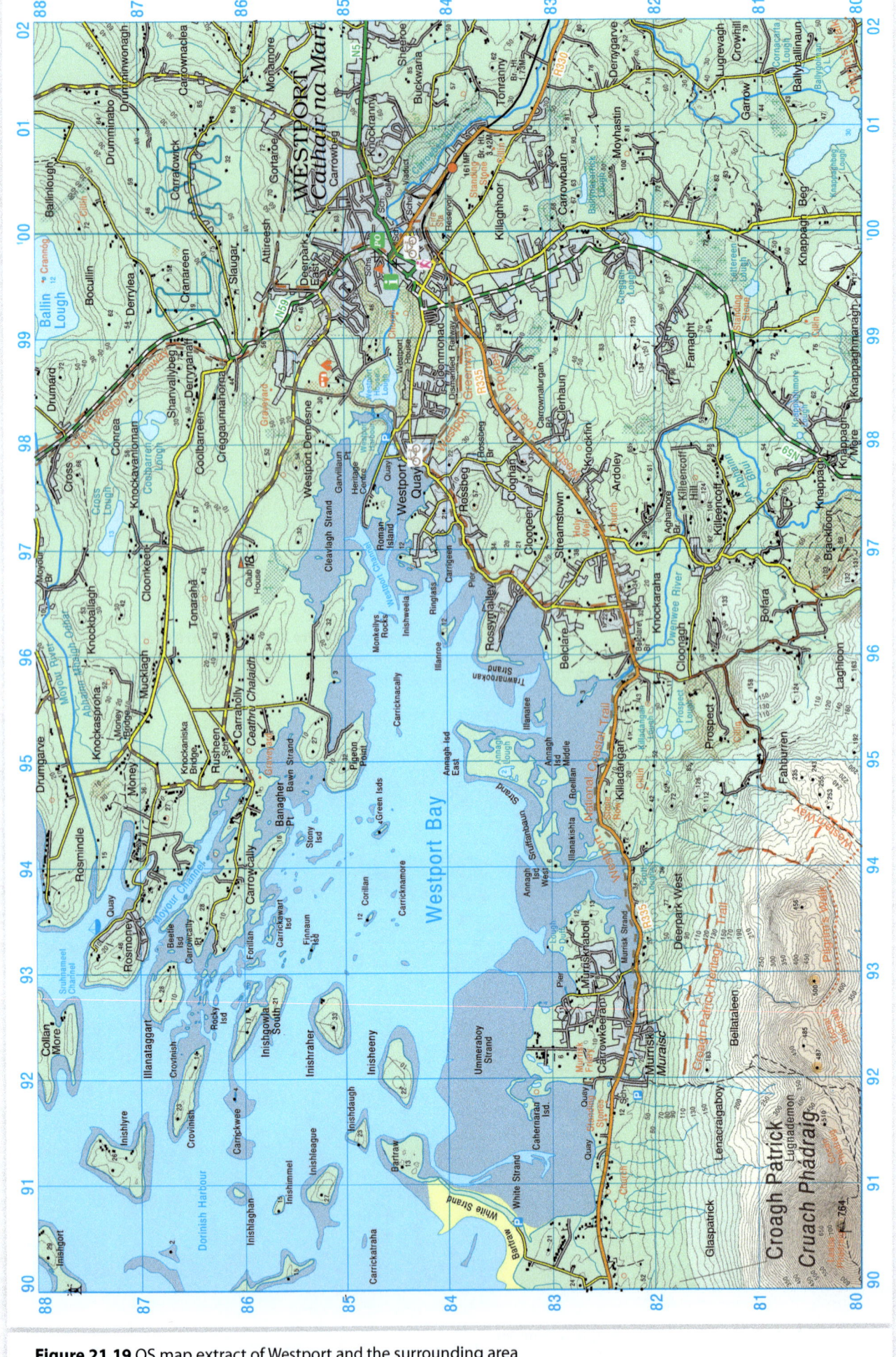

Figure 21.19 OS map extract of Westport and the surrounding area

Figure 21.20 Oblique aerial photograph of Westport

SHORT QUESTIONS: HIGHER LEVEL

Examine the OS map of Westport on page 434 and the aerial photograph of Westport on page 435 to answer the questions on pages 436 and 437.

1 Relief and landforms on an OS map (8 marks)

Examine the OS map extract of Westport and identify each of the following:

(i) The slope type at L 90 81
(ii) The drainage pattern at L 90 82
(iii) Two coastal landforms at L 90 83
(iv) Two fluvial landforms at L 97 80.

2 Historic development on the OS map (8 marks)

Examine the OS map extract. Identify and locate by grid reference **one** example of each of the following:

(i) Pre-Christian settlement
(ii) Early Christian settlement
(iii) Norman/Plantation settlement
(iv) Modern settlement.

3 Location on an aerial photograph (8 marks)

Examine the aerial photograph of Westport. Using accepted notation, write the correct location of each of the sections from the aerial photograph shown here.

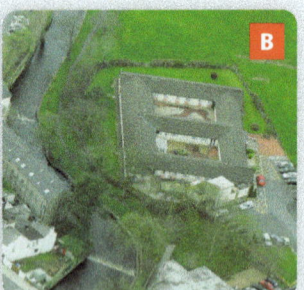

SHORT QUESTIONS: ORDINARY LEVEL

1 Ordnance Survey map (10 marks)

Examine the 1:50,000 Ordnance Survey map on page 434 and the legend on page 411. Name the features that can be found at each of the following grid references:

(i) L 983 846
(ii) L 969 860
(iii) L 996 879
(iv) M 013 838
(v) M 006 840.

2 Ordnance Survey map (10 marks)

Examine the OS map extract of Westport.

(i) Calculate, in kilometres squared, the area of the full map extract.
(ii) Measure the length, in kilometres, of the section of the N59 shown in the extract.

LONG QUESTIONS: HIGHER LEVEL

1. **Urban functions with aerial photograph** (30 marks)

   Name, locate (using accepted notation) and explain **three** different urban functions evident on the aerial photograph of Westport.

2. **Urban development with aerial photograph and OS map** (30 marks)

   Using the aerial photograph **and** the OS map extract, explain **three** reasons why the town of Westport grew up at this location.

3. **Rural settlement patterns with OS map** (30 marks)

   Identify, locate and explain any **three** rural settlement patterns in the area shown on the OS map extract.

4. **Economic development with aerial photograph and OS map** (30 marks)

   Using the aerial photograph **and** the OS map extract, explain **three** reasons why the town of Westport developed as the centre of economic activity for the region shown on the map.

LONG QUESTIONS: ORDINARY LEVEL

1. **Economic development with OS map** (40 marks)

   Examine the 1:50,000 Ordnance Survey map on page 434 and the legend on page 411. Imagine you have been given the task of finding a suitable location for a new large hotel within the area covered by the map.

   (i) State, using a six-figure grid reference, where you would locate the hotel.
   (ii) Explain **two** reasons why you chose this location.
   (iii) Describe **one** disadvantage of locating the hotel at this location.

2. **Sketch map of aerial photograph** (30 marks)

   Examine the aerial photograph of Westport. Draw a sketch map of the area shown on the aerial photograph. On it, **show** and **label** each of the following:
   - A bridge
   - Two churches
   - Two connecting streets
   - A large car park in the centre background.

3. **Urban development with OS map** (30 marks)

   Examine the OS map extract. Explain **three** reasons why the town of Westport grew up at this location.

Chapter 22
Satellite Images

UNIT 3 · GRAPH SKILLS & GI

KEYWORDS

› satellite image
› change over time

LEARNING OBJECTIVE

By the end of this chapter, you should be able to understand:
› How to interpret the use of satellite images of both physical and human landscapes.

Introduction

Satellite images are photographs that are gathered by a global satellite network. Some satellites orbit the Earth at regular intervals, while others stay in the same position in space.

ADVANTAGES OF SATELLITE IMAGES	DISADVANTAGES OF SATELLITE IMAGES
› Each image can cover a large area, showing up to 100 square kilometres per square centimetre of map. › Satellite images also provide more detail than regular aerial photographs, for example temperature and humidity of the atmosphere and temperature of the oceans.	› It takes a long time to process the large pictures using such a high resolution. › Ideal conditions also required over a large area. These include cloud cover and the position of the sun. If the conditions are not ideal, it may be days or even weeks until the satellite will return to the area that needs to be photographed.

Table 22.1

Uses of satellite images

Satellite images have many uses. The data that they provide can be interpreted to:
› Find out how a natural disaster has affected an area
› Reveal what type of vegetation is present and its current status
› Check on agricultural land use for grant purposes
› Study change over time, for example the effects of deforestation and ice melt
› Help forecast the weather
› Examine urban growth
› Assist in military operations.

GEOFACT

The Department of Agriculture uses about 6,000 satellite images per year to see if fields are being properly farmed.

Coastal landscapes

Atoll

This atoll (a circular island of coral and some sand dunes) is located in the Pacific Ocean, close to the equator. It completely encircles a lagoon that is 6 km in diameter.

Nukuoro is remote. It has no airstrip and a passenger boat calls only once a month. The tiny population of about 900 people speaks its own unique language. Fishing, animal husbandry and growing vegetables are the main occupations.

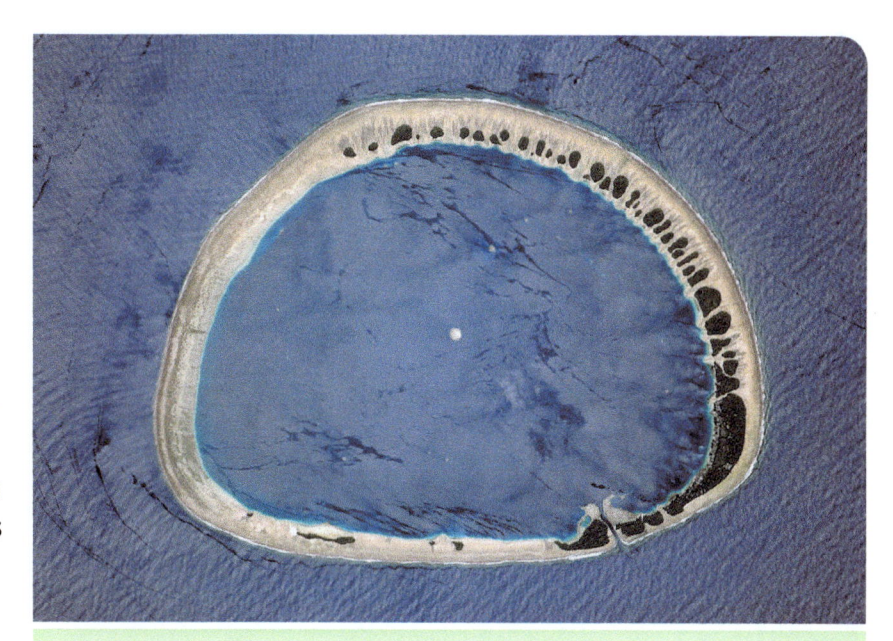

Figure 22.1 Nukuoro, an atoll in the Pacific Ocean

Lagoon

A narrow barrier island (an offshore bar that has risen above sea level) protects the lagoon of Venice from storm waves in the Adriatic Sea. Breakwaters protect the three entrances to the lagoon.

The city of Venice, with its red-tiled roofs, is built on an island and connected to the mainland by a causeway. What appears to be another causeway joining the island to the airport (right background) is actually the combined wakes of water taxis shuttling between them.

Figure 22.2 Venice is an island city, built in a lagoon

River landscapes

Mouth of the Amazon

This image shows the mouth of the Amazon where it flows into the Atlantic Ocean through a number of distributaries. The Amazon carries the largest volume of fresh water in the world, accounting for nearly 20% of the Earth's discharge into the oceans. Much of the sediment is transported far away from the shore.

Figure 22.3 Muddy mouth of the Amazon River

Meanders in Kazakhstan

The current course of the river is shown in green. The floodplain is shown here as a tangle of twisting meanders and meander scars. One section of the river has been straightened (canalised). The flow of water to the floodplain is controlled by a series of dams in the mountain valleys upstream.

ACTIVITY

Skills

Examine the satellite image of the river valley (below). Identify three landforms of deposition on Figure 22.5.

Figure 22.4 River valley in Kazakhstan

Mountain landscapes

Figure 22.5 The Aletsch Glacier in the Swiss Alps

The Aletsch Glacier

The Eiger, at almost 4,000 metres, is one of the higher peaks of the Alps. The Aletsch Glacier, with its range of medial moraines, flows south in its U-shaped valley from the cirques of the Eiger. The image also shows several hanging valleys, arêtes and pyramidal peaks.

Plate tectonics

This is a false-colour satellite image taken over East Africa. The African Plate is breaking up here.

As a result of the spread, a rift valley with a flat floor and steep sides has developed.

Volcanoes are often associated with spreading zones. Magma rising to fill the gaps reaches the surface and builds up cones. If one of the cones collapses following a violent eruption, a caldera is the result. Further spreading can fracture the volcanoes, which is evident on the two large volcanoes in the rift valley.

> **ACTIVITY**
>
> **Skills**
>
> Using the usual location terms for a photograph, locate an example of each landform listed in the *Aletsch Glacier* section on Figure 22.5.

Figure 22.6 Volcanoes in the African Rift Valley

CHAPTER 22 · SATELLITE IMAGES

Desert landscapes

Sahara and Arabian Deserts

A thick band of dust snakes across the Red Sea from Saudi Arabia (right) towards Egypt (left). The dust plume is hundreds of kilometres across and so thick that it completely hides the desert surface in places.

The Nile River Valley appears as a thick, fertile green band on either side of the Nile River as it flows north towards the triangular Nile Delta.

A tectonic fault that contains the Dead Sea can be seen in the centre background.

Figure 22.7 Sandstorm in the Sahara and Arabian Deserts

ACTIVITY

Skills
Identify (i) the Nile delta (ii) the floodplain of the Nile River and (iii) a tectonic fault on Figure 22.7.

Solar energy

One of the largest solar power plants in the world is located in the California deserts. It covers an area of 25 km² and is made up of 9 million solar panels. This source of clean, renewable energy produces enough electricity to power about 180,000 homes.

Other solar energy farms are also under construction in the area.

ACTIVITY

Skills
Identify a tectonic fault in the satellite image of the solar energy farm.

Figure 22.8 Solar energy farm in California

Figure 22.9 Volcanic cone and eruption in Japan

Volcanic activity

Central vent eruption

Figure 22.9 shows a volcanic eruption on one of Japan's many volcanic mountains. Note the ash column rising into the atmosphere and the pyroclastic flow rushing down the side of the volcano.

Fissure eruption

Figure 22.10 shows lava flowing from fissures beneath Iceland's largest glacier in 2015. This was the largest lava flow in Iceland for several hundred years. It now covers nearly 100 km^2.

Fresh lava is bright orange. Newly formed basaltic rock is black. The plume of steam and sulphur dioxide appears white.

Figure 22.10 Fissure eruption and lava flow in Iceland

Disasters

Forest fires

Hundreds of fires raged through woodland in Portugal in August 2016, as shown in Figure 22.11. The landscape had been left tinder dry by months of drought. High temperatures, strong winds and rough terrain produced what firefighters called a 'perfect storm'.

Landslides

Figure 22.12 is a satellite image of one of the largest landslides not caused by an earthquake. The landslide occurred in Myanmar (Burma) after a tropical storm drenched the area.

Over 150 mm of rainfall per hour fell as the storm moved in from the ocean. The intense rainfall triggered destructive flooding and numerous landslides.

Figure 22.11 Forest fires in Portugal

Figure 22.12 Effects of landslides in Myanmar

ACTIVITY

Discussion

Identify two dangers that the landscape in the satellite image (Figure 22.12) now poses for people.

Flooding

Figures 22.13 and 22.14 illustrate the Great Flood of 1993, when the flood control system of the Mississippi River and its tributaries failed. The upper drainage basin received almost double the usual average rainfall over a six-month period.

Figure 22.13 Before the flood

Figure 22.14 After the flood

Floods overwhelmed the system of dykes, levees, dams and other water control structures, leading to the greatest flood ever recorded on the Upper Mississippi. In St Louis, the Mississippi remained above flood stage for five months.

Deforestation

Change over time

Tropical forests are threatened by many types of farming, ranching and other human activities. One of the best ways to track those threats is by using satellites. These are two images of part of the Amazon forest in Peru taken less than twelve months apart. It is estimated that deforestation has taken place at a rate of roughly 250 acres per week. The newest threat to the Amazon forests is the clearing of land for palm oil plantations.

Figure 22.15 Before deforestation

Figure 22.16 One year later

Climate change

Arctic ice melt

These images show how the sea ice of the Arctic declined from 1980 to 2012.

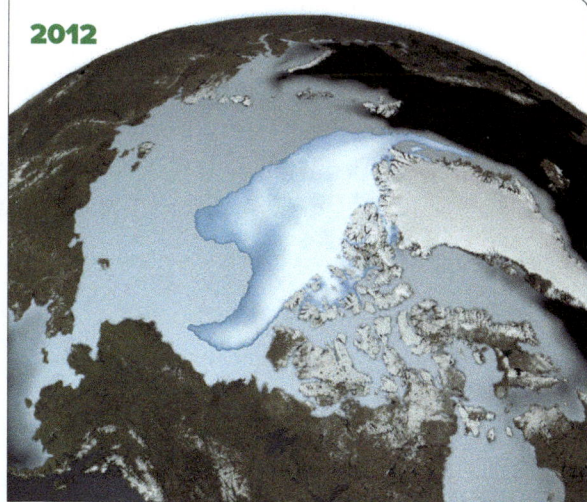

Figure 22.17 The old, thick ice (shown here as the bright white mass) is 'permanent' ice cover that should survive the summer melt season. However, its area is rapidly declining. Young ice that has formed over winter (shown here in light blue) just as quickly melts again in summer. Greenland is the land mass shown in grey.

Urban growth over time

Urban sprawl

The images in Figure 22.18 cover an area 50 km x 50 km. They show the growth of the Chinese city of Shenzhen over a ten-year period.

In the 1970s, Shenzhen was a small fishing village. The transformation to a modern city was rapid and widespread. It included expansion on land as well as reclaiming large areas of shallow sea. Today, Shenzhen is China's second largest port.

ACTIVITY

Discussion

Examine Figure 22.18. Describe the changes that have taken place in:

(i) The harbour area
(ii) The interior.

Figure 22.18 Large-scale urban development in Shenzhen

Hydro-electricity production

The Three Gorges

The Three Gorges Dam, built on the Yangtze River, is the world's largest hydro-electric power (HEP) generator. The dam was also built to control serious flooding in the lower Yangtze.

The dam is 2.4 km wide and holds back a 650 km-long reservoir. Almost 1.5 million people were displaced by its construction. Two issues have been identified with the dam. About 40 million tons of alluvium settle on the bed of the reservoir instead of being carried downstream. The dam is also built on a seismic fault.

Figure 22.19 The original river

Figure 22.20 The dams and reservoirs

Drought

California drought, 2012 to 2016

California gets one-third of its water supply from mountain snow melt. Figure 22.21 shows the situation in early spring. Most of the Sierra Nevada is covered in snow. The Central Valley is green, with growing crops. The coastal hills are also green from winter rain.

One year later, following a warm, dry winter, the snowpack was reduced to about 10% of normal. Everything to the west of the mountains is brown, as shown in Figure 22.22.

Under such conditions, California is prone to water shortages, crop loss and wildfires.

Figure 22.21 Snow-covered Sierra Nevada Mountains

Figure 22.22 Sierra Nevada in drought conditions

Extreme weather

Hurricane

Hurricanes are giant, spiralling tropical storms with wind speeds up to 250 km/hr. They also bring torrential rainfall.

Figure 22.23 shows Hurricane Matthew, which hit the Caribbean in September 2016. It was the first Category 5 hurricane in almost ten years and it lasted for twelve days. The hurricane formed in the Atlantic and moved west towards the Caribbean. It made landfall in Haiti and eastern Cuba. From there, it hammered the Bahamas. It then skirted the east coast of the USA before eventually dying away.

Figure 22.23 Hurricane in the Caribbean

There were more than 900 fatalities, most of them in Haiti. Vast regions were destroyed by the winds and coastal areas were flooded.

Low pressure system

The clouds over Western Europe have the menacing curl of a low pressure system, as shown in Figure 22.24. This particular storm lashed Britain and Scandinavia as well as parts of Germany and Russia with hurricane-force winds and intense rainfall. The storm also brought severe floods to Scotland and Northern England.

Irish weather

Winter anticyclone over Ireland

Low-pressure systems are common in Ireland in winter. Depressions move rapidly east, bringing strong winds and frontal rainfall to the country.

Occasionally the cold **anticyclone** over Europe extends its influence west to Ireland (as seen in Figure 22.25), giving dry, cold periods that can last for several days. Winter anticyclones allow the Earth to lose heat rapidly at night, so while the following morning may be bright and sunny, the ground is often hard with frost.

Figure 22.24 Low pressure system over Britain

Winter snow

Figure 22.26 is a satellite image showing snowfall over Ireland in December 2010. More than 30 cm of snow fell over a five-day period.

Minimum air temperatures fell below −15°C at some weather stations and maximum temperatures were below freezing on eight successive days in some midland areas.

The snowfalls caused major traffic chaos for both road and air transport.

Figure 22.25 High pressure system over Ireland

Figure 22.26 Snow-covered landscape of Ireland

Natural resources

Open-cast mining

The Rio Tinto mine is the largest open-cast mine in California. It covers an area of almost 60 km² in a desert landscape. Much of the mine workings were underground originally, but sixty years ago they changed to open-cast (or open-pit) mining. One of the world's richest borax mines, it has sufficient ore reserves to keep the mine in production until 2050. Borax is used in the manufacture of detergents, cosmetics, enamel and fibreglass.

Figure 22.27 Large-scale open-cast mining

Oil spill

Figure 22.28 shows the oil spill in the Gulf of Mexico, just off the Mississippi Delta. The spill began with the explosion of the *Deepwater Horizon* oil rig. The image shows the resulting spread of the oil spill. It was the largest oil spill in marine history and caused major environmental problems.

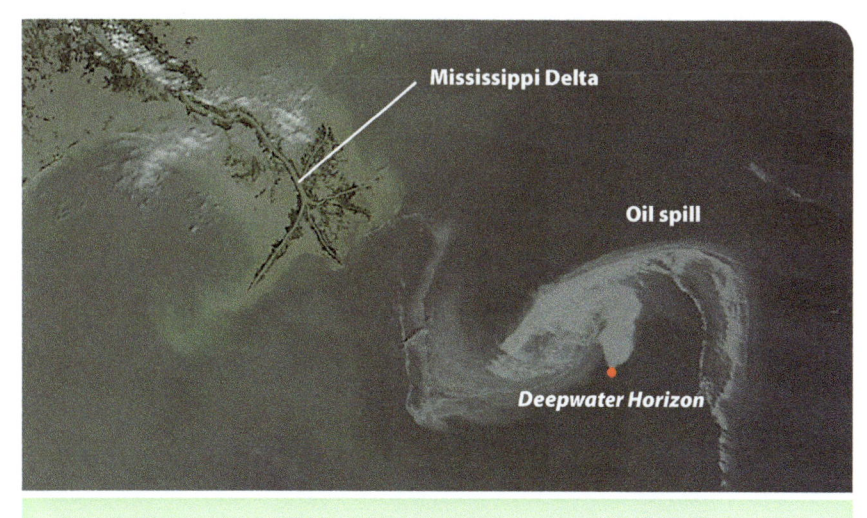

Figure 22.28 Oil spill following rig explosion in the Gulf of Mexico

PowerPoint Summary

Leaving Cert exam questions

SHORT QUESTIONS: HIGHER LEVEL

1 Satellite interpretation
(8 marks)

Examine the satellite images.

Match each of the letters **A**, **B**, **C** and **D** with the description that best matches it in the table below.

Description	Letter
Delta	
Open-cast mining	
Dust storm	
Forest fire	

2 Satellite interpretation
(8 marks)

Examine the satellite images.

Match each of the letters **A**, **B**, **C** and **D** with the description in the table below that best matches it.

Description	Letter
Deforestation	
Hydro-electric power station	
Nuclear power station	
River flooding	

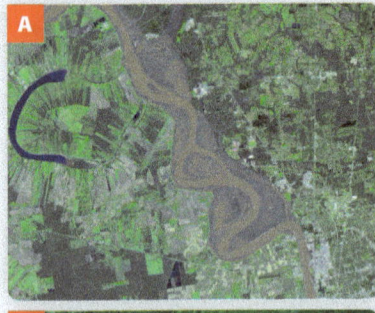

3 Satellite interpretation (8 marks)

Examine the satellite images below. Match each of the letters **A** to **D** with its correct description in the table below.

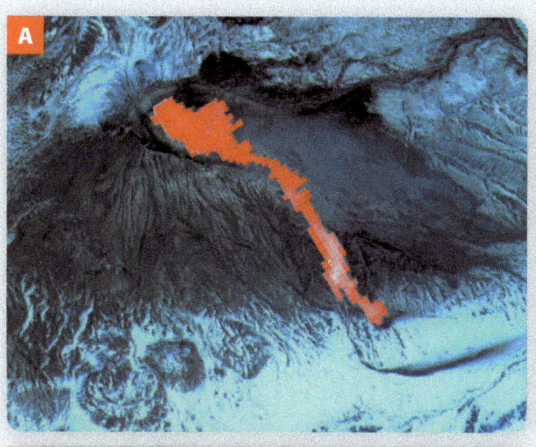

Description	Letter
Aswan High Dam	
A hurricane	
A recent lava flow	
Coastal sediments	

SHORT QUESTIONS: ORDINARY LEVEL

1 Satellite image interpretation (10 marks)

Match each satellite image with the most suitable description by writing the correct letter in each case in the table below. One has been completed for you.

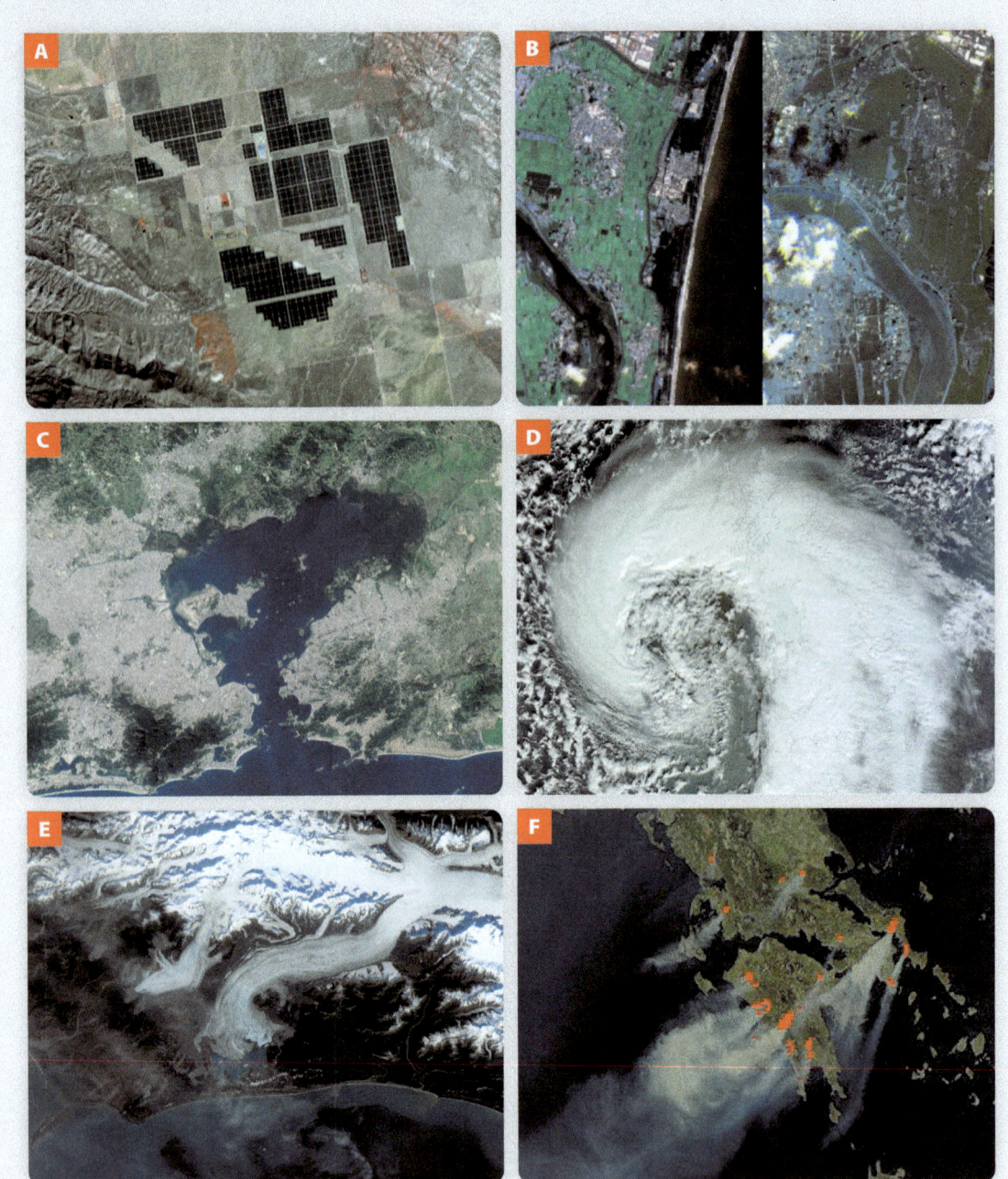

Description	Letter
Atlantic storm	
Retreating glacier	
Solar power plant in the desert	
Copacabana beach, Rio de Janeiro	
Before and after Japan tsunami, 2011	
Forest fires	F

OL

2 Satellite image interpretation (10 marks)

Match each satellite image with the most suitable description by writing the correct letter in each case in the table below.

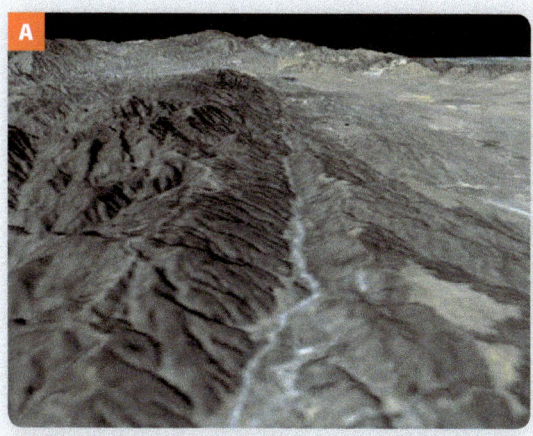

A

B

C

D

E

Description	Letter
Oil well burning in the desert	
Fiords in Norway	
Mining in the desert	
The San Andreas Fault	
Icebergs breaking from an ice sheet	

Chapter 23
Weather Charts

KEYWORDS

- meteorology
- synoptic chart
- isobars
- warm front
- cold front
- occluded front
- depression
- anticyclone
- radar chart
- wind rose
- isohyet
- isohel
- isotherm

LEARNING OBJECTIVES

By the end of this chapter, you should be able to understand:

- The symbols used on a weather map
- How these symbols are interpreted to get basic weather information
- How to read charts and diagrams that are used to present weather information.

Introduction

A weather chart illustrates the meteorological conditions over a specific region at a specific time. The chart is made by putting together many weather reports from different locations. The weather conditions are represented on the chart by coloured lines and symbols.

DEFINITION

Meteorology: The study of the atmosphere, especially weather and weather conditions.

Synoptic charts

A **synoptic chart** is the scientific term for a weather map. Synoptic charts provide information on the current weather conditions. This information is shown on the chart by using symbols. The key elements that make up a synoptic chart include:

- Isobars
- Fronts.

Synoptic charts are useful because they identify features such as **depressions** and **anticyclones**, which are associated with particular kinds of weather.

Isobars

An **isobar** is a line on a weather map that connects points of equal atmospheric pressure. Atmospheric pressure is measured in **millibars** (mb). Isobars are usually drawn at intervals of four millibars.

> When isobars are close together, the wind is strong.
> When isobars are far apart, the wind is light.
> The wind blows almost parallel to the isobars.

Weather fronts

A **weather front** is the boundary zone between two **air masses** that have different properties. For example, one air mass may be cold and dry and the other air mass may be warm and moist. Three types of front can be identified on a synoptic chart:

> Warm fronts
> Cold fronts
> Occluded fronts.

> A **warm front** means that a mass of warm air is advancing and rising up over a mass of cold air. This is because warm air is lighter than cold air. A warm front is shown on a weather map as a line with red semicircles.
> A **cold front** means that a mass of cold air is advancing and pushing underneath a mass of warmer air. This is because the cold air is heavier than the warm air. A cold front is shown on a weather map as a line with blue triangles.

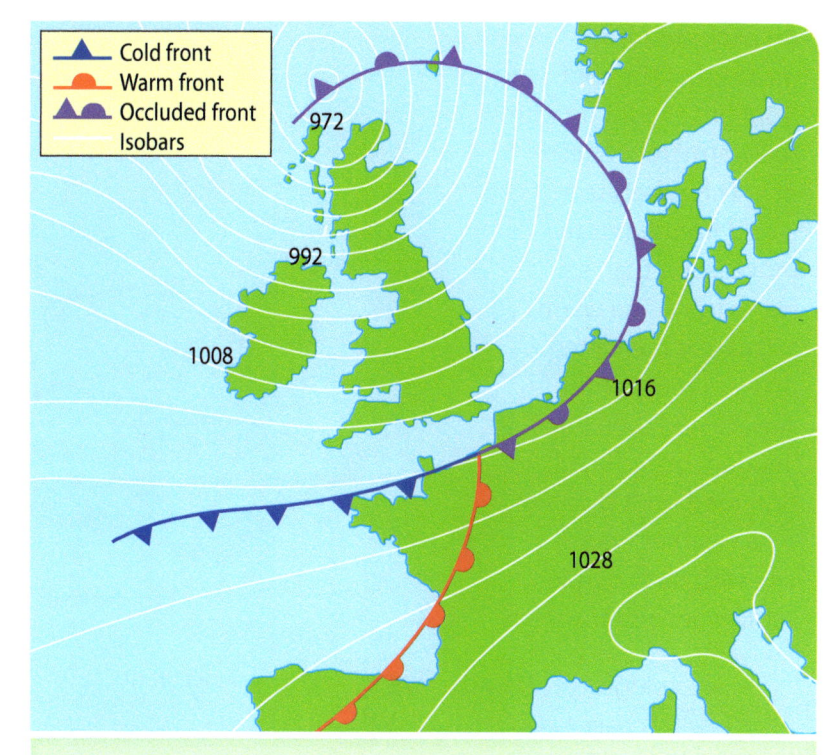

Figure 23.1 A synoptic chart of Western Europe

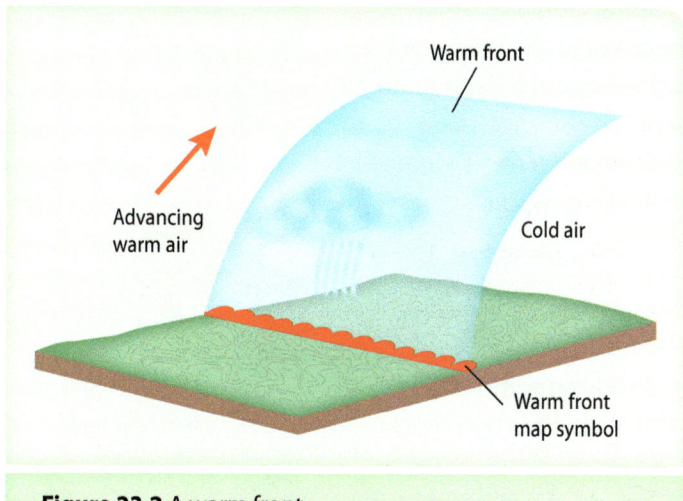

Figure 23.2 A warm front

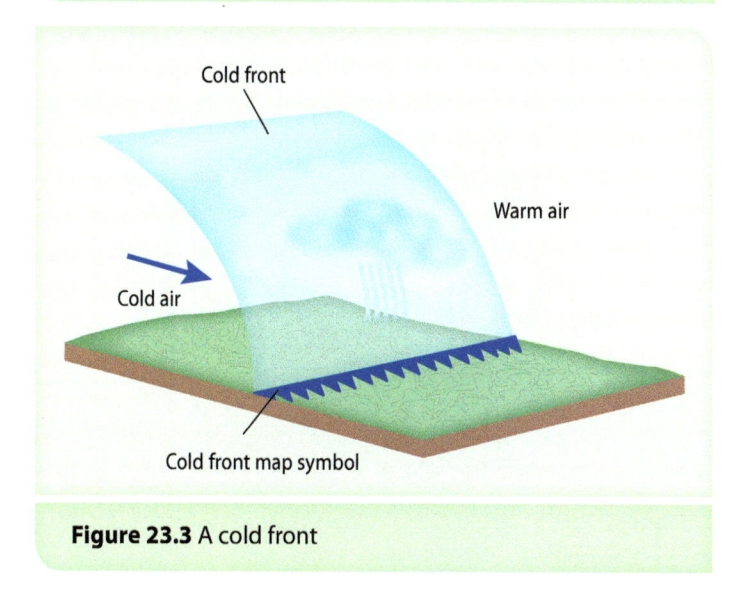

Figure 23.3 A cold front

> An **occluded front** means that the cold front has caught up with the warm front ahead of it. This is because a cold front tends to move faster than a warm front. The warm air mass is then lifted up from the ground surface and therefore 'hidden', or occluded. An occluded front is shown on a weather map as a line with both purple semicircles and triangles.

Figure 23.4 An occluded front

Depressions

A **depression** is an area of low atmospheric pressure. A capital L on a weather chart marks the centre of the depression. In a depression, warm air rises and cools. Condensation and perhaps precipitation occur.

Low pressure systems bring:

> Unsettled (changeable) conditions
> Cloudy conditions
> Strong winds that blow in an anticlockwise direction
> Periods of rain and possibly snow in winter.

A low pressure system over the North Atlantic Ocean brings rain and strong winds to Ireland and Britain. A very deep low pressure area lies in the centre of the spiral, just off the north-western coast of Ireland. Bands of cloud containing rain and thunderstorms extend over Britain.

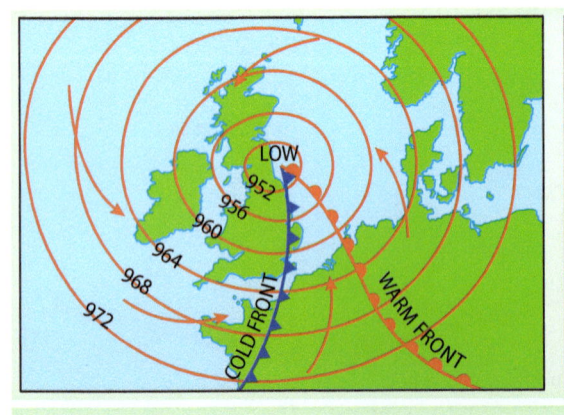

Figure 23.5 Characteristics of a low pressure system or depression

ACTIVITY

Skills

Examine the satellite image of a low pressure system. What direction are the winds blowing: clockwise or anticlockwise?

Anticyclones

An **anticyclone** is an area of high atmospheric pressure that can be thousands of kilometres in diameter. A capital H on a weather chart marks the centre of the anticyclone. In an anticyclone, cold air descends and warms up.

Anticyclones generally bring:

› Dry, settled weather
› Clear, cloudless skies
› Hot summer days with warm, starry nights
› Cold winter days with clear, frosty nights
› Calm conditions or light winds that blow in a clockwise direction.

This image was taken in winter. A high pressure system (anticyclone) over Ireland and Britain has resulted in skies that are largely clear of cloud. Many of the mountains of Scotland are snow-covered.

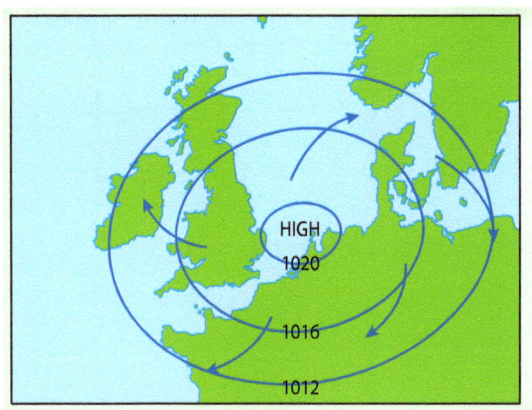

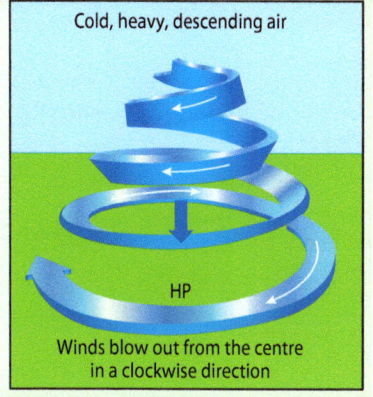

Figure 23.6 Characteristics of a high pressure system or anticyclone

ACTIVITY

Discussion

Examine the satellite image of a high pressure system. What weather conditions are being experienced over Ireland?

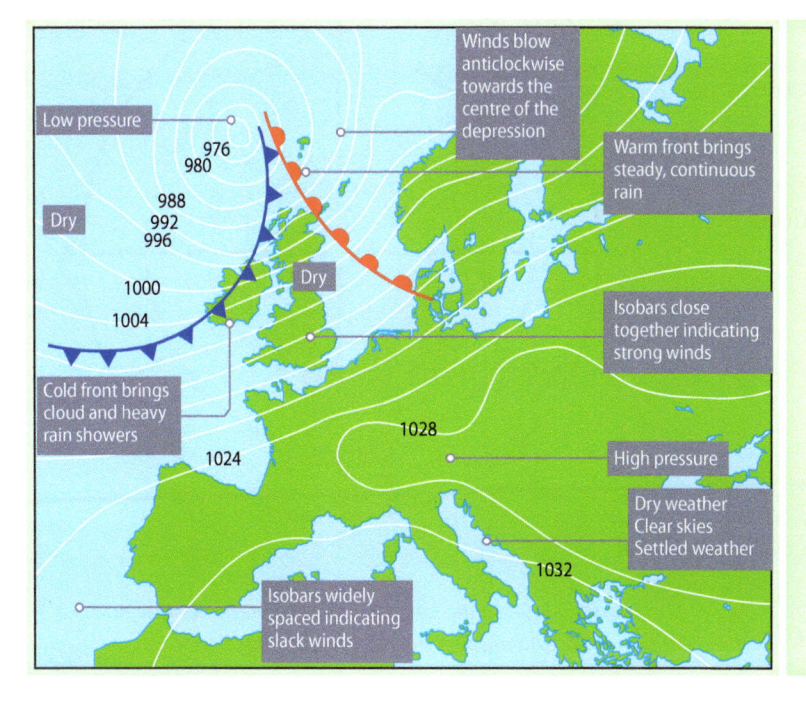

Figure 23.7 Summary of the weather conditions associated with a typical synoptic chart

CHAPTER 23 · WEATHER CHARTS   457

Wind charts

The information about wind that can be displayed includes its speed, direction and frequency.

Radar charts

A **radar chart** shows the wind frequency and the direction it blows from over time.

Figure 23.8 gives this information for the main meteorological stations in Ireland. It shows:

- The directions the wind blows from
- The percentage of time it blows from that direction (using the scale bar)
- The percentage of time when there is calm (small circle).

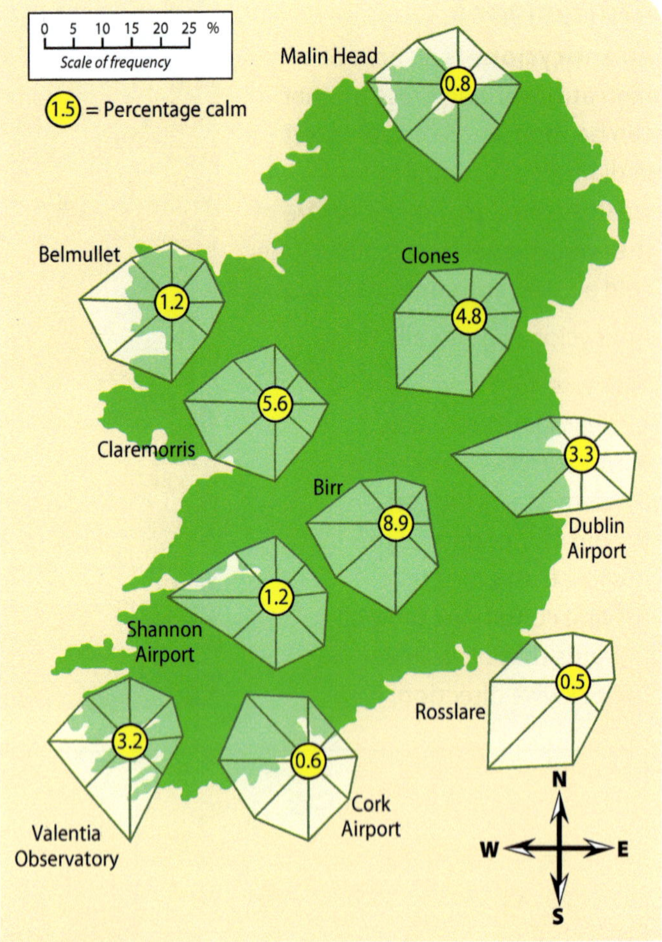

ACTIVITY

Skills

Examine Figure 23.8.
  (i) Which weather station experiences the greatest amount of calm conditions?
  (ii) What is the prevailing wind direction at Rosslare?

Figure 23.8 Wind radar chart for the main meteorological stations in Ireland

Wind rose

A **wind rose** shows the variations in wind speed and wind direction at a particular location over time.

Figure 23.9 gives detailed information on wind measurements at Valentia Observatory. It shows:

- The wind direction for that location, based on an eight-point compass
- How wind speeds varied in each direction
- The frequency (in percentages) of each of the above.

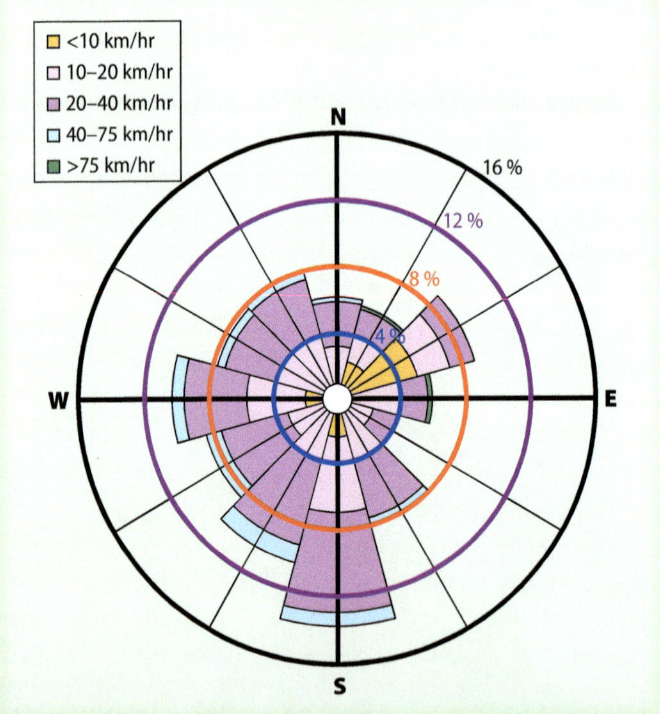

ACTIVITY

Skills

Examine Figure 23.9. What is the prevailing wind direction at Valentia Observatory?

Figure 23.9 A wind rose showing wind directions and variations in wind speed at Valentia Observatory

Precipitation maps

A **precipitation map** is used to show the annual average precipitation in an area over a period of time. Variations in precipitation are represented by the intensity of colour used on the map.

Isohyets are lines on a map that connect points that have equal amounts of precipitation during a given period of time. The boundary between any two shades on the map in Figure 23.10 represents an isohyet.

ACTIVITY

Discussion
Examine Figure 23.10. Explain two reasons why the greatest amounts of precipitation occur along the west coast.

Sunshine maps

Sunshine hours is the term that is used to describe the duration of sunshine in a given period of time. The duration is given in hours annually or hours per day. Sunshine hours can be represented in a number of ways.

Temperature maps

Temperature maps are used to show mean (average) temperatures across an area (see Figure 23.13 on the next page). The figures are usually calculated on a monthly basis.

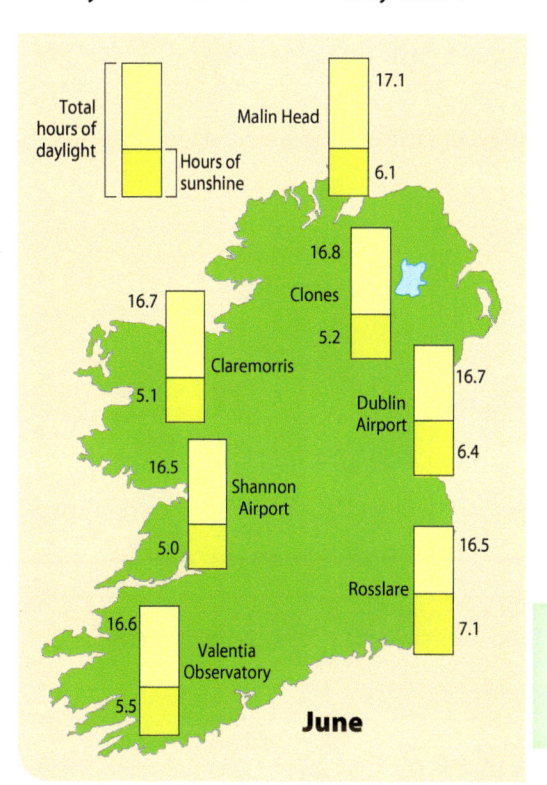

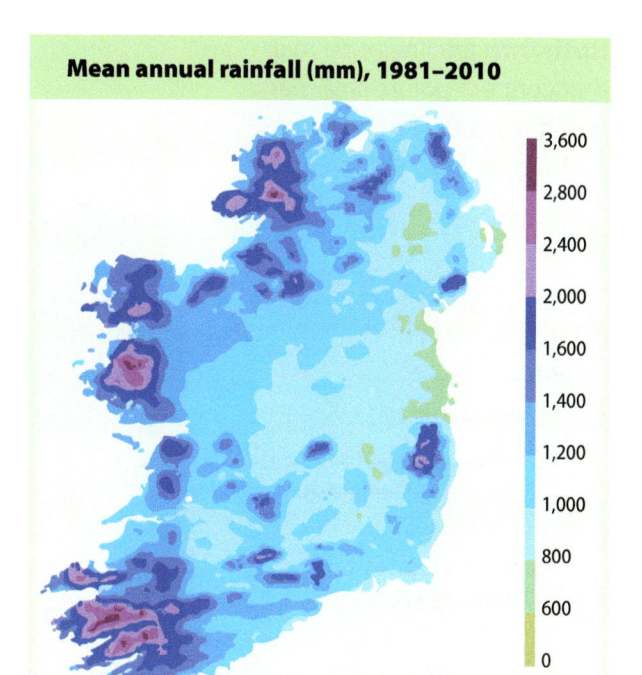

Figure 23.10 Mean (average) annual precipitation in Ireland between 1981 and 2010

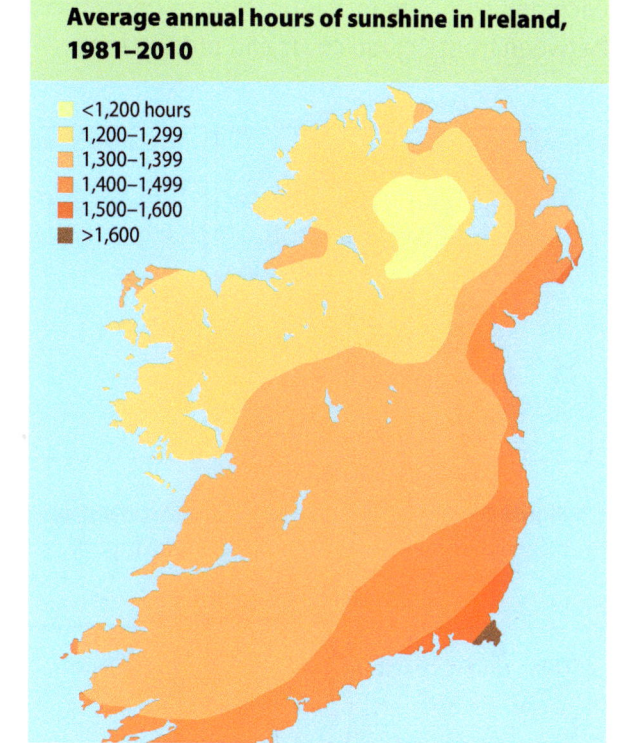

Figure 23.11 Total mean (average) hours of sunshine experienced in Ireland annually in the period 1981 to 2010. **Isohels** are lines on a map that connect points that have equal amounts of sunshine during a given period of time.

Figure 23.12 Mean (average) daily hours of sunshine during the month of June in selected locations in Ireland. The average hours of daylight are also given for each location.

Isotherms are lines on a map that connect points on a map that have equal temperatures for that period.

ACTIVITY

Skills

Examine Figure 23.13.

(i) What two regions have an average temperature above 16°C?

(ii) Explain one reason why this might be so.

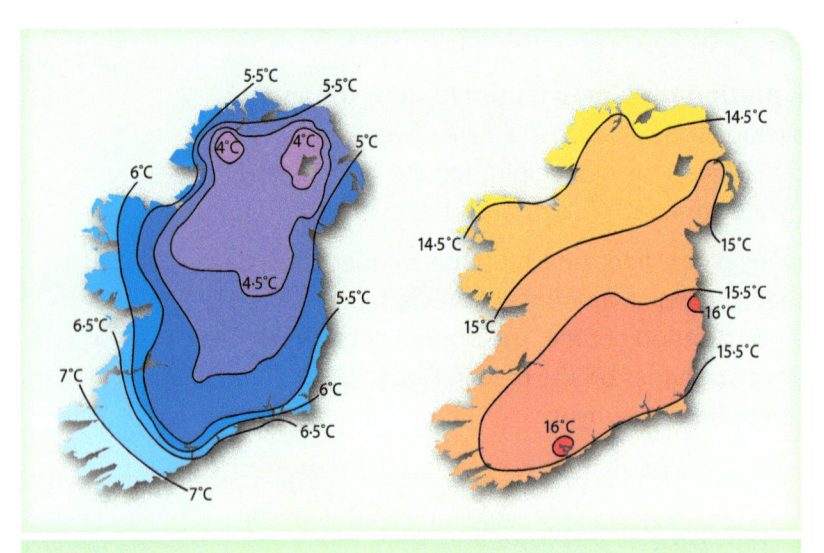

Figure 23.13 Average air temperatures in Ireland for January (left) and July (right)

Cloud and rainfall maps

Met Éireann publishes a series of weather maps on its website each day. Using them, it is possible to understand the link between fronts, cloud cover and precipitation.

ACTIVITY

Research

Look up Met Éireann Atlantic Charts on the internet.

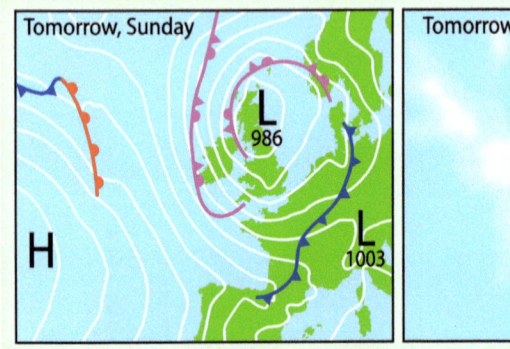

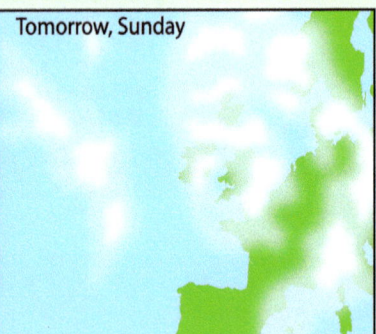

Figure 23.14 A depression, centred on Scotland, lies over Ireland. Synoptic map (left), with its accompanying cloud cover map (centre) and rainfall map (right).

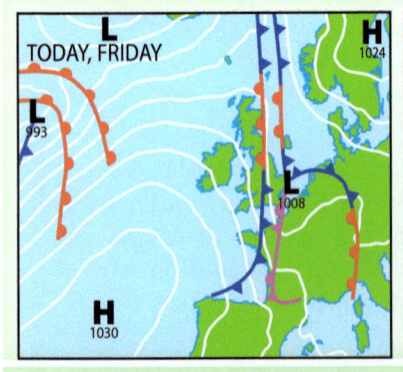

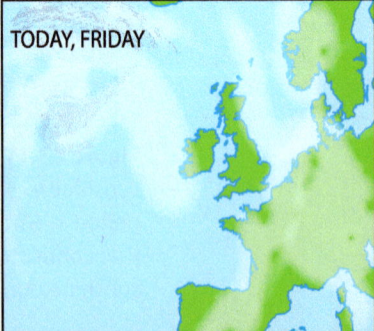

Figure 23.15 An anticyclone lies to the south-west of Ireland. Synoptic map (left), with its accompanying cloud cover map (centre) and rainfall map (right).

PowerPoint Summary

Leaving Cert exam questions

SHORT QUESTIONS: HIGHER LEVEL

1 Weather charts (8 marks)

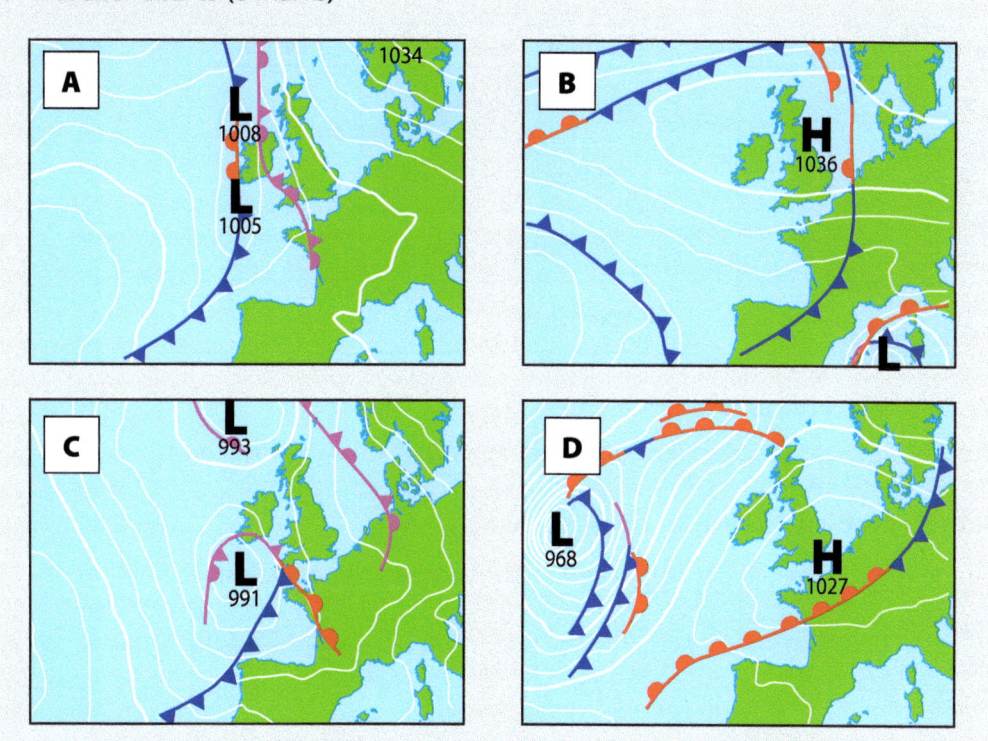

Examine the weather charts above and the cloud charts below.

Match each of the weather charts **A**, **B**, **C** and **D** with the cloud chart most associated with it by writing the correct letter in the space provided in each case.

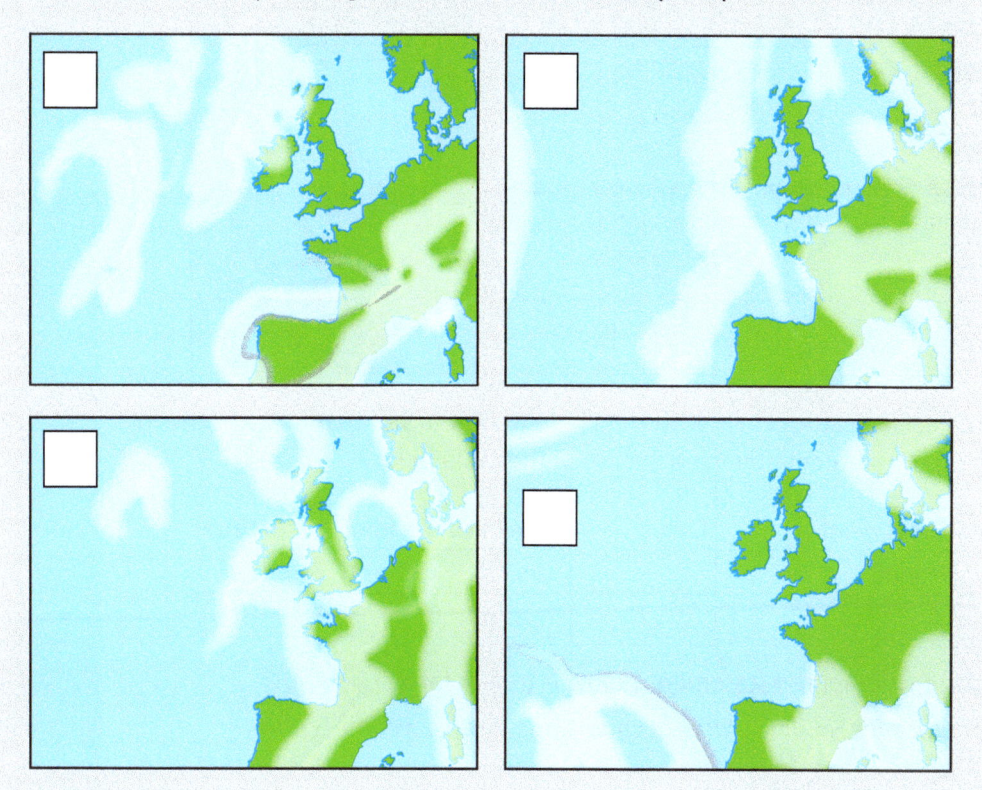

CHAPTER 23 · WEATHER CHARTS

SHORT QUESTIONS: ORDINARY LEVEL

1 Weather charts (10 marks)

(i) Match each of the weather chart symbols with the feature of weather that best matches it by writing the correct letter in each case in the table below.

Letter	Symbol
A	(warm front symbol)
B	L
C	H
D	(cold front symbol)

Feature of weather	Letter
High pressure system	
Cold front	
Low pressure system	
Warm front	

(ii) Indicate whether the following statement is true or false.

Isotherms are lines that join places of equal temperature on a weather chart.

2 Weather charts (10 marks)

Examine the weather charts below and answer each of the questions that follow.

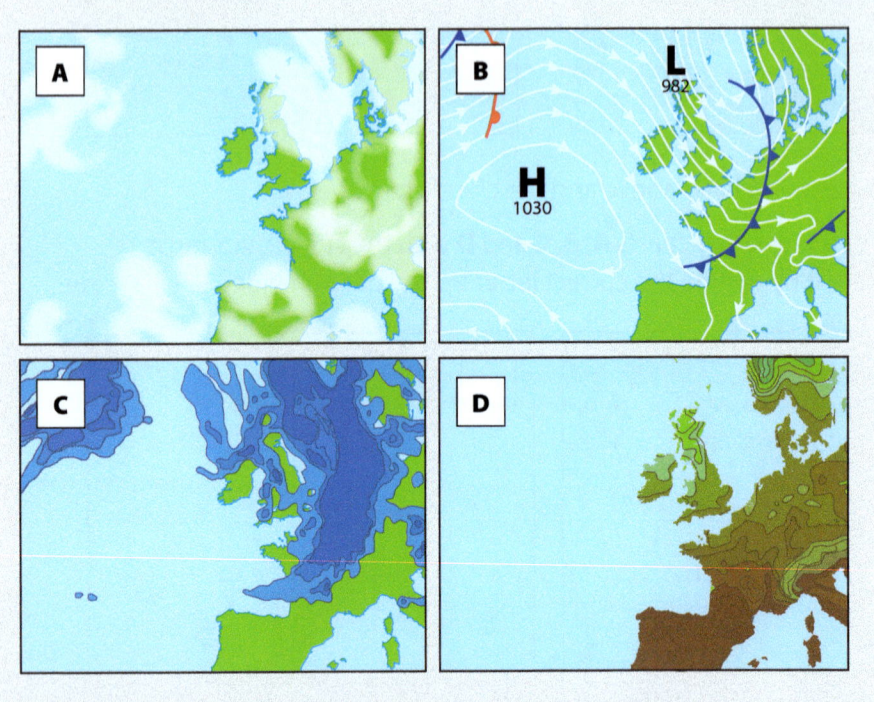

(i) Match each weather chart with the element of weather that it represents by writing the correct letter in each case in the table below.

Element of weather	Letter
Temperature	
Rainfall	

Element of weather	Letter
Cloud	
Pressure	

(ii) Indicate whether the statement below is true or false.

Isobars are lines joining places of equal pressure on a weather chart.

Chapter 24
Interpreting Graphs

KEYWORDS

- bar chart
- population pyramid
- trend graph
- climograph
- scatter graph
- pie chart
- table
- flowline map
- choropleth map
- triangular graph
- radar chart

LEARNING OBJECTIVE

By the end of this chapter, you should be able to understand:
- How to interpret and construct a wide variety of charts and graphs.

Introduction

Graphs are a simple but effective visual method of showing statistical information. You must be able to interpret them in order to answer examination questions. You will also need to create graphs so that you can present the results of your Geographical Investigation.

Bar charts

Bar charts consist of rectangular bars or columns that are drawn to scale to the frequency or amount that they represent. They are useful for showing comparisons between two or more pieces of data.

One axis shows the type of data that each column represents. The other axis shows a value for that type of data. Ensure that:

- The units on the value axis are drawn to scale
- The bars have equal width and are properly spaced
- The bars are labelled or identified by a key
- Each axis has a title.

There are four main types of bar chart:

> Simple bar chart
> Multiple bar chart
> Compound bar chart
> Divided rectangle.

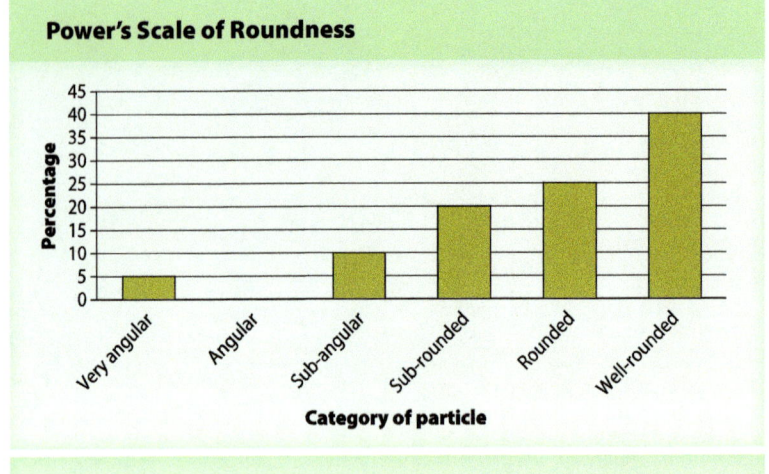

Power's Scale of Roundness

Figure 24.1a Simple bar chart. Each bar indicates a single value.

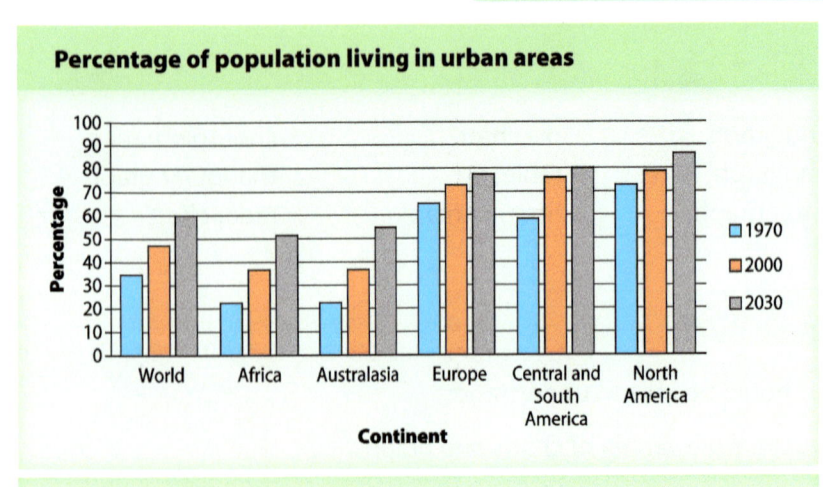

Percentage of population living in urban areas

Figure 24.1b Multiple bar chart. A number of variables are grouped together. This is an ideal way to show comparisons. A population pyramid is another type of multiple bar chart.

ACTIVITY

Skills

Examine Figure 24.1b.

(i) What percentage of Europe's population lived in urban areas in 2000?

(ii) In 1970, which continents had a lower percentage of urban dwellers than the world average?

(iii) What percentage of the world's population will not dwell in urban areas in 2030?

ACTIVITY

Skills

Examine Figure 24.1c.

(i) In what year was total emigration from Ireland highest?

(ii) In what year did the smallest number of Irish people emigrate?

(iii) How many non-Irish people emigrated in 2014?

Emigration from Ireland, 2006–16

Figure 24.1c Compound bar chart. Each bar shows two or more pieces of information. Information may be shown as totals or as percentages.

Energy sources in the USA, 2000 and 2015

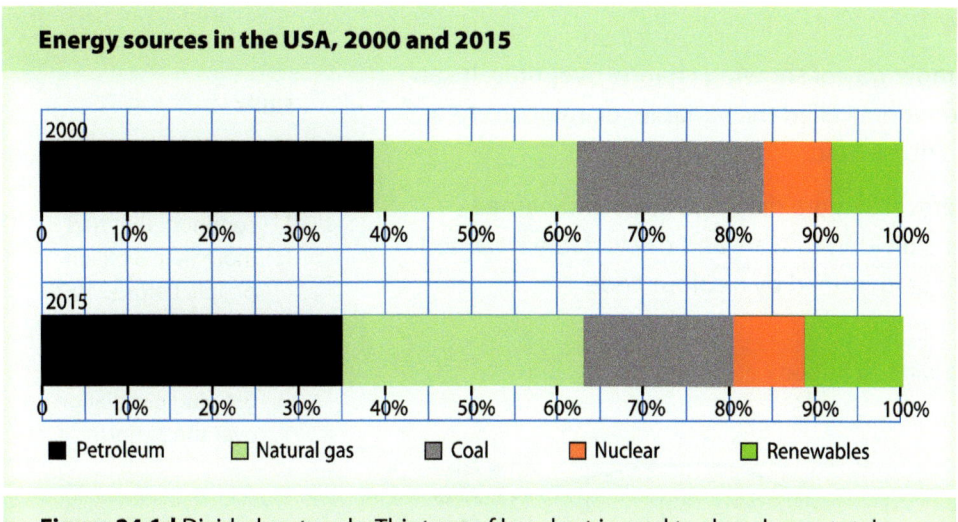

■ Petroleum ☐ Natural gas ■ Coal ■ Nuclear ■ Renewables

Figure 24.1d Divided rectangle. This type of bar chart is used to show how a total is divided into parts. As a result, figures are normally given in percentages.

Population pyramids

Ireland, 2014

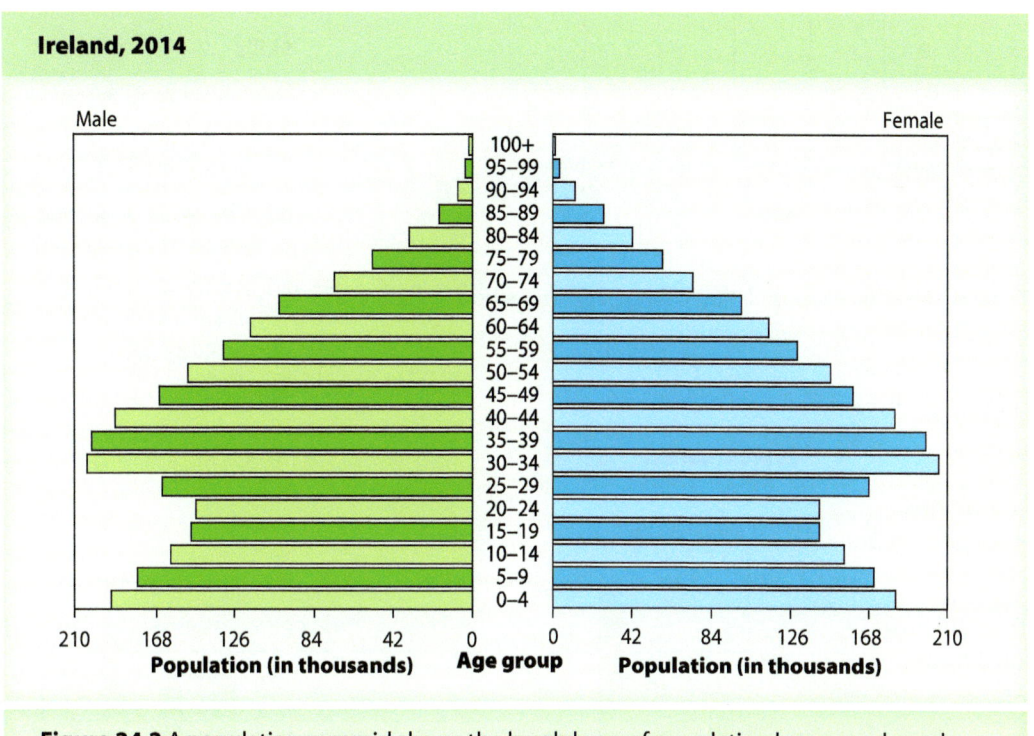

Figure 24.2 A population pyramid shows the breakdown of population by age and gender

A **population pyramid** is a type of bar chart. It shows the breakdown of a particular population in terms of age and gender.

› The horizontal axis is divided into two sections: males (left) and females (right).
› The scale used on the horizontal axis is either percentages or numbers.
› The vertical axis is divided into age groups, each with a five-year span.

ACTIVITY

Skills

Examine Figure 24.2.

(i) How many females are under 5 years of age?

(ii) What is the total population in the 5–9 age group?

(iii) Who has the longest life expectancy: men or women?

CHAPTER 24 · INTERPRETING GRAPHS   465

Trend graphs

A **trend graph** is a simple way of showing change over time. It can show one set of information (called the variable) or, more likely, a number of variables. Ensure that:

› The units on the vertical axis are drawn to scale and named
› The horizontal axis is divided to scale and the variable is named
› Each line is labelled or identified by a colour code.

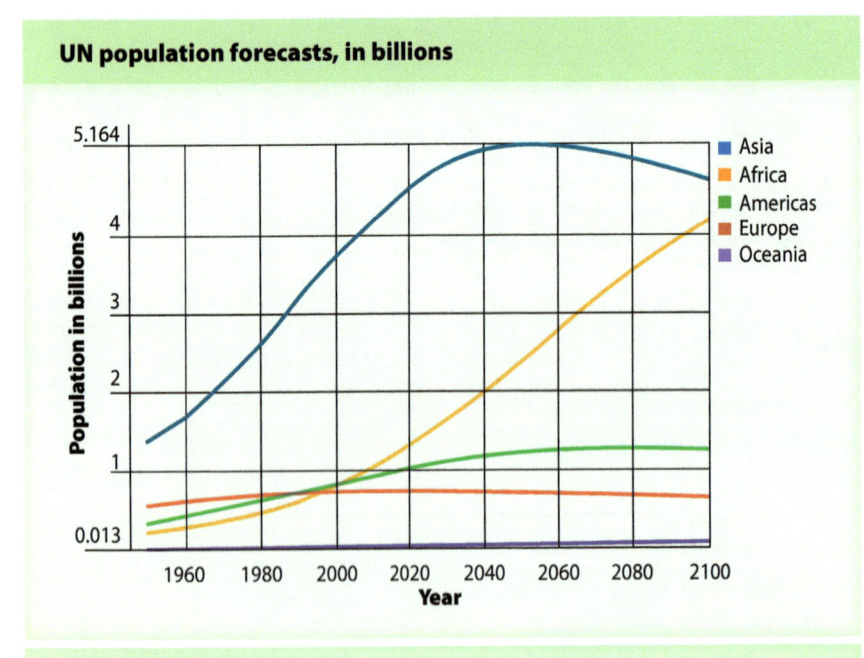

UN population forecasts, in billions

Figure 24.3 Trend graph showing population change and projection over time

ACTIVITY

Skills

Examine Figure 24.3.

(i) What is the only continent that had more than 5 billion people before 2100?

(ii) Which continent has the fastest-growing population over the period?

ACTIVITY

Skills

Examine Figure 24.4.

(i) What was the wettest month?

(ii) What was the highest temperature reached?

(iii) In how many months was precipitation below 45 mm?

Climographs

A **climograph** combines a bar chart and a line graph to show the monthly precipitation and temperature conditions for a selected place.

› Precipitation is shown by the bar graph.
› The line graph (trend graph) shows temperature.
› Each vertical axis has a different scale. One shows precipitation in mm (usually on the left) and the other shows temperature in °C.

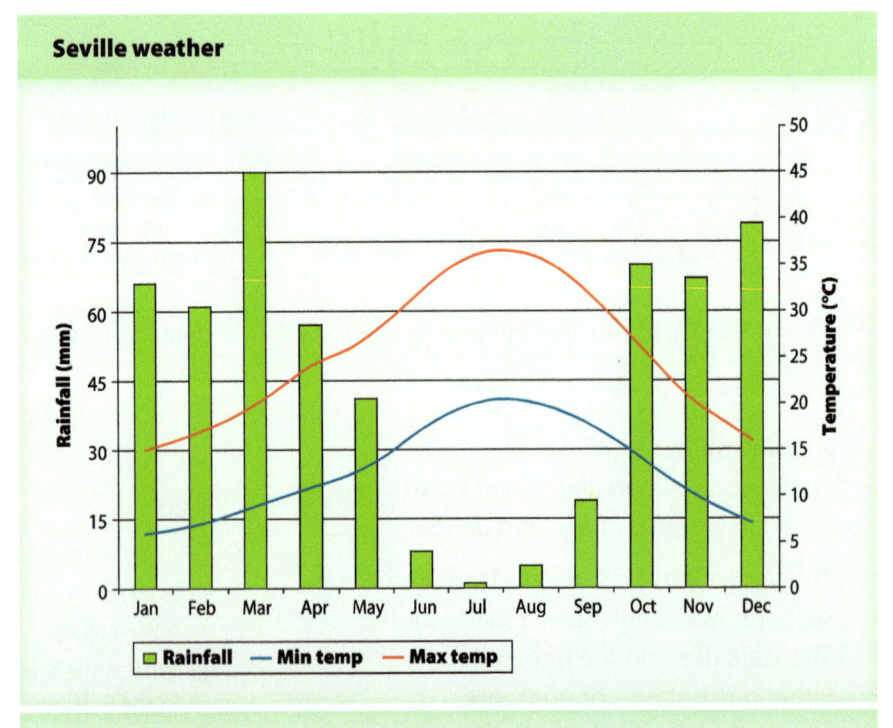

Figure 24.4 Climograph for Seville, Spain. This example shows both the average maximum temperature and the minimum temperature for each month.

Scatter graphs

A **scatter graph** shows how two sets of data are related to one another. These might include population size and the number of services, or distance from the source of a river and pebble size.

› The fixed element is drawn on the vertical axis.
› The variable element is drawn on the horizontal axis.

ACTIVITY

Skills

Examine Figure 24.5.
(i) What was the size in cm of the biggest pebble in the sample?
(ii) How many pebbles were sampled at each location?
(iii) What was the average size of the pebbles sampled at the HWM?

Particle size

Figure 24.5 Variations in particle size along a beach transect, drawn between the high water mark (HWM) and the low water mark (LWM)

Pie charts

A **pie chart** represents the proportion of each category as part of the whole.

› The pie is divided into slices. Each slice represents a category of data.
› By comparing the size of the slices, you can figure out the relative size or value of each category.
› The data is most commonly given in percentages.

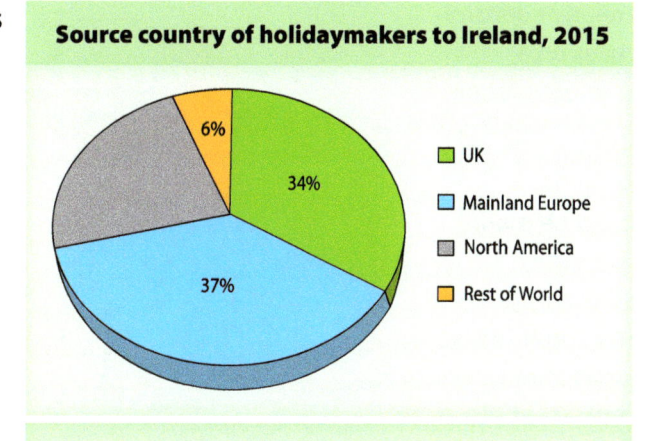

Source country of holidaymakers to Ireland, 2015

- UK 34%
- Mainland Europe 37%
- North America
- Rest of World 6%

Figure 24.6 Pie chart showing the source region of holidaymakers to Ireland

ACTIVITY

Skills

Examine Figure 24.6.
(i) What percentage of holidaymakers came from North America?
(ii) Calculate the number of degrees allocated to the UK and Rest of World combined (40%).

Tables

A **table** uses columns and rows to show the various items of data. A table can show a large amount of information. It is a simple way to record data that may later be displayed in another type of chart.

AVERAGE YOUTH UNEMPLOYMENT RATES (15 TO 24 YEARS)				
	2013	2014	2015	2016
Greece	61	57	50	50
France	26	23	25	23
Ireland	29	24	21	15
Czech Republic	16	17	15	10
Germany	8	8	7	7
EU average	24	23	21	19

Table 24.1 Simple table showing the variations in youth unemployment in six countries over four different time periods

CHAPTER 24 · INTERPRETING GRAPHS

Flowline maps

A **flowline map** can be used to show the movement of people or products between different areas. For example, it could show data about traffic flow, migration patterns or movement of goods (exports/imports) between places.

> Direction is indicated by an arrow.
> The size of the data can be indicated by varying the thickness of the lines.

Immigration to the USA, in hundreds of thousands

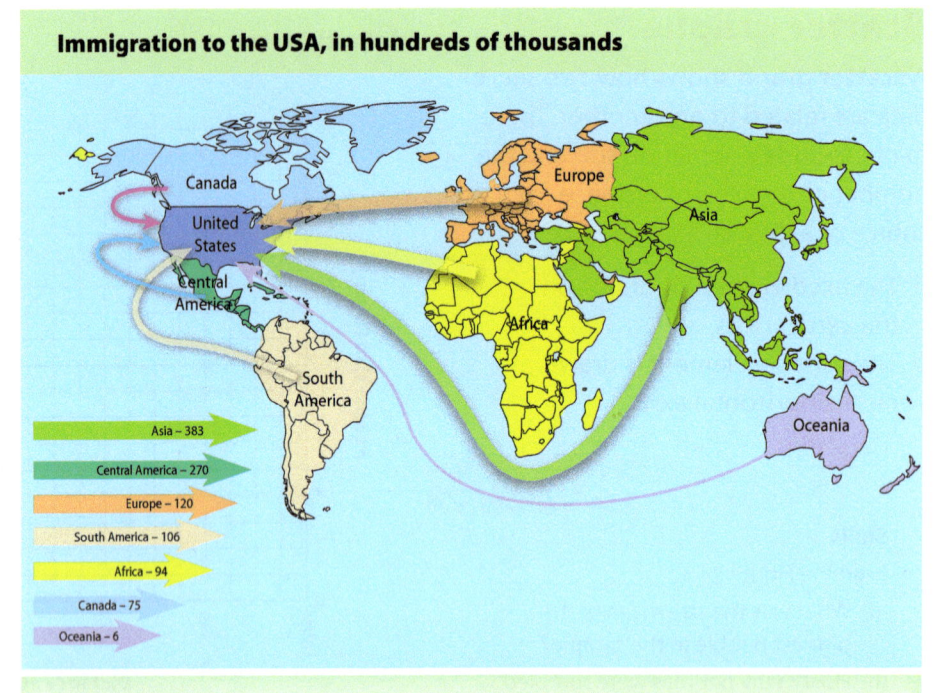

Asia – 383
Central America – 270
Europe – 120
South America – 106
Africa – 94
Canada – 75
Oceania – 6

Figure 24.7 Flowline map showing immigration to the USA in a particular year

Choropleth maps

A **choropleth map** shows relative density or change in an area. It focuses on a single theme, often related to population.

> It uses shading or colouring to display the actual difference or change.
> Classes or groupings should be made on a number of regular intervals.
> Choropleths have limited value because they suggest that conditions are constant within an area (colour). They also show sharp contrasts at the boundaries of areas, which may not necessarily be true.

ACTIVITY

Skills

Examine Figure 24.8.
(i) Which county showed the greatest rate of increase?
(ii) Name one county that showed a decrease in population.

Percentage population change by county, 2011–2016

% change
- <0
- 0–2
- 2–4
- 4–6
- >6

Figure 24.8 Choropleth map showing population changes in Ireland between the 2011 census and the 2016 census. Data is shown on a county-by-county basis. (Source: CSO)

Triangular graphs

A **triangular graph** is an equilateral triangle with each of the three sides divided into percentage scales.

> It is used to show information that can be broken into three variables.
> Each variable represents a percentage value. The three percentage values must add up to 100%.
> This type of chart could show information on many areas, for example mass movement (slide, flow creep), soil texture (clay, silt and sand content) or, as in this case, employment structure (primary, secondary, tertiary).

Economic activities

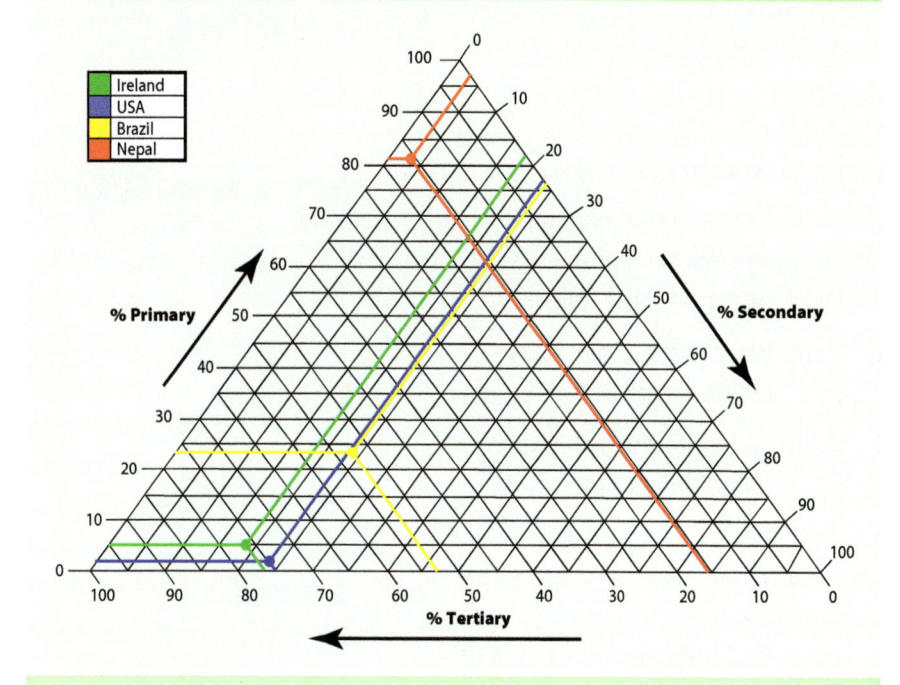

Figure 24.9 Triangular graph showing the breakdown of economic activities in four countries

ACTIVITY

Skills

Examine Figure 24.9.
 (i) Which country has the highest percentage of tertiary economic activity?
 (ii) What percentage of primary economic activity do (a) the USA and (b) Nepal have?

Radar charts

A **radar chart** is also known as a spider chart because of its appearance.

> It plots the values of a number of variables (in this case, age groups).
> Each fixed unit (in this case, countries) has a separate axis.
> Each axis starts in the centre and ends in the outer ring.

ACTIVITY

Skills

Examine Figure 24.10.
 (i) Which country has the highest under-14 population percentage?
 (ii) Which country has the highest 15–64 population percentage?

Differing balance between age groups in the population (%)

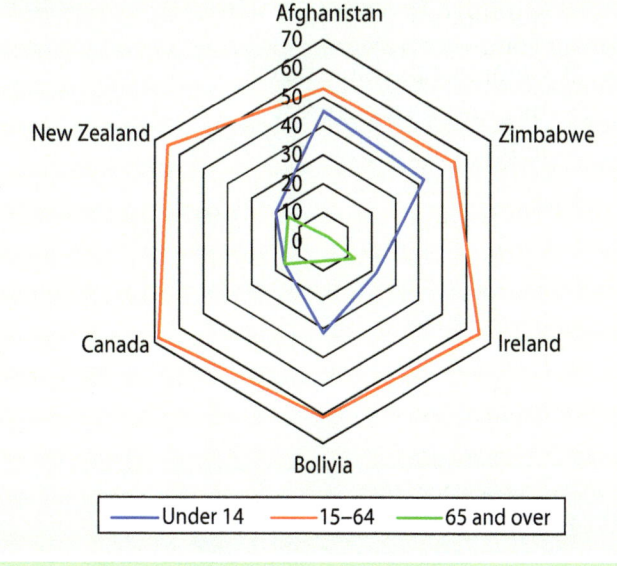

Figure 24.10 Radar chart showing the balance between different age groups in selected countries

CHAPTER 24 · INTERPRETING GRAPHS

PowerPoint Summary

Leaving Cert exam questions

SHORT QUESTIONS: HIGHER LEVEL

1. **Weather** (8 marks)

    Examine the map and answer each of the questions that follow.

    (i) What is the mean daily temperature at **A**?

    (ii) Calculate the approximate mean daily temperature range in Co. Kerry.

    (iii) What is the name given to the lines on a weather map that join places of equal temperature?

    (iv) Explain briefly why temperatures in the West of Ireland are usually higher than temperatures in the midlands in January.

Mean daily January temperature in Ireland

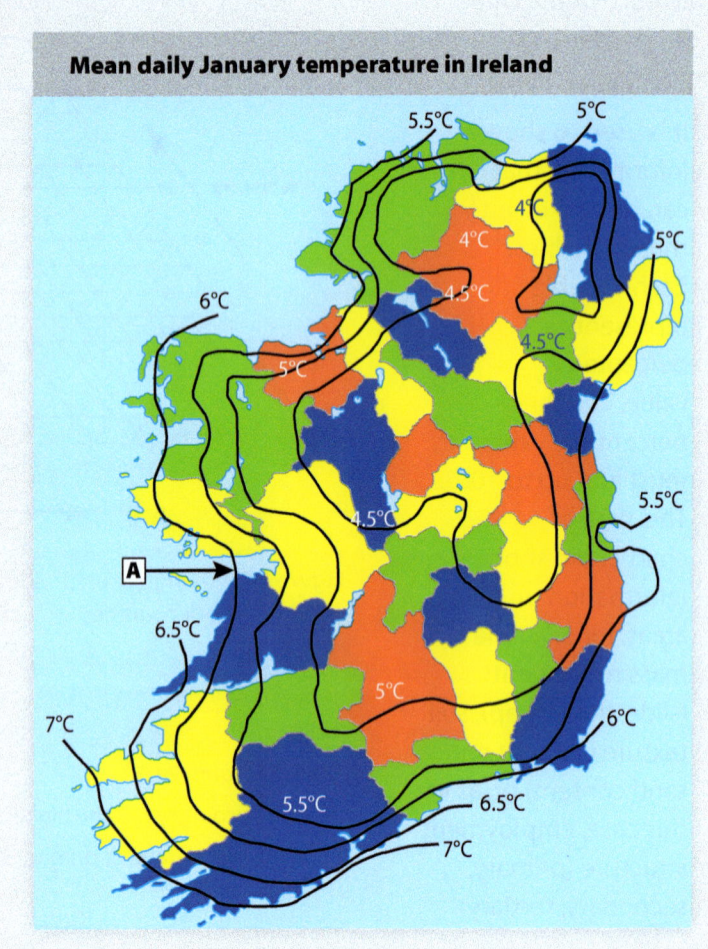

2. **Employment structure** (8 marks)

    Examine the triangle diagram and answer the questions that follow.

    (i) Complete the table below by inserting the correct letter in the grid.

Employment structure	Letter
Primary: 20% Secondary: 40% Tertiary: 40%	
Primary: 90% Secondary: 5% Tertiary: 5%	
Primary: 10% Secondary: 30% Tertiary: 60%	

    Employment structure

    (ii) What percentage is engaged in secondary activity at **D**?

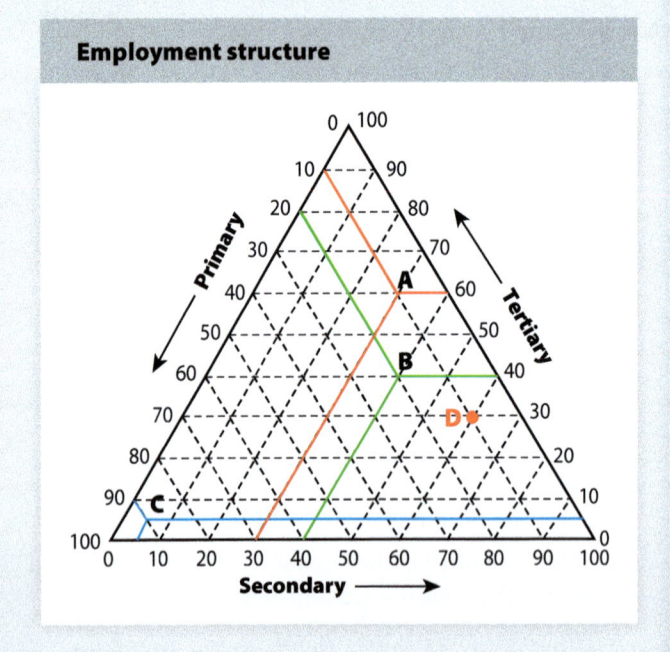

SHORT QUESTIONS: ORDINARY LEVEL

1 Weather statistics
(10 marks)

Examine the climate graph showing average temperature and rainfall levels for Dublin and answer each of the questions that follow.

Climate graph for Dublin

(i) Which month had the highest rainfall level?

(ii) Which month had the lowest rainfall level?

(iii) In which month was the highest average temperature recorded?

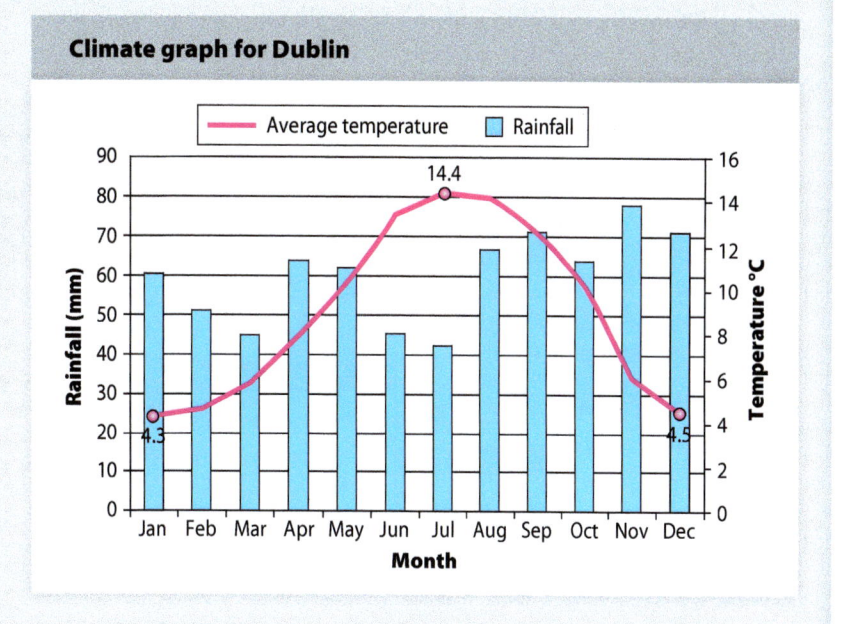

(iv) Did the average temperature fall below 0°C in any month?

(v) What was the average temperature range in degrees Celsius (°C)?

2 Population pyramid (10 marks)

Examine the population pyramid and answer the questions that follow.

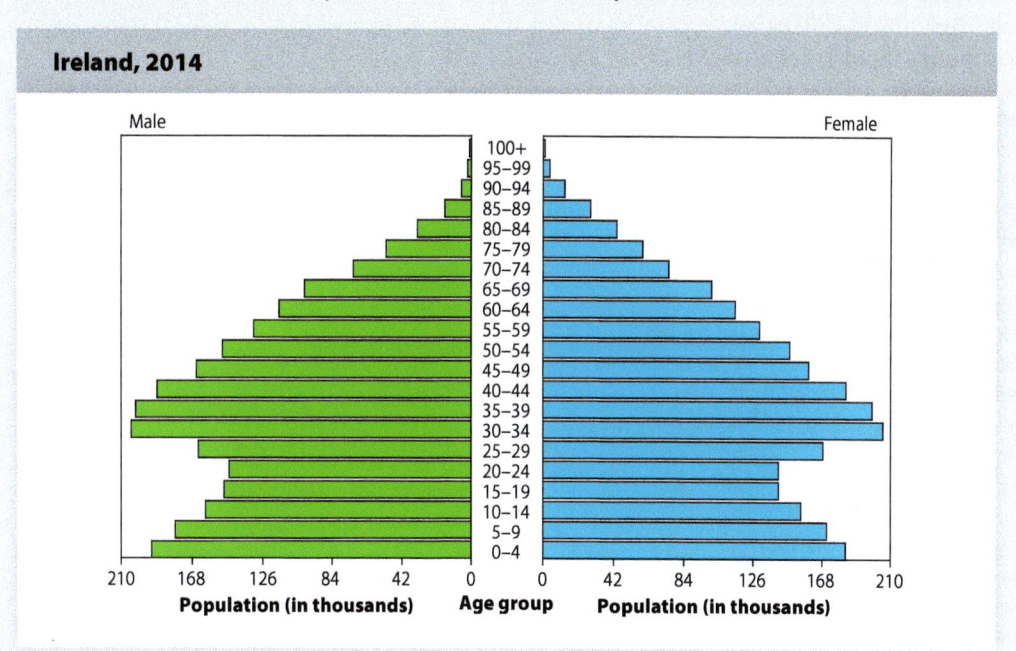

Ireland, 2014

(i) Are there more males or females in the 0–4 age group?

(ii) Which age group contains the greatest number of females?

(iii) How many females are under the age of 10 years, approximately?

(iv) True or false: Males over the age of 75 live longer than females.

(v) True or false: Each bar represents a five-year span.

LONG QUESTIONS: HIGHER LEVEL

1 Disposable income of Irish regions (20 marks)

Examine the graph and answer the questions that follow.

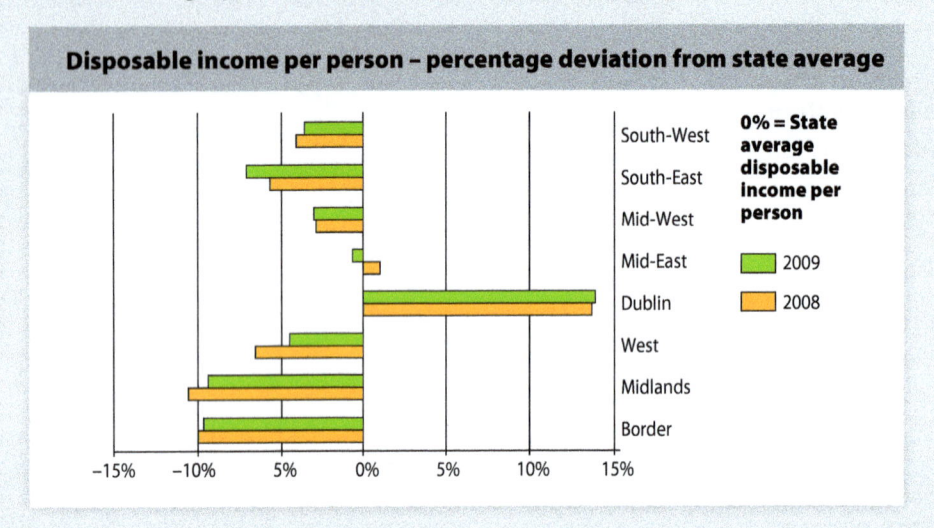

Disposable income per person – percentage deviation from state average

0% = State average disposable income per person

- 2009
- 2008

Regions (top to bottom): South-West, South-East, Mid-West, Mid-East, Dublin, West, Midlands, Border

X-axis: −15%, −10%, −5%, 0%, 5%, 10%, 15%

(i) How many regions had a disposable income per person below the state average in 2008?

(ii) Which region had a disposable income per person 10% below the state average in 2008?

(iii) Which region's disposable income per person was closest to the state average in both 2008 and 2009?

(iv) Which region had a disposable income per person above the state average in both 2008 and 2009?

(v) Explain briefly why this region had a disposable income per person above the state average in both 2008 and 2009.

LONG QUESTIONS: ORDINARY LEVEL

1 Tourism in Ireland (30 marks)

Examine the chart showing information regarding popular Irish tourist attractions in 2013 and answer each of the questions that follow.

Popular Irish tourist attractions, 2013

Attraction	Visitors
National Botanic Gardens	550,000
Book of Kells	588,723
National Gallery of Ireland	641,572
Cliffs of Moher Visitor Experience	960,134
Dublin Zoo	1,026,611
Guinness Storehouse	1,157,900
National Aquatics Centre	858,031
Tayto Park	435,000
National Museum of Ireland – Archaeology	404,230
Fota Wildlife Park	365,396

Source: Fáilte Ireland

(i) Name the **two** most popular Irish tourist attractions in 2013.

(ii) Name the tourist attraction with the least number of visitors **and** state how many visitors it received.

(iii) Calculate the difference between the number of tourists that visited the National Botanic Gardens and the number of tourists that visited Tayto Park in 2013.

(iv) Explain briefly **one** positive effect of tourism on Ireland.

(v) Explain briefly **one** negative effect of tourism on Ireland.

Chapter 25
Geographical Investigation

KEYWORDS

- Geographical Investigation
- Reporting Booklet
- primary source
- secondary source
- aims and objectives
- planning
- method/task/activity
- gathering information
- results
- conclusions
- evaluation

LEARNING OBJECTIVES

By the end of this chapter, you should be able to understand:

- How to plan and undertake your Geographical Investigation (GI)
- How to write up the Reporting Booklet.

Introduction

The Geographical Investigation is a field study where you learn through activity.

- It represents the practical application of some of the geographical skills listed in the syllabus.
- It is a core area of study and is compulsory for all students.
- It is worth 20% of the overall marks in the Leaving Certificate examination.

Choosing a topic

- A list of titles is issued to schools by the State Examinations Commission in Year 1 of the Leaving Certificate cycle. The list is also available on the SEC website (www.examinations.ie).
- The list of Investigation Topics is common to both Higher and Ordinary Levels.

The Reporting Booklet

- Although candidates may work in groups, each candidate must submit an individual report.
- Candidates are required to submit the report on the investigation using the official Geographical Investigation Reporting Booklet. This must be completed by mid- to late April in Year 2 of the Leaving Certificate cycle.

Sources of information

Information may be obtained from:

> Primary sources
> Secondary sources.

Primary sources

Primary source information is original.

> It is collected through individual or group work.
> Primary sources include observation, measurements, surveys, questionnaires, gathering samples, sketching, etc.
> Most primary data is collected in the field. This means that it is gathered during a trip to the investigation site.
> Ordnance Survey maps and aerial photographs may also be regarded as primary sources in the investigation.
> Primary sources should make up **at least 60%** of the information gathered.

Secondary sources

Secondary sources are any data that has been collected by someone else. It includes information collected using information technology (internet, DVDs, etc.) as well as from published sources (journals, books, maps, photographs, sketches, etc.).

> Other than essential references such as definitions and statistics, material should not be copied directly from the secondary source.
> All secondary sources used (books, journals, websites, etc.) should be acknowledged.

Note: Data that is gathered from secondary sources can be regarded as primary information, provided that it is processed further (for example, using census data).

Stages of the Geographical Investigation

> There are five distinct stages to the Geographical Investigation. This is reflected in the format of the Reporting Booklet.
> Each section of the booklet has a prescribed length (word count) and a specific mark weighting. These are the same for both Higher Level and Ordinary Level students.

Section 1: Introduction (50 words, 5 marks)

List **four** clear, simple statements outlining your aims and/or hypotheses.

> An **aim** is a brief statement setting out what you want to do.
> A **hypothesis** is a statement or theory that you can test during the investigation.

The aims or hypotheses should relate to the investigation. Each should be specific and qualified.

STAGE 1: INTRODUCTION	
Aim	**Hypothesis**
> To measure changes in the profile of the beach along a transect line.	> The beach profile changes as one moves from the foreshore and up across the backshore.
> To examine the distribution of shops and services within the central business district.	> Land use pattern varies within the central business district.
> To measure the discharge of the river at a number of locations.	> The discharge of a river will increase as one moves from the source to the mouth.
> To examine the impact of migration in the local area.	> Population structure in the local area has changed over the last five years.
> To investigate if material is transported along a stretch of coastline.	> Longshore drift is active along this stretch of coastline.

Table 25.1

Section 2: Planning (100 words, 5 marks)

List **four** points about how you prepared to carry out your investigation. Each point should be qualified (e.g. where/how/why?). These points might include:

> Decisions on what information you need to collect
> Decisions on the location(s) for the investigation
> The selection of methods to be used in gathering the information
> The design of questionnaires and recording sheets
> Devising your own street maps, etc.
> Organising equipment and practising how to use it in advance
> Writing letters, arranging interviews, etc.
> Specific reference to the revision of topics related to the investigation
> Advance investigation of weather forecasts, low tide times, etc.

STAGE 2: PLANNING
> We made a homemade clinometer using a large protractor, a piece of string and a small weight.
> We wrote a letter to the manager of three local factories asking if a small group could come to interview each manager.
> I revised the coasts chapter in my textbook. I concentrated on the main processes of erosion and the formation of a cliff and wave-cut platform.
> I used the internet to find out the times of low tide over the following two weeks as we waited for the weather to improve.
> We devised a set of eight land use categories and made a list of what buildings or businesses would be included in each of them.
> We visited the local library and got photocopies of old maps of the local area at 6-inch and 25-inch scales.
> We practised measuring gradient by using the equipment on the school driveway.

Table 25.2

Section 3: Gathering information (450 words, 40 marks)

This section deals with the reporting or description of the activities that you carried out while gathering the information.

> Gathering information must be **activity based**.
> You must describe **two** different **methods** or **tasks** that you used in gathering the information.
> A **method** of gathering may be a single activity, such as measuring.

STAGE 3: GATHERING INFORMATION – METHODS	
Investigation	**Methods**
> The impact of the process(es) of transportation and/or deposition on the formation of **one** coastal landform	> Measuring wind and wave properties > Measuring beach characteristics
> The impact of land use on traffic patterns	> Undertake land-use survey in the CBD/along a street or road outwards from the town centre > Measuring traffic type and frequency over time

Table 25.3

› A **task** is a group of relevant, linked activities. Any number of these activities can be combined to form one gathering task. This approach is more flexible and allows greater scope in the gathering process.

STAGE 3: GATHERING INFORMATION – TASKS	
Task	Activities
Measuring beach characteristics	› Measuring the changes of gradient along a transect line on the beach › Measuring beach fabric at a number of sites along the same transect line › Observing minor beach landforms such as berms, ridges and runnels
Undertaking a land-use survey	› Using a 1:1,000 street map/mapping › Recording › Observation › Interviewing › Counting › Sketching/photography › Measuring › Colour coding
Measuring the discharge of a river	› Measuring the width of the river › Measuring the depth of the river at fixed intervals › Calculating the cross-sectional area of the river › Measuring the average velocity of the river › Calculating the discharge

Table 25.4

When writing your report, you should provide a detailed or qualified account of how you gathered the information. Simple statements are not sufficient (e.g. I observed the features, I sketched the landform).

This account might include reference to:
› The use of instruments (their names, what they were used for, how and why you used them)
› The use of maps (how and why)
› Sketching (what and why)
› Explaining how you recorded the information (e.g. by including a sample of a partly completed recording sheet)
› Taking photographs and/or videos for later recall in the classroom
› Observations (what and why)
› Interviews
› Sketches and diagrams, provided they relate to the gathering of the information
› Research
› Sampling/testing.

Some other points to remember:
› Ensure that all the activities undertaken in this section are in line with the points that you made in your introduction and planning stages.
› Some aspects may be described by annotated sketches or diagrams, provided that they are activity based and illustrate the gathering process.
› Do not refer to any planning or preparation in this section. This information belongs in Section 2.
› Do not include any of your results in this section. This information belongs in Section 4.

Section 4: Results, conclusions, evaluation (400 words, 30 marks)

In this section, you should:

> **State four results.** Each result may take the form of any of the following: written statement, set of figures, map, sketch, chart, graph, table, etc. Ensure that each result relates directly or indirectly to the information that you have gathered in your investigation.

> **Draw four conclusions from the results.** A conclusion is a simple written statement that must be based directly or indirectly on the information provided by your results. It must also be relevant to the tasks completed in Section 3. Ideally, you should match your results with your conclusions.

STAGE 4: RESULTS AND CONCLUSIONS

Result	Conclusion(s)
> The wave count at Trabeg varied between eight waves and ten waves per minute.	> As the wave count was less than ten waves per minute, we can conclude that these are constructive waves.

> The land-use data for Market Street was:
  > Retail 60%
  > Offices 15%
  > Finance 10%
  > Residential 10%
  > Others 5%.
	> Land use in Market Street is dominated by various types of commercial activity.

> The velocity of the river meander was:
  > Inside bend 3 m/sec
  > Outside bend 5 m/sec.
	> The velocity of the river varies across the meander. The different speeds of the water is one factor that leads to both deposition (slip-off slope) and erosion (river cliff).

> Passenger car units (PCUs) totalled 240 from 8:00 a.m. to 9:00 a.m. There were only 82 from 9:00 a.m. to 10:00 a.m.	> The rush hour traffic had ceased by 9:00 a.m. > The presence of two schools near the survey location led to the traffic spike before 9:00 a.m.
> In-migration to the parish between 2011 and 2016 was 28 people, while 49 people left the parish.	> The decrease in population (68) in the parish was partially due to the high out-migration figures.

Table 25.5

> **Write four points of evaluation of your investigation.** Evaluation is a critical examination of your investigation. Its main purpose is to see if the objectives of your investigation have been met. As such, they should relate to the aims in Section 1 and the tasks completed in Section 3. This might include:

> Evaluating the aims/hypotheses that you started out with
> Commenting on the success and usefulness of the investigation
> Commenting on the limitations of the investigation
> Describing any reservations that you have about the methods you used
> Commenting on the reliability/accuracy/limitations of the results
> Making reasoned suggestions for improving and extending the investigation.

Points of evaluation do not have to be tied to either the results or conclusions. They must always be geographic in nature.

> **STAGE 4: EVALUATION**
>
> › If I were measuring the longshore drift again, I would get the average speed of eight floats at two different times. This would help to get a more accurate result than the one we got using four floats once.
> › I was happy with the results produced by the investigation. They fit my original hypothesis about transportation by both swash and longshore drift being the dominant process on the beach.
> › Our planning was poor because the tide had turned when we arrived on the beach. This gave us little enough time to undertake our tasks, especially as we undertook wave activities ahead of beach activities.
> › Our traffic survey was not representative of a typical day because we undertook all our counts within school hours. We did not do any in the early morning or during the evening rush hour.
> › We should have done a second practice run in using the clinometers and ranging poles, as some people in my group were not sure what they should do.
> › Undertaking measuring tasks on the river gave me a better understanding of fluvial processes compared to our classroom work.
>
> **Table 25.6**

Section 5: Presentation of results (20 marks)

There is a link between Section 4 and Section 5. In Section 4, credit is given for the actual results. Here, in Section 5, credit is given for the ways in which these results are presented in graphical form. Present your results in **two** or, preferably, **three** graphic forms. Remember that each graphic form should:

› Be different (for example, do not draw two bar charts)
› Have a title and labelling as relevant
› Match the results
› Appear in the appropriate graph pages in the Reporting Booklet.

There is a wide range of suitable graphic forms. See Chapter 24 for examples.

Appendix
Exam Terminology

Before your examination, you should become familiar with common command words. These are the key to understanding what the question really wants you to do.

The table below lists the command words that have been used in the Leaving Certificate to date.

> **HINT**
>
> Information on past examination papers and marking schemes is available at **www.examinations.ie**. Click on **Examination Material Archive**.

COMMAND WORDS IN EXAMINATION QUESTIONS	
WORD	**EXPLANATION**
Name	Point out and name from a number of possibilities. This command will generally be used in conjunction with 'Describe' or 'Explain'.
Identify	Same as 'Name'.
Describe	Say what something is like. Give a detailed account with specific geographic information to show your knowledge of the topic.
Outline	Give a general summary, referring to the main points. It is similar to 'Describe'.
State	Express or list the main points in clear statements. Use brief sentences, as there is no need to go into depth or detail.
Examine	Look at an issue carefully and in some depth. To examine is to do much more than to describe.
Investigate	Plan, inquire into and draw conclusions about an issue. It is similar to 'Examine'.
Discuss	Identify issues/key points. Present arguments for and/or against them and reach a conclusion.
Explain	Show, using evidence, how or why something happens. Answers to these questions should look to the reasons behind what is happening. This means that 'because' will be an important part of your answer.
Account for	Say why something is the way it is. Similar to 'Explain the reasons for' (see above).
Illustrate	Present information as a figure, picture, diagram or example.
Draw a diagram	For a question that asks for a diagram, you should present a drawing, chart, plan or graphic representation in your answer. Generally, you are expected to label the diagram and give the diagram a title. You could also add brief points of information.
Example	Questions are often worded with expressions such as 'with reference to an example you have studied', 'with reference to the Irish landscape', 'in any region studied by you', 'Irish landform', etc. This means that marks are reserved for naming a location where the feature under discussion is found or located.

Note: Some questions may use the command words 'Describe and explain'.

Index

Aasleagh Falls 144
ablation 196
   zone of 187
abrasion 102, 104,
   coastal 165–8
   glacial 189–91, 199
   river 139, 143–4, 146
accumulation, zone of 187
Achill Island 173, 281, 285
Adamstown 270
Aden, Gulf of 13
administrative regions 221
   France 228–9
   Ireland 227–8
aerial photographs 419–28
   camera direction 422
   comparing with OS maps 428
   high oblique 420–1
   information from 424–8
   line of sight 422
   location on 421
   low oblique 420–1
   sketch maps from 423
   types 420
   uses 419
   vertical 420–1
affirmative action 366
African Plate 11, 19, 26
agriculture
   Brazil 344–8
   Dublin region 253–4
   Mezzogiorno 321–2
   Paris Basin 298–301
   Western region 274–6
Aillwee Cave 106, 108

Aletsch Glacier 441
Alfa Romeo 326
alluvium 141, 148, 150
Alpine folding 25–6
Alps 441
Amazon Basin 342–3, 349, 357
   forests 445
Amazon River 137, 151, 342, 440
American Plate 12
Andes Mountains 17
Annestown 173
anticlines 24, 27
anticyclones 448, 457
Antrim, Co. 123
   coastline 214
Antrim–Derry Plateau 56, 64,
   74, 77, 82
apartheid 239
Apennines 319, 322–3, 329, 331
Apulia 319, 321–4, 331
Apulian Aqueduct 322
Arabian Desert 442
Arabian Peninsula 13
Aran Islands 77
Arctic ice melt 445
arcuate deltas 152
arêtes 190
Armorican folding 25–7
Arras 246
asthenosphere 4
asylum seekers 334
Athlone 201
Atlantic Forest 349–50
Atlantic Ocean 14–15, 19
atmospheric pressure 455

atolls 439
attrition
   coastal 165–6
   river 138–9, 143, 165
Autostrada del Sole 322
avalanches 127

backshore 172
backswamps 150
backwash 162, 170–2
Baile Ghib 232
Ballymun 271
Bandon River 27, 136
Bantry Bay 214
bar charts 463–5
Bari–Brindisi–Taranto industrial
   triangle 325
Barrow River 212
basal slip 187–8
basalt 64, 73–4
   landscape 82
Basilicata 320, 323–4, 332
basket-of-eggs topography 196
batholiths 58, 97
baymouth bars 175
bays 167–8, 170
beach(es) 172
   bayhead 167, 172
   cusps 173
   nourishment 180–1
   raised 213
   storm 172
Beauce 299
bedding planes 101–2
bedload 140

GEOGRAPHY TODAY

Belfast, Titanic Quarter 374
Belgium, languages in 233–4
Belo Horizonte 354
bergschrund 190
berms 172
biodiversity 344
bird's foot deltas 152
Blackwater River 27, 30, 136, 216
block mountain 28–9
Bloody Foreland 167
blowhole 169–70
Blue Lagoon, Iceland 67
bluff lines 147
bogflows (bogbursts) 124, 129
bogs, blanket 124
Bord Iascaigh Mhara 277
bottomset beds 151
boulder clay 195–7
boundaries, regional, changes in 385–7
brain drain 242
Brasilia 355, 362
Bray, Lough 189
Brazil 341–68
    African-Brazilians 365–7
    agriculture 344–8
    carnivals 358
    Central Plateau 342, 345–7
    climate 343, 346–7
    culture 365–8
    deforestation 350–1
    drainage 342
    fertility rates 359
    foreign investment 352–3
    gold 349
    Great Escarpment 342
    industrial triangle 354
    language 368
    life expectancy 359
    manufacturing 351–2
    markets 348
    metal ores 349
    migration 360–1
    mineral exploitation 348–9
    music 368
    native peoples 360, 365
    oil 348
    population 359–62
    race 365–6
    relief 342
    religion 366–7
    soils 347
    timber industry 349–51
    tourism 357–8
    transport 354–7
    urban development 361–2
    vegetation 343–4
Brazilian Highlands 142
Brexit 376, 383–4
    impact 384–5
    negotiations 384
Bride River 148
Brie 299
brownfield sites 427
Bull Island 176
Burren 77, 82, 96, 102, 110–13

calcite formations 107–8
calderas 55, 62
Caledonian folding 25–6, 73, 76, 78
California
    deserts 442
    drought 447
Campania 319–21, 323–4, 331, 335
Campos Basin 348
canalisation 156
carbonation 95–6, 102–4, 167
cardinal points 397
Carran Depression 105
Carrauntoohil 94, 190
Cassa per il Mezzogiorno 321–2, 325–6
Cavan, Co. 137
caves 106–8, 113 see also sea caves
caverns 106–8
cavitation 139, 146, 149
Celtic Tiger 286
Central Plain (Ireland) 77, 201
Cerrado 345–7
chalk 77
Champagne (region) 299
Champagne (wine) 299, 301
Channel Tunnel 246, 310
choropleth maps 468
Chrysler 326
cirques (corries) 189–90
city councils 227
Clew Bay 197
cliffs see river cliffs, sea cliffs
climate, of Ireland 225–6
climate change 445
climatic regions 224
climographs 466
clints 103
Clonmacnoise 201
closed depressions 105
Cloyne 106
coal 75
coast, hard and soft 177
coastal
    deposition, landforms of 172–6
    erosion 162, 164–70, 177–9
        factors 164
        landforms 165–70
        processes 164–5
    landscapes 439
    management 179
    processes 161–81
    recreation 178–9
coastline 161
    of emergence 213
    importance 177
    Ireland's 177–81
Coca-Cola 280
cold fronts 455
Cold War 386–7
Comeragh Mountains 27, 76
communes 228
compression 23, 25, 30
    air 165, 167–8
Cong Canal 105
conglomerates 75–6
Connemara 137
    lowlands 73
constructive boundaries 13
consumer industries 256, 279
continental
    break-up 13
    crust 2–4
    drift 9
    shelf 3
convection currrents 10
cool temperate oceanic climate see Western European climate
core regions 240–1, 296–317
Corrib gas field 84, 277–8
corries 203
Coumshingaun 189
county councils 227
Courtmacsherry 214
craters 54
Croagh Patrick 79, 94
cross-sections 403
cultural regions 221, 230
Curitiba 356, 361
Curracloe 173
customs union 378

INDEX

dams 154
Death Valley 94
deforestation 103, 445
    in Haiti 129
    in Brazil 350–1
deformation 23–4
deltas 151–2
    lacustrine (lake) 151–2
    marine (sea) 151–2
denudation 90–1
départements 228–9
deposition (river) 138, 141, 149
depressions 456
    frontal 226
Derrybrien bogflow 124
desert landscapes 442
deserts, hot 94
destructive boundaries 16
Devil's Punch Bowl, Killarney 189
dialect 230
dioxin emissions 326
discharge 137
distributaries 151
dolines 105
doming 23, 31
Donegal Bay 167
Donegal mountains 73
drainage 404
    basins 134–5
    superimposed 215
    patterns 135–7
        dendritic 135
        deranged 137
        radial 136
        trellised 27, 136
dripstone curtain 108
dripstone features 107–8
drought 447
Drumlin Belt 197
drumlins 196–8, 203
    drowned 197
    lee end 196
    stoss end 196
    swarms 196
Dublin Airport 265
Dublin Bus 265
Dublin city 385–6
Dublin Port 258, 266
Dublin region 252–71
    agriculture 253–4
    climate 253
    councils 386
    financial services 266–7

fishing 255
inner-city decline 271
inward migration 268–9
labour 258
manufacturing 256–60
market gardening 254
markets 260
physical processes 252
population 267–9
    structure 268–9
rocks and soils 252
tertiary sector 260–7
third-level education 259
tourism 260–2
transport 258, 262–6
urban development 269–71
urban sprawl 270
Dunloe, Gap of 136, 191
Dunmore Cave 106
Dunmore East 173
dykes 58

Earth
    core 3
    crust 2–3
    mantle 3
    plates 3
    structure 2–5
earthflows 124
earthquakes 12, 17 35–47
    see also seismic waves
    aftershocks 35
    cause 36
    damage, limiting 45–6
    deep focus 37
    depth 37
    early warning 41, 45
    effects 41
    epicentre 35
    focus 35
    forecasting 40–1
    foreshocks 35
    intensity 39–40
    Japan 37, 42–4
    magnitude 39
    Mezzogiorno 319, 329
    Nepal 42–4
    recording 39
    shallow focus 37
    tremors 35
East African Rift Valley 14
Eastern Europe 243
    boundary changes 387

eastings 396
economic redevelopment 246
EEC 378
Eiscir Riada 201
electronic engineering
    industries 256
Embrapa 345–6
endogenic processes 90, 208
Enterprise Ireland 257
Eriff Valley 30
erosion 19, 90–1, 101 *see also*
    coastal erosion, fluvio-glacial
    erosion, glacial erosion, river
    erosion, soil erosion
    differential 167
erratics 198
Errigal, Mount 79
esker ridges 201
eskers 200–1, 203
estuarine deltas 152
Etna, Mount 52, 55
Etna Valley 327
EU 260
    candidate countries 379
    development 377
    economic regions 240–4
    economic union 382–3
    enlargement 378–81, 387
        impact on Ireland 380–1
    and fishing 277, 302, 323
    Ireland's membership of
        286, 375–6
    members 378
    political union 383–5
    trade 378
Euralille 246
Eurasian Plate 11, 14, 16, 18–19, 26
euro 382
European Central Bank 383
Eurostat 259
eurozone 383
examination command words 479
exfoliation (onion weathering) 94–5
exogenic processes 90, 208

falls 126
fault lines 12
faulting 23, 28
    normal 28
    reverse 28, 30–1
    tear 28–30
    thrust 30–1
federal system 234

feldspar 97
fetch (waves) 162
Fiat 326
field study *see* Geographical Investigation
financial crisis 383
fiords 192
firn 186, 190
First World War 243, 377
fishing *see also* EU, overfishing
    Dublin region 255
    herring 255
    Mezzogiorno 322–3
    Paris Basin 301–2
    Western region 276–7
Flanders 233–4
flocculation 151
flood walls 155
flooding 444
floodplains 147–8
    depositional 148
    erosional 147
floodway areas 156
flowline maps 468
flows 124–5
fluting 103
fluvial processes *see* river processes
fluvio-glacial
    deposition 200–2
    erosion 199–200
    landforms 198
fold mountains 17–18, 25
folding 23–7
folds
    asymmetric 25
    overfold 25
    overthrust 25
    recumbent 25
    simple 25
    symmetric 25
Food Safety Promotion Board 376
foreset beds 151
foreshore 172
forest fires 444
fossils 77
freeze-thaw (frost wedging) 93–4, 102, 121, 190–1
frontier forests 349

GAA 377
Gaeltacht 230–2, 282
Galtee Mountains 27, 76
Galway, Co. *see* Western region

Galway Bay 167
Galway city 280, 285–6, 289–90
Ganges, River 151
GDP 314
Geographical Investigation 473–8
    information sources 474
    Reporting Booklet 473
    stages 474–8
        1 Introduction 474
        2 Planning 475
        3 Gathering Information 475–6
        4 Results 477
        5 Presentation 478
    topic 473
geomorphological regions 221
geos 169–70
geothermal energy 60 *see also* Iceland
Giant's Causeway 64, 82
Gioia Tauro 330
glacial
    advance 187
    deposition 195–8
    erosion 105, 188–9
        differential 192
        landforms of 189–92
        lateral 191
        vertical 191
    ice, movement of 187–8
    meltwater 199
    processes 185–204
    retreat 187
    spillway (overflow channel) 199
    stairway 192
    till *see* boulder clay
    transportation 194
    troughs 191
glaciation of Ireland 203–4
glaciers 186, 441
    advance and retreat 185, 187
    cirque 186
    continental 186
    piedmont 186
    valley 186
Glen of the Downs 199–200
Glendalough 191
Glendasan 191
Glenveagh 136, 191
Good Friday Agreement 239, 373, 376
gorges 105, 145
graben *see* rift valley

gradient 137, 402
granite 65, 73
    landscape 82
graphs, interpreting 463–9
Great Famine 286
Great Glen Fault 29–30
Greece 242, 383
greenfield sites 427
grikes 103
growth poles 325
groynes 179–80
Guerrero Gap 40

Haiti 129
harbour construction 178
Hawaiian Islands 57
headlands 167–8, 170
healthcare industries 256
Himalayas 18, 26, 37, 42, 186
historic settlement 405–6
Hook Head 169
horst *see* block mountain
Howth 175
Hurricane Katrina 156
hurricanes 447
Hwang Ho 141
hydraulic action 102, 104, 138–9, 146, 149, 164–5, 167–8, 199
hydro-electricity 446
hydrolysis 96–7
hyperinflation 351

IBM 256
ice
    blue 186
    formation 186
ice age 185–6, 203, 210
Iceland 14–15, 56
    geothermal energy 66–7
    hot springs 60
    volcanic activity 53, 59–60
ICT industries 256
IDA 257
IFSC 266–7, 271
igneous rocks 72–4
    extrusive 73
    intrusive 73
Iguazu Falls 145
Île-de-France 296
IMF 352, 383
Inch 174
Indian Plate 11, 18, 26
industrial decline 243–5

INDEX

Industrial Revolution 243
inlets 169–70
interglacial periods 185–6, 203
interlocking spurs 144
Intertrade Ireland 376
Ireland, Republic of, and Northern Ireland 375–7
Ireland West Airport Knock 284
IRFU 377
Irish landscape, formation 19
Irish language 230–2
Iron Curtain 386–7
Islamic region 236–7
island arcs 16
isobars 455
isohyets 459
isostasy 210–16
 coastal landforms of 213–14
 fluvial landforms of 211–13
isotherms 460
Itaipu Dam 354

Japan 16
 earthquake and tsunami (2011) 37, 42–4
joints 101–2

kaolin 97
karren 103
karst 77, 96
 landscape 82, 101–13
  lifecycle 108–9
Kazakhstan 440
Keimaneigh, Co. Cork 199
Kenmare Bay 214
Kilkee 169
Killary Harbour 28, 30, 144, 192
Kinsale, Old Head of 169
Kinsale Head gas field 84
knickpoints 211
Knockmealdown Mountains 214

laccoliths 58
lagoons 175, 439
lahars 53, 62
lakes
 kettle hole 202
 mort 149
 oxbow 148–9
 paternoster 192
 pro-glacial 199

land
 reclamation 178
 use 408–9
landforms 404
landscape
 cycle 209
 human and economic 405–9
 physical 404
landslides 122, 129–30, 444
language
 regions 230–4 *see also* Belgium, Gaeltacht
 survival 231
latifundia 321–2
lava 52–3, 443
 acidic 52–3
 basic 52–3, 56
 dome 55
 plateau 56
Leannan Fault 29–30
Lee, River 27, 136
Leinster Batholith 65, 73, 97
levees 150
 artificial 155
life science products 279
Liffey, River 147
light industries 256, 279
Lille 246
limestone 75, 77
 characteristics 101–2
 landscape 82, 102
 pavement 103
liquefaction 44
lithification 74
lithosphere 4
Loire, River 300
longshore drift 171
low pressure systems 448, 456
Lugnaquilla 65

Macgillycuddy's Reeks 27, 76
magma 10, 52
 chamber 52
Malaspina Glacier 186
Manaus 361
maps *see also* Ordnance Survey maps, sketch maps
 scale 393
marble 78–9
Marble Arch Caves 96, 108
market gardening 254

marram grass 173
mass movement 19, 90–1, 119–30, 165
 classification 120
 factors 119–20
 human influences 128–30
 processes 121–7
Matterhorn 190
Mauna Loa 57
Mayo, Co. 165 *see also* Western region
meander scar 149
meanders 146–9, 440
 incised 212
medical device production 279–80
Mediterranean climate (warm temperate oceanic) 224
Mediterranean diet 332
meltwater streams 200
Mercalli scale 40
Mercosul 353, 355
Merkel, Angela 383
Met Éireann 460
metamorphic rocks 72, 78
metamorphism
 contact (thermal) 78
 regional 78
meteorology 454
Mezzogiorno 242, 318–37
 agriculture 321–2
  modernisation 322
 climate 319, 328
 fishing 322–3
 hilltop towns 334
 infrastructure 325, 329
 life expectancy 332
 manufacturing 323–7
 migration 324, 333–4
 organised crime 324, 329
 population 331–4
 relief 319–20, 329
 soils 320
 tourism 327–9
 transport 329–31
 urban developments 334
Mid-Atlantic Ridge 14, 37, 56
Midlandian glaciation 204
mid-ocean ridges 14
millibars 455
minerals 72
mining, open-cast 449

Mississippi
   Delta 152
   River 150, 151
      system 153–6
Mitchelstown Cave 106, 108
Mizen Head 167
Moher, Cliffs of 165, 167
Moho 3
Monaghan, Co. 137
Monnet, Jean 377
monoculture 130
moraines 194–5
   englacial 194
   ground 194, 196
   lateral 194–5
   medial 194–5
   push 194
   recessional 196
   terminal 196, 204
mountain(s)
   block 28–9
   cone-shaped 54
   fold 17–18, 25
   landscapes 441
Moy, River 148, 150
mudflats 176
mudflows 125, 129–30 *see also* lahars
multinational companies 256, 279
Munster, South
   drainage system 215–16
   rivers 216
Munsterian glaciation 204

Naples
   image 337
   tourism 336
   transport 336
   urban development 336–7
nationalism 377
natural gas 83–5
   exploration 83
   formation 83
   production, in Ireland 84, 277–8
   impact 85
   usage, in Ireland 85
Nazca Plate 17
Neagh, Lough 28
Nepal earthquake (2015) 37, 42–4
Nevado del Ruiz 60, 125
New Orleans 156
Niagara Falls 145
Niemeyer, Oscar 362

Nile
   Delta 152
   River 151, 442
nivation 190
Nord 245–6
Normandy 299
North American Plate 11, 14, 19
North Atlantic Drift 226
North European Plain 222–3
   economy 223
   landscape 222–3
North-South Ministerial Council 376
Northern Ireland 373–4
   economic development 373–4
   education 239
   power-sharing 239, 373
   religion 238–9
   and Republic of Ireland 375–7
   tourism 374
   Troubles 373
northings 396
Nukuoro 439
nunataks 203
Nyos, Lake 60

occluded fronts 456
ocean trenches 16–17
   Peru–Chile 17
oceanic crust 2, 3
offshore bars 175
oil spills 449
old red sandstone 76
onion weathering *see* exfoliation
Ordnance Survey Ireland 392
Ordnance Survey (OS) maps 392–411
   calculating area 394–5
   colour layering 400
   communications/transport 405
   comparing with aerial photographs 428
   contour lines 400, 404
   direction 397
   Discovery Series 392–3
   gradient 402
   grid references 396–7
   height 400
   land use 408
   legend 411
   measuring distance 393–4
   National Grid 395–7
   settlement patterns 405–9
      historic 405–6
      rural 406–7
      urban 408–9
   slope 401
   spot heights 400
   tourism and leisure facilities 408
   triangulation pillars 400
   urban settlement 408–9
orogenies 25
outwash plains 202
overcropping, in the Sahel 130
overfishing 255, 277, 323
overgrazing, in Ireland 128–9
overhang 144
Ox Mountains 28

Pacific Plate 11–12, 16
Pacific Ring of Fire 51, 61
Pangaea 9, 19
Pantanal wetlands 357
Paraná River 347
Paris, Greater 315–17
Paris Basin 296–317
   agriculture 298–301
   aquaculture 302
   biotech industries 305
   climate 298, 300
   cosmetics industry 303
   deindustrialisation 306
   drainage 297
   fashion industry 302–3
   fishing 301–2
   inward migration 314
   manufacturing 302–6
      modern fields 304
   markets 300
   population 311–14
   relief 296–7, 300
   resources 304
   soils 300
   third-level education 304
   tourism 306–9
   transport 305–6, 309–11
   urban development 314
Paris Metro 310
peneplains 209
   South Ireland 214–16
peripheral regions 240, 242–3, 318–37
Pfizer 256, 259
pharmaceutical industries 256
physical regions 221
pie charts 467
pillars 107

Pinatubo, Mount 52, 59, 61–3
place names 405–6
plastic flow 189
plate boundaries 11–18, 37
    convergent 11, 16–18
        continental–continental 18
        oceanic–continental 17
        oceanic–oceanic 16
    divergent 11, 13–15, 36–7
    transform 11–12, 36
plate margins
    active 81
    trailing 81
plate tectonics 8–20, 441
plates 3
    collision 16
    movement 10
platforms, raised 213
plucking 188, 190–1
plunge pool 144
plutons 58
Po, River 151
point bar 146
polar front 226
poljes 105, 113
Pollaphuca Falls 144
pools 146
population pyramids 465
potholes 144
precipitation maps 459
primate cities 315
pyramidal peak 190
pyroclastic
    cloud 53
    flow 53, 62
    material 53

quartzite 65, 79

radar charts 469
Radió na Gaeltachta 232
rain
    convectional 298
    frontal 298
    maps 459
rainforests 343, 358
rapids 145
Ráth Chairn 232
Red Sea 13
reforestation 350
Reims 299
regional assemblies 228

regions 220–1 *see also* administrative, climatic, core, cultural, language, geomorphical, peripheral, physical, religious, socio-economic, sub-continental, urban interactions between 375–85
regolith 91, 119
religious regions 235–9
Renault 306, 352
representative fraction (RF) 393
RER 310
research and development 259
Rhine, River 152
Rhône, River 151
rias 214
Richter scale 39
ridge and valley landscape 24, 26–7, 136
ridges (coastal) 173
riffles 146
rift valleys 28–9, 441
Rio Grande 149
Rio de Janeiro 353–4, 362
river cliffs 146
river(s) 209, 211–13
    base level 142
    capture 216
        elbow of 216
    channel 138
        raised 150
    course 142–3
    erosion 138–9
        base level 209
        differential 144
        headward 145
        vertical 143
    flow 138
    gradient 142
    landscapes 440
    load 140
    long profile 142
    mature stage 142, 146–8
    old course 148
    processes 134–56
        impact of human activities 152–6
    rejuvenation 209, 211
    youthful stage 142–5
robber crops 130
Robinson, Peter 239

rock
    armour 180
    basins 192
    flour 189
    strata 74–5, 101–2
    type and landscape 82
rock cycle 80
    human interactions with 82
rockfalls 126
Rockies 26
rocks 72–82 *see also* igneous rocks, metamorphic rocks, sedimentary rocks
    distribution, in Ireland 80
    plutonic 73
    volcanic 73
rockslides 122
Roscommon, Co. *see* Western region
Rosses Point 173
Rosslare Harbour 178–80
rotation crops 299
rotational slide 190
rural
    functions 424
    land use 424
    settlement 406–7, 425
RUSAL 349
rust belt 245

Sahara Desert 94, 442
Sahel 130
St Helens, Mount 55
salt marshes 175–6
saltation 140
San Andreas Fault 12, 29
sand dunes 173–4
    protection 180
    restoration 180
sandspits 174–5
    recurved 174
sandstone 75–6 *see also* old red sandstone
Santos 353
São Francisco River 347
São Paulo
    city 354, 363–4
    state 345–7
Saône, River 151
satellite images 438–49
    uses 438
Scalp, the, Co. Dublin 199
scarps 28, 297

INDEX

scatter graphs 467
schist 65
Schumann, Robert 377
Scotland, Highlands of 242
Scottish Rift Valley 28
scree (talus) 93–4, 126, 189
sedimentary rocks 25, 72, 74
    inorganic 75–6
    organic 75, 77
sea arches 168–9
sea caves 168, 170
sea cliffs 165–6, 170
    inactive 166
    raised 213
sea-floor spreading 14–15
sea stacks 168–70
sea stumps 168–9
Second World War 243, 335, 376–7, 387
Seine, River 300
seismic gap 40
seismic waves 35–6, 38
    body waves 38
        P waves 38
        S waves 38
    surface waves 38
seismographs 39
settlement patterns 407
ShakeAlert 41, 45
shale 76
Shannon Airport 280
Shannon River 147, 148, 152
    system 135
Shannonbridge 201
shearing 23
Shenzhen 446
shingle 172
shore 161
sial 3
Sicily 322–4, 327–30, 332, 334
sills 58
sima 2
Single European Act 375
sinkholes *see* swallow holes
Skellig Michael 126
sketch maps 398
slab-pull force 10, 16
slash and burn farming 347
Slemish Mountain 52
slides 122
Slieve Bloom Mountains 31
Slieve League 94, 165, 167
slope types 401

slumps 122–3
    rotational 123
snow 448
snow line 186
socio-economic regions 221, 240–6
soil
    creep 121
    erosion 129, 320
soils
    alluvial 274, 300, 347
    brown earth 252, 274, 300
    gley 274
    limon 300
    loam 300
    peat 273
    terra rossa 347
solar energy 442
solution 102–4, 139–40
South American Plate 11, 17
spider charts 469
stalactites 107
    straw 107
stalagmites 107
STMicroelectronics 327
Strandhill 174
stratification 200
streams
    braided 202
    consequent 215
    emergent 105, 113
    misfit 216
    subsequent 216
striae 189
sub-continental regions 341–68
subduction 16–17
    zone 36–7
Suez Canal–Gibraltar shipping route 330
Sugar Loaf Mountain 79, 94
Suir, River 147, 216
sunshine maps 459
suspension 140
Sutton tombolo 175
swash 162, 170–2
Sweden, Northern 242
synclines 24, 27
synoptic charts *see* weather charts

tables 467
talus *see* scree
Taranto 326
Tari project 326–7

tarns 189–90
temperature maps 459–60
tension 23
terraces, paired 213
terracettes 121
TG4 232
TGV 246, 310
Three Gorges Dam 446
Tibetan Plateau 18
tombolos 175
topset beds 151
tors 65, 97
traction 140
traffic management 426
Tramore Bay 167, 176
transportation (water) 138, 170
tremors 35
trend graphs 466
triangular graphs 469
troika 383
truncated spurs 191
tsunamis 44, 45 *see also* Japan
turloughs 105, 113
Twelve Pins 136

Údarás na Gaeltachta 232
uplift 209
urban
    functions 409, 425
    growth 385–6, 446
    land use 425
    planning 427–8
    regions 221, 247
    renewal 246
    settlement 408–9
    sprawl 446
uvulas 105

Vaiont Dam rockslide 122
valleys
    dry 104–5, 113
    glaciated 136
    hanging 191
    U-shaped 191–2
Venice 439
Ventry 173
vertical exaggeration 403
vertical interval 402
Vesuvius, Mount 55, 320
volcanic activity 50, 443
    cycle of 52
    in Ireland 64–5
    predicting 59

volcanic eruptions 52
    central vent 54, 443
    effects of 60
    fissure 55–6, 443
    hot spot 56–7
volcanic gases 52
volcanic landforms 54
    extrusive 54–7
    intrusive 54, 58
volcanic materials 52
volcanic zones 50–1
volcanoes 17, 50–68, 441
    active 52
    composite 55
    dormant 52
    extinct 52
    and plate boundaries 50–1
V-shaped valleys 143

Wallonia 233–4
warm fronts 455
warm temperate oceanic climate *see* Mediterranean climate
waterfalls 144
watershed 134
Waterways Ireland 376
wave(s) 161–3
    constructive 163, 172
    destructive 162, 165
    refraction 163, 167, 175

wave-built terrace 166
wave-cut notch 166
wave-cut platform 166
weather, in Ireland 448
weather charts 454–60
    cloud 460
    depressions 456
    fronts 455
    rainfall 460
    sunshine 459
    temperature 459–60
    wind 457–8
weathering 19, 65, 90–1, 92–7, 101, 165–6
    chemical 91, 95–7
    physical (mechanical) 91, 93
Wegener, Alfred 9
West on Track 283
Western region (Ireland) 242, 272–90
    agriculture 274–6
    aquaculture 277
    broadband 279
    climate 274
    farm income 275
    fishing 276–7
    manufacturing 278–80
    natural gas 277–8
    population 284–7
    relief 273
    rocks and soils 273–4

    rural depopulation 285
    tourism 280–2
    transport 282–3
    urban development 288–90
Western European climate (cool temperate oceanic) 224–6, 298
Western Railway Corridor 283
wet-dry cycle 121
Wexford, Co. 123
Wexford Harbour 174, 178–80
Wicklow Head 167
Wicklow Mountains 65, 82, 136
    weathering in 97
Wild Atlantic Way 281
wind charts 457–8
    radar 458
    rose 458
wind gap 216

Yangtze River 446
Yellow River 141
Yellowstone National Park 55
Youghal 173

zone of saturation 106